LYDIA MARIA CHILD

Lydia Maria Child

A RADICAL AMERICAN LIFE

Lydia Moland

The University of Chicago Press   CHICAGO AND LONDON

The University of Chicago Press, Chicago 60637
The University of Chicago Press, Ltd., London
For more information, contact the University of Chicago Press,
1427 East 60th Street, Chicago, IL 60637.
Published 2022
Printed in the United States of America

31 30 29 28 27 26 25 24 23 22   1 2 3 4 5

ISBN-13: 978-0-226-71571-1 (cloth)
ISBN-13: 978-0-226-71585-8 (e-book)
DOI: https://doi.org/10.7208/chicago/9780226715858.001.0001

Library of Congress Cataloging-in-Publication Data

Names: Moland, Lydia L., author.
Title: Lydia Maria Child : a radical American life / Lydia Moland.
Description: Chicago ; London : The University of Chicago Press,
2022. | Includes bibliographical references and index.
Identifiers: LCCN 2022007565 | ISBN 9780226715711 (cloth) |
ISBN 9780226715858 (ebook)
Subjects: LCSH: Child, Lydia Maria, 1802–1880. | Women
abolitionists—United States—Biography. | Women social
reformers—United States—Biography. | Women authors,
American—Biography. | Authors, American—19th century—
Biography. | LCGFT: Biographies.
Classification: LCC HQ1413.C45 M65 2022 | DDC 326/.8092 [B]—
dc23/eng/20220223
LC record available at https://lccn.loc.gov/2022007565

♾ This paper meets the requirements of ANSI/NISO Z39.48-1992
(Permanence of Paper).

FOR MY FATHER AND MOTHER,
KEN AND BARBARA MOLAND:
LOVING PARENTS OF FIERCE DAUGHTERS
AND COMPASSIONATE SONS

Contents

Illustrations

A Personal Prologue

This is a story of never living your life the same way again.

I have always loved asking the big questions. What is justice? What is truth? What about beauty? How should we live? By some miracle, I have managed to turn this love into a career by becoming a philosophy professor. I have devoted happy years of my life to parsing claims made by scowling nineteenth-century German philosophers and analyzing confounding arguments with the help of smart students. I have found in philosophy guidance on how to be moral, clarity about political principles, and an exhilarating argument for the necessity of art.

But after the presidential election of 2016, I decided something had to change. I decided it was time to come home: to find resources to confront my country's new reality in our own history. On Inauguration Day 2017, I made my way to Washington, DC, in a van full of Colby College students, all of us ready to march in our nation's capital. As we left Maine behind us, I had another thought. It was time, I decided, to turn to women.

This was going to be a problem. In nineteenth-century philosophy, women would be scarce. But two months later, spring break found me at the Schlesinger Library for the History of Women in America at Harvard's Radcliffe Institute. I arrived with the criminally vague idea of researching the philosophical foundations of American abolitionism. I knew women had been powerful voices against slavery, but I didn't know who or how. But attacking an entrenched institutional evil, I imagined, must have entailed thinking philosophically. It must have required a clear articulation of concepts like justice, dignity, and humanity as well as a capacity to make arguments that changed people's lives. An obliging librarian produced a box of archived letters. Among correspondence by Elizabeth Cady Stanton, Louisa May Alcott, and Julia Ward Howe, one letter stood out.

The letter was clearly written by one activist to another. It was affectionate, firm, and principled. It balanced self-deprecating humor with gentle reproach. It deftly applied wisdom gained from a life of antislavery activism to the newer cause of women's suffrage. Its perfectly formed sentences testified to a clarity I craved. The handwriting was gorgeous. It was signed "L. Maria Child." I had no idea who that was. Reader, I googled her.

What I found stunned me. Lydia Maria Child had written the first book-length argument against slavery in 1833—a book so progressive in the cause of abolition and so scathing in its attack on Northern racism that Boston society ostracized her. She had been the first female editor of a major American weekly political journal. She had written a two-volume history of women and a three-volume history of religion. When she realized that her country needed guides to home economics, parenting, nursing, or aging, she wrote those too. She had tangled publicly with politicians and used her body to shield abolitionist speakers from violent mobs. When her marriage threatened to break her spirit, she risked scandal by living apart from her husband, managing nevertheless to forge a love story that ended only when he died in her arms. She even wrote "Over the River and through the Wood." How had I never heard of this woman?

Among all these accomplishments, one thing fascinated me most. That was the story of how Child, once incontrovertible evidence of slavery's evil awakened her conscience, had never lived her life the same way again. Living by her conscience made her a radical, unwilling to accept the conventional wisdom of her time and unable to abide by its norms. She had aborted a fledgling career as one of America's first female novelists. She had consigned herself to a life of poverty. She had lost friends and alienated family. Decades later, after a civil war had accomplished what abolitionist activism alone could not, she was still fighting. How had she done that? What had prepared her for that moment of conversion, and what had sustained the life of activism that followed? And what could the example of her life teach me about how to live my own?

* * *

Pursuing these questions took me on a multilayered journey. It took me physically to the grave of an eighteenth-century Catholic priest near Norridgewock, Maine. It brought me to the hallowed halls of the Boston Athenæum, a library that, for disputed reasons, had terminated Child's membership in the wake of her ostracism. It led me to the wood-paneled rare books room at the New York Public Library, where evidence of Child's paralyzing despair—brought about by professional failure and personal heartbreak—filled my eyes with tears. And it brought me to Wayland, Massachusetts, where Child lived the last decades of her life and where she died. There, at a Sunday service at Wayland's First Parish Church, I heard a choir sing her words, set to music by a local composer. When they finished, a parishioner lit a candle. The minister invited the spirit of Lydia Maria Child to join us, and I felt a chill run down my spine.

More metaphorically, my questions about Child's lifetime of activism took me on a journey through bad arguments in my country's history. I learned about the reasoning that granted Maine statehood in exchange for slavery's expansion in Missouri. I confronted the rationale within the abolitionist movement for forbidding women to speak. I worked through the arguments that average Bostonians used to keep from caring about slavery and the justifications that allowed Northerners to abandon newly emancipated Black men and women to their fate during Reconstruction. The arguments were bad, but they felt very familiar. They sound a lot like arguments we hear on other topics every day.

Through tracing these arguments, I learned about episodes in my country's history that, to my shame, were new to me. I learned about proslavery mobs in Boston, about Lincoln's persistent hope to send freed slaves out of the country, and about the origins of feminism's whiteness in battles over the Fifteenth Amendment. It has become a cliché for white Americans like me to be outraged at their own ignorance, so I will not rehearse my outrage here. Suffice it to say that confronting that ignorance through studying Child's life has been a memorable experience in humility.

In Child's example, I also found someone taking on some of moral philosophy's thorniest questions. What causes moral change? Is it appeals to reason, to sympathy, or perhaps to integrity? When is a problem moral and when is it political? What is the value of nonviolence, and what happens when those who have gained power through violence urge nonviolence on their victims? Child faced many questions that still haunt political engagement today. What does it mean to take the United States' radical commitment to human equality seriously, to weave it into your life as more than an empty slogan? When do we have a duty to disobey unjust laws? What should you do when who you are—in Child's case, a woman—is an impediment to your own activism? How do we balance personal duties with political duties, or love of individuals with commitment to principle? How do we push beyond our comfort zones yet know when to retreat?

These were philosophical questions. So was Child a philosopher? It seemed not. "Mrs. Child disclaims the character of a philosopher," one of her early reviewers wrote. This broke my heart a little. It echoed my own fears about philosophy's impotence in the face of injustice. But, the reviewer continued, "she knows how to teach the art of living well, which is certainly the highest wisdom." Philosophy, etymologically, is the love of wisdom. One of its earliest pronouncements is Socrates's insistence that the unexamined life is not worth living. Despite her protestations, her reviewer implied, Child was thinking philosophically. Making life worth living, for Child, meant facing her nation's greatest crisis and dedicating her life to meeting it. She loved her country enough to demand that it live up to its radical principles, and she took full responsibility for her part in doing so. She tried everything she knew and a lot of things she didn't know. Her understanding of her duty to protect her country's principles unified and sustained her life and made it worth living. Her resolve never to live her life the same way again had come from thinking philosophically: from being devoted to the art of living well.

As I started to absorb the brilliance of her example and the relevance of her story, it began to infuriate me that she was not better known. I could try to fix that, I thought. This prompted another question. Does the world need another white hero? The study of racial injustice in American history all too often focuses on white activists, concealing how Black Americans led the struggle not only for their own liberty but for American ideals more broadly. It tempts us to ignore how most white Americans were complicit in slavery and to neglect the ways many of us are complicit in racial injustice now. It encourages us to overlook cases in which white activists themselves perpetuate prejudice and privilege. Child was bracingly progressive for her time, but her failures are instructive. She didn't offer easy answers to problems of entrenched injustice, but she grappled with them honestly and passionately. On this topic, too, I learned from her. I learned both from the mistakes she made and from the fierce humility with which she always acknowledged that she, too, might be part of the problem. We might not need more white heroes, but I have come to believe that white Americans like me need more examples like hers.

* * *

When I began to write this book, I was in an enormous hurry. Child's example was so relevant, her voice so present, her advice so needed, that any delay in adding her to our national conversation felt unbearable. But here again her biography offered a lesson. After her conversion to abolitionism, Child had done the least rushed, least urgent thing possible: she had spent three years researching and writing a book. So I tried to slow down.

As I researched and wrote, current events unfurled in eerie parallel to Child's life. As I wrote about President Andrew Jackson's embrace of white supremacy, our populist president watched demonstrators chant neo-fascist slogans and claimed there were good people on both sides. Progressive organizations splintered around me as I documented the schisms in the abolitionist movement that set its cause back by at least a decade. As I wrote about the courageous struggles of a formerly enslaved woman to have her story of sexual assault be heard and believed, I watched influential men in America's halls of power refuse to believe a woman's more recent story of abuse. Protests insisting that Black lives matter electrified the country as I struggled to chronicle the systematic violence that had characterized American slavery. Finally, on a January afternoon in 2021, as I wrote about a violent insurgency that announced itself in 1861 by replacing the United States flag with its own, rioters in military gear paraded Confederate flags through the United States Capitol. In one photograph from that dreadful day, a Confederate flag unfurls just beyond a painting of one of the men Child converted to abolitionism: Massachusetts senator Charles Sumner. I imagined him witnessing the violence in the Capitol that day with a mournful lack of surprise. In 1854, he himself had lain bleeding on the Senate floor after being viciously beaten for his abolitionist beliefs. Charles Sumner knew something about violence in the Capitol.

I finished the first draft of this book as another president took office. This was reason for hope. Child advised caution. "Ever since I can remember, the country was just about to be *saved* by a presidential election," she wrote in 1856; "and every time, salvation has proved to be farther and farther removed." Indeed, the parallels between Child's biography and contemporary events have at times been deeply disheartening. Have we learned anything? Has anything really changed? In 1860, Child wrote to a fellow abolitionist that "no particle of scattered truth is ever wasted. The harvest will come in time."[1] Did she believe this? Should we?

I have often tried to imagine what Child would say if she too could witness the parallels between her America and mine. I think the answer has two parts. The first is that none of this would have surprised her. She knew her country's history and the powers of oppression too well. She knew how institutionalized evil could pair with moral complacency to perpetuate injustice. But the second conclusion is more hopeful. It might be true that none of this would have surprised her. But none of it would have stopped her either.

*　*　*

In spring 2017, all these thoughts lay in the future. As the semester ended, I was still trying to decide if I should write this book. I went back to Harvard. This time I knew who Lydia Maria Child was, and I knew what I was looking for. I knew that she and I shared a first name, and that it was a name she shared with several correspondents. At the Schlesinger Library, I ordered two boxes of files. I knew they would include several of her letters and a scrapbook of articles and images she had collected in her early antislavery years. I sat in the still, climate-controlled room waiting for them to arrive. The windows in the reading room are high. Settled among them are paintings of eminent women in America's history: artists, intellectuals, activists, entrepreneurs. Researchers around me shuffled quietly through boxes, taking pictures of priceless documents with their smartphones. My boxes arrived on a metal cart pushed by another obliging librarian. Only one folder allowed out at a time, she reminded me. I nodded. I pulled out the first one, laid it in front of me, and opened it. This time I was prepared for the even, elegant handwriting and the perfectly organized lines of text. I should also have been prepared for the first words, but I wasn't.

"My dear Lydia," she wrote.

I looked up past the eminent women and out through the windows. All right, I thought. Let's do this.

1

By an American

She didn't like her name.

Later in her life, someone asked why. "Suffice it to say," she replied, "that some associations of childhood make the name of Lydia unpleasant to me." It would not have been hard for some Lydia or other to make a bad impression: in nineteenth-century America, Lydias were everywhere. This Lydia herself had a great-grandmother, a grandmother, and an aunt by that name. As an adult, she would add a mother-in-law, a sister-in-law, a niece, and several namesakes to the chorus of Lydias around her. They were ubiquitous outside her family, too. Perhaps this is why her contemporary Ralph Waldo Emerson, whose second wife was named Lydia, rechristened her Lidian. The marriage went downhill from there.[1]

This Lydia would not wait for a man to rename her. By the time she was twenty, she had done it herself. But for now, Lydia Francis was the only name she had. And so until, by way of a religious quest and a complicated marriage, she became known to the world as L. Maria Child, Lydia Francis would have to do.

She was born on February 11, in Medford, Massachusetts. Medford was a small town on the Mystic River at the intersection of six colonial highways, about five miles northwest of Boston. The year was 1802. The American Revolution, with all its glory and uncertainty, was still in the recent past. The war was a vivid memory to her parents, who had both been ten years old when it started. Her father's father had fought against the British, distinguishing himself at the battles of Lexington and Concord by killing five enemy soldiers. Her mother's family had fled Charlestown during the Battle of Bunker Hill as the city burned behind them. There had been real poverty during those years—her father remembered that one winter, had a neighbor not shared extra potatoes with him and his nine siblings, they might well have starved.[2] But now the war was over. Her parents had been born British subjects, but now they were American citizens, free and clear.

And what kind of country was the United States of America? In many ways, it was too early to tell. When Lydia Francis was born, Thomas Jefferson, America's third president, was entering the second year of his first term in office. Already the country had weathered several crises that threatened its fragile union. Often those crises had to do with the fact that, despite Jefferson's own soaring rhetoric about the self-evidence of human equality, by the time he took office almost a million humans were enslaved in the country whose ideals he was pledged to defend.

Most enslaved people were in Southern states. But when the Revolution started, slavery still existed in all thirteen colonies. Their presence in the North was damning evidence of the evil pulsing through New World trade. For much of the eighteenth century, ships sponsored by New England port cities like Boston or Newport, sailed to Africa to trade goods for humans. Kidnapped Africans were then shackled in the holds of the ships and trafficked across the Atlantic to the Caribbean. Many were sold there to work the sugarcane fields; many more were sold in ports in the American South. There they were forced to work on sugar or tobacco plantations where the life expectancy of a slave was seven years. Those still unsold were shipped North, where their labor was extracted in forests and on farms, in shipyards and in woodshops. They could also be found in Northerners' homes, where they cooked, cleaned, minded children, and tended animals.[3]

The profit made by trafficking Africans could be used to outfit the next ship, and the cycle would begin again. If you were not rich

enough to fund your own voyage, you could buy a share in someone
else's and hope for the profits to return to you. If you were lucky,
you could make a fortune. Short of that, if you owned human chattel and managed them well, their free labor could boost you into
the middle class. As a result, the years 1700 to 1770 saw a 900 percent increase in the number of enslaved Africans in New England.
Boston newspapers regularly ran advertisements for their sale or
reports of their attempted escapes.[4] And so the bloody, torturous,
and highly profitable trade in abducted human capital continued.
It ensured generational wealth for many white Americans and
built the fledgling colonies into an economic power whose benefi-
ciaries shocked the world by declaring themselves free and waging
a successful war to prove it.

As her parents grew to adulthood, a combination of moral and
economic factors meant that slavery was waning in the North. But
it was essential to the South, where the entire political, social, and
economic order was structured around it. Southern delegates to
the 1787 Constitutional Convention staked their careers—and
the new country's existence—on preserving it. As representatives
from each state suffered in the Pennsylvania heat that summer,
compromise after compromise was struck to keep the union, including its slaves, together. In the end, the new Constitution did
not explicitly allow slavery; in fact, it never mentioned the word.
Northern politicians could, however plausibly, tell their constituents that the document had "antislavery potential." But it also gave
Southerners several guarantees of their "peculiar institution." In
tallying population, it allowed Southern states to count each enslaved person as three-fifths of a human, ensuring Southerners
congressional representation that maintained a balance of power
with the North. It permitted the new federal government to put
down slave insurrections and committed Northern states to returning any "persons held to service or labor" who tried to escape.
Only one of the Constitution's framers, Gouverneur Morris, explicitly condemned enslavement during the negotiations, declaring that if the South insisted on retaining slavery, North and South
"should take friendly leave of each other."[5] There were others who

thought slavery was wrong. But faced with a choice between their country's survival and slavery's end, they chose the former.

After the Revolution, slavery died a slow, reluctant death in New England. In other words, there was no cathartic, collective recognition by Northerners that slavery was wrong. In Massachusetts it eroded as enslaved people sued their owners and petitioned the legislature, challenging the state to take its post-Revolutionary constitution seriously, including the claim that "all men are born free and equal." Others did not bother to sue but simply left, knowing that the laws now worked in their favor and it would likely not be worth their enslavers' trouble to pursue them. Still others used the skills they had developed as woodworkers or bricklayers to buy their own freedom. Bowing to pressure from manumission societies formed by free Black citizens, some Northern states gradually emancipated slaves born after a certain date. There was also a small core of white allies—antislavery societies in New York, sympathetic lawyers in Boston, Quakers in Pennsylvania—whose efforts were having an effect. Some combination of these factors meant that by 1800, slavery in New England had essentially ended.[6]

But if it was shrinking in the North, slavery was exploding in the South. As new inventions made crops like cotton and tobacco more profitable, the demand for new humans to grow these crops increased as well. Opposition to slavery among Northern politicians also grew, sometimes for moral reasons but more often for political or economic ones. The growth of slavery increased Southern congressional representation, giving the South more political power. How could that be fair? And how was the North to compete with an economy based on free labor? When Jefferson signed the Louisiana Purchase in 1803, some New England politicians, alarmed that the new territory would expand slavery and so upset the precarious political balance struck over a decade ago, proposed leaving the Union. Perhaps they could form an alliance with England or Quebec.[7] Needless to say, this did not happen. But it was frightening evidence that someday, it might.

And so in 1802, when the Francis family's youngest child was born, the latest compromise was holding despite the egregious hypocrisy at the country's core. President Jefferson himself was living out this hypocrisy in his bed. That year, Jefferson's daughter Harriet was one year old. Her mother was Sally Hemings, one of Jefferson's slaves. Because American slavery was passed through the mother, the tiny, light-skinned Harriet was her father's slave as well.[8]

* * *

As her world began to take shape around her, little Lydia Francis began to recognize her immediate family. In addition to her parents, Convers Sr. and Susannah, there were four older children: James, Susannah, Mary, and Convers Jr. Of her siblings, probably Convers came into focus first. He was almost seven when she was born; one baby had died between their births. He seems to have taken being displaced by a younger child well, emerging early in his little sister's memories as affectionate and attentive even as other family members were perhaps too busy to mind her. Their father had by now fought his way out of poverty through the system of apprenticeship and had, at long last, become a prosperous baker. He was even famous: his "Medford crackers"—a buttery, crunchy, labor-intensive biscuit—were sold throughout the Northeast and exported in large quantities to England. The family lived in a two-story house across the street from the local cemetery, where at least one ancestral Lydia was buried. Next to their house was the bakery, a sign hanging in front for passersby to see.[9]

One of Lydia's earliest memories was of almost dying. Some "long, protracted" sickness had taken hold, and the doctor had given up. She had, she remembered, been "laid away for dead." What had that been like? Had she sensed her family sorrowing over her, her mother weeping but resigned, the room emptying as she fought alone against the fever or infection that was sapping her strength? Whatever it was, at some point her tiny body turned it back. Perhaps she opened her eyes in a dark room and became conscious of muffled activity downstairs. Or perhaps Convers was sitting there watching. Her illness had not killed her; it had made her stronger. Thereafter, her constitution was "hardy as an oak."[10]

Her parents were hardworking, frugal people. They had, she recalled, "small opportunity for culture"; there had been "nothing like literary influence in the family, or its surroundings."[11] There was, of course, religion. The Francis family, like most people in the town, were Congregationalists, which meant they were Calvinists. This in turn involved a crushing belief that humans were fundamentally sinful, in many cases destined for a very real and eternal hell. No one could evade suspicion of damnation, but if you were prosperous, you might convince yourself and others that God favored you. And so people like Convers Francis Sr. worked very, very hard to prosper, resulting in a work ethic that became as famous as the goods it produced.

It was the job of the Reverend David Osgood, minister of Medford's First Parish Church, to deliver this message of uncertain salvation to the town's sinful but striving inhabitants. Indeed, Lydia long recalled her minister's ominous weekly incantations along with his shining white hair. But it seems that by the time she was old enough to remember, his message had also softened. Like many near Boston, he was being drawn to an interpretation of Christianity—soon to be known as Unitarianism—that depicted God as more loving than punishing and humans as capable of both freedom and goodness. But whatever their minister's reformist tendencies were, Lydia's father never lost his belief in hell or his conviction that his children might go there. Once a month, she and Convers were sent to Reverend Osgood to recite the old-fashioned catechism that promised as much.[12] There she also encountered his daughters—Mary and Lucy—a few years older than she and clearly very bright. She must have watched the daughters of this learned man—growing up in a household full of books and ideas—with a mixture of admiration and envy. It seems that the fascination was mutual: well into adulthood, the Osgood sisters remembered the baker's daughter who recited her catechism in their home as exhibiting considerable spirit and spunk.

Fig. 1. Bridge over the Mystic River, Medford, Massachusetts. Courtesy of the Boston Athenæum.

Having overcome his own humble origins, Convers Francis Sr. was in a position to be generous with those still fighting for a place in American prosperity, and he was. His daughter later recalled how, the night before Thanksgiving, thirty "humble friends of the household," including "the washerwoman, the berry-woman, the wood-sawyer, the apprentice bakers," were summoned to the Francis residence for a dinner including "chicken-pies, pumpkin-pies . . . and heaps of doughnuts."[13] It was a model of liberality she never forgot. Then, on Thanksgiving Day itself, the Francis family apparently went over the river and through the woods to their grandfather's house, where there were cousins and sleighing and pumpkin pie. That memory stayed in Lydia's mind until she turned it into verse, putting Medford on the map not as the birthplace of one of America's fiercest reformers but as inspiring one of its most sentimental poems. There is still a river in Medford. There are no more woods.

What impressions of slavery did she have as she grew? Her father, one source reported, "detested slavery with all its apologists in all its forms." This may have been because he had witnessed its effects in Medford itself. A ten-minute walk from the Francis

Fig. 2. Ten Hills Farm (the Royall House), Medford, Massachusetts. The slave quarters are on the far left. Courtesy of Royall House and Slave Quarters/Theresa Kelliher.

home—over the same river and a bit farther through the woods— was an elegant residence known as Ten Hills Farm. Its owner, Isaac Royall Jr., had been born in Antigua, where his father, a native New Englander, had made a fortune in the slave trade. When the family returned to New England, they moved to Medford and brought the humans they enslaved with them. Royall had close ties to Britain and fled the country on the eve of the Revolution.[14] But the mansion remained, as did the long two-story building where his slaves had lived within earshot of their master's voice.

There is almost no record of what became of his slaves after he fled, but what *is* known is remarkable. Belinda Sutton, one of the Black women he left behind, later successfully petitioned the Massachusetts government for payment from the Royall estate as compensation for her lifetime of forced labor: clear evidence that Black Americans understood what "justice for all" entitled them to even if the founding fathers themselves would never see it that way. But the rest? Did they stay in Medford? Did Lydia Francis see them in town and hear them talk about their past? Did her father point out Ten Hills Farm to his children, recounting the shameful history of the money that built it? If he did, she never mentioned it. The Francis residence and bakery no longer exist, but the Royall mansion still does. So do its slave quarters. They are the only remaining example of their kind north of the Mason-Dixon line.[15]

There was another story of slavery in Medford that she must have known as well. At the turn of the century, a different Medford family had owned about twenty slaves. One, named Caesar, was sold to a Medford native named Mr. Ingraham who lived in the South. When Ingraham returned to Medford to visit some years later, he brought Caesar with him. Caesar had now experienced slavery in the South, and he did not want to go back. With some encouragement from Medford locals, he attempted to flee but was quickly caught, bound, and imprisoned by Ingraham on a Southbound ship. But in the commotion of his capture, Caesar had managed to alert sympathetic bystanders to his plight. Before the ship could sail, his allies appealed to the governor of Massachusetts himself to make use of new Massachusetts laws to obtain Caesar's freedom.[16]

This was exactly the kind of story that enraged Southern politicians. The North, they complained, had agreed to assist in returning fugitive slaves as part of the Constitution. That Massachusetts and other states had passed laws providing the kinds of loopholes that allowed Caesar to go free was evidence, they claimed, that Northerners had no intention of abiding by their pledge. As a girl, Lydia Francis would not have known about these legal technicalities. But she surely would have known of Caesar, who, a local historian reported, subsequently "worked at his trade in Medford several years with great approbation."[17]

The only childhood memory of slavery that Lydia Francis actually recorded was of celebrations that marked the end of the international slave trade. That end had come in 1808—a date that had also been set as part of the Constitutional Convention's compromise on matters regarding slavery. After this date, enslaved humans could still be bought and sold domestically, but there would be no more ships leaving the United States for Africa and returning with fresh supplies of stolen humans—at least not legally. Members of Boston's thriving Black community, which included both those born free and those who had somehow ended their enslavement, gathered to celebrate. The day began with a parade winding through downtown Boston and ending at the newly constructed African Meeting House, just blocks behind the Massachusetts Capitol. Speeches and a dinner followed. The date was then commemorated annually by Black Bostonians; as an adult, Lydia still remembered how viciously their celebrations were caricatured by Boston newspapers.[18] As to the African Meeting House, little did she know that some of the forces that would shape her life were already gathering in its modest rooms.

Ten Hills Farm, Caesar's escape, parades in Boston—through these and doubtless other incidents, Lydia fashioned an impression of slavery that was both complex and limited. She knew slavery had recently existed in her own world; she knew it still existed elsewhere; she knew some people were trying to end it, some to escape it, and some to preserve it. But in her developing young mind, it probably still felt distant, still abstract, still like nothing that could affect her life very much.

*   *   *

In due time Lydia was sent to a "dame school" run by one of Medford's spinsters, known to be a great drinker of tea and chewer of tobacco. She next attended the local grammar school where all the Medford children went, the girls safely separated from the boys. "Virtue hath its sure reward," the small schoolgirl wrote over and over in her copybook, tracing out the beginnings of what would become her beautiful handwriting.[19] That education was available at all, especially for girls, was certainly to Medford's credit. But it was minimal, just enough to ensure that new Americans could function in their self-assigned role as self-governing. Independence required self-sufficiency, which in turn required an ability to read and reckon and perhaps even to reason.

But though the official education on offer was limited, Lydia Francis had an advantage over other children. She had an older brother who loved books. In her earliest memories of Convers, he was never without one in his pocket, "poring over it, at every moment of leisure." Where this love came from was anybody's guess. There were very few books in their parents' house, and there is no evidence that the older Francis siblings shared Convers's passion. But he had teachers who took an interest in him. He also had a blind, religiously rebellious uncle to whom he was sometimes dispatched to read aloud.[20] To a young, intelligent, and curious mind, this must have been fascinating. So there were interpretations of the Bible other than Reverend Osgood's? There were other theories about heaven and hell, grace and punishment? It was enough to make Convers want to keep reading.

Then there was his little sister, watching him with adoring attention as only little sisters can. What was he doing? What book was that? What did those words mean? Perhaps Convers obliged her by recounting stories from novels the local teacher lent him. Perhaps he spun tales from history books or posed questions raised by their uncle's recent foray into Baptist theology.[21] Perhaps their parents were just as happy when Convers got their youngest child out from underfoot by reading to her. Soon she was reading to him; soon she was reading everything in sight. Convers was probably the first person to notice that his younger sister was extremely bright.

And so a kind of secret society was born next door to Medford's famous bakery. "When I came from school," perhaps from a long day of documenting virtue's sure reward yet again, "I always hurried to his bed-room, and threw myself down among his piles of books," Lydia recounted years later. For any texts beyond her "childish comprehension," she had a ready tutor. "'Convers, what does Shakespeare mean by this? What does Milton mean by that?'" she remembered asking. From all indications, Convers loved it. Her curiosity and admiration must have been a welcome relief from their parents' judgmental frugality. He was patient with his little pupil, only occasionally giving way to the universal tendency of older brothers to, as she put it, "bamboozle" their younger sisters with bad information. Until Lydia was called down to help hang wet laundry or Convers was needed to roll out the next batch of crackers, they existed blissfully "in a little world of our own, into which no one about us entered." It was a small vision of heaven. Recollection of those hours together, his sister wrote after his death, "is sufficient to fill me with gratitude to God for the gift of such a brother." "Such development as my mind has attained," she continued, "I attribute to the impulse thus early given by his example and sympathy."[22]

But the fact that the two youngest Francis siblings had to be "unearthed" from their intellectual preoccupations every time there was real work to be done soon became a source of tension. Being literate was fine, but the Francis family had a business to run, and Convers was needed. "My father," he later reported, "was a somewhat severe extractor of labor from his children."[23] It seems there were arguments. Their contours are not hard to imagine: their father had not, he was sure to remind his son, sacrificed his whole life to drag the family out of poverty just to have his youngest children fritter their lives away on books. Convers tried to reform, becoming passably good at the many culinary techniques necessary to make the bakery the transcontinental success it was. But his books always tempted him away again, and the arguments would resume.

Finally the family doctor intervened. "Mr. Francis," he advised the exasperated baker, "you will do very wrong to thwart the inclinations of that boy. He has remarkable powers of mind; and his passion for books is so strong, that he will be sure to distinguish himself in learning; whereas, if you try to make anything else of him, he will prove a total failure."[24] It was not exactly a ringing endorsement, but it had the desired effect. His parents gave up thinking he would be useful at home, so they did the next best thing: they sent him to Harvard.

When he left Medford for Cambridge, Convers Francis Jr. was sixteen years old, and Lydia was nine. The tiny world of ideas they had conjured into being evaporated. If her parents had been skeptical of the value of educating their promising son, they would have been adamant that no such value existed for their daughter. Most likely they thought that without his influence she could get back to the business of behaving like a girl. Perhaps attempts to encourage this redoubled.

But redirecting a wayward child takes energy, and energy was something their mother, Susannah, increasingly lacked. There's no record of when signs appeared of the tuberculosis that would kill her—when the coughing started or when exhaustion first drove her to her bed. But it was soon obvious that she was very sick. As she lay in her room, fretting restlessly about all the work left undone, perhaps her feverish mind hovered over each of her children. Her oldest three were already young adults: they would grieve for her, but they would be fine. Convers, inexplicably different though he was, seemed to be excelling as a baker's son among his country's intellectual elites. But Lydia? What would happen to Lydia? I wonder whether her mother was ever able to enjoy her youngest daughter's promise. Did she ever smile as this diminutive human struggled to keep up with her brother's lectures on Shakespeare? Did she ever laugh when Lydia's astonishing facility with language began to emerge? Did she notice the ferocity and independence that were, apparently, already evident and hope that they would serve her daughter well? Or did she only worry whether, as Lydia grew, there would be a place in the world for a woman too interested in books for her own good? In fact, Medford already had one of those: her name was Hannah Adams. In 1784, she had written a book on the history of religion: an intellectual feat unheard of for a woman and also widely condemned. The rumor was that Adams couldn't recognize herself in a mirror. Apparently this meant she had no vanity, which in turn made her not really a woman.[25]

A few months after her youngest daughter's twelfth birthday, Susannah Francis died. Decades later, Convers, by then a professor at Harvard's Divinity School, memorialized her in all the glowing terms a mother could wish for. "Of her I have the most grateful and affectionate recollections," he wrote. "Hundreds of instances rush to memory of the devoted, anxious care with which she watched over my welfare. Ever blessed with me is the remembrance of this excellent mother."[26] When he returned to visit her grave, remembering her early death still made him weep.

But Lydia, the Francis child whose words would become internationally famous, had almost none to spare for her mother. I have found only two exceptions. In one she remembers her mother's repeating a proverb to the effect that winter always comes early. In another she wishes her mother had had access to modern conveniences that would have made her life easier. But she never mentions her by name, and her reflections on her earliest years are bleak. She had spent her childhood believing that thieves "had changed me from some other cradle, and put me in a place where I did not belong," she wrote to Lucy Osgood decades later. "Cold, shaded, and uncongenial was my childhood and youth," she recalled: "Whenever reminiscences of them rise up before me, I turn my back on them as quickly as possible." But stories of motherless daughters haunted her fiction for her entire life. Among her possessions when she died, a lock of her mother's hair was carefully preserved, tied in a little loop with a small blue bow. "My mother, died—1813—48 years old," she wrote beneath it.[27] The hair had not yet turned gray.

The following year ushered in a period of breathtaking loss in young Lydia's life. Within months of her mother's death, both her maternal grandmother and her sister Susannah died. Her remaining sister, Mary, found a husband and moved to Maine. Her older brother James had long ago married and moved away. Convers was at Harvard. She and her father were alone.

Since he outlived his wife by over forty years, Convers Francis Sr. left a long record of his temperament. As an older man, he was irascible, impetuous, demanding, and critical. What was he like in his forties as a single parent trying to raise a headstrong, precocious adolescent girl? His Calvinism, with its dark visions of sin and hell, surely did not help. Nor did his continued alarm at her "increasing fondness for books."[28] The experiment did not last long. One year later, thirteen-year-old Lydia Francis was packed up and sent to Maine to live with her sister Mary. She would never live in Medford again.

*   *   *

Fig. 3. View of the northern part of Norridgewock, Maine, and the Kennebec River. Courtesy of the Boston Athenæum.

As an adult, she never recorded why she was sent to Maine or how she got there. There was a ship that went from Boston to Portland and a stagecoach from Portland into Maine's interior; perhaps that was how.[29] It would have been a terrible journey for someone so young to make alone, but she might have. After days of travel she finally arrived at Norridgewock, a picturesque settlement on the banks of the Kennebec River.

Her sister Mary Preston had just given birth to a baby, the first of five born over the next several years.[30] Mary certainly could make use of another pair of hands, and Lydia's later expertise in household matters suggests that her sister kept her busy. Norridgewock was well established, but provisions would have been in short supply and deliveries from elsewhere uncertain. Living in Maine meant knowing how to make do. By the time she returned to Massachusetts five years later, Lydia could sew beautifully and cook competently. She also could tell very good children's stories, a technique perhaps honed with one Preston child or another nestled in her lap.

The Preston family lived on the north side of the river, where there was a courthouse, a hotel, and a jail. Mary's husband, Warren Preston, was a lawyer from Massachusetts who had resolved to try his legal skills in the wider, wilder world of Maine. His professional position in the town meant that Lydia, perhaps as she helped her sister serve her husband's friends or tended a fire in the room where they talked, could listen in as they discussed pressing issues of the day.[31] Perhaps Warren, like Convers, enjoyed having a young, eager listener who would hang on his every word, always wanting to know more.

More important for Lydia's development, Warren Preston was helping Norridgewock found its first library and was serving as its librarian.[32] There's no record that the librarian's teenage sister-in-law borrowed books, but we know she was reading them. This is because in June 1817, the following letter burst out of the Maine woods, addressed to Convers, who was now studying at Harvard Divinity School. "My Dear Brother," it began:

> I have been busily engaged in reading "Paradise Lost." Homer hurried me along with rapid impetuosity; every passion that he portrayed I felt: I loved, hated, and resented, just as he inspired me! But when I read Milton, I felt elevated "above this visible diurnal sphere." I could not but admire such astonishing grandeur of description, such heavenly sublimity of style. I never read a poem that displayed a more prolific fancy, or a more vigorous genius.[33]

This is the earliest surviving letter by Lydia Francis. Its author was fifteen years old.

The letter continues, as does its precociousness. Although she liked Milton, she wanted to register a concern. "Don't you think," she mused to her brother, "that Milton asserts the superiority of his own sex in rather too lordly a manner?" As evidence for this charge, she cited a passage in *Paradise Lost* in which "Eve is conversing with Adam, [and] is made to say . . . 'God is thy law, thou mine: to know no more / Is woman's happiest knowledge, and her praise.'" Could that be right? Could woman's highest happiness, Lydia wondered, really consist in knowing as little as possible? The question was provocative, and she knew it. She hedged a little. "I feel satisfied that you will excuse a little freedom of expression from a sister, who willingly acknowledges the superiority of your talents and advantages," she assured him, "and who fully appreciates your condescension and kindness."[34]

Did Convers read the letter to his classmates, daring them to believe it came from his little sister? Either way, the letter certainly got his attention. His response does not survive, but her next letter to him conjures its stern rebuke. "I perceive," Lydia wrote, resigned already to a lifelong battle with her brother's conservatism, "that I never shall convert you to my opinions concerning Milton's treatment to our sex."[35]

The Maine woods were vast; compared with Medford's placid Mystic River, the Kennebec roared and swelled, sometimes sweeping away whole bridges as winter snows melted. She had always loved the springtime flowers and delicate birds in her parents' garden, but here in Maine nature was uncultivated and sublime. Her intellectual adventurousness kept pace with her surroundings: by this time, she was reading Sir Walter Scott. Scott's evocations of Scotland's magnificent landscapes, fierce heroines, and tragic conflicts were a perfect accompaniment to her new environment; they also appealed to her emerging personality. "In very early youth," she later recalled, "I loved scenes tinged with melancholy; they were a pleasant contrast to the excessive gayety of my own buoyant spirit."[36]

Scott's valiant female characters thrilled her so deeply that she again risked Convers's disapproval on the topic of gender. "In spite of all that is said about gentleness, modesty, and timidity in the heroine of a novel or poem," she wrote to him, "give *me* the mixture of pathos and grandeur" she found in Scott's heroines, complete with their "lofty contempt of life and danger." I imagine her rereading that sentence, remembering her audience, and deciding to hedge again. "In *life* I am aware that gentleness and modesty form the distinguished ornaments of our sex," she assured her brother. "But in *description* they cannot captivate the imagination, nor rivet the attention." In other words: she could acknowledge, at least for now, that modesty was a virtue in women. But she could not stand it in literature. Larger questions loomed here. What did that mean about the difference between men and women? Or about the difference between virtue in life and virtue in literature? She would have to think about that. For now, she was consumed by what she saw around her and felt within her. "You see that my head is full of rocks and crags and dark blue lakes," she conceded to Convers: a raw, teeming landscape for a restless, pulsing mind.[37]

Maine's history felt raw too. The year she arrived in Norridgewock, evidence of a gruesome chapter in this history was literally unearthed when a storm brought down a tree a few miles from town. Buried among its roots was a church bell that had survived the 1724 British massacre of Abenaki Indians and their French priest, Sebastian Rale. The British troops had attacked without warning and murdered some eighty people, among them dozens of women and children. The intention was to decimate the native population and scare off the French settlers who were allied with them. By the time the bell was rediscovered a hundred years later, both missions had been largely accomplished. The French had been driven into Canada, and the Abenaki had been reduced to a fraction of the mighty, populous people they had been.[38]

But they were still there, and Lydia Francis was curious. Somehow, in the midst of child care and household duties, she found time to seek them out in the hemlock forests near the river. She watched them dyeing wood strips and weaving them into baskets. She also joined them for meals and listened to their stories, absorbing a worldview and an aesthetic entirely different from her own. She met one of their chiefs and remembered, decades later, that his young warrior nephew reminded her of a god. She also recounted watching a native woman who had given birth the night before walk through the snow "with vigorous strides," a sack of potatoes on her shoulder and her baby on her back.[39]

These interactions apparently led the inquisitive teenager to a few conclusions. One was that the native peoples of America had been grievously wronged. If her later fiction is any indication, the story of the Norridgewock massacre, together with evidence of the hardship still endured by the survivors' descendants, clearly haunted her. But the other conclusion was that these native peoples were spirited, generous, and wise, possessing dignity and resilience that many in her own culture lacked.

*   *   *

The winters in Maine were brutal, and the summers were not much better. The second year she lived in Norridgewock, there was snow in June and frost every month of the year.[40] As Mainers struggled with epic blizzards and heaving ice, the sultry sugarcane fields of the South, and the enslaved humans who worked them, must have seemed a world away. But in 1819, the topic of slavery burst upon Maine residents in a way that would mark their, and their country's, history forever.

This was because Maine was still officially part of Massachusetts. Now, after decades of irritation with an alternately negligent and overbearing Boston government, it was staging its own bid for independence. Legal experts were consulted, newspapers opined, petitions were organized. Warren Preston, Lydia's brother-in-law, was among those who favored separation. No doubt she heard his reasons articulated in the lively debates that preoccupied the state's residents at the beginning of 1819. Finally a regionwide vote was scheduled. In July of that year a majority of Mainers voted to apply to Congress for statehood.[41]

Approval should have been a formality. Instead, Maine's request triggered a political crisis that quickly threatened the country's still fragile union. The United States consisted at this point of eleven free states and eleven slave states. Adding Maine would tip the balance in the Senate in favor of free states. Unwilling to allow this threat to their power, Southern legislators proposed making Maine's admission contingent on adding Missouri as a slave state. Maine's independence, it suddenly became clear, would have a moral cost: it would come at the price of expanding slavery. Mainers' political freedom would ensure other humans' physical enslavement.

Some Mainers, at least, reacted with horror, condemning the idea as the moral compromise it was. Delegates to Maine's Consti-

tutional Convention initially agreed that they would rather postpone independence than become "a mere *pack horse* to transport
the odious, anti-republican principle of slavery" farther into the
country. The *Portland Gazette* agreed, urging the delegation to
"hold fast to their political integrity, for as much as we wish success to the Maine Bill, we confess we had rather it would sink, than
bear up so wicked a freight as the slavery of Missouri."[42] But other
Mainers were not so sure, and their arguments are worth pausing over. In her career as an abolitionist, Lydia Maria Child would
have to fight every single one of them.

"We admit in the fullest manner that [slavery] is both a moral
and political evil," wrote two of Maine's prominent lawyers in another newspaper. "But having said this, it must be admitted on the
other hand that it is an evil too deeply seated to admit of an immediate cure. No man in his senses, thinks of emancipation. All
agree that it would be ruinous both to master and slave." There is
already a tension here. Why did slavery have to continue? Because
even though it was evil, it was too entrenched? Or because it was
not evil but rather beneficial, meaning that its end would be bad
for all involved? The lawyers did not pause to parse these nuances.
But one of them expanded on his reasoning in another letter: "If
I were a citizen of Missouri I should oppose slavery," he assured
a fellow lawyer. "But I do not feel that I have a right to dictate to
the citizens of that state the local policy which they shall pursue."
Then he apparently paused to reconsider. On second thought, he
concluded, he would not insist on ending slavery even if he did
live in Missouri. Surely it would be unwise to "legislate against the
wishes of the majority of the people in the state."[43] It is safe to assume that this "majority" of people did not include the ones who
were enslaved.

Yet another prominent Mainer, a future congressman, mixed a
stupefying instance of self-deception with a naked declaration of
self-interest. "I am for going as far as anybody to restrict slavery,
if it can be done without setting the United States on fire," he said.
But "the welfare of eight million of whites [is] of more importance

than a question about the black population," he concluded. Besides, "the preservation of the Union and the admission of Maine, [are] of more importance, than the doubtful right by the constitution to meddle with state sovereignty."[44]

As the debate raged and Mainers watched their hopes of independence dim, one more line of reasoning is worth considering. Whose fault was it, future Maine senator John Holmes asked, that some Mainers were suddenly so agonized about the fate of enslaved Africans thousands of miles away? The answer, he concluded, was a pamphlet circulated by a group of New Yorkers. This group called themselves abolitionists, and they had managed to convince some Mainers that slavery was wrong and should be stopped. Before these "abolitionists" had meddled, Holmes said, there had been no trouble. In fact, he had often, throughout his career, supported the expansion of slavery and "never received a letter in protest."[45] If Mainers' bid for liberation failed, he concluded, they would have abolitionist rabble-rousing to blame.

In the end, Mainers' desire for independence won out over their qualms about others' enslavement. The deal was struck, and the Missouri Compromise was approved. In March 1820, Maine was admitted as the United States' twenty-third state. The next year, Missouri was admitted as the twenty-fourth. As part of the compromise, slavery was prohibited anywhere above the thirty-sixth parallel, Missouri excepted. Northern politicians could assure their antislavery constituents that, despite the compromise, slavery would from this point on be contained forever. Apparently that was assurance enough for most white Northerners to go back to living their lives as before, and to forget again about slavery.

John Holmes proudly sent a copy of his defense of the compromise to the aging Thomas Jefferson, now enjoying his retirement at Monticello. Jefferson wrote back, praising Holmes's effective and persuasive reasoning. But about the question that Maine's bid for independence had broached—whether and how and where slavery should be allowed to expand—he was less sanguine. "This momentous question, like a firebell in the night, awakened and filled me with terror," he wrote to Holmes; "I considered it at once as the knell of the Union." The United States had won a "reprieve only," he said. The issue would be back.

Jefferson then paused to admire his own dislike of slavery. Like his Maine contemporaries, he was as much against it as anyone. "I can say with conscientious truth, that there is not a man on earth, who would sacrifice more than I would, to relieve us from this heavy reproach in any *practicable* way," he wrote. "The cession of that kind of property . . . would not cost me a second thought, if, in that way, a general emancipation and *expatriation* would be effected." Note the emphasis on "expatriation": in Jefferson's mind, even if Africans and their descendants could be emancipated, they would have to be sent away. But since neither freedom nor exile was possible, there was nothing to be done. "As it is," he regretted, "we have the wolf by the ear, and we can neither hold him, nor safely let him go. Justice is in one scale, and self-preservation in the other." It would all, he predicted, end badly. "My only consolation is to be," this founding father wrote, "that I live not to weep over it."[46]

Perhaps Jefferson actually believed there was no man on earth who would sacrifice more to end slavery than he would. It is also true that when he died six years later, he left behind over 150 slaves, 130 of whom were sold to pay the debts he had accrued living the life of a Virginia gentleman. Some of them were children who probably never saw their families again.[47]

* * *

How did Lydia Francis—with her sharp curiosity, her burgeoning wit, her love of wild landscapes and fierce heroines—absorb these debates as they swirled around her? In 1819, she was seventeen; we can imagine her, now a few years after her arrival in Maine, still weaving in and out among her brother-in-law's friends and colleagues as they dined in the Prestons' house, refilling their plates or glasses, listening all the while. What did freedom mean? What were the promises and perils of independence? What was worth compromising for what? When did politics trump morality or, as Jefferson put it, self-preservation weigh more heavily than justice?

Whatever thoughts she had, she apparently did not record them. This may be because as Maine's fate was being debated in the halls of Congress, Lydia Francis was embarking on her own bid for freedom. On March 12, 1820, three days before Maine officially became a state, she wrote an ecstatic letter to her brother. "I can't talk about books, nor anything else, until I tell you the good news," his sister wrote. No time for books: this must be big news indeed. "I leave Norridgewock, and take a school in Gardiner, as soon as the traveling is tolerable," she announced. "I hope, my dear brother, that you feel as happy as I do," she gushed. Then she quickly checked herself. "Not," she assured him, "that I have formed any high-flown expectations. All I expect is, that, if I am industrious and prudent I shall be *independent*."[48]

Gardiner was another Maine town along the Kennebec River, known for building ships and for harvesting the river ice that cooled Bostonians' iceboxes in the summer. Very little is known about her time as its schoolmistress except that, at least initially, she was elated. "I never was more happy in my life," she wrote to Convers after arriving. "I never possessed such unbounded elasticity of spirit. It seems as if my heart would vibrate to no touch but joy." Was educating Gardiner's youth really that thrilling? Or was she simply glorying in her liberation from the duties of life in Norridgewock? Perhaps it was more simple: Was she in love? Later in life she wrote of someone who had touched her heart during these years.[49] But she never names him, so we do not know.

Even if there is no proof of a romance, there is proof of a heady intoxication with new ideas. It seems that by this time, Lydia Francis had rejected her father's Calvinism. She was, in fact, later to describe herself as simply hating it: hating its evocations of hell, its images of human depravity, its claim that a just God could elect to save some humans and damn others. What kind of God would do that? What kind of justice would that be? But if she was rejecting Calvinism, where could she turn for religious structure? She could certainly have chosen Unitarianism. Convers had, by this time, been ordained as a Unitarian minister. She doubtless heard through him more about his church's gentler creed. But Unitarianism struck her as cold and cerebral. What she had discovered instead, much to her brother's dismay, were the teachings of Emanuel Swedenborg.

Swedenborg was an eighteenth-century European scientist and inventor who, later in life, claimed to have experienced divine revelations. God had revealed to him, he wrote, that the Bible was not literally true but rather a symbolic text to which Swedenborg was now being given the key. Based on his resulting analysis, Swedenborg rejected the assertion that God had been willing to torture his son in order to save a choice group of radically evil humans. Instead he claimed that the entire universe—including both natural and moral laws—was an expression of divine love. Everything was "coherent from things first to last," he promised, a beautiful unity of interlocking mysteries waiting to be deciphered. Humans, as part of this whole, were also divine, progressing toward ever greater perfection. Heaven, in turn, was simply an extension of this life but happier—a place where like minds congregated and lived in peace.[50] His was also an aesthetic vision, suggesting that poetry was an expression of divine love and poets were among humans' greatest prophets. Swedenborg had been widely denounced in Europe as a heretic, but by the nineteenth century his ideas had crossed the ocean and settled into a few small American congregations. Among them was one in Gardiner, Maine.

A religion based on love that called nature poetry and poetry divine? Lydia Francis was intrigued. She must have written as much to Convers, whose alarm prompted his sister to reassure him. "You need not fear my becoming a Swedenborgian," she wrote. The next sentence was less comforting. "I am," she continued, "in more danger of wrecking on the rocks of skepticism than of stranding on the shoals of fanaticism." Why was this eighteen-year-old describing her religious life in terms of a shipwreck? Was she really toying with a skepticism that, as everyone would have warned her, would lead to atheism? What kind of coherence would life have then?

She was, she admitted, looking for a safe harbor. She seemed to know what it would look like: "I wish I could find some religion in which my heart and understanding could unite," she wrote to her brother; "that amidst the darkest clouds of this life I might ever be cheered with the mild halo of religious consolation."[51]

Whatever combination of dark clouds, exultant independence, young love, and religious doubt characterized her time in Gardiner, it did not keep her there. Despite her early happiness, she stayed only a year. Perhaps it was just that a better opportunity beckoned. By now Convers had taken a parish in Watertown, an elegant Massachusetts town just west of Cambridge. As he settled into his new parish duties, he decided to invite his sister to join him there. She probably did not need to be asked twice. To have access to her brother's mind every day and, perhaps as important, to have access to his *books*: perhaps it sounded too much like Swedenborg's heaven to resist. Maybe they could re-create their little world. By late summer 1821, she had left Maine and taken up residence in Watertown.

Not long after moving in with her brother, Lydia Francis made a strange decision. She decided to be baptized. She had probably, as an infant, been christened in her parents' church, no doubt by the Reverend Osgood with his shining white hair. But now, apparently, she wanted to make her own spiritual statement. Even stranger: she wanted to be baptized in her old Medford church. Her father no longer lived there; her associations with Medford were, by her own description, dark and gloomy. But somehow she wanted to make her stand in its familiar sanctuary. Had she become frightened by her own religious curiosity? Had her ship indeed needed a quick and ready harbor? She was, she later admitted, "in search of a religion" at the time; she wanted to try "the ordinances"— traditional religious rituals like baptism and communion—to "ascertain whether they would help my spiritual growth."[52] Maybe in structure there would be peace.

But the nineteen-year-old Lydia Francis did not just want to be spiritually reborn: she wanted to be renamed. She no longer wanted to be Lydia Francis: she wanted to be Lydia *Maria* Francis. So she took this second name as a part of her baptism. As was common practice in the nineteenth century, she pronounced her new name "Mariah." Why Maria? She never says. But she did not just add it as a middle name: she wanted to use it. "My name is *Maria*," she wrote to a new acquaintance. Friends and family acquiesced and made the change—who knows how reluctantly and with what sighs of resignation at this new evidence of her independent streak.[53] As she stood before the congregation and heard Reverend Osgood speak her new name for the first time, did she feel a new self emerging? This too she never says. If Convers was there, he probably shifted uncomfortably in his pew, chafing under the Calvinist liturgy that he was, as a Unitarian minister, committed to opposing. If her father was there, he was probably puzzled but pleased. Maybe his wayward daughter—whatever he now had to call her—had found her way back home.

If this was anyone's hope, it was soon disappointed. Not a year later, the woman now known as Maria Francis had done what she had assured her brother she would not do: she had become a Swedenborgian. What had happened to push her away from the rocks of skepticism and onto the shoals of Swedenborgianism? It may, indirectly, have been Convers's fault: it may have been through him that she encountered Sampson Reed, one of his Harvard contemporaries. Reed had discovered Swedenborg through a fellow student who, intrigued by rumors about the forbidden author, had searched for his writings in Harvard's library, only to find them hidden in a dusty storage room along with a stuffed crocodile.[54]

Reed soon become a convert. In a much-circulated address in 1821, he put Swedenborg's ideas into language that would have gone straight to Maria Francis's heart. "Because God is love, nature exists," he claimed: "because God is love, the Bible is poetry." "The laws of the mind are in themselves as fixed and perfect as the laws of matter," he wrote five years later: "Eternity is to the mind what time is to nature." "Truth, all truth, is practical," he also promised. In other words, knowing the truth would *change* you: "Whether its effect be directly to change the conduct, or it simply leave an impression on the heart," he reiterated, "[truth] is in the strictest sense practical." Truth was also allied with beauty and science: "The true poetic spirit, so far from misleading any, is the strongest bulwark against deception," Reed wrote. "It is the soul of science."[55] It was an intoxicating mix.

Becoming a Swedenborgian was not quite like joining a cult, but it was close. Reed and other converts were forbidden to become ministers or start schools for fear of their heretical influence. No doubt Convers tried to reason with Maria. What would joining such a movement mean for her teaching career, assuming she wanted one? What would it do to her marriage prospects? What, he might have wondered, would his sister's unorthodox tendencies mean for his own reputation as a newly ordained minister?

If he indeed tried to dissuade Maria from going where her heart and mind led her, he failed. It was not the first time, and it would not be the last. She knew what she believed, and she would follow that belief regardless of its consequences. Decades later, she remembered how heady this period was. "I was young then," she wrote; "and all [Swedenborg] said seemed to me a direct revelation to his soul, from the angels." "I then '*experienced religion*,'" she recalled, "and for a long time lived in a mansion of glories." It felt, she remembered, like falling in love for the first time.[56]

She doesn't say exactly when this faith, too, began to crumble. It did seem increasingly implausible that Swedenborg's revelations could unlock *every* biblical mystery. "By degrees, I was constrained to admit that the golden key opened the way to *nothing*; though it turned smoothly in the lock, and was beautiful to look upon," she later wrote. But when she looked back at her time as a Swedenborgian, it was always with longing. If only she could recover "the un-doubting faith, the poetic rapture of spiritual insight, which I *then* enjoyed," she mourned later in life: "That church is my mother, and I would fain die in her arms, after all my wanderings." She knew the hope was in vain. "It cannot be," she concluded. "It was a state of childhood, and childhood *will* pass away."[57]

But many of her Swedenborgian convictions never left her. Until the end of her life, she remained convinced that the "natural world has its prototype in the *spiritual* world, from which it derives its existence." "Man, being a microcosm [of the universe]" she believed, "is connected with all above him, and all below him." Even as, decades later, she watched her country pitch into a civil war, she retained faith that there was a universal spiritual force progressing through both the spiritual and the natural world. She never lost her sense that life was a mystery to which humans had yet to find the key. She continued to hope that heaven would be a brighter reality where "only those are together whose states of mind and heart are similar."[58]

Her attraction to Swedenborg's theories led her to read Plato, and then to explore other religions. Her sense of wonder, mystery, and confusion fueled a lifelong desire, sometimes almost a desperation, to know *what it all meant*. What was the structure of the world? What kind of agency did humans have, and what kinds of responsibilities? What was justice, divine or otherwise? How were beauty and truth related, and how did one achieve either? She was hooked on the questions. But she never officially joined a church again.

* * *

Living with Convers meant being plunged into the social world of Harvard. Watertown's proximity to Cambridge made it relatively easy for his young, learned friends to visit. His parlor provided a perfect setting for several of them, including Ralph Waldo Emerson, to gather and discuss the new ideas of the day. In such a setting, a younger sister could come in handy. She could serve the men their drinks, or perhaps their dinner. That she did not always enjoy this role is clear: "We have just bid good night to a couple of the *moralizing* sons of Harvard," she complained in a letter to her sister in Maine, "and for whom, dreadful to relate, we have had to prepare a dinner, and perform the honours of the table." Still, it gave her the opportunity to hear them discuss Kant, or the latest theological controversy, or the upcoming election.[59] Did any of them remember her from her precocious letters? Did they want to know if she had read more Shakespeare, or if she still preferred

Homer to Milton? Did they ask whether she still disputed Milton's claim that a woman's happiness was to know nothing but her husband's law?

Even if Convers and his younger sister managed to re-create their little world, it was soon enough disrupted by the arrival of his wife. In 1822, he married the daughter of a respected minister from another town. His Watertown congregation bought the new couple a graceful brick parsonage just down the hill from the church, overlooking the Charles River. In a gossipy letter to her sister, Maria recounted weeks spent preparing the house for her brother's new bride: painting floors, filling feather beds, and stocking cabinets in preparation for the big day. In the end, the wedding had gone well. Their working-class father had known how to flatter his new daughter-in-law's erudite father.[60] He had behaved pretty much all right.

* * *

In 1824, Maria Francis had been living with her brother for three years. She had tried a few religions; she had socialized with intellectuals; she had made diligent use of her brother's growing library, poring over his collection of classical plays, English poetry, American history, and German philosophy. Whatever her remaining attachment to the Swedenborgian church, she found time to attend her brother's Unitarian services too. On one particular Sunday that spring, she returned to the parsonage after the first service of the day. She had listened to her brother preach and probably watched him greet his parishioners at the door as they filed out in their Sunday best. Maybe there had been a midday meal. There would be another service later in the afternoon.

To pass the time, Maria decided to read a recent issue of a literary journal called the *North American Review*. In it was an article assessing a new poem by two American authors, James Wallis Eastburn and Robert Charles Sands. The poem was called *Yamoyden, a Tale of the Wars of King Philip*. It portrayed in wrenching detail the apocalyptic conflict that had raged between New England settlers and Native Americans more than a century before. The reviewer quoted some of the poem's more powerful passages with approval, calling them "forcible and poetical."[61] But he was not entirely impressed. He found the poetry uneven and the poem's suggestion that Europeans were mostly to blame for the conflict objectionable. He did, however, grant the authors this much: they had shown the way out of one of the many conundrums facing the still newly independent United States. Americans had gotten out from under the British politically. But would they ever be able to declare independence *culturally*? Or were they doomed to a perpetual imitation of England's playwrights and novelists, always aspiring but never original?

How was a new country to build a new literature? All the ingredients were there in *Yamoyden*, this reviewer said: all you had to do was take your cue from Sir Walter Scott. The United States had a landscape to rival Scotland's. It also had, in its origins, a conflict with all the tragic potential an author could want: the struggle of European civilization against the inhabitants of the land it was determined to conquer. "Whoever in this country first attains the rank of a first rate writer of fiction . . . will lay his scene here," the reviewer declared. "The wide field is ripe for the harvest, and scarce a sickle has yet touched it."[62]

When she recalled this moment decades later, Maria Francis didn't even remember wondering if she could rise to this challenge. Instead, she just did it. The first chapter of a novel poured out of her mind and onto whatever paper was at hand in a matter of hours. Pen scratching furiously, she suddenly called to life a spunky young heroine named Mary Conant. This imagined Mary was the daughter of one of America's earliest European settlers; her black eyes flashed in rebellion against her father's Calvinist severity and softened at the sight of a young Englishman named Charles Brown. By the end of the chapter, Mary has sneaked out of bed and into the woods, used a pocketknife to draw her own blood and cast a spell there, and set in motion a love triangle between her, Charles, and a Native American warrior named Hobomok.

Before Maria Francis knew it, the church bell was ringing to gather Watertown's faithful for the day's second service. She must have looked up at the time, shocked, then hurriedly put away the papers and rushed up the small hill from the parsonage to the church.[63] Perhaps she slid into the pew flushed and breathless, earning reproving glances from other parishioners. Whatever the topic of Reverend Francis's second sermon, his younger sister probably had a hard time focusing.

"Maria did you *really* write this?" she remembered Convers wanting to know when she showed him her chapter. "Do you *mean* what you say, that it is entirely your own?" In fact, Maria had likely taken her cue from the work under review, which also featured an illicit romance between a white woman and a Native American.[64] The idea had not, in fact, been entirely original. But in the six weeks following, Maria bent the narrative in a direction that was indeed all her own.

The plot did not become less scandalous as it developed. In subsequent chapters, Maria imagined Mary Conant becoming wrongly convinced that her beloved Charles had died, blaming her father for his death, and taking her revenge by running away with Hobomok and becoming his wife. She imagined Mary's furious father disowning her, horrified that his daughter would degrade herself in the arms of a heathen. She imagined Mary bearing Hobomok's child, learning to be content with her life among his people, and in the end coming to love him.[65] But when Charles reappears unharmed, Hobomok voluntarily cedes his right to Mary and disappears, never to see her or his child again. In other words, the novel *Hobomok* included an insubordinate daughter, an indictment of a Puritan patriarch, interracial sex, a mixed-race child, and a kind of divorce. How many taboos could one book break?

More subtly, *Hobomok* broke another convention. When early American literature, such as it was, dealt with the native peoples the country was quickly displacing, there was usually a bloody but exultant ending. James Fenimore Cooper had yet to write *The Last of the Mohicans*, but he and others had already set its violent, conquering tone in earlier novels.[66] The message of such literature was clear: America's European settlers would triumph by overwhelming force, subjecting the people it called savages to brutal extinction. Hobomok, by contrast, makes a graceful and even gracious exit, ceding the woman he loves to the white man's prior claim. But his love for her is depicted as plausible and sincere, and her feelings for him are evidently real. Perhaps, Maria's plot suggested, the mixing of the races was not as unthinkable as the bigoted, bitter Calvinists in her novel believed.

But even if it was gentler, Maria's message to her readers about Native Americans was in the end not that different. It simply predicted another kind of extinction. Hobomok gives up his rights to his son, releasing him into a world of European refinement and education. Native peoples, his gesture suggested, were noble and resigned. They did not have to be overcome with force. When confronted by white settlers' supposed superiority, they would quietly slip away. This prediction Maria Francis had not so far doubted. As for Hobomok's son, renamed Charles after his stepfather: his creator gave him the most promising American future she could muster. She sent him to Harvard.[67]

Maria Francis continued to claim, however plausibly, that she had never intended to write a novel. But now she had. The next question was what to do with it. The obvious answer—publish it—entailed significant obstacles. The American publishing market barely existed: most authors simply printed books at their own expense and hoped to recoup their investment in sales. But, showing a combination of confidence and tenacity that would soon propel her onto the national stage, Maria Francis wanted to try. Where did she acquire the $450 needed to print a thousand copies? Whom did she convince that they would sell out at seventy-five cents each?[68] It's hard to imagine that it was her father. He had been skeptical enough about his daughter's reading novels: now she wanted to write one? A story about a dour Calvinist father who almost ruins his daughter's life? Unlikely. Perhaps it was Convers. Did the newlywed minister have to persuade his wife to lend this sizable sum to his inexplicably ambitious sister? Whatever the facts: somehow she got the money, and the exhilarating process of seeing her words take shape on the printed page began.

There was, of course, one more taboo to reckon with before the book went to print. *Hobomok*'s author was a woman. Female American authors existed, but they were rare. It was not clear what becoming one would mean for her reputation or her future. So as the book went to print, she needed to make a decision. Whom should she name as the book's author? It was not unusual at the time for writers to remain anonymous. That was probably the best option. So when *Hobomok: A Tale of Early Times* appeared in 1824, its author placed three simple words where her name could have been: "By an American." It was a phrase as full of mystery and promise as the country its author claimed as her own.

It would be wrong to say the book was a best seller. It was more complicated than that. *Hobomok* sold relatively well, but its first reviewer's praise was decidedly mixed. "This tale displays considerable talent," it began: "The author has an eye for the beautiful and sublime of external nature, and a heart for the tender and generous traits of the human character." As Maria read this sentence, her heart must have leaped for joy. But the reviewer was not finished. The novel's attempt to blend the historical and fictional was not convincing: the author "would have succeeded better had he made it entirely a work of fancy." This was no doubt disappointing, but at least Maria had the comfort of knowing that she had, so far, succeeded in in hiding her gender. But the reviewer had saved his harshest criticism for the end. After describing the book's main protagonist as a "high born and delicate female" who becomes the wife of an Indian chief and mother to a "semisavage," he judged the book's plot "not only unnatural, but revolting, we conceive, to every feeling of delicacy in man or woman."[69]

Unnatural and revolting. It would be hard to recover from that. Well, becoming an author had been an improbable idea to begin with. Perhaps she should just resign herself to teaching. But she was feeling stubborn and ambitious. She knew the book was good, but she knew that was not enough. She needed help, and she was motivated enough to ask for it. This involved taking advantage of something that, even in early nineteenth-century America, was already a force to be reckoned with: a Harvard connection.

Professor George Ticknor was one of Harvard's established luminaries. As a young man, he had studied literature in Europe, returning to Boston with the goal of bringing the best educational practices back to his native country. Maria had already met him through her brother, perhaps while serving one of the meals she so dreaded. Meeting George Ticknor was a little like meeting American royalty. He had spent time with everybody who was anybody in both Europe and America. He could regale his listeners with stories of staying with Jefferson in Monticello and conversing with Goethe in Germany. He and his wife were famous for the dinner parties and balls they hosted at their elegant mansion. Such was his social influence that some called Boston "Ticknorville" and his wife the closest thing the city had to a queen.[70] There was no more powerful character in America's infant literary scene: a positive word from him and an author would soar.

So she wrote to him. The letter is a masterful combination of aspiration, tact, and flattery. Someone had told her, she recounted, that he had praised her book. This had made her ecstatic. "There is nothing," she assured him, like "a soul excited by praise, and expanding over its own glorious visions." But her book was not selling very well. Would he, for the sake of a heart beating with "pure, youthful ambition," praise it just a little more? Preferably in public? "Your influence in the literary and fashionable world is very great," she acknowledged, "and a few words timely spoken by you . . . would induce many to purchase, who would otherwise regard the subject with a very natural indifference." How to excuse such naked aspiration? "I am aware that it is almost unpardonable to obtrude myself upon you," she admitted, "but I am certain it will afford you some pleasure to revive the hopes of a young and disappointed author."[71] And please, she implied in the letter's conclusion, say nothing about this to my brother.

George Ticknor was no fool. He would have known when he was being flattered. But perhaps the letter amused him. Perhaps he appreciated its candid assessment of his power and admired its author's sheer audacity. Perhaps his mind went a little further. Miss Francis was not just a prodigy; she was a curiosity. The literary worlds of Boston and Cambridge were always looking for fresh perspectives: sometimes the less polished, the better. It could be entertaining to have Convers Francis's little sister around.

Whatever his thoughts, Ticknor's actions were decisive. Soon another review of *Hobomok* appeared, probably on his instigation, and it was more positive. True, it still declared the plot to be "in very bad taste, to say the least." It also, however, suggested that the book's "animated descriptions of scenes and persons, its agreeable style, and the acquaintance with the history and spirit of the times which it evinces, have not received the credit due to them." But, the reviewer predicted, they would. *Hobomok*, he concluded, would "stand the test of repeated readings, and it will obtain them."[72] The book's sales improved. George Ticknor, it seems, had spoken.

2

A Love Not Ashamed
of Economy

Two portraits exist of Miss L. Maria Francis as she entered her
mid-twenties. The first is in words. Lucy Osgood, daughter of
Maria's childhood minister, later remembered the "L. M. Francis of 1826" as a "youthful schoolmistress of Watertown, making
baskets for May day; brushing the morning dew, & writing poetical compliments to accompany her flowers," embodying the
"same aspirations after good, the same impatience of wrong, the
same independence, originality & honesty" as she had always had.
Romantic, idealistic, impatient, independent: that all sounds
right. The second portrait is on canvas. An aspiring young artist
named Francis Alexander had, also in 1826, asked her to sit for
him. When the painting was finished, she seemed both pleased
and embarrassed. "The artist has *too much* genius," she worried
to her sister: "He wanted to make a Sappho of me, and to pour
over my very ugly face the full tide of inspiration." He was, she
feared, not the only one exaggerating her virtues. In fact, she confessed to her sister, "I have been too much caressed of late by a
flattering world." The praise, she hastened to add in case her sister was worried, was not going to her head. "The world," she de-
murred, "seldom smiled so graciously on one so little worthy of its
notice."[1]

Worthy or not, the world was indeed noticing both her and her
portrait. "I saw . . . at Alexander's room a portrait of Miss Francis,"

Fig. 4. Lydia Maria Francis, age twenty-two. Collection of the Massachusetts Historical Society.

young Mary Peabody wrote to a friend that same year. "I can compare the expression on her face to nothing but a tiger." Most likely this was not meant as a compliment. Miss Peabody was also not convinced that the artist, in giving Miss Francis this expression, had actually captured anything about its owner. "I think she must have 'called up a look' that minute," she mused, "for I never heard that she looked fierce."[2]

Well, she may not have looked fierce, but she was.

How to account for all this attention? What did she mean that the world was smiling on her? In short, Maria Francis's daring appeal to George Ticknor had succeeded beyond all her expectations. After *Hobomok*'s second review, others had quickly followed, as had the discovery of facts about its author's identity. "I should think more highly of the talent of the woman who could write 'Hobomok,'" one admirer gushed, "'than of any other American woman who has ever written, though to be sure it has its faults." "Say nothing of its faults," wrote another; "they are the faults of genius, and the beauties weigh them down." Soon the acclaim was near unanimous: everybody, one chronicler recalled, "felt the genius and power of the writer." Flattering letters began arriving from across the country, as did invitations to Boston's most exclusive addresses. Miss Francis had become, one observer reported, "almost a fashionable lion."[3] Whether tiger or lion, one thing was certain: Professor Ticknor's support had had its effect, and she was launched.

Early indications were that Ticknor's confidence had not been misplaced. By the end of 1824, in addition to collecting these accolades for *Hobomok*, Maria Francis had published another book. This time it was an anthology of writings for children called *Evenings in New England*. Apparently she had taken her experience minding her sister's children, combined it with what she had learned as a teacher, and put the results into a book. But *Evenings* was more than this: it was, like *Hobomok*, an attempt to answer a question about her country's future. Anthologies for children existed, but they were British: Didn't American children need one of their own?[4] In answering that question, Maria Francis sought to answer others: What kind of virtues did the new country need? What kind of stories should it allow to shape its children? What, in short, should American children be like?

She answered these questions by populating her book's pages with both glorious heroes of the Revolution and simple, honest characters from Maine. These stories guaranteed young readers that decency, ingenuity, and integrity were their American birthright, characteristic of every American from President Washington to the local farmer. *Evenings* also debuted a figure not coincidentally named Aunt Maria: a kindly and omniscient relation who could answer all her nephew Robert's questions—from what "personification" meant to how sugar is made from sugarcane—but only after he'd finished his chores. There were also facts: lessons about plants, a description of pearls, an explanation of rainbows. The natural science lessons came with a moral too: a rainbow should always remind us, Aunt Maria stipulated, that everyone has at least seven good qualities that can be focused into light.[5] The overall message was clear: American children should be useful, prudent, honest, and fair. They should treasure the ideals of freedom and equality they had inherited. Above all, they should work hard. And always, virtue would have its sure reward.

Evenings in New England, too, was ostensibly anonymous. But this time the author did not bother to hide her gender. In place of an author its title page read "By an American Lady." It earned Maria Francis "unqualified approbation," she reported to her sister.[6] Even today, it still feels very marketable.

But if American children were to be schooled in basic lessons of fairness, honesty, hard work, and compassion, some awkward facts needed explaining. To be an American child, the book made clear, required absorbing truths that would jar any child's sense of justice: that in the interests of this new country's future, Black humans were being enslaved and Native Americans were being forced to leave. How to explain this to children who were also being told that their country was founded on principles of freedom and equality? Maybe, during her time in Norridgewock, the Preston children had asked her just such questions. Maybe, to her embarrassment, she had found no good answers. She would not make that mistake again. By page 3 of *Evenings in New England*, she had named both issues. In subsequent chapters she confronted them head-on.

In a chapter titled "Indian Tribes," imaginary Robert asks his Aunt Maria a simple question: Where had all the Indians gone? Aunt Maria gives a sober reply: they had indeed transitioned from being a "numerous, brave, and generous people" to being almost extinct. "What right did we have to take away their lands?" Robert wants to know. We didn't take them, his aunt replies. "In most instances" they sold their land willingly: at the same time, she admits, "it is to be feared that they are too often cruelly imposed upon." Robert keeps up his interrogation. Why would America's president allow such cruelty? Well, Aunt Maria suggests, the president means well, but sometimes his subordinates behave badly. This bad behavior, she regretted, had often produced violent results. "Exasperated by these insults, the injured tribe will often go to war with our people, while we, ignorant of what they suffer, complain of them as a nation in whom we can put no trust." It was true that Native warriors were sometimes called bloodthirsty, Aunt Maria conceded to her nephew: but they were, quite simply, fighting in self-defense. "How I wish something could be done to make all the Indians as happy and prosperous as we are," Robert concludes. "It is indeed desirable," agrees Aunt Maria, but probably not worth much effort: "It is probable that in the course of a few hundred years, they will cease to exist as a distinct people."[7]

So much for those who were being forced to leave. As to those who had been forced to arrive, Maria Francis's young readers would have found one answer in a story ominously titled "The Little Master and His Slave."[8] Here again is Robert, this time venting his youthful fury on the South. "It seems to me," he declares to his aunt, that "the people at the southward must be very cruel, or they would not keep slaves as they do." This outburst earns him a stern rebuke. "Your opinion is very unjust, my child," Aunt Maria begins. True, slavery is an "indelible stain" on the country. "But it is not right to conclude that our southern brethren have not as good feelings as ourselves"; in fact, she informs him, "no part of our country is more rich in overflowing kindness and genuine hospitality" than the South.

To illustrate her point, Aunt Maria recounts a story about little Ned, an incorrigibly unruly slave boy whose misbehavior, by the author's telling, had finally earned him the whipping he deserved. But just as he is tied to a tree and the overseer raises his arm to strike the first blow, the master's son Edward, frantic with sympathy, throws himself between the Black boy's naked back and the whip. The overseer is too enraged to stop himself; Edward is saved from his own whipping only by his father's sudden arrival. When his father, surveying this disorderly scene, declares that Ned is a hopeless case and must be sold, Edward pleads to be allowed to keep him and reform him. His wish is granted; the reformation succeeds; the grateful Ned grows up to be Edward's most trusted servant.

Robert is impressed but not convinced. Despite this touching denouement, he confesses to Aunt Maria, "I cannot bear the idea of keeping slaves." "I am very glad you cannot," Aunt Maria commends him. She reiterates that slavery is the "greatest evil that we have to complain of in this happy country." But at this point in her life, the story's author was not willing to conclude that great evils demanded immediate solutions. "I have already told you, that it is dangerous to cure some kinds of sickness too suddenly," she tells her nephew: "It is so with slavery." It was better to wait and, in the meantime, never to forget "that our Southern brethren have an abundance of kind and generous feeling." Surely, since there "is so much to admire and love in their characters," they would soon free all their slaves themselves. Mollified, young Robert is, by the next page, willing to move on to learning about astronomy, which he pronounces "the most delightful study in the world."[9]

George Ticknor was a doting and affectionate father.[10] If he read this story to his children as he continued to assess Maria Francis's literary potential, he probably nodded with approval. That was about right. Slavery was unfortunate—distasteful, even—but probably the slaves who endured the pitiless punishments evoked in little Ned's tale deserved it. And probably most others were, like other slaves that appear in the story, cherished and coddled by families that provided for their every need. Ticknor was also, as we will see, an unapologetic believer that the African race was inferior and that slavery was their natural condition. But whatever the facts about the illness of slavery, it was imperative not to cure it too quickly. The health of the country depended on it.

Based on his assessment of the fascinating Miss Francis's literary output to date, Ticknor had taken her on as a kind of protégée. Her star continued to rise. "Praises and invitations have poured in upon me, beyond my utmost hopes," she wrote to her sister. There had been gifts, too: "Books, rings, pictures, trinkets, and an elegant India comb, 11$." As if to confirm Ticknor's faith in her, she quickly wrote a second novel. It was called *The Rebels, or Boston before the Revolution*. She dedicated it to Ticknor, but only after asking his permission.[11]

*   *   *

And so, through Ticknor, Maria Francis won passage into Boston's famous drawing rooms where the great and good—politicians, professors, businessmen, philanthropists, and their wives—met in rooms with high ceilings, heavy curtains, and oil paintings above the mantelpieces. She was a triple curiosity to them: from working-class origins, fresh from the woods of Maine, and a female author with a sharp wit. For a time, it seems that fitting herself to this world became her goal. The year 1826 found her teaching school in Watertown and living in a genteel boardinghouse at the foot of Boston's fashionable Beacon Hill that doubled as a kind of finishing school. Here she could learn French as well as dancing and drawing; she could also get to know other young adults in the social class she now apparently aspired to join. A sure sign of her arrival in these social spheres was her invitation to Boston's party of the century: a gala, sponsored by the governor of Massachusetts, to honor the Marquis de Lafayette, the French hero of the American Revolution. She was introduced to him; he kissed her hand; she vowed never to wash it off.[12]

Sometimes, after returning from these heady evenings of high culture, she took notes on the conversations she had witnessed. At one, a Mr. Manning held forth about exotic plants of Mexico. Maria's brother Convers, also present, told an amusing story about someone's claiming he would rather marry his Greek grammar textbook than Hannah Adams, Medford's notorious female historian. A Mr. Grater, after regaling the group with stories about strange fashions in Germany, made a pun that worked in three languages. "I [also] made a pun," Maria recorded in her journal, "but nobody heard it."[13]

Her new fame also brought her male admirers. One was Francis Alexander, the artist whose portrait of her had made such a fierce impression on Miss Peabody. "Do not smile!" Maria warned her sister after describing him as "young, unmarried,—and my *especial* friend." However especial he was, nothing serious came of their relationship. Another admirer was Nathaniel Parker Willis. Willis was clever and vain, an aspiring writer and unapologetic social climber. One contemporary remembers trying to decide if he was a fop, a dandy, or simply a coxcomb. He was the sort of man who could flick lilacs off of bushes with his silver-plated riding whip as he walked down a Cambridge street. He and the fascinating Miss Francis "struck up quite an intimacy," she later remembered. They would walk together on the Boston Common, he "in tall white hat, buff vest, and new light-colored French gloves," "looking down from his slender height upon my slender shortness." Decades later, long after he had declared her writing unfit for "delicate ears" and she had dismissed his fiction as "miserably trashy," their lives would intersect in ways neither could imagine: when she would help his housekeeper, a woman who had escaped enslavement, publish one of the most important slave narratives in American history.[14]

But for now, Maria Francis continued trying to negotiate her new social world. Occasionally someone would find a way to remind her that her father was just a baker. Other times she would mention it herself, only—later, quietly—to be advised not to. She received other kinds of advice too. "When I published my first book," she re-

Fig. 5. Nathaniel Parker Willis, one of Lydia Francis's early admirers. Their paths would cross in an unexpected way later in life. © The Trustees of the British Museum.

membered, "I was gravely warned by some of my female acquaintances that no woman could expect to be regarded as a lady after she had written a book." It would take only a few decades for this advice to sound ridiculous. By midcentury, Nathaniel Hawthorne was complaining about the "damned mob of scribbling women" that were outselling him.[15] But for now a serious female novelist was still essentially unthinkable. And, worse, she would likely be unmarriageable.

As she moved through some of the most genteel parlors in America's self-proclaimed City on a Hill, she probably heard a wide range of arguments about the news of the day. President John

Quincy Adams, a Massachusetts native, was mired in a confrontation with the governor of Georgia about the rights of Creek Indians to keep their native lands. Slavery was a factor here too: Georgians wanted the Creek banished in part because, having depleted their soil with too many crops of cotton, they needed more land. The Creek resisted; another Indian war loomed. Maria never recorded conversations she heard on this topic, but the range of opinions was probably limited. To most powerful white men of the time, Native Americans, as one historian has put it, "were deemed an obstacle to progress, to be handled roughly or decently, depending on one's principles."[16] Probably some within her hearing openly advocated extermination—the faster and more ruthless the better. Perhaps others, considering themselves more compassionate and progressive, argued instead that they should simply be moved west. I wonder whether Maria tried to join these conversations. She had opinions about Native Americans and probably more actual experience with them than most Bostonians. But however these conversations went, they likely had a predictable outcome. The Indians would have to go. Perhaps this was regrettable, but, as Aunt Maria assured Robert, it was probably inevitable.

It was not all sweetness and light at the top of the social world. "You must not think, dear sister," she wrote to Mary in Maine, "that I have not had vexations and afflictions. Just in proportion to my conspicuousness, I have had enemies, as well as friends,-and I have deserved them both." But some of the friendships she was forming would last her whole life. Abigail May, one day to be the mother of Louisa May Alcott, was one of them. Another was Louisa Gilman, a delicate brunette whose fiancé, Ellis Gray Loring, descended from one of America's oldest and richest families. Loring was already practicing law. He and Maria quickly forged an ardent friendship based on a shared love of ideas, art, and books. Soon she was as eager to see him as she was to see Louisa.[17]

Another exhilarating friendship was with Margaret Fuller, a woman several years Maria's junior but altogether her intellectual peer. Fuller had been given a wide-ranging education by her father. She was on her way to becoming one of the United States'

Fig. 6. Ellis Gray Loring. Collection of the Massachusetts Historical Society.

best-known female writers and, as a close friend of Ralph Waldo Emerson, a founder of the Transcendentalist movement. The two women decided to study together. Their chosen subjects were John Locke, the English philosopher whose empiricism was influencing the development of Unitarianism, and Germaine de Staël. Staël was a French author whose role in the French Revolution provided a thrilling view of women's political potential and whose writing on German philosophy was shaping the American literary scene. "I received your very characteristic note with great pleasure," Maria wrote to Fuller as their friendship deepened. "Like you, it was full of thought, raciness, originality, and queerness; and like you it excited the pleasantest emotions in my heart." Fuller re-

Fig. 7. Louisa Gilman Loring. Both Ellis and Louisa Loring were among Child's closest lifelong friends. Collection of the Massachusetts Historical Society.

ciprocated the admiration. "Her conversation is charming," she wrote of her study partner: "she brings all her powers to bear upon it; her style is varied, and she has a very pleasant and spirited way of thinking."[18]

With Ticknor's patronage also came contacts with publishers. Miss Francis's talents were obvious, and the idea of an "American Lady" helping to shape America's next generation was intriguing. Why not turn something like *Evenings in New England* into a periodical for children? Soon not one but two publishers had proposed it.[19] Maria hesitated. Was she sure she wanted a reputation as a children's author and not as the serious novelist she felt herself, at her core, to be? But the idea of a periodical, besides presenting an interesting challenge, promised something even more attractive: a steady income. She didn't record the process of putting together this periodical, how she decided what content to include, what balance of fact and fiction to strike, which scenes should be illustrated, what kind of type should be used. But in September 1826, the first issue of the *Juvenile Miscellany* appeared. It was a small, compact volume of about a hundred pages. She had written much of the content, but she had also gathered the best children's material she could find from other sources. She had marshaled other authors to contribute as well.

The *Miscellany* had unabashedly moral aims. "I seldom meet a little girl, even in the crowded streets of Boston," she wrote on the first page, "without thinking with anxious tenderness, concerning her education, her temper, and her principles." In case readers thought this a bit much, the young editor repeated herself: "Yes, *principles*! Children can act from good principle, as well as gentlemen and ladies." In the service of cultivating said principles, there were again stories extolling honesty, integrity, and independence. But there was also intrigue and fun. In the *Miscellany*'s pages, American children could find stories of foundlings reunited with parents, of faithful dogs and forbearing cats, and even one about a pig in a wheelbarrow. There were fanciful letters "written" by winter to summer, and from the letter *H* to the letter *K*. There was also a wealth of facts that any child could learn and then proudly recite: that Roger Bacon had invented gunpowder, that Dutch children had helped develop the first telescope, and that cocoa most definitely does not come from coconut trees. Aunt Maria was back, too, answering her nephew's questions about coral reefs in one issue and about oceans in the next. There were beautiful illustrations, woodcuts of Russian reindeer pulling sleighs and children gathered in a miniature *Pietà* around a dead robin. Perhaps best of all, there were the riddles at the end. Why was London like the let-

THE

JUVENILE MISCELLANY.

" The child is father of the man ;
And I could wish my days to be
Bound each to each by natural piety."
WORDSWORTH.

—NEW SERIES—

VOL. III.

BOSTON :
PUBLISHED BY PUTNAM & HUNT.

1829.

Fig. 8. Front cover of Volume III of *The Juvenile Miscellany*, which Child edited between 1826 and 1834. Courtesy of the David Ruggles Center for History and Education.

ter *E*? When is a door not a door? The *Miscellany*'s readers would have to wait for the next issue to find out.[20]

The *Juvenile Miscellany* was a sensation. "No child who read the *Juvenile Miscellany* . . . will ever forget the excitement that the appearance of each number caused," one reader remembered decades later. "I know what that shout means among the children," wrote an author from South Carolina: "The Miscellany has come." Far into their adulthood, readers would still write fan mail to its editor: "I don't know whether I ever told you with what delight I fed on your little Juvenile Miscellany long ago," wrote one; the *Miscellany* had been "the delight of my childish heart," enthused another. By the time New Year 1827 dawned, it had 850 subscriptions with more coming in every day.[21]

We might expect that, in modeling the *Juvenile Miscellany* on *Evenings in New England*, its editor would continue to educate her young readers about the two moral evils at their country's foundation. Concerning Native Americans, this proved true. The *Miscellany* regularly included stories that encouraged sympathy for and identification with Indians. They were members of a noble race that had been egregiously wronged, its editor urged. Good Indian boys and girls were just as hardworking and honest as their white counterparts.

But about slavery the *Miscellany* was silent: there were no stories, no dialogues, no poems or essays to remind young readers of what life was like for enslaved children in the South. The only evidence that slavery existed was in a section titled "Extracts from a Journal" in which a traveler, signing his name only "F.," describes seeing slaves on a trip to Baltimore. "It cannot be too much regretted that such a thing as slavery exists," the traveler admits, "but so far as concerns the actual situation of slaves at the South, I think New England prejudices have been more violent and unreasonable."[22] It was as if the traveler—who may, in fact, have been her brother Convers—was putting the arguments for the Missouri Compromise in a nutshell. Of course slavery was unfortunate; of course decent people regretted it. But what was the real problem? It was agitators in the North whose prejudices against slavery were unreasonable. Did the *Miscellany*'s editor include this traveler's account because those agitators were growing loud enough for even children to hear?

Whatever her thoughts on these topics, Maria Francis found herself marveling at her success as 1827 began. "No young lady

in Christendom can look back upon a year of pleasanter reminiscences," she wrote to her sister. "Friends kind, generous, and attentive, where I least expected it. Fortune smiling beyond my utmost hopes." She was now in Watertown again, living with Convers
and his wife and teaching school. Her prestigious Boston connections held. "The rich and fashionable people, who I thought would
consign me to oblivion as soon as I left Boston, and the first nov-
elty had worn off, continue as attentive as if I were their equal," she
marveled. The "as if" was telling. "Valuable gifts, jewels, beautiful
dresses pour in upon me, invitations beyond acceptance, admiring letters from all parts of the country."[23] Could she possibly still
be the same person she had been in the bakery in Medford or the
forests of Maine?

*　*　*

Despite the *Miscellany*'s success, Maria Francis still longed to be
taken seriously as a novelist. At least one person was doing that.
A new newspaper called the *Massachusetts Journal* had recently
published a glowing review of both her novels. "It has been said
that personal beauty is a good letter of recommendation," the reviewer opined. "We will add that a work, whose title page discloses
the fact that the author has previously written a tale so beautiful as
'Hobomok,' needs no letter of recommendation from anyone."[24] It
was a strange sentence. The intent was clearly to praise something,
but what? What exactly was being complimented for its personal
beauty here, *Rebels* or *Hobomok*? Or perhaps their author? Perhaps
it was all three. The reviewer was a man named David Lee Child.

Maria Francis and David Child had been introduced to each
other at Convers's Watertown parsonage in December 1824. Maria
was clearly intrigued. "Mr. Child," she wrote in her journal, "possesses the rich fund of an intelligent traveler, without the slightest
twinge of a traveler's vanity."[25] And where had he been traveling?
Well, that was an interesting story, and one that Mr. Child was
likely all too happy to tell her.

Like the Francis siblings, David Child had grown up in mod-

Fig. 9. David Lee Child, ca. 1825. "I do not know which to admire most," Maria Francis wrote in her journal after they met, "the vigour of his understanding, or the ready sparkle of his wit." By permission of the Beaman Memorial Library.

est circumstances. He was from the central Massachusetts town of West Boylston and, like Convers, had escaped his humble beginnings by being admitted to Harvard. His impressive intellect and facility with languages had attracted the attention of Henry Dearborn, an American diplomat headed to Portugal. David had accompanied him there in 1822, embarking—or so his impoverished parents probably hoped—on a lucrative diplomatic career.

Instead, within nine months David had quit his job and joined the Spanish army. Spanish reformers had been trying to install a constitutional government; the French king Louis XVIII, fearing this insidious spread of republican ideals, had sent his armies to stop them. David rushed to the Spanish reformers' defense, a kind of Lafayette in reverse, only to be involved in a general rout that left Spain securely a monarchy and David Child without a job. He had arrived back in Boston penniless but with some very good war stories, and with his honor intact.[26]

"He is the most gallant man that has lived since the sixteenth century; and needs nothing but helmet, shield, and chain armour to make him a complete knight of chivalry," an admiring Maria Francis wrote in her diary after meeting him again. Was there some irony here, a tiny admission that David's stories sounded somewhat embellished? Perhaps. But other times her admiration for this aspiring lawyer was simply heartfelt. "I do not know which to admire most," she mused, "the vigour of his understanding, or the ready sparkle of his wit."[27] Maybe she could just admire them both.

As for the impression she made on him, it fairly leaped off the pages of his journal:

The ethereal, high-souled, high-reaching Maria! the elegant, pure, powerful-minded Maria! . . . I know of no mind with which it seems to me, my soul could hold such sweet converse as with the eloquent, susceptible, correct, & brilliant spirit which animates the pleasing beautiful form of Maria. . . . She is the only lady in Watertown, who has made any impression upon me of a serious & enduring kind, i e to say of *a tender kind.*

"Eloquent, susceptible, correct, & brilliant"—and all of that in a "pleasing beautiful form"! That sounded like love, and he knew it. "I would love her dearly," he confessed, "if the fates were not adverse to it."[28] But what could those fates be?

Most likely, the problem was finances. David was thirty years old when they met, and financial stability had so far eluded him. He had been a teacher, a diplomat, and a soldier; now he was a journalist, a lawyer, and—after winning a seat in the state legislature—a politician. Surely one of those professions would turn a profit. But until then, David seems to have felt his lack of stability keenly enough to worry that it made him at least temporarily unmarriageable. If Maria Francis, meanwhile, detected his tender feelings and wondered why they were producing no results, she said nothing about it. But after two years had gone by and his attentions still had led to nothing, she began to predict that she would never marry.[29]

The two continued to encounter each other socially. Others later remembered them as a kind of Shakespearean Beatrice and Benedick, outdoing each other in competitive banter. "She had a great deal of wit, liked to use it, and did use it upon Mr. Child," one witness later recalled. At least one maiden aunt predicted that such teasing could only lead to marriage. In the midst of this repartee, Maria Francis also probably got the sense that Mr. Child had opinions that were decidedly edgier than those of many in his generation. He had no patience with religion. He had passionately progressive views about women's equality with men that she, despite her challenges to Convers, so far did not quite share. He was also antislavery: not just "as against it as anyone else," but in the sense that he thought something should be done to end it, and soon. He was a fierce supporter of the right of Native Americans to defend themselves. He was, she later reflected, "wide awake before I was."[30] Even as his controversial views became clear, they apparently did nothing to dampen her interest. Perhaps she simply thought he was right. Meanwhile, it seems she was tiring of the social life she had been so eager to enter: of the silk dresses, silver service, and complaints about the servants. It felt so much like an aristocracy. Wasn't that what the American Revolution had been fought to end?

Finally either David's optimism or his tender feelings overcame his hesitation, and he proposed. George Ticknor's teenage nephew George Ticknor Curtis later claimed the proposal had taken place in his mother's house while he eavesdropped. If his account is to be believed, the negotiations lasted four hours while David's horse, cold and hungry, angrily kicked at the front steps.[31] If this is true, what were they talking about? What doubts was she expressing, or what promises was she extracting? Did she hesitate to give up her independence or wonder what becoming Mrs. Child would do to her literary career?

The protracted proposal may have been a fiction anyway, an account penned decades later by someone eager to share insider knowledge about the notorious couple, true or not. Maria herself recounted only a letter of proposal received and answered and her conviction that she was "happy,—happy, *beyond my own imagination*": which, this successful fiction writer admitted, "is saying much." As for her betrothed, his enthusiasm again burst off the pages of his journal. "Yesterday eve, after an ineffectual attempt to see Miss L. M. Francis, I sat down & indicted a letter, in which I told her that I loved her, & was lying at her feet. Today I received an answer, which, much as I loved & respected her, has raised still higher my opinion of her. It was favorable. I am ACCEPTED; & am too happy." To his mother, he wrote that he was engaged "to one of the brightest & best of beings . . . to one who possesses the intellect of Johnson, the goodness & learning of Lady Jane Gray; & the attraction of Aspasia." He almost forgot to mention her name. But he knew his mother would approve of it: it was her name too.[32]

It took them almost a year to marry. It seems that David wanted to get his finances in order before taking the step, a goal that proved ominously elusive. He was ambitious, idealistic, persuasive, and charming—a combination perfectly suited for racking up debts. Did his fiancée know what she was getting herself into? To some extent she did. "Your brother has been so anxious to relieve all the distress in the world, that he has done himself wrong," she wrote to his sister. "I love him the better for it," she was quick to add, "but it makes me look forward to the expenses of housekeeping with anxiety and fear."[33]

Finally they concluded that living together would be cheaper. It was not a particularly romantic reason to set a wedding date, but it would do. Maria Francis invested $1,100 of her hard-earned money to furnish a small home for them on Harvard Street in Boston. It seems to have been a lavish enough wedding: the woman now known as Maria Child breathlessly reported to her sister that she had worn "a wedding gown of India muslin trimmed with white satin." Her brother performed the ceremony. There were thirty-five pounds of cake. Their wedding gifts included silver-plated candlesticks, a study lamp, a jar of pickles, and a keg of tongues.[34]

Then David and Maria Child retreated to their modest rented home. The same George Curtis who claimed to have witnessed their engagement was an early dinner guest, together with his mother. He remembered, with some disapproval, that the new Mrs. Child had "done her own cooking." There were no servants in sight. There was also no wine, and not even coffee. "This was the beginning of the married life of Lydia Maria Child, a woman of genius," Curtis recalled, "who, in a worldly point of view, ought to have had a different lot."[35] George Curtis was only sixteen at the time; it's not clear that he would have known what kind of "lot" a "woman of genius" deserved. But his mother, George Ticknor's sister-in-law, certainly would have. She probably passed the descriptions of the Childs' humble abode right along to Ticknor and to anyone else who would listen.

As she and her beloved exchanged vows under her brother's watchful eye, Maria had given David something more than a promise of lifelong love: she had given him the rights to everything she had published. She didn't have a choice about this, and neither did he. Because of something known as the law of coverture, all a woman's property passed to her husband once she became his wife. Ellis Loring, the young lawyer by now married to Maria's friend Louisa, liked to tease her about her lack of independent legal status. "When my friend Ellis Gray Loring wanted to entertain himself with seeing my face flush and my eyes kindle," she later remembered, "he used to repeat, 'a married woman is dead in the law.' To *me*," she lamented, "who felt so very much alive."[36] Coverture also meant that her income would be fair game to her husband's creditors. She knew David was in debt, and she knew that this threat to her income could blossom into a crisis at any moment. There is a steady drumbeat of worry about finances in her earliest letters as a married woman.

Still, she was earning $300 a year from the *Juvenile Miscellany*, and she was managing to sell stories to other publications too. In fact, as David was fighting for Native Americans in his editorials, his wife was developing a genre she would use for the rest of her life: what one of her biographers has called "protest fiction." From 1827 to 1829, she published four short stories with Native American themes that show a sharpening, if imperfect, sense that she had not done native people justice in her earlier publications when she had predicted their noble, self-sacrificing extinction.[37]

So for now, she had faith in him and in their shared mission. She was a writer; she could help him with his *Massachusetts Journal*. Soon she was doing just that, making the paper more family friendly by including some of her own stories and, somewhat worryingly, an article called "Hints to People of Moderate Fortune." David welcomed and encouraged his wife's involvement, thanking her in print for her "constant assistance." In championing his wife's intellect, he was truly exceptional for his generation. He loved her mind, and he wanted her to use it. She was still the "high-souled, high-reaching . . . powerful-minded Maria," but now—and how happy this made him—she was also his wife. She loved his mind, too. He was, she wrote, "my walking Dictionary of many languages, my Universal Encyclopedia." He was also "the most loving husband God ever bestowed upon woman": affectionate, devoted, tender, forgiving.[38] If his paper could just turn a profit, they would be all right.

But events, it seemed, were against them. Soon after their wedding, American politics took a dark turn. "I am not yet prepared to believe that the people of this republic are corrupt enough to choose by fair and honest votes, such a blot upon humanity as Andrew Jackson," Child wrote to her new mother-in-law in the early months after Jackson's election in 1828. But elected he was, riding a wave of populism and nationalist fervor. Jackson was a slaveholder and not, like other presidents from George Washington to

Thomas Jefferson, an ambivalent one. While others might profess to "hate slavery as much as anyone," he embraced its economic potential by owning and trading slaves himself and by protecting slavery's status in the nation he governed. He supported the extension of slavery into western states and made no secret of his intention to remove the Native Americans in his way, by force if necessary. He had won by sweeping the Southern states whose representation in the Electoral College, thanks to the Three-Fifths Compromise, was amplified by their slave populations.[39] Slaves were, in effect, being forced to vote for their continued enslavement.

Jackson's election had immediate financial consequences for the Childs. David's paper had backed his opponent, John Quincy Adams. When Jackson won, subscribers canceled in droves— "some from disgust of politics, some from vexation at being deceived in their expectations," Child speculated. David hurried back and forth between home and office. We can imagine him hastily eating his lunch as he recounted the latest outrage by President Jackson, who was quickly laying the foundation for removing the Cherokee, Creek, and other tribes from the South to make way for more cotton plantations. No doubt they talked over how to phrase his next editorial, with David most likely staking out an outraged, extreme position and Maria trying to moderate it. It was true that "Andrew, the Slavetrader," as David liked to call the president, was doing everything he could to support slavery's westward expansion. But saying it quite so bluntly might cost them subscriptions they could not afford to lose. It was not only their financial stability at stake: David had a business partner, George Snelling, who would also suffer if they could not stay afloat.[40] Perhaps David could be more diplomatic. Maybe he promised to try. Then he would dash back to the office. She must have smiled at his tall, retreating figure. He was, after all, her knight minus the chain mail. Still, the thought must have haunted her: What if he was tilting at windmills? What torment it must have been to watch their subscriptions fall, day after day, as they also began to absorb what Jackson's victory meant for the country and the causes they cared about.

There was another major concern: in addition to his financial

Fig. 10. President Andrew Jackson depicted as the heartless Shakespearean villain Richard III. Child pasted this sketch into her scrapbook sometime after Jackson's election in 1828. Courtesy of the Schlesinger Library, Harvard University.

problems, David was in legal trouble. Given his impetuousness and willingness to plunge into any fight, his newspaper provided him with a dangerous platform from which to enrage powerful people. He had done this twice the year before, accusing a prison overseer of fraud and a state senator of corruption. Both men had accused him of libel and sued. In January 1829, the cases went to trial within days of each other. Supporters rallied to his side, praising his "honest patriotism" and reminding his subscribers that no "republic can flourish without a constant reference to the political character of those who aspire to office." It seemed that he had a reasonable hope of winning; everyone, his wife wrote, assured her that he would be acquitted. Instead, he was found guilty in both cases. The fraud case came with a relatively modest fine of $15. The corruption case came with jail time.[41]

David appealed the decision and fought back in his newspaper. "Let the facts and evidence be examined," he wrote, "and we have no fear of the judgment which may follow." Some journalists tried to defend him on grounds of freedom of speech. Other people started calling him David "Libel" Child. Perhaps most terrifying, his legal fees amounted to almost $300. It was as much as Child earned in a year from editing the *Miscellany*. The financial anxiety was sometimes paralyzing. They took in boarders, which meant that on top of her editing, writing, and work for the *Massachusetts Journal*, Child was cooking and cleaning for strangers.[42] As for the legal proceedings, they could do nothing but wait. Their financial situation became dire, and the newly married Mrs. Child grew desperate.

The best evidence we have for this desperation is another letter to George Ticknor. Writing it was, she confessed in the first sentence, "the most painful task I ever imposed upon myself." Painful, indeed, to have to admit to this man she so deeply admired how badly her new husband was failing. But Ticknor had helped her before; perhaps he would help her now. So she poured out the humiliating truth: her husband needed $5,000. It was a staggering sum. If Ticknor could lend them a thousand, perhaps others could be persuaded to do the same. The paper could get back on its feet, and they would pay everyone back. She offered their furniture as collateral. She admitted, at the letter's end, that she had not told her husband she was writing. She clearly hoped Ticknor wouldn't tell him either.[43]

Perhaps Ticknor picked up a copy of the *Massachusetts Journal* to consider what he would be investing in if he were, once again, to come to his protégée's aid. If he did, it probably did not help. David was taking an uncompromising line on the injustice being done to the Cherokee in particular. "We call upon all men in this land, white, black, and red; bond and free, Christian and heathen to resist, as we will in our sphere, the murders and rapine, which are here meditated," David wrote as the Jackson administration moved forward with plans to forcibly displace the Cherokee to the West.[44] But, Ticknor might have objected in his mind, Georgia needed more land to grow cotton, and Northern mills needed that cotton to keep funding the country's prosperity. In short, the country needed more room, and treaties with native peoples hardly seemed a serious enough impediment when weighed against that demand.

And just what kind of resistance was David Child calling for? Here again the evidence would have been disconcerting to someone like Ticknor. "We have heard several respectable men say that they should deem it a duty *to take arms* to protect the Indians and to preserve public treaties inviolate," he had written. "If the administration does not respect the treaties of the United States and the rights of the Indians, but yield them up to the caprice and cupidity of the Georgians, then do we feel confident that a CIVIL CONTEST between sister states is not distant, and the sooner it comes the better."[45]

A civil contest? As in a civil war? In defense of *Indians*? If George Ticknor ever read these editorials, he probably put David Child's paper right back down. He was no fool, he would have assured himself. It's not clear that he ever responded to Maria Child's most recent request.

In fact, the couple's financial situation was even worse than Child had admitted. Their debt, according to one estimate, was closer to $15,000. Child stripped their budget down to the bone. They stopped accepting or issuing invitations. "It seems queer to me,—I used to go about so much," she wrote to her sister-in-law.[46] Her fashionable friends must have wondered where she had gone; she must have imagined them discussing her sudden absence from high-society events. Well, she was not sorry, or she told herself she was not. Both she and David had tried ascending from their humble origins to the bright light of Boston society. In the end, neither of them had really liked it. She could also feel proud that they were engaged in crucial reform work: he was fighting Jackson in the press, and she was helping. The least she could do was make their home life as pleasant as possible. Fortunately, she knew how to do this. She tapped into every economizing skill she had learned in Maine: mending instead of buying, choosing cheaper cuts of meat, leaving no scrap of food unused.

At some point it occurred to her that she was not the only woman trying to live on a budget. What if she were to share the tips and tricks that were helping them economize? Better yet: What if she were to publish them? And so, with incredible pluck, she tried to spin her financial anxiety into money by publishing one of the United States' first self-help books. It was called *The Frugal Housewife*. It had a subtitle, too, that seemed aimed right at the friends whose invitations she could no longer accept or reciprocate. Under the title, readers would find the following words: *For Those Who Are Not Ashamed of Economy*.

"The true economy of housekeeping," she wrote in the book's first sentence, "is simply the art of gathering up all the fragments, so that nothing is lost." What kind of fragments might those be? "Look frequently to the pails, to see that nothing is thrown to the pigs, which should be in the grease-pot," she admonished. "Look to the grease-pot, and see nothing is there which might serve to nourish your own family, or a poorer one." And then she was off, giving her readers advice on everything from sewing to pickling to roasting a goose. There were recipes for every conceivable vegetable and cooking instructions for every cut of meat. Bread was harder. "It is more difficult to give rules for making bread than for anything else," she conceded. There was also advice on eradicating cockroaches, storing vegetables, washing clothes, and maintaining personal hygiene. Brush your teeth, she advised her readers. Rum makes a very effective shampoo, she suggested. "Beer," she recommended, "is a good family drink."[47]

Again, readers in the United States had never seen anything like it, at least not written specifically for *them*. Child made the political importance of the book crystal clear. Although its advice was practical, its tone was aspirational. Citizenship begins in the kitchen, she suggested. Democracy requires self-reliance, and self-reliance requires knowing how to make your own soap. Living beyond one's means for the sake of public approval was no guarantee of advancement, she warned. That was not the worst of it: "More than that, it is wrong—morally wrong, so far as the individual is concerned; and injurious beyond calculation to the interest of our country. To what are the increasing beggary and discouraged exertions of the present period owing?" Child demanded. She had a ready answer. "The root of the whole matter is the extravagance of all classes of people! We never shall be prosperous till we make pride and vanity yield to the dictates of honesty and prudence!" In a later edition of the book she sharpened the point lest readers miss it: "Let any reflecting mind inquire how decay has begun in all republics, and then let them calmly ask themselves whether we are in no danger, in departing thus rapidly from the simplicity and industry of our forefathers." Which of her fashionable former friends was she thinking of as she wrote these sentences? Whoever they were, she was leaving them behind. "Books of this kind have usually been written for the wealthy," she wrote: "I have written for the poor!" She put it one more way: "I have attempted to teach how money can be *saved*, not how it can be *enjoyed*."[48] If her Beacon Hill acquaintances sensed she was targeting them, that's because she probably was.

The targeting, at least in some cases, was mutual. Her former beau Nathaniel Willis—the beheader of lilacs—was by this time editing the *American Monthly Magazine*. His review of *The Frugal Housewife* positively sneered. The book exhibited a "thoroughgoing, unhesitating, cordial freedom from taste," he wrote: "No word is used where there was a plainer or ruder one to be had." He had hoped, he told his readers, that since it was written by a "celebrated lady," there would be "glimpses of refinement." No such luck. Worst of all, its author had committed the unpardonable sin of describing all kinds of household drudgery and showing no "distaste to the task."[49] She seemed to *like* her hard work. She seemed not to aspire to find someone else to do it for her.

Willis could sneer all he wanted: Child's public loved the book. In its first three years, it was reprinted twelve times; a decade later, the total editions numbered twenty-eight. Like the *Juvenile Miscellany*, it was the kind of book that shaped people's memories of whole periods of their lives. Middle-aged women remembered how it helped them as they learned to keep house. As an old man, the radical abolitionist Thomas Wentworth Higginson remembered the illustrations in his mother's copy. He also remembered his childish disappointment that Mrs. Child's *Frugal Housewife* had advised his mother against spending money on *preserves*.[50]

We can be sure that there were no purchased preserves in the Child household. Theirs was a love propelled by a passion for ideas and, increasingly, a hatred of injustice. It was certainly not a love ashamed of economy.

＊　＊　＊

During the period when she was most famous for giving homey, domestic advice, there is also evidence that Child's political and religious views were becoming more radical. Just months before *The Frugal Housewife* appeared, she quietly published a book called *The First Settlers of New-England, or Conquest of the Pequods, Narragansets and Pokanokets, as Related by a Mother to Her Children.* Its stated goal was to show that "the treatment [Indians] have met with from the usurpers of their soil has been, and continues to be, in direct violation of the religious and civil institutions which we have heretofore so nobly defended." European settlers' behavior, she warned, is "subjecting us to have the finger of scorn pointed at us, for having so grossly violated the principles which form the basis of our government." Child also aspired, she told readers, to "impress our youth with the conviction of their obligation to alleviate . . . the sufferings of the generous and interesting race of men whom we have so unjustly supplanted." In the service of inspiring this better treatment, she delivered a book-length litany of peaceful gestures by the Pequod that were repaid by violence; grossly disproportionate punishments inflicted on captured warriors; whole Indian villages razed and their inhabitants sold into slavery.[51]

Child framed these appalling stories about early American history in a genre she had used before: as a dialogue between a kind but stern adult and inquisitive children whose sympathies lead them to ask hard questions. In this case, the conversation took place between a mother, who recounted the injustices, and two daughters, whose naive indignation functions like the voice of conscience. "Oh! Mother," little Caroline exclaims after one particularly horrific example of retribution against the Pequod, "it appears impossible that human beings could have been so altogether lost to the feelings of humanity, or that they could have been so grossly deceived as to imagine themselves entitled to the name of Christians." "I cannot think it possible that the settlers believed they were acting in conformity with the will of God in destroying the Indians," her sister Eliza declares after another gruesome episode: it "appears to me very wicked and profane to say, that they did so by God's assistance." "I think, mother," Caroline protests at yet another point, "it is somewhat extraordinary, that the colonists should complain with so much bitterness" about the Pequod's counterattacks "after they themselves had so inhumanly destroyed the dwellings, killed the people, and refused to comply with the request of the Pequods to lay aside arms."[52]

Unlike Child's earlier stories, the mother here does nothing to check her daughters' moral anguish. She does not rebuke them for doubting their fellow citizens' sympathies or assure them of their president's good intentions. At every turn she instead praises their indignation and confirms their worst suspicions. The result is a revisionist history of early America that contrasts native peoples' generosity with European hypocrisy and challenges whether Americans, given their behavior, have a right to call themselves Christians. It feels like a book written in the heat of outrage by someone whose faith in her country and its religion has been badly shaken both by learning about its past and by assessing its present.

There is a dark side to Child's bright outrage in this book. She blamed the Puritans' egregious behavior toward native peoples on Calvinism; then she blamed Calvinism on Judaism. All she knew of Judaism were Old Testament stories suggesting a vengeful and unjust God who chose some people to the exclusion of others. As long as Christians modeled themselves on this God and claimed to be his chosen people, they were likely, like the early settlers she described, to feel justified in destroying anything in their path. She wanted, she wrote, to rid Christianity of the "blight" of this Jewish foundation and let, as she put it, the "pure and undefiled" message of Jesus shine through.[53] Although she never fully renounced her biases against Judaism, later in life Child would seek to break down others' prejudices against the Jewish people in their midst. She would also do her imperfect but principled best to credit Judaism as one of the many ways humans seek truth. But at this point, she had not found her way to that better vision. So she repeated, in a book that urged tolerance, arguments that could only intensify her society's intolerance of Judaism.

At the end of the dialogue, the mother steers her daughters firmly from history to the present. "It is, in my opinion, decidedly wrong, to speak of the removal, or extinction of the Indians as inevitable," she concluded, just as President Jackson was doing exactly that. "I devoutly trust, that our Government will not again pusillanimously compromise with the sordid avaricious Georgians," she wrote of the Southerners whose generosity she had only recently praised. "The crisis admits of no delay," she urged. The same was true of the Jackson administration's resolve to drive the Seminole out of Florida. "If the Seminoles be not speedily relieved," she predicted, "they must perish in the swamps to which they have been driven, in the presence of *civilized Christian* people, who have solemnly pledged themselves to be their guardians and protectors."[54]

The First Settlers is an eye-crossing blend of outrage, persuasion, religious iconoclasm, and children's literature. Child paid to have it published and then did not promote it.[55] This was probably just as well: it never would have worked. Its framing as an educational dialogue for children meant that adults would never read it for themselves; its uncompromising attack on both American patriotism and Christian hypocrisy would have guaranteed that few mothers would read it to their children. It also, unsurprisingly, had no effect. In 1830, Andrew Jackson signed the Indian Removal Act, condemning tens of thousands of native people living in Georgia to relocation a thousand miles west in Oklahoma. Thousands died on the way of starvation, exposure, disease, and violence, in a decades-long American travesty that came to be known as the Trail of Tears. "I fought through the Civil War and have seen men shot to pieces and slaughtered by thousands," one Georgia soldier reported, "but the Cherokee removal was the cruelest work I ever knew."[56]

But whatever *The First Settlers* did not accomplish, it did set the tone for what would become Maria Child's trademark style of assailing her country's sins. It seemed, she had written to her sister just five years before, "as if the public was resolved to give me a flourish of trumpets, let me write what I will."[57] This conviction was about to be tested. The next time she took aim at one of the evils at her country's core, she would skip the children and go straight for their parents.

3

Let Us Not Flatter Ourselves

"The position of New England in 1829, was a most cheerless one for Freedom," recalled the abolitionist Maria Weston Chapman as she reflected on that year a decade later. "Everybody was, in some way or other, actively or passively, sustaining slavery; yet all disclaimed its existence, opposed all efforts for its extinction, and was 'as much anti-slavery as anybody else.'"[1] Until 1830, Lydia Maria Child perfectly embodied this contradiction. Her disapproval of slavery was sincere but vague. Surely it was not her fault, and probably it was none of her business. Like her contemporaries, she probably assumed that nothing could be done.

How do good people become complacent? It's not hard. Still newly married, the Childs were busy. Maria was editing the *Juvenile Miscellany*, supplying her young readers with stories, puzzles, and stern but spirited advice on how to behave. She was also hard at work on several new publications. With Ticknor's help, she had launched a series of volumes called the Ladies' Family Library, which consisted of biographies of famous women, including Germaine de Staël, whom she had studied with Margaret Fuller, and Madame Roland, the French writer and revolutionary. Two other forthcoming books fell into the self-help genre she was establishing and also targeted women. *The Girl's Own Book* aimed to compensate for the state of girls' education, which Child simply pronounced "bad." *The Mother's Book* advised mothers on everything from cradle to courtship. Readers seemed unworried about taking parenting advice from an author who herself had no children: the book sold out in weeks. Meanwhile *The Frugal Housewife* was being reprinted in an expanded version. Use citric acid for headaches, Child told her readers, and never expose dried herbs to the air. The new edition netted her $2,000.[2] This was no doubt encouraging, although even this triumphant sum could go only so far in paying David's debts. Meanwhile, the second libel suit remained unresolved, and jail time still loomed.

So the Childs were busy and preoccupied. In their everyday lives, there was little to remind them of atrocities in the South. This was not an accident. For decades, Northern civic leaders had kept slavery as far as possible from public consciousness. The Missouri Compromise was still holding, but whenever they sensed a challenge to their right to hold slaves, Southern politicians threatened to secede. Desperate to avoid the unthinkable, Northern editors, politicians, and religious leaders promoted restraint and discouraged agitation. They promised that slavery would wither away if slaveholders were not antagonized. The smallest challenges to this fragile peace were cause for concern. When Quaker abolitionist Benjamin Lundy lectured in Boston in 1828, the Reverend William Ellery Channing, one of Boston's most influential ministers, wrote to Senator Daniel Webster in alarm. Lundy had recounted his decades spent walking across the South, trying to persuade slaveholders to emancipate the humans they claimed to own. The "rashness of enthusiasts" like Lundy needed to be carefully contained, Channing warned, lest Northern consciences awaken and make trouble with the South. It would turn out that Channing was right to worry.[3]

Even white Northerners who were against slavery rarely favored its immediate abolition. There was, of course, the argument that slavery was a disease that should not be cured too quickly. Besides, the logistics were daunting. What was to become of the millions of people who had been traumatized, denied literacy, and deprived of autonomy? How was the Southern economy to withstand the loss of free labor, and what might its collapse mean for Northern industry? Anyway, many ministers assured their parishioners, Negroes were an inferior race, better off under the tutelage of white Christian masters than in barbarous, pagan Africa.

For those whose consciences remained uneasy, there was the American Colonization Society. Founded in 1817, this society's mission was to settle former slaves in Liberia, a newly formed African colony, or perhaps in Haiti. Its leaders represented a kind of unholy alliance between otherwise opposed camps. On one side were advocates of slavery who, finding that free, economically successful Black residents undermined claims about racial inferiority, wanted them gone. On the other side were opponents of slavery who thought sending freed slaves to Africa might pacify those who could not tolerate the idea of free Black people in their midst. The society had positioned itself as the reasonable alternative to the unimaginable chaos of emancipation. By 1832, all Northern states had passed some kind of resolution supporting its aims. If you were a progressive, well-meaning white American, you could support the ACS and feel you had discharged your duty to fight slavery. There is some evidence that, earlier in life, Child herself had done just that. In "The Little Master and His Slave," Child's 1824 story about the unruly Ned and the magnanimous Edward, imaginary Robert had aspired to just such a scheme. "If I had a little slave," he announced to his aunt, "I would send him to Hayti, where he might be as free and happy as I am."[4]

So complacency was easy. But as the decade drew to a close, there were ominous signs that it was also misguided. In 1829, a Black Boston merchant named David Walker published an explosive tract titled *An Appeal to the Coloured Citizens of the World*. Walker had grown up in the South. He bore witness to slaveholders "chaining and handcuffing us, branding us, cramming fire down our throats . . . beating us nearly or quite to death," all in pursuit of their own wealth. He denounced the American Colonization Society. "The greatest riches in all America have arisen from our blood and tears," he declared: "and will they drive us from our property and homes, which we have earned with our *blood*?" Drawing on ancient, medieval, and biblical history, he issued a sweeping condemnation of slavery. He excoriated Thomas Jefferson for his hypocrisy. Building on Christian texts, he reminded his readers that God was a God not only of love but of justice. Most shockingly, he prophesied vengeance. "My colour will yet," he promised, "root some of you out of the very face of the earth!"[5]

Walker sewed copies of his *Appeal* into clothes and smuggled them into the South. When they were found in the hands of literate Blacks, wide-scale panic ensued. From New Orleans to Savannah, those caught possessing the tract were arrested and imprisoned. Legislators in Virginia and Georgia proposed that distribution of such pamphlets be punishable by death. Not a year later, Walker—still in his thirties—suddenly died. Some suspected poison. David Child placed advertisements in his *Massachusetts Journal* soliciting evidence. The police declined to investigate.[6]

But if Walker's publication at least temporarily got the Childs' attention, their own problems quickly eclipsed everything. In February 1830, David lost his appeal in the second libel case. A few weeks later Maria Child's husband went to jail.[7]

With David incarcerated, the Childs could not afford to keep their home. Maria boarded with wealthy friends. For six months, her well-heeled neighbors watched her pass, carrying a tin pail to the local prison with meals for her husband. She must have felt prescient. "As riches increase, it is easy and pleasant to increase in hospitality and splendor," she had written in *The Frugal Housewife*; "but it is always painful and inconvenient to decrease." Winter's slush slowly gave way to spring's warmth. Did her watchful neighbors comment on how the promising Miss Francis had become the impoverished Mrs. Child? "It makes my heart melt and the tears come to think how sweetly you have borne yourself . . . in the severe trials which I have brought upon you," David wrote to her. It was not his first apology to his wife, and it would not be his last. But it worked. "My Dearest Husband," she responded, "I am very homesick for you."[8] When he emerged from jail six months later, they probably hoped the worst was over.

It was during this time of racial tension in the country and personal crisis for the Childs that a man arrived in Boston who would

Fig. 11. William Lloyd Garrison in 1833. Child included this image of Garrison in her scrapbook. Courtesy of the Schlesinger Library, Harvard University.

change their lives forever. William Lloyd Garrison was a tall, thin, bespectacled editor, just a few years younger than Child. He had recently moved to Boston fresh from his own stint in jail. He had been in Baltimore editing a newspaper owned by Benjamin Lundy—the very Quaker whose abolitionism had prompted Reverend Channing to write to his senator in alarm. Garrison had heard Lundy speak and been riveted by his personal sacrifice for a righteous cause. Once entrusted with Lundy's newspaper, Garrison quickly accused a powerful Massachusetts merchant of profiting from the slave trade and was convicted of libel. After his release, he did something even more radical. He read Walker's *Appeal*, and he listened to the Black community's passionate arguments against colonization.[9] He had become an unapologetic abolitionist, and he was spoiling for a fight.

The groundwork for organized abolition had been laid over decades by Black communities across the North. In the eighteenth century, free Black citizens had organized societies dedicated to ending slavery in New York and Philadelphia. More recently, Black leaders such as Prince Hall and Thomas Paul in Boston and the powerful Forten family in Philadelphia had been fighting for racial equality by petitioning the legal system and establishing organizations for the education of Black children. In Philadelphia, Baltimore, and Boston, Black Americans had organized "vigilance committees" to protect Black residents from being kidnapped and sold in the South. Throughout the North, Black people organized safe houses on the Underground Railroad to help fugitives escape to Canada. Rebellious Quakers had helped as well, most famously Benjamin Lay, whose activist theatrics had gotten him expelled from the more conservative Quaker communities in which some members still owned slaves.[10]

But in 1830, it was still true that to be an abolitionist—to argue for the immediate and complete emancipation of enslaved people without compensation to their enslavers—was to be a radical. Garrison embraced the role wholeheartedly and in print. He had come to Boston to start a newspaper devoted to immediate emancipation. He would call it the *Liberator*. Its first home was the cramped basement of the African Meeting House, the center of Black life in Boston, just blocks from the imposing dome of the Massachusetts Capitol. Some of the *Liberator*'s first financial supporters were Black leaders like James Forten; the Black community also sold subscriptions, bought advertising space, and wrote articles for its first issues. As he bartered for ink and borrowed money to buy paper, Garrison also looked for recruits—people who could help spread the gospel of abolition. He knew of Child's work. In Lundy's paper, he had already praised her as possessing a "genius as versatile as it is brilliant" and as being equal in wit and wisdom to Benjamin Franklin himself. He knew she was a talented novelist with a bent toward social justice. He knew she was capable of giving readers practical advice on how to change their lives. Maybe she would write for him. First, she would need to become an abolitionist. Soon after arriving in Boston, Garrison proposed that they meet.[11]

*   *   *

Decades later, Child still remembered Garrison's effect:

> I was then all absorbed in poetry and painting—soaring aloft, on Psyche-wings, into the ethereal regions of mysticism. [Garrison] got hold of the strings of my conscience, and pulled me into Reforms. It is of no use to imagine what might have been, if I had never met him. Old dreams vanished, old associates departed, and all things became new. . . . 'I could not otherwise, so help me God.'[12]

In other words, a conversion experience. A moment after which she could never live her life the same way again. A moment she had been prepared for, however unconsciously, by her curiosity, sympathy, and intellect, but a moment she neither could have predicted nor could now rescind. A conversion from apathy, or at least resignation, to urgency. Child doesn't record what Garrison said. But we can infer his message from the publications that had recently landed him in jail and inspired his enemies to label him a "second Walker." Africans and their descendants were humans and our equals. They were being enslaved by the millions in the most brutal conditions imaginable. Their enslavement was made possible by Northern complicity. The duty to end it was immediate. The only question that remained was how.[13]

There is a special kind of agony in a conversion experience: shame at what we did not see and a desperation to make it right. The enormity of the evil, suddenly obvious, made Child's former obliviousness unbearable to her. "In former years," she later confessed, "the colored population came and went before my eyes, like shadows. I never paused to reflect that they were, like myself, immortals pent up in the prison-house of time." It got worse. Not only had she failed to think of them as human. She—the novelist who prided herself on her vision and compassion—had never paused to consider "the dungeon assigned to them by the will of the strongest." Now their enslavement haunted her like the wicked thing it was. And she knew her anguish was nothing next to that of those whose plight she had, until recently, so easily ignored.[14]

But anguished self-recrimination is only part of conversion's force. There is also a kind of elation at seeing truth and feeling old falsehoods slip away. Child described this newfound vision as her own emancipation. She had been led, she wrote, "out of [the] Egyptian bondage of the world" and into truth. And like the best conversions, Child's revealed what, in her heart of hearts, she had always known. She believed in freedom and equality. She knew slavery was immoral and that a country that institutionalized evil was corrupt. But she had allowed herself to be lulled into complacency by excuses that she knew, deep down, were empty. "Thus we have gone on, year after year, thoughtlessly sanctioning, by our silence and indifference, evils which our hearts and consciences are far enough from approving," she lamented. No more. From now on, she would be free of apologies and equivocations. She would live by her own conscience. She would be her own master.[15] But she would never forget that while her own enslavement had been only metaphorical, for millions of human beings in the South, it was the only reality they knew.

The walk from the modest rooms she and David now rented to her publisher's office still wound through the same uneven, crowded streets. Couples still promenaded through the Boston Common, arm in arm. Her publishing deadlines still loomed, and David's debts still mounted. But everything was framed by new questions. Some were large and theoretical. Was slavery a moral problem or a political problem? Whose problem was it, the North's or the South's? Other questions were more personal. Did her new convictions change which political party she should support or what church she should attend? Would her friends think she had gone mad? Perhaps she should stop buying clothes made of Southern cotton. Perhaps she should forgo sugar grown on plantations. Then there was her career. Writing fiction while actual human tragedy gripped the South suddenly seemed frivolous. Publishing parenting manuals while masters raped their slaves and sold their own children felt grotesque. *All things became new.* In the midst of such anguish, remorse, exhilaration, resolve, and fear, it can be hard to know what to do next.

To orient herself in her new moral landscape, Child turned to what she knew best: books. It's not clear how she got them. Perhaps she returned to her brother's Watertown parsonage to consult volumes there; perhaps sympathetic friends like Ellis Loring or Samuel May borrowed books from private libraries like the famed Boston Athenæum that she, as a woman, could not access on her own. No doubt she also made use of articles in the *Liberator*, including those by Black Bostonians such as Sarah Douglass and Sarah Forten.[16] Whatever her sources, for the next three years, as she continued to live in a city that boasted all the trappings of power the young United States could muster, she immersed herself in the history, economics, and politics of her country's ongoing sin.

Imagine yourself, then, an educated and engaged citizen, learning these now-familiar facts for the first time. In travelers' journals, Child read harrowing accounts of slaves left in stocks until they were crippled; deadly floggings for minor infractions; escaping slaves shot or torn apart by dogs; pregnant women beaten until they miscarried. In legal bulletins, she read of Southern laws that excused slaveholders if their slaves died "of moderate punishment" and prohibited even free Blacks from testifying in court on their own behalf. As Massachusetts's famous politicians framed legislation on Beacon Hill, she pored over political histories showing Northern statesmen cowed and cowardly in the face of Southern slaveholders. As celebrated merchants struck lucrative deals in Boston's busy harbor, she studied assessments of slave economies that tallied financial gain against human suffering. As renowned intellectuals theorized across the river in Cambridge, she read biographies of Black scientists, poets, authors, and political leaders whose brilliance proved every assertion of "Negro inferiority" to be a lie.[17]

As she read, I imagine her experiencing another emotion: rage. She had been told that the African race was inferior. It wasn't. She had been persuaded that slaves were happy. They weren't. She had accepted the argument that slavery would wither away. It was alive and growing. She had, in short, been deceived by men who claimed to share her values but who, she now saw, had manipulated her ideals for political and economic gain. Those very men surrounded her now when she walked Boston's city streets: men she had once idolized, but whom she now saw as shoring up an institution that ranked among the most wicked in the history of the world. These same men had also told her there was nothing she could do about slavery. She would devote the rest of her life to showing that this, too, was a lie.

Fortunately, a partner in outrage waited for her when she returned home. David had immediately warmed to Garrison's principled positions and uncompromising style. He began devoting more articles in the *Massachusetts Journal* to slavery, including ones titled "The Slave Question," "The Slave Trade in the Capitol," and "Some of the Evils of Slave Labor." He also began reprinting articles from Garrison's *Liberator*, clearly allying himself with Garrison's more radical views. David also encouraged his talented wife to experiment with her new convictions in writing and—also radically for his time—supported her move into the masculine sphere of political prose. He made space in the *Massachusetts Journal* for her to catalog arguments used to justify slavery and to test counterarguments.[18] She began experimenting with more familiar formats as well. Arguments alone, Child was already sure, would never convert her fellow Americans. She would have to engage their sympathies as well, and this engagement would have to start early. An attentive subscriber to the *Juvenile Miscellany* in 1831 might have noticed an increase in stories by "Aunt M" evoking the sorrows of slavery for its young readers and saying nothing at all about sending emancipated slaves to Haiti.

As she experimented, the radical implications of her conversion crystallized. For even the most progressive Northerners, declaring that Africans and their descendants should be *free* did not imply that they should be *equal*. Child now accepted both. This committed her to affirming the slippery slope many Northerners feared: that emancipation would lead to demands that Black residents be given an education, citizenship, and even the vote. Then there was the question of interracial marriage. At first this was the proverbial bridge too far, even for Child. In 1831, she published an article condemning racial prejudice but calling mixed marriages "unnatural." Such "arguments from nature" were popular then as now, and they are almost always bad. Historically, they have kept peasants servile, women subjected, and Europeans in charge. They are often a sign that our better arguments have run out. They say, in effect, This doesn't feel right; it doesn't happen in my culture; it must not be natural. In a responding article, Garrison gently but firmly called Child out. Interracial marriage might offend taste, he wrote, but that is not the same as being unnatural.[19] And when prejudices change, tastes will too. Anyway, he might have added, Don't humans usually aspire to be more than "natural"?

Child kept thinking and reading, following her new convictions to their conclusion. She emerged from her self-education convinced of the twin iniquities of Southern slavery and Northern complacency. She was ready to advocate for the right of all Americans to marry whomever they chose. She had tested and honed arguments that she would use, to great effect, for the rest of her life. There's a lesson here. Even if you resolve never to live your life the same way again, center before you stretch. Gather your resources, find your arguments, get your facts straight. Uninformed enthusiasm helps no one.

But personal enlightenment also achieved no one's emancipation. What was a twenty-eight-year-old woman, herself politically disenfranchised and in precarious financial straits, to do?

How could she take on a monstrous, multifaceted evil that the best minds of her fledgling country had failed to defeat? David—at least when he was not incarcerated—had his journal and his legal practice. Garrison had his *Liberator*. Samuel May, a fellow convert and Unitarian minister, had his pulpit. What did she have? Child took stock of her talents and abilities. At some point during her research, she settled on the idea of a book: a book that would disseminate facts, dismantle arguments, and make it impossible for her readers to live the same way again.

It remained only to decide what kind of book it should be. Garrison's *Liberator*, now in its second year, was setting a tone of uncompromising extremism. "I am in earnest—I will not equivocate—I will not excuse—I will not retreat a single inch," the pugnacious editor wrote in his first issue, "AND I WILL BE HEARD." The *Liberator*'s volume was, in fact, proving too loud for the average reader. "Like a man who has been in the habit of screaming himself hoarse to make the deaf better," Margaret Fuller complained, "he can no longer pitch his voice on a key agreeable to common ears." Garrison was also publishing Black authors like Maria Stewart, whose indictment of slavery and the white culture that sustained it was very hard for your average white Bostonian to stomach. It was also true that the *Liberator*'s arguments were scattered, serialized over weekly issues that only the already converted read. The movement—if it was to become that—needed a centralized synthesis of calm argumentation that dismantled anti-abolitionist arguments and then showed readers how to change their lives. Ideally, it would come from someone readers knew they could trust.[20]

And so it became clear what Child had to offer the cause: her reputation. She had established herself as a reliable source of homey but aspirational advice. Her readers knew her to be frank but compassionate. They would listen to her as they would never listen to Garrison. But would they trust her through a transition from housecleaning tips to abolishing slavery? Would they follow her from treating dysentery to curing the disease at their country's core? Was it true, as she had written to her sister, that they would always follow her, whatever she wrote?

I imagine Child, perhaps at her kitchen table, searching for her book's first sentences. Perhaps she thought again of the powerful men she passed every day on the street: men whose arguments she knew and whose power she no longer feared. "Reader, I beseech you not to throw down this volume as soon as you have glanced at the title," she wrote, her handwriting graceful and even. "Read it, if your prejudices will allow, for the very truth's sake." She thought of the women who cooked from her recipes and read her stories to their children. "If I have the most trifling claims upon your good will, for an hour's amusement to yourself, or benefit to your children," she wrote, "read it for my sake." I imagine her looking around her frugal home, then turning back to her paper. "Read it," she wrote, "from sheer curiosity to see what a woman (who had much better attend to her household concerns) will say upon such a subject."[21]

So what did that woman say?

* * *

As spring 1831 ripened into summer, Child began synthesizing her accumulated evidence into a methodical destruction of the arguments, excuses, and equivocations that had, all too recently, kept her from seeing the truth. She played to her strengths. With a novelist's touch, she conjured images of slavery's brutality. With an educator's efficiency, she cited facts, figures, and studies and sought out images she knew would get her readers' attention. As a pioneer of the American self-help tradition, she encouraged her readers to rely on their own thinking just as they could rely on their own cooking. But she also left these sanctioned female spheres far behind, wading vigorously into economics, politics, legal theory, and history. With firm precision, she anticipated her readers' objections and refuted them one by one. It was as if she was determined to clear the underbrush of bad moral arguments and leave her readers open to the clearest moral pitch she could make. Africans and their descendants are human. Enslaving humans is evil. The time to end the evil is now.

As she wrote, she also listened. Sometimes she visited one of

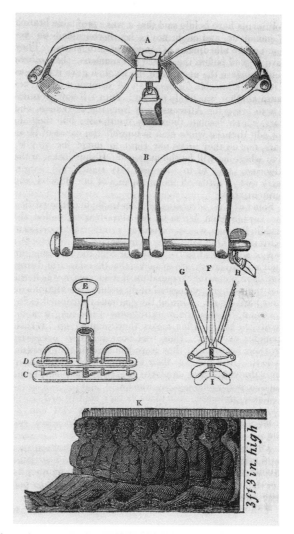

Fig. 12. "Slave Physical Restraints," illustration in Child's *Appeal in Favor of That Class of Americans Called Africans*, 1833. Child's willingness to include both descriptions and images of the torture enslaved people endured violated most Northerners' sense of propriety. Courtesy of the New York Public Library.

Boston's many churches and heard ministers describing slavery as God's plan. Even the Swedenborgian minister she had previously admired proved so bigoted against Black people that she could no longer stand his preaching. In stagecoaches, she heard fellow travelers boast of refusing to worship with Black congregants or sit with them on trains. And then, back at her desk, she met her readers where they were, taking on arguments that should have been irrelevant but, given her audience, were not. Some should make us cringe. Consider her assurance that free economies are more efficient than slave economies. This should be, and is, morally beside the point. No economic gain can justify enslavement. Or consider her assurance that "if we were accustomed to see intelligent and polished negroes, prejudice would disappear." Here is an argument we will encounter at every step of Child's activist career, an argument that would prove both deeply flawed and deeply harmful. It has two parts: the first is that white Americans will respect Black Americans just as soon as they are "respectable." The second is that "respectable" implies assimilating to white culture as quickly and as thoroughly as possible. For many in Child's activist circles, there would never be room to value any other way of being. The Black abolitionist Mary Ann Shadd Cary would later condemn this "disposition to make black appear white" among white abolitionists. It was "the most prominent feature of the times," she wrote, and it was poisonous.[22] This indictment should sound familiar. All too often, it holds against white activism today.

Then, in August 1831, white Americans' worst nightmare about slavery burst into their waking realities. An enslaved man named Nat Turner, believing that God had called him to free his people, led other slaves in a violent revolt. "INSURRECTION IN VIRGINIA!" blared Boston papers. Over the next seven weeks, Turner and his men terrorized the Virginia countryside, killing fifty-one white people, including Turner's owner and his family. As federal troops searched for him, hundreds of slaves were tortured in interrogations or killed by vengeful mobs. Turner was finally captured and hanged.[23]

The Southern press, recycling an already familiar argument, blamed abolitionists in general and Garrison in particular. One Washington paper demanded that the *Liberator* be shut down and the "instigator of human butchery" at its head be punished. The state of Georgia offered $5,000 for Garrison's arrest and extradition. Garrison fired back, at least metaphorically. He was a pacifist, he insisted. He had never advocated violence in this cause or any other. Turner's revolt had simply exposed Southerners' description of happy slaves as a lie and their justice system as a sham. Eminent Boston clergy tried to rein Garrison in, offering to support his movement if he would give up his "fantastical notions and be guided by us."[24] No thank you, said Garrison.

David Child, by contrast, was not a pacifist. As evidenced by his rush to join the Spanish army in its struggle for liberation, he believed that violent oppression justified violent response. In his *Massachusetts Journal*, he defended Turner's right to revolt. Oppressed peoples in Virginia, like oppressed peoples everywhere, "have a right to assert their 'natural and inalienable rights,'" he wrote. "We will never swerve from this principle," he promised.[25] Subscriptions to his journal continued to fall.

Maria Child kept writing. We honor our forefathers for rebelling against tyranny, she reminded her American readers. Surely rebelling against tyranny was exactly what Turner and his men were doing. "Why do we execrate in one set of men, what we laud so highly in another?" she asked. She also used Turner's actions to confront another bad argument. We have been told, she wrote, that slavery is "a lamentable necessity" since "insurrections would be the inevitable result of any attempt to remove it." Unpacked, this argument went something like this: We have behaved so badly that, if we stop behaving badly, our victims will demand justice. Therefore we must continue behaving badly. But Child had done the research, and she could reassure her readers that their fears were unfounded. "Slavery causes insurrections," she explained: "emancipation prevents them." In Chile, Colombia, and Mexico, where liberation had been immediate and permanent, she reported, not a hair on the head of a white person was harmed. Not only was emancipation the moral solution, she promised her white readers. It was the safe solution.[26]

This was all well and good, but it was also what philosophers call one argument too many. If the right thing to do is to free slaves because they are humans and humans should not be enslaved, they should be freed whatever the threat to their enslavers' safety.

Past injustice also does not justify future injustice. Child knew this, and she wanted to get her readers to the right argument. So she soothed their fears, but she also showed that these fears were, again, morally beside the point. "Duties are ours," she told them; "events are God's."[27] In other words, do the right thing and let the consequences take care of themselves. Did this feel daunting? "My life upon it, a safe remedy can be found for this evil, whenever we are sincerely desirous of doing justice for its own sake," she promised her readers. You can do it, I hear her saying. There is nothing heroic about it. All you have to do is live up to the beliefs about freedom and equality you already profess to have.

As she wrote, Garrison continued on his mission to convert as many people as possible to abolition. A small community began to form. They included the lawyer Samuel E. Sewall and his wife Louisa; John Greenleaf Whittier, who would soon become one of America's most beloved poets; the Unitarian minister Samuel May; and the German poet Charles Follen and his wife Eliza. The Lorings were also among them, with Ellis offering both legal and financial support to Garrison's *Liberator*. Child never forgot the electrifying effect of being around fellow converts newly dedicated to "the missionary work" of spreading the gospel of abolitionism. It seemed, she later recalled, that "the Holy Spirit did actually descend upon men and women in tongues of flame." Antislavery, she added, "introduced me to the noblest and best of the land, intellectually and morally, and knit us together in that firm friendship which grows out of sympathy in a good but unpopular cause." They had been, she thought, "a mighty smart set."[28]

By late 1831, Garrison believed he had enough converts to constitute a society. He recruited David to help. As Child worked on her manuscript, she watched her husband collaborate with Garrison to found the New England Anti-Slavery Society. It wasn't easy. Since Turner's rebellion, the stakes for abolitionists had risen. Declaring yourself an abolitionist now meant being open to the accusation that you supported Turner's violence. It was also difficult to decide how extreme a stand the society should take. Was it better to embrace more modest goals—proposing compensation to enslavers for their loss of labor, perhaps, or suggesting gradual emancipation over several decades? Or was it better to stake out a position that was principled and true and hope that its rightness would eventually attract supporters? On this question David was uncharacteristically gun-shy, fearing that endorsing immediate emancipation would alienate crucial support.[29] Garrison disagreed: articulate the truth, he insisted, and others will follow.

It took even a dedicated group of abolitionists four agonizing meetings to agree on a name and a prologue to their constitution. Finally, on an icy January day in 1832, the group gathered in the basement of the African Meeting House. With members of Boston's Black community looking on, consensus was reached and the society came into being. Ellis Loring and David helped draft its founding documents. "We hold that man cannot . . . be the property of man," their constitution declared. "We hold that whoever retains his fellow man in bondage, is guilty of a grievous wrong."[30] Today these sentences might sound like a simple statement of truth. But everyone present knew they amounted to the declaration of a kind of moral war.

David quickly regained his usual headlong enthusiasm. He became one of the society's most active members, chairing meetings, presenting resolutions, and giving speeches. At the society's first anniversary, he gave a breathtakingly combative speech titled "Despotism of Freedom, or The Tyranny and Cruelty of American Republican Slave-Masters, Shown to Be the Worst in the World." It was later published as one of the first tracts of the New England Anti-Slavery Society. In the end, it was just as well he had something to occupy him: only one month after the New England Anti-Slavery Society was founded, his *Massachusetts Journal* failed for good.

Child sometimes went with him to the society's meetings, but she didn't speak. No women did. For now, they deferred to an allegedly biblical injunction against women's speaking to audiences that included men. But in the next years, the movement would begin to attract women who had something to say. Their silence would not last much longer. Their insistence on being heard, and

Fig. 13. African Meeting House, Boston, where the New England Anti-Slavery Society was founded in 1832. Courtesy of the Boston Athenæum.

the resistance they met, would soon throw the abolitionist movement into crisis.

＊　＊　＊

All that lay in the future. For now, Child was homing in on her closing argument. As luck would have it, she had a new resource for this last stage of her research. Despite being, by its own description, "a man's institution, jealously guarded," the Boston Athenæum had recently offered her free borrowing privileges. She was one of the very first women to be granted this honor, and it was not uncontroversial: one member had described "the raising of the masculine eyebrows, provoked by the unaccustomed sight" of one of her few female predecessors; another complained that the presence of women caused "frequent embarrassment to modest men." "Please accept my warmest acknowledgments for your kindness and generosity in granting me free use of the Athenaeum

Library," she wrote in response to the invitation. "It is a privilege of which I have often felt the need, and which I shall prize very highly."[31] Little did the trustees know that one of the first uses their newest female member would make of their holdings was to take aim at one of the things they treasured most. Little could they have guessed that, after chronicling slavery's origins, history, politics, and horrors, Child had one more target: her own hometown.

"While we bestow our earnest disapprobation on the system of slavery," her final chapter begins, "let us not flatter ourselves that we are in reality any better than our brethren of the South." True, slavery had been outlawed here, "but the very spirit of the hateful and mischievous thing is here in all its strength." She herself had witnessed Black Americans in Boston being denied hotel rooms, chased from pews by indignant parishioners, blocked from trades by jealous workmen. She recalled racial slights in the halls of power and racial slurs in the streets. A violent mob elsewhere in the North, she recounted, had recently burned a school for Black children to the ground. Worse still, Northerners write and speak "as if the prejudice against skins darker colored than our own, was a fixed and unalterable law of our nature." It was another bad argument from nature, and Child was not having it. The truth, she reported, was bleaker: "We made slavery," she wrote, "and slavery makes the prejudice." Where must white Americans' contribution to ending slavery begin? Not in the hallowed halls of Congress. Not in the committee meetings of the American Colonization Society. Not in the mosquito-infested forests of Liberia, where the mortality rate among "returned" Africans was among the highest of any migrant group in recorded history. It would have to begin in the hearts of white Americans willing to examine their apathy and eradicate their bigotry. "The removal of this prejudice is not a matter of opinion," Child admonished her readers. "It is a matter of duty."[32]

A final refuge for her readers remained. It likely took the form of a protest we still hear today: Perhaps it is true that slavery makes prejudice. But I didn't make slavery; I never owned slaves.

Of course hooligans and the occasional politician let their prejudice get out of hand. But I do none of those things.

What does it take for institutional injustice to survive? It takes a culture. I may not set the school on fire or shout racial epithets in the streets. But if I participate in a culture that tolerates such behavior, a share of the responsibility is mine as well. This is doubly true if I am proud of that culture. One generation removed from the Revolutionary War, Child knew she could count on fierce pride in America's new democracy. But pride in our country's achievements is meaningless if we refuse responsibility for its failures. Credit accrues, but so do debts.

Perhaps all this blame felt unfair. And it is true: actually enslaving humans is worse than insulting them, building industry on their stolen labor, or turning a blind eye to their anguish. But the latter acts enable the former. Proof of responsibility is not measured only by intentions. It is also measured in outcomes. "If the free States wished to cherish the system of slavery for ever, they could not take a more direct course than they now do," Child wrote in Boston in 1833. A 2017 study revealed that the current median net worth among white Bostonians was $247,500. Among non-immigrant Black Bostonians, it was $8. Let us not flatter ourselves.[33]

*   *   *

For Maria Child's literary career, the year 1833 had a heartbreaking trajectory. In July of that year, the *North American Review*, the same journal that had launched her career, published a retrospective of her publications. It was the country's most prestigious journal, and it dedicated a remarkable twenty-five pages to discussing the "Works of Mrs. Child." The first paragraph must have been thrilling. What kind of woman, the reviewer asked, should be crowned the "first woman of the republic"? The answer: the woman who "wrote the most useful books." Based on this criterion, he continued, "we are not sure that any woman in our country would outrank Mrs. Child." "Few female writers, if any, have done more or better things for our literature," he wrote.

The reviewer next gushed over a "genius" who could communicate as beautifully with children as the *Juvenile Miscellany*'s editor did. This ability showed "remarkable power of invention" and was "one of the best proofs of the author's capacity for higher things." He marveled at the international sensation *The Frugal Housewife* had been, calling it "a more revolutionary book than any other that Mrs. Child has written." No aspiring housewife would be caught without it, he asserted, and its hints were "worth perusal once a month." He also credited *The Girl's Own Book* and *The Mother's Book* with advancing the crucial cause of women's education.

But this remarkable woman's talents were not limited to practical works. The reviewer was full of admiration for the Ladies' Family Library series and Child's ability to present a "speaking portrait" of the women in each volume. *The Coronel*, a collection of pieces she had published in 1832, showed that her fiction was also excellent; some of her lines were "full of as high and strong poetry as has appeared in our country." In fact, Mrs. Child seemed to "be graceful alike in telling a village story, and in giving a receipt for the kitchen; to be at home in the prose and the poetry of life; in short, to be just the woman we want for the mothers and daughters of the present generation." "We trust that Mrs. Child will continue her useful labors, and have no doubt that they will be received with constantly increasing favor," the review concluded. I wonder if, as Child read this, it was with a sense that the reviewer little knew just how wrong this last prediction was.[34]

This was because sometime earlier in 1833, Child had left the small house in Roxbury where she and David, after another move, had settled, and had made her way to the city. With her, she carried a manuscript titled *An Appeal in Favor of That Class of Americans Called Africans*. She eventually arrived at the offices of her publisher, Allen and Ticknor, a few blocks from Boston Common. In their hands, her hundreds of handwritten pages would slowly be converted to type. Soon her words would be public. As the printers laid out her text and inserted her images, what she was risking became ever clearer. In the *Appeal*, Child was attacking her nation's economy, threatening its unity, and defying its religious leaders. She was calling her politicians hypocrites and her neighbors racists. Her defense of interracial marriage staked out a position that would soon trigger some of the worst rioting New York had ever seen. The audacity of the *Appeal*'s every page was exacerbated by the fact that its author was a woman. As she checked her manuscript one last time, did she wonder if she had gone too far?

If she did, she left no record. But she concludes her *Appeal* bracing for scandal:

> By publishing this book I have put my mite in the treasury. The expectation of displeasing all classes has not been unaccompanied with pain. But it has been strongly impressed upon my mind that it was a duty to fulfil this task; and worldly considerations should never stifle the voice of conscience.[35]

At some point, maybe in a noisy, inky printing office, Child must have taken one last look at her *Appeal*. Then she resigned herself to its fate and walked away.

*   *   *

The backlash that followed the *Appeal*'s publication likely surpassed Child's most pessimistic predictions. The British reformer Harriet Martineau described Child as a "lady of whom society was exceedingly proud before she published her Appeal, and to whom society has been extremely contemptuous ever since." "Mrs. Child was denounced," her fellow reformer Samuel May later wrote: "The politicians and statesmen scouted the woman who had presumed to criticize so freely the constitution and government of her country. Women had better let politics alone." Ministers warned against her, May also recalled, predicting "evil and ruin to our country, if the women generally should follow Mrs. Child's bad example, and neglect their domestic duties to attend to the affairs of the state." Other rebukes were more personal. Some friends publicly denounced her; others quietly avoided her. Her brother James resented the embarrassment his sister's radical views caused him; their relationship never really recovered. One Bostonian proudly refused to read the *Appeal* because he feared it would make him an abolitionist. Another threw the book out of the window with a pair of tongs.[36]

The consequences for her career were quick and cascading. Her readers expressed their outrage by shunning not just the *Appeal* but all of her writings. Southern bookstores began sending her publications back. *The Mother's Book* went out of print. Even sales of *The Frugal Housewife* sputtered. "Her works were brought with avidity before," Martineau recalled, "but fell into sudden oblivion." She went from being "almost at the head of journalism at the time," recalled another source, to being "assailed opprobriously and treated derisively." Journals whose approval she had craved and won turned hostile. One lamented that "the most talented female in America" had "espoused the hopeless and unpopular cause of the slave." Sarah Hale, one of the writers she had recruited to write for the *Juvenile Miscellany*, furiously criticized the *Appeal*'s author as "wasting her soul's wealth" in radicalism and "doing incalculable injury to humanity." In one of the last letters Child received before her death, her lifelong friend John Greenleaf Whittier was still trying to reckon up the price she had paid. As the abolitionist movement began, he recalled, "some had little to sacrifice but I always felt, my dear friend, that thee had made the costliest offering to the cause. For thee alone, of all of us, had won a literary reputation which any one would have been proud of."[37]

I think what must have hurt most was the *Miscellany*. There had already been some trouble here: in the previous year, Child had published stories with antislavery themes that may well have displeased some parents. In January 1833, there had apparently already been rumors that she was resigning. At that point, Child had assured her young fans that she did not have "the slightest intention of leaving them until they leave her." A year later, now that its editor had outed herself as a full-blown abolitionist, they were

indeed leaving. Child was forced to resign. "Writers are respectfully requested to send no more contributions for the Miscellany,
as it is about to be discontinued, for want of sufficient patronage,"
read a notice in spring 1834. "After conducting the Miscellany for
eight years, I am now compelled to bid a reluctant and most affectionate farewell to my little readers," read a notice in the next. "I
part from you with less pain," Child bravely wrote, "because I hope
that God will enable me to be a medium of use to you, in some other
form than the Miscellany."[38]

How are we, generations later, to understand her public's reaction? The answer has many layers; here I will focus on just one.
George Ticknor, as everyone in Child's world knew, was the un-
questioned high priest of Boston's high culture. He took his position as its protector and promoter very seriously. Boston was, after
all, America's City on a Hill, a beacon of justice, cultivation, and
propriety. The principles of Boston, Ticknor asserted, "are right,
and its severity towards disorganizers and social democracy in all
its forms, is just and wise. It keeps our standard of public morals
where it should be." Public morals, in Ticknor's view, included a
justification of slavery. Accordingly, he kept those admitted to his
circle on a very tight leash: he was the person, one witness noted,
before whom "all have to deferentially bow on this subject of slavery." Southerners were frequent guests at his mansion across from
the State House: no doubt that helped.[39]

Garrisonian abolitionists were unquestionably just the sort of
"disorganizers" Ticknor feared. By claiming that Africans and
their descendants were human beings and the equals of whites,
they were subverting religious and political leaders. By publicly
discussing torture and rape, they were violating fixed norms of social decorum. By amplifying voices in the Black community, they
were encouraging people like Maria Stewart and David Walker in
their stinging rebukes of American culture. None of this could be
tolerated. "To Ticknor," wrote one of his biographers, "the abolitionist virus was a disease fatal to the republic, and must be quar-
antined."[40]

Quarantining such a virus, in Ticknor's world, happened through ostracism—through refusing to socialize with or even speak to those who had dared to transgress social expectations. It's important to understand why Ticknor was sure this would work. Ostracism was a bet that losing access to the goods high society offered—the fine food and wine, the proximity to the rich and powerful, the thrill of an invitation to the event of the season—would be more than most people could bear. If the ostracism took sufficient hold, its victims could be shut out of their churches and dismissed from their jobs. Business contracts and political connections would dry up. Access to capital or publishers would cease.

But Ticknor's refusal to brook dissent on the subject of slavery was not just because he feared the dissolution of Boston society. He also held viciously racist views. Africans were a "shiftless, inefficient race of men," he claimed. They were not just inferior: they were a problem. This was because white people hated them and wanted to keep them down. "The black race is more and more a disturbing element in our political system," he wrote, "and therefore, we—the white race, to protect ourselves[—]increase their disabilities in different ways, and, on the whole, render their position everywhere less favorable." White Americans' determination to increase their good fortune at Black Americans' expense, Ticknor believed, left only two solutions. He was brutally honest about this. "I see," he wrote, "no alternative left for [the Black man] except emigration or extermination." By emigration, Ticknor meant what the American Colonization Society meant: that anyone with black skin would be sent away. "If they cannot be forced to go, they will be exterminated. A war of the races will, in some form or other come on, and the black race, as the inferior, will be its inevitable victims."[41]

No explicit records exist of how Child's ostracism began. Did Ticknor, after seeing the *Appeal*, send her word never to approach him again? Or did he wait until the next time she wrote to him and return the letter unopened? Most likely she never gave him the chance. She did not need to be told that her time as his protégée was over. As to the rest of Boston high society: Ticknor would have made it clear to them that David and Maria Child were out. Ostracism worked only if society presented a united front. Those who disobeyed would face their own punishment. And so, less than ten years after she arrived, Child was turned out of the society in which she had risen so quickly and shone so brightly.

If the response of Boston's elites was outraged horror, however, the reaction within the antislavery community was ecstatic. "That such an author—ay, such an *authority*—should espouse our cause," the early abolitionist Samuel May wrote, "was a matter of no small joy, yes, exultation." Hopes were high that Child's stature could boost the cause everywhere, even in the South, where she "was extensively known" and "her books commanded a ready sale." Perhaps this was the movement's breakout moment when they would go from fringe to mainstream, invited into people's kitchens by *The Frugal Housewife*'s author herself. In addition to their jubilation, May admitted, there had also been some surprise. "We had seen her often at our meetings," he recalled, "but we did not know that she had so carefully studied and thoroughly mastered the subject. Nor," he confessed, "did we suspect that she possessed the power, if she had the courage, to strike so heavy a blow."[42]

Well, she may not have looked fierce, but she was.

The Childs' financial situation was now even more dire. Since the *Massachusetts Journal* had failed, David was both without a steady income and being hounded by creditors sure they would never recover their investment. And now Child had sacrificed the literary reputation that might have saved them. Things would get worse before they got better. Soon anti-abolitionist mobs would rage from Pennsylvania to Maine. Child would find herself shielding abolitionist speakers with her body, spiriting them out of the city, and hiding them in safe houses. Through it all, neither she nor her husband would make enough money to keep them solvent. And yet violence and poverty would not be the greatest challenges to her conversion. She could not have known this, but the end of slavery was still thirty years away. Nothing threatens a conversion like delayed change. Life gets in the way. Old habits get in the way. Failure and discouragement and defeat get in the way. Never living the same way again, it would turn out, would be the challenge of Lydia Maria Child's life.

* * *

I imagine a genteel Boston dinner party at which Convers Francis, Child's beloved brother, is asked awkward questions about his sister's new book. He answers as best he can. He returns home to his vast library, now among the largest in greater Boston, paralyzed by soul-searching. Had he indeed gone wrong in cultivating a young girl's intellect, just as his parents had worried? What harm had he unleashed on the world by lending his little sister Milton and Shakespeare? He wrote her a letter, which is now lost. But Child's response conjures its admonishing tone. "You ask me to be prudent, and I will be so," she concedes. But, she quickly warns, it is too late for "what the world calls prudent." "I have examined the cause of the slave too thoroughly, and felt his wrongs too deeply, to be prudent in the worldly sense of the term," she wrote. I imagine Convers Francis reading the letter, then closing his eyes, head in his hands.[43]

I imagine tearful children being told they will no longer be receiving the *Juvenile Miscellany*, since their beloved Aunt Maria had turned out to be a dangerous radical. But while their less tolerant parents were not looking—trusting perhaps too easily in a familiar author—the damage had been done. "I well remember," an early reader of the *Miscellany* wrote to Child decades later, "the zeal with which it was circulated, by a little group of schoolgirl abolitionists, of which I had the honor to be one." We can only imagine what rippling effect those schoolgirls had on their society as they grew to adulthood and raised children of their own. Other effects of Child's efforts we do not need to conjecture. Thomas Wentworth Higginson, one of the financers of John Brown's bloody abolitionist insurrection twenty-five years later, gave Child credit for his youthful conversion to antislavery work. Massachusetts senator Charles Sumner, too, cited Child's influence in starting him down the road of passionate abolitionism that would lead, decades later, to his being beaten unconscious on the Senate floor.[44]

And what of the proud Bostonian who refused to read the *Appeal*, fearing it would make him an abolitionist? He was a respected colonizationist minister whose income depended on keeping his wealthy congregation happy. His wife and daughter had been converted by Child's arguments.[45] I imagine them emboldened by the *Appeal*'s female author. I envision the minister harried by antislavery arguments as he sat at dinner, pursued by evidence of racial equality as he tried to escape to his bedchamber.

How many more people among Boston's polite society sat at dinner parties, hearing their hosts rage at Mrs. Child's audacity, wondering to themselves whether she was right? Among the outraged parents who canceled their subscriptions to the *Juvenile Miscellany*, how many had second thoughts? How many hearts were softened and minds awakened, so that when an opportunity for action materialized, people were ready? We will never know, and Child never did either. But people do not throw ineffective books out of windows with tongs.

4

Of Mobs and Marriages

The first few times I read Maria Child's response to her brother's letter—her defiant reply to his call for prudence—I thought his concern was primarily for his sister's reputation. Perhaps also for his own. But one day it dawned on me. The letter had been written in 1835, two years after the *Appeal* was published. By then, Convers would probably have resigned himself to her radical opinions and reduced social status. But the intervening years had also witnessed a dramatic and dangerous shift in abolitionists' fortunes. By then, their opponents had tried ignoring them, chastising them, ostracizing them, and legislating against them. None of these tactics had worked. And so in 1835, a year that became known as "the mob year," anti-abolitionists had turned to violence.

Convers, I now realized, no longer feared only for his sister's reputation; he feared for her life. Here is how her letter continues: "Firmness is the virtue most needed in times of excitement. What consequence is it if a few individuals do sink to untimely and dishonored graves, if the progress of great principles is still onward? Perchance for this cause came we into the world."[1]

An "untimely and dishonored grave"? Convers must have blanched. It had clearly not been enough for his younger sister to throw away her reputation and, with it, her livelihood by writing an incendiary book. Now she seemed intent on putting herself in physical danger. Most likely, he did not know the half of it.

* * *

The first years after her *Appeal* had passed quietly enough. The Childs were still living in a tiny home called Cottage Place—which they laughingly called "Le Paradis des Pauvres"—in Roxbury, a few miles from the heart of Boston. So far David was holding his creditors at bay: by what means is unclear. It must have felt like a stay of execution; they both must have known that it could end at any time. Child never forgot this little home, which, although she did not know it, was to be their last together for many years. Much of what is now Boston was then water, and their house was right on its edge. The moonlight played on the waves as they went to bed; the garden on the side of the house overflowed with flowers. Not far from them lived Louisa and Ellis Loring, who by now had a baby girl named Anna and a big gray cat. Child remembered long, luxurious breakfasts and electrifying, wide-ranging discussions, cementing the two couples' friendship as well as their dedication to abolition.[2] So the Childs continued to exist in a vertiginous mix of financial insecurity and domestic happiness, social ostracism and burgeoning friendship.

One day, not long after her *Appeal* had been published and their ostracism had begun, Child received a surprising visitor. The Reverend William Ellery Channing had walked the mile and a half from his home on Boston's genteel Mount Vernon Street to their humble lodgings on the waterfront. Channing was the concerned Unitarian minister who had written his senator to warn that the influence of abolitionist Benjamin Lundy had to be stopped before it spread. He was another of Boston's most influential men. A grandson of a signatory to the Declaration of Independence, he had refined tastes to match his long American pedigree. He was both a beloved preacher and a prominent theologian. By the time he arrived in Roxbury, he was hot and tired. Despite the warm weather, he had brought his coat, just in case.[3]

Child must have felt apprehensive. What did the famous clergyman want from her? Why would he make this arduous journey instead of asking to see her in his church offices? Channing had a reputation for being thoughtful and reform-minded, but he was, in his own way, also a conscientious protector of Boston's status quo. He had discouraged his parishioners from joining antislavery societies, warning that the misguided message of abolition would damage the church's unity and undermine its authority. So what he said next must have stunned her. "He expressed great joy at the publication of the 'Appeal,'" she later wrote. It had, he told her, "aroused my conscience."

They talked for three hours. One tense moment occurred when Channing ventured to suggest that perhaps she had gone too far. Wasn't it true, he proposed, "that slavery existed in a milder form in the United States than elsewhere"? "I was fresh from the bloody records of our own legislation, and was somewhat vehement in my opposition to this statement," Child recalled. We can imagine her reciting piece after piece of gory evidence, countering each of Channing's efforts to "moderate [her] zeal" with her research and her passion. It was, apparently, a full and frank conversation between the middle-aged theologian and the young reformer. Before he left, to her further shock, Channing "urged me never to desert the cause through evil report or good report," she wrote. He also mused that her book had made him wonder if he should write something on the subject as well.[4]

It would be wrong to say that Channing never lived his life the same way again. He would always be a moderate, and his reluctance to champion their moral clarity would prove a constant source of exasperation to abolitionists. Having been given an opening to him that day in Roxbury, Child was regularly dispatched by her coadjutors to try to win him over more fully. After one meeting, she reported that "he had progressed . . . considerably since I last conversed with him" but "still betrayed his characteristic timidity," beginning almost every sentence with "I am doubtful" or "I am afraid." When he indeed published a pamphlet titled *Slavery* in 1835, Garrison denounced it in the *Liberator* for its tepid gradualism and modest ambitions. But there is no doubt that many of Channing's readers were moved from complete ignorance or apathy about slavery to more moderate positions because of his writings. That afternoon in Roxbury also marked the beginning of a complicated bond between Child and Channing that persisted through many tortuous twists in abolitionism's progress. One observer reported that when Channing once heard "aristocratic ladies, seated in one of the handsomest drawing-rooms in Boston" mocking Child, he put her detractors to shame by predicting that she would be proved right.[5]

But if Channing remained chronically unconvinced, other readers of Child's *Appeal* were not. One evening, Ellis Loring later recalled, a "very talented and agreeable young gentleman" called on him and Louisa. This visitor had, he told them, been reading the *Appeal*, and it "had made a strong impression on him." Apparently they too had an intense conversation about the book and its arguments. "When he bade us good evening," Loring recalled, "he said, with a charming smile, that he didn't know but he should be obliged to come out an abolitionist." The man's name was Wendell Phillips. Phillips was a lawyer, a former student of Channing's, and, it turned out, a stunningly gifted orator. He did indeed become an abolitionist. Within a few years, he had abandoned his law practice and joined the movement as a full-time speaker and agitator, known as "abolition's golden trumpet."[6] It's not clear when he and Child first met, but their lifelong friendship ended only when he spoke at her memorial service, thanking the woman who had changed his life.

Sometime in these early years of the movement, Child also met Francis and Sarah Shaw. Francis Shaw had been born into a powerful Boston merchant family that had recently become one of the wealthiest in the nation; his wife Sarah, herself born into great affluence, was beautiful, curious, and intellectually vivacious. Both had grown disillusioned with their wealth and the exploitation of labor in the West Indies and the American South that fueled its growth. By the 1830s, Francis Shaw had left his father's business and dedicated himself to reform. Both were eager supporters of progressive theology and found kindred spirits in other radical thinkers. Somehow they met the Childs and were drawn, possibly through them, into abolitionism. The two couples formed a bond

Fig. 14. Wendell Phillips, the abolition movement's "Golden Trumpet," was converted to antislavery views by Child's *Appeal*. Courtesy of the National Portrait Gallery.

that would sustain them through decades of activism and through the sacrifice of the Shaws' only son at the head of a troop of Black soldiers at the height of the Civil War. "You have been the greatest blessing of my life," Child wrote to Sarah Shaw after almost forty years of friendship. "I believe all the flowers of my soul would have been submerged in mud, if it had not been for you."[7]

As these alliances formed and friendships flourished, Garrison continued to expose the horrors of American slavery in the *Liberator*, week after exhausting week. Money was always scarce. Con-

Fig. 15. Francis George Shaw. Collection of Staten Island Museum.

verts always seemed too few. Despite their insistence that he be silenced, Garrison was still relatively easy for his enemies to dismiss: too fringe, too ultra, too fanatical. Until, suddenly, it wasn't possible to dismiss him at all.

* * *

In the mid-1830s, abolitionism exploded from the periphery of Americans' consciousness into the mainstream. At the beginning

Fig. 16. Sarah Blake Sturgis Shaw. The Shaws were also among Child's closest life-long friends. Collection of Staten Island Museum.

of 1833, there were four antislavery societies across two states. By the end, there were forty-seven spread across ten states. Four years later, there were over a thousand local societies with a collective total of 100,000 members.[8] The movement also was gaining support from influential allies. Among them were Lewis and Arthur Tappan, wealthy New York businessmen who had bailed Garrison out of his Baltimore prison cell just three years before. In 1833, Arthur Tappan, Garrison, and others formed the American Anti-Slavery Society, or AAS, a centralized national organization that operated out of New York. It soon had more than seventy agents in the field. Agents gave speeches, raised money, met with local societies, and tried to increase the numbers of the converted. Teamed with such powerful supporters and a growing network of like-minded reformers, Garrison suddenly seemed less like a voice crying in the wilderness and more like the general in an advancing army.

What had happened? The abolitionist movement owed its astonishing growth to two principal weapons. The first was its orators. Abolitionist speakers—Garrison, Wendell Phillips, and a young Lane Seminary student named Theodore Dwight Weld—often conducted their meetings like evangelical revivals, delivering fiery sermons about slavery's evils that left their listeners convicted of their sin and desperate to change. Like Child, these converts used the language of religious conversion to describe the transformative commitment they were making to ending slavery.[9] Like Child, they cycled through agony and elation. Also like her, many of them would never be the same again.

The second weapon was the steam-powered printing press. Combined with new techniques for manufacturing and cutting paper, these new presses sharply increased production and decreased expense. New York abolitionists jumped at the opportunity to mass-produce antislavery books and pamphlets, reporting in 1835 that they were able to produce nine times as many publications for only five times the money. The year before, they had printed 120,000 individual pieces of literature. This year they produced over a million. And they got creative. The AAS inundated the country not just with newspapers but with antislavery "kerchiefs, medals, emblems," and even chocolate wrappers. Their materials included illustrations that illiterate slaves could easily understand. In Maryland, an enslaved boy who would one day rename himself Frederick Douglass began to hear his fellow slaves whisper the word "abolitionist" and wondered what it meant.[10]

The flood of publications hit the South in summer 1835. The outcry was immediate. "The unexpected evil is now upon us," future US president John Tyler warned a Virginia audience. "A society has sprung up whose avowed object is to despoil us of our property" and to destroy "our political paradise, the Union of these States." Worse, he claimed, the society was encouraging slave insurrections, "sharpening the dagger for midnight assassination." Several Southern states passed resolutions demanding that Northern legislatures prohibit the distribution of abolitionist publications. South Carolina senator John Calhoun argued that mailing antislavery publications to the South violated the "law of nations" because it meddled with slaveholding states' independence. Still the publications kept coming. Southern postmasters, complaining that their offices were "literally filled" with abolitionist publications, appealed for help. New York's anti-abolitionist postmaster sympathized, so he simply stopped sending the publications south. He wrote to President Jackson's postmaster general asking whether this was legal. Probably not, came the response, but do it anyway. "The President, the Secretary of State, the Secretary of War and the Secretary of the Navy entirely concur with me in my general views of this subject," the postmaster added.[11]

But now the abolitionists had the country's attention. New measures to repress them were called for. Across the country, citizens decided to take the law into their own hands. Throughout 1835, violence against abolitionists increased, surged, and spiked. There was plenty of precedent for violent conflict in the United States, but this kind of unrest felt new. "What is the meaning of all this?" asked a *New York Herald* writer after one mob attack. Was it possible that the abolitionists, whom he called "a few thousand crazy-headed blockheads," had "actually frightened fifteen million people out of their senses"? Mobs have "pervaded the country from New England to Louisiana," marveled a young Illinois lawyer named Abraham Lincoln; "they are neither peculiar to the eternal snows of the former nor the burning suns of the latter."[12]

The violence focused on the abolitionists' two greatest strengths: their speakers and their printing presses. As of 1835, abolitionist lecturers regularly confronted mobs. Sometimes mob participants simply made so much noise that the speaker could not be heard. Often they threw eggs or bricks, and sometimes things got more serious. Mobs occasionally set fire to the abolitionists' meeting places or even their homes. In 1838, a mob burned Pennsylvania Hall, built by the Pennsylvania Anti-Slavery Society, to the ground three days after it opened. Not content to stop there, they attacked a Black orphanage and a Black church. In 1836, a stone-throwing mob accosted abolitionist orator Theodore Weld, leaving him with a concussion that helped end his speaking career.[13]

Mobs also regularly attacked abolitionist newspapers. In Alton, Illinois, in 1837, the abolitionist editor Elijah Parish Lovejoy had just received his fourth printing press—the first three had already been destroyed by anti-abolitionist rioters—when a mob set fire to his building. This time Lovejoy decided to defend himself. Shots were exchanged, and Lovejoy was killed. Even as his friends tended to his corpse, mob members stayed to smash his printing press with hammers and throw it in the river.[14]

Who *were* these people?

Convers Francis blamed the masses. Democracy, he wrote to his sister, was the "mother of evil," encouraging passions and delusions of grandeur in every street-corner hooligan. Child disagreed. The problem was not uneducated workers or illiterate immigrants. "The majority of their voices would be on the right side if the question were fairly brought before them," she wrote to Convers. The problem lay elsewhere. "We should be little troubled with mobs," she assured him, "if people called respectable did not give them their sanction."[15]

She was right. Anti-abolitionist mobs were not usually spontaneous groups of enraged street thugs. They were organized and led, as one Boston paper favorably put it, by "gentlemen of property and standing"—doctors, lawyers, merchants, bankers, judges, and politicians. These were often middle-aged men whose families were wealthy and whose American heritage was long. They were also men who had the most to lose in a society whose manufacturing base was changing and whose social order was shifting. Many were members of the American Colonization Society.[16]

How do we know all this? Because mob organizers took attendance at their meetings. They also passed resolutions and laid out strategies. Sometimes they issued warnings. Those "engaged in the unholy cause of annoying our southern neighbors," one handbill in Philadelphia advised, could "prevent a resort to violence" only by ceasing to publish their paper. Other times they issued invitations to working-class members of their cities to join them at a certain time and place. In some cases they insisted that the American Anti-Slavery Society's "system of operations" was "un-American," and that abolitionists had forfeited due process and police protection by being traitors to their country.[17] In other words, these groups targeting abolitionists were not really mobs. They were not just hooligans whose uncontainable outrage suddenly crystallized into action. They were groups of otherwise upstanding citizens engaged in premeditated extrajudicial violence.

This violence drew widespread praise from politicians, journalists, and police. In one case a riot raged until the police chief decided it had "done enough damage" and—only as the violence threatened those beyond its abolitionist targets—now risked "harming innocents." One New York newspaper suggested darkly that a forthcoming abolitionist convention should be put down by "the law of Judge Lynch"—in other words, that attendees should not be arrested and tried but should simply be executed by the mob. After Lovejoy's murder, the attorney general of Massachusetts told an audience at Boston's famous Faneuil Hall that his attackers should be praised for following the example of Samuel Adams by using violence to protect their country. In his 1835 annual message, President Jackson himself praised the "strong and impressive" Northern response to abolitionists, calling for "severe penalties" to suppress abolitionists' "unconstitutional and wicked" actions.[18] It was a dog whistle few could mistake.

How had abolitionists so enraged these non-slaveholding gentlemen of property and standing? Let us count the ways. Abolitionists, Child among them, were threatening to undermine both economic and political stability. They were disrupting traditional channels of authority, going over the heads of husbands, ministers, and politicians and appealing directly to women, children, and both free and enslaved Black people. They were using "heart-rending stories and horrifying pictures" to stir up feminine passions. Sewing circles, one politician lamented, were being turned into antislavery clubs. Abolitionists were also believed to be in the pay of England as part of a plot to sow dissent and undermine American democracy. President Jackson called abolitionists "emissaries from foreign parts" who had "dared to interfere" in American sovereignty.[19]

Let us also be honest. Participants in these mobs were not objecting only for political and economic reasons. Most viscerally, Northern anti-abolitionist mobs were racist. In particular, the idea of interracial marriage—it was called "amalgamation"—drove them nearly mad. A series of New York mobs in July 1834 was triggered by fabricated rumors that abolitionists had married Black women or adopted Black children. During the worst of these mobs, rioters held off the National Guard for three days as they destroyed the largely Black neighborhood of Five Points. In white neighborhoods, special destruction was reserved for homes and churches of ministers reported to have presided over interracial marriages. On the fourth day of rioting, the American Anti-Slavery Society published a handbill that disclaimed "any desire to promote or encourage intermarriages between white and colored persons."[20] The violence subsided. It was an ignoble retreat.

Racial violence against free Black Americans in the North was nothing new. It was already well established and sanctioned, haunting free Northern Blacks, as one author put it, "from cradle to grave." It was not, as anti-abolitionists liked to claim, the fault of the abolitionists for stirring up hatred. It also served as its own justification. Anything as vicious as Northern prejudice against Black Americans, one colonizationist argued, was obviously "an ordination of Providence, and no more to be changed than the laws of nature."[21] There it was again: another bad argument from nature.

Another familiar argument is at work here as well. It has to do with the idea of a backlash. What, this argument asks, did abolitionists expect? If you antagonize powerful oppressors, you have only yourself to blame for whatever happens next. This is especially true if the oppression is so systemic and entrenched that resistance appears irrational. Slavery, in other words, was lamentable, but resistance was unreasonable. So when Black people or abolitionists resisted, the argument went, they deserved whatever furious response they got.

And what of the accusation that abolitionists were to blame for exciting "violent" prejudices? It's important to think this accusation through. No one in Garrison's abolitionist movement had done anything remotely violent. They were writing and speaking: engaging in time-honored American rights. But accusing those who resist oppression of violence, however metaphorical, is itself a time-honored way to silence them. If what Garrison and Child were doing felt violent, that was only because they were speaking directly and clearly, calling out people who thought of themselves as good for participating in evil. And insofar as David Walker had threatened retribution or Nat Turner had carried it out, were *they* not the backlash to the violence inflicted on them and their fellow Black Americans? If white Americans continued to enslave and degrade Black Americans, was it not *they* who should have seen a great reckoning coming? Who, we might ask, gets to be the backlash?

As the "mob year" came and went, violence against Black businesses, churches, and schools raged on, depriving free Blacks of generations of capital and education—exactly the trappings of respectability whites claimed to need in order to accept them. Black activist Susan Paul, in an 1834 letter to the *Liberator*, protested the "cruel prejudice which deprives us of every privilege whereby we might elevate ourselves—and then condemns us because we are not more refined and intelligent." This paradoxical dynamic would prove to be a favorite tactic of white supremacy, extending through Reconstruction to Jim Crow and beyond by means of unfair housing prices, corrupt lending practices, and lack of educational opportunity. The effects of these injustices are still evident today in income and education disparities. Since 1989, a bill sponsored by Black legislators has been introduced in the House of Representatives every year, proposing a commission to study whether reparations are owed to the Black community for these generational losses. As of 2021, no such commission had been formed. Perhaps this is not surprising. "The doctrine of leaving the injurer to decide when and how reparation should be made to the injured," Child wrote in 1834, "forms a very precarious basis for civil rights."[22]

In the summer of 1835, as mob violence was at its peak, Maria Child found herself in the center of the storm. The legendary abolitionist orator George Thompson had arrived in the United States on a speaking tour. Thompson especially enraged anti-abolitionists because he was British. He confirmed their worst fears about English intervention in American democracy: he had come, some claimed, "on purpose to split the American Church, and divide the American Union," to "promote civil war here, and thus overthrow our blessed institutions." At almost every stop, anti-abolitionists harassed him. He was evicted from a hotel in New York, driven out of his lodgings in Augusta, Maine, pelted with eggs and stones in Concord, Massachusetts. His enemies were right to be afraid. When he was allowed to speak, Thompson was electrifying. He left a trail of newly converted abolitionists in his wake. David Child's sister-in-law, hardly a radical, found Thompson to be a "gentlemanly, delightful man." "If he staid here another day," she declared, "he would make me an abolitionist."[23]

Next on Thompson's tour came Boston, where tensions were already high. On August 1, he was scheduled to speak at Julien Hall, a downtown venue used for public meetings, exhibitions, and the occasional boxing match. Thompson had already received death threats. On the day of his speech, Child arrived at the hall uneasy, and it quickly became clear that her fear was well founded. A "line of men in fine broadcloth"—well-dressed gentlemen of property and standing—were ominously exchanging "nods and glances" with "truckmen, in shirt sleeves"—with, in other words, working-class Bostonians they had recruited to join them. Her fear of these men was personal: David was also scheduled to speak. But the would-be troublemakers had eyes only for Thompson. The veteran abolitionist faced them from the podium with stoic composure. He began his lecture: "Such burning torrents of eloquence as he poured forth, I never before listened to!" Child later remembered.

His words "scorched like lightning," burning abolitionists and their opponents alike. As he finished, the mood turned ugly. "The heart of every abolitionist beat with a quickened pulse, for Thompson's safety," she wrote. "The stairway and entry were lined with desperate-looking fellows, brandishing clubs and cart-whips."[24]

The abolitionists had a plan, and it involved women. Female abolitionists, Child among them, quickly encircled Thompson, appearing to engage him with fervent questions. The glowering faces jostled closer, but Thompson's foes seemed unwilling to lay hands on the women to get to him. Chatting all the way, the tight group moved slowly toward an opening in the curtain. Thompson slipped through. The women stood there as if waiting for him to reappear. The would-be mob circled uneasily. David tried to distract a ringleader he knew as the barkeeper of a local tavern by engaging him in conversation. "My heart, meanwhile, throbbed so violently, that I felt I should sink upon the floor. But we did not sink, any of us," Child later wrote. Meanwhile, friends positioned behind the curtain hurried Thompson out a back door and into a waiting carriage. By the time anyone noticed he was gone, it was too late. Thompson had escaped.[25]

But Boston was no longer safe. The Childs volunteered to smuggle Thompson to New York. What followed were among the most harrowing few weeks of Maria Child's early life. She and David accompanied Thompson on a boat "full of Southerners": "Had I committed some monstrous crime," she wrote to a friend, "I could not have performed this journey with more uncomfortable sensations." They arrived to find New York a tinderbox. "Private assassins from N. Orleans are lurking at the corners of the streets, to stab Arthur Tappan," she continued, "and very large sums are offered for any one who will convey Mr. Thompson into the slave states." Concluding that any address in Manhattan would be unsafe, the fugitive group continued to the home of abolitionist sympathizers in Brooklyn. They stayed inside, away from windows. "I have not ventured into the city," Child wrote to Louisa Loring, "so great is the excitement here. You can form no conception of it— 'Tis like the times of the French Revolution where no man dared trust his neighbor." They soon learned that a flyer claiming Thompson was staying at Lewis Tappan's home was circulating in Manhattan. It exhorted New Yorkers to seize Thompson's "body forthwith and bring him before me" to be "dealt with according to my Code of Laws." It was signed "Judge Lynch." It included Tappan's address.[26]

Their Brooklyn hosts were frightened. It was only a matter of time until Thompson's real whereabouts were discovered and the mob arrived at their door. Early the next morning, David left to escort Thompson back to Boston and from there to John Greenleaf Whittier's farm in Haverhill, Massachusetts. Years later, Child recounted her "hurried farewell" to both men in the "morning twilight" as they rushed to catch the four o'clock boat.[27]

Child stayed on, but her presence was still a threat to her hosts. If somehow she was recognized, "it might naturally be reported that Thompson was in the same house." The mob would likely not have the courtesy to ask if he was truly there before attacking. She relocated to a hotel room near Brooklyn's Bath Beach and stayed there alone. "Never, before or since, have I experienced such utter desolation, as I did the few days I remained there," she later wrote. "It seemed to me as if anti-slavery had cut me off from all the sympathies of my kind." She sat on the beach, looking past Staten Island to the "surging sea" beyond. Behind her, Manhattan seethed. "Violence, in some form, seems to be generally expected," she wrote to Louisa.[28]

In the end, the violence erupted first in Boston. Again the incident involved women. In October, a rumor spread that Thompson was not only in Boston but scheduled to address the Boston Female Anti-Slavery Society meeting at abolitionists' downtown headquarters. Anti-abolitionist merchants published a flyer calling on "the friends of the Union" to amass at 46 Washington Street "to snake out . . . the infamous foreign scoundrel Thompson." It offered $100 to the first person who laid "violent hands on Thompson, so that he may be brought to the tar-kettle before dark." Nervous downtown shopkeepers begged the mayor to call off the meeting. When he didn't, the usual gentlemen of property and standing be-

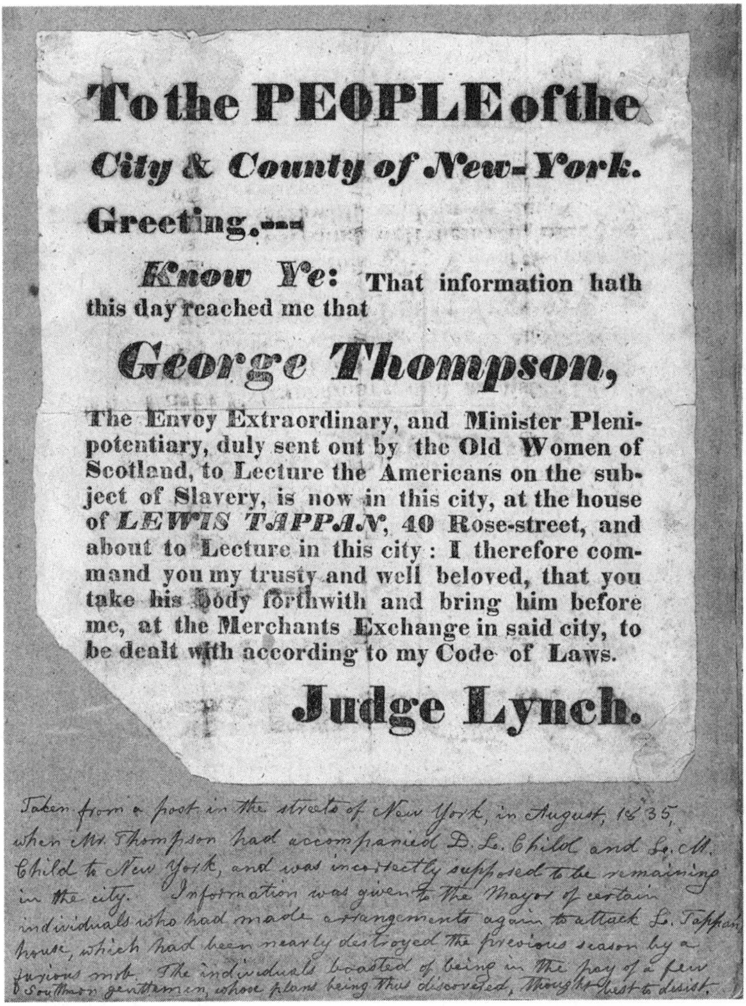

To the PEOPLE of the City & County of New-York.

Greeting.—

Know Ye: That information hath this day reached me that

George Thompson,

The Envoy Extraordinary, and Minister Pleni-potentiary, duly sent out by the Old Women of Scotland, to Lecture the Americans on the sub-ject of Slavery, is now in this city, at the house of *LEWIS TAPPAN*, 40 Rose-street, and about to Lecture in this city : I therefore com-mand you my trusty and well beloved, that you take his body forthwith and bring him before me, at the Merchants Exchange in said city, to be dealt with according to my Code of Laws.

Judge Lynch.

Taken from a post in the streets of New York, in August, 1835, when Mr. Thompson had accompanied D. L. Child and Mr. M. Child to New York, and was incorrectly supposed to be remaining in the city. Information was given to the Mayor of certain individuals who had made arrangements again to attack L. Tappan's house, which had been nearly destroyed the previous season by a furious mob. The individuals boasted of being in the pay of a few Southern gentlemen, whose plans being thus discovered, thought best to desist.

Fig. 17. A flyer encouraging a mob to form and lynch British abolitionist George Thompson in August 1835. Child pasted it into her scrapbook, adding a descrip-tion of her involvement in protecting Thompson in New York City. Courtesy of the Schlesinger Library, Harvard University.

gan to gather; Boston workers, clerks, and shopkeepers came to join them. At some point, the news spread that not Thompson but Garrison was scheduled to address the women. The crowd seemed not to mind that its quarry had changed. There was talk of captur-ing Garrison and extraditing him to Savannah.[29]

The streets filled. The women who managed to force their way

through the crowd gathered in the society's auditorium. A few aspiring hooligans pushed into the entryway; others began rattling
doors and throwing garbage through the transom. It was now
clear that if Garrison spoke, there would be a riot. The women decided only to transact the society's business and to reschedule the
lecture. Garrison left the auditorium for an office at its back. As
the meeting began, howls for his lynching from the street below
drowned out the secretary's report. Boston's mayor burst in, demanding that the women leave before a serious riot started. "If
this is the last bulwark of freedom," Maria Weston Chapman replied, "we may as well die here."[30] The mayor was not interested in
creating martyrs, especially female ones. He escorted them out.
The mob roared insults as they passed. Unfortunately their departure meant that Garrison was now alone in the building.

It didn't take the mob long to find him. Bellowing their intent to
hang him in the Common, they tied him up and dragged him into
the street. Just as it seemed that Garrison would achieve the martyrdom he so openly courted, two sympathetic truckmen suddenly
appeared like guardian angels, fought off the mob, and rushed him
into city hall. The mayor arrived to find a bruised but unbowed
Garrison in ripped clothes and crushed spectacles, his neck encircled by a sagging noose. He put Garrison in the only place he was
sure he could protect him: the jail. The next day he charged Garrison with disturbing the peace. Sensing a press opportunity, Garrison autographed the walls of his jail cell and went home ecstatic.[31]

The Boston *Atlas* blamed abolitionists for the riot. The *Patriot*
complained that this was what happened "when women turn reformers." The *Commercial Gazette* praised the "gentlemen" who
had defended their country from abolitionist radicals. Media in
other cities also took notice. A Cincinnati newspaper praised Bostonians for dragging Garrison, whom they accused of being "the
Missionary of Britain, and probably the hired stipendiary of the
[king] himself," through the streets. Directly preceding an anti-
abolitionist riot the following year, a Cincinnati town meeting
passed a resolution praising "the noble and fearless example set
us" by the Boston mob, whom it described as patriots acting "*with-*

Fig. 18. A depiction of an anti-abolitionist mob ransacking the Anti-Slavery Society offices on Washington Street in Boston. The mob dragged William Lloyd Garrison through the streets and threatened to lynch him on Boston Common. Courtesy of Digital Commonwealth.

out the sanction of law, but in the plentitude of the justness of their cause."[32]

Child was still in New York. It must have been harrowing. Two of her fellow abolitionists—Maria Chapman and Garrison—had barely survived violent mobs. Several others, in the wake of the violence, had temporarily fled Boston. Thompson was not yet safe. At some point, the news arrived that a young seminarian from Massachusetts named Amos Dresser had been caught in Nashville with antislavery literature, including one of Child's publications. Authorities accused him of plotting a slave insurrection and publicly flogged him. Did Child wonder how much of this violence was the result of her *Appeal*? It was working: Was it working too well? "My faith has at times been so weak, that I have started, and trembled, and wept," she wrote.[33]

* * *

As it happened, Maria Child had other reasons to weep. The fact was that the Childs were not just accompanying Thompson to New York: months before, they had decided to accompany him back to England after his United States tour. Child's writings had caught the attention of English abolitionists who had invited them both to move to England and work for the movement there. What excitement Child must have felt. David had lived abroad, but she had not. England offered her a chance to write for a more receptive audience and to repay some of their debts. Antislavery collaborators raised money for their journey. Female abolitionists in Lynn and Salem presented Maria with a watch inscribed "To their friend MRS. CHILD, the true, the noble, the irreproachable, who made the first 'APPEAL' in behalf of the AMERICAN slave": an attribution that, however touching, unfortunately neglected to acknowledge David Walker's earlier *Appeal*. The Childs sold most of their belongings, packed up the rest, and bid tearful farewells to admiring friends.[34]

And then, as they waited on the pier to board the ship, David was arrested.

If only he had been arrested for his radical views. There would have been dignity in that. The truth was less flattering. David owed money to George Snelling, his business partner from the *Massachusetts Journal*. Hearing that the Childs were about to sail for England and fearing their departure would decrease his chances of being repaid, Snelling had arranged to have David detained.[35] This disaster was, in fact, just the latest in a series of professional setbacks for David, all bearing his trademark combination of idealism and imprudence. In 1835, thinking perhaps that he should put his law degree to work now that his journalism career had ended, he had offered to represent a group of sailors from a Spanish ship called the *Panda* who had been accused of piracy. Several of them were Black, and David, no doubt correctly, was convinced they would not get a fair hearing. As it became clear that his clients had very little chance of winning and even less of paying, Child had warned him: "You must *think* of this; though you know me well enough, to know that I would not allow it to weigh very much in the balance with human life."[36]

Fig. 19. A pocket watch given to Child by "anti-slavery Ladies" in Lynn and Salem, Massachusetts. It is inscribed: "To their friend MRS. CHILD, the true, the noble, the irreproachable, who made the first 'APPEAL' in behalf of the AMERICAN slave." Courtesy of the Medford Historical Society & Museum.

The quick pivot in her sentence is striking. Please be prudent, she says. Of course the sacrifice will be worth it, she continues. If it works, she implies. This sounds like an echo of a chronic argument. Its pattern goes something like this: David has another passionate, well-intentioned idea for saving the world. He rushes in. His wife's first impulse is to follow. She loves him, and his cause is just. Their joint activism is at the foundation of their marriage. But scheme after scheme fails and their debts grow. Her alarm registers to him as a lack of faith or, worse, a weakening dedication to the cause. When her caution is vindicated, shame propels him at the next target with renewed energy. Aware of his wounded pride, she compensates by asking no questions. The scheme fails. The next time around, her hesitation feels like an accusation. She hastens to assure him it's not. But in a way it is. And then the cycle begins again.

David's defense of the *Panda* crew was partially successful—five of the twelve sailors were acquitted. A motion for a retrial failed. David fought on. In one of the couple's more bizarre escapades, he sent his wife to Washington, DC, to plead with Andrew Jackson for clemency. As she traveled from Boston to the capital during a frigid February, she must have known this was a fool's errand. Indeed, Jackson was unmoved, and Child returned humiliated. Those judged guilty were hanged. David's clients' inability to pay added to their debts. The case also cemented his reputation as a reckless, stubborn, and ultimately ineffective lawyer. He never practiced law again.[37]

In 1835, as George Thompson sailed to England without them, the question was what to do next. David avoided jail this time, but Snelling had filed a lawsuit to recover money David owed, and the case threatened to drag on indefinitely. For a year, David flailed, turning from one idea to another, the more improbably heroic the better. Perhaps he could take over a New York editorship. Maybe they should move west to Illinois—a prospect Child dreaded but braced herself for. He became obsessed with the burgeoning war between Mexico and the Republic of Texas. Perhaps nostalgic for his youthful freedom fighting in Europe, he wrote to a Mexican official offering to raise a military corps of Black soldiers. At one point, Child announced to friends that they were moving to Mexico to live in an interracial frontier settlement run by Benjamin Lundy. This settlement would prove once and for all, Lundy hoped, that Blacks and whites could live together peacefully and productively. True, Child admitted to their alarmed families, there was a war going on in Mexico. But the proposed settlement, David had assured his wife, was far from the conflict. This turned out to be false. Before they could leave, Texans invaded and conquered the entire region. The plan was scrapped.[38] Meanwhile, unable to afford a home of their own, they boarded with others and then—oh, the shame of it—separately with their respective families.

Very few of David's letters survive, but evidence of his shame during this period is abundant in letters from his wife. "Dear husband, do not be discouraged," Child wrote as he traveled to Boston to confront his legal woes. "'Better days are coming'—even in *this* world." She soothes his ego: "Few men have done more good in the world than you have done. Few are more *truly* respected, though thousands are more popular." She attributes his failures to his good intentions: "The errors you have committed have been entirely errors of judgment. How much more bitter would be the retrospection, if you had to look back upon crime, and willful wrong!" She assures him that she doesn't mind their shared sufferings: "God knows that I consider my union with you his richest blessing. . . . I had rather be your wife without a cent in the world, than to possess millions, and not be your wife."[39]

And she apologizes: "I weep when I think how selfish and unreasonable I have often been." She assures him of her love and—perhaps more important—her respect: "You have been to me a most kind, considerate, and forgiving husband; and I have ever loved and respected you with my whole heart." There is evidence of darker dynamics at work as well. "*Do* you love me?" she asks. "God only knows how deeply and tenderly I love you, and how often the tears start from my eyes because I cannot relieve your troubles." She begs him to join her at her father's home. She has assured her father that she will pay room and board for them both. "*Do* come, if you love me," she begged. He never did.[40]

By this time, they were probably both struggling with another sorrow. The Childs had now been married for several years. At some point it became clear to them that they would not have children. It's not clear why; reproduction and infertility were among the nineteenth century's inscrutable mysteries. So they probably never knew, and neither will we. The ironies were inescapable and cruel; the Childs would have no children, and the author of *The Mother's Book* would never be a mother. For a while Child kept hoping, putting together an album of lovingly sketched flowers for a daughter named Rosa-Maria who, she finally admitted, would never join them. Eventually she gave the album to a niece instead. Sometimes she acknowledged that she could help the cause better without children to distract her, and this made her grateful. But other times, the soft curls of other people's daughters made her heart ache: more, she insisted, for David than for herself.[41]

As she waited for her husband to right himself, shuttling from location to location and plan to plan, harboring her own sorrows all the while, Child also wrote her third novel. Perhaps more surprisingly, she found a publisher willing to take a chance on her again. Set in ancient Greece, *Philothea* is vintage Child: smart, witty, imaginative, philosophical. It includes lively discourses on the nature of reality, the essence of love, and the promise of an afterlife. Like *Hobomok*, it weaves social critique through an elegant plot. In the age of Andrew Jackson, it critiqued demagogues. It supported abolition by probing the distorted psychology of slavery.

But the heroine, Philothea herself, is enough to make you weep. She is beautiful, brilliant, artistic, and good. But she renounces her intellectual gifts and devotes herself to living in poverty with her grandfather, preferring loyalty and truth to fame and wealth. The book's other female characters, who pursue knowledge or reputation, suffer punishing fates. Philothea marries her childhood love only after he is physically incapacitated by illness. His paralysis enables him to see visions of truth hidden from others. Philothea lovingly records these visions as she nurses his feeble body. When he dies, she dies as well.

The biographical parallels are almost unbearable. A husband who sees the truth but who is debilitated and demands constant care. A wife who sacrifices her talent to promote his vision. Women punished for ambition, for wanting to be more than the chaste facilitators of others' brilliance. As if all this were not enough, the book is dedicated to Child's supportive but admonishing brother Convers. There were additional indignities. For legal reasons, its copyright was in David's name, and its proceeds went to her father, to repay money the Childs owed him.[42]

Here is what else hurts: the public loved it. You can almost hear the collective sigh of relief. The beloved author was back, duly chastened. One reviewer called it brilliant, celebrating the "pleasure at meeting [Child] again in the calm and gladsome light of literature" after a deviation he had witnessed "with some surprise and more regret." Henry David Thoreau checked it out of Harvard's library and copied pages from it into his journal. Her fellow female abolitionists also loved it, gathering at Louisa Loring's to hear Child read it aloud. Edgar Allan Poe wrote that *Philothea* placed its author in "new and most favorable light," calling the book an "honor to our country, and a signal triumph for our countrywomen." He especially thought it would be appropriate to use in "female academies."[43]

It is hard not to feel cynical about this. How useful to find a female author affirming the absolute value of women's self-sacrifice. How convenient to point to a woman chastened by her ambition and repenting through her fiction. In short, *Philothea*'s readers praised the book for all the wrong reasons. I wish they hadn't loved it so much.

* * *

A few months after *Philothea* was published, David had a new plan. Abolitionists were beginning to sense that simply articulating arguments against slavery was not enough. Different tactics were needed, among them economic ones. How could abolitionists strike a blow at the heart of what made slavery so profitable and therefore intractable? Some of them happened upon an idea: there was evidence in France that a certain kind of beet could produce sugar. If this were done on a wide enough scale, perhaps beet sugar could undermine cane sugar production and the demand for slave labor it created. Investors decided to try, but they needed someone to go to Europe to learn the process. Perhaps because of his experience abroad and his facility with languages, they asked David to go. Apparently this time Snelling did not object, so David accepted the invitation and sailed for Europe in October 1836. Alone.

"My poverty, but not my will, consented to remaining behind, while one I loved so much was going where I so much wished to go," a heartsick Maria Child wrote to her sister-in-law as David crossed the ocean without her. While he toured Belgium and France, Child lived with her father. His dismal Calvinist outlook had not changed, and now he had an additional weapon. He had warned his daughter of her prospective husband's financial insecurity, and he had been right. This left Child in the unenviable position of living, as a married woman in her thirties, with a crabby, aging, vindicated parent. She insisted on buying her own firewood.[44]

Once in Europe, David all but vanished. In six months, he wrote to his wife three times. His letters mostly contained updates on his abolitionist projects for Child to pass on to the *Liberator*. After becoming something of an embarrassment to his abolitionist allies, how good it must have felt to report, through his wife, that new abolitionist friends "rained down on him" in Europe. After all his financial failures, how invigorating to describe himself as "blessed beyond expectation in the objects of his voyage" and being met with "utmost liberality" in France and Belgium.[45]

But the letters fail to answer basic questions about his whereabouts or his finances. They are alarmingly short on affection. Abandoned and uncertain, Child cycled through emotions: envy, resentment, anger, fear, pride, guilt, loneliness, longing. She was "out of sorts with matrimony." She was "gloomy almost to madness." She was pessimistic about David's success, sure "that his customary bad luck will follow him in everything." Yet she also bargains with the universe for his return: "If I can only be with my husband again, I shall never more express any dissatisfaction with him, if he shoots all the birds in the country, and sets the house afire beside." He said he would return in May, then June, then August. "His future plans are involved in entire uncertainty," she confessed to his sister.[46] That, at least, was certain.

What was going on? One of Child's biographers has suggested that David's shame at his professional failures was exacerbated by his wife's successes.[47] Perhaps this, combined with his guilt at having brought her down with him, drove him away from her. This seems right. It is not difficult to imagine them locked in a pattern of recrimination and reconciliation that he was all too happy to flee. There is plenty of evidence—mostly from her apologies—that they had quarreled about finances. Whatever the causes, David withdrew from his wife emotionally. How clear this was in his own mind—whether the distancing was intentional or merely the unconscious result of the distractions of travel and activism—is difficult to assess. It also feels hard to forgive.

But it is also hard, I find, not to sympathize with them both. Resisting institutional injustice is hard on a marriage. David never, to my knowledge, questioned his wife's intellect or sought to rein her in. But challenging social norms is exhausting. It is no wonder there were periods of retreat: hers through her fiction and his through absence.

As she negotiated these heartaches, Child continued to refine her abolitionist arguments, publishing them through the Anti-Slavery Society in formats targeted for maximum effect. From 1834 to 1836, she published no fewer than four important anti-slavery works. Three are short, succinct pamphlets that answered specific questions about abolition: *Authentic Anecdotes of American Slavery*; *Anti-Slavery Catechism*; and *The Evils of Slavery, and the Cure of Slavery*. These writings could be produced, distributed, and sold cheaply. Again they show Child anticipating her readers' objections and patiently but firmly deconstructing them. If the enthusiastic reviewers of *Philothea* had looked a little further, in other words, they would not have been so sanguine about Mrs. Child's return to the fold.

The fourth publication, *The Oasis*, was both more ambitious and more devious. Published in 1834, it was modeled on a popular literary genre called the annual. Annuals were a kind of *Juvenile Miscellany* for adults, combining histories, poems, illustrations, and stories. They were a popular holiday gift for readers who wanted to be both educated and entertained. In *The Oasis*, Child included all of the annual's traditional genres—some written by her, some by others—but with a revolutionary uniting theme. Every piece focused on shifting her readers' opinions about slavery. "Bear with me, my countrymen, while I again come before you with an unwanted message," it began. What was that unwanted message? "I wish to familiarize the public with the idea that colored people are *human beings*—elevated or degraded by the same circumstances that elevate or degrade other men," she wrote. Was that really so much to ask?

Unlike the *Appeal*, *The Oasis* privileges narrative over argument. Here her readers found inspiring biographies of Africans and poems featuring enslaved mothers desperate to save their children. One of its chapters presented an emancipated slave's testimony in his own words. Hoping to shame prideful Americans used to admiration from abroad, Child featured foreigners' outraged accounts of Southern slavery. Child is at her best when she depicts African civilizations with noble roots and a noble present, superior in many respects to the European cultures that have enslaved them. She is at her worst when she backtracks on the question of interracial marriage, reassuring nervous white Northerners who apparently feared that emancipated slaves would immediately arrive in their parlors and demand to marry their children. Emancipation will instead *prevent* amalgamation, she promises, by no longer allowing masters to impregnate their slaves with impunity.[48] As usual, Child is unsparing in her description of the torture and depravity slaves endured. It sometimes feels like every cruelty devised by humans is chronicled here, page after bloody page.

In other words, *The Oasis* made a strange Christmas present. Indeed, it did not sell well. As for Child's attempt to package her radical message in an innocuous format, at least one reviewer was not fooled. "Mrs. Child," he raged, "has prepared poison in the shape of an Annual. . . . She has insidiously endeavored to steal upon the early impressions of the mind" to introduce "error under the treacherous form of amusement." This treachery should stop, he warned: "We should suggest to the authoress to return to her usual species of composition, fiction." But on another reviewer, it appeared to have exactly the effect Child intended. Despite disagreeing with Child's politics, the reviewer predicted that readers would still respect and admire a woman "who ventures so fearlessly and yet so unassumingly, in the profitless cause of philanthropy." He praised Child's "excellent sense" and "fine imagination." He even declared her writing free of "fanaticism." Perhaps Child's message was easier to hear in narrative form. Perhaps her audience was shifting. "Both in New York and Philadelphia the tide is obviously turning in our favor," Child wrote.[49] Probably it was a little of both.

It had been a heady and humiliating few years. "From no other point of view, but our present lowly one, could either of us see so distinctly the numerous errors of our past lives," she wrote to David. "Present disappointments and discouragements, severe as they now seem, will make both of us better fitted to perform the mission whereunto we were sent." Meanwhile, her strong sense of the sufferings of others continued to motivate her. "*Every* shackle on *every* human soul not only arrests my attention, but excites the earnest inquiry: 'What can *I* do to break the chain?'" Child asked.[50] Chained though she was to a loving but unreliable husband, her resolve never to live the same way again had held. So far, her conversion had sustained her.

5

How Does It Feel
to Be a Question?

During Child's early abolitionist years, as mobs battled antislavery speakers and she wrestled with how to be in her marriage, another question emerged that, in a sense, synthesized the two struggles. It had to do with what it meant to be a woman.[1]

Like many of abolitionism's controversies, this one can be traced to the *Liberator*. In 1832, Garrison's paper had celebrated its first anniversary by announcing a new feature called the "Ladies' Department." "The fact that one million of the female sex are reduced, by the slave system, to the most deplorable conditions . . . ought to excite the sympathy and indignation of American women," Garrison wrote. Indeed, he suggested, white women had some catching up to do. Black women had recently founded the "Afric-American Female Intelligence Society of Boston" whose philanthropic aims he lauded and whose constitution he reprinted as an inspiration. To drive home his point, Garrison included an essay by Black abolitionist Maria Stewart calling her community to action. "How long shall the fair daughters of Africa be compelled to bury their minds and talents beneath a load of iron pots and kettles?" Stewart demanded. "Sue for your rights and privileges," she continued, addressing Black women in particular. "Know the reason you cannot attain them. . . . You can but die, if you make the attempt; we shall certainly die if you do not."[2]

In the next years, women took up the challenge and several female antislavery societies formed. The first was organized in February 1832 by Black women in Salem, Massachusetts. Another, also of Black women, formed in Rhode Island five months later. In October 1833, twelve women—eleven white and one Black—gathered in Boston and voted the Boston Female Anti-Slavery Society, known as BFASS, into existence. One of its first official acts was to invite Lydia Maria Child to join.[3]

Child hesitated. The invitation was flattering. It was a clear affirmation of the value of her work, and it came from people she admired. But the invitation raised uncomfortable questions. One concerned the nature of political change. Were associations—with their interminable meetings, issuing of reports, election of officials, personality conflicts, and compromise—the best way to fight slavery? Or were they a way for Northerners to feel they were doing something while doing nothing? Child had only recently declared herself independent of arguments and compromises that she now realized were wrong. She had determined to follow her conscience. Joining an organization felt dangerously conformist.

The second issue was the *F* in BFASS. Why a *female* society? Child had just sacrificed her reputation and livelihood by daring to speak on masculine subjects. Did she really want to go back to sewing circles? "The plain truth is, my sympathies do not, and never have, moved freely in this project," she wrote to BFASS president Charlotte Phelps.[4] Larger questions also loomed. What did a female-only society suggest about the role of women? What could women do that men couldn't? More to the point: What *could* women do that men wouldn't *let* them do? Was there such a thing as a woman's sphere? What, in the end, was a woman? There were several theories on offer. Perhaps women were just like men, only usually smaller and less intelligent. Or maybe they were essentially different, destined by nature for domesticity, passivity, and sympathy. Did either of these theories explain what women were? If not, what might?

As Child began to confront these questions in her abolitionist work, it was still 1834. She still had her Athenæum borrowing privileges. So she went back to the library. Her new topic was no less revolutionary than the last: having done what she could to educate readers about the history of slavery, she now wanted to educate them about the history of women. If her culture had misled her about women the same way it had misled her about slavery, she wanted to know that. In the Athenæum, where "masculine eyebrows" surely reached new heights as the notorious Mrs. Child consulted its holdings, she began gathering information about Chinese marriage rituals, Turkish dowries, and female African warriors. Soon she was making plans to write a book: she would call it *The History of the Condition of Women in Various Ages and Nations*. In the meantime, she reluctantly paid her membership dues to BFASS and threw in her lot with other female abolitionists.

This group of women soon included Maria Weston Chapman, who—although her courage in the face of the Boston mob still lay in the future—quickly proved herself a force to be reckoned with. Chapman was wealthy, fierce, and beautiful. One admirer described "golden hair which might have covered her to her feet" matched by a "brilliant complexion, noble profile, and deep blue eyes" that were "vivified by courage, and so strengthened by upright conviction." She was "the very embodiment of heroism"; she was "unrivaled." She also came with a posse of younger sisters: Caroline, Anne, Deborah, Lucia, and Emma. All of them had "warm hearts, clear heads, wit, [and] human spirit," not to mention "the virtue which every woman should have if she possibly can, beauty." They were consummate socialites: their calendars were full, their dinner parties epic, their attire newsworthy. Some simply called them the "House of Weston." Forced to care for an alcoholic father and shiftless brothers, they took a dim view of men. "We have been much tried with little Henry," Anne wrote to Deborah after babysitting their nephew. "He acts like sin; we think it is because he is in boy's clothes."[5]

The Westons descended from early Massachusetts settlers and were well established among Boston's great and good. Female philanthropic endeavors were nothing new to them, but antislavery activism was. Like Child, they had been converted by Garrison. Unlike Child, their comfortable social and financial situation insulated them to some extent from the social censure that followed.

Fig. 20. Maria Weston Chapman. Collection of the Massachusetts Historical Society.

But their radical commitments markedly lowered their status and made the five younger sisters essentially unmarriageable.[6] It's not clear that they minded.

The sisters quickly devoted their formidable organizational talents to BFASS. The society started small; at first the members simply attended lectures and concerts in support of antislavery efforts. Unlike most female benevolence societies, which often reinforced religious and racial divisions, BFASS included wealthy Unitarians and middle-class Congregationalists, Black women and white women.[7] And now, as Maria Child—however reluctantly—paid her dues, it included an infamous author.

Child was warmly folded into the Westons' fierce sisterhood. Soon she was making her way from "Le Paradis des Pauvres" to the elegant Chapman townhouse just south of the Boston Common to meet the sisters before BFASS meetings. How did it feel to arrive dusty and disheveled after the long walk from Roxbury and have one of the Chapman servants take her wrap at the door? Probably her discomfort quickly evaporated as she crossed the threshold into the busy, buzzing parlor where she was sure to find some Weston sister or other preparing an antislavery petition, John Greenleaf Whittier being quizzed about his latest abolitionist poem, or Garrison himself practicing an upcoming speech. Here her opinion was eagerly solicited and her expertise valued. Probably this enthusiasm extended to her research as well. It's not hard to imagine her discovery in the Athenæum's book stacks that some Africans attributed white skin to a "leprous disease" prompting lively discussions among the sisters about standards of beauty and the origins of prejudice. The same would have been true of her report that Roman women, in ways that would have been familiar to every member of BFASS, were not allowed to hold property without the agreement of a male guardian.[8] Learning how their condition differed from that of women at other times and in other places must sometimes have been exhilarating to Child's new friends. Sometimes the similarities must have been downright depressing.

As the huddle of dynamic women walked the short distance from West Street to the BFASS meeting, Child must have marveled.[9] Out of the ashes of her former social life, she had found a new community of like-minded women who were smart, powerful, and motivated in ways that made her former socialite friends seem pale and frivolous. They cared about issues beyond marriage and fashion, and, like her, they were willing to sacrifice for what they thought was right. Together the Weston sisters formed the kind of in-group—loyal, gossipy, conspiratorial—that could make you feel invincible. It was also the kind of group that could make you tremble to be an outsider.

BFASS needed both money and a wider base of supporters. Child, who had at least temporarily suspended her ambivalence about working in a female society, had an idea for how to get both. "Anti-Slavery Ladies—Attention!" read a notice in the November 22, 1834, issue of the *Liberator*. Women were invited to make items to be sold at a fair being organized by "MRS. CHILD and other ladies" for the benefit of the New England Anti-Slavery Society. It was *The Frugal Housewife* with an activist twist. Not only could Americans do their own spinning and sewing; now they could do them in support of a noble cause. "Let the articles combine utility with adornment," the announcement counsels: "Ladies, use your needles in the cause of bleeding humanity."[10] Because these activities fell squarely into a sphere of female expertise, the fair raised no unsettling questions about the role of women.

Between trips to the Athenæum, where she diligently took notes about women in civilizations as distant as the Philippines, Syria, and Sumatra, Child now enlisted the help of women in her own. As the day of the fair approached, she and Louisa Loring met at anti-slavery headquarters on Washington Street to set up tables, set out items, and hang banners. "Remember them that are in bonds, as bound with them," read one. "We trust in the power of truth," proclaimed another: "The truth shall make us free." The fair's aims were serious, but its presentation could be playful. Flatiron holders for sale were tagged "anti-slave-*holders*." A homemade flag was labeled "Stripes on the banner, none on the back." At the entrance, shoppers were asked "not to handle the articles, which, like slavery, are too '*delicate*' to be touched." The all-day fair took place in December, just in time for Christmas. It was "more successful than any of the ladies had anticipated," the *Liberator* reported, raising "*three hundred dollars*."[11] It went so well that the next year Maria Chapman took it over, turning it into an annual event that steadily increased in ambition, size, and popularity.

The potential of female antislavery societies was becoming clear. In the next years dozens more were formed, from Pennsylvania to Maine to Ohio. Impressed, the more conservative New York-based American Anti-Slavery Society also issued a call for women to organize themselves into societies of their own. There, they were told, they could "hush the awry passions of political and personal strife" and exert their "soothing and gentle influence amidst the wildest of the storm."[12]

Garrison had something less soothing in mind. The *Liberator* urged women to make use of their capacities, "whether moral, political, civil, or religious, or all combined," to fight slavery. "Some of you may, perhaps plead the effeminacy of your sex, and some—mental inferiority; but oh! this is nothing else than vain mockery," proclaimed a contributor to the "Ladies' Department." Let the "justice of the cause," another author pleaded, "shield you from the pointed darts shot from the bow of prejudice by the oppressors of female moral activity."[13]

The *Liberator* did not, however, confine itself to metaphorical exhortations. It also provided practical advice for the increasing number of women who, like Child, had converted to abolitionism and now were determined to convert others. Sometimes in the form of sample dialogues, it coached women on how to counter the neighbor who was too busy, the friend who feared her husband's disapproval, the in-law who had visited Virginia and gave eyewitness accounts of apparently well-treated slaves. Soon these tactics were having an effect. "My wife and grown up daughter," one farmer complained, "have got a notion out of some tract they have been reading, that we ought not to eat rice, nor sugar, nor anything that is raised by the labor of slaves." In at least one case, women honed their argumentative skills by "read[ing] aloud 'Mrs Child's chapter upon prejudices'" from the *Appeal*.[14]

Indeed, some reflection on prejudice was needed, and not just by those yet to be converted. Many female antislavery societies were open to Black women. In some, these women immediately took leadership positions and remained lifelong members. But there is painful evidence of discrimination that kept many of them out. Some antislavery societies simply banned Black women. Some declared membership for "ladies" only, then defined "lady" in a way that could only mean white. "Even our professed friends have not yet rid themselves of prejudice," mourned Black abolitionist Sarah Mapps Douglass. Not surprisingly, many Black women chose to form their own organizations, far from the insulting hypocrisy of their supposed allies.[15]

Even the societies' focus on abolition had problematic undertones. White women sometimes found it easier to sympathize with those who were enslaved by others in faraway states than with free Black women in their midst. It was easy to condemn slaveholders while ignoring the prejudice that shut Black women out of their own churches, schools, and hospitals. Some white women wanted to fight slavery, but without being required to treat their Black neighbors too "familiarly." Black women identified this hypocrisy and called it out. "Tell us no more of southern slavery," Maria Stewart charged her white coworkers, "for with few exceptions . . . I consider our condition but little better than that."[16] Again the problem is familiar. It is indeed sometimes harder to address local problems in which we are complicit than faraway problems that appear to be someone else's fault. As Child had asserted in her *Appeal*, Southerners were right to accuse Northerners of hypocrisy on this point.

Child often showed herself more sensitive to these tensions than most. When Susan Paul, the daughter of a prominent Black minister and a charter member of BFASS, could not obtain housing because of her race and fell into debt, she came to Child for help.[17] Child's own financial position was too precarious to pay the sum Paul owed, but she quickly appealed to others on Paul's behalf. I especially admire this. Child had gained Paul's trust over years of collaboration. She had put herself in a social position where she could understand and react to the real needs of those who suffered from the prejudices she condemned. She had cultivated benefactors who trusted her reputation and responded to her requests. She was using her privilege to get Paul what she actually needed. Northern racism was still alive and strong, but Child had made life better for at least one of its victims.

Women continued mobilizing, expanding both their numbers and their activities. They were also becoming skilled at petitioning Congress by carrying documents door-to-door for their fellow citizens to sign. These petitions protested the annexation of Texas, laws against interracial marriage, the expansion of slavery into Arkansas, and the persistence of slavery in Washington, DC. By one count, women delivered twice as many petitions to Congress in 1836 as men did, sending their delegates approximately 33,000 signatures on the subject of slavery alone. Soon the number of abolitionist petitions became so overwhelming that the House of Representatives passed a "gag rule" preventing the petitions from ever reaching the floor.[18]

The steady success of female antislavery societies did not stop Child and other Boston women from attending the general Massachusetts Anti-Slavery Society meetings as well. There they encountered an atmosphere decidedly different from the productive solidarity of their female-only meetings. "Let women keep silence in the church," the apostle Paul had said in the first century AD, and the phrase had stuck. Just to be safe, the admonition had been extended to apply to all public gatherings. This provoked some awkward scenes. Several women, the abolitionist minister Samuel May reported, by this point counted as "presiding geniuses" of the antislavery movement. At MAS meetings, they often proposed "the wisest measures" and suggested "most weighty thoughts, pertinent facts, apt illustrations." But they could not, he recalled years later and still with apparent frustration, "be persuaded to utter [these thoughts] aloud." Instead they would whisper their insights to someone who was—May himself puts the phrase in scare quotes—"allowed to speak in the assembly": in other words, to a man. "Repeatedly in those early days," he recalled, "did I spring to the platform, crying, 'Hear me as the mouthpiece of Mrs. Child, or Mrs. Chapman, or Mrs. Follen,' and then convulsed the audience with a stroke of wit, or electrified them with a flash of eloquence, caught from the lips of one or the other of our antislavery prophetesses."[19]

So which was it? Were they allowed to speak or not? May was not the only man who wanted the antislavery prophetesses to break their silence. They were not above scolding the women if they refused. At a New York meeting in 1836, Lewis Tappan told Child that "you really ought to make an effort to overcome your reluctance, when you reflect . . . how much the audience will be interested, if you allow me to announce that Mrs. Child of Boston is about to address them." Theodore Weld declared it wrong of Child "to let any foolish scruples stand in the way of doing so much good." Still she refused. It wasn't that she didn't think she would be good at it. She had once recounted to a friend that, in an argument over slavery in a stagecoach, she had "burnt [her opponent] up like a stroke of the sun, and swept his ashes up after him," a verbal drubbing that became the talk of the town. It was also not that she had nothing to say, or that she did not want to say it. "Oh, if I was a man, how I *would* lecture!" she lamented to Louisa. "But I am a woman, and so I sit in the corner and knit socks."[20] She knew she could speak. She *wanted* to speak. *Others* wanted her to speak. So why did she stay silent?

Child's earlier biographers have offered a range of reasons. Perhaps she was, again, afraid of upstaging her husband. When asked, David insisted that he would be "ashamed of himself now and forever" if he stood in the way of her speaking.[21] But deeper psychological considerations might have been at work. Or perhaps—despite her stagecoach triumph—Child just didn't like addressing audiences in public. Both interpretations are plausible. Here's another one. Like most members of oppressed groups, Child knew better than those in the dominant group around her—in her case, men— what risks violating a social norm entailed. Perhaps it was true that, had she been a man, she would have lectured. But she wasn't, and she knew that mattered. It's also possible that her Athenæum research was making all too clear to her the opposition women often faced if they rejected tradition. She knew such a challenge to authority risked bringing down the antislavery movement, and she was right.

In 1835, Maria Weston Chapman's defiance in the face of the Boston mob confirmed her as the leader of BFASS and her home as the nerve center of Boston abolitionism. The already industrious House of Weston reached ever higher levels of productivity. The sisters swarmed in and out of their eldest sibling's home, editing journals, collating petitions, pricing items for the next antislavery fair. The home itself served as a post office, meeting place, hostel, and occasionally as a refuge for fugitive slaves. The eminent historian George Bancroft arrived one evening to visit Chapman's husband but quickly fled when he found the house occupied by "a squad of blue-stockings and abolitionists; both of whom are my abhorrence." By this point, Chapman was editing BFASS's annual report, which she originally called *Right and Wrong in Boston*. Like the *Liberator*, *Right and Wrong* made bracing reading. Chapman took aim at clergy, politicians, and journalists who opposed abolition. She happily named names. She also perfected a tone of ironic outrage. To someone's description of a slaveholder as a "sincere, and humble Christian" she simply added "(!!!!)." The poet James Russell Lowell christened her the "Joan of our Arc." Her enemies, noting her influence over Garrison and imagining more devious motives, had begun calling her Lady Macbeth.[22]

It was in this heady atmosphere of solidarity and productivity, as Child was finishing *The History of the Condition of Women*, that the Athenæum terminated her free borrowing privileges. The trustees, she later recalled, had written her a letter "informing me that at a recent meeting they had passed a vote to *take away* my privilege, lest it should prove an inconvenient precedent." The accuracy of this account has been disputed, and its timing—two years after the *Appeal*—is strange.[23] Had the Athenæum's leadership gotten wind of the controversial nature of Child's new research and determined that enough was enough? Or had it simply taken a while for some trustee's displeasure with the *Appeal* to have an effect? Or did Child later in life simply misremember details of what had happened? Whatever the truth, the Westons jumped into outraged action. If the Athenæum was going to revoke Child's free membership, her friends would buy her one—assuming the Athenæum would allow that.

Deborah breathlessly wrote to Anne about their eldest sister's efforts: "Maria is very busy about Mrs. Child," she confided. "The facts are these. Mrs. Child is writing a book & she can't go on with it, because the directors of the Athenaeum library have revoked the permission which they gave her some years ago to take out what books she chose. . . . [T]hese books she *must* have, or give up her book. So Maria has taken it in hand." Membership dues were $100, Deborah reported, and "Maria has raised $75 since yesterday, so we think she will succeed."[24]

Women raising money to help a woman write books about women—the rush of solidarity was intoxicating. On receiving the funds, Child professed herself "moved even to tears." "I have never in my whole life, met with anything that gratified me more, or affected me so deeply," she wrote. But was she even in a position to accept the money and buy the membership? It seemed not: "We are obliged to leave our present residence," she wrote, "and when my husband left home, he was quite undecided between several plans, some of which would remove us to an inconvenient distance from the Athenaeum." Indeed, two months later the Childs left for New York with George Thompson, en route, as they thought, for England. Somehow, even without her books, Child finished her two-volume history anyway.[25]

Or did she? Despite its length and scope, *The History of the Condition of Women* feels strangely incomplete. Unlike the *Appeal*, there is no preface daring her audience to read it, no conclusion exhorting action and predicting scandal. In fact, the first edition includes no preface or conclusion at all. Amid exhaustive reports of dress and adornment, swaddling practices, and punishments for adultery, there is almost no commentary. Child had collected thousands of anecdotes about how women cooked and sewed and fought and mourned. Surely it was striking to her to read that in some Hindu cultures the woman is ruled by her mother-in-law, that in Egyptian religions women were allowed to perform sacred ceremonies, and that a woman was credited with introducing smallpox inoculation to England after returning from a journey to Turkey.[26] But what did she make of it all?

Some readers were puzzled. "From her did we anticipate somewhat more of the philosophy of history," one wrote. In other words, What did all this information *mean*? From historical sources not unlike Child's, philosophers from Herder to Hegel had, not long before, drawn grand conclusions about the meaning of history and human progress. George Bancroft—he of the abhorrence of blue-

stockings and abolitionists—had recently made his name arguing
that history had culminated in the republican achievements of the
United States. Child had reached no such conclusions. Her first
volume had started with Asia and Africa; the second discussed
Europe and America but ended with women of the South Sea Is-
lands, undermining any suggestion that history culminated with
her own culture. If her intent was to resist a triumphalist American account of history, however, she never says that either. "We
only regret," her reviewer continued, that "in these volumes she
should have transcribed so much, and written so little."[27] What had
happened?

Perhaps Child had harbored greater ambitions for the books.
Perhaps she imagined, having accumulated this wealth of information, that she would show what it meant for how women should
be treated and how women should live—that she would synthesize
her research into the kind of searing argument found in the *Appeal*. Perhaps she ran out of time as she and David fled with George
Thompson to New York on their way, they hoped, to Europe. Even
after their European plan failed, losing her Athenæum privileges
and finding herself made itinerant by David's business failures
may have caused her to despair of completing a final analysis. Perhaps for all these reasons she simply published it as it was.

But if Child herself is to be believed, none of these was the main
reason. A decade later, the books were published in a new edition.
Now there *was* a preface. But far from delivering the philosophical synthesis her reviewers had wished for, Child went out of her
way to refuse to provide one. "This volume is not an essay upon
women's rights," she wrote, "or a philosophical investigation of
what is or ought to be the relation of the sexes. . . . I have simply endeavored to give an accurate history of the condition of women, in
language sufficiently concise for popular use. Those who reflect on
this highly interesting and important subject will find in the facts
thus patiently collected much that will excite thought, and many
materials for argument."[28]

If we detect defensiveness here, possible reasons are clear
enough. In her *Appeal*, Child had woven her research into incisive

arguments for a radical cause. She had paid dearly for it. Perhaps she felt psychologically unable to withstand social opprobrium on yet another front. This time she would simply deliver the facts and let others do the rest. Perhaps she simply felt uncomfortable advocating for a group she herself belonged to. "If I must, at the bidding of conscience, enter the arena and struggle for human rights, I prefer they should be the rights of others, rather than my own," she once confessed.[29] It is a laudable sentiment. But praising women for their self-sacrifice is a time-honored way to cultivate their submission. How much has it hindered women, then and now, from achieving their own good?

There's one more possibility. Perhaps Child drew no conclusions because she simply didn't have any. The truth of slavery's evil had hit her like a thunderbolt. No such clarity about women's rights had emerged. What did it mean to be a woman? Child still wasn't sure.

*   *   *

But Maria Child was not one to let large unanswered questions get in the way of action. Throughout these years, she continued her efforts with other BFASS members to expand women's sphere of antislavery activity. In 1836, they tried another new tactic. It was summer, and "sojourners from the south," as Maria Weston Chapman put it, were arriving in Boston in droves.[30] In other words, it was tourist season. With vacationing Southerners came the people they enslaved. And with those slaves, members of BFASS had concluded, came an opportunity to advance the cause.

Southerners had a constitutional right to their slaves, and Northerners had a legal duty to return them if they fled North. But the Constitution's Fugitive Slave Clause said nothing about whether enslaved humans temporarily brought North by their owners were required to return. This left open the possibility of prying them away from their enslavers so that they could claim their freedom. In the 1836 edition of *Right and Wrong*, Chapman recounted three episodes in which members of BFASS had done just that. The most famous of these concerned a six-year-old girl named Med.

The incident began when someone alerted Child to the presence of a Black girl at 21 Pinckney Street, just behind the State House. The girl was staying at the home of Thomas Aves, whose daughter, Mrs. Samuel Slater, was visiting from New Orleans. She had not been there before. Was she Mrs. Slater's slave? To find out, BFASS members first needed to confirm her presence. "I will not fill this sheet with particulars," Child later wrote to a friend. "Suffice it to say, the way was opened for us." Med's mistress later complained that BFASS members had entered her house under the pretext of recruiting for Sunday school. However devious, the plan worked: the little girl, they now knew, was indeed there. The women then engaged a lawyer to issue a writ of habeas corpus so Med's status could be ascertained.[31] Yes, the hearing confirmed, she was a slave. BFASS then hired Ellis Loring to sue for her freedom.

At stake was the possible liberation of countless enslaved people brought North in the company of their masters. If, in other words, the judge ruled that Med could go free, any slave brought North by a master could be freed as well. But also at stake was the fate of a six-year-old girl whose mother, it turned out, was still enslaved in Louisiana. Loring offered to drop the suit if Med's owners would manumit her and bring her back to her mother as a free child. They refused. In fact, Child recounted, it emerged during the trial that "Med was to be sold on her way back to New Orleans, to pay the expenses of her mistress's journey to the North."[32] Either way, Med would likely never see her mother again.

In his arguments before the judge, Loring acknowledged this cruelty. But he was clear about its origin. The responsibility for Med's plight, he asserted, belonged "wholly to that odious system, which is continually breaking up the domestic ties. It is slavery and not freedom that is separating mother and child. An inveterate, deep-rooted abuse puts anything within its sphere in a false position. Any attempt to rectify it, on either a general or a partial scale, produces incidental and temporary disorder." This, to my mind, is beautifully put. Injustice on the scale of human enslavement creates countless irresolvable and tragic moral dilemmas in its wake.

But Loring had concluded that in Med's case, this was "no reason for standing still." True, there was the question of whether six-year-old Med *wanted* to be free. Here Loring's reasoning is much more problematic. If Med "were able to form an intelligent wish," he argued to Chief Justice Lemuel Shaw, "she would prefer freedom to slavery." But she wasn't able to form such a wish, he claimed; she was too young. What about the mother? Was freeing the child an injustice to her? Loring seems not to have hesitated. "Not if she desires the good of her child," he confidently concluded.[33] In other words, there was no description in Loring's mind under which Med's mother would be justified in wanting her daughter to return if returning meant a life of enslavement.

In a precedent-setting decision, Judge Shaw decided for Loring. Med was free. Southerners could no longer bring people they enslaved into Massachusetts and expect to take them back to the South. More important, the decision implied that Black Americans could claim legal protection equal to that of whites—a status that held in Massachusetts until Loring's case was overturned by *Dred Scott v. Sandford* in 1857. In the meantime, Southerners took their revenge by vacationing elsewhere. Boston newspapers castigated abolitionists for damaging the hotel industry.[34]

Loring was clear that the victory belonged to BFASS. "I have never doubted that the Female Anti-Slavery Societies were a very valuable addition of power to us," he wrote in a letter published in *Right and Wrong*, "but it is a very pleasant assurance to see, year after year, tangible proofs of it." BFASS rejoiced. Med was rechristened Maria: after which one—Chapman, Child, or both—remains unclear.[35]

But this story does not end well. Nineteen months later, Loring wrote to the Samaritan Asylum for Colored Orphans, clearly alarmed at reports of Med's (or was it Maria's?) failing health. He offered to pay for a full-time nurse and to send his own physician. "I feel a strong interest in her, & most earnestly pray that she & her mother may, one day, be reunited, *in freedom*," he wrote to her caregivers. But six months later, she was dead. Loring paid for her gravestone; Child wrote the inscription. It fell to Child to inform Judge Shaw of Med's death. Shaw confessed he was still haunted by "the cruelty of separating a child from its parents." Please, Child wrote to Loring afterward, find a way to reassure Shaw that "Med received every possible kindness" before she died.[36]

Was this the protestation of a guilty conscience? Had Child and her BFASS conspirators done enough for Med/Maria after wresting her from her enslaver's clutches? What else could they, should they, have done? Did Child, still longing for a daughter, ever imagine adopting her? Probably not. She and David were, so Child thought, about to leave for Illinois, or England, or Mexico, none of them promising places to raise a Black child. What about the others? Could all the good intentions of the women of BFASS have saved a young girl, effectively orphaned, alone in a foreign society whose prejudices against her were perhaps different but no less poisonous? Had she been asked if she wanted to stay? Or if she wanted a new name? And what of her mother—did she ever learn her daughter's fate? Was she ever allowed to communicate with her again? Med's short, free life was not necessarily worse than a long enslaved life would have been. That fact is a testament to the horrors of slavery. But it also testifies to the limitations of good intentions.[37] Child might have helped her fellow abolitionists understand the condition of some women, but she, Loring, and other members of BFASS were apparently unable to imagine that an enslaved woman like Med's mother might have understood her daughter's condition better than they.

∗   ∗   ∗

The publication of Child's *History of the Condition of Women* coincided with the emergence of two more antislavery prophetesses. Angelina and Sarah Grimké were South Carolina natives who had renounced their slaveholding pasts and dedicated their lives to abolition. Angelina had already written an electrifying tract titled "Appeal to the Christian Women of the South," which called on

Southern women to take responsibility for ending slavery in their midst. Most copies sent to Southern ports were burned before they could reach their intended audience, but the letter's rhetorical force and moral clarity, coming from an eyewitness to slavery's brutality, newly galvanized Northern women.[38] Sarah had followed by writing an "Epistle to the Clergy of the Southern States" that extended the sisters' plea to church leadership. But their captivating writing was not the Grimké sisters' real potential. It turned out that both of them, Angelina especially, could *speak*.

Abolitionist leaders knew a good thing when they saw it. In 1836, both sisters were trained as agents by the American Anti-Slavery Society in New York and dispatched on speaking tours. They started small, addressing ardent groups of women in modest parlors. Soon audiences became too large for private residences, so they moved to meeting rooms. Curious men began to attend. The first time Angelina saw one in the audience, she paused. To continue speaking would be to break precedent and invite censure. She kept speaking. Soon the sisters were filling churches, then lecture halls. Sometimes several times a week, they riveted audiences with eyewitness accounts of slavery. "I have seen it—I have seen it. I know it has horrors that can never be described," Angelina cried from the podium. She "swept the chords of the human heart with a power that has never been surpassed and rarely equaled," wrote Wendell Phillips, himself by now fully established as one of the movement's most powerful orators. Angelina was keenly aware of the power she wielded. "My auditors literally sit some times with 'mouths agape and eyes astare,' so that I cannot help smiling in the midst of 'rhetorical flourishes' to witness their perfect amazement at hearing a woman speak in the churches," she wrote to Theodore Weld.[39]

In February 1838, Angelina, with Chapman by her side and Child in the audience, became the first woman to address the Massachusetts state legislature, an event Child called "a spectacle of the greatest moral sublimity I ever witnessed." Later that spring, she lectured at the Odeon, one of Boston's largest theaters. Child was ecstatic. Not only were all three thousand seats filled, but the

Odeon management's willingness to hold the event suggested that their cause was becoming mainstream. Angelina spoke for two hours: "The whole audience," Child wrote to her mother-in-law, "seemed to hang on her every word." "Think of this, compared with the time when a few women were mobbed in their small room at 46 [Washington St.]!" she marveled.[40] Finally, it seemed, the men who had reproached Child for her silence were getting what they wanted.

But some members of the public were less impressed by women's expanding activism. Newspapers called them a "parcel of silly women," "petticoat philanthropists," and a "mortifying spectacle." In their proper sphere, the *Boston Courier* asserted, women were "lovely as the evening star"; but when inspired to leave that sphere for realms they could not understand, very little could "outmeasure the evil that might follow." Women were now everywhere they were not supposed to be, it seemed, sometimes behaving badly. "We hope that Anti-Slavery Society Ladies will cease so far to forget the dignity and delicacy which should mark the deportment of their sex," wrote the Reverend Joseph Tracy. "Perhaps they will say that they cannot *see* why clapping and hissing in public meeting is any more unbecoming in them than in men; to which our only reply is, that if they cannot *feel* the difference, we are very sorry for them." That "our females should have come forth from their retirement—from the holiness of the fireside, the protection of their household goods—to mingle in scenes like this," lamented a writer for the *Boston Courier*, "it is, it must be, but a dream. Oh deliver me from its agony."[41]

Public mockery only intensified the women's solidarity. They were also expanding their aims. "I had a long talk with the brethren on the rights of women," Angelina wrote to Weld after a lively evening at the Chapmans', "and found a very general sentiment prevailing that it is time our fetters were broken. L. M. Child and Maria Chapman strongly supported this view; indeed very many seem to think a new order of things is very desirable." Their confidence grew as well. When Weld offered to assist with an upcoming meeting, Angelina replied that "when women got together, they

Fig. 21. Theodore Dwight Weld, Angelina Grimké Weld, and their three children. "My auditors literally sit some times with 'mouths agape and eyes astare,' so that I cannot help smiling in the midst of 'rhetorical flourishes' to witness their perfect amazement at hearing a woman speak in the churches," Grimké wrote to Weld the year before they married. Courtesy of William L. Clements Library, University of Michigan.

found they had *minds* of their own, and could transact their business *without* his discretions," a rebuke that did not stop her from marrying him the very next year.[42]

The achievements of local female antislavery societies had convinced Chapman that a national meeting was needed. So she organized one. Christened the "Anti-Slavery Convention of American Women," it took place in New York in May 1837. It would be the first nationally organized political gathering of women in the country's history, and possibly the first racially mixed meeting on the national level as well. Local societies from New Hampshire to Ohio selected delegates to make the arduous trip to Manhattan. Who would go from Boston? Child was an obvious choice, but she was ambivalent. The meeting would involve travel and expense; and she was beginning, it seemed, to tire of meetings. "Mrs. Child had obstinately refused to go," Anne Weston complained to her sister Deborah right before Child—no doubt under pressure from Chapman but also having decided it was her duty—changed her mind and went anyway.[43] Never living her life the same way again continued to be hard to navigate.

If Child was ambivalent about her attendance, her abolitionist sisters were not. They quickly voted her one of the convention's vice presidents. It also turned out she had a lot to say. Except for Angelina Grimké, no one proposed more resolutions. The convention's minutes read like a record of classic Child concerns. One of her resolutions countered the objection that many slaves were well treated. The "great question" was not "one of treatment, but of *principle*," the resolution asserted. No "compromise can be made on the score of kind usage, while man is held as the property of man." No doubt thinking of Med, she proposed a resolution urging that all Northern states repeal laws guaranteeing Southerners ownership of slaves they brought North with them, and another that "the right of trial by jury may be granted to all persons claimed as slaves." Child was also still working on her fellow Northerners' prejudices, including the prejudices of those in attendance. She proposed a resolution to "use all our influence in having our colored friends seated promiscuously in our congregations" and pledging to "take our seats with them."[44] The convention also took a strong stand against ministers who refused to condemn slavery.

Child and the other officers left at least one anonymous attendee from New Hampshire overcome with admiration. "Their work was truly arduous and in performing it, they displayed a spirit of wisdom—a noble, generous disposition of the heart—and real magnificence of mind," she reported to the *Liberator*. The collaboration must have been electrifying. The elegant, sharp-tongued Weston sisters; the determined, uncompromising Black abolitionist Grace Douglass; the Grimkés, whose modest gray Quaker apparel set off their fiery pronouncements; and Child, earnest and eloquent in her habitually unfashionable dress. The meeting also made clear that another new leader was emerging in Abby Kelley, a Quaker schoolteacher whose physical courage and rhetorical brilliance would soon become legendary. All were discovering untapped powers of persuasion and mobilization in themselves and others. "Hitherto many of them had only heard of each other by the hearing of the ear, but now they enjoyed the satisfaction of seeing each other, face to face, and hearing from each other's lips, 'thoughts that breathe and words that burn,'" the New Hampshire delegate continued in the *Liberator*. Angelina Grimké put it more directly. "We Abolitionist Women," she wrote, "are turning the world upside down."[45]

Child had come ambivalent and left a leader. She would have written to David recounting it all, but he had by now embarked on his European adventure, and she had no idea where he was.

Less than a month after the national convention, the General Association of Congregational Ministers had had enough. "We invite your attention," they wrote on June 27, 1837, in what became known as "The Pastoral Letter," "to *the dangers which at present seem to threaten the* FEMALE CHARACTER with widespread and permanent injury." "The power of woman is in her dependence flowing from the consciousness of weakness which God has given her," the clergy explained. When instead "she assumes the place and tone of man as a public reformer . . . she yields the power which God has given her for her protection, and her character becomes unnatural." Ah yes, unnatural. But that was not all. The ministers also deplored the tendency of abolitionists to sow "*alienation and division*" in their congregations by insisting that clergy condemn slavery and leaving in protest if they did not. "*Your minister*," they wrote, "is ordained by God to be your teacher." Deference and subordination were the only acceptable responses. It turned out that other clergy had grievances too. One group aired them in yet an-

Fig. 22. Abby Kelley. From the collection of Worcester Historical Museum.

other appeal (this time "of Clerical Abolitionists on Anti-Slavery Measures") that explicitly blamed the *Liberator* for this breakdown in women's decorum.[46] The war between Garrison and the clergy was officially on.

Garrison reacted as only Garrison could: with moral justification and rhetorical excess. There could be no doubt, he wrote, that the time had come to fight "for the rights of woman to their utmost extent." If freeing both women and slaves meant tearing down "the crazy superstructure . . . [of] man-enslaving religion," then so be it. This was shocking enough. But Garrison went on to accuse his opponents of being "hirelings, blind leaders of the blind, dumb dogs that cannot bark." He was just warming up. They were also "wolves in sheep's clothing" and "hindrances to the march of human freedom." "Their overthrow is registered on the scrolls of destiny," Garrison prophesied. More moderate voices began to despair. "I believe in my heart that we have all over valued Garrison," wrote Gamaliel Bailey to James Birney. "And as to himself, pride has driven him mad."[47]

For their part, women like Child, the Weston-Chapmans, and the Grimkés were past being silenced by the clergy. They had, as Chapman wrote, "been too long accustomed to hear the Bible quoted in defense of slavery, to be astonished that its authority should be claimed for the subjugation of woman the moment she should act for the enslaved." In serialized letters to the *Spectator*, Sarah Grimké responded to their critics with a carefully reasoned defense of women's rights, using Child's *History of the Condition of Women* to shore up her arguments. Chapman's response had, we might say, more rhyme than reasoning:

> Confusion has seized us, and all things go wrong,
> The Women have leaped from "their spheres,"
> And, instead of fixed stars, shoot as comets along,
> And are setting the world by the ears! . . .
> They've taken a notion to speak for themselves,
> And are wielding the tongue and the pen;
> They've mounted the rostrum; the termagant elves,
> And—oh horrid!—are talking to men![48]

Chapman titled her poem "The Times That Try Men's Souls."

But Bailey and Birney were not the only male abolitionists who were becoming uneasy. The antislavery cause had just begun to move from the radical fringes to the mainstream.[49] Real change—perhaps even emancipation—seemed within their grasp. The clergy's support was critical, and the clergy were, in effect, offering the abolitionist movement a deal. They would join ranks in fighting for the slave, but only if the women were sent back home. The debate now also had a catchy name: it was called the woman question.

It had been easy to be open-minded as long as it was convenient. But now men who had thrown themselves at anti-abolitionist mobs suddenly feared to allow a woman to mount the podium. As is often the case, responsibility for accommodating prejudice fell to its victims. Until now, abolitionist men had argued that their female allies were being overly cautious. Now, apparently, they were being overly zealous. Messages to this effect were dispatched. "Mrs. Child came in & brought a letter she has just got from Mr. Birney," Caroline wrote indignantly to Anne. "He appeals to the *magnanimity* of women," reminding them "that the wrongs & sufferings of the slaves are greater than those of women"—asking them, in effect, to stand down for the good of the cause. "You never saw," she concluded, "such a piece of malicious twaddle as his letter was."[50]

As women's stunning successes in petitioning, fund-raising, and legal battles, not to mention their physical bravery in the face of violent mobs, were met with admonitions to muzzle themselves in deference to others' bigotry, their own lack of freedom was becoming clearer. Some white women began to compare their condition to that of slaves, a claim whose absurdity did untold damage to the possibility of true solidarity with Black women.[51] Insofar as women *did* accurately analyze their lack of freedom, it may have been because Child's *History of Women*, despite its claims to neutrality, had pointed it out to them. However widely the condition of women varied, lack of control over their own destinies was a worldwide constant. In cultures where women were cherished, they were restricted. In cultures where they were demeaned, they were restricted. Any exceptions only suggested what was possible if these restrictions could be lifted. But evidence also showed that battles necessary to lift them could be both long and deadly.

Just two years after its publication, Child's book was being used in exactly the way she had intended. She had delivered the facts, and others were drawing the conclusions. Here are some examples. Sarah Grimké: Men have "made slaves of the creatures God designed to be their companions and coadjutors in every moral and intellectual improvement." Angelina Grimké: "The time has come for woman to . . . no longer remain satisfied in the circum-

scribed limits with which corrupt custom and a perverted application of Scripture have encircled her." Maria Weston Chapman:
"What is the sphere and duty of woman, it rests with each one for
herself to interpret." And again Sarah Grimké: "All I ask of our
brethren is, that they will take their feet from off our necks, and
permit us to stand upright."[52]

The woman question went from being a distraction to being a
litmus test and then a wedge issue. "Garrisonian" women—the
Chapman-Weston faction, the Grimkés, and, more distantly,
Child—were given a choice. They could abandon women's rights
and keep fighting for the enslaved people. Or they could stop fighting for the enslaved people and fight for women. This was a false
choice, and Child knew it. She fought hard to stay out of the trap.
The Grimkés had not, she insisted in an open letter to the *Liberator*, introduced the "foreign topic" of women's rights into the abolitionist movement. It had been introduced for them. It was the
obstacles men had put in the Grimkés' path that made the "estab-
lishment of women's freedom" suddenly "of vital importance to
the anti-slavery cause." She had hoped it would not be necessary
for women "to *talk* about our rights, but simply go forward and *do*
whatsoever we deem a duty." "In toiling for the freedom of others,"
she had trusted, "we shall find our own." This trust had proved unfounded. Men determined to silence women had only themselves
to blame for the controversy now roiling their movement.

Child was eager to stop asking the woman question and get back
to work. "I now, as ever, would avoid any discussion of the woman
question in anti-slavery meetings, or papers," she confessed. And
she did not deny anyone's right to disagree with her, or anyone's,
behavior. "But when a man advises me to withdraw from a society
or convention, or not to act there according to the dictates of my
own judgment," she wrote in the *Liberator*, "I am constrained to
reply: 'Thou canst not touch the freedom of my soul. I deem that I
have duties to perform here. I make no onset upon your opinions
and prejudices; but my moral responsibility lies between God and
my own conscience. No human being can have jurisdiction over

that.'" "What a woman!" wrote one *Liberator* reader in response.[53] If only anybody knew what that meant.

Child's careful arguments fell on deaf ears. Increasingly impatient male colleagues continued to ask the "radical" women to withdraw, out of deference to clergy and for the good of the cause. When that didn't work, they laid plans to block them. It was not just abolitionist men who were nervous. Other women were, too. Several BFASS officers belonged to more conservative Congregational churches. The brilliant, irrepressible Westons made them feel uneasy and more than a little bullied. When the esteemed author Catharine Beecher wrote in a public essay addressed to Angelina Grimké that "whatever . . . throws a woman into the attitude of a combatant, either for herself or others . . . throws her out of her appropriate sphere," some of them feared she was right. In short, abolitionist women were not a monolith.[54] Oppressed populations never are, nor should we expect them to be. But until now abolitionist women had agreed to differ about what it meant to be a woman. They could tolerate each other's opinions for the greater good of ending slavery. But the clergy's opposition had forced a moment of decision. The woman question demanded an answer.

In October 1837, Maria Chapman, as the foreign correspondence secretary of BFASS, submitted the annual edition of *Right and Wrong*. This year its subtitle read: "With a Sketch of the Obstacles Thrown in the Way of Emancipation by certain Clerical Abolitionists and Advocates for the Subjection of Woman." The report recounted, in combative detail, the year of controversy. It quoted at length from the Pastoral Letter as well as from other incendiary sermons designed to put women in their place. There was no shortage of exclamation marks. Alarmed, the society's officers, most of them more conservative women, asked Chapman to soften the tone. When she refused, they appended a preface stating that they "cherish[ed] the most serious objections" to parts of the report. Chapman resigned in fury. A bitter, multiyear power struggle ensued. The society never fully recovered. It was all very painful. "Deeply, deeply do I feel the degradation of being a woman," Child wrote to the newly married Angelina Grimké Weld as the conflict raged. "Not the degradation of being what *God* made woman, but what *man* has made her."[55]

On the one hand, the woman question had emerged too late. Many of the women it sought to silence went on to fight with renewed energy for the rights of others and for their own. On the other hand, it is never too late to weaken a movement by sowing internal dissent. If this sounds like a familiar theme from the history of progressive movements, it should.

*   *   *

In late fall 1837, Child's involvement in the woman question was abruptly interrupted. David had returned. There is no record of their reunion—no description of Maria flying down the pier into his arms; no account of how he explained his long silences and longer absence. Decades later, after his death, Child discovered evidence in David's diary that he *had* missed her.[56] Why had he not communicated that better? Perhaps it didn't matter. They were reunited, and David was ready to sweep his wife up into his next adventure. On his travels, David assured her, he had mastered the process of making sugar out of beets. Together they could undermine plantation sugar and weaken the slave trade. That spring, they loaded their meager belongings onto a stagecoach for a two-day journey. They were moving to central Massachusetts. The Childs were going to farm.

6

On Resistance

At its beginning, May can feel like another cruel month in Massachusetts. Mornings are cold, trees are bare, and the promise of spring can seem like a mockery. Bundled against the chill, the Childs traveled west, watching Boston and its outlying towns disappear in the distance. One hundred miles later, they passed from the Holyoke mountain range into a wide, flat glacial plain. Here the Connecticut River descends from hills and gorges in the north and broadens into a valley. On the other side of the river, the land rises again toward the town of Northampton. In 1838, Northampton was picturesque and prosperous, already a popular destination with travelers looking for clean air and quiet streets. The topsoil in the valley is nine feet deep. Theoretically, it is good for farming.

The last time the Childs had bid farewell to friends, it was, everyone thought, to take up positions abroad as celebrated reformers in London. Their friends had been admiring and maybe a little envious, at least until the trip was aborted by David's arrest. This time must have felt different. What did their Boston community think as the Childs moved west? Undermining planation sugar was a noble goal. The fight against slavery was turning into a protracted, many-pronged struggle. All modes of resistance were needed. But where exactly was Northampton? And had either of the Childs farmed before?

Growing sugar beets entailed all the risks of farming: inclement weather, invasive insects, the neighbors' hungry cows. But it

Fig. 23. Thomas Cole, *View from Mount Holyoke, Northampton, Massachusetts, after a Thunderstorm—The Oxbow* (1836). Courtesy of the Metropolitan Museum of Art.

also entailed the risks of entrepreneurship. No one had ever made sugar from beets in the United States. Processing David's crops would require expensive machinery that would be hard to find and harder to fix. There would be no experienced local labor base, no neighboring farmers to advise on replacing a part or eradicating a pest. Even if the beets were successfully grown, harvested, and processed, would people switch from a time-tested pantry staple to an experimental one? How would the sugar be packaged, or marketed, or sold? The company that had promised to pay David's expenses in Europe and his start-up costs in the United States had gone bankrupt. If this seemed a bad omen, he chose not to heed it. He borrowed more money to buy machinery, and the Childs set to work.[1]

"Labor in the open fields and streets is rarely performed by women [in America], unless it be by foreign peasantry lately arrived in the country," Child had written in *The History of the Con-*

dition of Women. But here she was, in the earliest morning hours, helping her husband weed the one-acre plot of rented land that was all they could afford. As she looked up from the damp earth, perhaps the rising sun drew Child's thoughts east toward Boston. In the quiet of the dawn, "when all the world, except the birds, are asleep," even Garrison's thundering voice must suddenly have felt like a distant echo.[2]

Child's writing was supposed to keep them afloat until David's beets could turn a profit. This was a risky strategy for someone whose public was now skittish. Could she write in the midst of all the dirt and manure and weeds? What would she do without a library? Did she even have a desk? Until they could afford their own home, they were boarding with a local family on one of Northampton's main streets. Their landlords were Calvinists—their dour outlook all too familiar—whose taste in home decor ran to portraits of scowling ministers in blackened frames. They were honest, kind, and practical, Child reported, but also "so narrow, so uninformed, so bigoted." As long as it was summer, she could delight in the "majestic hills, the broad clear river." But she missed the ocean and Boston's intellectual edge. When Abby Kelley, who was enduring a punishing schedule of antislavery speaking and facing frequently hostile audiences, wrote envying Child her country paradise, Child was quick to correct her. "A succession of trying circumstances led us here, and I ought to be thankful for the blessings with which I am surrounded," she wrote. "But I am in fact more home-sick than I ever was in my whole life."[3]

Far from her publishers, she struggled to control her copyrights and keep her literary prospects alive. Maybe *The Girl's Own Book* could go into another edition. Maybe she could put together stories from the *Juvenile Miscellany* into a new edited volume. Or maybe she couldn't. "I have been so long out of the way of children," she wrote to one publisher, "and life is getting to be such a deep and serious matter to me, that I do not feel as if I could ever again succeed in that kind of writing."[4] There is, in fact, no record that anything came of these schemes.

The area surrounding Northampton was home to settled wealth

that predated the Revolution. Ten families, known locally as "the River Gods," controlled its capital and dictated its culture. The Childs' arrival caused a minor sensation. The beloved-turned-notorious author of *The Frugal Housewife* a resident of Northampton! Residents were curious. "When I first came here," Child reported to Caroline Weston a few months after their arrival, "'the upper circles' were decidedly disposed to patronize me." That had quickly changed. When she made it clear that she would use her popularity to talk about abolitionism, she could feel their enthusiasm cooling.[5]

Indeed, as spring planting began, the Childs were tilling difficult soil metaphorically if not literally. While they were initially well received by the "upper classes," "the kind of welcome we expected, viz. from abolitionists, has been very scanty," Child confessed. "I was told that two thirds of the town were abolitionists. It may be so, but they keep wonderfully to themselves."[6] The reality, they soon learned, was bleaker. Northampton was full of people who claimed to be abolitionists but who cared more for religious conformity and the appearance of respectability than for ending slavery. Reform work here was going to be a challenge. Sometimes the hardest people to convert are those who think they are already saved.

In her more optimistic moments, Child was grateful that Northampton allowed her to use her powers of persuasion more productively than among her like-minded Boston friends. She proudly recounted some of her verbal jousting to those back home. Anne Lyman, wife of a local judge, was an early sparring partner. Mrs. Lyman "seems determined that she *will* get acquainted with me, though she is the very embodiment of aristocracy," Child wrote to the Lorings: she "hates republics, hates democracy in every form, and of course hates reforms of all sorts." Slavery was sure to come up, and Child was ready. "Both of us were as direct and energetic as loco-motives under high pressure of steam; and, coming full tilt from opposite directions, we sometimes ran against each other with a clash," Child reported. "But no bones were ever broken." She had already, she added, deduced which antislavery arguments might work best with Mrs. Lyman's husband.[7]

She was also determined to make her new posting useful to her fellow laborers in Boston. Letters raced back and forth across the Holyoke mountains. Sometimes they read like spy reports, sometimes like accounts from a mission field. To William Lloyd Garrison, Child recounted who was posing as an abolitionist but acting like a colonizationist, who called abolitionists traitors, what arguments had worked to unsettle the local minister. To Theodore Weld, who was collecting data for a book about slavery, she detailed who was doing business with slaveholders, who boasted of participating in anti-abolitionist mobs, who professed to be "glad Lovejoy was shot."[8] The list of those implicated from this charming riverside town was long and damning.

Child also had more opportunities to interact with slaveholders themselves in Northampton than she had elsewhere. "The Hotels here [are] full of Southern travelers, attracted by the beauty of the scenery," she wrote to Weld. In principle this did not alarm her. "With regard to intercourse with slave-holders, far from shunning it myself, I seek it diligently," she reported to the Shaws. "Many and many an hour's argument, maintained with candour and courtesy, have I had with them; and they have generally appeared to like me, though my principles naturally seemed to them stern and uncompromising. I am not so intolerant as to suppose that slaveholders have not many virtues, and many very estimable qualities."[9] These conversations can't have been easy, but Child was determined. It was another small but persistent form of resistance.

But in the Childs' own neighborhood, things became more complicated. As luck would have it, across a small courtyard from their boardinghouse window was the elegant home of a Mr. Napier, a former slave auctioneer who had moved North but still did business in the South. Mr. Napier was "irascible on the subject of Anti-Slavery," Child reported, and he was powerful. He paid a sizable portion of the local minister's salary. As a consequence, no antislavery speakers or announcements were allowed in church for fear "it should drive Mr. Napier out of town." Worse, the man taught Sunday school, enthusiastically instructing his pupils that "the Africans are descendants of Ham, and that God has expressly ordained them to perpetual slavery." It perhaps goes without saying that he was president of the local chapter of the American Colonization Society. Child began strategizing. "If only I could get somebody to help me hammer on their consciences, I should be glad," she wrote. She was not optimistic. "He is too rich—employs too many people—and unfortunately builds a *church* with his stolen timber." Meanwhile, Mr. Napier insisted on praying "loud enough to be heard all round the neighborhood."[10] Between his noisy devotion and her hosts' pious silence, their new home must have felt foreign indeed.

There's very little evidence that Child was able to write in these months. Occasionally a fan letter, a request for an autograph, or hate mail from the South would remind her of her former literary status. Once a little girl nearly brought her to tears by handing her a bouquet of flowers she had picked "for the author of the *Juvenile Miscellany*." Those early days of literary success felt very far away. But even if she could not write, she took flights of intellectual fancy whenever she could. "It is not *me* who drudges," she wrote to her brother in the midst of their farmwork. "It is merely the case containing me. I defy all the powers of earth and hell to make *me* scour floors and feed hogs, if I choose meanwhile to be off conversing with the angels." Fortunately, one local minister was more to Child's intellectual taste. "He has been to see me," Child wrote to Louisa, "and though I left my work in the midst, and sat down with a dirty gown and hands somewhat grimed, we were high up in the blue in fifteen minutes. I promised to take a flight with him from the washtub or dish-kettle any time when he would come along with his balloon." A philosophical conversation in a muddy field was a far cry from the Chapmans' drawing room or the Lorings' breakfast table.[11] But as far as intellectual stimulation went, it would have to do.

*   *   *

Northampton's isolation must have made news that reached them shortly after their arrival all the more shocking. In May 1838, Maria

Weston Chapman, William Lloyd Garrison, and the newly married Theodore and Angelina Grimké Weld had all convened in Philadelphia for the second Anti-Slavery Convention of American Women. The convention was to be held in the newly completed Pennsylvania Hall, a two-story structure built by abolitionists tired of being denied venues for their lectures. Given its purpose, the building itself was a provocation in this southernmost of Northern ports, where cotton picked by slaves was unloaded for transfer to factories in Providence or Hartford or Lowell. That the hall's inaugural conference featured the despised Garrison and female lecturers made the provocation worse. Now-familiar posters calling on citizens to interfere with the convention, *"forcibly if they must,"* began to circulate.[12] Once again, violence was expected.

The first evening had been bad enough. Chapman's speech—her first in public—had been interrupted by a mob that, Garrison later reported, burst in "yelling and shouting as if the very fiends of the pit had suddenly broken loose." As Angelina Weld and Abby Kelley took their turns at the podium, bricks crashed through the windows. "What is a mob?" Angelina shouted above the splintering glass. "What would the breaking of every window be? Any evidence that we are wrong, or that slavery is a good and wholesome institution? What if that mob should . . . commit violence on our persons—would this be anything compared with what the slaves endure?"[13]

The next evening, the mob returned and swelled to ten thousand. The Boston delegates must have had a sense of déjà vu as the mayor arrived, ordered them to leave, then abandoned the building to its fate. Rioters quickly broke through the locked doors, hacked up window blinds and the podium, and piled them in the middle of the floor. Newly installed gas pipes were "torn from the walls, placed in the vicinity of the wood work, and fired." Soon, the *Philadelphia Inquirer* reported, "the whole building was wrapped in flames, which diffused a lurid light around . . . . Every window vomited forth its volume, and the roof cracked, smoked and blazed." Firefighters arrived to protect adjacent buildings, but "not a single [water] pipe was directed at Pennsylvania Hall," the *Inquirer*

Fig. 24. Pennsylvania Hall, built to host abolitionists' meetings, was burned to the ground in May 1838, just days after its completion. Courtesy of the Library of Congress.

testified. By morning the building had been reduced to rubble. "A more complete wreck than the building now exhibits," the *Inquirer* concluded, "could scarcely be conceived."[14]

In the midst of the jostling, yelling, flying bricks, and lighted torches, the unthinkable happened: Maria Chapman collapsed. Her friends hurried her onto a New York train. By the time they reached Connecticut, she was delirious. A doctor was summoned; her husband rushed to her side from Boston. Garrison reported that she was now "a raving maniac" and that there was "no hope for her recovery."[15] Salacious newspaper reports hopefully agreed. It was called a nervous breakdown; it was called brain fever; it was called exactly what she deserved for acting like a man.

As ambiguous reports from Philadelphia slowly reached Northampton, Child was frantic. The news "completely over-whelmed me," she wrote, "and I have been in a fever of anxiety to obtain further news." She clearly feared the worst. "Where shall I find faith that the anti-slavery work will go on without her?" she

despaired of her longtime friend and ally. Chapman was "one of
the most remarkable women of the age," Child mourned. "How I
have loved and admired her."[16]

What a relief it must have been to receive a long, newsy letter
from Chapman's sister Caroline, full of spirited reassurances
about Chapman's health. Perhaps Child read the letter standing
outside the post office on Main Street, still dusty from an afternoon's labor. Chapman was improving, Caroline wrote: now would
Child please help with damage control? An insane abolitionist was
exactly what the movement's adversaries needed, and the Weston
sisters were not going to let them have it. Of course, Child assured
her, and set to work. In long, patient letters to friends and family, she refuted rumors about Chapman point by point. She had
not defied her husband; he supported her right to speak. Nor had
she abandoned her children; they were merely being cared for by
friends. The excitement had not caused the fever; it had merely
exacerbated an existing illness. Chapman was not in an insane
asylum but "at home writing me very agreeable and rational letters."[17] From the political backwater of Northampton, Child had
her friend's back. The in-group was still intact.

Meanwhile, in Philadelphia, an investigative committee criticized the mob. But it concluded that abolitionists were to blame
for the violence. They had promoted "doctrines repulsive to the
moral sense of a large majority," and they had gotten exactly the
backlash they deserved. In other words, authorities concluded,
there were good people on both sides. Chapman recovered, much
to her enemies' disappointment. Perhaps she was simply too busy
to go mad, one admirer speculated. Her Anti-Slavery Fair the next
Christmas included table ornaments made from the charred remains of Pennsylvania Hall.[18]

* * *

The conflagration in Philadelphia took place just months after Elijah Lovejoy had been shot to death by an anti-abolitionist mob. In
other words, violent defenses of slavery were not declining. In the

end, even the most despised abolitionists—Garrison, Frederick Douglass, the Grimké sisters, Abby Kelley, Theodore Weld, the Childs—would die of natural causes after long lives. But no one knew that at the time. On the contrary, a martyr's death was looking more likely by the day. "I warn the abolitionists, ignorant, infatuated, barbarians as they are, that if chance shall throw any of them into our hands he may expect a felon's death," vowed South Carolina congressman James Henry Hammond. "No human law, no human influence, can arrest his fate. The superhuman instinct of self-preservation . . . pronounce[s] his doom." Abolitionists, this elected official predicted, could be "silenced in but one way— Terror—Death."[19]

As it happened, William Lloyd Garrison had been thinking a lot about violence, human law, and self-preservation. As he was rushed out of Pennsylvania against his will by friends concerned for his life while the ruined hall still smoldered, how could he not? His thoughts turned philosophical. In whose cause was violence justified? The country's? Liberty's? The slaves'? His own? As antislavery agents throughout the North were pelted with manure, thrown out of second-story windows, and forcibly ejected from trains, Garrison's answer was increasingly: none of the above.[20]

He had long been drawn to pacifism. He had always opposed wars of aggression. More radically, he was a member of the American Peace Society, which opposed even wars fought in national self-defense. All war, this society declared, was *contrary to the spirit of the gospel.* In any case, they claimed, "defensive" wars were usually wars of aggression in disguise.[21]

If even national self-defense was unjustified, what about personal self-defense? Didn't each individual have the right to fight back if attacked? Garrison thought not. He himself had not resisted the mob that dragged him through the streets with the intent of hanging him in the Boston Common. He had been dismayed to learn that Lovejoy had exchanged fire with his attackers. Lovejoy was a martyr, Garrison admitted, but "strictly speaking" not "a Christian martyr."[22] American Anti-Slavery Society agents, who still canvassed the North speaking and distributing abolitionist literature, were trained not to defend themselves against mobs. On personal nonresistance, then, Garrison was clear. But as violence against the cause increased, Garrison was coming to even more radical conclusions.

What, he had begun to ask himself, was the basis of government? The answer was force. Philosophers at least since Hobbes had defined the state as a political entity with a monopoly on legitimized violence. The history of nations—including his own—seemed to be one long history of war. And what had Jesus said about force? He had told his followers not to use it, even in self-defense. They were to "resist not evil," but to turn the other cheek. Jesus had modeled this nonresistance in his life as well as in his submission to a brutal and humiliating death.

If all earthly government was based on force, what legitimacy could it possibly have? Perhaps none at all. The problem, Garrison began to conclude, was not just that the United States Constitution needed to be reformed to outlaw slavery. It was that there was a constitution at all. Any human government now seemed to him a breach of fundamental truth. This raised uncomfortable questions about political participation. What was voting if not sanctioning and perpetuating this illegitimate force? The only justified law was God's, and that law could not be found in secular governments or church doctrine. One of Garrison's favorite preachers recommended that Americans simply "abandon human government and nominate Jesus Christ for the Presidency, not only of the United States, but of the world."[23] This was not meant ironically.

Early in his reforming career, Garrison had voted. But now he stopped and urged others to do the same. He also helped found a new organization called the Non-Resistance Society. Its founding documents read: "We cannot acknowledge allegiance to any human government. . . . As every government is upheld by physical strength, we therefore voluntarily exclude ourselves from every legislative and judicial body, and repudiate all human politics."[24]

Behind Garrison's nonresistance was another fundamental philosophical commitment. Abolitionists, he now believed, needed to advocate for *all* truths in order to pursue any particular truth. In other words, attempts to end slavery without attention to other issues of justice—women's rights, workers' rights, the use of violence—would fail. Until society was reestablished on a peaceful, just foundation, its violent nature would simply reassert itself in another form. Even if slaveholders emancipated the humans they claimed to own today, slavery would rear its head in another form tomorrow. Garrison began advocating a "universal emancipation" that would "liberate humans from the dominion of man." He would now, he announced, extend the purview of the *Liberator* to include questions about "the cause of peace."[25]

Garrison's position raised more questions than it answered. If the country's most justice-minded citizens refused to engage politically, surely that left the field entirely open to their less scrupulous opponents. How would this not result in more oppression, more injustice, more suffering? To some, Garrison's withdrawal looked less like an embrace of truth than an abdication of duty. To others it looked like simple selfishness and self-absorption. By following this line of thought, Garrison could congratulate himself on his purity of conscience while others did the dirty work of compromise and persuasion. Garrison was unmoved by all these objections. The progress of truth had to start somewhere, he thought. He would start it in the only place he could truly control: his own heart.

When Garrison's more moderate allies read his resolution in the *Liberator* about withdrawing from politics, they must have despaired. First the woman question, and now Garrison was going to tell people not to *vote*? Several of Garrison's Black supporters began to worry as well. Perhaps all truths were connected, but the more abstract and utopian his concerns became, the less relevant they seemed to the realities of slavery. It also did not help that some of Garrison's earliest supporters were drawing the opposite conclusion. These included Lewis and Arthur Tappan, the wealthy New York brothers who, a decade earlier, had bailed him out of the Baltimore jail. Far from thinking that politics was illegitimate, they had concluded that political engagement was abolition's only hope. Together with others, they began laying plans for a political party whose sole objective would be emancipation. They also began laying plans to wrest control of the American Anti-Slavery Society from its most notorious spokesman.

In faraway Northampton, Child also read the *Liberator*. Chilly spring mornings had given way to sticky summer afternoons, and farmwork in the valley intensified. As she weeded rows of beets, perhaps she tried to sort it all out. She certainly agreed that truths were interconnected. That conviction she still retained from her Swedenborgian years. "It needed, indeed, but a common portion of far-sightedness to foresee that a struggle for the advancement of any principle of freedom would inevitably tend to advance *all* free principles; for they are connected like a spiral line," she wrote. She also agreed that all physical resistance was unjustified and that politics rested on "such a thoroughly bad foundation" that she wouldn't vote even if she was allowed to.[26]

But Child had never shared Garrison's wholehearted Christian faith, though she often wished she could. It was clearly a source of comfort to him and others. And she was deeply drawn to the message of radical peace that Jesus had preached and his church had, in so many ways, betrayed. She always spoke of Jesus's teachings with respect, although she laughed when David suggested that Jesus would have been more interesting if, like the Hindu god Krishna with his flute, he had "taken an interest in the fine arts." She also agreed that a peaceful revolution had to start somewhere and thought that somewhere might be her. "The conviction returns upon me, and daily gains strength," she wrote to Abby Kelley, "that if but *one* human being earnestly and perseveringly sought to reach perfect holiness, the emanation from him would purify the world. There is overwhelming solemnity in this thought of our individual responsibility."[27]

But did this responsibility require rejecting human government altogether? "Up to a certain point my perceptions are clear, and my convictions strong, on the subject," she wrote to Kelley. "I follow the straight road, till I see the no-government question in the distance . . . and there I stop." For Child it was "the old problem that has puzzled the world eighteen hundred years" since Jesus's

death. "*Can* individuals living in the midst of a wicked world conduct [themselves] precisely as they would, if . . . earth was made
a Heaven?"[28] Brought down to the dusty earth of the Connecticut
River Valley, the question meant something like this: Is it possible
to live a good life within a corrupt system? Does participating in an
unjust government—by voting, exchanging money, paying taxes,
getting married—make us complicit? What was the value of living
a spiritually upright life while millions of humans were physically
enslaved? Was it enough to set a good example and hope the world
would follow?

These were difficult questions. So when Kelley urged Child to
attend the first meeting of Garrison's Non-Resistance Society in
Boston, she badly wanted to go. "The Peace Convention," she wrote
wistfully, "is unquestionably the greatest event of the 19th century.
Posterity will marvel at the early adoption of such transcendental principles." Nevertheless, Child would not attend. "The simple
reason is that we must be very economical," she wrote, "and trav-
elling is expensive."[29]

As they planted, or watered, or mended fences, the Childs also
mulled over these issues together. True to his days as a liberation
soldier, David remained a "defensive war man"—committed to the
idea that wars in self-defense were justified. "My dear husband
cannot quite give up his good opinion of war in certain cases,"
Child wrote to Ellis Loring, "but he is continually writing and saying things that make grand pegs for me to hang future arguments
upon."[30] Maybe David heard his arguments critiqued as his wife
tried to steady the horse he was harnessing or while they dug pits
to store the beets until they could be processed. David still loved
his wife's mind. He must have loved her all the more for keeping
their intellects alive in the midst of the now knee-high beet leaves.
Child's letters to friends brim with adoring descriptions of her heroic husband. As hard as the work was, at least they were doing it
together. They could laugh together, too. When Mr. Napier's high-
decibel prayers became intolerable, David drowned him out with
an accordion. Their grim Calvinist hosts must have wondered

what they had gotten themselves into by renting rooms to these radical, aspiring farmers from the faraway big city.

But as summer tourism hit its stride, neighborhood matters took a more serious turn. Mr. Napier's niece, a Mrs. Gasden, arrived from South Carolina on holiday. She was accompanied by an enslaved woman named Rosa. After Med's case, slave owners knew to be careful. But they had found ways not only to continue their Northern vacations but to use them to provoke abolitionists. A "happy slave" who *could* run away while in the North but didn't was a triumph, especially if abolitionists had tried to "coax her away" and failed. Mrs. Gasden had apparently come prepared to play this game with Northampton's most notorious abolitionist and had induced Rosa herself to participate. Rosa "repeatedly hemmed very loud, when near me," Child reported, quickly suspecting that Rosa had been "instructed to throw herself in my way, in order to boast of her happy slavery, and laugh at my useless efforts to make her in love with freedom."

So Child took another tack. She wrote an eight-page letter to Mrs. Gasden, deploying her arsenal of arguments against slavery. In the envelope, she placed a copy of her *Anti-Slavery Catechism* and Angelina Grimké's *Appeal to the Women of the Nominally Free States*. She crossed the courtyard, left the package next door, returned to her room, and waited. The contents of the entire envelope, Child reported with some mischievousness, were "sent back in about two hours, in great wrath." But a small victory had been won: "I afterward learned that the whole family had the benefit of hearing the letter, except Mr. Napier who *would* not hear it." At least he did not throw it out of the window with tongs. But the incident was, as Child wryly reported, "quite a blow up."[31] The silence at her hosts' supper table that evening must have been especially strained.

The intrigue escalated. Rosa herself soon appeared at Child's door in her own state of indignation. She complained, Child said, that her mistress "told her that I called her a well-fatted pig, and her children puppies." Child corrected the record. "I easily convinced her, by reading the letter, that I had said nothing about her, but compared the happiness of slaves to that of well fed pigs; and spoke of them as liable to be sold like dogs." Rosa apparently listened: "The influence of truth and kindness on my part had its effect," Child reported. She came to visit Child again. All the while she insisted that she was not a slave but had been told to "*say* she was a slave." Which was she: a happy slave or not at all a slave? "Here is a pretty piece of duplicity somewhere," Child mused to Caroline Weston.[32]

Her intuition was right. Two weeks later, Rosa had "open[ed] her heart fully to me; and oh, what a tissue of meanness and falsehood her disclosures reveal!" Rosa *was* a slave, and not a happy one. She was trapped in a situation as distressing as it was common. An earlier owner had given Rosa to a granddaughter and specified in her will that Rosa be freed after this granddaughter's death. But the question of who owned Rosa had become mired in a family dispute, and the will had conveniently been lost. Rosa would almost certainly remain enslaved if she returned to the South. She wanted her freedom, and she knew this Northampton holiday was her chance. But her children, who, according to the will, should also have been freed, remained enslaved in South Carolina.[33]

We can only imagine Rosa's tortured indecision. Child promised to find "a good home for her, if she chose to take her freedom."[34] But why should Rosa trust this white stranger? What would she do to support herself if she stayed? She knew she could not ultimately protect her children even if she returned: they could be sold away from her at any moment. But if she remained, who would offer them even the little protection she could give if she returned? If she did not return, would they ever forgive her?

With Rosa's permission, Child wrote to Angelina Grimké Weld. Angelina knew people in South Carolina from her days as a slaveholder there. Perhaps she knew of a way to force Rosa's owners to honor the will. Perhaps she knew someone who could appeal to their humanity or shame them into fulfilling the grandmother's wishes. As they waited for Angelina's answer, Mrs. Gasden prepared to return home. Time was running out. "At one time, I think the balance would have turned in favor of remaining in Massachusetts," Child reported. By this point, Mrs. Gasden was suspicious, and Rosa was closely watched. And just at that moment—Was it a coincidence?—Rosa received a letter from her daughter, pleading with her to return. She and Child had one last stolen meeting. Rosa's heart, Child reported, "seemed almost torn in two by the struggle between contending feelings." But by the time her mistress was ready to leave, Rosa had made up her mind. "I saw her no more," Child reported, "until I saw her follow her mistress into the stagecoach that conveyed her away from freedom."[35] Perhaps Child witnessed this wrenching scene from her boardinghouse window with its view down Main Street. Rosa had chosen her children and returned with her mistress to slavery.

Child did not give up immediately. She continued to inquire about legal resources and moral pressure available near Rosa's home. But she was also aware that her efforts could backfire. What kind of retaliation would Rosa suffer if it emerged that she had confided in a Northern abolitionist who was now meddling in her enslavers' affairs? Sometimes, Child had learned, white people's good intentions could have deadly consequences. Ultimately, she knew, there was very little she could do.

In the end, Rosa suffered the fate of so many enslaved people: she faded out of recorded history. Was she allowed to live out her life with her children? Or was she sold away from them, or they from her? Did she ever think of the strange white woman who had spoken to her so earnestly and promised so much? Did she live to regret her decision? No one knows. Meanwhile, the Napiers publicly boasted that Child had tried and failed to "coax [Rosa] away from her beloved mistress." "They must know this is untrue," Child mused, "but Christians that will steal will lie also."[36]

On the topic of helping visiting slaves to freedom, David took a more direct, headlong approach. When he encountered a Black man at the Mansion House, Northampton's most prestigious hotel, he simply asked him if he was free, quite clearly implying that, if not, he would help him become so. This did not go over well with the hotel's owner. "I dislike slavery as much as you do," he groused at David, "but then I get my living by slave-holders."[37]

*　*　*

The layers of resistance to abolitionism were becoming distressingly clear. Slavery's defenders were proving more wily, tenacious, and unscrupulous than Child and her allies had anticipated. Abolitionists had produced pamphlets; the postal service had refused to deliver them. They had sent petitions to Congress; Southern senators had passed a gag rule ensuring that they would never be heard. They had won enslaved people the legal right to claim freedom when brought North; enslavers had made it emotionally impossible for many to do so. For every action they took, there was an equal and opposite backlash. "When we first unfurled the banner of the *Liberator*," Garrison admitted, "we did not anticipate that, in order to protect southern slavery, the free states would voluntarily trample under foot all law, order, and government" and that "nearly every religious sect, and every political party would side with the oppressor." This had worrying consequences for even the most committed abolitionists, who were, as one of Child's biographers puts it, prepared for quick martyrdom but not for decades of ostracism. Never living the same way again was becoming a chronic struggle. "What think you of the prospects of Anti Slavery, dear brother," Child wrote to Weld. "Shall we keep the steam up till the work is done? I am disheartened sometimes."[38]

More specifically, it was looking as if Garrison had been wrong to stake his movement on what was called "uplift suasion." Uplift suasion was the theory that if Black people became respectable, white prejudice would evaporate. Garrison had not invented this theory: Black and white leaders had preached varieties of its aspirational message for decades. But he had been its most recent and vocal prophet, and his converts, Child among them, had diligently spread its gospel. An articulation of its essence was even written into the constitution of the AAS. "This Society shall aim to elevate the character and conditions of the people of color," it read, "by encouraging their intellectual, moral, and religious improvement, and by removing public prejudice."[39]

For anyone paying attention, uplift suasion had obvious problems. It made it easy to hold Black Americans responsible for the prejudice they suffered. Never mind that education and employment opportunities that might have made "respectability" possible were closed to them. If prejudice continued, the argument suggested, they had only themselves to blame. If they would just dress neatly, talk softly, and—most important, their socially conservative benefactors urged—*stop going to theaters*, all their problems would be solved.[40] Garrison knew that uplift suasion was problematic in these ways, but it paired irresistibly with his nonresistance. It promised a future in which there was no fight but everyone won. Black Americans would emerge as refined, educated citizens. White Americans, in turn, would emerge cured of their racism.

Black New Yorker Peter Paul Simmons was beginning to have other, darker suspicions. If uplift suasion was sincere, he pointed out in an 1839 speech, it was disastrously naive. The situation of Northern Blacks had not improved in the decades that it had been urged on their community as the only way to thrive. "Our people were slaves then and are the same today," he lamented: "This northern freedom is nothing but a nickname for northern slavery." Where had education, for instance, gotten the few Black Americans who were allowed to get it? No higher-skilled or professional jobs were open to them, leaving them "nothing but learned paupers" who were then reproached for taking work that degraded them even further.

The consequences of uplift suasion on Black Americans' psyches, Simmons also argued, had been its own disaster. The "soft manners" Black people had been advised to cultivate in the hopes of improving white people's behavior—the modestly averted eyes, the harmless, ready smile—were humiliating. The perpetual need to signal deference had sapped Black Americans' confidence, Simmons mourned, prompting them to put white men "at the head of even our private affairs." In other words, uplift suasion had persuaded Black Americans to turn over their futures to white "friends" who exhorted patience, promised transformation, and overwhelmingly failed to deliver.

But Simmons had a deeper fear. Why, he asked, were white people so interested in moral and intellectual uplift? Why had they never recommended political or physical action? Because, he concluded, only the latter would work, which was the one thing white people feared most. "There is no such a thing as elevating a nation of people by good morals," Simmons insisted to his audience. "It is contrary to common sense or any plan . . . laid down in record." In other words, Simmons, like Garrison, had observed that no government on earth had been established without physical and political struggle. But he had drawn the opposite conclusion. It was not that government was illegitimate. It was that physical and political struggles *were* legitimate. Anyone who told Black Americans otherwise, Simmons concluded, was trying to suppress them. White Americans' obsession with the "moral elevation of our people," he warned, is "nothing but a conspicuous scarecrow designed expressly, I may safely say, to hinder our people from acting collectively for themselves."[41]

"We have been a people more deceived than any nation of people under the sun," Simmons concluded, his voice no doubt rising in anger. "Physical and political efforts are the only methods left for us to adopt." To remain passive would be to "raise another generation of slaves." No more, he commanded his listeners. "We must show ACTION! ACTION! ACTION!" he demanded. "This we study, this we must physically practice," he urged. Once this was accomplished, he promised, "we will be in truth an independent people."

Simmons was not alone. In the following years, other Black abolitionists such as Henry Highland Garnet and James McCune Smith would make similar arguments. If being an abolitionist required nonresistance, Garnet argued against Garrison in 1843, "then I do not hesitate to say that your abolitionism is abject slavery."[42]

Were people like Child listening to people like Simmons? It's not clear. Garrison continued to claim that uplift suasion would work, sometimes in the same breath as he acknowledged it was fail-

Fig. 25. Frederick Douglass, ca. 1850. Courtesy of the National Portrait Gallery.

ing. Other abolitionists, including some Black leaders, continued to support its arguments. A case in point, at least initially, seemed to be Frederick Douglass, the young slave who had wondered what abolition meant and, in 1838, had escaped to the North and begun a new life. He had come to Garrison's attention soon thereafter as an extraordinarily promising speaker. With the support of the American Anti-Slavery Society, Douglass began touring the North, holding audiences spellbound with tales of the hypocrisy and sadism that defined Southern slavery. By 1841, he was touring with Garrison himself as Garrison preached the gospel of nonresistance, using Douglass as evidence of a Black man who, despite the scars on his back, had nothing but "forgiveness in his heart." Years later, in his best-selling 1855 biography *My Bondage and My Freedom*, Douglass himself described even the moment when he physically battled an enslaver who tried to whip him in nonresistant terms. "Every blow was parried," he said of this life-and-death struggle, "though I dealt no blows in turn. I was strictly on the *defensive*, preventing him from injuring me, rather than trying to injure him," he assured his readers.[43] White audiences flocked to hear Garrison praise this brilliant Black orator's supposed willingness to always, only, resist without force.

But Douglass would not allow himself to be portrayed in this way forever. Fortified by arguments like Simmons's and by his own evaluation of the reach of white racism and the failure of uplift suasion, Douglass would eventually break with Garrison and openly embrace political action and physical resistance as necessary for emancipation. Garrison would never quite forgive him.[44]

By the time she and David had lived a few years in Northampton, Child's own understanding of the question of nonresistance had also become more complicated. After the burning of Pennsylvania Hall and a year among Northampton's River Gods, Calvinists, and vacationing slaveholders, she had come to doubt that Black respectability would transform white people's behavior enough to bring about emancipation. "I have ceased to believe that public opinion will ever be sincerely reformed . . . till long after emancipation has taken place," she wrote to Henrietta Sargent. Even then, she predicted, "for generations to come, there will be a very large minority hostile to the claims of colored people."[45] This still left room to hope that uplift suasion *after* emancipation would achieve what uplift suasion *before* could not. Surely once all Black Americans were free, they could achieve dignity and respect. *Then* white Americans—however slowly—would lose their prejudice. Uplift suasion could still work: just later. Indeed, Child would continue, well beyond the Civil War, to try to convince Black Americans that the end of prejudice depended on their ability to make themselves respectable to the white people around them. I sometimes think that she and other Americans, then as now, simply could not stand to believe otherwise.

The delay of uplift suasion's success left a larger question. If emancipation could not be achieved by white people's voluntarily giving up their prejudices, what *would* work? Child made a shocking confession to Kelley. She was beginning to doubt that nonresistance could end slavery. "Much as I deprecate it," she confessed, "I am convinced that emancipation must come through violence."[46] And who would engage in this necessary violence? At least at this point, Child didn't say.

Child was not only beginning to doubt the effectiveness of Garrison's nonresistance; she was also watching it scare others away from the cause. Garrison was, quite simply, getting too far ahead of his base. From her Northampton post, she tried hard to translate for the coastal elites. It was not easy. Northampton abolitionists, she reported, were "honestly, sincerely frightened at the bearing of the Peace principles on governments," she wrote to Caroline Weston. What, indeed, was your average resident of Northampton to make of the claim that the Revolutionary War was a mistake, the United States Constitution was illegitimate, and voting was immoral? That Garrison and others were endorsing these views confirmed moderates' worst fears about abolitionism's radical core. Meanwhile, Garrison published attack after attack on dissenting allies in the *Liberator*. "Oh! how my heart is grieved by these dissentions!" Child wrote. "I wish our dear and much respected friend Garrison would record them more sparingly in his paper." "I suppose," she conceded loyally, "he thinks it necessary." Rural abolitionists, she warned, "have a very dim idea of what all the quarrelling is about," and the festering rancor was doing "immense injury to the cause."[47]

*   *   *

The winter of 1838 set in. Their little room got no light and was too small to receive guests. David usually worked late at the processing factory he had constructed, cleaning, grating, pressing, and filtering the beets they had produced. This meant that Child often spent her evenings, she reported, *"entirely* alone." Early suppers in her hosts' cold dining room must have been a trial. "Calvinism sits here enthroned, with high ears, blue nose, thin lips, and griping fist," she complained to Ellis Loring. Probably Child ate quickly and retreated to their room. To pass the dark, lonely hours, she read a history of the Norman Conquest and compared translations of Goethe. She wrote to the Massachusetts legislature supporting the repeal of laws against interracial marriage. She also wrote letters pleading with their feuding friends to reconcile. "Let us work shoulder to shoulder, and the victory is won," she wrote in an open letter to the *Liberator*. "Fix your eye singly upon the *slave*," she urged.[48]

The evenings passed slowly. The Lorings sent her a lavish package of gifts. It included a little image of a medieval saint that reminded her of the heroine of her *Philothea*. She was embarrassed to admit how much she loved it. "I have been in a desert, and my soul has been very thirsty," she wrote. But their generosity also pained her a little. She took it, probably correctly, as evidence of their concern for her finances. She was proud enough that that hurt. A letter from Maria Chapman hurt a little too, at least judging from Child's slightly defensive response. Chapman was not to worry, Child wrote. "My husband," she assured her friend, "is very remarkable for mastering difficulties, and doing whatever he tries. His soul has been almost worried out of him by want of funds, and by delay after delay occasioned by cheap machinery; but he has made perfect sugar; and finds his skill in no way deficient to the task he has undertaken."[49]

Some of this was true. David *had* made sugar from beets. He was the first American to do so, according to the Mechanics Institute, which awarded him a silver medal, a diploma, and $100 for his success. In the *Liberator*, Garrison hailed David's "invaluable work" for the cause. David was also managing to sell some of his sugar, and he had plans for improving his production process for the next season. He had even written a book, *The Culture of the Beet, and the Manufacture of Beet Sugar*, which instructed would-be beet

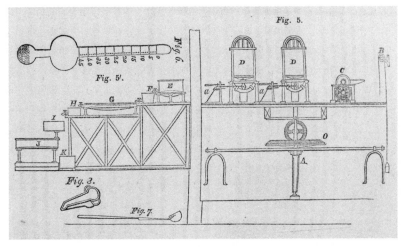

Fig. 26. David Lee Child included this illustration of machinery needed to process sugar beets in his 1840 book *The Culture of the Beet, and Manufacture of Beet Sugar*. Courtesy of the Boston Athenæum.

farmers on everything from planting to machinery to ideal sources of fertilizer. "Whenever we find good husbandry," he advised his readers, "we find that manure is the soul of it."[50] But every bit of money he made, plus all of his wife's literary earnings, went to pay for farming expenses. Worse, his old business partner had resurfaced, as had several creditors.

As winter finally ended and the weather warmed, David was obliged to go to New York to try to settle his legal matters just as their second season of planting began. "The loss of these ten days is a serious disaster," Child wrote to Louisa, adding that her husband was "anxious, and more depressed than I have ever seen him." "I do not feel as if I ought to leave him till he gets some sugar into the market, and feels in better spirits," she wrote in April 1839. She was, she admitted, consumed with anxiety about money. "I must *earn* something this summer," she agonized: "I am willing to do *anything*." I imagine her getting up in the morning, determined that this day would be different. She was the author of *The Frugal Housewife*: surely she could figure out something. But one avenue after another closed. She could not teach school since at any moment she was "liable to be called away to follow Mr. Child's fortunes." Writing was wasted effort since her radicalism had "cut off [her] profit as an author." Maybe she could work for a publisher, editing manuscripts or coloring maps. Perhaps she could sell candy made from the sugar David had produced.[51] Once again, it all felt very desperate.

In June, Child went back to Boston, apparently hoping that being nearer to schools, libraries, publishers, and intellectual stimulation would mean she could somehow earn something. David promised to join her soon. But for now, he stayed behind.

∗   ∗   ∗

Initially Child boarded with friends. Weeks went by, and then months. Was she wearing out her welcome? She feared the answer was yes, so she finally rented rooms without her husband. "The first night I came here I was all alone," she wrote to him from her new quarters. "How lonesome I *did* feel! How I *did* long for you!" Memories of their years together in Boston came to her "like blessed angels in my path, and I fervently thank God for the rich experience of your tenderness." But if she was thankful, she was also wounded. That he failed to join her was "a very grievous disappointment," and there was no evidence that the feeling was mutual. Her frustration developed an edge. It seemed, she wrote, "as if in everything connected with *you* I was to be forever disappointed." That was too much. She backpedaled. "And you know very well that what is *not* connected with you has very little interest in my eyes," she quickly added.[52]

David, as always, needed just a little more time. "I do not see when I can come to Boston; it cannot be under 4 weeks. If I can get my sugar moults within ten days it may be a little less," he reported to his wife. "I am sorry for this," he assured her, "but you know under what disadvantage I am compelled to do everything." Success was within his grasp: "I am going to make a great number of *1 lb loaves* expressly for samples, for which there is great demand. I think I can sell a thousand of them." His apologies were laced with optimism. "It is a dreadful hard time that you have," he wrote to his forlorn wife, "but I expect you will rest on a bed of roses by and by." Meanwhile, she wrote to his creditors explaining the situation and asking for more time—sometimes with his knowledge, and sometimes not.[53]

Child rallied and made the most of her time in Boston. By the time David finally joined her in October, she was attending Emerson's lectures in Cambridge and Margaret Fuller's "Conversations" for women in Boston. How good it must have felt to be among like-minded intellectuals, women and men, learning and thinking about the newest theories of the day. She was also busy preparing for Chapman's ever more elaborate Anti-Slavery Fair and writing stories to be included in *The Liberty Bell*, Chapman's more successful version of Child's own *Oasis*. Apparently she now had a desk. She and Chapman were in fact thick as thieves, serving on several committees together and in high demand for their organizational and rhetorical talents.[54]

But it was increasingly looking as if not even these talents could keep their beloved organizations together. In both the AAS and BFASS, conflict had gone from bad to worse. The woman question still seethed. Garrison's nonresistance increasingly rankled. His opponents now wanted an abolitionist association that explicitly welcomed clergy, excluded women, and embraced politics as a force for change. In short, they wanted Garrison out. Some Black leaders rallied to Garrison's side, declaring him the "true friend of the slave"; others agreed with the Tappans that it was time to pursue political means. Months of "disagreeable, mortifying, and discreditable collisions" followed.[55] Their details need not detain us here. They can be summed up in a few images.

In April 1840, after years of disputed elections, contested meeting minutes, and quarrels about money, more conservative women in BFASS resorted to a final suicidal tactic. Unable to wrest power from the Weston-Chapmans and unwilling to continue the society under Garrison's influence, they proposed a surprise resolution. "Whereas, for some time past," it read, "the harmony of this society has been disturbed and its usefulness impeded by differences of opinion. . . . And as this state of things is painful to us as individuals, as friends of the slave . . . Resolved, that the Boston Female Anti-Slavery Society, be by the act of adjourning, *Dissolved*." Maria Chapman and her sisters were stunned. Over their furious protests, the president declared the resolution passed. Yet again the unthinkable had happened: the House of Weston had been outmaneuvered. Both factions quickly convened their own new associations. That year at Christmas, the groups held competing abolitionist fairs.[56]

Weeks later, the American Anti-Slavery Society held its annual meeting in New York. This would be a showdown between Garrison and his opponents, and everyone knew it. Hundreds flocked from Boston to New York to support him; hundreds more arrived to oust him. The society's chairman was Arthur Tappan. Perhaps thinking longingly of Garrison's time in the Baltimore jail and regretting his role in ending it, Tappan sent word that he was withdrawing from the association and would not attend the convention. When the meeting opened and Abby Kelley was nominated for the executive committee, Lewis Tappan and others made it clear that they would not tolerate a woman in the society's leadership. "In Congress the masters speak while the slaves are denied a vote," responded Kelley. "I rise because I am not a slave." When votes in Kelley's favor prevailed, Lewis Tappan and others walked out. By the next day, they had formed the American Foreign and Anti-Slavery Society.[57] The acronyms proliferated. In Boston alone, one could be a member of BFASS, MFES, MAS, AAS, and AFAS. Abolition's enemies rejoiced.

Many factors had contributed to the schism, but Kelley made an easy target for the backlash. John Greenleaf Whittier, a lifelong abolitionist, accused her of being the "bombshell that *exploded* the society." He compared her to Eve, Delilah, and Helen of Troy all rolled into one. He wanted to be progressive, but he had had enough. "The last exploit of my good friend Abby . . . is too much for me," he confessed to a friend. "I am getting rather off from woman's rights."[58]

Whatever combination of biblical and mythical she had achieved,

Kelley was also now an elected official on the executive committee. So, after the next round of votes, was Lydia Maria Child.[59] But the honor was bestowed in absentia. Child was not in New York. She was back in Northampton, where she and David were, against all odds, planting the next crop of sugar beets. It was true: he had persuaded her to try again.

But with what money? Hadn't they only recently been destitute? Who in their right mind would have lent this noble but flawed enterprise more funds? The answer is enough to make you despair. Child's father had agreed to give his daughter her inheritance in advance so she and David could buy their own Northampton farm.[60] The sacrifice this required on Child's part is unimaginable. She had already mortgaged what was left of her early literary career against David's sugar beet experiment. Now she was borrowing against her future as well. It is a tribute to his powers of persuasion, her love for him, and her desire for his success. It is also a tribute to her desperate resolve to resist slavery in every way she could. Maybe postal campaigns, petitions, uplift suasion, and all the rest weren't working. But maybe economic resistance, in the form of sugar beets, still could.

So even though the one hundred acres David had bought was locally known as the "Seeger Swamp," she called it an "excellent farm." Despite fearing that David would collapse from "laboring in the hot sun, day after day," she was optimistic. "I hope we shall prosper," she wrote to his mother. "We work hard enough for it, in any event." The next year passed much as the first had: backbreaking work, social isolation, financial disaster. Her father moved in with them as a condition of the advance on her inheritance. Then he moved out because he and David made each other miserable. Convers Francis Sr. "could not abide" David's habit of reading aloud to his wife at night since literature, he pointedly claimed, "always leads to beggary." "Dear Mr. Child has borne all manner of provocations with wonderful calmness and patience," Child wrote to Louisa, "never giving a hasty word, though continually fretted at, even when he was trying the most to please; but I never saw any-

thing take down his natural cheerfulness, as this trial did." Ultimately the Childs returned the money they owed her father and
instead borrowed from David's brother to make ends meet.[61]

From across the tree-covered mountains, they heard agonizing details of the fallout of the abolitionists' split. Friendships
forged in the early years of activism splintered. Staunch allies became "pealers," pealing away from Garrison's society and joining
the Tappans'. Former associates worked to undermine each other's newspapers and steal each other's supporters. It was, in short,
ugly. Abolitionism as they had known it was dead, concluded Theodore and Angelina Weld as they retreated to a farm in New Jersey.[62]

Child continued to defend Garrison and to report back to her
Boston allies whenever the endless work of farming allowed. But
the infrequency of her letters was making Maria Chapman uneasy. She wrote to Child once, twice, then a third time. She got no
response. Now she began to fear the worst: that Child's silence
suggested weakened resolve. Finally Child wrote back. A "mass of
household cares and hourly trials" had kept her from responding,
she confessed, and she was sorry. Then she took Chapman's para-
noia straight on. "Have you begun to suspect that I am a 'pealer'?"
she asked. "Have no fear. My detestation of the mean, vile treachery [of Garrison's opponents] deepens daily." Child sensed an even
deeper worry. "Do you suspect me of indifference to the cause?" It
was true, Child admitted, that the all-consuming farmwork made
it harder to stay engaged. But no, she was not indifferent. She was
not quitting. She would write something for the next *Liberty Bell*.
She was working hard to get subscriptions for the *Liberator*. She
had recently spent hours explaining to a neighbor why religious
disagreements should not impede abolitionism. She apologized
again for not writing. "I *am* ashamed of my silence," she confessed.
But she also teased a little: "If you had had the wit not to have written, *I* should have written in order to get an answer." "But what mo-
tive had I, you foolish sister, when your letters came without the
asking?"[63]

At the end of that year's harvest, it was clear that David's farming experiment had produced that classic entrepreneurial para-

dox: a profitless success. "Handsomer or better flavored brown sugar we never met with," the *Journal of Commerce* pronounced. "If such sugar can be produced at the same price as cane or maple, it will have a great run. We conceive that Mr. Child," the report continued, "is rendering an important service to the American public, and we hope to himself also." The possibilities were still intoxicating. Imagine: something that could do good for the American public, the antislavery cause, and himself. Today, sugar beets make up 30 percent of all sugar consumed.[64] David's was just an idea whose time had not yet come. No wonder he wanted to try again the next year.

But the fact was that they were broke. A new desperation crept into Child's letters. "Of all the trials I ever met," she wrote to Louisa, this one was "the most intolerable." The work, the isolation, the poverty; her father's censorious attacks on David, resentment of their happiness, and angry departure: it was too much. "If there were no other escape from such a position," she confessed, "I might escape in drunkenness or suicide."[65] Something had to change.

Perhaps ironically, change arrived as a consequence of the abolitionists' schism. The American Anti-Slavery Society, still reeling from the defection of Garrison's enemies, wanted its own newspaper to compete with theirs. Someone needed to move to New York to be its editor. Why not Lydia Maria Child?

7

The Workshop of Reform

To understand how this ended, it's important to know how it began.

The newspaper Child was asked to edit was called the *National Anti-Slavery Standard*. Like the American Anti-Slavery Society itself, the *Standard* had become mired in the controversy and infighting of the past several years. Now, with the split behind them, the society's executive committee wanted to take the paper in a new direction. They wanted an editor who could steer the paper away from partisan bickering and transform it into a "good family anti-slavery newsletter" that would "gain the ear of the people at large." "The general feeling is that we have had too much of fighting," Abby Kelley acknowledged. "There is now an opening for something better."[1]

It is hard to imagine a more qualified editor than Maria Child. She had editorial experience from the *Juvenile Miscellany*. In the *Appeal*, she had shown herself able to master politics, economics, history, and philosophy. She had a national reputation, however controversial. Her literary talents could make hard truths compelling; her refusal to look away from evil would help convince her readers of the need for change. Perhaps, AAS leaders—Garrison, Chapman, and Loring among them—suggested, she and David could be coeditors. He too had newspaper experience and solid abolitionist credentials. And surely it was time they gave up farming: in fact, maybe taking on the *Standard* could save the Childs from going bankrupt. Perhaps it was time to move from Northampton to New York and trade farming for editing.

But it quickly became clear that editing the *Standard* would mean leaving David behind. Once again, he needed just a little more time. His entreaties echo through his wife's letters to their friends. "He has never yet fairly tried the Beet Sugar experiment," she explained to Francis Shaw. "He has never had the machinery to do so, until now." Surely, things were about to turn around. A "good many acres are now well prepared for sowing, and the machinery is all in readiness. In this state of things, I could not bear to have him throw all up, without having even tried the experiment."[2]

And so it was decided. He would stay in Northampton and try one more time. She would go to New York to earn money for him. When friends praised her for shouldering the enormous job of editing the *Standard* in the name of abolition, she was brutally honest about her true motives. If she had to leave home to work, she was glad that her labor would be for a good cause. But only "love for my husband, and the hopes of earning a home" reconciled her to her new task. And that, she concluded with her trademark scrupulousness, "is all the praise I deserve for 'devotion to the cause.'"[3]

In retrospect, it would be all too clear. She had taken the wrong job for the wrong reasons. But for now, Child agreed to edit the *National Anti-Slavery Standard*. She made her terms explicit. She would "have nothing to do with fighting and controversy." She would "confine myself to appeals to reason and good feeling" and "aim more at *reaching the people* than pleasing the abolitionists." Just as important, she warned the executive committee, she would act according to her own conscience, editing the paper as she saw fit and not as others dictated. Kelley assured her that they accepted these terms. "You are just the editor we want," Child remembered her saying. "We need oil upon the waves."[4] The deal was settled. The salary for the year would be $1,000. It was not much, but it was far more than their beets were worth.

Northampton had been hard, but leaving it was worse. Despite the drudgery and the failure, there had been moments of domestic happiness, "glimpses of real sunshine," she told Louisa. When they were together, David doted on her, showering her with affection, praise, and gratitude. "What has wealth or fame to offer," she mourned to Francis Shaw as she prepared to leave, "compared with a friend whose welcoming smile and kiss is always ready, and who verily *thinks* you the wisest, best, handsomest, and above all, the dearest person in the world?"[5] But a decade of marriage had taught Child that separation was likely to lead to neglect, emotional withdrawal, and promises to join her followed by failure to arrive. No wonder she dreaded it.

The angry rupture with her father had left them without a house. So as Child prepared to leave for New York, she helped David move into a little shack near the former oil mill where their manufacturing equipment was installed. She spent her last days in Northampton trying to make the hut a home: scrubbing, dusting, and stocking David's chest with newly mended summer shirts. The day of departure arrived. She missed the stagecoach because of the weather. The next one never came; apparently it no longer ran on Sundays. Each delay meant one more day with David; each felt "like a reprieve from being hanged," she told Louisa. But finally a coach arrived in good weather and on schedule. She said one last good-bye to her husband and climbed in. The Holyoke mountains receded in the distance. Despite herself, she had come to love these mountains. They now seemed to her the "face of a wise and loving friend," providing "clear visions of inward light, guiding me in my spiritual pilgrimage."[6] Now she was leaving them, and her husband, far behind.

Several days and multiple transportation mishaps later, she found herself deposited alone in the throbbing melee of Manhattan. Somehow she made her way to the Lower East Side. There, on Eldridge Street, she would board at the home of Isaac Hopper, a Quaker abolitionist. Hopper was a kindred spirit, a lively, quick-witted man whose lifelong struggle against slavery had made his home a well-used stop on the Underground Railroad. His wife was warm and hospitable in her earnest, austere way. Child's rooms were comfortable and clean. They looked out on a tiny garden with two graceful trees. There were no grim Calvinists or proslavery

Sunday school teachers in sight. She arrived in early May, just as flowers were beginning to appear in the little parks that dotted the city.[7]

But she had brought with her a Bostonian's disdain for New York, and she was already looking forward to leaving. The air in New York was dirty, the streets were dangerous, the people were hurried and aggressive. And the juxtapositions were harsh. A boat docked in the harbor called the "Fairy Queen," she recorded with incredulity, transported dead hogs. New York was, in short, "a frightful place." "Oh, Louisa!" she wrote to her friend in Boston, "how dreary it is to be here alone, and leave Mr. Child there alone. I hope at last, when I've worked my passage, I shall get settled in our little rural home, never to see N. York more."[8] One year, $1,000, and enough.

Her first issue of the *National Anti-Slavery Standard* was scheduled to appear on May 20. She had only weeks to prepare. Her experience editing the *Juvenile Miscellany* surely helped as she met with printers, examined typefaces, and contacted distributors. Somewhere in these early weeks, perhaps at a desk in the Hoppers' home or in the offices of the American Anti-Slavery Society, she wrote her first editorial. "Such as I am, I am here—ready to work, according to my conscience and ability," she told her readers: "promising nothing, but diligence and fidelity; refusing the shadow of a fetter on my free expression of opinion, from any man, or body of men; and equally careful to respect the freedom of others, whether as individuals or societies." "I have great confidence in you," Ellis Loring wrote to her from Boston. Then he added: "I think your position will be a difficult one."[9] If she felt any pride when the first issue rolled off the presses with her name on the masthead, she gave no indication.

The task of editing the *Standard* was crushing. Every issue consisted of four enormous pages, twenty-six by nineteen inches, each containing six columns of minuscule type. Week after week, it was Child's job to fill them. This meant soliciting some contributions and rejecting others, soothing one author's bruised ego and correcting another's poor spelling. But these tasks were nothing com-

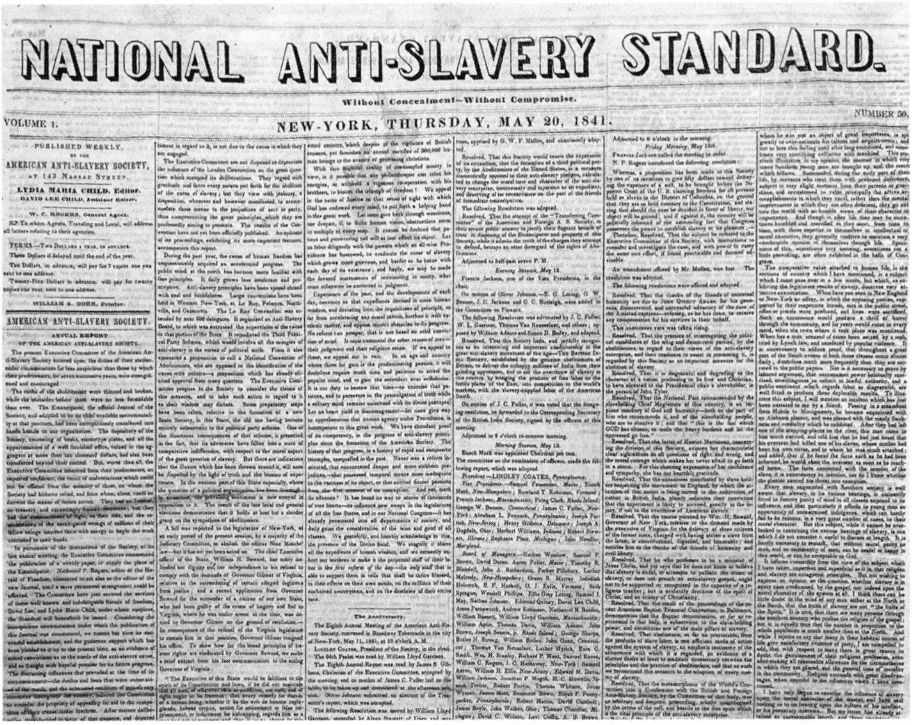

Fig. 27. The first issue of the *National Anti-Slavery Standard* to appear with Lydia Maria Child's name on the masthead, May 20, 1841. Courtesy of Historic Northampton, Northampton, Massachusetts.

pared with the conceptual challenge presented by the paper's mission. How, in four weekly pages of tiny type, do you change minds and convict hearts, steering your nation toward eradicating a cancerous evil at its core?

Child quickly settled on a complex, multilayered strategy. Readers of the *Standard* could, first of all, count on becoming informed. In the paper's opening pages, they could read articles gleaned from other publications that documented national and international political developments as they pertained to slavery: laws passed, speeches given, treaties signed. They could also read about antislavery activity: the AAS annual meeting agenda; the mob that had interrupted Abby Kelley's address in Rhode Island; where to send items for Maria Chapman's antislavery fair. Child made sure to in-

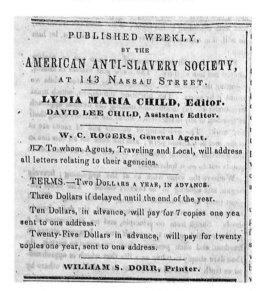

PUBLISHED WEEKLY,
BY THE
AMERICAN ANTI-SLAVERY SOCIETY,
AT 143 Nassau Street.

LYDIA MARIA CHILD, Editor.
DAVID LEE CHILD, Assistant Editor.

W. C. ROGERS, General Agent.
To whom Agents, Traveling and Local, will address
all letters relating to their agencies.

TERMS.—Two Dollars a year, in advance.
Three Dollars if delayed until the end of the year.
Ten Dollars, in advance, will pay for 7 copies one yea
sent to one address.
Twenty-Five Dollars in advance, will pay for twenty
copies one year, sent to one address.

WILLIAM S. DORR, Printer.

Fig. 28. *National Anti-Slavery Standard*, May 20, 1841, detail. As assistant editor, David's name appears below his wife's. Courtesy of Historic Northampton, Northampton, Massachusetts.

clude reports from the Black community as well, giving notice of a journal edited by the Black abolitionist David Ruggles, reprinting speeches by Frederick Douglass, or documenting the activities of vigilance committees charged with protecting fugitive slaves from recapture. She also helped readers learn how to argue. "The A, B, C, of Abolition," a column regularly reprinted from a like-minded paper, armed her readers with conversational tactics to rebut the claims that "negroes" were not human, that slavery could not possibly be so very bad, or that surely there was nothing wrong with trading with the South.[10]

The *Standard* would also leave readers outraged. Child again let slaveholders speak for themselves, reproducing advertisements for runaway slaves in Washington, DC, or from slave auctions in Virginia. Her landlord, Isaac Hopper, contributed a regular column titled "Tales of Oppression," in which he detailed appalling evidence of the physical and mental torture he had witnessed among fugitive slaves. Disgraceful treatment of Black Americans, Child was always quick to remind her readers, was not unique to the South. When Frederick Douglass and a white abolitionist challenged segregated seating in the Eastern Railroad Company and were physically thrown from the train in Lynn, Massachusetts, she gave full coverage to the event and the unrest that followed.[11]

But Child also made sure her readers felt encouraged. The cause was progressing; their efforts were not in vain. Some fugitive slaves, she assured them, were making it North. In 1841, a successful slave revolt on the *Creole*, a ship bound for New Orleans from Virginia, freed over one hundred enslaved humans. Also that year, New York repealed a law that allowed slaves to be held there by Southern slaveholders for up to nine months. In 1842, Massachusetts repealed a law forbidding interracial marriage. "This change is to be attributed to the progress in public sentiment, occasioned by previous agitation of the subject," the *Standard* told its readers. In other words, the effort to change people's hearts and minds was working. "Political action will inevitably follow *moral* influence, as the shadow follows the substance," the *Standard*'s editor promised.[12]

But in addition to all this informing, alarming, and encouraging, Child wanted her readers to feel they had been addressed as whole people: human beings who wanted to fight slavery but who also had other interests. All truths were interconnected, she told them; the more that readers searched for wisdom in all areas of life, the closer they could come not just to eradicating slavery but to transforming society. So she used the *Standard*'s columns to answer questions on many readers' minds. What was this new philosophical movement called Transcendentalism? What was phrenology? What about mesmerism? Who were Mormons? She also never forgot that her readers were embodied beings in need of practical advice, so she included household and farming tips worthy of *The Frugal Housewife*. Feed your animals regularly. Don't drink too much coffee. Use spearmint to keep mice out of your closets. She also taught readers how to avoid buying products made with slave labor.[13] "Free Labor Store: Everything for Sale but Principles!" a frequent advertisement read.

Perhaps more than anything, Child wanted her readers to feel that wherever you were on the antislavery spectrum—cautious or zealous, measured or impatient—there was room for you in the movement. Yes, the abolitionist cause had recently seen its tensions. "Were you an abolitionist in the good old days?" she asked her readers. "Are you disappointed that duty and this high joy no longer go together?" Weary reformers from Maine to Maryland probably nodded their heads. But infighting was normal, she assured them. Moral visionaries from Tacitus to Jesus to Luther had all faced squabbling and backbiting as their movements grew. Every association has its "go ahead" advocates—those like Garrison, who raced from one extreme position to the next—and its "stop there" proponents—those like Channing, whose caution sometimes looked like cowardice. Neither position had a lock on truth: "All conservative minds are not necessarily narrow and base, nor all reforming minds honest and true," she wrote.[14] Both positions were needed. So which one were you? Child asked her readers. Whatever the answer, there was work for you to do. There was also room for you to grow—to push beyond your caution and channel the knowledge the *Standard* provided into effective action. Everyone could contribute in their own way, each according to their conscience.

The best vehicle for such contributions, Child assured her readers, was still the American Anti-Slavery Society. It was, she admitted, easy to look at recent discord and conclude that such societies had outlived their usefulness. Not so, she declared. "I think there never was a time when their agency was more needed, or when so many channels were opened for efficient action," she wrote in her second issue. Opponents of slavery should all think of themselves as part of a larger force gathering momentum through the AAS and pulling others into its wake. Quitting now would be disastrous. "Tell the experienced dairy-woman to stop her agitation when the feathering cream gives token that the butter *begins* to come; but do not tell us that anti-slavery societies have done their work, and are no longer needed," she wrote. The split had been painful, but it was over. "Fear nothing," she concluded, "but be strong, and of good cheer."[15] She might just as well have been saying this to herself.

With any luck, readers would close the *Standard* feeling energized, convicted, entertained, and informed. It was a tall order.
Child did it almost entirely alone. Technically David was her assistant editor: his name appeared beneath hers on the masthead.
Occasionally an editorial would arrive from the fields of Northampton, signed "DLC," opining about Senator Daniel Webster's scandalous compromising or the proposed annexation of Texas.[16] But
there was no question of David's taking part in the daily grind of a
weekly publication. All of that Child did without him.

Did she know she was the first woman to head such an endeavor?
It's not clear. But it *is* clear that she felt the weight of her gender.
"I suppose you are aware that, from the beginning, I have had the
entire charge of the paper, unassisted by any individual, and you
may well suppose that a woman is obliged to take more pains than
a man would do, in order to avoid any inaccuracy or oversight in
state affairs," she wrote to Chapman. She was not above pointing
out her disadvantages to men, either. "Have the goodness to remember," she wrote the Eastern Pennsylvania Anti-Slavery Society to explain a slow response, "that in addition to what men
editors have to perform, I am obliged to do my own washing and
ironing, mending and making, besides manifold stitches for my
husband's comfort."[17] Women who are the first at anything are often expected to work silently and gladly, so I doubt the committee
wanted to hear this. Characteristically, Child wanted them to hear
it anyway.

Some early signs were good: "Well *done*! Faithful, dear Maria;—
your beginning in the *Standard* is all & just what it should be;—
brilliant, true, heavenly-spirited," cheered Ellis Loring. "I feel
hope and courage flowing in upon me, in full steam." Coming
from Loring, whose mind and spirit Child so cherished, this was
wonderful praise. The *Pennsylvania Freeman* declared that "in
neatness and beauty of mechanical execution, [the *Standard*] is
equaled by very few papers." It singled out Child's editorials for
praise, calling them "animated and animating . . . liberal in their
spirit and free from uncharitableness in their temper." From most
quarters, Child wrote, she heard "nothing but encouragement and

approbation." Antislavery agents on lecture tours reported that sales were brisk. When she started, the *Standard* had 2,500 subscribers. After two years the number had doubled.[18] It turned out, to no one's surprise except perhaps her own, that Maria Child was good at this.

But for all the early accolades, there were also warning signs. The *Standard* was, Child soon learned to her horror, deeply in debt. It often did not have funds to pay for paper or printing. At an early executive board meeting, Black members of the committee— apparently assuming that, like other white abolitionists such as Gerrit Smith or Arthur Tappan, the *Standard*'s new editor was independently wealthy—complained that her salary was too high. She could not bring herself to correct them. She watched her dream of $1,000 toward David's debts evaporate. "I have been crying, like a fool, today," she confided to Ellis when these facts became clear. The debts were only part of the problem. Because the *Standard* depended on subscriptions and on funds raised by local antislavery societies, themselves often badly organized and short of cash, its income frequently could not cover even her reduced salary. After the first three months, she had been paid only $20. After six months, she had been paid a meager $300.[19] She was trapped by a predicament anyone employed by a nonprofit knows: her passion for the cause made her feel too guilty to demand her due. Her motivating hope—that her work for the *Standard* would relieve her husband's financial distress—was clearly unfounded. She had come for money that was not there.

Just as worrying was an ominous silence from the Boston Garrisonians who had urged her so passionately to take the position. "I observe Garrison gives no indication, public or private, of interest in the *Standard*," she wrote to Loring. The Weston sisters were similarly noncommittal, and "Mrs. Chapman, in her letters, gives no opinion whether the paper is now advancing the good of the cause, or not." Probable reasons for this silence were not hard to imagine. For all their protestations about wanting unity, Garrison and his allies were still seething about the past year's events: resentful at their opponents' betrayal, eager to settle the score. Very early on, Child took a heavy pen to one of Abby Kelley's reports, editing out its attacks on one of Garrison's enemies. When Maria Chapman used language insistent enough to "draw wine out of a turnip" demanding that she call out another opponent, Child refused. Meanwhile, when Arthur Tappan raised money for the legal defense of the kidnapped Africans who revolted on a ship called *La Amistad*, she praised him. When Gerrit Smith gave a speech at the convention of the newly formed Liberty Party, she published it.[20]

Arthur Tappan and Gerrit Smith! They stood for everything the Garrisonians opposed—political engagement, clerical involvement, and the repression of women. Child disagreed with Tappan and Smith on these topics too. But she had committed herself, as the editor of the *Standard*, to presenting a variety of approaches to antislavery and letting readers decide for themselves. There was, she continued to insist, room for everyone in the movement. That's what leaders of the American Anti-Slavery Society wanted. Wasn't it?

But here was the most worrying sign during Child's early months at the *Standard*: she hated it. This is not an exaggeration. "I hate it, with an inconceivable and growing hatred," she raged to Ellis Loring after only four months on the job. "This reading of papers and pamphlets, and poring over Congressional documents, is perfectly intolerable, unless sustained by the conviction that I am doing some good to the anti-slavery cause." One week the Quakers were angry with her; the next week it was the Baptists. "I question the morality of letting one's soul thus be ground up for cursed reform!" she despaired. Cursed reform: this was strong language. "Excuse the word—nothing else would express my feeling," she apologized. Still, she would not deny that she was miserable. "How I do long to get out of this infernal tread-mill!" she mourned. "How I do long to be re-united to my dear husband, and have some quiet, domestic days again!" But at least one reason to stay remained. "Nothing *but* Mr. Child's pecuniary distress would keep me here another month," she fumed to Gerrit Smith.[21] But the pecuniary distress continued, so she soldiered on. Column by column, week by week.

After long days of editing, writing, proofreading, and wondering how she would pay the printers this week, Child must have left the AAS headquarters at 143 Nassau Street with her head spinning. The streets between her offices and the Hoppers' austere home were no quieter, nor did they provide any peace of mind. Child's path north toward Eldridge Street led her past city hall's imposing columns, then alongside the internationally notorious Five Points slum. Here teeming tenements now housed the thousands of immigrants newly arrived in New York's biggest immigration wave to date.[22] Every kind of illness, poverty, and wretchedness was on display. If Child walked south from headquarters instead, Wall Street, already a juggernaut of American financial power, was only blocks away. It was a perfect place to witness intersections of American power and powerlessness, the potential of a free society packed tightly against its cruelest effects.

But as she was jostled by carriages, street musicians, reeling drunks, and begging children, a strange thing began to happen. She began to see beauty. And even as she discharged her editorial duties, she began to write about this beauty too. For reasons she never articulated, her thoughts took the form of impetuous, intimate letters addressed to an unspecified interlocutor.

The first letter begins simply. "You ask what is now my opinion of this great Babylon," Child wrote, as if picking up in the middle of a conversation. It was true, she admits, that once the mere thought of New York had prompted a "long string of vituperative alliterations, such as magnificence and mud, finery and filth, diamonds and dirt." But, she continued, "though New-York remains the same, I like it better." Why? "I have lost the power of looking merely on the surface," she confided. "Every thing seems to me to come from the Infinite, to be filled with the Infinite, to be tending toward the Infinite."[23]

Firefighters were no longer merely firefighters. Instead they filled her with "thoughts about mutual helpfulness, human sympathy, the common bond of brotherhood." Street musicians were no longer a tuneless nuisance to be tolerated. Instead, her heart "saluted" them for their "cheering voice of poetry and song." Battery

Park, at the tip of Manhattan where the city meets the harbor, was no ordinary city park. Instead, it too was a "symbol of the Infinite," its restless waters resembling the "eager, unsatisfied aspirations of the human soul." The letter ends with a plea to her anonymous interlocutor: "Blame me not, if I turn wearily aside from the dusty road of reforming duty, to gather flowers in sheltered nooks, or play with gems in hidden grottoes," the beleaguered editor wrote. "The Practical has striven hard to suffocate the Ideal within me, but it is immortal, and cannot die. It needs but a glance of Beauty from earth or sky, and it starts blooming into life, like the aloe touched by fairy wand."[24] On August 19, 1841, she included this dreamy, ethereal reflection in the *Standard*'s editorial section. A week later she wrote another one. Soon they were one of the paper's regular features. She called them "Letters from New York."

The "Letters" became Child's creative escape from the ongoing drudgery of editing a weekly newspaper. If their effusive reports were to be believed, Maria Child could be pulled into wistful philosophical ruminations about anything: the brick wall opposite her window, the neighbor's new red roof, a flock of doves flying before her on Broadway. At sunrise, she went to the Battery again to see "earth, sea, and sky, kiss each other, in robes of reflected glory." She watched the ships "stretch their sails to the coming breeze, and glide majestically along—fit and graceful emblems of the Past; steered by Necessity; the Will constrained by outward Force." In the hardworking steamboat, she saw the "busy, powerful, self-conscious Present" and "man's Will conquering outward Force." In the physics of the new Croton Aqueduct she saw again the "stern old conflict between Necessity and Freewill."[25]

"Letters" also became a vehicle for her almost frenzied curiosity about her newly adopted city. To her still unnamed correspondent, she reported experiences that stretched her readers' imaginations and engaged their sympathies. In a Methodist church on Elizabeth Street, she witnessed a doubly shocking sight: a Black woman preaching. On Crosby Street in September, she watched a rabbi blowing a shofar on Rosh Hashanah. In her walks throughout the city, she watched "Catholics kneeling before the Cross, the

Fig. 29. Broadway, New York City, 1840. Raphael Tuck & Sons. Museum of the City of New York.

Mohammedan bowing to the East, the Jew veiled before the ark of the testimony, the Baptist walking into the water, the Quaker keeping his head covered." Some of these practices she found strange or alienating, but she just as often checked her prejudices and returned to a theme she would articulate with growing conviction in the coming years: all religious faiths were in some way expressions of the divine. The point was to honor each, to "look at truth as *universal*," and to discover "the great central ideas common to all religious souls."[26]

She also used her "Letters" to talk about race. Like many of her contemporaries, Child was sometimes obsessed with trying to determine what the existence of different racial groups *meant*. What did various skin colors, eye shapes, and hair types reveal about human beings? Did they suggest that humans were fundamentally different, or could those differences be explained by tracing different histories, geographies, and traditions? Here Child was clear: all humans, she insisted, were "children of the same Father."[27] But like philosophers from Rousseau to Kant to Hegel, Child sometimes speculated about "ages" that humans were passing through and the races that had predominated in each. This is almost never a good idea. The results are almost invariably racist. One European philosopher after another had determined that Africans and indigenous peoples were backward, barbarous, and inferior beyond redemption, their "ages" left far behind in the progress of humanity writ large. Such "scientific" theories were happily absorbed and redeployed by those eager to justify the exploitation of Black labor and the theft of indigenous peoples' land.

As to Child's own philosophizing on this topic, there is good news and bad news. The good news is that when she conceived of world history in "ages," she did not imagine Europeans coming out on top. Instead, she thought that Africans would lead the way to a "Spiritual Age" that would surpass the current "Intellectual Age," which was overly dominated by European efficiency and skepticism. She also refused to think of any race as irredeemably savage or backward. Instead she was at pains to show that it was often European culture that best exemplified barbaric cruelty: enslavement of Africans and decimation of Native American tribes being two prime examples. All too frequently, she reminded her readers, white civilizations exported patterns of cruelty to other cultures, then blamed those cultures for adopting them. "We must not teach as superiors," Child admonished, but instead must "love as brothers," striving together to obey the "law of love" exemplified by Jesus and too often broken by those who claimed to follow it.[28]

But in looking forward to the "Spiritual Age," Child also essentialized Africans, claiming they were inherently musical, docile, and childlike. Unlike many of her contemporaries, she found these characteristics worth emulating rather than denigrating. But there is no question that such stereotyping has done untold damage. Child was also willing to entertain some of her contemporaries' more bizarre theories regarding what the shape of the skull suggested about the capacities of the mind. "The facial angle and shape of the head, is various in races and nations," she wrote, acknowledging those scientists trying to deduce intelligence from bone. These angle measurements indeed appeared to her to correspond to levels of cultural sophistication, with the angle between the European forehead and chin suggesting higher development.

But these were not natural or irrevocable differences, Child insisted; they were "the *effects* of spiritual influences, long operating on character." Exposure to the "more harmonious relation between the animal and the spiritual" produced by the Judeo-Christian tradition "would gradually change the structure of [Africans'] skulls, and enlarge their perceptions of moral and intellectual truth."[29]

Frederick Douglass once called such theories "scientific moonshine," pointing out time and time again the harm they did to Black Americans. I like to think that the fierce humility Child always exhibited would, today, allow her to see that. She was certainly willing to consider that she might be part of the very problems she was committed to solving. How much harm had she herself done, she asked in another letter, "by yielding to popular prejudices, obeying false customs, and suppressing vital truths"? "I know not," she confessed, "but doubtless I have done, and am doing, my share. God forgive me. If He dealt with us, as we deal with our brother, who should stand before Him?"[30]

The "Letters" also show Child widening her reformist sensibility to include other injustices on ready display on New York's streets. Always she sought to redirect her readers' disapproval of vice to the systemic injustices that produced it. Unlike those who attributed poverty to poor character or ethnic inferiority, Child laid the blame squarely on the greed and exploitation symbolized by nearby Wall Street. "When, oh when," she lamented, "will men learn that society makes and cherishes the very crimes it so fiercely punishes, and *in* punishing reproduces?" She called out the sexual hypocrisy ruining the young women she saw on the streets. The very men who made prostitutes of these women, she lamented, "sit in council in the City Hall, and pass 'regulations' to clear the streets they have filled with sin." She despaired about the cruelties of capital punishment and the inhumanity of prison conditions on Blackwell's Island. "Society[,] with its unequal distribution, its perverted education, its manifold injustice, its cold neglect, its biting mockery," she lamented, had robbed the imprisoned of "the gifts of God." "I will not enter into an argument about the right of society to punish these sinners," she wrote, "but I say she *made* them sinners."[31]

"Letters" also became the vehicle for some of Child's most philosophical speculations. What, for instance, was the relation between spirit and matter? How were music and color related? What about minerals, plants, and animals? What was the value of sorrow? How were past and future connected? What was beauty, and how were its different manifestations related? What happens after death?[32] What was electricity, and what did it tell us about hidden forces shaping our world? Her writing was experimental and educational, wide-ranging and intimate, confessional and convicting. It was, in effect, a new genre. Her readers had never encountered anything like it.

There is evidence that some of them complained. What was the *Standard*'s new editor doing imagining fairies at the Battery at midnight? What were treatises on Mormons or electricity doing in an antislavery newspaper? But other readers loved "Letters": loved being addressed as the famous author's familiar "you," loved being invited to speculate and philosophize, loved being allowed to participate, however vicariously, in the great human experiment of New York City.

*   *   *

An observant reader of the *Standard* may also have paused to wonder at something else. Often the author of "Letters" was not alone. It was a "we" who paid sixpence to board a boat to Hoboken and spoke in hushed tones of a girl murdered there. It was a "we" who visited Greenwood Cemetery in Brooklyn, who marveled at the Battery at midnight, who purchased a white willow basket before returning to the boat, arriving home just before nine.[33] Someone was accompanying Maria Child on her New York sojourns. Perhaps such a reader occasionally wondered who that someone was.

The answer might well have raised a few eyebrows. Child's companion was John Hopper, the twenty-six-year-old son of Isaac Hopper, Child's landlord. Young Hopper was a fledgling businessman and an aspiring law student.[34] As a member of the Hopper family, he had been raised among ten siblings, all of whom had witnessed their father's often heroic efforts on behalf of fugitive slaves. But mostly, he was an excitable, earnest, romantic young man, filled with yearning for the sublime. He was also clearly smitten by the famous author boarding with his family. His, too, was a poetic soul under duress—smothered, in his case, by a Quaker father who considered beauty at best a waste and at worst a sin. Perhaps over the small rituals of family meals or in snatched conversations in a common hallway, he and Child had discovered a shared enthusiasm for the wonder and mystery of the world.

He asked her to accompany him on his habitual midnight walks to the Battery—outings that, to Child's surprise, his father tolerated. Her delight in this small excursion led to others. Soon he was reading poetry aloud to her in parks while she wove oak garlands. He began showering her with little gifts: flowers, musical scores, engravings. Early in July, they took a boat to Brooklyn and ate a picnic "dinner" of oranges and cake. Soon they were inseparable. He napped on her couch as she wrote letters. When the stresses of editing and the pangs of homesickness overwhelmed her, he tried to console her as she wept. When she proved inconsolable, he retreated to his own room in tears. "As for his kindness," Child wondered to Ellis Loring, "I never saw anything like it; I think he lives for nothing else but to devise ways and means for my happiness."[35]

Their mutual affection blossomed into a relationship that both found electrifying but neither could quite define. Sometimes she described him as a brother. Before long she was calling him her son. Soon thereafter—this was "the best joke of all," Child wrote—he was calling her, a woman thirteen years his senior, his daughter. He also called her his "little Zippy Damn."[36] I wish I knew how to explain that, but I don't. Clearly, as they say, it was complicated.

Brother, son, father, friend . . . lover? The question begged to be asked, so Ellis Loring asked it. Or at least he warned Child that other people probably would. It was, he hardly needed to remind her, not exactly conventional for a married woman and a much younger man to be parading through moonlit parks on summer nights. This she found amusing. "I accept your caution," she conceded, "though the idea of the need of it made me smile. My charms were *never* very formidable," wrote the almost forty-year-old author, "and at this period I think I can hardly endanger a young man of 26, passionately fond of the beautiful." Still, she admitted, the relationship was serious: "If there is danger in being absolutely necessary to each other's happiness, for the time being, we are both in great peril." She also issued a warning: "You who want to sustain the *Standard* may as well be thankful that it is so, for I absolutely would not stay in N. York, away from my husband, if I had not him to walk with me, read to me, bring me pictures, and always greet me with a welcoming smile." This barely veiled threat would not have reassured those worried about Child's reputation, to say nothing of her apparently vulnerable heart. So she repeated her denial: "That I can disturb *his* peace seems to me scarcely possible; and he will not *mine*, except the pain of parting from a friend sometimes makes us regret that we ever formed the acquaintance."[37]

Her claim that she could not bear to remain separated from David without John's companionship was telling. The fact was that John reminded her of David, and this made her miss David even more. "I have many a home-sick and husband-sick hour," she wrote to Loring. "The ingenious kindness, and perpetual vicinity of John sometimes increases this sad feeling. His thousand little deliberate attentions remind me so much of Mr. Child, and yet are so insufficient for the cravings of a heart so fond of domestic life as mine." To David himself, her letters were both loving and plaintive. "Best Beloved of my Soul," she wrote him: "I received your dear, kind letter . . . and it was a real refreshment to my heart. . . . It was so tender—so loving." In the letter's margins, she added: "I have not dreamed since I came here. I wish I could dream of you."[38]

It was both mysterious and all too clear. Child knew by this point that she would never have a son of her own. Her father had recently abandoned her in anger, leaving her homeless and nearly bankrupt. Her husband, whom she still adored and whom John resembled, had transformed from an ambitious champion of the good into an ongoing disappointment. John had appeared, as if by magic, to fill the void each of these sorrows had created. Before long she was reporting to Loring that "my affections have gotten so entwined around [John], that it would almost kill me to leave him." With almost comic implausibility, she added: "I do hope that things will so happen that David and he and I can live together, and bless each other."[39] As I said, it was complicated.

But for now, she and John both lived in the Hoppers' small boardinghouse while David toiled away in Northampton. When, six months after arriving in New York, she finally was able to set aside her editorial duties to make the long journey to see her husband, the visit was "one of almost unmixed pain." She found David living in squalor, so thin and pale from hard work that she barely recognized him. None of her efforts to arrange the little hut were visible. How had her brilliant, charismatic husband become incapable of caring for himself? Had there been some kind of psychological breakdown, brought on the chronic stress of a fading dream? Or by shame at his own failures and his wife's successes? Whatever the cause, Child threw herself into saving her husband from himself. She was "overwhelmed with hard work while there," she wrote to Loring, but soon her efforts had the desired effect. David's "health and spirits mended astonishingly during the short time of my sojourn," she reported.[40] She could not have known this, but she and David were embarking on a new pattern. He would work himself sick while separated from her, return to her to be healed, then head back out, almost like a man possessed, to work himself sick again. Then the cycle would begin once more.

But this time, Child believed that their weeks together, however painful, had yielded a way forward. Perhaps as she cooked for him, mended his shirts, and again tidied the shanty, they talked. Perhaps she used his destitution as evidence that their period of separation had to end—to persuade him to quit the farming experiment at the end of the year and join her. "We have plans in which both of us agree, which I think will have a happy result," she wrote to Loring after returning to New York. "They involve long separation; but at the end of the road, I see a light."[41] He needed her. She could heal him. If they could just be together, they could be happy.

Child returned to New York determined to make the *Standard* "a first-rate paper" that would get out of debt, pay her salary, and finally fund her husband's dream. In her lodgings at the Hoppers' home, she was "comfortable as a poodle on a Wilton rug," she reported to Francis Shaw, settled in a "cheerful, sunny room" with an efficient stove and a comfortable rocking chair. "If only it were not for this dreary separation from my dearly-beloved husband, I should be right happy; as it is, I generally feel cheerful and hopeful."[42] Whatever their plan was, it energized her. It also never materialized.

Returning to New York also meant being immediately embroiled in conflict. The Quakers were upset when she criticized them; their enemies were upset when she did not. There were angry letters to the editor complaining that her pacifist stance was too obvious. Others complained that she kept it hidden. Each letter itself presented a conundrum. Should she print it in the next issue of the *Standard* or not? If she did, one faction would complain and cancel their subscriptions in a rage. If not, the other faction would do the same. With every decision, so much was at stake—for her professional and personal life, surely, but more important, for the cause of abolition. "There is more responsibility rests on my shoulders, than ought to rest on one little woman," she wrote to Ellis. "I am harassed with the thought that I may not pursue the best course for the good of the cause; or that I may neglect to give sufficient attention to some important aspect of it. Then this tumultuous din of politics plagues me like the tooth-ache."[43]

And what was more worrying, the silence from Boston had turned into complaint. Nathaniel Rogers, one of Garrison's allies, "has never liked the *Standard* since I had it," she wrote to Ellis; "Garrison's want of cordiality is obvious enough; and Abby Kelley is out of sorts with it." Chapman complained as well, at one point writing Child three separate letters insisting that she call out one of their opponents. Chapman, Child sardonically reported, was willing to make her friend the editor a deal: "The shortest paragraph would answer, and I might choose my own language," she wrote, "provided I would make it clear to all the people that I considered him a *knave*."[44]

The particular complaints masked a deeper difference. Kelley, Chapman, and Garrison were now advocating for what was known as "come-outism": the demand that abolitionists should "come out" of any organization that did not explicitly condemn slavery. Kelley herself had left her Quaker church in 1841 over its refusal to do so. As for Garrison, "No Union with Slaveholders" was already included on the *Liberator*'s masthead. Garrison made it clear in his editorials that the "union" in question was not just with the South: it was with anyone in any organization that did not make antislavery part of its mission. This meant churches, social groups, or political parties. The time had come, this group of abolitionists had decided, to stop defending people's right to be moderates. It was time to eject lukewarm abolitionists from antislavery societies, to insist that to be anything short of radical was to be complicit. In 1841, Kelley endorsed a resolution of the Rhode Island antislavery association stating that "every person who is not an out-spoken and out-acting abolitionist . . . is a dangerous member of the community."[45]

Why did Child object to this? She was clearly not opposed to taking deeply unpopular stands and urging others to do the same. She herself had "come out" of society in ways that had involved enormous personal loss. In some ways, she had sacrificed more, for instance, than the still wealthy Chapmans or the still influential Shaws. For over a decade, she had argued to her fellow white Northerners that their apathy made them complicit in evil and that their good intentions would not exonerate them. And in almost all matters of substance, she agreed with Garrison and his allies. Like them, she advocated immediate emancipation without compensation; she abhorred the idea of an abolitionist political party; she was a passionate supporter of peace principles. What, then, did the deepening disagreement come down to?

First, it was a matter of consistency. Only recently, Garrison's enemies had tried to make nonresistance a litmus test. They had demanded that Garrison publicly renounce his position or leave the movement. Garrison's allies, Child and Kelley among them, had defended Garrison's right to fight slavery in the way he chose. But now Kelley wanted to make "coming out" such a test. Child had opposed the former, and she now opposed the latter. "I object to the application of tests or rules concerning individual duties on this, or any other matter," she wrote. In fact, Child was watching the harmful effects of such tests play out in her own home. In 1842, Child's landlord Isaac Hopper, as well as her colleague at the AAS, James S. Gibbons, had been expelled by their Quaker congregation for their association with the *Standard* after the paper criticized of one of its members.[46] Child watched her friends suffer their community's rejection, grieved by the personal pain it caused and the damage it did to the antislavery movement.

If there ever was a cause in which moral shaming and absolutism were appropriate, surely the eradication of slavery was that cause. In other words, if ever Kelley's tactics were justified, surely they were justified here. But this, Child was sure, did not mean such tactics would work. More effective, she believed, was the position she had articulated in the *Standard*: every movement had its Garrisons and its Channings. Both were necessary; both were welcome. This did not mean tolerating lukewarm abolitionism. Every week in the *Standard*, Child tried to move moderate readers toward a clearer view of their more radical duties. But she wanted to do this by making them feel included and heard. Kelley, by contrast, seemed intent on exclusivity. "I am grievously tried with Abby Kelley's resolutions," she wrote. "It seems as if the devil helped her to drive away all the tender-spirited and judicious from our ranks."[47]

As to what all this meant for herself as editor, in Child's mind the answer was simple. "The views of a large majority [of the AAS] are by no means coincident with my own, on many subjects; but there is sufficient identity for me to manage their organ without interfering with their conscientious freedom, or in any degree violating my own," she explained to one group of critics. This, to her, was just a matter of doing the job she had agreed to do. "I have neither the right, nor the wish, to make the paper a vehicle of my own opinions, as distinct from theirs; therefore I am silent about many things which I should probably advocate in a paper of my own."[48]

Maintaining this delicate balance was not easy. "I have an increasingly uncomfortable sense of being fettered by being the organ of a *Society*," she confessed to Ellis. "I am not certain whether one *can* fill such a position without injury to his own soul. At all events, it injures mine," she concluded. This somber assessment was followed by a heretical thought that was in sharp contrast to her stated views as the *Standard*'s editor. "Have not *societies* done about all they *can* do for the cause?" she asked. "I have the same faith in the efficiency of combined action that I ever had; but I see many signs that make me think [the AAS] has nearly *done* its work on this subject." She added a speculation that, it would turn out, was prescient: "Should you do any the less [for abolition], if you were not a member of any society?" she asked. "I should not."[49]

The toll all this was taking on Child was becoming painfully obvious. By January, she was despondent. "I never before was so much troubled with anxiety," she confided in Loring, sure as ever of his sympathetic response. February was worse. Infighting was making her "for the first time, deliberately sorry that I ever had anything to do with anti-slavery associations," she confessed. "In view of all the things I am thinking," she wrote to Loring, "I am thinking some person can be found for this post fitter than I am." Who, she wondered, would have the right skills and perspective to navigate these treacherous waters with less damage to their soul? "I am sadly weary of this lonesome life," she confessed to Louisa Loring. "Our mortal span is too brief to be thus wasted, for the sake of money."[50]

*   *   *

Maria Child had a lifelong aversion to being photographed. But during these years in New York, she consented to have her silhouette done by Auguste Edouart, a French artist famous for his lively, evocative images of royalty, politicians, and commoners alike. It

Fig. 30. Auguste Edouart, silhouette of Lydia Maria Child, 1841. Courtesy of the National Portrait Gallery.

is the only image we have of Child as she approached forty years old. She is seated and solitary, shrouded in black. In her hand is a book, but it's not clear that she's reading it. Her gaze seems fixed on something far ahead. She looks very still. Both present and absent, both there and not there, signifying herself without being herself. "When you call upon me 'to define my position,' I do not clearly understand whether you mean me, L. M. Child, or me, the editor of the *Standard*," she wrote to a group of impatient critics. "Write to me soon," she begged at the end of a long, plaintive letter to Ellis Loring. "To me, *myself*, I mean."[51]

* * *

Loring was alarmed enough at her desperate tone that he staged an intervention. He shared her melancholy letters with mutual acquaintances and asked them to write to encourage her. Suddenly, instead of weighing her down with complaint, her mail was full of good wishes from old friends. There were letters from Wendell Phillips, Henrietta Sargent, Eliza Follen, even from Maria Chapman.[52] Child was chagrined. Had she really seemed that needy? More to the point, had Ellis not understood that her despair was confidential?

Still, the supportive letters helped. One in particular is striking: it was from William Ellery Channing. By now it had been almost ten years since Child had been dispatched to try to persuade the eminent Boston clergyman to support the cause and had despaired of moving him out of his complacency and into reform. He must have known that she had considered him at best a tepid abolitionist: indeed, she had said as much in print. But Channing had, in the intervening years, taken his own stand, essentially relinquishing his pulpit at the Federal Street Church when his congregation opposed his increasingly antislavery views.[53] Now, from his own kind of banishment, Channing wrote to encourage Child.

"I had heard so often of your brave endurance of adversity, and was conscious of having suffered so little myself for truth and humanity," wrote the now sixty-two-year-old preacher to the forty-year-old editor, "that I almost questioned my right to send you encouraging words." Could this explain why Child had felt so abandoned? Had she presented such a brave front that no one thought she needed support? If that were true, Channing was now willing to make up for it. Her need had shown him "that I can do more than I believed by expressions of esteem and admiration." It was, he acknowledged, the least he could do. "If I can lift up and strengthen such a spirit," he asked, "how can I keep silent?"

He made clear that he sympathized with her struggle. "I understand fully your language when you speak of *reform* as your *workshop*," Channing wrote. "I fear I understand it too well; that is, I am too prone to shrink from the work," he added. "Reform is resistance of rooted corruptions and evils, and my tendency is to turn away from the contemplation of evils," he confessed. "My mind seeks the good, the perfect, the beautiful," he continued. "You see I am but poor material for a reformer." But Channing was not going to stop there. "On this very account the work is good for me. I need it; not, as many do, to give me excitement . . . but I need it to save me from a refined selfishness, to give me force, disinterestedness, true dignity, and elevation." Child must have heard an echo of her own agony in Channing's honesty. Unlike Garrison and Chapman and even her own husband, she did not relish conflict. For ten years, she had looked evil in the face, but now she was tired. She longed to look away—to return to the beautiful thoughts that had fed her soul in her youth, before Garrison's burning words had changed her life.

Perhaps Channing sensed this. He ended his letter with a gentle admonition. "We must be something *more* than reformers," he urged her. "We must give our nature a fair chance. We must not wither it by narrow modes of action." It must have felt to Child as if he were looking into her soul. "Let your genius have free play," he urged her. "We are better reformers, because we are calmer and wiser, because we have more weapons to work with, if we give a wide range to thought, imagination, taste, and the affections." Her chosen road was hard, he acknowledged. "But trial brings strength," he assured her. "You need not fear."[54]

Something else is striking about this letter. The copy that survives is not in Channing's handwriting, it is in Child's. In other words, she copied it out herself. The first time I noticed this, I wondered if she had returned the original to him for his own records. If so, she clearly wanted a copy to keep. Was this so she could fix Channing's words in her mind and allow them to ease her heart? Did she keep it in a drawer to reread when exhaustion threatened to overwhelm her yet again? But later, another conclusion occurred to me. Channing died only seven months after writing this letter. Child had copied it out for publication in the *National Anti-Slavery Standard* as a tribute to the renowned minister. The original, apparently, she indeed wanted to keep: a way, perhaps, for Channing's words to offer solace when he himself no longer could.

In the meantime, the collective encouragement of her friends worked. Child's next letter to Louisa reads like a battle cry. "When my *will* is roused, unreproved by conscience, I too am a giant!" she wrote to her friend. "These are proud words for a little woman," she admitted, "but my vision is clear that the *Standard ought* to be carried high, and *will* be." It was, she again confessed, brutal to be separated from David. But "when I reflect . . . how few in our ranks combine earnest love for the cause, with clear vision and cautious discrimination, I feel as if I were raised up for this crisis." It helped that she could now boast of "presenting weekly portions of truth to 16,000 readers; for at the lowest estimate, as many as that read the Standard." Sixteen thousand readers! It was an extraordinary number, representing close to five thousand subscriptions, many more than the *Liberator*'s more modest three thousand.[55] Surely that was worth whatever daily discouragements the *Standard*'s editor faced. At least for now.

Child also replied to Chapman's encouraging letter. She acknowledged that Chapman had sent it on the eve of a trip to Haiti, undertaken in the vain hope of improving her tubercular husband's health. "It touched my heart that you should stop, at *such* a time, to comfort my despondency," Child wrote to her friend. Then she paused to offer some reassurance to both Chapman and her sister Caroline. "In your parting letter," Child wrote, "you seemed to forebode some new division among us; and Caroline's letter seems to imply some such thought in her own mind. Rest you easy. No division will ever come through *my* agency," she promised. She ended the letter by sending best wishes to Chapman's husband and—perhaps remembering evenings of loving solidarity at the Weston home—"to your sunny troop of sisters."[56]

8

On Quitting and Not Giving Up

As Child rededicated herself in New York to holding the movement together, Garrison was in Boston, finding new ways to get out ahead of it. After decades of watching the South parry each of the abolitionists' efforts with ever more diabolical defenses, Garrison had run out of patience. Worse, a series of legal decisions guaranteeing slavery's existence had convinced him that the US Constitution not only was as illegitimate as any other human-authored political document would be; in an echo of Black abolitionist James W. C. Pennington, he was calling it a "covenant with death, and agreement with hell."[1] And if the Constitution was morally corrupt, he concluded, so was the Union it had called into being.

At antislavery society meetings around the Northeast, Garrison began proposing resolutions that made this clear. "Resolved," read one, "That the union of Liberty and Slavery . . . is a moral impossibility . . . and, therefore, the American Union is . . . a hollow mockery instead of a glorious reality." "Resolved," it continued, "That the time is rapidly approaching when the American Union will be dissolved in form as it is now in fact." "Resolved," read yet another motion, "That the safety, prosperity and perpetuity of the non-slaveholding States require that their connexion be immediately dissolved with the slave States in form, as it is now in fact." Perhaps in an effort to comfort those who might be alarmed at the idea of the end of their country as they knew it, Garrison added another resolution: "Resolved, That the consequence of doing right must ever be more safe and beneficial than those of doing wrong; and that the worst thing Liberty can do is to unite with Slavery, and the best thing is to withdraw from the embraces of the monster."[2] After decades of trying to reform the country, he concluded, it was time to quit. It was time, in short, to dissolve the Union.

It was a radical position on an old question. In the half-century since the country's founding, the threat of secession had continued to be a standard weapon in Southern politicians' arsenal. More recently, however, it had entered congressional records as a threat from the North. In January 1842, Massachusetts representative and former US president John Quincy Adams had submitted to Congress a petition from a town called Haverhill requesting "a dissolution of the Union." They could no longer, the petitioners claimed, countenance the fact that their resources were being "drained" for the benefit of slaveholders and so helping to perpetuate slavery's existence.[3] As a matter of conscience, they wanted out.

Southern congressmen, apparently unbothered by the hypocrisy of their position, called Adams a traitor and wanted him censured, expelled, or worse. In the hearings that followed, Adams engaged in a two-week tirade against slavery. Given that a "gag rule" had prohibited any petitions against slavery from being considered by Congress since 1836, this was itself a major accomplishment. The attempt to discipline Adams failed, but not before newspapers had broadcast his arguments across the country. Garrison was thrilled. Adams had achieved a "signal victory," Garrison rejoiced, and had "frightened the boastful South almost out of her wits."[4]

For all but the most pure-minded abolitionists, however, disunion raised agonizing questions. Had it really come to this? Was George Washington's fervent hope—that the Union hold strong—to be betrayed already, while the last Revolutionary War veterans still lived? Other questions were more philosophical. What, in the end, did it mean to be an American? Did it mean loyalty to ideals or to an identity? It was true that breaking with the South might feel better to an abolitionist: at least your tax money would no longer be used to capture fugitive slaves. You would no longer feel the shame of belonging to a country that was betraying its fundamental principles in obvious and atrocious ways. But if your primary goal was not just the eradication of slavery in your country but its eradication period, it wasn't clear that disunion would accomplish that. Without the North to check its slaveholding ambitions, would the South recommence the international slave trade? Would it institute yet more savage laws to control its enslaved population? Was that even possible? Whatever the answers to these questions, one thing was clear: abolitionist pressure from the North seemed to be having no effect whatsoever on the South. When was it time to quit?

Soon, Child thought. In a March 31, 1842, editorial in the *National Anti-Slavery Standard* titled "The Union," she asked her readers to confront some sobering truths.[5] To begin with, she agreed with Garrison that the Union was in fact "a sham, not a reality." The betrayal had started early. "In framing the Constitution, our fathers compromised a principle of freedom, and they knew it," she wrote. The consequences of this tainted beginning had reverberated ever since. "Despotic institutions cannot, by any device of man, or agency of the devil, be made to mix with free institutions. When brought into *juxtaposition*, they *will* clash," she wrote. But instead of being roused to action by a betrayal of their principles, Northerners had been lulled into complacency. By what? "The natural action of reason and conscience have been spell-bound by the name of The Union," she lamented. And complacency, she warned her readers yet again, was corrupting. "To keep up the appearance of union, the American people are fast becoming accustomed to the relinquishment of those real principles, on which free institutions *must* rest, if they exist at all." The net result was both demoralizing and shameful: the North had been blinded by loyalty to an ideal that had long since been betrayed.

Union with the South, Child continued, "compels the free States to direct partnership with great and extensive wrong." Northern taxpayers funded the government's enforcement of the laws that made slavery possible. Their participation in the census sanctioned a practice that counted slaves as less than human.

Their military service assured Southerners that slave insurrections would be crushed. "In point of fact," Child urged, "we are the standing army of the South. . . . Without our help, southerners would not even *try* to sustain their peculiar institutions." Northern complicity had also helped slavery expand. "Calculating on *our* partnership," Child claimed, the South "has gone deeper and deeper in the ruinous business." As always, Child was willing to accept the moral responsibility this complicity implied, and she wanted others to do the same. "Honor among thieves," she told her readers, "requires that we should not leave [the South] alone to grapple with bankruptcy and insurrection." The North, in other words, owed it to the South "to bring her *out* of the condition *into* which we have helped to bring her."

But it was becoming increasingly clear that the South wanted no such help. Southern politicians continued to prevent antislavery petitions from reaching Congress. Their arguments in support of slavery were becoming both more creative and more hardened. They also continued to fight for slavery's expansion—into Texas, Missouri, Kansas, even a newly organized territory called California. Given this reality, the prognosis was grim. "When collision after collision occurs, people must needs pause and ask, 'Is *this* Union?'"

In the face of this deep complicity, what were a citizen's duties? Some, Child speculated, would conclude that personal action would be enough. Perhaps "each individual citizen can absolve *himself* from partnership, by withdrawing from all connection with the government." That would mean no taxes, no census, no military service. What else, Child could have asked, might such withdrawal require? Refusal to use the postal service, send your child to a publicly funded school, or travel public roads? How many people would take such drastic steps? Would it make any difference? And wouldn't total withdrawal violate other civic duties? This is a problem philosophers sometimes call collective responsibility. To what extent are we implicated in society's wrongs even if we object to them? Was it enough, as Child had done, to make enormous personal and professional sacrifices? Or did an evil on this scale demand more? What does it take to remain innocent within a guilty society?

Whatever the answer, the day of reckoning was fast approaching. "Let every man ask himself," Child urged: "Does the Union answer any of the purposes for which it was intended? Or is its power made to sustain slavery alone? If the latter be true, how far am I implicated in the gigantic system of oppression and fraud? If implicated, how can I best extricate myself, with the least injury to my fellow-creatures, and the least danger to the welfare of my country?"

The questions were wrenching, but the answer, to Child, seemed ever clearer. It was time, she urged her readers, to explore options for a "peaceable dissolution of the Union." Perhaps the Constitution could simply be amended and the North could go free—free to establish a republic that would remain true to its principles. Above all, bloodshed should be avoided. Surely that was possible.

Garrison liked Child's column so much that he reprinted it in the *Liberator*. A few weeks later, he upped the ante as only Garrison could. In an editorial on April 22, 1842, he reminded his readers of the upcoming annual meeting of the American Anti-Slavery Society in New York. "Many important topics will be presented for consideration at the meeting in New-York," Garrison promised. "The first of these, in importance, is the duty of the REPEAL OF THE UNION between North and South." Then Garrison declared himself "for measuring the humanity, patriotism, and piety of every man by this standard."[6]

New York newspapers pounced, gleefully reprinting Garrison's words and declaring that abolitionists had finally shown themselves for what they were: traitors. The *New York Courier and Enquirer* ominously predicted that the Anti-Slavery Society meeting would be inconsistent "with the peace of the city." The *New York Sun* hinted darkly that any discussion of disunion would not be allowed to "reach the final question." A New York judge known for his hatred of abolitionists promised that his court would do all it could to convict any "agitators" who had the audacity to discuss doctrines of such "treasonable import." "Mob fever" was once again on the rise.[7] The AAS meeting would make an easy target.

*   *   *

It's not clear where Child was when she learned of Garrison's editorial and the New York papers' rabble-rousing. Just weeks before, much of the Hoppers' neighborhood had burned down. Everyone was safe, but everything was disrupted, and nerves were still on edge. Meanwhile, arrangements for the annual meeting loomed. There were last details to include in the *Standard* about travel, lodging, and scheduling. Child's next editorial needed to be typeset in time for the same edition. But at some point, the news reached AAS headquarters. There's no record of who read it first—Child or the chairman of the AAS executive committee, J. S. Gibbons; there's no account of either of them bursting into the AAS offices or hurrying to the other's house, the editorial in hand. But it is clear that they experienced it as an emergency. We know this because they rushed to act.

On May 3, a notice appeared in several New York papers.[8] "The Executive Committee of the American Anti-Slavery Society have seen with regret," it read, "that certain publications in the Boston *Liberator*, have been so construed as to commit the society in the public view, in favor of an object which appears to them entirely foreign to the purpose for which it was organized, viz: *Dissolution of the Union*." "This committee," it continued, "declare that they have not, at any time, either directly or impliedly authorized such publications; and that it is no part of the object of the American Anti-Slavery Society to promote the dissolution of the Union." It was signed by J. S. Gibbons, chairman of the committee, and L. M. Child, recording secretary.

The editor of the *Standard* rebuking the editor of the *Liberator* in hostile New York papers? Garrison's enemies were ecstatic. His allies were astonished. Child's readers were confused. Hadn't she only recently, with her customary eloquence, argued much the same position? Were she and Gibbons now forbidding discussion of disunion at the AAS meeting? Were they suggesting that disunion was antithetical to the AAS's purposes? In short, the notice caused a sensation up and down the Eastern Seaboard. It became known as "the disclaimer."

Garrison took the disclaimer personally. It would have been hard not to. One of his oldest allies had rebuked him publicly, to the delight of his opponents. He had read the notice, he confessed, with "unfeigned surprise, deep mortification, and extreme regret." He was not the only one opposed to Child's decision. Ellis Loring wrote to Child to protest. David did too, suggesting that "we must 'back out of the mistake as well as we can.'"[9] Child was unmoved. It had not been a mistake, and she was not backing out of it. And anyway, who, suddenly, was "we"? If others wanted to apologize to Garrison, they were welcome to. She, on the other hand, would do it all again.

Why? To anyone who would listen, Child tried to explain herself. Garrison's editorial had created three problems. The first was impending violence. To this, Child was resigned. She had already removed her "few valuables to a place of safety" just in case.[10] But if the meeting was mobbed because of Garrison's editorial, it would have been mobbed for a mistake: disunion was *not* the first item on the meeting's agenda. That Garrison had claimed it *was* gave evidence of the second problem. His own and others' impressions frequently to the contrary, Garrison was not the spokesman of the American Anti-Slavery Society. He was not authorized to announce their meeting's agenda. And he was *certainly* not authorized to declare disunion "a duty" and the standard by which every AAS member's "humanity, patriotism and piety" would be judged. What was this if not another litmus test—suspiciously like the one Garrison had recently rejected by claiming his right to be a nonresistant? For Child, there was a third, more personal reason. Garrison's editorial was a repudiation of her claim that there was room for people of many convictions to work together against slavery. True, she had urged her readers to consider the possibility that the time for disunion had come. But she wanted them to make the decision themselves, according to their own consciences. Garrison wanted to dictate; she wanted to persuade.

Garrison announced that since he had been accused of meddling in the meeting's agenda, he would *really* not meddle: he wouldn't even come. Garrison's not coming to the AAS meeting would be like a presidential candidate's not coming to his own party's convention. His absence would be looming, and it would certainly be blamed on Child. As people prepared to travel to New York from Vermont, Ohio, and Pennsylvania, some must have worried. Would the meeting even take place, lacking its unofficial leader? If it managed to start, would it simply be shut down by torch-wielding mobs determined to silence traitors? The owners of the meeting venue certainly thought so: they threatened to back out of their contract, leaving AAS members scrambling to find another location.[11] Was the society about to split again, two short years after surviving its last schism? Whatever happened, would Maria Child be to blame?

The most stinging rebuke of her actions arrived just as the meeting was about to begin. It came in the form of a letter from Maria Weston Chapman. Chapman, clearly, was furious. How dare Child reproach Garrison publicly and forbid discussion of disunion? Was she afraid of a mob? Frightened of a little controversy? Did she feel the need to coddle the Quakers? Was she too timid to offend moderates like Channing? Or was the problem, Chapman openly suggested, that Child wanted her readers to like her and so refused to endorse Garrison's extreme position? Maybe what Child needed, Chapman fumed, was just to go off and have a good cry.

I imagine Child finishing the letter and putting it in a drawer. Then I imagine her leaving her still-smoldering neighborhood to walk the several blocks through lower Manhattan in time for the annual convention to begin.

What was the three-day meeting like for Child? She already had legendary status in the movement. Her stature had grown since taking on the *Standard*. Attending abolitionists would have known who she was, perhaps pointed her out to each other as she passed. But now their whispers of admiration may have been tempered with gossipy disapproval. She must have felt this as the meeting opened. She was probably sitting in the Broadway Tabernacle's immense sanctuary as one of Chapman's allies insisted that Garrison's response to her disclaimer be read into the minutes.[12] Did she fume? Was she resigned? Why did she not defend herself on the record? Did she try to explain herself in small groups of sympathizers, or did she isolate herself from those who might want to argue? Did she wonder if she herself was about to be censured, officially rebuked, or even fired?

In the end, things went all right. Garrison did not come, but the meeting continued. There was no mob. Child was not asked to resign. Instead, the society's minutes record a lively, searching debate. Some insisted that the AAS commit to supporting disunion. Others protested that the United States Constitution had done and could still do good. Still others argued that if the AAS was to be a moral institution, not a political one, it could take no position on a political matter such as disunion. Another faction maintained that the North could better influence the South by remaining part of the United States. Finally, after several hours, the whole subject was tabled.[13] The meeting adjourned, and abolitionists from all corners of the free states returned to their homes energized and emboldened.

Garrison was quick to forgive his old ally. For all his fire and brimstone, Garrison could be generous and even gentle. Now almost forty years old, he was the father of a large, lively family and had been leading the abolitionist movement for over a decade. He had seen it through explosive growth and paralyzing crisis. He knew what an asset Child still was to the cause they both loved, and from all indications he genuinely liked and respected her. So from his *Liberator* offices a few months later, he took the occasion of Child's second anniversary at the *Standard* to praise her to the skies. "It would not be easy to name another person in the crowded ranks of anti-slavery, who has made greater sacrifices, or exhibited superior moral courage or devotedness, in the cause of emancipation," he wrote. "Mrs. Child has very few superiors as a writer," he continued: "Her style is clear as crystal, and elegantly simple;

combining that rare quality, practical good sense, with great poetic beauty." Garrison also perceptively described his longtime co-adjutor's character. "Between her fondness for literary pursuits and her sympathy for the oppressed, there is a visible struggle," he wrote, "and each in turn receives its due share of attention, to the relief of her heart, and the gratification of her intellect." For her part, Child went out of her way in her next editorial to commend Garrison's "clear, moral perceptions, and unbending integrity." He still had, she assured him and her readers, her "unreserved confidence and respect."[14]

But there was still unfinished business. The day after the meeting began, Child sat down to answer Chapman's letter. "I received your vehement letter on the 8th," she wrote to her friend, "and smiled at the great fluster you were in." Somehow I doubt that Chapman, on reading this, smiled back. Child went on to defend herself, patiently but thoroughly, from Chapman's many accusations. No, she had not refused to allow the disunion question in the *Standard*. She only insisted that it be done in a "rational and manly style" and without "cat-hauling." No, she had not gone out of her way to rebuke Garrison. She had only tried to clarify that he could not set the meeting's agenda. And no, she had not published the notice out of fear of a mob. She had published it because she found Garrison's assertions untrue and his insistence on disunion as a litmus test unreasonable. "I am not willing to be mobbed for *him*," she stipulated, "though I am for any *principle* that we hold in common." This was likely not the assurance of unconditional loyalty Chapman was looking for.

Finally, Child confronted Chapman's insinuation that she cared more for her popularity than for the cause. "I care not the turning of a copper," she wrote, "whether the Channingites and the Quakers approve my course, or not." So far, from Chapman's point of view, so good. But Child was not finished. "I care *as* little whether the Chapmanites and the Garrisonites . . . give me a blowing up; I am glad that they should do it, if it is any relief to their minds." "Chapmanites"? Chapman must have flinched. Child was still not done. In the letter's last paragraphs, an edgier, colder tone emerges. "You say we 'must not *prescribe* to each other,'" she wrote to her friend. This demand Child could only meet with sarcasm. "I thought so too," she continued, "when I read that a set in Massachusetts were going to measure every man's 'humanity, patriotism, and piety,' by their willingness to dissolve the union."

A "set in Massachusetts"? And again: "Chapmanites"? There, she had said it. Child had long chafed under Chapman's well-intentioned bullying, and she had reached her limit. She would no longer play the game on Chapman's terms, and she was ready to make that clear. "An agitator I am not, and never will be," she declared. One more sentence to drive the point home: "Every day that I live, I thank God more and more, that he gives me the power and the will to be an *individual.*"

Booksellers had begun proposing projects to her, opening up the possibility of a return to the literary world. If Chapman and others were unhappy with her handling of the *Standard*, she would happily accept those offers. She was not, she improbably insisted, threatening to resign. "I merely wish it understood that I am emphatically an *individual*," she repeated, "and that you must choose your agent with reference to the work you want done. Remembering always," she could not help but add, "that I am eager to jump out of the tread-mill."[15] She signed the letter, folded it, addressed it, and sent it. Then she returned to her work. The next issue of the *Standard* was about to go to press.

Maria Chapman received the letter at her home in Boston. She was not amused. Always efficient, she habitually labeled incoming correspondence with the author's name and a brief record of the letter's subject matter. On the outside of Child's letter, she summarized its contents as follows: "Mrs. Child. Evidence of the influence of Dr. Channing, William Jay & the Tappans, in alienating her mind from the line of duty."[16]

*   *   *

The summer of 1842 passed. Child stayed in New York, interspersing grueling weeks at the *Standard* with trips to the "vernal forests" of Long Island or to enjoy the "luxury of pure breezes" on Staten Island. She continued to chronicle these trips in "Letters from New York," weaving her delight in nature through descriptions of Native American history, praise for charities that benefited old sailors, and wonder at her first encounter with a kaleidoscope. John Hopper, it seems, was often at her side. There were more moonlit walks through Battery Park. Once a flute, heard over the waves, "called us back with such friendly, sweet intreaty, that we could not otherwise than stop to listen to its last silvery cadence." "We lingered and lingered," Child wrote.[17] David stayed in Northampton, getting the new beet seeds into the fertile ground, then struggling again to transform the harvested crop into sugar.

But by October, it finally became clear even to David that his farm was failing. Whatever he wrote communicating this to his wife has been lost, as have any expressions of guilt or sorrow or anger they exchanged as a consequence. It was also becoming clear that the second part of their plan—that she would support the farm by editing the *Standard*—was failing as well. The board of the Massachusetts Anti-Slavery Society, Chapman and Garrison among them, had recently insisted that the AAS send more agents into the field. This was duly if reluctantly done, with the result that the *Standard* was again deeply in debt. Child sent a scathing letter to the Massachusetts board, protesting that the printer, landlord, and paper maker had again not been paid. She had again forgone much of her salary and had spent the past three months with thirty-seven and a half cents in her pocket. She was badly in need of new winter clothes.[18] Still the directive came from Boston to expand, but the promised money to support the expansion never arrived. This policy seemed calculated to drive Child away. Was it?

In December 1842, David Child declared bankruptcy. The little they had would be auctioned off to pay their debts. As always, Ellis Loring helped them with the legal details. "My anti slavery watch, two rings from my husband, various little keepsakes of very trifling value, and some forty or fifty books, *gifts* to me, can I not honestly save them to myself, somehow?" Child wrote to Loring as bankruptcy proceedings commenced. The answer, it seemed, was no.[19]

Relations with Boston Garrisonians continued to disintegrate. Abby Kelley was now advocating for come-out-ism to be official AAS policy. She called it the "tee-total" pledge. "I cannot express the degree of my dislike, of my utter abhorrence, of this come-out-ism," Child wrote to Loring. "It seems to me irrational, unphilosophic, impracticable, mischievous in its effects, and excessively tyrannical in its operation." In the *Standard*'s pages, she fought back. Why is it, she asked, that whenever anyone perceives "some new application of anti-slavery truth, he is not content to follow his own conviction in honest freedom, but is straightway desirous that the body of abolitionists should endorse it"? Why must people who decline to do so be "branded as compromising" or accused of "treachery"? No one, Child insisted, had a monopoly on truth. "I see fragments of truth in all, and the whole of truth in none," she insisted. One person might think it a duty to quit his church over its proslavery attitude; "another may honestly think that he can do more good by remaining within the association, and exerting his influence to purify it." No person could decide for another. Insisting otherwise would simply drive people away. In fact, it was driving her away. "If I may judge of the application of tests to other minds by the effect they have on my own," she confessed, "I certainly should draw a most unfavorable conclusion."[20]

This editorial must have incensed Abby Kelley and Maria Chapman. Child had not quite named names, but her targets were obvious. She had rebuked Garrison, and now she was rebuking them. In March 1843, Abby Kelley wrote to Gibbons that "L. Maria Child has disgraced and degraded the *Standard*."[21]

∗   ∗   ∗

In the spring of 1843, Lydia Maria Child took three decisive steps.

On May 4, readers of the *Standard*, turning to page three, would have seen the motto WITHOUT CONCEALMENT OR COMPROMISE that, as usual, announced the beginning of the editorial section. But what followed was far from usual. The first editorial was simply titled "Farewell." In it the *Standard*'s editor announced her resignation and defended, for the last time, her policy of inclusion. "I have had a constant aim to elevate and enlarge the soul. I have purposely avoided what would have been popular among sects, and parties, and patriots." That aim no longer correlated with the aims of the AAS, so she was resigning. But although she was quitting her job, she assured her readers, she was not giving up. "To those who have found strength, refreshment, or consolation, in anything I have written, I will promise that my pen shall be busy in other departments of usefulness." But her time at the *Standard* was over. "The freedom of my own spirit makes it absolutely necessary for me to retire," she wrote. "I am too distinctly and decidedly an individual, to edit the organ of any association."[22]

Child left before a successor could take her place. It fell to an anonymous interim editor to comment, in the next week's edition, on "the retirement of 'L. M. C.'" "Her labors have been more generally acceptable to the mass of abolitionists," this editor wrote. "Whilst striving to be impartial, she has, at the same mo-than those of any other writer. I say this, because, as she told us in her 'Farewell' of last week, that ment, incurred censure from either party for favoritism towards the other."

I'm afraid that's exactly what it said. In other words, it included a glaring editorial error. The editor—do we want to call him that?—continued. "Perhaps she has been too free in the expression of her own views," he opined, "—too rigidly just between parties, to win the decided approbation of either." But, he insisted, "her pathway has been followed by generous and warm affections—not entirely free of thorns—but always strewn with abundant flowers."[23] It was insulting and painful. In a way, it didn't matter. I am very sure Child never saw it. She had washed her hands of the *Standard*, and she was moving on.

The second step was more personal. Two weeks later, on May 19, Maria Child wrote to Maria Chapman. She addressed the envelope to Chauncey Place, where Chapman was staying with her in-laws. It was one of the homes where Child had spent hours in cozy solidarity and energizing conversation with Chapman and her bustling family. But this time, her letter included no gossipy affection or friendly needling, and also no patient defense of her position. There was also no salutation. "I have just received your note about the Fair, and will attend to it as requested," the note began. The next sentence was as abrupt as it was shocking. "Please take off my name from the list; as I have retired from the anti-slavery cause altogether." The next sentence contained a warning. "I write promptly, because I would rather it should be quietly left off, than to have it inserted, and then taken off." In other words, she was willing to go quietly and spare the movement another messy feud. But if Chapman failed to remove her name from the list of fair sponsors, she would protest, and their split would become public. There was one more sentence referencing her husband's movements: "Mr. Child will probably be detained in Northampton two or three weeks longer, by the bankrupt process, auction, &c," she wrote. Why this was relevant will soon become clear. Then the letter concluded, simply and abruptly: "Yrs respectfully, L. Maria Child."[24]

Chapman received the letter and read it. Below Child's careful handwriting, she wrote four simple, damning words: "A revelation of character."[25] She filed it among her other letters. It would be more than a decade before the women corresponded again.

The author of the *Appeal* retiring from the antislavery cause: What did this mean? Child had to assume that her defection would be the subject of wagging tongues in the very parlor where she had once been a welcome guest. It was true that to Chapman, Child had been blunt to the point of rudeness. To others who heard the news and wrote to protest, she was more nuanced. "When I said I would have nothing to do with reforms," she wrote to Loring, "I merely meant with the organized machinery. I will work in my own way, according to the light that is in me." From now on, she wrote to Francis Shaw, she would "make literature the honest agent of my conscience and my heart."[26] She was quitting, but she was not giving up. She would simply stop doing what she hated for the cause she loved. Instead, she would channel that love into projects she could fully embrace. Surely that would benefit both her and the movement for which she had sacrificed so much.

A final decision remained. It concerned her marriage. "I have made up my mind not to follow David's movements any more," she wrote to Louisa in February 1843. She would stay in New York, make a living as an independent author, and let her husband "experiment where he will." That was not all. "I have resolved to separate my pecuniary affairs entirely from David's," she wrote to Ellis in June. "I mean to keep my earnings out of the way," she clarified, no longer "pump[ing] water" into the sieve of his doomed financial schemes. She was determined to take back this part of her life. "I *can* put a stop to it; and I will put a stop to it," she wrote in August. She was also desperate. "[I] must put a stop to it, or die."[27]

She was not asking him to leave. She was not seeking a divorce. She was not giving up. If he wanted to return on her terms, he could do that. She would, she told Louisa, "prepare a home always in readiness for him."[28] But she would not be in her marriage the same way again.

New York laws regarding women's property rights were more liberal than Massachusetts laws, but they still did not permit a married woman to manage her own financial affairs. If she wanted to separate her finances from David's, Child would have to find another man to be her legal surrogate. Now forty-one years old, Child asked Ellis Loring to fill this role.[29] How humiliating it must have been to ask. But from now on, whatever she earned would be hers, at least if Loring let her have it. Fortunately, he always did.

What had happened between David and Maria Child to force this rupture? Only months before, there had been real signs of affection and hope. What had been the last straw? Child doesn't tell us, but here is my theory. It had to do with David's next financial scheme. As it became clear that his farm was failing, David had come up with another plan. His wife was unhappy editing the *Standard*; perhaps he should try.

I sometimes try to count the ways this idea would have tormented Child. Two years earlier, David had declined to accompany her to New York. More times than she could count, he had promised to join her and failed to arrive. He had been unavailable to help with the arduous task of editing the *Standard* when she needed him most. Now that she was essentially being forced out, he was going to move to New York and take it on. As a solution to their financial problems, the idea was ludicrous. Thanks to the demands for expansion made by Chapman and others, the *Standard* was once again mired in debt. David himself was a walking financial disaster. Under his direction the *Standard* would be less capable than ever of paying an editor's salary. There was no way this position would support him, much less them.

More was at stake than money. Child correctly predicted that David would do exactly what she had just sacrificed her job and friendships to prevent. He would turn the *Standard* into a partisan paper. As it turned out, she was not alone in this assumption. In fact, Child at some point learned, Maria Chapman herself was behind David's scheme. She had begun urging him to take over the *Standard* precisely because of his old reputation as David "Libel" Child: because he was known to be combative where his wife was appeasing.[30] The AAS executive committee, in other words, no longer wanted "oil upon the waves." They wanted someone to churn the water up.

Chapman's apparent willingness to recruit Child's husband even as she edged Child herself out was brazen, but perhaps it was not shocking. Intrigue and manipulation were what Child had come to expect from the House of Weston. But David's willingness to cooperate with Chapman must have felt like a betrayal. He was siding with the very people she had just broken with. His willingness to do so was a repudiation of both her and her vision for the *Standard*. Reformulated more bluntly, Child's newly former friends had recruited her husband, of all people, to undo her two years of backbreaking work. And why had she done the work—the reporting, the proofreading, the editorializing, the recruitment— that had ended in unemployment and shattered friendships? She had done it for him—for him and for the farm that had failed and left them destitute once again.

When she stopped and thought about it, it must have become clear to Child that David had failed at everything he had tried in their fourteen years of marriage—the *Massachusetts Journal,* his law practice, the aborted Mexico commune, the farm. There must have been humiliation in this, too—the humiliation of loving someone so flawed and of having believed him so many times. Editing the *Standard* would likely prove no different from his other schemes. There must have been agony in this as well. If he succeeded in his new role, he would do exactly what she had tried so hard to prevent. And if he failed, he would have failed. Again.

Child was not the only one convinced that David's editing the *Standard* would be a disaster. Abby Kelley and Maria Child no longer agreed on much, but on the topic of David's incompetence, they were, ironically, united. Kelley was aghast at Chapman's proposal. David Child had "some-how a killing influence on every thing he touches," she warned. "We shall all go over the dam if he takes [the *Standard*]; Heaven avert such a catastrophy [*sic*]."[31] But Chapman, as usual, prevailed. David prepared to take the post.

This toxic combination of humiliation, betrayal, desperation, and exhaustion could easily have justified Child's decision to separate from her husband. But was there something more? Years later, in a letter to her beloved friend Sarah Shaw, Child referenced a deep humiliation that originated in her time in New York. But she begged Shaw not to be too curious. Please, she wrote, "don't *speak* of these open wounds in my soul, by way of ascertaining what they are or from what hands they came." Even if Shaw asked, Child would never tell: "Don't you know, dear, that our *severest* experiences, those from which we suffer *most* and *longest*, are hidden even from our dearest friend, known only to God and our own souls?" To Loring, she wrote that "if you knew a thousandth part of the secret causes I have had for anxiety, you would not wonder at the restlessness to which you have alluded."[32] These are strong words. What other crippling shame had Child endured? Had there been infidelity? Had David had done something illegal? Had he defrauded a lender, cheated on their taxes, lied to a friend about a loan?

If there was such a secret, both Childs took it to their graves. In the end, I think it is unlikely. David was incompetent, but not a criminal. Nor, I think, was he unfaithful; there is never any indication from them or others that he had a wandering eye. As to the other obvious possibility—that Child's relationship with the young John Hopper had burst the banks of all their imagined relations and become an affair—I doubt this, too. Child was both too devoted to her husband and too bound by her conscience to betray her marriage. This does not mean there could not be deep emotional damage resulting from her attachment to John. There will be more to say about that later.

So when I imagine Child's decision to leave, I do not picture a new betrayal or an explosive discovery. Instead, I imagine a final, wrenching iteration of an old, exhausting argument. Perhaps it happened during one of his rare visits to New York. Perhaps Child confirmed her husband's worst fears: she had lost faith in him and his schemes. Perhaps she wept as she confessed that he had worn her down. Perhaps she quietly, firmly, told him that she was done. Maybe he tried to persuade her to give him one more chance; maybe he didn't. Perhaps he turned away in silent anger; perhaps he walked out and slammed the door. He also might have simply shrugged and walked away, preoccupied with his new plans, sure that this time he would succeed.[33]

Whatever the particulars, it must have broken her heart. She honestly loved him, and she loved him for traits that were honestly good. Despite years of chronic tension, there was deep affection on both sides. But sometimes the people we love most make our lives unbearable. For much of the next decade, David and Maria Child lived apart.

A final indignity remained. On June 6, 1843, a notice appeared in the *Hampshire Gazette*. "By order of the District Court of the United States, Massachusetts District, will be sold at Public Auction . . . all the right which David L. Child of said Northampton, a Bankrupt, has of redeeming the following described mortgaged personal property." The list of auction items included "1 Yoke Cattle, 2 Cows, 1 hog, 1 Ox Sled, 1 Cart, 9 Hoes, 3 Shovels, two stone Hammers . . . 30 Sheep and about 20 Lambs and 3 Hives Bees." Also

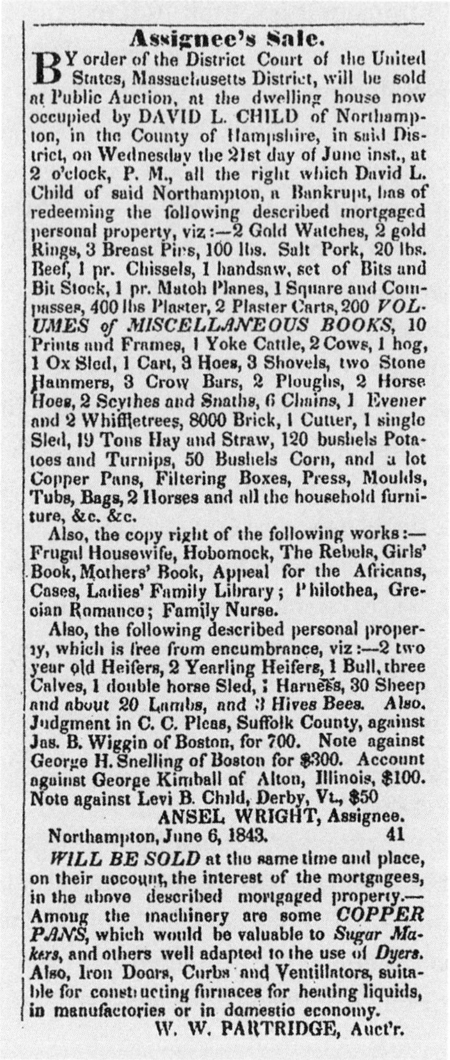

Assignee's Sale.

BY order of the District Court of the United States, Massachusetts District, will be sold at Public Auction, at the dwelling house now occupied by DAVID L. CHILD of Northampton, in the County of Hampshire, in said District, on Wednesday the 21st day of June inst., at 2 o'clock, P. M., all the right which David L. Child of said Northampton, a Bankrupt, has of redeeming the following described mortgaged personal property, viz :—2 Gold Watches, 2 gold Rings, 3 Breast Pins, 100 lbs. Salt Pork, 20 lbs. Beef, 1 pr. Chissels, 1 handsaw, set of Bits and Bit Stock, 1 pr. Match Planes, 1 Square and Compasses, 400 lbs Plaster, 2 Plaster Carts, 200 *VOLUMES of MISCELLANEOUS BOOKS*, 10 Prints and Frames, 1 Yoke Cattle, 2 Cows, 1 hog, 1 Ox Sled, 1 Cart, 3 Hoes, 3 Shovels, two Stone Hammers, 3 Crow Bars, 2 Ploughs, 2 Horse Hoes, 2 Scythes and Snaths, 6 Chains, 1 Evener and 2 Whiffletrees, 8000 Brick, 1 Cutter, 1 single Sled, 19 Tons Hay and Straw, 120 bushels Potatoes and Turnips, 50 Bushels Corn, and a lot Copper Pans, Filtering Boxes, Press, Moulds, Tubs, Bags, 2 Horses and all the household furniture, &c. &c.

Also, the copy right of the following works :— Frugal Housewife, Hobomock, The Rebels, Girls' Book, Mothers' Book, Appeal for the Africans, Cases, Ladies' Family Library ; Philothea, Grecian Romance ; Family Nurse.

Also, the following described personal property, which is free from encumbrance, viz :—2 two year old Heifers, 2 Yearling Heifers, 1 Bull, three Calves, 1 double horse Sled, ; Harness, 30 Sheep and about 20 Lambs, and 3 Hives Bees. Also, Judgment in C. C. Pleas, Suffolk County, against Jas. B. Wiggin of Boston, for 700. Note against George H. Snelling of Boston for $300. Account against George Kimball of Alton, Illinois, $100. Note against Levi B. Child, Derby, Vt., $50

ANSEL WRIGHT, Assignee.

Northampton, June 6, 1843.   41

WILL BE SOLD at the same time and place, on their account, the interest of the mortgagees, in the above described mortgaged property.— Among the machinery are some *COPPER PANS*, which would be valuable to *Sugar Makers*, and others well adapted to the use of *Dyers*. Also, Iron Doors, Curbs and Ventillators, suitable for constructing furnaces for heating liquids, in manufactories or in domestic economy.

W. W. PARTRIDGE, Auct'r.

Fig. 31. Notice in the *New Hampshire Gazette* of a public auction of the Childs' possessions after David Child's bankruptcy in 1843. The copyrights to many of Lydia Maria Child's books are included in the sale.

for sale were "*COPPER PANS* which would be valuable to *Sugar Makers*." A separate paragraph made clear that this was no ordinary farming family who had fallen on hard times. For sale were also "the copy right of the following works:—Frugal Housewife, Hobomock, The Rebels, Girls' Book, Mothers' Book, Appeal for the Africans... Philothea, Grecian Romance; Family Nurse." The author of these books was unnamed. The sale took place on Wednesday, June 21, at 2:00.[34]

In the end, it's not clear that her copyrights sold or that they were even for sale. Some of them were in her father's name, not David's, and so would have escaped the auction block.[35] But in a way it doesn't matter. The humiliation of seeing her books, the product of her labor and her mind, listed for auction along with cows, shovels, and hammers, all as a result of her husband's failures, must have been searing.

＊　＊　＊

During this period, despite its layers of shame and loss, a lightness enters Maria Child's letters. There is more equanimity, less agony. This relief would not last; a short time later, the consequences of her decisions would make her doubt that her life was worth living. But for the moment she felt brave and free. She would not go back to apathy and complicity. She would still not live her life the same way again. She would simply change course. She would try something different.

In fact, she had been laying the groundwork for something different already. Her "Letters from New York" had been successful. Perhaps she could publish them as a book. Before long the *Letters*—complete with their flights of fancy, philosophical asides, wide-eyed wonder, and imaginative evocation of New York's teeming variety—were in her readers' hands. The volume sold out in months and was reprinted ten times in the next seven years. Decades later, Frederick Douglass went out of his way to praise it, confirming too that she was still working for the cause, but in her own way: "She always managed to infuse ["Letters" with] a spirit of brotherly love and good will, with an abhorrence of all that was unjust, selfish and mean," Douglass remembered, "and in this way won to anti-slavery many hearts which else would have remained cold and indifferent."[36]

How good it must have felt. She had shown readers her real self:

her mystical, philosophical, searching self. They had loved it. Lucy Osgood, daughter of Child's childhood minister Reverend Osgood, wrote from Medford to tell her that she had not changed a bit. The "L. M. Francis of 1826" and the "L. M. Child of 1843" were "but one and the same person," Osgood assured this now middle-aged friend of her youth.[37] The two women renewed their attachment and remained faithful correspondents for the rest of Osgood's life.

Child wrote a second volume of *Letters from New York*. She also began writing fiction for popular periodicals. She published a collection of short stories called *Fact and Fiction*. And she returned to writing for children. "Over the river, and through the wood," one poem began, "To grandfather's house we go!" Young readers across the country cheered as the poem's protagonists tumbled through snowdrifts, tussled in snowball fights, and kissed their red-cheeked cousins. "Hurrah for the fun! Is the pudding done? Hurrah for the pumpkin pie!" her diminutive protagonists rejoiced. She could not have known it, but Lydia Maria Child had just written her most famous words.[38]

Some of her stories and essays from this period had antislavery themes, but most did not. Here, too, I think Child was trying something different: hoping that since all truths were interconnected, she could help her readers toward antislavery sentiments by encouraging a wider embrace of humanity. And when she was not writing, she was fighting injustice wherever she found it with her signature combination of indignation and resolve. She advocated for a woman accused of killing her abusive husband. She sought gainful employment for a woman who otherwise would have gone to jail. She agitated for prison reform. When a Unitarian minister resolved to free his slaves and needed places to settle them, she found positions for five of them.[39] She was indeed pursuing the same good, but in a different way. Instead of synthesizing broad arguments for a wide readership, she now focused on concrete actions that benefited particular individuals.

But it is important not to misdescribe this. After a dozen years of headlong involvement in the antislavery movement, Child took a very long break. After her nightmare at the *Standard*, she pre-

28 THE NEW-ENGLAND BOY'S SONG.

Over the river, and through the wood—
When grandmother sees us come,
She will say, Oh dear,
The children are here,
Bring a pie for every one.

Over the river, and through the wood—
Now grandmother's cap I spy!
Hurra for the fun!
Is the pudding done?
Hurra for the pumpkin pie!

Fig. 32. Illustration of "The New-England Boy's Song about Thanksgiving Day," 1845, in Child's *Flowers for Children II*. Courtesy of the Library of Congress.

dicted, it would take "great quantities of music, and blossoms, and serene engravings, to restore me to my former self." So she set about nurturing her artistic core, throwing herself into the New York arts scene, attending concerts, visiting galleries, befriending artists. Music—Mendelssohn in particular—especially moved her. When her literary efforts brought in money, she bought a piano and learned to play. She formed another passionate friendship, this time with an internationally famous Norwegian violinist named Ole Bull. She resumed her acquaintance with Margaret Fuller, who had moved to New York to pursue journalism. Their

shared passion for art and social reform drew them closer together, with Fuller writing of Child that she was "so entertaining"
and that "her generous heart glows through all she says, and makes
a friendly home around her." Meanwhile, Child grew attached to
New York and its anonymity, cherishing the freedom to walk un-
recognized by strangers and unseen by former friends.[40] The New
York she had hated had become the refuge she craved.

She was not the only nationally known white abolitionist forced
to regroup and reorient in this period. The Grimké sisters, Theodore Weld, Samuel May, Isaac Hopper, and even some of the
Weston sisters retreated, in one way or another, for large parts of
the next decades, each struggling—certainly psychologically and
often physically—with the toll their abolitionist work had taken.[41]
Emancipation was taking far longer than any of them had expected: although they could not have known this, it was still over
two decades away. Any individual body could take only so much.

All this is true. It is also true that while their most passionate
allies regrouped, those enslaved in the South continued to suffer
daily atrocities. We should also remember that white abolitionists
could take breaks: blend into the anonymity of New York streets,
pursue neutral means of employment, retreat to the countryside
to consider racial injustice from a distance. For Black activists,
there was no such retreat. Prejudice in every part of the North
continued unabated, from segregated public transportation to restricted job and educational opportunities to the constant threat
of being kidnapped and sold into slavery. The resulting physical
and mental suffering took a terrible toll on Black leaders such as
Frederick Douglass and David Ruggles. Later in life, Child came to
regret the pause in her activism. "Conscience twinges me now and
then, that I ever turned aside from . . . duty, to dally in primrose
paths," she admitted.[42] She would spend the last decades of her life
atoning for this lapse.

A more charitable reading of this period is that she was refuel-
ing, refocusing, readying herself to emerge again when the time
was right. "I am passing through a spiritual transition, and like the
lobster, when a new shell is forming, I protect my thin skin by hid-

ing away in the crevices of rocks," she wrote to Francis Shaw.[43] This would have been cold comfort to those enduring the daily torment of prejudice and enslavement. But it is a testament to the limits of individual human endurance in the face of institutionalized evil.

John Hopper, whom she had settled on calling her "adopted son," continued to be Child's closest companion. Their mutual affection showed no signs of abating. "I hardly care what happens to me, if I can only manage not to be separated from John," she wrote to Loring. David flitted in and out. True to her promise, Child made room for him in her small quarters at the Hoppers' home whenever he needed shelter. For a brief period her dream that she, David, and John could live together came true. But David's time in New York did not last long. After six weeks of editing the *Standard*, he was accused of libel. After one year, subscriptions had plummeted. He resigned and returned to Northampton. Alone. When he asked his wife to accompany him, she said no.[44]

9

First Duties First, and How to Do Your Second Duties Too

Sometime in 1846, John Hopper met a young woman named Rosa De Wolf and fell in love. Her parents objected to his abolitionist origins, so they did what any reasonable couple would do. In March 1847, they eloped.[1]

Child had met Rosa. She knew John was in love. She knew it was time for him to attach himself to a woman his own age who was, more to the point, unmarried. Still, the news, Child wrote, hit her like a "thunder-bolt." John and his bride would soon be returning to live in his father's house. That house was also Child's home. She immediately made plans to move. Probably the lack of space was not her only reason for leaving. "I hope I shall be *near* John, but I shall not try to think of living *with* them. . . . We shall be more likely to *continue* excellent friends, if we make our arrangements independent of each other," she wrote to Susan Lyman. The newlyweds protested: how genuinely is hard to tell.[2] Child refused their pleas that she stay with them. Essentially, she fled.

*   *   *

Her flight marked the beginning of six years of disruption, isolation, and depression. Child shuttled from one temporary housing situation to another, moving first to rural New York, then back to New York City, then to a rented farm in Massachusetts. Sometimes David joined her, often when he was sick and needed nursing. Always when he recovered, he left. He tried farming in Northampton again. He worked on the railroad in Tennessee, then Ohio, then Alabama. He threatened to go to California to look for gold. Sometimes she had to rely on friends to tell her where he was. When his mother wrote asking how to reach him, she had to confess that she had no idea.[3]

Shame isolated her from old friends and kept her from making new ones. How many people knew how intense her relationship with John had been? Did those who knew pity her now, a middle-aged woman abandoned by both her husband and the younger man to whom she had opened her heart? What would she say when people asked her where David was, or what he was doing, or why they were not together? She became prickly, abrupt, sometimes rude. She wanted to be left alone and then was hurt when no one wrote. She took up cursing, or at least she claimed she did.[4]

Sometimes she cherished her isolation; sometimes it haunted her. Often it seemed to strengthen her conviction that her life had been a failure. "All the time, I am weighed down with the miserable consciousness of having lived in vain," she wrote to Sarah Shaw. "All my efforts seem to me so poor, that in glancing back upon them, I feel a profound contempt for them, and for myself." She knew such thoughts only intensified her hopelessness, but she did not know how to stop them. "This state of mind of course kills any power there might be to do better; and for *that* I also reproach myself. It is a diseased state; but how to get well?"[5]

Her book sales had been good, but they were tapering off. Her publisher warned that she was not communicating with her public enough to keep them engaged. To this she replied that she had "lost interest in the world. Of literary ambition," she added, "I am sorry to say I have not one particle." She had also become acutely aware of how difficult it was for her, as a woman, to make her living by writing. "It is of no use for me to make more than enough to feed and clothe myself decently," she wrote to Francis Shaw. "I cannot make a position for myself, as *men* can." Maybe it didn't matter anymore. "I am indifferent to the game of life, and weary of the battle," she wrote. "As for what I am doing, I am eating and sleeping; and that is nearly all. My aspirations have all come down to a warm blanket, a cup of tea, and a quiet corner to die in." When her sister Mary, with whom she had shared happy, busy years in Maine, died in 1847, she wrote to her niece expressing as much envy as sorrow.[6]

There were bright spots. She deepened her friendship with a young Spanish woman named Dolores who shared her love of beauty, and she developed an intense attachment to a budding sculptor named Harriet Hosmer. Sometimes when David stayed with her, wherever she was, they would have a glimpse of old happiness. She tried to work against slavery when she could. When she was living in New Rochelle, New York, fugitive slaves would sometimes arrive at her door; she gave them money and sent them on their way with letters of introduction that got them one step closer to freedom. Over and over, she resolved to count her blessings and cheer up. But it is hard to change your outlook in unchanged circumstances. "I hope you won't blame me for being sad," she wrote to Louisa. "I know I have many more blessings than I deserve." "I do assure you that I *try* hard to be humble and patient, and to look away from the dark side of things," she promised. "I think the old heart would still spring up again, if the eternal pressure could only be a *little* raised from it. Let us hope."[7]

But they were long, demoralizing years. "I have never been so *much* depressed in spirits as I have this winter," she confessed in 1850. Memories from her struggle at the *Standard* haunted her. "The experience of the last eight years has terribly shaken my faith in human nature," she confessed to Loring. Decades later, memories from this period were still too painful to recount. "Let the silence of the grave rest over them," she wrote to Sarah Shaw. "Perhaps flowers will bloom above them some day."[8]

Writing was a kind of torture, and not only because she had lost interest in the literary world. As it turned out, Child was undertaking her most demanding scholarly project yet: she was writing a history of religion. It was an almost obstinately imprudent decision. The book would be unorthodox: "I am going to tell the plain unvarnished truth, as clearly as I can understand it, and let

Christians and Infidels, Orthodox and Unitarians, Catholics and Protestants and Swedenborgians growl as they like," she wrote to her brother Convers.[9] In other words, it would probably upset her public again. It would confirm their worst suspicions: that some-one who went in for radical abolition would embrace all kinds of heresy. For all those reasons, it was also unlikely to earn her any money. But she was going to write it anyway.

Why do this to herself? One biographer has suggested that Child turned to writing about religion as penance for falling in love with John Hopper.[10] I doubt it. She had committed no sin; she had simply engaged in an unconventional friendship that had brought her joy but whose ending, as she had always predicted, had caused her real pain. I think it was instead a response to the desperate disappointment of having broken with a cause that she loved so deeply and for which she had sacrificed so much. The splintering of the abolitionist movement raised a searing question with new urgency: Is there progress in the world? Have religious beliefs evolved, or are humans doomed to perpetual superstition and strife? Was there any certainty that the antislavery cause would prevail, that women would cease to be a question, that racial prej-udice would disappear? Because if not, darker questions were rel-evant. Here was one: What was the point of living?

The disruption and isolation continued. She had dreams of Da-vid's death and premonitions of her own. The latter were strong enough that she put her financial affairs in order and burned hun-dreds of her letters. She had already chosen a cemetery: it was a "burial-place for the colored people" close to her latest temporary home.[11]

*   *   *

To read the letters Child wrote in this period is almost to forget that slavery existed. She was, it seems, so overwhelmed by per-sonal struggle and so crushed by disillusionment that she barely registered events that otherwise would have occupied her com-pletely. Among these was the Compromise of 1850. The United

States' rapacious appetite for land and resources was pushing the nation's boundaries steadily westward. With each expansion came the question whether slavery would expand as well. Many thought this question had been settled by the 1820 Missouri Compromise that Child had heard so much about as a teenager in Maine. That compromise had concluded that slavery would not extend north of the thirty-sixth parallel, with the exception of Missouri. But now Southern states again threatened to secede unless demands for slavery's expansion were met. Kentucky senator and master negotiator Henry Clay struggled throughout the summer of 1850 to craft a series of provisions that would stave off this disaster. Finally he proposed a set of compromises that he thought would keep the country together. He proposed that California be admitted as a free state; that the slave trade but not slavery itself be abolished in Washington, DC; and that Congress pass something called the Fugitive Slave Act.[12]

That the proposed compromise included this law was more evidence of the simmering tension between North and South. Consistently and in increasing numbers, enslaved people were doing whatever was necessary to escape to the North. Enslavers' financial losses were estimated at $200,000 a year in the Border States alone. It was a staggering sum in the nation's young economy. The affront to Southern pride was also costly. States like Massachusetts, Vermont, and Pennsylvania continued to pass personal liberty laws that made recapturing a slave difficult and expensive. Southerners in pursuit of lost property often found themselves spending more on travel and legal fees than the fugitive was worth.[13]

The new law intended to address this tension, allowing the South to save face as much as money. Instead of subjecting slave owners to a lengthy legal process, it gave local commissioners—until now fairly low-level officials—complete power to adjudicate fugitive slave cases. These commissioners were paid more if they returned the fugitives than if they freed them, a fact that almost defies belief but is, unfortunately, true. The new law also prohibited Black detainees from testifying in their own defense or acquiring legal representation.[14]

After a summer of intense negotiation, the law was passed on August 23, 1850. President Millard Fillmore signed it into effect. Boston's cotton magnates, deeply invested in Southern trade, breathed a sigh of relief. The Union was safe. Business could continue. Boston greeted news of the compromise with a hundred-gun salute.[15]

The effect of the Fugitive Slave Act on the Black community was immediate and devastating. Thousands of fugitives who had settled in Northern states escaped to Canada, emptying out whole neighborhoods and churches almost overnight.[16] We do not understand the legacy of slavery unless we to pause to think of capital lost, businesses shuttered, communities broken, families torn apart as those who could, fled, and those who were too feeble, or too tired, or simply too tenacious, stayed behind. Entire communities of free Black Northerners were now also in danger. Given that no Black people were allowed to testify in their own defense, even those born free could easily be kidnapped, falsely claimed as someone's property, and then disappear forever into Southern enslavement. Solomon Northup's 1853 memoir *Twelve Years a Slave* documented one such case that predated the new law; how many cases there were both before and after its passage we may never know. Faced with this ever-present threat, many free Blacks also simply left for Canada and never returned.

Thousands more, building on arguments by David Walker and Peter Paul Simmons, decided to stay and arm themselves. Vigilance committees patrolled Black neighborhoods, working to identify would-be kidnappers. Bills describing these agents were posted, and the community was put on alert. "If any man approaches my house in search of a slave and I do not lay him a lifeless corpse at my feet," Black abolitionist Martin Delany wrote, "I hope the grave may refuse my body as a resting place." Black orator Samuel Ringgold Ward exhorted his community to make enforcement of the Fugitive Slave Act the "last act in the drama of a slavecatcher's life." Frederick Douglass warned that if the law was enforced, people should expect to see the "streets of Boston running with blood"; Ward assured his Black neighbors that any blood shed would not be theirs. Short of violence, the Black community found other ways to frustrate fugitive hunters' aims. They reported with astonishing speed to courthouses where fugitives were held and amassed in raucous opposition at fugitives' hearings. In one case, they harassed a slave hunter, ringing the doorbell of his hotel until he appeared at the door holding a pistol. They then had him arrested for carrying a weapon. Black women often took a leading role in these protests. Sometimes white women lent their support as well.[17]

Generally speaking, the reaction among white Northerners covered the spectrum. Some rejoiced at the mass exodus; no doubt some moved quickly to take over Black businesses and abandoned real estate. Others recognized that the number of escaping slaves was evidence that slavery was untenable. But so, to many, was the idea of living alongside free Black people. Several states, including Illinois, Oregon, Indiana, Iowa, and Wisconsin, passed laws restricting Black settlers or forbidding them entirely. Where then were free Blacks to go? "Back" to Africa, said some. Colonization societies again gained traction, as did ever more creative arguments to justify their aims. Perhaps, one such argument went, this was all part of a divine plan. God had allowed Africans to be enslaved in order to convert them to Christianity. Now it was time to send them back to Africa to convert others.[18] If this seemed circuitous for a divine strategy, that appeared not to bother them. Neither did the hypocrisy of claiming that African descendants were incurably immoral on the one hand and destined to be missionaries on the other.

But the Fugitive Slave Act began to awaken another reaction among Northerners who had remained mired in the uncommitted discomfort so familiar from Child's early writings. These were Northerners who thought slavery was probably wrong, and certainly unfortunate, but largely a matter for Southerners to manage among themselves. The Fugitive Slave Act changed that. Northerners assisting fugitives in any way—including clothing or feeding them—could now be punished by a fine of $1,000 and six months in jail. Another of its provisions stipulated that any citizen, North or South, could be forced to assist in catching escaped slaves. In other words, as one historian has put it, the Fugitive Slave Act suddenly made "the average citizen into a slavecatcher."[19]

This intrusion on their freedom galvanized white Northerners in a way that the plight of the fugitives themselves could not. Some who had not yet allied themselves with abolitionists now did so. Ralph Waldo Emerson, long a tepid abolitionist at best, weighed in with righteous indignation. So did Henry David Thoreau. In Boston, 3,500 people gathered at Faneuil Hall to hear Frederick Douglass, Wendell Phillips, and Charles Lennox Remond condemn the law. Members of the legal community rallied, promising to fight it in court and to aid captured fugitives whenever possible. Many more fought the law by other means. Some communities refused to fill commissioners' posts or so shamed those who complied with the law that they were rendered ineffective or quit. Syracuse declared itself a "free city" and dared federal officers to enforce the law within its boundaries. Some clergy, this time, protested as well.[20]

Opposition to the Fugitive Slave Act was sometimes dramatic and occasionally violent. In October, barely six weeks after the law had been passed, Georgia slave catchers arrived in Boston to recapture William and Ellen Craft, a couple whose spectacular escape several years earlier had made them household names. The Black community organized and managed to drive their pursuers out of the city. When a fugitive named Shadrach Minkins was arrested and jailed in February 1851, Black Bostonians broke into the building in broad daylight, rescued Minkins, and spirited him to Canada. In September 1851, a Maryland slave owner was shot and killed in Christiana, Pennsylvania, while attempting to recapture the humans he claimed to own.[21]

These incidents were a triumph for the Black community, a boost for abolitionists, and a humiliation for law enforcement. Southern slaveholders howled that their suspicions had been confirmed: the North had no intention of honoring the Compromise of 1850, and the federal government had no intention of enforcing it. Threats of disunion resumed. President Fillmore was under pressure to show that he was serious. The next time there was an opportunity, he was ready. In April, a fugitive named Thomas Sims was arrested in Boston. He was immediately put under massive federal guard, and a chain was wrapped around the courthouse where he was imprisoned. A plot to rescue him through an upper window failed. Abolitionists tried to purchase him, but his owner refused to sell. He was returned to Georgia, publicly flogged, and sold into Mississippi.[22]

*   *   *

Child watched all of this through a fog of depression and helplessness. Her avenues for action were closed. She no longer had an editorial column in which to express her outrage and sway public opinion. She could no longer raise funds with her cohorts at BFASS. If she were being generous to herself, she could have taken pride in undeniable evidence that her writings were having an effect. Wendell Phillips's electrifying speech rallied a thousand people to Sims's defense at Tremont Temple. Thomas Wentworth Higginson had helped organize attempts to rescue him. Charles Sumner, the newly elected senator from Massachusetts, was fighting for the repeal of the Fugitive Slave Act. All three men credited Child with converting them to the cause. But as they thundered, plotted, and legislated, Child found herself sidelined, defeated, and alone. Work on her book on comparative religions was not going well. Was this a surprise?

Help, ironically, came through loss. In her most recent home, a borrowed farmhouse outside Boston, word reached her that Isaac Hopper, whose family she had boarded with during most of her nine years in New York, was dying. Child traveled to New York to be with him one last time. As his large family gathered around him, his restless mind turned to his fellow Quakers who had banished him for his abolitionism. How many times, over the years, had he and Child comforted each other about friendships betrayed, alliances broken, careers compromised, all in the name of their principles? He understood Child's heartache better than most. He murmured her name. She bent close to hear him. "Tell them I love them *all*," he whispered. And then he was gone.[23]

Why leave this message with Child? Because, it turned out, she had promised to write his biography. In doing so, Hopper had given Child the gift of a duty to fulfill. It was a duty that could draw her out of her misery by challenging her to undertake something she could do well: write in the service of the cause she still loved. He had also given her another gift, the example of someone willing to forgive allies who had betrayed him. That second challenge would take more time, but she could start on the first one now.

Child gladly put aside her work on religion. For Hopper's biography, she had two sources. The first was "Tales of Oppression," the column he had serialized in the *National Anti-Slavery Standard*. For two years, it had appeared under the masthead that bore her name. As she sorted through the individual columns, choosing which stories to include, the memories must have been intense. The second source consisted of notes she had hastily and secretly jotted down when, while living with Hopper and his family, she had heard him telling stories of his exploits to his grandchildren. Now the question was how to synthesize these sources. How to weave together a story of someone's life? How to capture another person's spirit, vision, energy? She had done it before, years earlier, in the Ladies' Family Library series that had introduced readers to women like Germaine de Staël and Lady Russell. Hopper's life felt different. She struggled to pinpoint how. Finally it came to her. "This biography differs from most works of the kind, in embracing fragments of so many lives," she told her readers. "Friend Hopper lived almost entirely for others; and it is a striking illustration of the fact, that I have found it impossible to write his biography without having it consist largely of the adventures of other people."[24]

Most of those people were Black. True, it *is* a biography of Hopper. Every story features the wily, rambunctious Quaker who looked like Napoleon and acted like Robin Hood, who was capable of being thrown through a window by slave hunters, dusting him-

Fig. 33. Isaac Tatem Hopper. Collection of the Massachusetts Historical Society.

self off, entering through another door, and whisking their prey to safety. But Child made Hopper's antics the frame of a much bigger story: the story of enslaved people taking their freedom. Child arranged these stories to emphasize both the reasons individuals ended their enslavement and the strategies they used to do so. As to reasons: the enslaved Ben Jackson, for instance, could not "reconcile [slavery] with the justice and goodness of the Creator, that one man should be born to toil for another without wages."

So he escaped. James Poovey, having learned to read, concluded from the New Testament that his enslavement was antithetical to the Golden Rule. So he refused to work, causing his enslaver such trouble that he eventually gave up and let Poovey go. Another fugitive named William Anderson was less philosophical but equally justified. He just wanted, he reported, to "try whether he couldn't do something for himself."[25] He fled Virginia for Philadelphia and found work with a merchant.

As to the strategies: some fugitives, after fleeing, blended into the lumberyards of Philadelphia with new names and invented histories. Some joined a ship's crew and escaped to a life at sea. Some fled to England, or Canada, or Sierra Leone. If their masters pursued and found them, their tactics were equally resourceful. One willingly surrendered, then got his master drunk and escaped again. Another positioned himself carefully, tripped his master with a chain, and fled into the woods. Some bought guns and simply threatened to shoot.[26]

The stories do not always end well. Some fugitives killed themselves rather than be recaptured. There is abundant evidence of bodies wrecked and minds destroyed. There are heartrending betrayals and separations. One man, after his successful escape, risked returning to his plantation, desperate to find his children. They had been sold South. He returned without them and died of despair. Other fugitives were captured, flogged, sent back, and never heard from again. "This was done in a Christian country," Child reminded her readers, "and there was no law to protect the victim."[27]

Hopper's biography was also another kind of admonition to white Americans. He had been assisting escaped slaves since before the turn of the century. Black Philadelphians had come to treat him as a first responder, a white ally who could be relied on to help them or find others who could. He was the person they would turn to when they were arrested, if they knew of a fugitive hidden somewhere, if they heard that a free Black man was being tortured in the hopes of making him betray his enslaved family's hiding place. Hopper sometimes hid fugitives in his own house and sometimes arranged for others to harbor them. Often he raised money to buy their freedom or simply paid off their enslavers himself. In legal hearings, he made ingenious arguments that flummoxed slave hunters and amused judges.[28] If one man could do all these things, surely more people could do some of them. Hopper was a one-man answer to the question of what your average person could do to fight slavery. The answer was anything and everything.

Child used Hopper's life to one more purpose. The stories that together made up Hopper's biography offered real-life evidence of the truth behind Harriet Beecher Stowe's blockbuster novel *Uncle Tom's Cabin*, published only the year before. The novel's unprecedented success in awakening Northerners' consciences to slavery had made it a target of Southerners eager to prove that it was built on exaggerations and lies. Hopper's life proved Stowe's fiction true, Child told her readers. "Her descriptions are no more fictitious, than the narratives within by Friend Hopper. She has taken living characters and facts of every-day occurrence, and combined them in a connected story, radiant with the light of genius, and warm with the glow of feeling," Child wrote.[29] Stowe had supplied the narrative arc; Hopper, through Child, could ground that arc in fact.

Ellis Loring, ever Child's able financial adviser, secured very favorable terms for the biography from a new publisher. But Child made it abundantly clear that she would take none of the profit. She would not, she vowed, "put Friend Hopper up for sale" in that way. All proceeds would go to Hopper's widow and children. It was the right thing to do. It also left her as impoverished as ever. I imagine Loring both admiring and exasperated. No one knew better than he how desperate her financial situation was and how heavily her poverty sometimes weighed on her. But he also knew better than to argue. The biography was published and went on to be Child's best-selling antislavery work.[30]

Isaac Hopper, we should remember, had not only been Child's landlord, mentor, and friend. He was also her beloved John's father. As Child worked with the publisher, choosing typeface, epigrams, and images, she corresponded with John. They are the only letters between them that survive, and they are all business. Yes, she thought a particular sentence could be simplified. No, she would not add an appendix. Was it difficult to transact professional matters from a distance with the man she once thought she could not live without? If it pained her, she never said so. *Send it to the printer already*, she finally insisted when the still-grieving son suggested another round of edits. It was time, it seemed, to let go.[31]

* * *

As she wrote Hopper's biography, Child was still essentially itinerant. But as the book went into publication, an unlikely plan emerged. Child's father was now eighty-seven years old. It's safe to assume that age had not made him less cranky. But his frailty and loneliness tugged at Child's conscience. She had spent the previous winter caring for him and was convinced that he could not manage the next one alone. No one else—including her two brothers— would care for him as she could. And despite his disapproval of her husband, her profession, her passions, and her activism, he loved her "better than he loves anything else in this world," she thought. She had also become more forgiving of his faults. "He has been a kind father to me, according to the measure of his knowledge and ability," she conceded. It would feel right to care for him.[32]

David meanwhile had tried and failed at yet another farming scheme. He was exhausted; he had been ill again; he had nowhere else to go. If they all lived together, they could economize. But wouldn't reuniting with David simply plunge her back into the financial chaos that had caused their separation in the first place? Maybe not. Child extracted a promise from her husband that he would not "spend a dollar with out first consulting me."[33] Her property was safely in Ellis Loring's name; even if David were to break his pledge, her own finances were no longer at risk. With those safeguards in place, perhaps her literary earnings could keep all three of them afloat. It seemed worth a try. In December 1853, she and David moved into her father's farmhouse on a small plot of land in Wayland, Massachusetts.

Illness, failure, finances, and an aging father: it was not exactly a recipe for a romantic reunion. Would it work? By Child's description, it did. Years later, after David's death, she composed a little remembrance book. It detailed their courtship and marriage, excerpting diaries and letters that testified to their newborn love for each other. It acknowledged the years of separation and hardship. "I throw a veil over these sad memories," Child wrote. Then she continued:

> At last . . . we made a humble home in Wayland, Mass'ts, where we spent twenty two cozy years, entirely alone, without any domestic, mutually serving each other, and entirely dependent on each other for intellectual companionship. . . . He was the most loving husband God ever bestowed upon woman. In his old age, he was as affectionate and devoted as he was when he was the lover of my youth; nay, he manifested even more tenderness.[34]

When I read this passage in the archives at Cornell University, I was skeptical. I hope I didn't roll my eyes, but I might have. After decades of unexplained absences, financial irresponsibility, and emotional neglect, had David really reformed so completely? I thought not. Probably Child, widowed and nostalgic, was glossing over the truth about her late husband. Probably she was forcing a fictional happy ending onto a drama of disappointment. I expected that a careful look at her later letters would reveal that the hurtful patterns of negligence and recklessness had continued.

But in the end, I think she was right. There is no evidence from this point on that he was wasteful or callous or allowed idealistic schemes to imperil their finances. True, he was still often oblivious and a magnet for bad luck: there was the time he missed the Boston train both coming and going; the time he lost all four shirts she had sewed for him; the time he apparently forgot to look both ways and was hit by a speeding wagon. But for the rest of their lives, their letters to each other teem with endearments, gratefulness, and affection. She was his "darling Mariequita" and his "Blessed Heart"; he was her "Davidito" and her "Dearly Beloved Mate." "Oh how I miss the dear little causeries that we carry on unawares in our quiet home," he wrote to her during one of their infrequent separations. "Good, kind, generous, magnanimous soul! How I love you," she wrote back. She thanked him for the kindling he had split for her before he left. "I don't," Child improbably concluded, "deserve that you should be so kind to me."[35] After twenty-five years of marriage, including ten of painful separation, David and Maria Child had found a way to live their love for each other.

I will admit that David remains a mystery to me. How had this passionate, articulate lawyer, journalist, and activist become incapable of caring for himself? Why, well into his fifties, had he felt driven to undertake ever more demanding physical labor that wrecked his health without improving his finances? How had this man who, by many indications, loved his wife, valued her mind, and wished for her success, managed to handicap her career and cripple her spirit? Why had almost everything he tried ended in humiliation? Caroline Weston may have said it best when commenting on one of his failures: "I *hope* it is *mere* folly and stupidity," she said: "but it looks so much like *perversity*."[36]

In the end, we don't have to understand him. Child loved him, and whatever she relinquished for this love was clearly worth it to her. They began to settle their belongings into the tiny bedroom and shared parlor. She did not know this at the time, but she and David would live in this house for the rest of their lives. At the age of fifty-one, she was finally home.

This was the good news. The less good news was that she was home with two men whose combined needs would define the rest of her life. What of her literary ambitions, such as they were? What of her desire to live freely and independently, surrounded by beauty? Apparently none of it mattered much anymore. "The strong affections, which have made me expend all my resources so unreservedly for those I love, find solace in being the object of supreme importance to the two beings who depend on me for their

Fig. 34. The Childs' Wayland home. Courtesy of Digital Commonwealth.

daily happiness," she wrote to Marianne Silsbee. "This tendency is ingrained in my nature, and has been the source of my greatest virtues, and my worst mistakes." The sacrifice came with some relief. "I am very weary of conflict and disappointment," she admitted; "and in the performance of duty there is rest."[37]

That only prompted another question. What about her duties to the millions of enslaved human beings who still—still!—suffered the same unimaginable fates? What about duties to her country as it stumbled ever further into complicity with evil? It is another classic philosophical problem: When do our duties to those we love outweigh our duties to the greater good? Child had shown herself uniquely, powerfully able to shift public opinion on the topic of slavery. Her silence was undoubtedly a loss to the movement. There is plenty of evidence that this fact tormented her. But for now, her first duties, she had decided, were to the men who needed her. As to the other duties: somehow she would find a way to fulfill them too.

*　　*　　*

Child settled into her new life. Although not as remote as Northampton, Wayland was isolated. It took both a stagecoach and a train to travel the twenty-odd miles to Boston, and there was only one return coach each day. The town was generally sleepy and conservative, but it had a good abolitionist minister and one of the country's first free public libraries. Her father's house was a one-mile walk from the town center, which included two churches, a school, a town hall, and a general store. The house was small, but behind it were two ponds and a gentle hill. In the summer, the ponds were full of water lilies; in the winter, the sun sparkled on the ice. Their first year there, Child planted a garden and laughed at a squirrel that insisted on eating cherries in its most picturesque corner. Her father quickly came to depend on her completely, carrying on in an "extraordinary fashion" if anyone else tried to care for him. His behavior—including increasing dementia that rendered him unreliable and paranoid—made both visiting others and having visitors impossible. Occasionally, news of the busy world reached her. Charles Sumner, who was establishing himself as the country's most uncompromising abolitionist senator, sent her "California flower-seed" for her garden, reminding her that her influence was inspiring him ever onward. This assurance, she wrote back, made her heart sing.[38]

That December, as she began this next stage of her life, Child took another momentous step. For the first time in over a decade, she attended Maria Weston Chapman's Anti-Slavery Fair. As she walked into the decorated hall with its glittering merchandise, earnest atmosphere, and thieving little boys circling the refreshment

Fig. 35. Charles Sumner, ca. 1850. Courtesy of the Metropolitan Museum of Art.

stand, she must have wondered what kind of reception she would get. People she had not seen in years milled about, going from table to table, buying gifts and exchanging gossip. They seemed happy to see her. It was, she reported, "a real heart-warming to find how much I was cared for." Eventually, she and Maria Chapman began corresponding again. There is no record of their first words to each other, but whatever their content, they were enough for the two women to renew their collaboration. Chapman resumed hounding Child to do whatever she asked, and Child resumed trying to resist. Before long, Child was back to not wanting to go to the fair but doing it anyway.[39] Child continued to find Chapman's rhetoric divisive and her tactics extreme, but she was often more amused than critical. Sometimes she was even admiring. She was on record saying that all types were needed in the struggle against slavery, and that it was impossible to deny that Chapman was, in her own way, often a force for good. Perhaps the old warmth never fully returned. But mutual respect, it turned out, could sustain a friendship too.

Her biography of Hopper finished and her domestic arrangements finally stable, Child returned to her work on religion. Hauling books from Boston libraries onto the train and then onto the stagecoach was arduous. The many demands of preparing meals, mending clothing, preserving food, and caring for an aged parent were often all-consuming.[40] But in the moments when she could write, she absorbed herself completely in Hindu religious festivals, the travails of early Christians, the ecstasies of Muslim mystics. After a few stolen hours at her desk, she would look up and be surprised to see quiet fields and David's woodpile instead of the temple in Jerusalem or the Egyptian pyramids. Once again, there had never been an American book quite like this, one that tried to assess religions first on their own terms and then against the advance of spiritual progress. The work was strenuous and not always pleasant. Sometimes it felt as if she were on a "pilgrimage of penance, with peas in my shoes."[41] But finally, she was done. *The Progress of Religious Ideas, through Successive Ages* filled three volumes and ran over twelve hundred pages.

What, at the end of all this scholarship, was the verdict? Was religious thought progressing or not? Here as so often, Child combined faith in humans' goodness with realism about their flaws. First the goodness. In describing the book's aim to Lucy Osgood, Child wrote: "I perceive that an immense good has been done to the human race by *religion*, by which I understand practical love and truth toward our fellow-beings, and humble reverence with regard to the infinite and incomprehensible, which we call God." Evidence of this love and reverence was abundant in all religions, *Progress of Religious Ideas* showed. God had not, she told her readers bluntly, imparted truth only to Christianity. It was arrogant of Christians to claim otherwise. Jesus, she argued, was simply the purest articulation of what all religions were trying to express.

And what had he articulated? An uncompromising sympathy with the most vulnerable. He had asked his followers "to sacrifice time, talent, and wealth, for the benefit of remote and degraded classes of people, from whom no return of advantages could be expected," Child wrote.[42] Insofar as Christianity *did* represent progress, that was why.

Insofar as it did not, universal human weaknesses were to blame. "Human nature," she argued against champions of racial hierarchy, "is everywhere the same, and in all ages has had the same wants and the same aspirations, and been liable to the same infirmities." Humans were forever contorting truth by turning it over to priests, claiming to have captured it in a book, or trying to contain it in ironclad rituals. To focus on minutiae of doctrine and historical fact distracted them from compassion and reverence. Humans too often, in other words, exchanged religion for theology and stifled feeling with thought. The result was millennia of strife and a perpetual threat to the progress of truth. Christians were as guilty of this as anyone. Their treatment of Jews was a "blot." Medieval Europe had created a caste system as rigid as any in Asia.[43] And then, of course, there was slavery. If Christians had received the truth most fully, Child concluded, they had also betrayed it most egregiously. She had never been one to flatter her readers.

As the book was published, Child again braced for scandal. This time there was none. Far from being outraged, her public seemed grateful. Warm, enthusiastic letters from ordinary readers arrived in a flood—a better response, she thought, than to any of her other works. Three months after its publication, the trilogy had paid for itself. Several people whose opinion she valued expressed amazement. *Progress* was nothing less, Lucy Osgood marveled, than a "broad foundation upon which to build a philosophy of religion." "Mrs. Child's book is especially valuable, and in a high degree creditable to her love of truth, her generous spirit, and her faithful industry," the *Christian Examiner* wrote. Her reviewers agreed that there was nothing like it in English. The abolitionist minister Samuel May proclaimed from his pulpit that Child's history was "the most valuable contribution to an enlarged, charitable and true theology, that has been made by any one in our country." Even Child's brother Convers, now a theology professor at Harvard, guardedly approved, only protesting—how could he not?—that surely theology was good for *something*. Theodore Parker, another abolitionist minister who had himself suffered professional ostracism for his revisionist work on Christianity, was astonished. *The Progress of Religious Ideas* was "*the* book of the age," he declared: "and written by a *woman!*"[44]

No doubt there is also much to criticize in Child's assessments. Her scholarship was heroically impartial for her time, but her preference for Greek and Christian worldviews is unmistakable. Criticism from Child's peers, by contrast, went in the other direction. The author, some complained, had not shown Christianity triumphant enough. There was little evidence of the *progress* of religious ideas here, one reviewer wrote. Child's book was simply a "geography of heathenism"; it failed to trace a clear line out of pagan darkness and into Christian light.[45] These critics were correct: that, indeed, was the narrative she had refused to give. Exactly this refusal was what made her book so radical. Perhaps that in itself was progress enough.

* * *

As the Childs adjusted to life together in Wayland, the next front in the conflict over slavery opened up on the prairies of the increasingly populated Midwest. Kansas and Nebraska were both territories applying for statehood; at issue was whether they would be admitted as slave states or free. From most Northerners' point of view, once again, the Missouri Compromise meant that this should not have been a question. But some Southern politicians had concluded that the 1850 Compromise invalidated the Missouri Compromise. A new policy was needed. Illinois senator Stephen Douglas, together with other legislators including South Carolina senator Andrew Butler, proposed legislation known as the Kansas-Nebraska Act. The act was passed in the Senate on March 3 and in the House of Representatives on May 22, 1854. It was scheduled to go into effect on May 30. Among its provisions: immigrants to both Kansas and Nebraska would be allowed to settle, by popular vote, whether or not they would admit slavery.[46]

On May 24, as the country prepared for the act to become law, a fugitive slave named Anthony Burns was arrested in Boston. Tensions again were running high. Boston's mayor mustered every soldier in the city to guard the streets surrounding the courthouse. Abolitionists called a meeting at Faneuil Hall. Again, Child's converts led the charge. Wendell Phillips exhorted the meeting's attendees to barricade the courthouse unless they were ready to consider themselves citizens of Virginia. Higginson, tired of rhetoric, simply brought two hundred men from Worcester to Boston, armed them and others, and used a beam to batter down the courthouse door. Once inside, he and his men fought hand to hand with guards until someone drew a gun and a police officer was shot. Higginson escaped with a scar that marked him for the rest of his life. Burns remained incarcerated. The rescue attempt had failed.

That Burns had been a slave was never really in question, so the commissioner's verdict was a foregone conclusion. What was less clear was whether one of the remaining plots to rescue him would succeed. After Higginson's raid, President Franklin Pierce was leaving nothing to chance. Once the verdict was announced, all of Boston was converted into a military zone. City, state, and federal forces amassed to ensure that Burns would be returned to Virginia without incident. On the day he was to be conveyed to a ship sent expressly for the purpose by President Pierce himself, Boston streets were blocked off. Businesses were ordered to close. Cannons were loaded. Cavalry and artillery stood at the ready. Fifty thousand Bostonians turned out to watch their tax dollars being used to force a man back into slavery. The intention to humiliate Boston felt clear. Burns was returned to Virginia, then sold into North Carolina.[47]

Child followed Burns's rendition with pain and humiliation. "I should be willing to pour out my blood, like water, if I could do anything to arrest the downward course of things," she wrote to Francis Shaw. When her longtime friend Marianne Silsbee referred to

Fig. 36. The arrest of Anthony Burns—who had escaped enslavement in Virginia but been recaptured in Boston after the passage of the 1850 Fugitive Slave Act— provoked a sensational trial and rescue effort in 1854. Courtesy of the Library of Congress.

Burns with a hateful epithet and complained that it was a "ridiculous fuss" about one Black man, Child was so enraged that the two stopped corresponding. But many Bostonians who had, until now, remained either uninformed or apathetic were stunned to see the lengths to which the federal government was willing to go to force Northern compliance with Southern laws. The sight of a solitary Black man, led in chains through the narrow streets by dozens of armed soldiers, left many Bostonians distraught. *Uncle Tom's Cabin* had ensured that everyone could imagine the horrors

Fig. 37. To prevent his rescue by abolitionists, a massive military guard was assigned to convey Burns to a waiting ship, sent by President Pierce himself, which carried him back to slavery. Courtesy of the New York Public Library.

that awaited a slave sold South. Amos Lawrence knew he spoke for many Bostonians when he reported that after seeing Burns led away, they had gone to bed "old-fashioned, conservative, Compromise Union Whigs and waked up stark mad Abolitionists."[48]

Amos Lawrence, as it happened, was no ordinary Bostonian. He was one of the city's most successful businessmen, owner of a mercantile company that had built its fortune on cotton.[49] In other words, he had a financial interest in slavery's existence. But Burns's rendition convinced him that slavery was wrong and had to be fought. For the next battlefront, Lawrence needed to look no further than the Kansas-Nebraska Act, which had become law between Burns's arrest and his escort back to slavery. If Kansas was going to remain free, Northerners opposed to slavery would have to move there and vote. Populating Kansas would take hardy, dedicated settlers, able to survive the hardships of frontier life. Lawrence himself did not fit that description. But the settlers would need money. That he could take care of.

Soon Lawrence was funding the Massachusetts Emigration Aid Company, founded with the express purpose of populating Kansas with enough abolitionists to win a popular vote and keep Kansas free. The call went out, and hundreds of aspiring settlers volunteered. The company financed their transportation, provisions, and housing; it also promised to establish a printing press, schools, and churches. Early scouts were dispatched, most notably a former medical doctor named Charles Robinson. The first settlers began arriving in Kansas in July 1854. A second group, including women, children, and musicians, left Boston on August 29, 1854, to great fanfare, including a hymn written by John Greenleaf Whittier. After the long and treacherous journey, the emigrants settled in a valley near the Kansas River. They started building a town and named it in Lawrence's honor.[50]

None of this, unfortunately, is to say that antislavery emigrants to Kansas were fully on the right side of history. Many of them were displacing native peoples with the same callousness and conviction of superiority that Child had been criticizing since her days with the Abenaki in Maine. And while some who came from New England, like Robinson, were genuine abolitionists and also supported citizenship and voting rights for Black men, others believed that keeping Kansas free of slavery was completely compatible with keeping it free of Black residents. An early resolution among "Free-Staters" prohibiting Black settlers was put to public vote and passed with 1,287 votes in favor and 453 against, adding Kansas to the list of territories with such openly racist regulations.[51] The consequences of these policies would shape Black Americans' experience in western states long after emancipation.

But for now, the focus was on keeping slavery out of Kansas. The first test of Amos Lawrence's endeavors came in the territorial election of November 1854. It was a debacle. It had not been lost on proslavery forces that Free-Staters were amassing in Kansas. A call went out to stop them, by force if necessary. Paramilitary groups of Missourians calling themselves "Border Ruffians" streamed into Kansas leading up to election day. They harassed antislavery voters and threatened to hang judges. They themselves voted in droves, with the result that sometimes the number of votes cast in a given precinct outnumbered the registered voters.[52]

To no one's surprise, the proslavery forces won the election. As the resulting proslavery legislature enacted laws in Lecompton, their chosen capital, Charles Robinson and his allies declared the election results void and announced that they did "not feel bound to obey any law of [the Lecompton legislature's] enacting." Robinson convened a competing political convention in Lawrence. There, Free-Staters wrote their own constitution and, as one historian puts it, "openly rebuked, ignored, or simply disobeyed legislation repugnant to them."[53] By 1856, the territory of Kansas had two capital cities, two legislatures, and two governors.

By early May, President Pierce had had enough. Robinson was indicted for treason. The indictment also called for "forcible resistance" to the "inflammatory and seditious character" of Lawrence's two Free-State newspapers. It singled out the town's newly completed Free State Hotel, which it called a "strong hold of resistance to law." Pierce assured Free-Staters that they could expect to confront "any available force of the United States" if they continued in their defiance. In response, residents of Lawrence closed their schools, shuttered their churches, built up their defenses, and prepared to fight. "It looks very much like war & I am ready for it & so are our people," wrote Robinson. Amos Lawrence added another item to his list of supplies for the settlers: rifles.[54]

On May 19, 1856, a thousand miles away from the Lawrence settlers, Charles Sumner rose in the United States Senate to deliver a speech. It was titled "The Crime against Kansas." Its intent was to protest the violence and voter fraud proslavery forces were perpetrating in Kansas. He had memorized his five-hour speech and had copies made in advance, ready to be sent to constituents. "Not in any common lust for power did this uncommon tragedy have its origin," pronounced the forty-five-year-old senator, his six-foot frame towering above the podium. "It is the rape of a virgin Territory, compelling it to the hateful embrace of slavery; and it may be clearly traced to a depraved desire for a new Slave State." The sexual imagery was shocking enough, but Sumner reserved special

Fig. 38. The remains of the Free State Hotel in Lawrence, Kansas, after its destruction by pro-slavery forces in May 1856. Courtesy of the Kansas State Historical Society.

insults for Senator Andrew Butler from South Carolina, who had helped write the Kansas-Nebraska Act. Butler, Sumner said, "has chosen a mistress to whom he has made his vows, and who, though ugly to others, is always lovely to him; though polluted in the sight of the world, is chaste in his sight—I mean the harlot, slavery."[55]

Two days later, on May 21, David Atchison, a former Missouri senator, also gave a speech. His audience was a band of some 750 Border Ruffians who had amassed outside Lawrence, Kansas. "Gentlemen, officers & Soldiers! This is the most glorious day of my life!" he shouted. "I know you will never fail, but will burn, sack & destroy, until every vistage [*sic*] of these Norther[n] Abolitionists is wiped out." Under the command of Sheriff Samuel Jones, the proslavery forces marched into town, positioned cannons on the main street, and opened fire. When it became clear that the Free-Staters were outnumbered and would offer no resistance, the

SOUTHERN CHIVALRY — ARGUMENT versus CLUB'S.

Fig. 39. The caning of Charles Sumner on the United States Senate floor, May 1856. Courtesy of the New York Public Library.

looting began. "Every house in town was plundered," an eyewitness recorded, "and the women and children driven off." The only casualty was a proslavery man who was hit by falling masonry, but hordes of ruffians broke through doors, burned photographs and letters, and threw furniture out of windows. They destroyed printing presses and pitched them into the river. They burned the Free State Hotel almost to the ground. The assault became known as the Sack of Lawrence.[56]

The next day, in Washington, DC, Charles Sumner sat alone at his desk in the Senate chamber at the end of another legislative session. He was approached from behind by Preston Brooks, a congressman from South Carolina and a relative of Andrew Butler's. Brooks had come to avenge Butler's honor after Sumner's verbal attack. Before Sumner could rise to defend himself, Brooks clubbed him with a gold-headed cane until Sumner collapsed, bloody and unconscious, beneath his Senate desk.[57] He regained consciousness and was helped from the scene, but he soon collapsed again. His wounds became infected; some newspapers reported that he hovered between life and death. If he survived, doctors warned his horrified Massachusetts constituents, it could be with severe mental impairment.

Americans were attacking Americans on the prairies of Kansas and in the halls of Congress. The country convulsed in mutual accusation. Sumner had deserved it, cried Southern papers. Brooks had simply done his duty by restoring both his family's and South Carolina's honor. From all over the South, admirers sent Brooks new canes. Northern newspapers denounced him as a coward who, unable to defend himself with argument, had revealed the true core of Southern "honor" by resorting to violence. If Northerners continued to submit to such outrages, the *New York Tribune* despaired, "we have lost the noblest attributes of freemen, and are virtually slaves."[58]

The attacks and counterattacks were not only verbal. Two days after Sumner's caning, a radical abolitionist named John Brown and his band took revenge for the Sack of Lawrence by dragging five proslavery Kansans from their beds and murdering them in cold blood. In August, proslavery forces retaliated by attacking Brown's settlement and killing his son Frederick.[59] Had the war begun?

* * *

Isolated in Wayland, Child was shaken to her core. Her words had turned Sumner toward abolitionism: Was he now to die for those beliefs? Or, worse, survive but with his mind in ruins? For the first time in her life, she felt murderous rage: ready to rush to battle like Joan of Arc or simply assassinate people in their homes like the French Revolution's Charlotte Corday. At night, her fitful sleep was interrupted by visions "of murdered men in Kansas, or of Charles Sumner, bleeding and dying." Her anguish became physical; she complained of "suffocation of the heart" and "throbbings of the brain."[60]

Her first thought was to rush to Washington and offer to nurse Sumner. As an older, trusted female friend, she could do that. Except that she couldn't. "If I had not been chained to my aged father,

I verily believe I *should* have done it," she wrote to the Lorings' daughter Anna. "As it was, I could not." Nursing Sumner was not all she wanted to do. If only she herself could join the Free-Staters in Kansas. She knew she was capable of hard physical work. She could have survived prairie existence: she was, after all, still the author of *The Frugal Housewife*. But her father's health made that plan, too, unthinkable. "The thought of those poor suffering emigrants from Kansas presses on heart and brain, so that I lie aware many hours in the night, revolving hopes and fears, until it seems as if it would *kill* me to be compelled to remain inactive much longer," she wrote. Was there nothing she could do? She could, and did, recommence her arguments with strangers on public transportation. When a young man in the stagecoach opined that Sumner was to blame for his own caning, she did not hold back. "I will not *repeat* what I said," she told Louisa. "But I *tell* you it thundered *itself*." But that could not possibly be enough. "Oh, it seems as if I should *die* of inaction at this crisis," she lamented.[61]

Clearly, Child's long-dormant energies had reawakened. And though she was limited by her domestic duties, she now found ways to channel those energies. The Lawrence settlers had lost everything: they would need clothes if they were to survive the next winter. She wrote to a friend who was a textile merchant, begging him for fabric. Then she roused the women in her quiet town to sew it into clothing. David, too, was stirred to action. For the first time in years, he put his rhetorical talents to work. By fall he was touring New England, lecturing and raising money for the New England Emigrant Aid Society, sometimes accompanied by a spokesman from Kansas itself. He wrote Child loving, energized letters. "Darling Blessed Mariquita," one began, "How I do miss my mate!" In the evenings, with David away lecturing and her father finally asleep, Child stayed up late, sewing. Soon the women were done and sent a crate of clothing to Kansas, along with $60 they had raised and a rousing letter of support from Child.[62]

The clothing still did not feel like enough. There had to be something else she could do. In the end, Maria Child did what she had so often done; she met the crisis at her desk. Looking out at fields bordered by classic New England stone walls, she imagined herself in Kansas. In her mind, the woods and meadows of Massachusetts became the waving grass of western prairies. And when she transitioned from imagining the landscape to populating it, she imagined women.

The result was a story called "The Kansas Emigrants." It features two female protagonists: the fierce Kate, who eagerly moves to Kansas with her husband to keep it free, and the timid Alice, who fearfully accompanies her husband out of love and duty. Through their eyes, Child imagined the jolting wagon ride, the rivers almost too full to ford, the plates and trinkets from home broken on the rough roads. She envisioned the dirt floors, the freshly cut timber, the satisfaction of seeing a town grow from a dream into reality. And then she funneled her nightmares into vivid descriptions of honorable New England settlers harassed by brutish Missouri thugs. Child depicted the abolitionists as clinging to nonresistance, sure it would work, waiting for assistance from Northern states that was slow to come.

The story ends with Lawrence in flames: its churches smoldering, its famous hotel ransacked, its residents huddling in the ruins of their homes. Its only gleam of hope is Alice's dying vision of a future Kansas, with "church-spires, and beautiful houses, windows glittering in the sunlight," populated, peaceful, and—most important—free.[63] Why is Alice dying? Her husband is dead, shot in the back by lawless enslavers for being an abolitionist. Like Child's heroine Philothea two decades before, Alice cannot survive the grief of her husband's death. She does her duty, and then she dies.

As she wrote, Child must have wondered: Which was she? The fearless, heroic Kate who smuggles kegs of gunpowder through enemy lines and brandishes a pistol while rescuing supplies from her burning home? Or the clinging, fragile Alice, who renounces herself for her husband and whose only contribution to the cause is her dying vision? There is no doubt which of her creations Child envied: oh, to *act* as Kate did, to stride forcefully across the prairie grasses, to risk her life for her principles! There is also little question which fate Child feared: the trembling Alice, fulfilling her duty and leaving behind nothing but visions in the air.

٭٭٭

Child's New York literary connections, however strained by her long silences, still held. "The Kansas Emigrants" was serialized in Horace Greeley's *New York Tribune* in late October and early November. Its publication was timed to lead up to the national election on Tuesday, November 4, 1856.

The 1856 presidential candidates reflected a country in political turmoil. James Buchanan, a proslavery Democrat, was being opposed by candidates from two fledgling parties. The first was former president Millard Fillmore, now representing the anti-immigrant, anti-Catholic Know-Nothing Party. The second was a dashing young veteran, surveyor, and explorer named John Frémont. Frémont was a senator from the new and still mythical-sounding state of California. He was the first presidential candidate to be put forward by a new political party called the Republicans. His hair was full and wavy, his wife was vibrant and beautiful, and he had literally struck gold on his California property. Most important, he was unapologetically antislavery. He had vowed, if elected, to aid the Kansas emigrants. Child admitted that she was smitten. "For the first time in my life, I am a *little* infected with *political* excitement," she confessed to Mary and Lucy Osgood. "For the sake of suffering Kansas, and future freedom in peril, I *do* long to have Frémont elected. Don't *you*? Let's *vote*!"[64]

The last sentence was, of course, a joke. The Nineteenth Amendment, which finally permitted at least white women to vote, was six decades in the future. But for now, the still disenfranchised Maria Child focused on the progress that Frémont's candidacy represented. It could not be denied, she wrote to Sarah Shaw, "that an *Abolition* principle is the big wave which has taken Frémont on its back, and is floating onward in the open light of day. . . . We old abolitionists may well feel repaid for twenty five years of labor, discouragement, unpopularity, and persecution, since our principles, at *last* begin visibly to sway the masses. I, for one, thank God that I live to see it."[65] For their part, Southern Democrats warned, not for the last time, that the election of a Republican would mean civil war.

The last installment of "The Kansas Emigrants" was published two days before the election. Its political message was simple: Vote Republican. Child was not above making this very explicit. Alice's dying vision of a free Kansas included a local hill rechristened Free Mont. A vote for Frémont was a vote for that vision, a redemption of all the Kansas settlers had suffered.

David was still on the lecture circuit. Child threatened to dress in his clothes and vote for him if he was late. He arrived in time to vote and to carry his fragile father-in-law to the polls to cast his final ballot. "My *first* vote was given for Washington, and my *last* shall be given for Frémont," Child's father declared. Abolitionists everywhere held their breath. But when all the votes were counted, Buchanan had won. Neither the abolitionists' arguments, nor Frémont's charisma, nor Child's story, had been enough. The ninety-year-old Convers Francis wept.[66]

His daughter was more philosophical. She had never really gotten her hopes up: she had thought too carefully and studied her fellow citizens' apathy and prejudice for too long to expect too much. That almost a million Americans had voted for the Know-Nothings, showing themselves more interested in ending immigration than in ending slavery, was no surprise to her. But there was no denying that the election made things bleaker than ever. It assured the South of another four years of executive power, legislative advantage, and Supreme Court nominations. "Our ship is sinking, my friend," she wrote to Parke Godwin. "It is not reserved for the United States to be a beacon-light for the world, as we have proudly hoped." The only way to redeem America's potential, Child continued to think, was to dissolve the Union as quickly as possible. Perhaps a new Northern republic, freed of its duties to the South, could take up the country's failed promise. "*How* this will happen, I cannot foresee; for the South understands her interest too well to secede from the Union," Child predicted, "and there is not virtue enough in the North to do it."[67]

Despite the dreariness of the election's outcome, David soon left again to continue fund-raising for Kansas. "How melancholy I felt, when you went away 'in the morning darkness'!" Child wrote to him, hoping the letter would reach him wherever he was. She returned to caring for her father. As Thanksgiving approached, his health began to deteriorate. Child spent days at his bedside, feeding him with a spoon and sleeping so little that she feared she was hallucinating. The nights became long, solitary vigils. "Here I am alone with the stars, while the old man lies there waiting for his prison-gate to open," she wrote to Louisa. As his death approached, she imagined her own release. "I want to rush out into infinite space," she confessed. "I think nothing will satisfy me but trying my freedom by chasing a comet through the universe, or riding on the flash of the Aurora." But when he finally breathed his last, she was bereft. "I almost cried myself blind," she wrote to Sarah. "I would willingly be fettered to his bedside for years, if I could only hear that voice again." But the voice was silent, and her duty was done. "Thank God," she confided in Loring, "I *never* disappointed him."[68]

∗   ∗   ∗

What could possibly guide her life next? For three years, her path had been clear. Her emotional energy had been consumed by someone to whom she was everything. "Now the occupation of my life seems gone," she mourned.[69] Would she ever matter that much to anyone again?

Her father's death forced her to take emotional stock of her life. What she saw was bleak. The years of not leaving her father's side, combined with her own shame, withdrawal, and poverty, had left many of her friendships in tatters. In doing her duty to him and the cause she loved, had she neglected her friends? She feared the answer was yes, so she set about trying to change that. She wrote to Whittier asking if any wrongdoing of hers had prevented him from replying to her latest letter. When he wrote back to say he simply hadn't received it, she was more relieved than she could say. Then there was the matter of not having guests. "I believe I have pursued a mistaken course all along, about inviting my friends," she wrote to Louisa. She tried to explain. She and David lived so humbly that she had thought visiting them could only be an imposition on her wealthier acquaintances. "And so I have allowed myself to appear unhospitable and unsocial, when in my heart there is nothing I wouldn't delight to do to promote the happiness of those I love," she confessed.[70]

Her argument with Marianne Silsbee over Burns's return to slavery also weighed on her. What were her duties to this friend? Child settled on the duty to explain. She had, she wrote to Marianne, seen too many people fail in the duty to fight slavery because they were afraid of alienating their friends. She had vowed to be different. "Again and again, I have said to myself, 'Take care! Maria Child! Take care! Don't allow this pleasant friendship, and these kind attentions, to draw you away from the advocacy of an unpopular cause. Let no one mistake, for a moment, your willingness to lay upon *that* altar anything and everything that renders life agreeable.'" "Such has been my normal state of mind," this veteran abolitionist explained, "for twenty five years."[71]

Of all the evidence of Maria Child's radicalism, this confession hits me the hardest. To guard oneself so vigilantly against joy or openness; to view every friendship as a temptation and every kindness as a trap: it was no wonder Child's activism had left her depleted and alone. It was no wonder she felt vulnerable and bereft in the decade when the cause that guided her life had ebbed so low. It is usually futile to argue about who has sacrificed most for what cause. Activism is not a contest, and whatever privation Child experienced will always pale against what Black Americans fighting slavery suffered. But when I consider this admission and Whittier's statement that "No woman in this country . . . sacrificed so much for principles as Mrs. Child," I think I at least know what he was trying to say.[72]

Was it too late to rebuild this and other friendships? Child wanted to try. Having explained her position, she tried to imagine how it appeared to others. "You could not understand this state of mind, dear friend," she continued to Silsbee; "for, in the first place, the subject had not been kept so *near* to your large kind heart, by frequent interviews with fugitives, during twenty-five years." If Silsbee was paying attention, she would have noticed an admonition here: the reason she hadn't been outraged, her friend was suggesting, was that she hadn't been paying attention. But Child was ready to take some responsibility for the tension, too. "I did not remember this, as I ought, and I pray your forgiveness, if I seemed to strike against you with a sharp collision, in return for your many proofs of love. I love you truly," Child concluded, "and that is a fact."[73]

It was again time for the Anti-Slavery Fair. Did she have friends there? It seemed so. In the midst of all the bustle, some people wanted to update her about the latest news from Washington. Others took her off for cozy chats in the corner. This generally felt reassuring. Child stayed a few days in Boston, going to the theater and visiting friends. Charles Sumner, now six months into his recovery, came to see her. He seemed frail but resilient; her relief was immense. She left Boston sure that her time of mourning was over. But when she got off the Wayland coach in the frigid darkness on New Year's Day 1857 and found the house empty and cold, her grief for her father overwhelmed her again. "Always when I went to Boston, he watched anxiously for the return of the stage, and had a bright fire for me," she remembered to Marianne Silsbee. "The old face lightened up as I entered, and he exclaimed cheerfully, 'You're welcome home, Maria!'" But now the house was silent. "It seemed," the still-grieving daughter wrote, "as if it would kill me."[74]

∗　∗　∗

The winter months passed slowly. The news was always bad. On March 6, two days after swearing in James Buchanan as president, Supreme Court Chief Justice Roger Taney issued a decision in the case of *Dred Scott vs. Sandford*. The court had been asked to rule whether Scott, who had been born enslaved but lived in free states with his enslaver, was free. No, said Taney in the 7–2 majority opinion. Scott was still a slave. But Taney did not stop there. The Constitution, Taney claimed, protected slavery. Period. This meant that Congress could not limit its expansion. Neither could the popular vote. Both the Missouri Compromise and the Kansas-Nebraska Act were, it now seemed, unconstitutional. Taney was still not done. African descendants, he added, had no "rights which a white man was bound to respect." "The Negro," he concluded, "might be justly and lawfully reduced to slavery for his benefit."[75]

We are often told that the South began the Civil War in order to protect states' rights. The irony of that claim should now be clear. The *Dred Scott* decision, as Child and many others pointed out, was in "direct opposition to the decision of the Supreme Court of Massachusetts." It nullified decisions like the *Med* case that limited how and for how long slaves could be kept by Southerners in the North. It also undermined long-standing laws guaranteeing that Black men could enter into legal contracts, become citizens, and vote. What, after this decision, did being a free state even mean? Apparently very little. There was, Garrison mourned, not "yet an inch of truly Free Soil in the nation." And given this sweeping legal victory, where would the South stop? Nowhere, both abolitionists and Republican politicians began to warn. Unless Northerners resisted, they should expect nothing less than a Southern invasion and the final loss of their own liberties. Black abolitionist Charles Remond declared that it was time to save "the American people" from the "American Government." Child agreed. "If the old Commonwealth don't rise in her moral strength, at this attempt to lay the yoke on *her*," she wrote, then the spirit of the Puritans was once and for all dead, "and we must all drift together toward a military despotism." The only hope, she wrote to Sarah Shaw, was that Southern politicians "have got rope enough, and they will hang themselves."[76]

The days began to lengthen over the ponds beyond their cottage; the worst of the winter was over. Child continued trying to rebuild her circle of friends. She looked around at the little home that now, thanks to her father, they owned. His bedroom was vacant. For the first time in her life, she could comfortably have guests. Old anxieties quickly resurfaced. What would her genteel Boston friends think of her tiny parlor and modest furnishings? She had no servants to wait on them as their servants waited on her. She would have to make their meals and turn down their beds herself. Would she even have time to enjoy their company? Would they go away shaking their heads, confiding in other friends about the Childs' poverty, compensating again by sending her expensive gifts— chairs, desks, dresses—that both pleased and pained her?[77]

But she had resolved not to isolate herself. She painted and wallpapered her father's old rooms, sending David to Boston so he would not be in her way. The bedroom was transformed, and then the parlor. She hung the image of a Venetian palace that the Shaws had given her and the reproduction of Raphael's *Sibyls* other friends had sent her from Rome. Finally she was ready for guests. Marianne Silsbee visited, as did Convers's wife Abigail. Sarah Shaw, Child's "friend most beloved," came too.[78] Making herself vulnerable to others' judgment wasn't easy. But visit by visit, some of Child's loneliness eased.

More than anyone, she wanted Louisa and Ellis Loring to visit. She continued to arrange her few precious objects, imagining how they would react to each one.[79] She could never re-create the lavish breakfasts the two couples had enjoyed in their early days in Roxbury when Anna had toddled among them. But she could make them feel welcome and loved. She could show them that despite her modest means and her sometimes stubborn solitude, she was capable of fashioning a cozy home.

This hope would never be realized. One day a letter arrived on the six o'clock stage. Child took it inside, opened it, and almost collapsed. Ellis Loring was dead, taken by an illness so severe and yet so brief that she had not even known he was sick. He had been only fifty-five years old. It was an "overwhelming blow" that "for a time seemed to crush all life and hope out of me," she wrote. Ellis was irreplaceable. "In my worldly affairs, and in my moral doubts, he disentangled all knots, and straightened all crookedness," she remembered. For him—this trusted moral, financial, and legal guide—her resolve to put her shame aside and open her home had come too late. Their thirty-year correspondence went quiet. Was it possible that someone so present, so alive, was simply gone? "My dear friend Ellis . . . *where* is he? What is he *doing*? Above all, does he know what *we* are doing?" she demanded. The questions were as urgent as they were unanswerable. "Oh," Child mourned, "this dreadful silence!"[80]

*　*　*

The country settled into a wary standoff. Tensions in Kansas ground on, erupting in the occasional bloody skirmish. Vigilance committees throughout the North guarded Black communities from slave catchers and kidnappers. In October 1858, Abraham Lincoln debated Stephen Douglas for a US Senate seat from Illinois, assuring voters that although slavery was wrong, "I am not nor ever have been in favor of making [Black people] voters or jurors." Black and white populations could never live together equally, he said, "and I as much as any other man am in favor of having the superior position assigned to the white race."[81] He said many other quotable things that were progressive and uplifting. By the end of his life, his views of Black Americans had evolved. But we must acknowledge that he said this, too. Let us not flatter ourselves.

Child too settled into an uneasy calm. She visited the grieving Louisa and was distressed at how little she could help. She nursed David through a life-threatening bout of the rheumatism that would plague him for the rest of his life. She published a short-story collection called *Autumnal Leaves* that included "The Kansas Emigrants" and a poem about death called "I Want to Go Home." As she negotiated the often conflicting demands of being both author and housewife, national developments were never far from her mind. "The South plays with us, like the cat with a mouse," she wrote to Sarah Shaw. "We are permitted to amuse ourselves with the idea that we are to obtain our freedom; but the tiger is watching us closely all the while, and is sure to grip us at last." Disunion, she still maintained, was the only remedy. But what would finally rouse the public to take such a radical step? "If the Kansas outrages, and the assault on Charles Sumner could not arouse the Free States to *unanimous* resistance to Southern tyranny, we have no reason to suppose that any event which may hereafter happen will sufficiently arouse them," she concluded. "Probably such an exciting combination of circumstances will *never* occur again."[82]

10

Keep Firing

Shortly after midnight on October 17, 1859, Lewis Washington was asleep at Beallair, his elegant plantation home, five miles from Harpers Ferry, Virginia. The night was cold and rainy. Washington was a great-grandnephew of George Washington himself and had both status and wealth to match his Revolutionary pedigree. His home was situated on 670 acres of land. He had inherited priceless objects from his famous relation, including a sword given to the country's first president by Frederick the Great and a pistol given to him by Lafayette. He was also a slave owner and kept careful records of the humans he bought and sold as well as those he hired out to profit yet further from their labor.[1]

Now one of those slaves, he thought, was disturbing his sleep by calling his name in the hallway outside his bedroom. Drowsy and in his pajamas, Washington opened the door to find not his slave but a group of armed strangers. Among them were three Black men. One of the white men spoke. "You are our prisoner," he said.[2]

Washington was ordered to dress and prepare to leave. While they waited, the men raided his collection of guns. They forced him to hand over both Frederick the Great's sword and Lafayette's pistol to a Black man named Osborne Anderson. He asked what his invaders intended. When they said it was to free all the slaves in the South, he thought they were joking. Perhaps it was just the kind of thing a thief with a sense of humor would say.[3]

Washington was led outside, where his own carriage awaited

him. A Black man he did not recognize was at the reins. Behind the carriage was a wagon in which several of his slaves sat. Washington climbed into the carriage, and the small caravan started forward. They traveled a short distance to another plantation. Washington's captors broke into the house, roused its owner from his bed and, amid the screams of his family and servants, forced him into the carriage. Seven of his enslaved men were also loaded into the wagon. The caravan started forward again. It was still dark, still raining.

The enlarged group now entered the deserted town of Harpers Ferry and headed toward the armory at its edge. Nearby was the arsenal, where the federal government's store of weapons, produced at the armory, was kept essentially unprotected. Once there, the captives were hurried inside and herded into the guardroom. Other heavily armed men were stationed there, some Black and some white. One of Washington's captors pointed to a gaunt, bearded man who was giving orders. "This is John Brown," he said. "Osawatomie Brown of Kansas," the bearded man added, as if to clarify.[4]

To be taken from your bed in the middle of the night and find yourself a hostage of John Brown: it was the stuff of Southern nightmares. Ever since he and his men had murdered proslavery Kansans in revenge for the sacking of Lawrence, Osawatomie Brown—named for the Kansas town from which he launched his raids—had been one of the country's most wanted men. President James Buchanan had personally offered a reward for his capture.[5] Now here he was in Harpers Ferry, handing out pikes to Washington's slaves.

*   *   *

Who was this John Brown, and what was he doing?

Brown had pledged to fight an "*eternal war* with slavery" when, still a boy, he had witnessed a slave his own age being beaten mercilessly with a shovel. He also, very early in life, had embraced violence as a just punishment for a nation that sanctioned such atroc-

Fig. 40. John Brown. Courtesy of the Library of Congress.

ity. He had been inspired by the methods of Black revolutionaries Toussaint L'Ouverture in Haiti and Nat Turner in Virginia as well as by Black vigilance committees' armed rescue of fugitives in Northern cities. He had tried to publicize the writings of Black leaders Henry Highland Garnet and David Walker, including their calls to action rather than words.[6] He had come to see himself as a disciple of these Black crusaders for justice and as the equivalent of an Old Testament prophet visiting vengeance on a guilty people.

For years, Brown and several of his sons had operated in Kansas, engaging in open warfare with antislavery forces. At one point he had executed a daring raid into Missouri to free enslaved people, then arranged for them to flee all the way to Canada. But by 1858, Brown had bigger designs in mind. He had written a "Provisional Constitution" that was intended to "amend and repeal" the United States Constitution and proclaim a new, more just republic. The constitution's preamble declared slavery to be "none other than a most barbarous, unprovoked, and unjustifiable war of one portion of its citizens upon another portion."[7] Brown had also concluded that rescuing slaves and then fleeing to the safety of the North was no longer enough. Instead, he would invade and occupy federal property within the South itself.

Brown's strategy was simple and implausible. He and his twenty-one men, five of them Black, would seize the Harpers Ferry armory complex and distribute its thousands of weapons to locally enslaved people, who, upon hearing of the raid, would flock to join them. Brown would then lead a mass insurrection. He imagined hundreds, then thousands of escaping slaves taking up the stolen weapons, retreating into the hills of Virginia and then Pennsylvania, and waging guerrilla warfare against any resistance. He began amassing the weapons necessary for the raid at a farmhouse outside Harpers Ferry. Initially, he found support for his plan within both the Black and white abolitionist communities. Black entrepreneur Mary Ellen Pleasant and the "Secret Six," including Thomas Wentworth Higginson and Gerrit Smith, provided funding. Brown was not just raising money. There is some evidence that both Pleasant and Harriet Tubman herself had begun recruiting locally enslaved people to wait for Brown's signal and join the raid.[8]

Earlier on the night of October 16, while Lewis Washington still slept, Brown and his men had easily overpowered the armory's few guards, then waited for word to spread and insurgent slaves to join them—waited, in one of Brown's favorite phrases, for the "bees to swarm." They did not. It is not hard to imagine why. Brown, possibly out of fear that his plans had been betrayed, had started the raid eight days ahead of schedule. Any potential insurrectionists who had been alerted by Tubman or Pleasant were not ready. Those who heard about Brown's actions only as they happened had even less reason to "swarm." Why should they trust a wild-eyed white man whose plan, even if they had had time to prepare, sounded deranged? "They would have been perfect fools had they demonstrated any willingness to join him," Black preacher J. Stella Martin later declared. "They have learned this much from the treachery of white men at the North, and the cruelty of white men at the South, that they cannot trust the white man, even when he comes to deliver them." In fact, several Black Americans who knew the situation best, including Frederick Douglass and Henry Highland Garnet, had already concluded that Brown's tactics would not work. When Douglass, months earlier, tried to persuade Brown that his plan was doomed, Brown stopped listening.[9] Even if some of the best minds and bravest hearts of the Black community were against it, Brown was going to try it anyway. Which is how he found himself, by the afternoon of October 17, with a dwindling number of men guarding forty hostages in a federal armory with every escape route closed off.

But as far as the residents of Harpers Ferry knew, there were hundreds of insurgents inside the armory and thousands more crawling the hills outside. The first news of the raid, frantically telegraphed by a train conductor trying to pass through to Maryland at 7:05 a.m., read: "Express train bound east, under my charge, was stopped this morning at Harper's Ferry by armed abolitionists. They say they have come to free the slaves and intend to do it at all hazards." "It has been suggested," the telegraph continued, that "you had better notify the Secretary of War at once." This incredible news was received by W. P. Smith, the master of transportation at Baltimore. Smith replied: "Your dispatch is evidently exaggerated and written under excitement. Why should our trains be stopped by Abolitionists, and how do you know they are such and that they numbered one hundred or more?" "My dispatch was not exaggerated," the conductor retorted. "I have not made it half as bad as it is."[10]

As dawn broke, the news began to spread. Panic spread too. Harrowing headlines quickly transfixed the nation. One described a

"Negro outbreak in Virginia" involving "750 fully armed men"; another described a "gang of 150 whites" in full revolt. Yet others reported an "extensive Negro conspiracy" and a "general stampede of slaves."[11] Again Americans faced the question: Had the war begun?

Harpers Ferry civilians gathered what weapons they had and tried to dislodge Brown. When several were shot in the attempt, it became clear that Brown was serious. The casualties on both sides mounted. Brown's son Oliver was shot and died quickly; his son Watson was soon dying a slow, ghastly death from a stomach wound. Dangerfield Newby, a formerly enslaved man who had joined Brown's band in hopes of freeing his wife and children before they were sold South, was shot in the street. His body was mutilated by enraged onlookers. "I want you to buy me as soon as possible for if you do not get me some body else will," his wife had written him short months before. "Their has ben one bright hope to cheer me in all my troubles that is to be with you," she continued. After her husband's death, she and their children were sold into Louisiana.[12]

As the situation at the armory intensified, the hostages, Washington included, were moved to the nearby enginehouse. There they awaited their fate. The situation was unprecedented in American history, and there were no military commanders in the vicinity prepared to handle an insurgency. A call for help went out to Washington, DC. The man who answered the call was a fifty-two-year-old colonel named Robert E. Lee.[13]

Lee arrived and took charge of an ill-prepared group of marines who had been stationed nearby. He gave Brown a final opportunity to surrender. Brown refused. Lee's men, using a ladder as a battering ram, crushed the engine-house door and rushed in. In the resulting melee, several of the raiders were killed, but Brown himself—miraculously—was captured alive. So were four of his men, including Shields Green, who had been born into slavery, and John Anthony Copeland, a free-born Black man whose experience rescuing fugitive slaves in Ohio had made him one of Brown's most valuable fighters.[14]

Fig. 41. Dangerfield Newby, one of five Black men who participated in John Brown's raid on Harpers Ferry in October 1859. Courtesy of the West Virginia Archives and History.

Brown's raid had failed, just as Douglass had predicted. But his failure was so spectacular and his behavior thereafter so extraordinary that he changed the terms of the debate forever. He had once stormed out of a Boston antislavery meeting muttering "Talk! talk! talk!—that will never set the slave free."[15] Now words were all he had, and he would use them to wage a new kind of war.

"How do you justify your acts?" demanded Senator James Mason of Virginia, who had rushed to Harpers Ferry as soon as

Fig. 42. Robert E. Lee leading US Marines in storming the enginehouse where Brown and his men made their last stand. Courtesy of the Library of Congress.

he heard the news. "I think, my friend, you are guilty of a great wrong against God and humanity," replied Brown, who, having been moved to a nearby office, lay still bleeding on the floor. "I say that without wishing to be offensive," added the man who hours before had tried to start an insurrection. He paused. "I think I did right, and that others will do right who interfere with you at any time, and all times. I hold that the golden rule, do unto others as you would that others should do unto you, applies to all who would help others to gain their liberty." Then he issued a warning. "You had better—all you people at the South—prepare yourselves for a settlement of that question that must come up. You may dispose of me very easily; I am nearly disposed of now; but this question is still to be settled—this Negro question I mean—the end of that is not yet."[16]

Lewis Washington got back both his enslaved men and his great-granduncle's weapons. Robert E. Lee returned to Washington, DC, downplaying the raid as the folly of a small-minded fanatic. But efforts to resume life as usual were made difficult when Brown's stockpile of weapons, including "rifles, revolvers, bayonets, swords, and ammunition," was found, along with "tents, blankets, axes, knives, boxes of clothing, and almost a thousand pikes." Brown had also left behind copies of his provisional constitution and maps identifying vulnerable communities deeper in the South. In short, as Lee himself put it, Brown and his men had gathered "all the necessaries for a campaign."[17]

It looked, in other words, like preparation for civil war. Henry Wise, governor of Virginia, made sure his fellow Southerners understood it as such. For weeks after the attack, he gave speeches from Harpers Ferry to Richmond, warning of things to come. He had Brown's treasonous documents transcribed into newspapers. His was a call to arms to Southerners everywhere, warning them of a larger Northern conspiracy to rob the South of its freedom and its way of life. "My fellow citizens," he urged them, "you must not imagine that this invasion was so insignificant, or that Commander Brown was mad because his force was so small." He also petitioned President Buchanan to have several men named in Brown's papers arrested, including Frederick Douglass.[18]

Meanwhile, plans were quickly made to try Brown and his four surviving men. Charges had to be brought, lawyers engaged, juries assembled. Since the raid had taken place in Virginia but concerned federal property, questions of jurisdiction were complicated. That Copeland and Green were Black added another layer of complexity. Brown and the other white men could be accused of treason, but as the *Dred Scott* decision had made clear, Black men were not citizens. Could a noncitizen commit treason? Apparently not. The Black men were charged only with murder and inciting a slave rebellion.[19] In a way, it didn't matter. The penalty was still death.

Governor Wise was also deluged with letters, some demanding that Brown be immediately shot, others pleading for his pardon. Still others, coming from medical schools, began bargaining for use of the Black men's bodies after their hangings.[20] In the midst of everything, Wise took the time to read a letter that arrived from Wayland, Massachusetts. "Governor Wise," the letter read: "Enclosed is a letter to Capt. John Brown. Will you have the kindness, after reading it yourself, to transmit it to the prisoner?" Perhaps the governor scanned the letter to see who would be making such a request. At the bottom of the paper, he would have found the answer in careful, clear writing. The letter was signed "Yours respectfully, L. Maria Child."

Did he recognize her name? Given that she had been notorious in proslavery circles for almost thirty years, he might well have. Even if not, the rest of the letter's contents provided plenty of evidence of the kind of interlocutor he was dealing with. "I have been for years an uncompromising abolitionist," Child wrote to Wise. But "believing in peace principles, I deeply regret the step the old veteran has taken." Even if she rejected Brown's means, she certainly approved of his ends. "If I believed our religion justified men in fighting for freedom, I should consider the enslaved everywhere as best entitled to that right," she wrote. But the goal of her letter was not to argue with the governor about slavery. She was writing because she wanted his permission to come to Virginia. John Brown, she continued, "needs a mother or sister to dress his wounds, and speak soothingly to him. Will you allow me to perform that mission of humanity?"[21] Her father's health had prevented her from nursing Charles Sumner. But now she was free, and she wanted to nurse John Brown.

A known abolitionist visiting a state newly and justifiably paranoid about agitators in its midst? And on a mission to "speak soothingly" to a man who had just terrorized the Virginia countryside? It was an audacious request. Governor Wise scanned the letter to Brown that Child had included. Child repeated to Brown that she did not endorse his methods. "But I honor your generous intentions—I admire your courage, moral and physical. I reverence you for the humanity which tempered your zeal," she wrote. "In brief," Child assured the prisoner, "I love you and bless you." Would Brown, she asked, allow her to come and care for him as he awaited trial?[22]

Governor Wise must have shaken his head in amazement. No doubt he had always believed the worst of abolitionists, but to see

Fig. 43. Virginia governor Henry A. Wise. Courtesy of the Library of Congress.

this evidence of their sympathy for Brown must have felt outra-
geous in a whole new way. To his credit, he nevertheless arranged
for the letter to reach Brown. He also took the time to respond to
Child's request himself. Of course she could come to visit Brown, he
wrote in reply. "Why," he somewhat disingenuously asked, "should
you not be so allowed, Madam?" Massachusetts and Virginia were
not at war, he reminded her, and the Constitution permitted any
United States citizen to enter Virginia. If she were concerned for

her safety in a state where hostility toward abolitionists was admittedly running high, he would, he gallantly offered, personally ensure her safety. Yes, he would do this even if she were coming to minister "to one who whetted knives of butchery for our mothers, sisters, daughters and babes."

He took time to lecture her a little, too. Virginians, he reported, found abolitionists' surprise at Brown's actions absurd. "His attempt was a natural consequence of your sympathy," Wise wrote, "and the errors of that sympathy ought to make you doubt its virtue from the effect on his conduct. But it is not," the governor magnanimously concluded, "of this I should speak."[23]

Satisfied that he had put this misguided fanatic in her place, Wise prepared to mail the letter to the return address in Wayland. Then he apparently had another thought. He made copies of Child's letter, together with his own reply. Then he sent them to the press.

*　*　*

In Wayland, Child had packed her bags and was awaiting Brown's summons. "My thoughts are so much with Capt. John Brown, that I can scarcely take comfort in anything," she wrote to Garrison. "I would expend all I have, to save his life. Brave old man! Brave and generous, though sadly mistaken in his mode of operation." "Night and day, I think of scarcely anything else but Capt. Brown, and of those who may possibly become implicated with him, by misconstruction of letters, or otherwise," she wrote to Sarah Shaw. "No use to try to write about anything else. I can't do it."[24]

Meanwhile, Brown's hasty trial was nearing its conclusion. On October 31, he was found guilty of treason, conspiracy, and murder.[25] Two days later, he was sentenced to death by hanging. When asked if he had anything to say, Brown found that he did. His words seared themselves into history:

Had I so interfered in behalf of the rich, the powerful, the intelligent, the so-called great, or in behalf of any of their friends[,] . . .

every man in this court would have deemed it an act worthy of reward rather than punishment. . . . I believe that to have interfered as I have done, as I have always freely admitted I have done, in behalf of His despised poor, was no wrong but right.

Brown's justification for his violence was, in his terms, something Child had always deeply admired: it was consistent. If violence was sometimes justified in fighting oppression, the case of enslaved humans in the South was a perfect example of a justified case. And if fighting for one's own liberation was, in such cases, noble, how much *more* noble was fighting for the liberation of others? Brown was living Christian truth as he understood it, combining God's promise to avenge injustice with Jesus's admonition to suffer for the downtrodden. "Now," Brown continued, "if it is deemed necessary that I should forfeit my life for the furtherance of the ends of justice, and mingle my blood further with the blood of my children and with the blood of millions in this slave country, whose rights are disregarded by wicked, cruel and unjust enactments, I submit. So let it be done!"[26]

After his sentencing, Brown returned to his cell and continued his war of words. As his execution approached, he wrote dozens of letters to admirers and critics alike.[27] One of his first letters, dated November 4, was to Child.

"My Dear Friend—Such you prove to be, though a stranger—your most kind letter has reached me, with the kind offer to come here and take care of me," he wrote. But, he assured her, he was much recovered from his wounds and being well cared for by his jailer. "Allow me to name to you another channel through which you may reach me with your sympathies much more effectually," he suggested. Then he listed his surviving family members: his wife, his small daughters, his dead sons' wives, the other sons who survived but had lost everything fighting in Kansas. "Now, dear friend, would you not as soon contribute fifty cents now, and a like sum yearly, for the relief of those very poor and deeply afflicted persons?" She could, and more; before long, Child was raising money for Brown's family while remembering, as many did not, that the Black members of Brown's vanquished band also needed financial support.[28]

During these days, Child received Governor Wise's response. That was surprising enough. Probably Child was vexed by its supercilious tone and high-minded scolding, but what did it matter? Wise had guaranteed her safe travel if Brown wanted her to come, but it seemed that he did not. The incident could have ended there. Instead, the surprises continued. On November 12, Child was astonished to find both her letter and Wise's response "blazoned" in the *New York Tribune*.[29]

Now I imagine Child in a perfect rage. Her letter had been addressed to Wise, intended to be "a private affair."[30] The governor had published it without her permission. Her candid, personal letter was now open to public scrutiny. Worse, it was paired with a response that dripped with the kind of chivalrous condescension that she hated and indulged in the kind of rationalizing she despised. If Governor Wise had intended to infuriate Maria Child, he could not have found a better way to do it.

But I don't imagine her enraged for long. Instead, I imagine her quickly realizing that Governor Wise had given her the gift of a "very large audience." She would, she swiftly resolved, seize the opportunity "to impress some powerful facts on their minds." He had access to the press, but so did she. If John Brown was waging a war of words, Maria Child could help fire the next round. "The fact is, I want to shoot the accursed institution from all quarters of the globe," she wrote to Maria Chapman. "I think, from this time till I die, I shall stop firing only long enough to load my guns."[31] On November 19, an article appeared in the *New York Daily Tribune* titled "Lydia Maria Child's Reply to Gov. Wise."

It was civil of him, Child's letter to the governor began, to remind her of her constitutional right to visit Virginia. So much for pleasantries. "I was also aware of what you omit to mention, viz.: that the Constitution has, in reality, been completely and systematically nullified whenever it suited the convenience or the policy of the Slave Power," she wrote. If Wise was not clear as to what those crimes against the Constitution were, she was happy to remind him. There was Southern censorship of antislavery publications. There were lynch mobs and corrupt judges. There were unpunished brutalities committed against anyone "who happened to have black, brown, or yellow complexion." There were massacres and robberies in Mexico, committed to ensure slavery's expansion. Finally, there was the fact that Wise and his fellow Southerners regularly threatened to secede from the Union. "With these, and a multitude of other examples before your eyes," Child admonished the governor, "it would seem as if the less that was said about respect for constitutional obligations at the South, the better." She could put it another way. Did Governor Wise wish to accuse John Brown of treason, robbery, and murder? Brown would have no trouble, Child concluded, finding "ample authority for such proceedings in the public declarations of Gov. Wise."

And who exactly was to blame for Brown's actions? Was it, as Wise had claimed, a "natural" consequence of abolitionist teaching? On the contrary, Child countered: Southerners had done it to themselves. They had denied Northerners the right of petitioning; they had forced them to accept the Fugitive Slave Act; they had beaten Charles Sumner on the Senate floor; they had "robbed, outraged, and murdered" in Kansas. Southern behavior had in fact been better at rousing Northern indignation against the South than Garrison's and Phillips's rhetorical skills combined. "You may believe it or not, Gov. Wise, but it is certainly the truth that, because slaveholders so recklessly sowed the wind in Kansas, they reaped a whirlwind at Harper's Ferry."

Child had one more point to make. "The people of the North had a very strong attachment to the Union," she conceded; but "you have weakened it beyond all power of restoration." Most Northerners would now "rejoice to have the Slave States fulfill their oft-repeated threat of withdrawal from the Union," she assured Wise. Finally, she quoted Shakespeare at him. "'Go, gentlemen,'" she concluded: "'Stand not upon the order of your going, But go at once!'" "Yours, with all due respect," the *Tribune*'s readers read in the letter's final words, "L. Maria Child."[32]

* * *

Margaretta Mason was not a native of the South, but by 1859 she had lived in Virginia most of her life. Three decades earlier, at the age of twenty-three, she had married her childhood sweetheart, James M. Mason. By all accounts it was a happy marriage, complete with eight children, a stately mansion, and plenty of slaves that they preferred to call servants. The Masons considered themselves kind masters. In all her years, their daughter Virginia later recounted, she never saw her parents mistreat a slave. On the contrary, they considered their duty to care for and train the humans they owned as second only to their duties to their own children. Their slaves were so few, and so many of them were too old or too young to work, Virginia Mason speculated, that in fact the family probably would have been financially better off without them.[33] Keeping these humans enslaved, she implied, was actually an act of charity on her parents' part. Their consciences, in short, were clear.

Margaretta Mason watched as her intelligent, ambitious husband was elected first to the Virginia House of Delegates, then to the US House of Representatives, and finally to the US Senate. He had helped draft the Fugitive Slave Act and pressed for its inclusion in the Compromise of 1850.[34] When news of Brown's raid reached him, he raced to the scene and, with Governor Wise, was among Brown's first interrogators. When the Senate commissioned a report on the raid, he was chosen to write it. Through his letters to her and during his visits home, his wife, then, had had a front-row seat to the raid and its aftermath. And Margaretta herself, often at home alone with their young children while her husband was in Washington, was one of the Southerners into whose hearts John Brown's raid had struck unmitigated terror.

It is no surprise, then, that Child's exchange with Wise, now public and circulating widely, would reach her and enrage her. What is more surprising is that on November 11, Margaretta Mason took up her own pen and took the war of words one step further.

"Do you read your Bible, Mrs. Child?" the letter began. "If you do, read there, 'Woe unto you, hypocrites, for, rest assured, in the day of Judgment it shall be more tolerable for those thus scathed by the awful denunciation of the Son of God, than for you.'" Margaretta Mason's reasons for thinking Child would end up in hell were obvious. "*You* would soothe with sisterly and motherly care the hoary-headed murderer of Harper's Ferry!" she seethed: "A man whose aim and intention was to incite the horrors of a servile war—to condemn women of your own race . . . to see their husbands and fathers murdered, their children butchered, the ground strewed with the brains of their babes." And Brown would have succeeded in this butchery, Mrs. Mason continued, if he had found as many sympathizers in Virginia as he seemed to have in Massachusetts.

Margaretta Mason's accusations of hypocrisy went further, and they focused on an oft-repeated accusation against the North: that poor Northerners, including Black Northerners, were worse off than slaves. "Would *you* stand by the bedside of an old negro, dying of a hopeless disease, to alleviate his sufferings as far as human aid could?" she demanded. "Did *you* ever sit up until the 'wee hours' to complete a dress for a motherless child, that she might appear on Christmas day in a new one?" "Do *you* soften the pangs of maternity in those around you by all the care and comfort you can give?" The answer, Mrs. Mason was sure, was no. "*We* do these and more for our servants, and why?" she raged. "Because we endeavor *to do our duty in that state of life it has pleased God to place us.*"

If Governor Wise was willing to guarantee Child safe passage to Virginia, Mrs. Mason was not. "Keep away from Charleston," she warned, then added what was perhaps the most damning insult she could muster. No one who deserved "the name of woman," North or South, should dare to "read a line of your composition, or to touch a magazine which bears your name in its lists of contributors."[35]

Maria Child, several of her contemporaries reported, had striking eyes. They sparkled; they danced; they blazed. What did they do as she read Mrs. Mason's words, challenging her honor as a Christian, a Northerner, and a woman? Did they widen? Did they narrow? Did they flash? This we will never know. But we do know that soon after Margaretta Mason's letter reached the Childs' home in Wayland, it was also broadcast to thousands of readers in Virginia newspapers.[36]

* * *

On December 2, John Brown was taken from his prison cell and guided into a wagon. In the wagon was his coffin, on which he was instructed to sit. The bulky vehicle lurched forward. The weather was unusually warm. "This is a beautiful country," Brown said as the wagon traversed the rolling Virginia hills. "I have not cast my eyes over it before."[37] Brown and his jailers soon arrived at a carefully constructed and massively guarded scaffold. Robert E. Lee, Governor Wise, and Senator Mason stood in attendance. So, as it happened, did a young actor named John Wilkes Booth who, five years and a civil war later, would murder his president.

Brown was helped from the wagon and mounted the scaffold. He extended his bound arms to his executioners in an awkward handshake. They put the hood over his head and the noose around his neck. For a few moments there was silence. Then the trapdoor opened under his feet, and John Brown passed from notoriety into martyrdom.

Two weeks later, his Black co-conspirators were hanged as well. "This morning, for the last time, I beheld the glorious sun of yesterday rising in the far-off East," John Anthony Copeland wrote to his parents, "and now as he rises higher and high bright light takes the place of soft moonlight, I will take my pen, for the last time, to [w]rite to you." As officers took him from his cell hours later, he said: "If I am dying for freedom, I could not die for a better cause. I had rather die than be a slave."[38] His words, unlike Brown's, were quickly forgotten as, following his death, he passed from notoriety into obscurity.

Brown's death was marked in Boston by a massive commemoration at Tremont Temple. Although some white abolitionists continued to mix praise for Brown's aims with disapproval of his actions, Garrison and his allies had quickly seen the potential

Fig. 44. John Anthony Copeland, one of the Black men who fought with John Brown, was hanged on December 16, 1859. Courtesy of the West Virginia Archives and History.

Brown's execution had for the movement and were determined to make the most of it. For weeks, the *Liberator* had been extolling Brown's courage and conviction. Prominent Bostonians like Emerson joined in, calling Brown "the new saint" who would make "the gallows glorious like the cross." While many continued to call Brown a traitor or question his sanity, such praise suggested that the tide of sympathy continued to turn toward abolitionism. Four thousand spectators were expected at the Tremont Temple meeting to hear a full roster of abolitionist orators: people who, until very recently, had been considered public enemies.[39]

Child arrived early from Wayland to help Garrison with preparations for the evening's memorial. But she spent the day of Brown's execution with Black Bostonians at a South Boston meetinghouse. "I could not have elsewhere found a scene so congenial to my tender state of mind," she recalled. "*There* was no doubt of his sanity, no division of opinion concerning the reverence and gratitude due to his memory. He was the friend of their persecuted race, and he had proved it by dying for them." The day was filled with hymn singing and fervent prayer, the intensity of which Child found unsettling even as she recognized the "force of earnest feelings" behind it. "One old man, who informed the Lord that he 'had been a slave, and knew how *bitter* it was,'" she wrote, prayed with great fervor: "'And since it pleases Thee to take away our Moses, Oh Lord God! raise us up a Joshua!' to which was responded 'Amen.'"[40]

* * *

The next day, with the singing and praying still ringing in her ears, Child boarded the Fitchburg train back to Stony Brook, and then the stagecoach to Wayland. I imagine her looking out the window as miles of snowy fields rolled by. Perhaps others in the coach shared their reactions to Brown's execution; perhaps she engaged with them, perhaps she didn't. Perhaps as the distance shortened between her and her small Wayland home, Child's mind shifted away from imagining Brown's last moments and toward the letter she had not yet answered when she left for Boston to mark his death. She turned Mrs. Mason's denunciations over in her mind. Mason had accused her of supporting murder in the South and of committing hypocrisy at home. She had broadcast these accusations to a national audience. Perhaps the words still stung; perhaps the anger burned brighter. But Child soon realized that Mrs. Mason's insults had given her, once again, something to offer the antislavery movement. The combination of letters from Governor Wise and Mrs. Mason, she later wrote to a friend, had granted her "a grand chance to do mischief." At some point in the days after Brown's death, she resolved to "do it with all diligence."[41]

What resulted was an eleven-page response to Mrs. Mason that distilled Child's twenty-five years of fighting against slavery into one sustained, scathing argument. There was the incredulity that men calling themselves Christians would rape their female slaves and enslave the children born as a result. There was the mockery of a legal system that allowed only whites to testify and sanctioned "moderate punishments" from which slaves died. As evidence of the brutality inevitably resulting from one human's holding absolute power over another, Child simply quoted an enslaver advertising a fugitive slave: "Runaway, a negro woman and her two children. A few days before she went off, I burned her with a hot iron on the left side of her face. I tried to make the letter M." Child left her readers, including Mrs. Mason, to imagine the smell of burning flesh and the desperate physical struggle that had made tracing out a simple letter so difficult.

What other key antislavery points, Child wondered, could she use Mrs. Mason's letter to communicate to her readers? There was the question of whether the Bible condoned slavery. This was easy: if Mrs. Mason could quote her Bible, so too could abolitionists. Child went on to cite no fewer than eighteen biblical passages condemning enslavement. Next there was the question of free speech. Northern newspapers regularly published arguments in favor of slavery, Child wrote, while Southern newspapers suppressed those against it. Their own correspondence, Child predicted, would be a case in point: "Your letter to me is published in Northern papers, as well as Southern; but my reply will not be allowed to appear in any Southern paper," she wrote. This was not only contrary to the American commitment to free speech, it also betrayed a weakness: "The despotic measures you take to silence investigation, and shut out the light from your own white population, prove how little reliance you have on the strength of your cause."

Despite lofty questions of biblical interpretation and free speech, however, Child had not forgotten that Mrs. Mason's attack had also been more targeted. "To the personal questions you ask me," Child wrote in the letter's concluding paragraphs, "I will reply in the name of all the women of New England. It would be extremely difficult," she continued, "to find any woman in our villages who does *not* sew for the poor, and watch with the sick, whenever occasion requires." As for Christmas dresses: "We pay our domestics generous wages, with which they can purchase as many Christmas gowns as they please; a process far better for their characters, as well as our own, than to receive their clothing as a charity, after being deprived of just payment for their labor." There was one more point Child wanted to make. "I have never known an instance where the 'pangs of maternity' did not meet with requisite assistance," she assured Mrs. Mason. But there was a difference: "here at the North," she wrote, "after we have helped the mothers, *we do not sell the babies.*"[42]

Sixteen days after Brown's execution, Child wrote to Horace Greeley, publisher of the *New York Tribune*. "I send you a letter from Mrs. Mason, first sent to me, and soon after published in the Virginia papers; also my reply to it," she wrote. "I want you to publish them both together if you can." Indeed he could. Soon thereafter, "Letter of Mrs. Mason" and "Reply of Mrs. Child" appeared together in the *Tribune*. They were quickly copied in newspapers throughout the free states and "blazoned by all manner of anathema in the Southern papers." The *Liberator* reprinted the letters together with Child's correspondence with both Brown and Wise. The American Anti-Slavery Society then issued the entire set as a twenty-eight-page tract. It cost five cents; before long, an astonishing 300,000 copies were in circulation. Child personally sent Mrs. Mason a copy.[43] As far as we know, there was no reply.

The pamphlet, now known as *Correspondence between Lydia Maria Child and Gov. Wise and Mrs. Mason*, had begun as a personal response to another body's pain. It had grown into a searing cry of rage and sorrow, laced with wit and underpinned with sarcasm. In its combination of heartbroken indignation, mournful desperation, fury, and pride, it found an immediate echo.

Child returned to Wayland from another trip to Boston to find an avalanche of letters. They arrived from Maine and New Orleans, from Minnesota and Rhode Island, from friends and strangers alike. "Thanks thanks for your letter to Captain Brown," Emerson quickly wrote. "I bless you for that letter it is so perfect—so wise, so true, so eloquent, so full of life & spirit—so moving & yet so calm," gushed Eliza Follen. "It is not often that I read anything on the extreme abolition side of the slavery question with such hearty unmixed satisfaction and sympathy," wrote William Armstrong from New York. "Hundreds of thousands will read your letter with the same appreciation, though but few may think to tell you so," he added. A Hindu man wrote to Child with similar thanks, delighting her by writing his and her names together in Sanskrit. Garrison was ecstatic: Child, he exulted, had "pulverized" Wise and "used up" Mrs. Mason. A copy of the letters in every home, he thought, would abolish slavery "by the majesty of moral power without the aid of invasion or insurrection." The adulation did not come only by mail: when attendees at a Republican Party meeting heard that Child was staying in the area, they insisted on visiting her to get a look at the woman who "fired hot shot at Gov. Wise."[44]

There was hate mail too. "You can hardly conceive of the violence and obscenity of those I receive from Virginia," Child marveled to Chapman. "I did not suppose that even slavery could produce anything so foul." But mostly there was resounding sympathy and gratitude. Bryant Bartlett, identifying himself as "the representative of a million humble American freemen," wrote: "Mrs. Child, from the depths of a grateful heart, I thank you. And more, I reverence you, for your most noble, patriotic, Christian, and yet womanly reply to Mrs. Mason's characteristic letter, with a depth of feeling, and grateful warmth of heart that my humble pen can but feebly express." "We know, by your communication to the Governor of Virginia, that your heart throbs in unison with ours," a Black man wrote from Ohio. "When it is convenient, will you send us your likeness? We desire it to occupy a place in our best room, with Capt. John Brown, whose likeness we already have."[45]

More than one person saw in Child's correspondence the successor to her *Appeal*. "Your first book awakened many a soul that had never thought on the subject before—& this letter is doing the same work," wrote one. Child's earlier writings had "stirred my heart, and aroused my thought; and made me, as you have thousands of others, your debtor," wrote another, concluding simply: "I am happy . . . to thank you, as I do most heartily, for what you have done for me." "Every body I have seen praises to the skies your letter to Mrs. Mason," reported Lucy Osgood.[46] The line about not selling the babies, she added, was an especially good hit.

The letters continued to pour in. Child was "almost crazed" trying to answer them. But they presented a priceless opportunity to encourage allies and fight adversaries, so she replied to them all as fast as she could. "You would clap your delicate little hands, if you heard my curt reply to an old fogy, who implored me to remember the 'sacredness of our Constitutional obligations,'" she wrote Chapman: "Any pro-slavery hand that touches me receives a torpedo shock." "Before this affair," the fifty-seven-year-old author wrote to one friend after another, "I thought I was getting old and drowsy; but now I am strong as an eagle."[47]

Before this incident began to fade in her readers' minds, there was one more charge Child wanted to make. But it was not a charge against Governor Wise or Mrs. Mason. It was a charge against her sympathetic readers, and against herself. So in the midst of all the praise and grateful enthusiasm, she stopped to write a column for the *Liberator*. It was far too easy, she wrote, to claim to support Brown's mission while disapproving of his violence. Instead, she admonished, "it would be more profitable for us to inquire of ourselves whether we, who believe in a 'more excellent way,' have carried our convictions into practice, as faithfully as he did *his*."

And what, again, were those convictions? "*We* believe in *moral influence* as a cure in the diseases of society," Child reminded her fellow Garrisonians. "Have we exerted it as constantly and as strenuously as we ought against the giant wrong? . . . Do we bear our testimony against it in the parlor and the store, the caucus and the conference, on the highway and in the cars? . . . Do we withhold respect from ministers, who are silent concerning the mighty iniquity? Do we brand with ignominy the statesmen, who make compromises with the foul sin, for their own emolument?" The answer all too often was no. Child then laid responsibility for Brown's violence, and more possible violence to come, at her readers' feet.

"And because *we* have thus failed to perform our duty in the 'more excellent way,'" she predicted, "the end cometh by violence; because come it *must*."[48]

If John Brown could die for his principles, misguided though we might find his violent means, the least others could do is fight to change hearts and minds in every way possible. How hard is that? As many of us know all too well, it is harder than it should be. And then when violence comes, Child thought, we are among the guilty.

* * *

The feverish energy inspired by Brown's raid drove Maria Child through all of 1860. It seemed a space for change was opening, especially in Virginia, where the price of slaves had fallen as a consequence of widespread doubts about slavery's future. Child was determined to fill this space. She first published a tract on the safety of immediate emancipation titled *The Right Way, the Safe Way*.[49] She followed it with another tract called *The Patriarchal Institution, as Declared by Members of Its Own Family*. Here she compiled more evidence of slavery's evil from the South itself, then framed it with cutting irony. Sadistic punishments inflicted by slave owners appeared under the heading "Southern Proofs of the 'High-Minded Character' Produced by Slavery." Accounts of desperate escape attempts appeared in a section titled "Southern Proofs That Slaves Are 'Happy and Contented.'"[50]

Child then collected the addresses of hundreds of slaveholders in Virginia and began sending her tracts to every one of them. Most, she assumed, would be thrown away, but perhaps a few would find open minds. Occasionally she received hopeful feedback: "There is a great work going on, and your Tract exactly meets the wants of the time," one reader wrote. "Emancipation will take place in Virginia sooner than anybody *out of* the State supposes. Pray send in your Tracts." She did not need to be asked twice. Letters raced between her and her publisher as she demanded more copies faster than he could print them. Back and forth to the Wayland post office she went. Soon she had sent more than a thousand packages. It was both a financial and a moral investment. "I get a few encouraging responses," she wrote to Lucretia Mott, "and I cherish the hope that much of the seed, which now seems to fall on barren soil, will produce fruit in the future."[51]

Also in 1860, Child wrote a forty-page tract titled *The Duty of Disobedience to the Fugitive Slave Act*. By one description, it was ten years too late: the law in question had now been on the books since 1850, and untold numbers of fugitives had already been returned by Massachusetts officials to their enslavers in the South. But when the law had first been passed, Child had been too mired in depression and helplessness to respond. It was time to make up for that now. She chose a specific target: new legislators. It was an audacious choice. How could she persuade men who had just sworn to uphold the law that they must break it? Child assembled her usual barrage of religious, legal, and personal arguments. She also fashioned a dark narrative and placed her legislators at its center. "Suppose your father was Governor of Carolina and your mother was a slave," she began. Imagine, she suggested, that your mother is sold because your father's wife hates her. Imagine that you are whipped as a boy for trying to read, and then whipped as a young man for trying to protect the woman you love from being raped by your master, who is also your father. Imagine that you somehow save money to buy your own freedom, only to have your new master—who is also your half-brother—steal it in order to buy your wife and make her his concubine.

Imagine all this, she urged, then imagine that, hearing your enslavers swear their particular hatred for Massachusetts, you resolve to get there. You find your chance and escape; you hide in swamps, are bitten by snakes, chased by dogs. You arrive in Massachusetts and breathe the free air. But only briefly. "Suddenly," Child asked her legislators to imagine, "you find yourself arrested and chained. Soldiers escort you through the streets of Boston, and put you on board a Southern ship, to be sent back to your master. When you arrive, he orders you to be flogged so unmercifully, that the doctor says you will die if they strike another blow."[52]

If they had followed Child this far into her alternate reality, her readers were likely ready for her verdict. "Shame on my native State! Everlasting shame!" Child cried to her representatives. "Have we no honest pride, that we so tamely submit to this? What lethargic disease has fallen on Northern souls, that they dare not be as bold for Freedom as tyrants are for Slavery?"[53] State-sanctioned evil did more to undermine the sanctity of the law than breaking this particular law ever could, she concluded. The only way for legislators to uphold their oath of office was to refuse to return people to slavery. The duty to uphold law in general, in short, paled beside the duty to disobey the Fugitive Slave Act in particular.

Child's determination to atone for her silence when the Fugitive Slave Act was passed did not end with attempts to convict her legislators. In fall 1860, she heard that Thomas Sims, one of the fugitives who had been returned from Boston to the South, had been put up for sale by his North Carolina owner. She jumped at the chance to right the wrong her native state had done. She drafted fund-raising letters, determined "that as Massachusetts had sent him into slavery, Massachusetts should bring him back." She would write a hundred letters if necessary, she said; she would stand outside the Massachusetts State House and beg for donations all winter if she had to. In the end, it was both easier and harder than she thought. After only eighteen letters, an anonymous donor—who turned out to be the US marshal responsible for returning Sims to the South—offered to pay the entire amount. "I got it! I got it! I got it!" Child rejoiced to Sarah Shaw. But as hostilities between North and South escalated, negotiations with Sims's owner broke down. In the end, Sims would remain enslaved until the Emancipation Proclamation took effect in 1863.[54]

* * *

On November 6, 1860, Abraham Lincoln was elected president of the United States. In response, the American flag was lowered in Charleston, South Carolina, and a state flag was raised in its stead. On December 20, South Carolina voted to secede. Outgoing US president James Buchanan used his State of the Union Address, and an argument from nature, to blame abolitionists. "The long-continued and intemperate interference of the Northern people with the question of slavery in the Southern States," he lamented, "has at length produced its natural effects."[55] If abolitionists were to blame, they needed to be punished. Anti-abolitionist mobs in Boston resumed. Furious businessmen, politicians, and workers, all of whom saw life as they knew it threatened by attempts to end slavery, convened to vent their wrath wherever abolitionists spoke. The Childs were present for two of these mobs.[56] Apparently they had traveled from Wayland for the occasion.

The last time Maria Child had faced a mob, she had been in her thirties. Now she was almost sixty. What did it feel like to put her older body—a little stiffer, a little stouter, her hair white and her foot rheumatic—into the fray? David was closer to seventy and in much worse health. But there was no question of either of them staying home, much as Child would have preferred it. "I would rather have given $50 than attend," she wrote to Sarah Shaw. "But conscience told me it was a duty."[57]

Some of the details were depressingly familiar from thirty years ago. There was the sleepless night as she imagined what would happen the next day and the secretive gatherings to plan escape routes before the speeches began. There were the moments when people she admired and cherished—in this case, Wendell Phillips and Frederick Douglass—rose and tried to speak. Then there were the "gentlemen of property and standing" combined with "street roughs" who rushed into the meeting hall "yelling, screeching, stamping, and bellowing." There was, again, an anti-abolitionist mayor who told the abolitionists to leave rather than using his police to protect them. There was the moment when she and Maria Chapman, united again, surrounded Wendell Phillips to lead him to safety. And there were the Black Bostonians beaten and trampled as they tried to bear witness to the wrongs of slavery. Many of them also fought back. When one mob rushed Frederick Douglass and attempted to drag him from the stage, he fought them off, one newspaper reported, like a "trained pugilist."[58]

"My heart beat so, that I could hear it," Child wrote to Sarah

Fig. 45. An anti-abolitionist mob in Boston in 1860. Courtesy of the Library of Congress.

Shaw of her emotions during one of the riots. One eyewitness, however, observed no such fear. In the midst of all the chaos, a man named E. Hayward had identified the diminutive abolitionist. "Mrs Child," he reported to a friend, "was 'tumbled up and down' somewhat" in the melee. But, he continued, she "left the field a victor" in not one way but two. She "illustrat[ed] her Bunker Hill by collaring a burly rioter," he testified, and then proceeded to demonstrate "her Non-resistance by preaching a broad cloth-Plugugly into immediate repentance."[59]

It is a record as fanciful as it is telling. Nowhere else do we find descriptions of Child laying hands on anyone, much less "collaring" someone in the midst of a mob. It is also difficult to imagine even this champion arguer converting a rioter to antislavery as people broke chairs over each other's heads and bricks smashed windows around her. But I do not doubt that there is a grain of truth in Hayward's testimony. His description pays tribute to both the physical courage and the intellectual brilliance for which Child, by now, was famous. It was a combination that allowed her to keep firing, now and for the rest of her life, in every way she knew how.

*　*　*

Meanwhile, desperate attempts continued to compromise with South Carolina and prevent other states from seceding. A Thirteenth Amendment to the Constitution was proposed guaranteeing that the federal government would never interfere with slavery again. Rumors that proslavery Northerners were plotting a coup to remove Lincoln and replace him with someone more acceptable to the South abounded. By February 8, seven states had seceded and approved a provisional constitution declaring themselves the Confederate States of America. The contrast with John Brown's provisional constitution could not have been starker. Confederate Vice President Alexander Stephens proclaimed that the new government of the South "rests upon the great truth, that the negro is not equal to the white man; that slavery—subordination to the superior race—is his natural and normal condition." The fact that the South had "thrown off an old government and formed a new" marked the beginning of "one of the greatest revolutions in the annals of the world," he declared. Not only that, this revolution was "signally marked, up to this time, by the fact of its having been accomplished without a single drop of blood."[60]

11

On Delicate Ears and Indelicate Truths

But before the war: a story, and a story about a story.

In 1853, Harriet Jacobs was a forty-year-old Black woman living in Cornwall, New York, in a fourteen-room mansion overlooking the Hudson River. She worked as a housekeeper and nurse for the family of Nathaniel Parker Willis. Willis was the former friend of Child's, the beheader of lilacs, who had denounced *The Frugal Housewife* for its humble hints. His youthful ambitions had been realized: he was now an extremely wealthy magazine writer. Jacobs had worked for Willis since before the death of his first wife, caring for his motherless daughter as Willis grieved. Willis now had a new wife, Cornelia, and the couple had two small children of their own.[1] These children were also now in Harriet Jacobs's care. They called her Hattie.

Jacobs had not always been a free woman. As she went about her daily routine of preparing for Nathaniel Willis's distinguished guests, attending to his wife, and caring for his children, she carried with her the physical and emotional scars of her enslavement. Willis and his wife knew she had been enslaved, but they did not know the full story. Neither did they know that, at night in her upstairs room in the servants' quarters, while listening for the cries of waking babies or the call of their parents, she was writing it down.

* * *

"I was born a slave," Jacobs wrote in the manuscript's first sentence, "but I never knew it till six years of happy childhood had passed away." She had been born in North Carolina in 1813. Her mother and Margaret Horniblow, her mother's mistress, were "foster sisters": they had both been nursed by Jacobs's grandmother. As children, they had played together; as adults, Jacobs's mother had served Miss Margaret faithfully. Their mutual affection had ensured that young Harriet enjoyed a childhood unimaginable to most slaves. Jacobs's father was an accomplished carpenter, owned by another family but allowed to live with his wife and children in what Jacobs recalled was a comfortable home. "I was so fondly shielded," she remembered, "that I never dreamed I was a piece of merchandise." Looking back, Jacobs recognized signs of the fragility of their situation in her father's repeated efforts, before his early death, to buy his children's freedom. He had reason to worry. Jacobs's uncles and aunts had all been sold away from her grandmother, some never to be seen again.[2]

When Jacobs was six years old, it became clear that her mother was dying. At her deathbed, Miss Margaret promised no harm would come to Harriet and her brother. Initially she kept her oath. In the years that followed, she cared for the motherless girl herself, treating her almost like a daughter. She taught her to sew and even to read and write. This was something of a risk: teaching a slave to read was illegal, punishable in North Carolina by a fine of up to $200. But after six more years, Miss Margaret also died. Now older and wiser, the eleven-year-old Jacobs knew at the funeral that her life hung in the balance. Perhaps her mistress had freed her in her will. She had, after all, promised Jacobs's mother she would care for her children, and Miss Margaret had, Jacobs remembered, shown "many proofs of attachment to me."[3]

But freeing young Harriet apparently would have been one kindness too many. Instead, Miss Margaret had given Jacobs as a gift to her niece, then three years old.[4] In effect, Jacobs had been deeded to this girl's parents. In her narrative, Jacobs calls them Dr. and Mrs. Flint.

The horrors of her new situation quickly became clear. The

Flints habitually indulged in nonviolent cruelties: forbidding slaves to visit family, depriving them of adequate nourishment and clothing, spitting in the cook's cuisine when it failed to please them. They were proficient in violent cruelty as well. Mrs. Flint, Jacobs wrote, was physically fragile, but she had nerves so strong "that she could sit in her easy chair and see a woman whipped, till the blood trickled from every stroke of the lash."[5]

And Jacobs's new master, Dr. Flint, was a sexual predator. He had already fathered eleven children among his female slaves. When one woman's husband apparently dared to protest, Flint had him strung up in the workhouse and whipped until gore stuck to the walls. He then sold him, his wife, and the baby to a slave trader. "You *promised* to treat me well," the enslaved mother pleaded to Flint as she was led away. "You have let your tongue run too far; damn you!" he replied. Such merciless brutality could lead to other kinds of viciousness as well, as white women enraged at their husbands' sexual conduct vented their fury on their husbands' victims. Jacobs once witnessed a "young slave girl" giving birth to a lighter-skinned child. Her jealous mistress stayed in the room, taunting the laboring teenager as the birth slowly killed her. The baby was already dead.[6]

Jacobs, as a budding adolescent, soon became Dr. Flint's target. The assault began on her ears. As she went about her daily tasks, carrying out her mistress's orders, he cornered her in hallways and pantries and whispered his sexual fantasies to her. Jacobs had been taught modesty and decency by her pious grandmother; now Flint assailed her with "stinging, scorching words; words that scathed ear and brain like fire." "He tried his utmost to corrupt the pure principles my grandmother had instilled," she recalled. "He peopled my young mind with unclean images, such as only a vile monster could think of."[7]

In 1858, the Georgian legal scholar Thomas Cobb discussed the embarrassing rumor that Southern masters raped their slaves. "Every well-informed person at the South . . . knows that the exercise of such power for such a purpose is almost unknown," he protested. "The prevalence of the evil is attributable to other causes.

The most prominent of these is the natural lewdness of the negro." Jacobs experienced this power dynamic differently. "I would rather drudge out my life on a cotton plantation . . . than to live with an unprincipled master and a jealous mistress," she wrote. For a beautiful young woman fully in her master's power, "it is deemed a crime in her to wish to be virtuous."[8]

Initially, Flint's assaults emboldened Jacobs: "never before had my puny arm felt half so strong," she wrote as what she called the "war of my life" began. "My master had power and law on his side; I had a determined will. There is might in each." She treated Flint's advances with contempt, turning from him with "disgust and hatred." At first, her master tolerated this treatment. Perhaps he even enjoyed it. Perhaps it made the chase all the sweeter. But he soon made it clear that the game would last only so long. He called her into his office on a pretext to suggest there was "a limit to his patience." He told her how lucky she was that he hadn't raped her. "I was made for his use," she remembered his whispering, "made to obey his command in *every* thing. . . . I was nothing but a slave, whose will must and should surrender to his." When she rejected him again, he raged, swearing "by heaven and earth that he would compel me to submit to him." He also promised to kill her if she told her grandmother. He needn't have worried. His vile words alone had made her feel complicit and ashamed, unable to turn to her grandmother for help.[9]

Flint's pursuit of her became obvious; her mistress began to hate her. Mrs. Flint extracted a detailed account of her husband's adulterous advances from her teenage slave. With Jacobs present, she then confronted her husband, revealing Jacobs as her source. When Dr. Flint denied everything, her mistress wanted her whipped for lying. Dr. Flint knew better than to permit this. Jacobs's grandmother was a beloved, respected, and well-known free Black woman whose anger in front of a watching community—both white and Black—he could not risk. "As a married man, and a professional man, he deemed it necessary to save appearances in some degree," Jacobs recalled. "How often did I rejoice that I lived in a town where all the inhabitants knew each other!" she added.

"If I had been on a remote plantation, or lost among the multitude of a crowded city," she assured her readers, "I should not be a living woman at this day."[10]

The harassment continued. When Jacobs fell in love with a free Black man in their town and asked permission to marry him, Flint hit her for the first time. "You have been the plague of my life," he shouted at her. But he promised to give her a second chance. He also promised to cowhide them both if he saw them speaking to each other and to shoot the young man in question if he caught him on his property.[11] "Poor, foolish girl!" he lamented. "You don't know what is for your own good. I would cherish you. I would make a lady of you. Now go, and think of all I have promised you."

"I did think of it," Jacobs promised her readers.[12]

⋆   ⋆   ⋆

Decades later, as a forty-year-old woman writing in stolen moments while the Willis household slept, Jacobs still struggled to articulate what happened next. How many times did she try to put the story on paper? How many times did she tear it up, resolving either to lie or to stop writing entirely? "If it was the life of a Heroine with no degradation associated with it," she wrote to a friend, leaving the sentence unfinished. But somehow she kept writing, turning at this pivotal moment to address us directly. "And now, reader, I come to a period in my unhappy life, which I would gladly forget if I could," she wrote. "The remembrance fills me with sorrow and shame. It pains me to tell you of it; but I have promised to tell you the truth, and I will do it honestly, let it cost me what it may."[13]

She returned to her narrative. At a certain point, Flint's obsession with Jacobs became common knowledge in the town. Another white man, a local lawyer she called Sands, saw an opportunity. He approached the desperate girl as she ran errands and asked about her plight. "He expressed a great deal of sympathy, and a wish to aid me," Jacobs recalled. He said he wanted to see her. He began to write her letters. Jacobs was, she remembered, flattered and grateful, "encouraged by his kind words." Sands was well respected in the town; he had money; he was not married. His attentions were different from Flint's—he was gentle, courteous, refined. He was also educated and eloquent: "too eloquent, alas, for the poor slave girl who trusted in him," Jacobs admitted. "By degrees," she remembered, "a more tender feeling crept into my heart." At some point, Sands's eloquent sympathy turned suggestive, then seductive. Jacobs began to see a choice emerging. Was it, she began to wonder, "less degrading to give one's self, than to submit to compulsion"? Was there something "akin to freedom" in such an act? These were difficult questions, but of one thing she was sure. There was something sweet in imagining Flint's rage if she took another white man as a lover.[14]

There was one more final, decisive calculation. Any children she would have by Flint would also be his slaves. They would likely be sold to avoid further enraging his wife. Children she would have by Sands would be different. As her children, they would still belong to Flint. Slavery, by law, passed through the mother. But surely, reasoned the fifteen-year-old Jacobs, their father would buy them and free them. Perhaps, if she were the mother of his children, Sands would do the same for her.[15] Before long, she was pregnant.

"Pity me, and pardon me, O virtuous reader!" Jacobs wrote in her servants' quarters, high above the Hudson, alone with her memories. "I know I did wrong. . . . No one can feel it more sensibly than I do. The painful and humiliating memory will haunt me to my dying day." To be forcibly raped would have been forgivable. But Jacobs knew that her actions looked like a choice. Choice opened her up to blame. But what choice had she really had? She hazarded a defense. "You never knew what it is to be a slave," she pleaded with the imagined reader standing over her in judgment against the midnight stars. "I feel that the slave woman ought not to be judged by the same standard as others."[16]

The birth of her first child almost killed her. Even worse, Flint's fury did not have the desired effect. To the contrary, he vowed never to sell Jacobs to anyone. His wife, by contrast, promised to kill Jacobs if she ever saw her in her house again. Disgraced, Jacobs was sent to live with her grandmother. When Flint learned she was pregnant with a second child, he meted out the traditional punishment for whores: he cut off all her hair. "When they told me my new-born babe was a girl," Jacobs reported after her second delivery, "my heart was heavier than it had ever been before. Slavery is terrible for men; but it is far more terrible for women."[17]

Flint continued his campaign of terror and flattery. In one fit of rage, he threw her down the stairs. In another, he hurled her son across the room. Then, contrite, he offered to free both her and her children if she would take him as a lover. She treated this offer with the contempt it deserved. This provoked Flint to pronounce a punishment worse than death: he sent her and her children to one of his farms to be "broke in" as plantation slaves. Days later, Jacobs jumped out a window and disappeared. With her, her brother later wrote, it had become a matter, "in the language of one of our fathers, [of] 'liberty or death.'"[18] She left her children behind.

Actually, it is more complicated than that. By abandoning her children, she saved them. In planning her escape, she had predicted that without their mother, her children would be too much trouble to care for on the plantation. This proved true. Flint put them up for sale. Their father bought them. That part of this tangled web of human psychology she had correctly foreseen. The second part of her hopes remained unfulfilled. Sands did not free them. He sent his children, still enslaved but now to him, to live with Jacobs's grandmother and await his further decision.[19] When I imagine this man, I sometimes try to imagine how he felt about himself. I fear that he was proud of himself for being so magnanimous, so progressive, so much better than Flint.

As for Jacobs, a small, ingenious network of unimaginably brave people—Black and white—cooperated to hide her. First she hid in a friend's house; then in a swamp; then in the home of a sympathetic white woman who was herself a slaveholder; and finally, in the eaves of her own grandmother's house, just blocks from Flint's residence. The risks to the white members of this multilayered conspiracy were considerable. The risks to the Black members were far worse. For a Black person in North Carolina, aiding a fugitive slave incurred a mandatory death penalty. It goes without saying that the risks for the fugitives themselves were unthinkable. Not long before Jacobs disappeared, an escaped slave from a neighboring plantation had been caught, whipped, washed with brine, and imprisoned inside a cotton gin, where he died. By the time his corpse was recovered, it had been gnawed by rats.[20]

Flint searched for Jacobs like the obsessed man he was. His surveillance made it impossible for her allies to move her to safety. So under the eaves of her grandmother's house she stayed. The space measured nine feet long, seven feet wide, and three feet high. She could not stand or move freely. Weeks stretched into months. In the summer she almost suffocated; in the winter she nearly froze. She whittled a small hole in the roof through which she could see her children playing and hear them ask when she was coming back. She became violently ill. More than once she almost lost her mind. Still it was considered too dangerous to move her. In the end, Harriet Jacobs stayed hidden in this space for six years and eleven months.[21]

It is an unbelievable story. I mean that in two ways. We describe any number of things that are amazing, extraordinary, or astonishing as unbelievable. But for some of her readers, Jacobs's story would prove unbelievable in the more literal sense. They could not, would not, believe it had happened. A lecherous master who refuses to rape? A plot to escape one white man's lust by bearing another white man's children? Seven years in an attic? Jacobs knew this was a risk. "I hardly expect that the reader will credit me, when I affirm that I lived in that little dismal hole . . . for nearly seven years," she wrote. "But it is a fact."[22]

Finally, in 1842, Jacobs's allies succeeded in transferring her from her grandmother's home onto a boat to Philadelphia. The rest of Jacobs's story—how she evaded Flint's many attempts to recapture her, was reunited with her children, and finally obtained freedom—is no less extraordinary than the beginning. It is a testament to her own astonishing bravery but also to the organized determination of the Black community to protect one of its own. But I want her to tell the rest of her story. Her narrative is called *Incidents in the Life of a Slave Girl: Written by Herself*. Every American should read it; it is one of our most important national stories. It is in stories like these that we truly learn who we are, and why.

But I will mention one more moment from Jacobs's memoir. On landing in Philadelphia, the ship's captain, himself part of her network of rescuers, introduced her to the Black minister of a local church who was the next link in the chain of people moving fugitives northward. He and his wife took Jacobs in during her first days on free soil. He asked her story, and she told him. She included the truth about her children's parentage. Her reasons for this honesty are heartbreaking. "If he was desirous of being my friend," she wrote, "he ought to know how far I was worthy of it." The minister listened without judgment, but then he gave her some painful advice. "Your straight-forward answers do you credit," he said; "but don't answer every body so openly. It might give some heartless people a pretext for treating you with contempt." "That word *contempt*," Jacob confessed, "burned me like coals of fire."[23] It would be years before she would trust anyone with her story again.

When she finally did, the person she unburdened herself to was Amy Post, a white Quaker abolitionist. The two women had met through abolitionist circles in Rochester, New York, where Jacobs was helping her brother, who had also escaped, run an abolitionist reading room. Slowly, over many meetings, Jacobs had come to confide in Post. Years of accrued shame and secrecy made confessing her story even to this trusted friend almost more than Jacobs could bear. "Even in talking with me," Post later wrote, "she wept so much, and seemed to suffer such mental agony, that I felt her story was too sacred to be drawn from her by inquisitive questions, and I left her free to tell as much, or as little, as she chose."[24] Finally, Jacobs told her everything. Jacobs's trust was not misplaced. Post heard her with sympathy and without judgment. And then, apparently not long thereafter, Post had another thought. Tell your story to others, she urged Jacobs. Tell it for the cause.

The 1850s were the beginning of a boom in the genre of the slave narrative. Frederick Douglass was already at work on his second biography, *My Bondage and My Freedom*; as many as eight other former fugitives were also working on their accounts of escaping slavery. But none of these authors were women. Female fugitives were much less common. Often slaves fled in their physical prime; for women these were also their childbearing years. Pregnancies and small children made escape that much more improbable. Douglass and others had testified to the abuse their enslaved wives, sisters, and mothers suffered. But there had never been a book-length slave narrative written by a formerly enslaved woman herself.[25] It was time, Post urged Jacobs, for that to change.

Jacobs's letters to Post make clear what she stood to lose. "I never would consent to give my past life to any one for I would not do it with out giving the whole truth," she wrote. But the whole truth involved deep sexual shame that could compromise the respectability that Jacobs knew was the condition of white Northerners' respect. This included abolitionists. Since escaping, she had "avoided the Antislavery people as much as possible because I felt that I could not be honest and tell the whole truth." But through Post's urging, she had come to feel another source of shame. If telling her story "could help save another from my fate," she began to worry, "it would be selfish and unchristian in me to keep it back." As she helped the growing Willis family move from New York City to their new mansion on the Hudson, she weighed this additional shame against her new duty. Finally, duty won out. "I have tried for the past two years to conquer it and I feel that God has helped me," she wrote to Post.[26] She was ready to tell her story. The question was how.

Thanks to Nathaniel Willis's growing eminence as a writer, his wife was extremely well connected in the literary world. Carefully, Jacobs approached Mrs. Willis for advice. She had good reason to trust the mistress of the house. Cornelia Willis had played a crucial role in Jacobs's final escape from her master after the Fugitive Slave Act put her at risk of recapture. She had even put herself and her children at some risk in the effort. Jacobs described her as a true friend, raised up to aid her when her own community no longer could. Now Cornelia Willis enthusiastically endorsed her employee's literary ambitions and offered to use her connections to help her realize them. She suggested going straight to the top:

approaching Harriet Beecher Stowe, the author of *Uncle Tom's Cabin.*[27] Perhaps Stowe would take an interest in Jacobs's story and help her write it.

Jacobs must have thrilled at the thought. Perhaps, she reasoned, she could also be of help to the acclaimed author. Critics of *Uncle Tom's Cabin* continued to accuse Stowe of exaggeration and fabrication. She was hard at work on *A Key to Uncle Tom's Cabin*, which aimed to provide "facts, reports, trials, legal documents, and testimony of people now living South, which will more than confirm every statement" in the original novel. Perhaps Jacobs could help authenticate details, proving that Stowe's imagined horrors were all too real.[28]

Then Jacobs had another idea. Stowe was about to leave for England to meet with prominent abolitionists there. Perhaps she would take Jacobs's daughter, Louisa, with her. Jacobs had managed, against terrible odds, to get Louisa an education, and she was now an attractive, accomplished young woman. She would make a "very good representative of a Southern Slave," her mother thought, and could perhaps herself "do something for the cause." Maybe spending time with Louisa would also help interest Stowe in Jacobs's story. By spring 1853, Mrs. Willis had approved of the idea and written to Stowe.[29]

Amy Post also wrote to Stowe on Jacobs's behalf, sketching the outlines of her story and vouching for her character.[30] This was painful but necessary. To expose Jacobs's sexual shame to a world-famous author was a terrible risk. But Stowe had written with great compassion about the wrongs suffered by female slaves. *Uncle Tom's Cabin* included sympathetic portraits of enslaved women who had made wrenching sexual compromises, sometimes to protect their children. Surely she would respond with the same sympathy to someone who had lived the reality she had only imagined.

Stowe was probably, at this point, the most famous woman in America. Demands on her time and philanthropy were overwhelming; perhaps that explains some of what followed. But Stowe's response is a kind of manual of what not to do as a white ally. In her response to Mrs. Willis, she said she could not take Louisa with her. This was reasonable enough—having a young companion on a transcontinental journey would not necessarily have been pleasant. But she added another reason. As a former slave, Louisa would be "pett[ed] and patrioniz[ed]" by antislavery activists in England, Stowe feared: in essence, she predicted that Louisa would be spoiled by the attention. Worse, she said she could not help Jacobs write her memoir but would be happy to use parts of it in her own work.[31] Even worse, she forwarded Post's letter, including the details about Jacobs's past, to Cornelia Willis, asking Willis to verify that Jacobs was telling the truth.

The problem was that Willis did not yet know the full truth. Out of delicacy, she had never asked about the father of Jacobs's children. Now she knew. A painful, humiliating conversation between the forty-year-old housemaid and her twenty-eight-year-old employer followed.[32] The worst-case scenario did not materialize. Willis did not blame Jacobs: to her credit, she saw past the violation of female propriety to the true violation, that of a young woman's integrity by two men with unthinkable power over her. In this Jacobs was fortunate. Other Black women employed in the North had no doubt been fired for similar revelations.

But the outrage of Stowe's indiscretion remained. And indeed, Jacobs saw Stowe's abuse of her trust for what it was. She also saw her insinuation about Louisa for the racial humiliation it was. "Think, dear Amy," she wrote to Post, that "Mrs Stowe thinks petting is more than my race can bear?" She permitted herself some bitter irony. "What a pity," she wrote, "we poor blacks can't have the firmness and stability of character that you white people have."[33]

But Stowe's disrespect crystallized something for Jacobs. Until now she had imagined telling her story to a famous author and allowing that author to shape it into literature. Now she resolved that it would be "a history of my life entirely by itself." Such a history would "do more good" than a literary treatment would, she concluded. In fact, Jacobs now realized, her story "needed no romance"—no embellishment or enhancement. Both Jacobs and Willis wrote to Stowe communicating this new plan, pleading with her not to use Jacobs's story in her own material. Stowe made one more mistake. She never wrote back.[34]

* * *

For the next five years, Jacobs struggled to write her story herself. She worked in secret. Cornelia Willis clearly now knew that Jacobs wanted to share her story, but asking a famous author to tell it and telling it herself were different things. And while Cornelia had proved herself a staunch ally in the encounter with Stowe, her husband was another matter. Jacobs knew better than to cause difficulties between them.[35]

Nathaniel Willis had by now become even more successful. His newest publication, the *Home Journal*, was a chatty, breezy periodical, full of celebrity news and aimed at readers who aspired to respectability and class. Willis had used his sizable fortune to build Idlewild, the fourteen-room mansion that Jacobs now helped manage. He envisioned it as a writers' retreat both for himself and for other authors. Perhaps, he hoped, Idlewild would produce the next great work of American literature. Every room boasted a dramatic outlook on the river and the mountains beyond it, "each view being a separate picture set in a frame of unfading foliage," as his architect put it. Guests could luxuriate over long, gossipy breakfasts, ride horses, wander down mountain paths. Willis sometimes chronicled these adventures in a series in *Home Journal* called "Letters from Idlewild." Occasionally these letters referenced "our intelligent housekeeper," even calling her our "household oracle." Did Jacobs read these letters in copies of the magazine that guests left strewn around the house? If so, did she recognize herself in Willis's descriptions?[36]

As Jacobs waited on his guests and cared for his children, Nathaniel Willis was turning some of his travel writings that had appeared in the *Home Journal* into a book. Among the adventures included was a trip to the South. On a Virginia boat, he reported, he had encountered a "bevy" of newly purchased slaves on the way to

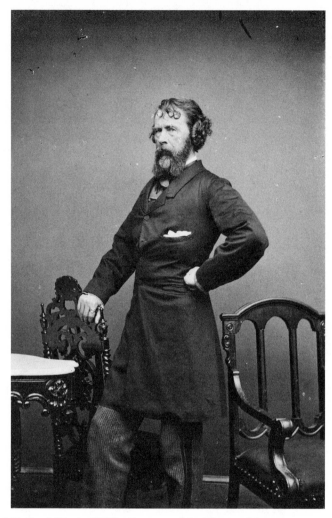

Fig. 46. Nathaniel Parker Willis. Courtesy of the Library of Congress.

Arkansas with their new master. "[A] better conditioned or more contented company of working-people I never saw," Willis declared. He studied them closely. "I looked in vain for any sulkiness, or abstraction, or other sign of brooding or hidden pain or sorrow," he reported. Whatever any one of them might be suffering, he concluded, "seemed overbalanced by the blessed consciousness that the cares of the day were no business of his." If his housekeeper Hattie happened to bring him coffee as he gazed out at the valley,

Fig. 47. Idlewild, the mansion owned by Nathaniel Parker Willis, where Harriet Jacobs served as a housekeeper and wrote the narrative of her escape from slavery. Willis's celebrity status prompted the publishers E. & H. T. Anthony to include this image in their set of stereoscopic views entitled "Beauties of the Hudson." Courtesy of the Library of Congress.

conjuring this scene of happy enslavement for the *Home Journal*'s readers, did he pause to wonder whether he should ask her for her own account of slavery? Not likely. He finished the anecdote, labeling it "Negro Happiness in Virginia." He knew his audience well: Southern papers soon declared that the *Home Journal* was one of the only Northern papers Southerners could trust.[37]

Above her employer's study at night, Jacobs wrestled with her memories of Dr. Flint's depravity and Mrs. Flint's cruelty. She concluded, no doubt correctly, that her employer would not be supportive of her project. She could not risk asking for time away to complete it. So between sewing dolls for Willis's children, cleaning up after his lavish open-estate parties, and caring for his wife through her next pregnancy, Jacobs continued writing when she could. Finally, the manuscript was complete. "I have left nothing out," she wrote to Amy Post, "but what I thought—the world might believe that a Slave Woman was too willing to pour out—that she might gain their sympathies."[38]

I want to pause for a moment with this devastating sentence. Jacobs, she tells Post, had left nothing out *except what she worried readers would object to as too explicitly an appeal for their sympa-*

thy. In other words: Jacobs knew that if readers thought she was including too much blood, or abuse, or trauma—if they felt their sympathies were being manipulated or overtaxed—they would turn away. Her narrative already included accounts of bloodcurdling torture and brutal sexual assault. What in the world, with her readers' limited sympathy in mind, had she left out? What accounts of starvation, rape, or sadism had she omitted out of fear that it would be too much?[39] Or did the self-censored passages instead describe her children's sobs as they begged to know where their mother was, or her grandmother's tears as she tried to comfort them? What details had she committed to paper and then destroyed, fearing her readers would judge her for trying to get the very least she deserved—their unmitigated sympathy?

I imagine Jacobs circulating among the Willis's guests as she served them, observing the politicians, authors, and businessmen who had come to Idlewild to enjoy great beauty and think great thoughts. I also imagine her watching their wives, knowing they could well be the readers whose response to her story could destroy her life. The project of framing herself, night after night, with their judgment in mind must sometimes have been excruciating. It's hard to believe it did not eat at her soul. But it was a project that many fugitive slaves, including Frederick Douglass, faced as white audiences insisted that fugitive slave stories strike an impossible balance: they should be true, but not too honest; bloody, but not too gory; titillating, but not indelicate.[40] And the stories should always end with gratitude to white saviors for their rescue, to white audiences for their sympathy, and to God for his deliverance. Requiring victims to tell their stories exactly to suit our tastes imposes a terrible burden on them. And it betrays a terrible selfishness in us. To the extent that we carry on this practice today, we perpetuate the cruelties at its heart.

*   *   *

With her manuscript completed, Jacobs began to look for a publisher. She approached one after another, both in England and in the United States.[41] Each one declined. Rejection is humiliating for any author; for Jacobs it must have been crushing. What were they rejecting? Her writing or her story? Which would be worse? Perhaps her fears had been all too well founded. Perhaps her story was too complicated, too raw, too indelicate for any reader's delicate ears. Perhaps she had, just as she had feared, miscalculated her appeal for sympathy and caused her readers to turn away.

Even interested publishers had conditions. One offered to take the book only if Jacobs included an endorsement from either Harriet Beecher Stowe or Nathaniel Willis. She tried Stowe again with no success; asking Willis, given his proslavery sympathies, was out of the question. She approached another publisher. This one had another stipulation. They would publish it, they said, but only if it included a preface by Lydia Maria Child.[42]

Sometime in the summer of 1860, William C. Nell, a Black author and publisher, arranged for the former fugitive and the famous abolitionist to meet at Anti-Slavery Society headquarters in Boston. These offices were just down the street from the city hall that had shielded Garrison from the mob twenty-five years before. Jacobs felt enormous trepidation at "approaching another Satellite of so great magnitude." She had been burned before. At some point Maria Child appeared, probably hot and disheveled from the laborious trip from Wayland. Perhaps she was wearing her now notoriously unfashionable bonnet. The women were a decade apart in age: Jacobs nearing fifty and Child nearing sixty. Their lives had been dramatically different in almost every way. But the meeting went beautifully. "Mrs C," Jacobs reported to Post, "is like your self a whole souled Woman." "We soon," she continued, "found the way to each others heart."[43]

* * *

"I have been busy with your M.S. ever since I saw you," Child, back in Wayland, wrote to Jacobs on August 13. "I have very little occasion to alter the language, which is wonderfully good for one whose opportunities for education have been so limited." The last phrase was clearly meant as a compliment. Did it nevertheless make Jacobs wince a little? Child continued. "The events are interesting, and well told," she assured Jacobs: "The remarks are also good, and to the purpose."[44] What a relief it must have been to read this: after years of secretive writing and publishers' rejections, she had found an enthusiastic reader who recognized both her literary talent and her story's potential.

Child's next sentences make it clear that she had not only agreed to write the preface, but had offered to edit the entire book: to shape it, mold it, improve it. "I am copying a great deal of it," she wrote to Jacobs, "for the purpose of transposing sentences and pages, so as to bring the story into continuous *order*, and the remarks into *appropriate* places. I think you will see that this renders the story much more clear and entertaining."[45]

Paragraph order, sentence structure, narrative trajectory: all of these are standard suggestions coming from an experienced editor. What is striking here is that, as regards the book's *content*—Jacobs's sexual history, her long imprisonment, her improbable escape—Child never flinched. She believed Jacobs and wanted others to do the same. This, we should remember, entailed some risk. Southerners would never let abolitionists forget that they had championed James Williams's 1838 slave narrative only to have it withdrawn after some of its details proved fictitious. John Greenleaf Whittier had helped edit the book, and his reputation had been badly damaged as a result. If Jacobs's account were less than entirely true, the same thing could happen to Child.[46] But Child seems not to have hesitated. She had quickly and fully committed herself to staking her reputation on getting Jacobs's story told.

Her concern now was to help shape Jacobs's narrative in hopes of winning the widest possible readership. She had a few ideas about how to do this. Could Jacobs, she asked, send more details about "outrages committed on the colored people" in the wake of Nat Turner's insurrection? And the last chapter, Child advised, should simply be cut. It was about John Brown. "It does not naturally come into your story," she wrote, "and the M.S. is already too long." Better to end simply with her own freedom and her grandmother's peaceful death. She then promised to send her edits to Jacobs "wherever you direct, a fortnight hence."[47]

Jacobs's response has not survived, but she clearly complied with both of Child's recommendations. In the published version of her narrative, appalling details about slaves tortured and murdered in the wake of Nat Turner's rebellion duly appear; the chapter about John Brown does not. Child's next letter to Jacobs, a month later, details the contract she had negotiated with the publisher. Things were clearly moving forward. The two had discussed Jacobs's visiting Child in Wayland to talk over more changes, but now Child thought that was unnecessary. "I have promised to correct the proof-sheets," she wrote, "and I don't think it would be of any use to the book to have you here at this time."[48]

Child exerted herself for the book with her usual energy, also becoming, in effect, Jacobs's literary agent. Matters became complicated as it emerged that the publisher was in financial trouble. If it went bankrupt, the book might never be published. Child hustled. She wrote to friends in other towns—New Bedford, Newburyport—asking if they thought booksellers would commit to selling it if they somehow got it printed anyway. If not, perhaps individual readers would pay for it by subscription. She asked the American Anti-Slavery Society to publish Jacobs's book instead; when they declined, she pressured Wendell Phillips to use a special fund to preorder a thousand copies in the hopes of persuading the publisher to increase the initial run. Perhaps the thousand copies, Phillips suggested, could be distributed to AAS agents to sell on their speaking tours. Child passed this information on to Jacobs, also writing to Phillips that if the publisher could count on that many sales, it ought to be willing to pay the author well.[49]

Child had also written the promised introduction. "The author of the following autobiography is personally known to me, and her conversation and manners inspire me with confidence," she assured her readers. The author was employed by a "distinguished family in New York, and has so deported herself as to be highly esteemed by them." Those who know her, Child continued, would never doubt her, however unbelievable details of her story might be. Why? Because, clearly, she was *respectable*. Child was at pains to assure her readers that the work was Jacobs's own. "At her request, I have revised her manuscript," she wrote; "but such changes as I have made have been mainly for purposes of condensation and orderly arrangement." "I have not added any thing to the incidents, or changed the import of her very pertinent remarks. With trifling exceptions," she pledged, "both the ideas and the language are her own."[50] This claim, too, Jacobs's readers would soon find unbelievable.

Child then came to the sensitive part. "I am well aware that many will accuse me of indecorum for presenting these pages to the public," she wrote, "for the experiences of this intelligent and much-injured woman belong to a class which some call delicate subjects, and some indelicate." This was a coded warning: the book, Child wanted readers to know, was about sex. "This peculiar phase of Slavery had generally been kept veiled; but the public ought to be made acquainted with its monstrous features," she wrote. "I willingly take the responsibility of presenting them with the veil withdrawn," she continued. "I do this for my sisters in bondage, who are suffering wrongs so foul, that our ears are too delicate to listen to them."[51]

Jacobs and Child arranged to meet once more to review the final draft. As Jacobs prepared to make the journey to Massachusetts, Cornelia Willis suddenly miscarried. Jacobs could not leave her. Child would have to finish the last edits alone. Even in cases involving the most mundane material, this is an author's worst nightmare. For someone in Jacobs's position, it must have been excruciating. "I know that Mrs. Child will strive to do the best she can more than I can ever repay," Jacobs lamented to Post, "but I ought to have been there that we could have consulted together, and compared our views—although I know that hers are superior to mine yet we could have worked her great Ideas and my small ones."[52] It was a poignant reflection of an author's sorrow at losing control of her manuscript.

Their challenges were not over. Despite Child's efforts to secure advance sales of the book, the publisher went bankrupt. Jacobs's only option now was to self-publish. Apparently with savings from her years of employment with the Willis family, she came up with half the money. It's not clear where the other half came from. Perhaps she paid it in installments; perhaps Child and others helped. Finally, in the early weeks of 1861, the book was out.[53] A reader opening its front cover would first have seen its title page: *Incidents in the Life of a Slave Girl: Written by Herself*. Below that: "Edited by L. Maria Child." Below that, where the publisher should have been: "Boston: Published for the Author. 1861."

The author's name was nowhere to be found. The reader was left to wonder. Who was this slave girl who had written a book herself? In the first-edition copy I looked at in the Boston Athenæum, someone had tried to help. Beneath the title, a name is lightly penciled in: Linda Brent. Indeed, in other editions, the book's spine simply read "LINDA" in gilt letters.[54] Who was Linda Brent? A reader turning to the first chapter would quickly have understood: she was the book's protagonist. She was the six-year-old whose mother had died, the eleven-year-old given to new masters, the teenager assaulted by Dr. Flint, the mother hiding under the eaves. All those things happened to, and were recorded by, Linda Brent.

Sometime during the process of editing, in other words, Jacobs had decided to publish the book under a pseudonym. Or had she?

*   *   *

The story of Jacobs's friendship with Child, as we will see, did not end with the publication of her book. But the story of the narrative they had brought into the world was not over yet either. By the turn of the century, both Child and Jacobs were dead, and the fact that a real-life woman stood behind the character of Linda Brent was fading from collective memory. By the mid-twentieth century, scholars were openly speculating that *Incidents in the Life of a Slave Girl* was in fact not, as the book's subtitle claimed, *Written by Herself*. The plot was too refined and complex, and the sentences were too sophisticated, to have been written by a former slave. It must have been written by someone else, a fictional evocation of an imaginable but unlived life. Probably there had been no Dr. Flint, no hiding place beneath the eaves, no miraculous escape to the North. Who could have imagined such a life, written it down, and gotten it into print? The answer seemed all too easy; it was right there on the title page, in the guise of the editor's name. Who else could have written it but Lydia Maria Child?[55]

The author whose biography she had helped publish erased by history, a real woman's sufferings negated into fiction: Child would have been appalled. In the end, it took decades of twentieth-century research and a stunning combination of scholarly tenacity and good luck to reverse this mistake.[56] That story, too, is worth reading in its own right. But now the truth is established. Harriet Jacobs existed, and the major events of her life have been corroborated. Dr. Flint was James Norcom, the local physician; Mrs. Flint was his wife, Mary Matilda Norcom. Jacobs's grandmother was Molly Horniblow. Mr. Sands was Samuel Tredwell Sawyer, an attorney who later served in Congress. The town where all this took place was Edenton, North Carolina. That Jacobs escaped and Norcom pursued her was confirmed by the discovery of an advertisement he placed in the newspaper offering $100 for her capture. As part of the advertisement, he went out of his way to protest that Jacobs had run away without "known cause or provocation."

Since these discoveries, the case of Harriet Jacobs has produced a wealth of scholarship. It is searing, searching, and brilliant. All Americans should read it, too. Collectively, it is a scathing analysis of the evil always below the surface when one group of humans has full power over another. It asks us to consider how Black bodies have been represented and how white readers demand they be represented. It weighs the danger of voyeurism against the necessity of confronting grisly truths. It raises questions about consent and choice, about power and coercion. It uses Jacobs's writings to probe our attitudes toward motherhood, sympathy, and language. It challenges us to think about what it means to be an ally and what it means to be complicit. Through Jacobs's life, in other words, scholars have probed our most tortured questions about

Fig. 48. Dr. James Norcom. Photo by the North Carolina Museum of History.

race, gender, power, and their intersection in the fabric of our nation's history.[57]

*   *   *

Some of these scholars have also raised questions about Child.

Child's correspondence with Jacobs sometimes feels patronizing and abrupt. Her editorial suggestions sound too much like

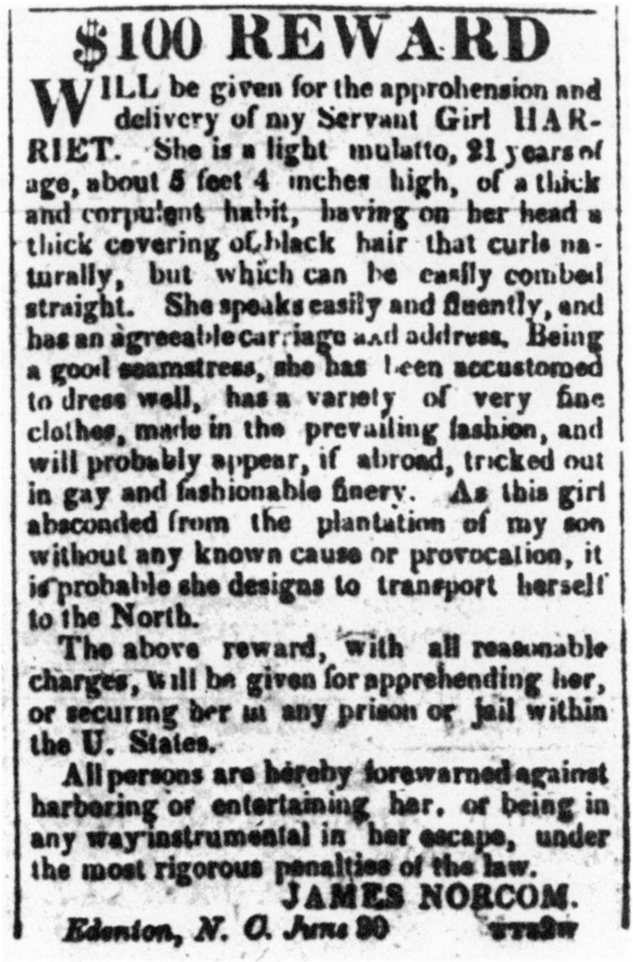

$100 REWARD

WILL be given for the apprehension and delivery of my Servant Girl HARRIET. She is a light mulatto, 21 years of age, about 5 feet 4 inches high, of a thick and corpulent habit, having on her head a thick covering of black hair that curls naturally, but which can be easily combed straight. She speaks easily and fluently, and has an agreeable carriage and address. Being a good seamstress, she has been accustomed to dress well, has a variety of very fine clothes, made in the prevailing fashion, and will probably appear, if abroad, tricked out in gay and fashionable finery. As this girl absconded from the plantation of my son without any known cause or provocation, it is probable she designs to transport herself to the North.

The above reward, with all reasonable charges, will be given for apprehending her, or securing her in any prison or jail within the U. States.

All persons are hereby forewarned against harboring or entertaining her, or being in any way instrumental in her escape, under the most rigorous penalties of the law.

JAMES NORCOM.

Edenton, N. C. June 30

Fig. 49. Reward offered for the capture of Harriet Jacobs. Courtesy of the State Archives of North Carolina.

commands. And how much of Jacobs's manuscript, in the end, had Child in fact rewritten? Her own account seems to shift: sometimes she says she changed almost nothing; sometimes she claims that she altered quite a bit.[58] The balance of evidence, to my mind, suggests that her changes were not substantial, but concerns remain. Is this yet another example of a white woman's taking too much control over a Black woman's story? Who, for instance, decided to change character names and place-names, and who determined that Jacobs should publish the book pseudonymously? Here the evidence is disturbing. "I use fictitious names in the book," Child wrote to Whittier in April 1861, "lest the Southern family, who secreted Linda some months, should be brought into difficulty."[59] The reasoning here is sound. Other fugitives, including Frederick Douglass, had also taken steps in their autobiographies to shield allies left behind. But what was Child doing using the first person to describe decisions about someone else's book?

Imagine for a moment that publishing the book under a pseudonym was Child's idea and that Jacobs, willingly or unwillingly, agreed. How did it feel to Jacobs to watch her name disappear from her own memoir, to be rechristened, possibly by her editor, then to watch the men who had abused her vanish behind fictional names? And although Child could not have predicted this, the pseudonyms made it possible, before long, for readers to doubt that any of the book's protagonists, innocent or guilty, had even existed. What if, instead of courageously facilitating the book's publication, Child had robbed Jacobs of her autonomy yet again? What if, in attempting to make Jacobs's voice heard, Child had silenced her?

Here is another question. Not a year before her first interaction with Jacobs, Child had been tirelessly publicizing John Brown's martyrdom. Why, then, did she essentially forbid Jacobs to include her chapter about John Brown? What did Child mean by asserting that "nothing could be so appropriate to end with" as Jacobs's grandmother's death and that, by contrast, Brown did "not naturally come into your story"?

There are several possibilities; here is the one that seems most likely to me. Ending with her grandmother's inspiring and peaceful death suffused Jacobs's narrative with the kind of sentimental maternalism that her most likely readers—white women, perhaps the very ones luxuriating at Idlewild—would both expect and find comforting. It was uplifting; it was moralistic; it affirmed, as one scholar puts it, "a nonviolent, matrilineal story of self-sacrifice and moral rebirth." Concluding with Brown's death, by contrast, would have ended the story in the masculine political sphere. Worse, it would have ended with a Black woman acknowledging that violence might, in the end, be necessary in order to free her "sisters who are still in bondage."[60]

In what way would such an ending not be "natural"? There is plenty of evidence in Jacobs's biography that she resisted her pious grandmother's injunctions to peaceful submission. Indeed, Jacobs had won her freedom *not* by submitting, but by escaping. She also recounts several instances of her own and others' defiance—both physical and psychological—in the face of their tormentors' abuses. After the Supreme Court's *Dred Scott* decision, Jacobs mourned to Post that Black people would now need to forget patience and embrace a new motto: "Might—and Strength—Liberty—or Death."[61] There was, in other words, plenty to make a chapter on Brown a logical outgrowth of Jacobs's own words. Child did not, or would not, see that. In short, Child had made an argument from nature, and it was, as usual, bad.

If it is true that Child wanted the book to end on a morally uplifting, nonviolent note—that only such an ending seemed "natural" to her—the desire clearly had deep roots in her own beliefs.[62] As the Civil War approached, Child continued to cling to an almost pathological hope: that examples like Jacobs's long-suffering grandmother would win out; that virtue and respectability would be rewarded; that the peaceful and the domestic would triumph over the violent and the political. Her insistence that Jacobs remove the Brown chapter positioned Jacobs's narrative squarely in the personal as opposed to the political realm. Child still wanted to inspire Northerners to a vision of moral progress deeply influenced by nonresistance. It's not clear that Jacobs shared those commitments.

But if Jacobs ultimately went along with Child's advice in order to conform to literary conventions her readers could accept, she also brilliantly subverts those conventions. Some of the most exciting scholarship about Jacobs shows how well she knew the literary traditions in which she was writing—both other slave narratives and the norms of sentimental fiction—and undermined them with carefully placed moments of resistance.[63] Other scholarship challenges our attachment to truth and transparency by suggesting that Jacobs, for tactical reasons, indeed changed facts in her story, signaling this strategy in a way Black readers might recognize even if white readers did not.[64] Did Child notice that while Jacobs followed many familiar literary conventions, she also deviated from them in significant and calculated ways and wrote with different audiences in mind? Was she aware of Jacobs's pointed mockery of white women's self-indulgent sentimentality? Did she notice that Jacobs managed to call not only for sympathy but for outrage? Did she see how Jacobs subtly rewrote the expected plot, refusing to romanticize white men's objectification of a Black woman's body? Was she aware that, in doing all this, Jacobs was insisting on confronting her readers with a different message than they expected and inventing a new genre through which to do it?[65]

Whether or not Child noticed these subversions, she clearly did not edit them out. If she did notice them, perhaps she calculated that they were likely to have a greater effect if embedded in an unthreatening genre, including a nonviolent end. Perhaps Jacobs's memoir was, in Child's mind, another example of "a troop of horses shod with felt"—an explosive message readers would not see coming and so could not escape. Perhaps editor and author, in an unrecorded meeting or a lost letter, agreed on this plan, hoping that Jacobs's readers would accept, almost despite themselves, the book's more disturbing truths. Perhaps it was also an acknowledgment on both their parts that there were things a Black woman could not say directly but could make her readers feel. Child herself had suffered her readers' censure when she had said too much. Perhaps she wanted to shield Jacobs from a similar fate.[66]

How did Jacobs experience Child's editorial advice? There's no doubt she was grateful. The two stayed in touch, seeking each other out in Boston when both were there, corresponding when they were apart. Jacobs was one of the few friends Child invited to stay in her home. Jacobs continued to turn to Child for help with other matters, and Child continued to promote Jacobs's book, including insisting that people believe its contents.[67] But even genuine gratitude and friendship are not incompatible with sorrow over lost agency or discomfort with a heavy-handed editor. Perhaps Jacobs was convinced that eliminating the John Brown chapter was wise. She may have disagreed but felt powerless to object. She may have been genuinely unsure. All these possibilities exist in any author-editor relationship.[68] But this was not just any author-editor relationship. The power differential was substantial. For all her sympathy and all her own social vulnerability, Child was still a white woman with ties to the literary world that Jacobs needed. How much choice did Jacobs feel she had?

As several scholars point out, she certainly had some choice, and she had already shown herself ready to use it. In refusing to allow Harriet Beecher Stowe to co-opt her narrative for Stowe's own purposes, she had asserted her choice against an even more famous author. She could also have refused Child's suggestions and continued to look for another publisher. She did not.[69] Instead, she spent her precious, hard-earned savings to publish the book herself. After it appeared, she made enormous efforts to get it into the hands of her public. The early months of 1861 found her traveling the Eastern Seaboard, no doubt in bitter cold, promoting her book from Boston to Philadelphia. Child helped, personally sending copies of the book to friends, along with letters recommending it. But it was Jacobs who did the hard work of bringing her message directly to readers: meeting with local activists, procuring letters of introduction from prominent abolitionists, persuading members of the Anti-Slavery Society to sell copies to their members. Sometimes she signed copies of her book with her fictional name: Linda Brent. She was also aware of the danger that Child would be credited with too much and fought to prevent this misunderstanding: she wrote to Post that she had promised to "tell no one what [Child] has done . . . it must be the Slaves own story," she continued, "which it truly is."[70] Her actions on the book's behalf suggest that she was proud of it, claimed ownership of it, and believed it could do the work she had spent so much emotional energy creating it to do.

And indeed, reviews were favorable. Abby Kelley, writing from an abolitionist lecture tour in Ohio, declared it "simple and attractive," commenting that "you feel less as though you were reading a book, than talking with the woman herself." William Nell, in the *Liberator*, praised this account of the "complicated experience in the life of a young woman" whose incidents "shine by the lustre of their own truthfulness." Just as important, a reviewer in England who had seen the original manuscript before Child's edits reported that the published version was "substantially the same" as the original draft and pronounced that it was "sure to effect more good for [Jacobs's] brethren and sisters still in bonds."[71]

But sales were modest. The reasons were perhaps all too obvious. Child complained that "the Boston booksellers are dreadfully afraid of soiling their hands with an Anti-Slavery book; so we have a good deal of trouble in getting the book into the market."[72] Perhaps Jacobs's narrative, despite both women's efforts to calibrate the book's subject to readers' sympathies, was still too indelicate for delicate ears.

* * *

What does this episode say about Child? It is a testament to her life of engagement and activism that Jacobs found in her a "whole souled woman" who, unlike Stowe, was willing to help her tell her own story. It shows Child at her resourceful best, using connections, concocting schemes, moving on to the next plan when the first failed. It shows her, here as so often, to be both a radical and a pragmatist: willing to publish what others would not, but still working to make the book's story palatable to a wider audience, pushing the boundaries without pushing them down. What is admirable about Child's part of this story is that she used the knowledge and power she had to amplify Jacobs's voice.

Yet it makes sense to me that some scholars point to the publication of *Incidents in the Life of a Slave Girl* as another instance of a powerful white woman's interfering with a Black woman's story. I wish Child had been less imperious, more sensitive to a vulnerable author's needs. It also makes sense that other scholars worry that in focusing on questions about Child's role, we repeat the mistake that early twentieth-century scholars made: we focus on the white protagonist rather than the Black one. In the end, the story about Jacobs's story rehearses some of the questions at the original story's core: the convoluted nature of power and consent; the fight over who gets to tell what; the complex network of actors and allies needed to break through silence, even in an imperfect way.[73]

It is always risky for biographers to imagine how their subjects would comment on the present. But let me hazard a speculation here. Far from bristling at these questions, I think Child would have welcomed them. It would be part of the fierce humility that she practiced all her life. She would not have been surprised that her own prejudices and aspirations sometimes got in the way. Just as she tried to uncover others' unconscious prejudices for them, surely she would have been glad to have her own brought to light. It is the least that white people seriously wanting to fight racism can do. Even scholars critical of Child have generally been willing to concede that she acted in "good faith."[74] We should not be surprised that good faith is often not enough. And when it is not, we should be willing to reassess.

Without Child, we would most likely not know Jacobs's story. Much more important is that without Jacobs, there would be an unbridgeable gap in the history of enslaved women. Jacobs's autobiography is now regularly taught next to Frederick Douglass's. It is used in political science, sociology, history, women's studies, and African American studies courses. Nathaniel Willis's dream that Idlewild would produce a great American literary work was fulfilled, just not in the way he imagined.[75] Jacobs's narrative is a priceless record not only of one woman's perseverance against unthinkable odds, but of the layered contortions that often result when that woman tries to give a history of what happened, written by herself.

I said this chapter would tell a story. Was that the right word? It is not just a story: it was someone's life. I'm sure that in telling it, I have foregrounded my own priorities and imposed my own perspective. I have calibrated my account to elicit sympathy—deciding how much violence to include, how much suffering to describe—but no doubt not exactly as Jacobs would have done it.

Fig. 50. Harriet Jacobs in 1894. By permission.

Jacobs's work should be allowed to stand on its own. I'll repeat myself. Every American should read it. That is the least that Jacobs's life, and what she did to document it, demands.

*   *   *

On March 4, 1861, just weeks after Jacobs's book appeared, Abraham Lincoln was inaugurated as the sixteenth president of the United States—states that were, after the series of secessions initiated by South Carolina, no longer so united. Lincoln was still determined to find a compromise that would achieve what he held to be his paramount duty: to restore the country to its original unity. He used his Inaugural Address to promise that he had "no purpose, directly or indirectly, to interfere with the institution of slavery in the South where it exists."[76] Despite these assurances, on April 12, 1861, newly designated Confederate soldiers fired on United States soldiers at Fort Sumter in Charleston, South Carolina. Finally, the war had begun.

Samuel Sawyer, the father of Jacobs's children, soon enlisted in the Confederate army. The Childs' nephews, George and William Haskins, enlisted on the Union side. So did Child's beloved friend Sarah Shaw's son, Robert Gould Shaw. "It seems as if it would be more than this guilty nation *deserved*, to get rid of its blasting curse without going through more suffering than we have yet dreamed of," Child wrote. "We of the North have been so persistently selfish, we have been so deaf to all warnings and admonitions of the Lord, that it must needs be that we should suffer for it."[77]

12

A Warning or an Example

The beginning of the American Civil War put nonresistance abolitionists like Maria Child in an almost unbearably paradoxical position. They were still against war. But now that one had started, they did not want it to stop. They needed this particular war to last long enough to achieve the one thing that, in their eyes, could make it worth fighting: not just another compromise to preserve the Union, but the emancipation of the four million human beings still enslaved in the South. The halting, tortuous road to this goal and her president's role in achieving it would define Child's experience of the war that ravaged the country for the next four years.

Early signs were not good. Even as the first battles showed that Southern states were in deadly earnest about their determination to break away, Lincoln remained convinced that his highest duty was to bring them back. If that meant continuing slavery, so be it. He was very clear about this. "If I could save the Union without freeing *any* slave I would do it, and if I could save it by freeing *all* the slaves I would do it; and if I could save it by freeing some and leaving others alone I would also do that," he wrote in an open letter to *New York Tribune* editor Horace Greeley. He himself, he continued to maintain, wished that "all men every where could be free."[1] It was possible that winning the war would achieve this. He would welcome that. But pursuing slavery's end was not what he had sworn to do. He had sworn to preserve the Union.

Preserving the Union meant enticing the rebel states to return by assuring them that their human property would still be protected by United States law. It also meant pacifying the Border States—slaveholding states such as Missouri, Delaware, Maryland, and Kentucky, that had so far not seceded—with similar assurances. In the lead-up to the war, then, United States policy was clear. First, if any slaves attempted to take advantage of wartime chaos to stage an insurrection in the South, American soldiers would help crush their attempt "with an iron hand."[2] Second, the Fugitive Slave Act would remain in force. The beginning of the war, in other words, in no way guaranteed that slavery would end even if the North was victorious.

The Union army's determination to protect enslavers' property was made brutally clear to the enslaved themselves. In March 1861, United States army lieutenant Adam J. Slemmer was the commanding officer at Fort Pickens in Pensacola, Florida. One morning, he was astonished to find several fugitive slaves who had arrived at the fort during the night. They had escaped their masters and fought their way through thirty miles of swampland. Somehow, he marveled, they had arrived "entertaining the idea that we were placed here to protect them and grant them their freedom." No such thing, he assured them. Instead, he reported, "I did what I could to teach them the contrary." He then commanded his men to return them to their enslavers.[3]

The incident made national news. Maria Child was beside herself with rage and sorrow. "I have raved and I have wept about that Fort Pickens affair," she wrote to Sarah Shaw. "God knows I *want* to love and honor the flag of my country, but how *can* I, when it is used for *such* purposes?" she mourned. "Every flap of the stars and stripes repeats to me the story of those poor slaves who, through great perils and sufferings, succeeded in making their way to Fort Pickens, strengthened by the faith that President Lincoln was their friend, and that his soldiers would protect them. They were chained and sent back to their masters, who whipped them till they nearly died under the lash." If the choice were between country and justice, Child would choose justice every time. "When such things are done under the U.S. flag, I cannot and will not say 'God bless it!' Nay, unless it ceases from this iniquity, I say deliberately and solemnly, 'May the curse of God rest upon it! May it be trampled in the dust, kicked by rebels, and spit upon by tyrants!'"[4]

As Child called down curses on her country, her Wayland neighbors began preparing to fight for it. On a balmy evening in April, the town voted to organize a military company of all the town's able-bodied men. Soon they were drilling every Wednesday in their black felt hats, frock coats, and dark pants, probably on the same town green where Revolutionary soldiers had drilled not quite a century before. Wayland also quickly organized a Soldier's Relief Society for women to meet and work for the cause.[5] Soon Child's neighbors were gathering to sew bandages and clothing and to gossip about the sensational news arriving daily from Washington, DC.

Child agonized. She could not, would not, support the war as long as Union soldiers were being used to return slaves. "I wait to see how the United States will deport itself," she resolved. "When it treats the colored people with justice and humanity, I will mount its flag in my great elm-tree, and I will thank you to present me with a flag for a breast-pin; but, until then, I would as soon wear the rattlesnake upon my bosom as the eagle." The mood in town was tense. At a "fashionable meeting" organized to determine how best to aid the war effort, David got up to insist that the United States also had duties to assist slaves. He was, Child reported, "very violently treated, and almost mobbed." He was told the war had "'nothing to do with the damned [slaves]; the war was to preserve the *Union*, that's what they were fighting for, and they wouldn't hear a word about the [slaves].'"[6] I am sanitizing this. Instead of "slaves," Child's neighbors used the most hateful racist language they could muster.

If the only thing that would destroy Lincoln's hope for compromise was a Confederacy emboldened by Union defeats, Child was ready to hope for that. "Success to Jeff. Davis," she wrote about the Confederacy's president, "till he goads the free States into doing from policy and revenge, what they have not manhood to do from justice and humanity!" "Yes," she affirmed, "I have said that we *needed* defeats, and that I hoped they would come, to teach us the lesson we needed, and were so slow to learn." What a wretched hope it was. It meant, in effect, willing the deaths of young men, among them the sons of relatives and friends. She wept as she watched a neighbor's son march off to war. Of the seventy-two Waylanders who left, twelve would never return.[7]

The practice of using Union army soldiers to return fugitives to their masters was made more complicated in May 1861, when three enslaved men—Frank Baker, Shepard Mallory, and James Townsend—escaped from their Virginian master, Confederate colonel Charles Mallory. They arrived at Union-held Fort Monroe in Virginia and asked to be taken in. General Benjamin Butler, in command of the fort, faced a question similar to the one Lieutenant Slemmer had faced in Florida. What were these men, legally speaking, and what was he to do with them? The difference was that by now the war had started, and Virginia had seceded. If Virginia were indeed part of a foreign country, as she herself claimed, surely the Fugitive Slave Act was no longer in force within her borders?

More to the point, as far as Butler was concerned, the three men told him they had fled when they learned that Mallory intended to send them to South Carolina to help build Confederate fortifications. Surely, Butler reasoned, he was not required to return property if that property would then be used in an effort to defeat his own army. Besides, the beleaguered general admitted, "the men were very serviceable and I had great need of labor in my Quartermaster's Department." In other words, he had a fort to run, and he could use their help.[8]

Lincoln's secretary of war reluctantly approved Butler's reasoning, but on the condition that Butler refrain from actively stealing Virginians' slaves, and providing he put to work any fugitives who arrived at the fort. So Butler sent Colonel Mallory a receipt for the men, redeemable for their return when the war ended. He also offered to return them if Mallory would come to the fort and take an oath of allegiance to the United States. Needless to say, Colonel Mallory did not oblige.[9]

What did the three men feel as they were put to work for the Union army? Did they feel that their status was different, their future brighter? Or did they feel they had simply exchanged one master for another? No record survives. For his part, Butler had more thinking to do. It was, he worried, unclear what to call these fugitives. They were no longer slaves, at least for the moment. They were definitely not citizens. Nor were they exactly refugees or prisoners of war. Butler finally settled on a novel designation. He would call them contraband: goods illegally smuggled across enemy lines. Baker, Mallory, and Townsend were, in a sense, now the legal equivalent of the cotton, tobacco, and lumber illegally brought North by disloyal Confederates. The irony, of course, was that this contraband had smuggled itself.[10]

The name stuck. The self-smuggling continued. Short months later, almost a thousand fugitive slaves were living in the first "contraband camp" near Fort Monroe. Their numbers now included women, children, and elderly men—people who could hardly claim to have been pressed into Confederate service or to be useful to Butler. Butler was not an abolitionist, but he decided to let them stay anyway. "As a question of humanity," he mused, how "can I receive the services of the father and mother and not take the children?" How, indeed? But there were other questions. Where would these "contrabands" live? What would they eat? What would they wear? Who would care for the many among them who arrived emaciated and sick? In short, what was to be done with them?[11]

At last: a cause to which Maria Child could devote her wartime energies. When the news from Fort Monroe reached Wayland, she threw herself into meeting every "contraband" need she could possibly imagine. She collected and mended secondhand garments for them. She used leftover scraps of cloth to make made hoods for the women and wool caps for the men. She had heard that many of the women could sew but had nothing to sew with, so she sent needles and buttons and thread. Child did not want only to meet their physical needs, she wanted them to learn as well. She gathered all the fugitive slave narratives she could find, restitching the pages and pasting images from old copies of the *Liberator* to make new covers "as nicely as if I were doing it for Queen Victoria." She collected picture books for children and rebound them as sturdily as she could.[12] For more advanced readers, she included copies of *Uncle Tom's Cabin* and her own writings about peaceful emancipation in other parts of the world. After weeks of work, the collection of supplies was ready to send. Child also included "a letter of encouragement and sympathy." The letter does not survive, but it is not hard to imagine Child at her desk, pouring her heart into it. Finally, an opportunity to speak directly to these humans whose agonies she had been imagining for so long and whose future kept her awake at night. Did any of the inhabitants of Fort Monroe ever hear the words directed to them by this faraway white woman? If so, what did they make of her encouragement and sympathy? I hope that, if they did hear it, they found it comforting. It also might have been somewhat bewildering.

Child was also keenly aware that meeting these humans' needs for food, shelter, and sympathy was not enough. Newly freed men and women would need job skills; they would need capital; they would need land. She also knew that they were not fighting only for their physical survival; they were fighting against the widespread expectation that they would fail. Only recently liberated from an indescribably traumatic reality, without adequate resources or education, these contraband humans bore the additional burden of convincing skeptical white Americans that they were capable of self-sufficiency. If they failed, arguments for their inferiority would be strengthened; what little opposition there was to slavery would weaken. How to prevent this? Child was full of ideas: perhaps they could be given farms to manage or be employed in a chair factory where they could earn a percentage of the profits. She thought up economic schemes and wrote to rich friends to try to fund them. "Projects for employing these poor creatures, so that they can have a share of profits proportioned to their labor, occupy my thoughts more than half the time," she wrote to Francis Shaw.[13]

There was one more thing she longed to do but could not: actually go there and help. The call to travel to Fort Monroe and assist the work there was so strong that it overpowered almost all her hesitations except one: David. He had been alarmingly ill in the past months, and his dependence on her was more pronounced than ever. "David's constitution is so shattered, that nothing but great quiet and regularity keeps his physical machinery in tolerable order," she wrote to his sister. "It is for his sake that I live as I do. I should myself like much better to be more in the midst of things. But I am thankful for our quiet . . . nest, and contented in it. It is lucky," she concluded, "that I am so, since I could not raise income enough for two to live in any other way."[14] And so she stayed.

∗   ∗   ∗

Meanwhile, Child's awful hope that Confederate victories would keep the North from winning too quickly was being fulfilled. In July 1861, 35,000 underprepared and overconfident Union troops confronted 30,000 Confederate soldiers at the First Battle of Bull Run. Union forces were quickly outmaneuvered, broke into panic, and retreated in disgrace to Washington, DC. The reports from the front were grisly. "Night and day, I am thinking of those poor soldiers, stabbed after they were wounded, shot after they dropped down from fatigue," Child wrote to Henrietta Sargent. "My heart bleeds for the mothers of those sons." Even worse was the thought that they might die in vain: "And shall all this awful havoc be made, without removing the *cause* of the war? Without abolishing the detestable institution, which will *always* be marring our prosperity and troubling our peace, so long as it is allowed to exist?" Child had not recovered faith in her country's flag. "If the U.S. flag does not represent the ideas of justice and freedom, it is to me merely a striped rag, and they are welcome to trample on it who are so inclined." "If we *must* have the noble structure *pulled* down about our ears by the blind giant Slavery," she mused, "I hope the poor negroes will have a rollicking good time over its ruins."[15]

The humiliating defeat at Bull Run had one silver lining. It had become clear that the North would have to deprive the South of all the resources it could if it wanted to win the war. In August 1861, Lincoln responded by signing the first Confiscation Act. Any enslaved people being used to aid the Confederate cause could now be taken from their owners and held as federal property.[16] What this meant for the future was anybody's guess. But for now it meant that not only self-smuggling slaves could become government property: any enslaved person being used in the war effort against the Union could as well.

Was this progress? Probably. Legal limbo in a refugee camp was arguably preferable to Southern enslavement. Still, Child was distressed. What would happen after the war was over if slaves had been freed not because slavery was wrong but because the North needed labor? What consequences would that have for Black Americans' treatment by the white population? "This entire absence of a moral sense on the subject, has disheartened me more than anything else," she wrote to Gerrit Smith. "Everything *must* go wrong, if there is no heart or conscience on the subject." What the nation needed instead was a simple confession: "We are verily *guilty* concerning our brother; for generations, we have been accomplices in robbery and murder; we have assisted in trampling on the helpless; and we ought to cease forthwith this partnership with iniquity."[17] However necessary such a confession was, Child knew it was unlikely.

The legal emancipation of American slaves continued its slow progress. In August 1861, John Frémont—the former presidential candidate who had won Child's heart, now commander of Union troops in Missouri—forced the issue again. In a sweeping proclamation made all the more shocking because he had not consulted his president, Frémont declared that enslaved people belonging to anyone in Missouri who had taken up arms against the United States "are hereby declared free men."[18] Not contraband, not confiscated, but free.

Child was jubilant. At last, she wrote, someone was willing to "acknowledge the slaves as 'men.'" She felt sure that joy over this declaration would inspire others like it. "If he *has* taken a step so bold and so wise," she wrote to Lucy Osgood, "the hour has struck at *last*. The contagion will spread like fire on the prairies." Antislavery allies everywhere would be enthused and emboldened; the war would gain a moral purpose and perhaps achieve a glorious conclusion. But was the news too good to be true? "I rejoice with trembling," she added, "for I am afraid that the next newspaper will contradict the report."[19]

She was right to worry. Lincoln was convinced that Frémont's proclamation would cause the slave states that had remained loyal to the Union to join the Confederacy. Missouri, Delaware, Kentucky, Maryland: if one seceded, the rest would probably follow. Then the North would lose the war. He wrote to Frémont asking him to modify his proclamation. Frémont sent his wife from Missouri to Washington to deliver his answer to Lincoln in person: no, he would modify nothing. Lincoln was stunned. Her husband, he told Jessie Frémont, "should never have dragged the Negro into the war."[20] A month later, Frémont was dismissed from his position. Missouri slaves were still, or perhaps we should say again, the legal property of their enslavers.

To see full emancipation proclaimed by an American officer and then rescinded by her president: after thirty years of struggle, it was almost too much for Child to bear. Lincoln's overruling of Frémont evoked some of the angriest letters in her sixty-year correspondence. Here is one example: "I should like to have Jeff Davis take Mr. and Mrs. Lincoln, and Seward, and Smith all prisoners," she wrote to Sarah Shaw of her president, his wife, and members of his cabinet. She would also, she declared, be "gratified by having a bomb-shell burst in the White House." Lincoln's long, skinny neck looked to her perfect for hanging. She fought to refrain from throwing stones at a local sign with his name on it. She was careful not to say such things in public, but she felt them as strongly as she had felt anything. "Thank God the Rebels *won't* be conciliated," she fumed. Let the battles continue and the death toll mount until the United States was forced to do by necessity what should long ago have done "by an act of justice and humanity!"[21]

It is a full and furious letter. At its end, Child seemed suddenly to remember to whom she was writing. Sarah Shaw's son, Robert Gould Shaw, was now fighting with the Second Massachusetts Infantry. The Shaws were ardent abolitionists: they had been allied with the Childs in the antislavery struggle for thirty years. They supported the war for the same reasons Child did. Still, Robert was their only son, and his chances of survival became more tenuous with every Union defeat. Child scrawled a quick, regretful post-script upside down on the letter's first page: "When you read my cold, philosophical way of talking about the crisis, you will say 'Ah, she has no darling son gone to the wars,'" she predicted. "True, dear Sarah. If I *had*, I am afraid I should be very weak."[22]

The first wartime Thanksgiving came and went. "David and I were all alone," Child wrote to Lucy Osgood, "but, as he wanted to *play* Thanksgiving, I made a plum-pudding, and stuffed a turkey, after the manner his mother used to do it." The two lifelong warriors for justice sat near the fire in their small home, and David read aloud while his wife knitted. By now, there were army regiments led by abolitionist officers such as Thomas Wentworth Higginson and James Montgomery. For *these* soldiers she would knit mittens until her fingers ached. "I have been knitting a pair of suspenders for Col. Montgomery," she wrote to a niece with better access to Boston shops. "Will you buy a pair of straps and fasten them on the suspenders, after I send them to you. I would not get *dandy* straps but real strong, stout ones." When she sent the mittens and suspenders off to Montgomery's Kansas Brigade, she also enclosed copies of Harriet Jacobs's memoir for the colonel to distribute to his troops.[23]

As she knitted, larger questions about history and her nation's part in it continued to consume her thoughts. Would the North win? Did it deserve to? "Thus far, the U.S. have been acting so basely against the slaves, that it seems as if God could not think us *worthy* of saving, as a nation," she wrote to David's sister. "Perhaps we are destined to be a *warning* to future nations, having proved ourselves too wicked to be used as an *example*."[24]

* * *

Other aspects of life went on as usual. The American Anti-Slavery Society's anniversary meeting took place in January, complete

with its exhausting socializing and feral little boys yet again ma-
rauding the concession stand. Wayland and its environs were
both sleepy and "coppery," Child complained: in other words, full
of "Copperheads," Northerners all too eager to compromise with
the South and be done with the war. The Childs moved uneasily
in their community, searching for the difficult balance between
being good neighbors and being honest. This sometimes resulted
in tense exchanges. Once, as they traveled to Boston by horsecar,
someone recognized Child and decided to lecture the famous abolitionist on the importance of forgiving the South. Northerners
should never, he coached her, "say a word to our Southern brothers
that they had been rebels." Fine, Child retorted, as long as freed
slaves were counted among our Southern brothers too. Better to
leave the slavery question alone, her interlocutor explained to her.
"I'd kill it first, and *then* let it alone," David chimed in.[25] Probably
the rest of the ride passed in awkward silence.

Far away, the wartime carnage escalated. Every newspaper
dropped at the foot of their elm tree brought lists of the dead. There
was poetic justice, Child found, in the fact that having long consented "to the shooting and burning and torturing of the colored
woman's sons," white women's sons should now be suffering the
same. But abstract poetic justice weighed lightly against concrete
human suffering. In April, Child watched the body of a Wayland
soldier carried past her house to the home of his devastated widow.
In July, the paper reported that Robert Gould Shaw's regiment
had been involved in heavy fighting in the Shenandoah Valley. She
rushed to write to his mother for news but found she could not:
"Such a shuddering came over me, that I *could* not write. There are
sorrows so appalling, that the mere thought of them takes away the
breath of the soul," she wrote. Near her, as she agonized and knitted, was a picture of Sarah's son. "So gentle and so gentlemanly!"
she wrote to his mother.[26]

As the nation's fate hung in the balance, simple joys became precious. "The steel-colored river is rippling brightly in the sunlight,
too busy playing with the breezes to reflect the blue arch above it,
flecked with fleecy white clouds," Child reported to Lucy Searle.

"This is," she admitted, "a beautiful world." In their garden, Child befriended a squirrel that came every day to eat on the wall outside the kitchen window. Then it disappeared. "When so many mothers are mourning for their sons, not knowing where or how they died, I am ashamed to say that I have cried a little for the loss of my squirrel," she admitted. "All innocent and peaceful things seem *peculiarly* attractive, in these times of bloodshed and hatred; and I cannot help mourning." A small loss could also quickly turn to foreboding. "My hopes of emancipation as the result of the war, grow feebler every day," she confessed. No less heroic a figure than Harriet Tubman, visiting the North between her forays to free slaves in the South, sought to reassure Child. It didn't matter what Lincoln did or didn't do, Tubman argued: whatever it was, God was guiding him. Child was still not sure. If slavery continued after the war, she had decided, she would move to Switzerland.[27]

One morning, Child answered a knock on the door to find herself looking at a woman's back. When the woman turned, Child saw a black face and sightless eyes. She was, the blind woman explained, a poet traveling the country, supporting herself by selling her poems and doing odd jobs. She had heard that Child was "a friend to her people" and had written against slavery, "for which she hoped the Lord would bless me." The Childs invited her in, and she spent the night. The next day Child paid her a dollar for her poems and gave her the names of other sympathetic people along her road. David gave her a flower from the garden. "Bless his soul!" the blind woman said. Child walked with her until she was well past the house of a notoriously racist neighbor. They said good-bye, and Child watched her erect form disappear into the distance. "It made me think of the Catholic legends of those who ministered to beggars, and found afterward they had entertained the Lord Jesus," Child wrote wonderingly to Henrietta Sargent. "*Spiritually*," she concluded, "such legends are true."[28]

Even far from the bloody battlefields, the war was taking a terrible toll. Towns like Wayland strained to meet their recruitment quotas as their already enlisted men fought in gory, disastrous confrontations such as the Second Battle of Bull Run and the Battle of Fredericksburg. Women whose husbands were at the front struggled to harvest crops and run businesses, desperately hoping the men would return before their families were ruined. Desertions increased as early hopes of a quick war were dashed and the numbers of wounded, dead, and captured began to defy belief.

There was an obvious solution to this shortage of Northern soldiers: the thousands of military-age Black men who by now had flooded contraband camps near Union forts throughout the South. But in the minds of many white Americans, the idea of armed Black men remained unthinkable. The paradoxical nature of the prejudices was telling: Black men, the argument went, were on the one hand too lazy and cowardly to be soldiers. On the other hand, they were naturally violent and ungovernable and therefore too dangerous to arm. The press was full of dire predictions of what would happen if Lincoln allowed Black men to fight. Would there be mass defections in the army ranks? Would this be the final straw that pushed the Border States into the arms of their rebelling neighbors? The answer to both, Lincoln feared, seemed to be yes. So when Union general David Hunter enlisted former slaves in his regiment, Lincoln overruled him. When General John Phelps attempted to form fugitive slaves into regiments, he was told to use them for manual labor instead. Finding that this made him feel too much like a slave driver, Phelps resigned.[29]

In despair, Child again turned to her desk. In September 1862, she wrote a widely published open letter to her president. "It may seem like a violation of propriety for a woman to address the Chief Magistrate of the nation at a crisis so momentous as this," Child began. Violation or not, Child first spent several paragraphs discussing wartime policy, then rounded on Lincoln with indignation and shame. "Shall I tell you," she asked her president, "what I said when cold water was thrown on the spark of enthusiasm kindled by the brave, large-hearted Gen. Hunter?" Yes, she would tell him. "Oh, what a misfortune it is to have an extinguisher instead of a Drummond light in our watchtower, when the Ship of State is reel-

ing under such a violent storm, in the midst of sunken rocks."[30]
How, she demanded, could Lincoln justify overruling his generals
when they had right on their side?

It's fair to say that Child knew little of the bigger game Lincoln
was playing as he tried to win a war and keep what remained of the
country together, all while staying within what he thought was his
legal power. She had always hated politics, so of course she hated
the intricate political calculations Lincoln slowly played out as it
seemed, day by day, that the possibility of emancipation receded.
It would always be the job of reformers, as she sometimes put it, to
hold politicians at the "point of a moral bayonet": to be sure they
never forgot to consider what was right as well as what was legal.[31]
This letter is a case in point. "If you *can* thus stifle the moral enthusiasm of noble souls; if you *can* thus disappoint the hopes of poor,
helpless wretches, who trust in you as the appointed agent of their
deliverance, may God forgive you!" Child concluded. "It will," she
predicted, "require *infinite* mercy to do it."

As it happened, Lincoln had been doing his own bargaining for
God's mercy. By now Lee's army was in Maryland, within striking
distance of Washington, DC. One more Confederate victory could
spell the end of the war. Sometime early that fall, Abraham Lincoln
addressed his creator. He had, he later told his cabinet, "made a
vow, a covenant, that if God gave us the victory in the approaching
battle, he would consider it an indication of Divine will, and that
it was his duty to move forward in the cause of emancipation."[32]
When Union forces repelled Lee's advance in the apocalyptic Battle of Antietam on September 17, 1862, it seemed that God had kept
his side of the bargain. It now remained for Lincoln to fulfill his.

As fulfillments of sacred vows go, Lincoln's feels unbearably half-
hearted. The initial Emancipation Proclamation, signed on September 22, 1862, reads like a study in equivocation. It reiterated
that the object of the war was to restore the Union, not to end slavery. It promised compensation to cooperative slaveholders. It reflected Lincoln's belief that emancipation could be legally justified
only as a military necessity, not as a matter of justice.[33] In slave
states that had remained loyal to the Union, it left slavery intact.

And the proclamation was, in effect, only a threat. If the rebelling states laid down their arms by December 31, all would be forgiven. Slavery could continue.

The proclamation included one more major proviso. It continued to express hope that Black men and women, once free, would leave. Before issuing the proclamation, Lincoln made a last-ditch effort to persuade Black leaders to commit to doing just that. Perhaps if they would promise to emigrate, emancipation would be more palatable to both Northerners and Southerners who continued to claim they would not tolerate free Black families in their midst. Calling these leaders to the White House, Lincoln spoke to them in brutally honest terms. "There is an unwillingness on the part of our people," he told them, "for your freed colored people to remain with us." He admitted that this was harsh. But, he continued, it was true: "I cannot," he confessed, "alter [this fact] if I would." Would they, in light of this information, finally renounce their "selfish" opposition to colonization? Perhaps, he speculated, separation would come as a relief. "I do not know how much attachment you may have toward our race," Lincoln said frankly. "It does not strike me that you have the greatest reason to love them." Could they find fifty, even twenty-five respectable Black families who, at the government's expense, would move to Liberia or Central America and encourage others to do the same?[34]

Some Black leaders, like Martin Delany, had in fact come to a similar conclusion and were organizing for emigration. But the leaders Lincoln had assembled did not share Delany's opinion. So they absorbed Lincoln's insult as best they could and went back to consult with their communities. When the content of Lincoln's proposal became public, protests broke out throughout Black communities in the North. A week later the answer came back: no, they would not emigrate. "Shall we sacrifice this, leave our homes, forsake our birthplace, and flee to a strange land to appease the . . . prejudice of the traitors now in arms against the Government?" demanded one incredulous group in Philadelphia. Frederick Douglass was not at the meeting with Lincoln, but his words on colonization perhaps best sum up their response: "Our minds are made up to live here if we can," he said, "or die here if we must." Not even such clear resolve extinguished Lincoln's hope. The "effort to colonize persons of African descent," he promised in the first Emancipation Proclamation, "with their consent, upon this continent, or elsewhere, with the previously obtained consent of the Governments existing there, will be continued."[35]

For all these reasons, Maria Child found the September Emancipation Proclamation deeply disappointing. "I was thankful for the President's Proclamation, but by no means jubilant," Child wrote to Henrietta Sargent at the end of September. "I confess to having all along painfully felt a want of moral grandeur in the process of emancipation now going on. God is accomplishing a great work by the meanest tools." Child was also suspicious of the three-month delay. "I cannot divest myself of some misgivings concerning contingencies that may possibly occur before the 1st of January," she wrote. "Three months is ample time for rebels at the South, and traitors at the North, to mature their plans. My belief is that there is a deeper game being played than the people are aware of." As an example of what this deeper game might be, rumors abounded that General George B. McClellan, commander of the Army of the Potomac, had delayed pursuing Lee's retreating troops after the victory at Antietam in hopes of achieving a compromise that would allow Southerners to keep their slaves.[36]

If the South won, slavery would continue. If the North won too quickly, slavery would also continue. So there was still nothing left but to hope the war would grind on until emancipation was achieved. "I see too plainly that rapid and easy success is our greatest danger. Because I truly love my country, and am earnestly desirous for its welfare, I pray to God that the victories may not come too fast," Child wrote to Sarah Shaw. But for all her principles, Child was not callous. "When I think of all our soldiers are suffering, and of the thousands of hearts that are breaking for their sakes, my own prayer gives me a pang, as if it were something wicked and monstrous. Thus the inward struggle goes on, as I sit here alone making lint and bandages."[37]

So the agony of being a war-supporting pacifist continued. It was all the more acute since the Childs now had two nephews in the Union Army. "I reverence you for the unselfish step you have taken," Child wrote to Willie Haskins, David's sister's son. What words, she must have wondered, could she offer this young man to urge him to keep fighting, and for the right reasons? Did it feel different trying to convey these imperatives to someone she loved whose life was on the line? Nothing less than the moral future of the country was at stake, she assured him: "Apologizing for despotism, and yielding inch by inch to its aggressions, had caused a great decline in the spirit of Liberty among us," she wrote; "and had not our downward course been arrested by this war, I think our free institutions would have been effectually undermined, and completely destroyed." She was even willing to admit that Lincoln was not entirely at fault for this: "The *people* were not prepared to sustain him" in any opposition to slavery; "they had become too generally demoralized by long subservience to the Slave Power." But even the people's resistance would not be strong enough to stop the progress of freedom, she promised. "It is wonderful how the wise Providence of God has so managed events, as to push us continually forward in the right direction, against the most stubborn resistance of our will. In view of this, I cannot otherwise than trust that all is coming out right, at last.... I feel confident that the *great* Battle of *Freedom* will surely be won. It is worth living for, worth dying for, my young friend."[38]

We don't know where Willie Haskins was when he received this letter from his famous aunt. Perhaps he read it while waiting in line for his army rations, or later by the light of a campfire. Perhaps he read it aloud to others in his regiment or passed it around to his tentmates. If he did, how did they respond? When his only brother George died two months later of an illness caught in an army camp, did he think of Child's promise that it was in a cause worth dying for? Child wrote to him again: "Your noble-hearted brother did not sacrifice his young life, for any sectional or small idea," she promised. "For, say what we will, this is a war to decide whether this is to be a free country."[39] Willie kept the letter. Did it help him shoulder his weapon once more and aim it at the hearts of his countrymen?

* * *

The three months between Lincoln's threat of emancipation and its execution ticked by. The Confederates showed no signs of taking Lincoln up on his final offer to preserve slavery. The path to emancipation seemed clear. But would Lincoln actually do it? Or would he find some other reason to hesitate, one last olive branch to hold out to the rebelling South?

In case he did indeed follow through, massive celebrations to greet news of emancipation had been planned in Boston for January 1. Midnight on December 31 had passed with no word from the White House. Noon came and went on New Year's Day with still no word. This was not a good sign. It was also not a good sign that the waiting crowds had self-segregated. Black Bostonians amassed at Tremont Temple, where Frederick Douglass and Charles Lenox Remond delivered rousing speeches. White Bostonians gathered at Music Hall to listen to Beethoven and to hear Ralph Waldo Emerson read. It was a fancy gathering, with Boston's great and good turned out in hopes of momentous news. William Lloyd Garrison was also there, no doubt wondering at how fashionable his once despised cause had become.[40]

Evening came, and still there was no announcement from Washington. What was happening? Had Lincoln changed his mind? Had the South capitulated rather than lose its slaves? It was eight o'clock, then nine, then ten. Orators and musicians tried to distract the increasingly anxious crowds. Finally it happened: messengers raced to both venues to deliver the news. Lincoln had signed the final proclamation: four million enslaved people were officially, immediately, free. In Music Hall, Garrison and Harriet Beecher Stowe were wildly cheered; in Tremont Temple, Frederick Douglass led ecstatic and weeping Black Bostonians in song.[41]

Where, in the midst of all this rejoicing, were the Childs? They had been invited to join the throng at Music Hall but had stayed home. They dreaded the ice, she hated crowds, and travel was always a threat to David's health. It also seems that Child was not in a celebratory mood. "The little jet of joy in my heart soon subsided," she wrote to Sarah Shaw, "and left only a sprinkling of tears."[42]

How was this possible? How could the freeing of millions of human beings, an outcome she had worked half her life for, not make her heart overflow with joy? There were a few reasons. It was true that the wording of the proclamation showed improvement over its first draft: "Upon this act, sincerely believed to be an act of justice, warranted by the Constitution, upon military necessity," Lincoln had written, "I invoke the considerate judgment of mankind, and the gracious favor of Almighty God." At least he had conceded that justice was involved, not only military expediency. But that was all the acknowledgment of slavery's immorality that Lincoln, mindful that the Proclamation was a legal document and not a moral one, felt he could afford. No one, Child mourned, was willing simply to say: "The black man has been wronged; give him his rights."[43]

More concerning still, "The number who sincerely and heartily acknowledge the equality of the races is still very small," she wrote. Even if the North was victorious, what would happen in a country newly reformed but with no acknowledgment of its grievous sin? It was also true that over a million people remained enslaved in the Border States as part of Lincoln's latest attempt to keep those states from joining the rebellion. Included, in a brutal irony, were those at Fort Monroe who had been among the first contrabands.[44] It felt, in short, like a hollow victory, and one destined to carry the country's evil forward in another form.

Adding to these sorrows, two of Child's friends had recently lost sons in the war—young men she remembered as children with affectionate nicknames and flaxen curls who were now dead on bloody battlefields. "I want to wish you a happy new year," she wrote to Shaw, whose son, they both knew, might well be next. "But how can we speak of a happy year, when this dark thunder-cloud hangs over our heads, and no one knows on whom the bolt may fall?"[45]

*   *   *

Indeed: it seemed that winter that death was all around. Several of Child's friends had recently died of old age or disease. David's bouts of sickness sometimes left her wondering how much time he had left. Then her brother Convers fell ill. She made the arduous sixteen-mile trip to Watertown as often as she could to nurse him. When it became obvious that he would not recover, she stayed at his side. As she sat by his bed, the memories flooded in: the two of them sprawled among his books during hours stolen from family chores; his patient attention to her questions about Shakespeare and Milton; his concern over her early radicalism; his gentle teasing and warm companionship. Now the mind that had sparked her own was wrecked by opium as her brother's body failed. But his death, in the end, was gentle. "I have not a want in the world," he murmured to his sister on his last day: "Blessings upon blessings!" For this she was thankful. But losing this companion of her childhood "tore me all to pieces," Child wrote. "When one is past sixty," she confessed to Elizabeth Cady Stanton, "the heart does not rebound from the pressure of such heavy weights so easily as it does in more elastic years."[46]

What, after all, was the point of an aging, weakening body that could not fight in battles or nurse in hospitals? "My hair is white," she wrote to a friend she had not seen in many years; "and Time, bringing its usual allotment of afflictions and chagrins, has cut the lines deep on my forehead and mouth." How often she wished she could offer her aging body in exchange for the life of a friend's young son. What did it mean to be in life's twilight, to feel that one's best days and best thoughts were over, to feel helpless and useless while one's friends died and one's country battled for its life? Child tried turning to books for answers. Surely there were volumes of inspiration and guidance for this stage of life, anthologies of cultural wisdom to guide her now. She came up with nothing. "As a people," she concluded, "we Americans are far too negligent of the *old*."[47] As at so many points of her life, Maria Child had identified a problem: now she resolved to do something about it.

And so as young, hot blood flowed on battlefields like Fredericksburg and Vicksburg, Child turned her attention to the slow stiffening of aging bodies. The idea of another book formed quickly in her mind. It would be a cheerful book: one that promised new joy in old age and helped readers achieve that joy. She set about collecting poems about life's twilight by Tennyson and Wordsworth. She wrote stories of friends growing old together and of married couples finding peace with each other at last. She reminded her readers of artists who had produced their greatest works in their last years. Old age had other advantages, she urged. Proximity to death revealed truths unavailable to youth. It freed one from petty anxieties and drew one's attention to higher things. As she had done in every stage of her career, she also gave practical advice. Eat sparingly but regularly. Chew slowly. Always get exercise, always go outside. No more tobacco, only a little wine. Be useful. Be engaged. Be curious. Don't worry about going bald or needing spectacles.[48] And most especially, don't fear death, which is only a passage to a better, truer life. Much of this advice she collected in a chapter titled "Letter from an Old Woman, on Her Birthday." The "old" here was relative: when *Looking toward Sunset* was finally published, Maria Child was only sixty-two.

*　*　*

In June 1863, an unusual event occurred in the Child household: an overnight guest arrived. Sarah Shaw had come to spend a few days with her treasured friend. Child's reluctance to have visitors in their cramped and humble lodgings had not lessened, and her discomfort as she saw her home through Sarah's eyes must have been acute. The Shaws were still among the wealthiest families in the Northeast. They had graceful, magnificent homes on Beacon

Hill and Staten Island. They collected art; they vacationed in Europe. They socialized with Boston's elite, including Massachusetts governor John Andrews.

Fortunately, there was more room for guests now. For a while, the household had included a few boarders, presumably to help meet expenses. But they had recently moved out, so the Childs were, for the first time in decades, alone in their own home. Maria Child spent hours fixing up the house just as she liked it. When her friend alighted from the coach, Maria took her on a tour of the tiny home, lovingly introducing her to each object: small replicas of famous artworks; a little basket made of shells; an inspiring bust of the violinist Ole Bull. What she lacked in riches, she could make up for in affection. "[My] little playthings," she murmured to Sarah: "I love 'em."[49]

But the focus of their visit no doubt quickly turned to more serious topics. Sarah Shaw had come to Wayland fresh from one of the most momentous days of her life. She had just watched her son, Robert Gould Shaw, parade in front of their Beacon Hill home at the head of a regiment of Black soldiers on their way to deploy to the South. In six short months, Robert Shaw had gone from being just another member of the Massachusetts Second Infantry Regiment to representing one of the most vexing questions of the war. Should Black Americans be allowed to fight? If so, could they?

How had Robert Gould Shaw, at only twenty-five years old, come to embody this question? It had not been easy. He was not much of an abolitionist. Short years before, he had regarded his parents' lifelong crusade against slavery with an adult child's weariness. "Because I don't talk and think Slavery all the time, and because I get tired . . . of hearing nothing else," he complained to his mother, "you say I don't feel with you, when I do." He was also not an obvious soldier. He had joined the war out of a sense of duty combined with the lack of a better life plan. Ending slavery was not his priority; he did not even care much about saving the Union. But after an only moderately distinguished career in the war, he had been asked by the governor of Massachusetts to take on the unimaginably difficult task of commanding New England's first regiment of Black soldiers. Why ask someone of moderate conviction and talent to do this? Because raising a regiment would take money. Shaw's parents were both abolitionists and rich. So Shaw got the offer of the commission, hand delivered from the governor by his father.[50]

At first he turned it down. He wanted to stay with the men he had forged blood ties with in legendary battles such as Cedar Mountain and Antietam. He also did not feel equal to undertaking one of the greatest social experiments of the war. The scrutiny of a Black regiment would be intense. The skepticism would be palpable. The ridicule would be vicious. If he failed to train his men to military standards—if they lacked discipline or fled from battle—he would help confirm the widespread belief that Black men were too cowardly, or lazy, or stupid to behave like soldiers. His letters show that Shaw shared some of these prejudices. No wonder he hesitated. But two days later, to his parents' immense relief, he changed his mind. After a massive recruitment effort led by Black leaders such as Frederick Douglass, Martin Delany, and Mary Ann Shadd Cary, a full regiment of Black men reported to Colonel Shaw for training at Readville, Massachusetts.[51]

These Black soldiers were not fighting for their freedom. They were already free. They were fighting for the freedom of their fellow African descendants enslaved in the South. Some had been born in the North and knew the South only from horror stories. Some had escaped slavery and knew all too well what they would find there. As they learned fighting formations and how to fire their weapons, it was not only death they faced. A fate worse than death undoubtedly awaited them if they were captured alive. What kind of torture would be reserved for Black men who dared to take up arms against white men? What kind of degradation would be inflicted on Black men who had presumed to be free? What price would they fetch on an auction block as they were sold into slavery, possibly—if the South won the war—forever?

Shaw subjected his men to brutal punishment when they learned too slowly or obeyed too reluctantly.[52] Anything short of absolute excellence was too risky. We sometimes hear the claim that Black Americans have to be twice as good as their white counterparts to secure opportunities or recognition or respect. But these Black Northerners were not competing for jobs or rewards. They were competing for the privilege of dying for the country that, even as they left the businesses they had started, the schools they had founded, and the families they loved, continued to deny that they were fully human.

Now, as her son and his men boarded the military transports that would carry them into the Deep South, Sarah Shaw was in Wayland. As the two women sat, perhaps looking over the pond in the lengthening June daylight, Sarah must have described to her friend the spectacle of her son on horseback, parading his troops down Beacon Street, past the State House and his parents' residence, with his one thousand Black soldiers in glorious lockstep behind him. The largest crowd ever assembled in Boston had come out to see them off. For white abolitionists still sure that uplift suasion would defeat prejudice, the sight of Black bodies in uniform, marching in tight, disciplined rows, was ecstasy. Garrison wept. The devoted pacifist John Greenleaf Whittier admitted that even he was moved by the military spectacle. Perhaps Sarah Shaw described how her son halted his troops briefly in front of the balcony at 44 Beacon Street where his parents and his new wife stood, held up his sword and kissed it, then marched his men onward.[53]

Their visit ended, and Sarah left. The next day was a rainy Sunday. Child spent the morning in her garden, transplanting seedlings while the soil was moist. Probably her mind was full of the waving flags and echoing footsteps evoked by her friend's description of her son's march to war. The gardening left Child tired, and she decided to lie down. This was rare; usually David napped after lunch and she did not. But David wanted to finish their transplanting while the rain continued. He returned to the garden. When he looked up from the newly dug dirt an hour later, he saw half their house in flames.

His frantic screams awakened his wife. Child jumped up and rushed to the bedroom door. The knob scorched her hand. She ran into the next room, where the smoke was so thick that she could see nothing. She stumbled down the front stairs but could not find the door latch. Somehow she forced her way out. Neighbors quickly assembled and fought to extinguish the fire. Others helped Child form a human chain reaching from inside her little parlor to the open air. With part of the house still on fire, Child hurriedly passed them one item after another: a photograph album, the shell basket, pictures from the walls, all her little "playthings."[54] Finally the fire was out. The neighbors took her precious objects home with them for safekeeping. David and Maria Child were left standing in the rain in front of their smoking home, an aging couple clinging to each other as they realized they had been granted a little more time together.

It is entirely possible for the bloodiest war in one's nation's history to be raging and nevertheless to look at the charred wallpaper in one's home and weep. Indeed, it seems that briefly, anyway, something inside Maria Child snapped. Her decades of frugality, her tiny indulgences, her desperate longing for a home: all reduced to a smoldering, soggy mess. The cause of the fire was never discovered. The Shaws sent money to help them rebuild, begging her to accept it. She did. "At this time, I confess my energies are somewhat paralyzed. I felt afraid, last week, that I was going to have a nervous fever," she reported to them. "I felt wrenchingly weak, in mind and body." It was finally time, she thought, to rest: perhaps to travel, to see something beautiful, to escape. "My soul and body absolutely need rest and refreshment, and so do David's; and I am going to use up some of your bounty in going a pleasuring," she promised the Shaws.[55] Nothing short of an imminent nervous breakdown could have made her accept money from friends. But accept it she did.

Then she sent it back. The Shaws should, she insisted, give it to someone who needed it more. And there would be no pleasuring. The house needed guarding; the fruit needed harvesting; the garden needed tending.[56] They had begun making plans for renovations, and workers were in short supply. They had to stay there in case any became available. Once the workers finally arrived, they started the job, made a mess, and disappeared. Apparently, some things never change.

As the Childs tended to their ruined home, the Civil War reached a turning point on the fields of Gettysburg, Pennsylvania. For three days in early July, the Union army struggled to block Lee's northward invasion. Several Wayland men fought among them. "No words can describe the excitement of those days of terrible conflict," Wayland shoemaker Edson Capen Davis reported: "The rushing of the infuriated men, with the ghostly forms of the dead, and the scarcely less revolting sight of the mutilated but still living ones, made a scene that will remain vivid so long as memory lasts." Davis survived with only bullet holes through his clothes. Another Wayland soldier, Sumner Aaron Davis, was less fortunate. Rushing forward to seize a fallen banner, he was shot in the chest. His fellow soldiers carried him to a nearby shelter where he slowly bled to death. On July 4, Wayland resident Alpheus Wellington wrote to his family from the front. "Perhaps you would like to know how I have spent the nation's birthday," he mused. "It has rained most of the afternoon; but we have been engaged in burying our dead." He wondered if they had been to Boston to see the Independence Day fireworks. He himself, he wrote, had seen all the explosions he ever wanted to see.[57]

But despite the fields full of Union dead, Lee's advance had been repulsed. Gettysburg was in Union hands. Northerners everywhere rejoiced. One of the Childs' neighbors later remembered the elation felt even in distant Wayland:

> Mr. Child came down to my father's house, wild with excitement, and asked for our great flag. Tying this over his shoulders, he climbed to the top of one of the great ash trees in front of the house-an incredible feat even for a young man-and there, sixty feet in the air, he lashed the staff to the tree, and with the flag blowing over him, and with his white hair streaming to the wind, he sang the "Star Spangled Banner," as loudly as his strong lungs could sing it.[58]

I imagine David's wife standing under the tree, with their house still a blackened mess, both laughing and wringing her hands.

Her husband swayed sixty feet in the air, singing. What could go wrong? This time, nothing did.

A week after the victory at Gettysburg, the worst race riots in United States history broke out in New York. For months, tension had built as working-class whites watched rich Americans buy their way out of the draft while their own sons were sacrificed on faraway battlefields or came home emaciated and maimed. On July 13, 1863, ten thousand protesters marched through lower Manhattan, pausing to set fire to the draft office at the corner of Forty-Sixth Street and Third Avenue. A newspaper office was attacked; an armory was pillaged. Soon telegraph poles were being pulled down and trolley tracks pulled up. And then the mob began to direct its rage at another, more vulnerable target: the Black workers and businesses they perceived as an economic threat. Boys ran through the streets, throwing bricks through the windows of Black-owned houses and businesses as a signal for the surging mob behind them to vent their fury there. An orphanage for Black children was set on fire. By the afternoon, Black men were being hanged on street-corner lampposts, their fingers hacked off after they strangled. Others were beaten to death and thrown in the East River. By the end of the three days of rioting, more than one hundred Black Americans had been murdered, and New York's Black business community had been destroyed. So much for the argument that if Black Americans would just work hard and be independent, white Americans would welcome them as fellow citizens.

Added to the horror Child already felt at this latest sign of racial loathing was her concern for her friends. Early on, the mob had targeted the homes of known abolitionists, among them Isaac Hopper's daughter Abby Hopper Gibbons. Soon there were rumors that five hundred rioters were roaming Staten Island, where Sarah and Francis Shaw lived. "How anxious I am for you!" she wrote as the rioting entered its third and fourth day. "Oh, darling Sarah and dearly beloved Frank, *do* come away from Staten Island, unless order is soon and completely restored! I have no peace, thinking of the peril you are in."[59]

* * *

As his parents braced for the mob and Black men were lynched on the streets of lower Manhattan, Robert Gould Shaw, a thousand miles away on a South Carolina island, was being given a choice. His regiment had seen action for the first time only the day before, withstanding an attack by a much larger Confederate force and acquitting themselves with honor. Ordered soon afterward to join other Union forces on nearby Folly Island, they arrived tired, wet, and hungry after an all-night march in a thunderstorm. But when Shaw reported to commanding General George Strong, he was told that a regiment was needed to lead the charge on nearby Fort Wagner in just a matter of hours.[60]

It was the opportunity Shaw and his men had longed for. Fort Wagner was just south of Fort Sumter. If they could take Fort Wagner, Fort Sumter would be within their grasp. With Fort Sumter defeated, Charleston—the birthplace of the Confederacy—would be within reach. Black soldiers helping take Charleston: the symbolism was impossible to resist.[61] On behalf of his exhausted regiment, Shaw accepted. In the few hours before dusk, his men prepared to prove their worth to the world by throwing themselves into what would prove to be an unwinnable fight.

There is some evidence that General Strong saw this moment as Shaw did: an opportunity for Black soldiers to prove their discipline, courage, and humanity. There is also evidence that others saw it differently. "Well I guess we will let Strong put those d——d negroes from Massachusetts in the advance," General Truman Seymore said. "We may as well get rid of them, one time as another." "I trust God will give me strength to do my duty," Shaw wrote after accepting Strong's challenge. "If I could only live a few weeks longer with my wife, and be at home a little while, I might die happy, but that cannot be. I do not believe I will live through our next fight."[62]

On the evening of July 18, the Black soldiers of the Massachusetts Fifty-Fourth Regiment stormed down the beach behind their white colonel. Confederates opened fire, and bodies began to fall.

Fig. 51. Colonel Robert Gould Shaw. Courtesy of the Library of Congress.

Shaw ordered a double-quick march. The soldiers reached the fort under heavy shelling and rushed up the parapet. Shaw scaled the rampart and stood briefly above his men, urging them forward. Then a Confederate bullet exploded in his chest, and he fell to the ground, dying as his men streamed past him toward the fort.

The fighting raged for hours, with more than half the Massachusetts Fifty-Fourth, now under Captain Luis Emilio, at one point gaining access to the fort. Finally, they were forced to retreat. White reinforcements, led by General Strong, repeated the attempt and were also repulsed, with Strong badly wounded. In the end, 272 of the 600 Black men who began the attack were killed, wounded, or taken prisoner.[63]

The next day, Confederate soldiers began throwing the Union dead into a mass grave. Shaw's body was found among them. What to do with him? Confederate General Johnson Hagood gave the matter some thought. He could have followed common practice: ordered the dead colonel returned to his family or buried in a separate grave, as befitted an officer. Instead, he ordered the worst humiliation he could imagine. Shaw was thrown into the same sandy ditch as his fallen men, their Black bodies falling on top of their white commander, their blood mingling with his. "Our darling son, our hero, has received at the hands of the rebels the most fitting burial possible," Shaw's father wrote. "The poor benighted wretches thought they were heaping indignities on his dead body . . . they thought to give an additional pang to the bruised hearts of his friends." But, he continued, speaking also for his wife, "we would not have him buried elsewhere, if we could." A month later, Union soldiers captured the fort. Shaw's body remained where it had been thrown.[64]

In the North, praise for the Fifty-Fourth was resounding. They had not won the battle, but they had fought with all the discipline, bravery, and nobility that their race was supposed to lack. Shaw was quickly transformed into a martyr and a hero. A sculpture of him mounted on his horse, with his men beside him, now faces the Massachusetts State House, just blocks from where his parents watched him march away. But we should pause in our grief for this "blue-eyed child of fortune," as the philosopher William James later called him. Shaw died honored by a country that had always honored him. His Black soldiers died still not knowing if their sacrifice would rid their country of the evil that had defined their lives and demanded their deaths.

"Oh darling! Darling! If the newspaper rumor be true, what I have so long dreaded has come upon you," Child wrote frantically to Sarah Shaw as the news reached Wayland. What to say to one whose loss was so devastating, so severe? "If your beautiful and brave boy has died, he died nobly in the defense of great princi-

Fig. 52. William Harvey Carney (ca. 1864). Carney, who was born enslaved, fought with the Massachusetts Fifty-Fourth at the Battle of Fort Wagner and was awarded the Medal of Honor for saving the flag despite the regiment's defeat. Courtesy of the Smithsonian National Museum of African American History and Culture.

ples, and has gone to join the glorious army of martyrs," she began. "Such a son in the spirit-world is worth ten living here for themselves only." This might be true, but what mother would want to hear it? "Ah, darling, my words fall coldly upon your bereaved heart," Child predicted.[65] Perhaps, in fact, there was nothing to say.

In the midst of her aching grief for her friend's loss, Child did not forget to mourn the fate of Shaw's Black soldiers. She did not want others to, either. "To think of those brave devoted men, after their exhaustion by hunger, fatigue, and the hard labors of battle, sent to Charleston, to be insulted and tortured by ferocious tyrants, and then sold into slavery!" she wrote in the *National Anti-Slavery Standard*. Her grief for her friend, she wrote to Anna Loring, together with "my anxiety about those of the Fifty-Fourth, who were taken prisoners, [has] been harder for me to bear, than anything which has occurred during the war."[66]

* * *

Another wartime Thanksgiving passed; New Year 1864 dawned. Child continued to sew caps for soldiers, taking care that they covered the neck "to keep the cold winds out." She also continued to fight against slavery in print whenever she could: "I write to the 'Tribune' about [the slave]; I write to the 'Transcript' about him; and I write to the President and Members of Congress about him; I write to Western Virginia and Missouri about him, and I get the articles published too," she wrote to Lucy Searle. In her isolated Wayland cottage, she was also receiving eyewitness reports from a different kind of battlefront. In spring 1862, Harriet Jacobs had left the safety of Nathaniel Willis's employment to assist her fellow former slaves who were streaming by the thousands into contraband camps throughout the South. "The misery I have witnessed must be seen to be believed," Jacobs wrote to Child from Virginia, describing conditions among the refugees. Diseases raged and rations were short. Hundreds of these freedom seekers, Jacobs reported in the *Liberator*, died still clothed in the "filthy rags they wore from the plantation."[67]

Jacobs mourned the effects of psychological and physical abuse all too obvious in the recently enslaved humans around her. But there were also signs of hope, and Jacobs wanted to share this hope with Child. From a camp in Alexandria, Virginia, that was housing seven thousand refugees, she reported that those who were healthy and able were working hard. "Within the last eight months seven

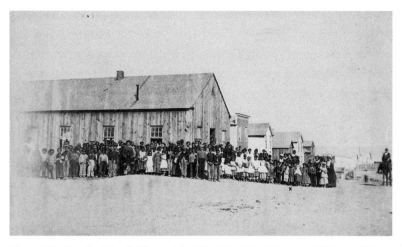

Fig. 53. The Jacobs School, Alexandria, Virginia, 1864. Courtesy of Emory University.

hundred little cabins have been built, containing from two to four rooms," she reported. Schools had already been established, both for children and for adults, and the community had chosen Black teachers and leaders—a sign of their desire for self-sufficiency. Jacobs was particularly proud of a recent community meeting that had taken place. "I wish you could have been at that meeting," she wrote to Child, no doubt conscious that Child would be hungry for evidence that these newly emancipated humans were showing signs of respectability. "Most of the people were slaves, until quite recently, but they talked sensibly, and I assure you that they put the question to vote in quite parliamentary style."

The camp's children provided even more vivid hope. Even those who only months earlier did not know the alphabet could now sound out multisyllable words. "Slavery has not crushed out the animal spirits of these children," Jacobs reported. "Fun lurks in the corners of their eyes, dimples their mouths, tingles at their fingers' ends." She ended with words that must have warmed Child's heart: "Thank you for your letter. I wish you could have seen the happy group of faces round me, at our little Fair, while I read it to them." Before long, Jacobs and her daughter had secured a lease on a small property to begin educating their charges in earnest.

It was called the Jacobs School.⁶⁸ Child arranged to have Jacobs's letters published in the *National Anti-Slavery Standard*, securing both patrons and funding for Jacobs while also assuring her fellow white Northerners that respectability, and the end of white prejudice, were surely just a few schools away.

In April 1864, the Senate passed the Thirteenth Amendment, which, if approved by the House and ratified by the states, would abolish slavery. Human enslavement had also by now been outlawed in Washington, DC. Perhaps because of these slow but sure legislative victories, Child had begun to reassess her president. It helped that Lincoln had recently published a remarkable open letter in which he disclosed his reasoning in stark, humble terms. "I am naturally anti-slavery," the president affirmed, adding, in a phrase that must have resonated in Child's soul, "if slavery is not wrong, nothing is wrong." But he had not, he once again repeated, been elected to make his own conscience the law of the land. His oath of office had committed him to preserving the Union.

Then the president explained several of the decisions that had grieved Child so deeply. When Frémont had declared slaves free in breach of Missouri law, the emancipation of those slaves was not yet necessary to save the Union. When General Hunter had attempted "military emancipation," the same was still true. But finally, after the Border States had ignored all his offers of compensated emancipation, "I was, in my best judgment, driven to the alternative of either surrendering the Union, and with it, the Constitution, or of laying strong hand upon the colored element," Lincoln explained.

Laying strong hand upon the colored element! It is a euphemism for the ages. Apparently, it meant drastically increasing the enlistment of Black soldiers. He had taken this step out of desperation, Lincoln continued, fully aware that it could trigger popular revolt or mass military desertions. But it had not. On the contrary, it had resulted in "a gain of quite a hundred and thirty thousand soldiers, seamen, and laborers. These are palpable facts," Lincoln advised skeptics, "about which, as facts, there can be no cavilling. We have the men; and we could not have had them without the measure."

There it was, plain as day: the benefit of emancipation had been the addition of Black bodies to stop Southern bullets.

Lincoln was willing to own the blunt calculus of it all. "In telling this tale I attempt no compliment to my own sagacity," he wrote. "I claim not to have controlled events, but confess plainly that events have controlled me." He concluded with a statement that Child herself could have written. "If God now wills the removal of a great wrong, and wills also that we of the North as well as you of the South, shall pay fairly for our complicity in that wrong, impartial history will find therein new cause to attest and revere the justice and goodness of God."[69] In that case, the United States would, as Child had put it, serve as a warning.

In her Wayland home, where workers again tramped in and out making repairs to the half-burned house, Child read Lincoln's letter and was moved. By now, she had abandoned hope that emancipation would be understood as a moral triumph; she was resigned to the fact that it had been achieved only as a military necessity. Much as she hated that fact, she appreciated Lincoln's explanation. She declared the letter an "honest, unaffected, sensible statement." "Abraham Lincoln is a 'slow coach,' and I have often been out of patience with him," she acknowledged. "But I believe he is a thoroughly honest man." In the end, she admitted in an open letter in the *Standard*, "he was the very best man that the moral condition of the American people admitted of being elected." Elsewhere she put it more simply: "He is a better president than we deserve."[70] Perhaps it was faint praise, but, like the man it paid tribute to, it was honest.

It was still true that Lincoln's proclamations and the Senate's amendments could do little on their own. Only one thing could ensure that emancipation would be permanent and universal: that formerly enslaved persons would be, as the proclamation declared, "thenceforward, and forever free." The North had to win the war. "I have never dreaded the battles," Child wrote to Lucy Osgood, "as I do this Spring."[71]

∗　∗　∗

On June 15, 1864, the soldiers of the Massachusetts Thirty-Fifth Division, with several Wayland men among them, began a months-long effort to capture the strategically crucial town of Petersburg, Virginia. The initial Union attack pitted US soldiers against a rebel regiment led by Child's former nemesis, Virginia governor Henry Wise. It failed. What happened next defies belief. Union generals resolved to dig under Confederate lines and pack the tunnel with explosives. On July 30, the explosives were detonated, killing several hundred Confederate soldiers and leaving a path for Union troops to press on toward Petersburg. But the commanding officer was drunk and failed to convey instructions to his men. Instead of marching around the crater left by the explosion, they marched into it, making them easy targets for Confederate soldiers who massed on its rim. A troop of Black soldiers was sent in after them as reinforcements. The battle turned into a rout.[72] As news of the humiliating Union defeat circulated, the Black soldiers were gleefully blamed in the press.

"We went in the morning with . . . hopes of victory, and came back utterly defeated to occupy the same lines we had left," Wayland resident Frank Draper reported to his family. "It was enough to take the stiffness out of anyone to see the chance of success lost by mismanagement," he wrote, adding, in what must have been one of the war's great understatements: "There was a blunder somewhere." In the midst of his grief for his fallen comrades, Draper paused to refute the reports of Black soldiers' cowardice. "The Colored Division is made to shoulder the lion's share of the blame of the disaster," he wrote. Don't believe everything you read, he advised his family. "To deny that the colored division broke and ran is not my purpose at all. They did run, and so did I, and so did hundreds of others, but not until circumstances had become so desperate as to make many a veteran wish himself out of it." "I am indeed whole in every limb, but how I escaped is and always [will] be to me a miracle," Draper wrote, concluding simply in a postscript: "The Wayland boys are all right."[73]

The news of the defeat, including the "horrible slaughter of the poor blacks; and the bad use that the copperheads would make of their panic," again kept Child up at night. Sleepless under distant stars, she fought against despair. The weight of meaning, of life and death, pressed in. "Sometimes I am oppressed and appalled by the mystery of my own existence; realizing what a small and vanishing point I am between two infinities, I feel lonely and frightened," she confessed to Sarah Shaw. "For such states of mind I find but two modes of cure; prayers to God, and active co-operation with my fellow creatures, which is praying with my *hands* as well as my heart."[74] I imagine her lighting a candle and going back to her knitting.

Lincoln desperately needed a military victory before the November elections. Finally, after two years of humiliating losses, he named Ulysses S. Grant commanding general, and the victories began to accrue. Atlanta fell to Sherman; Sheridan swept through the Shenandoah Valley; by November, Grant was pushing toward the Confederate capital in Richmond. Still, Child fretted as election day approached. She had by now so reversed her opinion of Lincoln that she regretted being unable to vote. In the end, Lincoln won easily. "I am a happy woman since the election," Child admitted. "He has his faults, and I have sometimes been out of patience with him; but I will say of him that I have constantly gone on liking him better and better."[75]

The series of Union victories and Lincoln's election were not the only good news that November. Child's book about aging, *Looking toward Sunset*, had finally been published. Its success far surpassed her expectations. Before the end of the year, it had sold four thousand copies. It would go through twelve more printings during her lifetime.[76] Once again Child had anticipated a need her fellow Americans hardly knew they had. In the face of so much young death, there was clearly comfort in thinking of old life.

Child knew exactly what she would do with the money. "Few human beings have been happier than I have been since January came in," she wrote to Anna Loring. "My book is a success, and the proceeds were vowed to the Freedmen." "To comfort old folks with one hand, and give out the proceeds to the suffering and the wronged with the other, is what I call the highest kind of recreation," she concluded. "No prince or nobleman can discover, or invent, any mode of enjoyment equal to *earning* with one hand and *giving* with the other."[77]

The first four months of 1865 altered the world with lightning speed. On January 31, the House of Representatives passed the Thirteenth Amendment, bringing slavery one step closer to legal extinction. In March, Lincoln was inaugurated for a second term. In early April, the Confederate capital of Richmond fell and Jefferson Davis fled. Days later, Grant's army, including several Wayland soldiers, finally broke the siege of Petersburg, cutting off Lee's chances of success. By mid-April, the war was over and Lincoln was dead.

Child's response to her president's murder was both tempered and true to her most cherished hopes. "The assassination of our good President, shocked and distressed me," she wrote to Sarah Shaw. But five minutes later, she had found reason for hope. "Dreadful as this is, perhaps it is only another of the wonderful manifestations of Providence," she speculated. "The kindhearted Abraham, was certainly in danger of making too easy terms with the rebels," she mused. "Perhaps he has been removed, that he might not defeat his own work, and that another, better calculated to carry it to a safe and *sure end*, might come into his place."[78] The person newly designated to complete Providence's work, it seemed, was Lincoln's vice president Andrew Johnson. Child thought early signs were promising. Johnson was a Southerner but not an aristocrat: perhaps he was perfectly suited to reshape the postbellum South. Child was impressed with his honesty and sincerity. "Providence has placed that respectable trust in his hands, and perhaps he will better finish the work, his upright and careful predecessor began, and carried forward so well. Yet"[79]

The letter breaks off there. Whatever second thoughts Child added have been lost. And whatever they were, they would have paled next to the bitter betrayal Child and other abolitionists would feel when Andrew Johnson systematically dashed their hopes for a racially just society. The next battlefront would open soon, and Johnson would, in effect, become the opposing general. The question of whether the 600,000 dead Americans would leave behind them a new birth of justice or a new system of oppression was not yet answered. Neither was the question of whether the traumatized country would prove, from the viewpoint of history, to be a warning or an example.

The Wayland soldiers returned home. On the Fourth of July 1865, the town held a celebration for them, including speeches, hymns, and fireworks. Alpheus Wellington, who had written so movingly about Gettysburg, was not there to see them; he had been shot on the final march to Richmond and was buried where he fell. Another soldier was luckier. "Found everything as it should be," he wrote in his diary. "Am glad to become a citizen once more. Intend to remain one as long as possible." Wayland's most famous resident, having lived to see the end of a three-decade struggle to free four million human beings from enslavement, had a similarly modest goal. "I intend to purchase a new bonnet," Maria Child wrote to a friend. "I have not had one for five years."[80]

13

No Time for Ovations

It might seem that this story should be over. In many of our history books, it is. The war was won, slavery was abolished, the country was moving on. American principles of liberty and independence had prevailed, and the country could go back to being a beacon to other nations. No doubt many Wayland citizens thought exactly this. Perhaps they expressed their righteous relief to the veteran abolitionist in their midst when they encountered her at the library or the general store or in the pews of Wayland's Unitarian church. If they did, they probably did not get the reply they were expecting.

"When people ask me if I am not thankful to have lived to see justice done to the negro," Child reported in the *National Anti-Slavery Standard*, "I reply, 'If I *do* live to see justice done to the negro, I shall be thankful.'"[1] I imagine the Waylanders receiving this response feeling rebuked, puzzled, perhaps a little defensive. The North had poured out blood and treasure to win this war. Even if, for most of them, ending slavery had not been its initial aim, the fact was that the slaves were now free: free from tyrannical masters, free to find family members who had been sold away, free to work and live by their own wages. They were free, in short, to pursue happiness. What more could they want? I imagine Child's fellow Waylanders walking away, shaking their heads. Some people, it seems, are just never satisfied.

Child was so far from being satisfied that she surprised even herself. "If I had been told, thirty years ago, that Slavery would be abolished in my day, I should have anticipated such enthusiastic joy as would set me half crazy," she wrote to Sarah Shaw. But "what with the frightful expenditure of blood; emancipation's being forced upon us by *necessity*, instead of proceeding from the repentance of the nation; and the shameful want of protection to the freedmen since they have been emancipated; there has been no opportunity for any out-gushing of joy and exultation." She could, she found, only "rejoice with trembling." Not even the new bonnet helped.[2]

We now know Child was right to tremble. The end of the Civil War was followed by a bloody, decade-long game of cat and mouse in which the federal government would look away long enough for the South to break out in raging violence against Black Americans. When the abuses could no longer be ignored, it would intervene and impose some kind of order. Then it would look away again. There were, after all, other problems to deal with: wars with Native Americans, the largest economic contraction in the country's history, labor unrest as monopolies and industrialization shattered workers' confidence in economic justice. Women were also intensifying their crusade for equality, and new waves of immigrants were forcing another reckoning with what it meant to be American. With the federal government preoccupied by one or more of these crises, Southern anti-Black violence would spike again. The cycle would repeat until finally, in the wake of a contested election in 1876, Washington looked away for good. This period of upheaval is known as Reconstruction, and its struggles would define the rest of Lydia Maria Child's life.[3]

* * *

What kind of country had the martyred Lincoln left to his successor? Postwar questions were daunting. What would the terms of peace be? Would Jefferson Davis be tried for treason? Would General Lee be hanged? When would Southern politicians be allowed back into Congress, and what would they do when they got there?

Who would pay for wartime devastation in the South, and how could the nation's economy recover without unpaid labor?

Speaking of unpaid labor: What would the country do with the hundreds of thousands of newly emancipated humans huddled in refugee camps around Union army bases? What about the millions more just learning that they were free? How would they be housed, fed, and protected from the fury of defeated Confederates? One answer came in the formation of the Freedmen's Bureau, a federal agency established to assist in the transition from slavery to freedom. As if to guarantee failure, the agency was initially set up to last for only one year and had no budget.[4]

Some questions were more philosophical. What did the end of the war *mean*? Among abolitionists and at least some others in the North, it meant the triumph of principles: of antislavery for one, but also of a free labor system that encouraged self-reliance and individualism. For many in the South, it meant no such thing. It simply meant that the North had had more industry, more weapons, more ships, more soldiers. Might had made right. So while many Northerners saw the war's end as ushering in an era of progress, many in the South simply wanted their old lives back.

The end of a civil war also presents a paradox for a democracy. When hundreds of thousands of citizens have recently tried to destroy the country, surely allowing them to vote anytime soon would be national suicide. Even if Jefferson Davis and Robert E. Lee escaped the gallows (which indeed they did), should they be reinstated as regular citizens? If so, what would guarantee that they would not restore the very conditions Northern soldiers had just given their lives to abolish? With these questions in mind, restrictions were put in place to determine who could participate in postwar governments and who could not.[5] But every election that excluded former Confederates strengthened the South's accusation that the federal government had become an occupying force and American democracy a dictatorship.

Meanwhile, the country began grappling with the meaning of the Thirteenth Amendment. "Neither slavery nor involuntary servitude, except as a punishment for crime whereof the party shall have been duly convicted, shall exist within the United States, or any place subject to their jurisdiction," it read. Slavery could now never be reinstated by any particular state. All Americans, except those convicted of a crime, were free. It would not take long for new laws to begin criminalizing Black men in overwhelming numbers, effectively enslaving them again. But for now, an even more basic question predominated. What, in the wake of the Thirteenth Amendment, did "liberty for all" mean?

It certainly did not mean justice for all. Freedpeople would never be compensated for the lifetime of labor that had been stolen from them or for the physical and emotional torture many had endured. Many of them would never find their children, spouses, or parents again. Most were left with no source of income to secure food or clothing. The United States Congress would not apologize for slavery until 2009, and even that apology came with the caveat that it authorized "no claim against the United States." In other words, no actual compensation should be expected.[6] Never mind all that: already the main concern of many Northerners was that freedpeople not become dependent on the government for handouts. Newly emancipated slaves, in short, soon confronted the fact that many white Americans thought they had already been given everything they were owed.

Liberty also did not mean equality. That Black people should not be enslaved did not, in most Americans' minds, imply that they should be citizens or vote. Nor did it guarantee property rights or the right to go to court, sue for damages, or engage in contracts. It did not even guarantee the right to choose where to live: several western states continued to pass laws expelling Black settlers or prohibiting new ones from entering.[7] And liberty certainly did not entail social equality, meaning admission to theaters or churches or public transportation. Black Americans would have to fight for every one of these rights, and many white Americans would fight back every step of the way. Some of these fights are still not over.

In the face of these realities, freedpeople were overwhelmingly clear about two things that were, at a minimum, necessary to make their freedom real. One was land. Land would allow them to grow food, establish homes, and begin to build financial security. And there was, as it happened, plenty of land available. Entire plantations had been abandoned by Southern aristocrats as they fled advancing Union armies, their fields left unused and overgrown. In some areas, the experiment was already being tried. In South Carolina, thousands of acres of Confederate property were being farmed by formerly enslaved people as early as 1861.[8] But what would become of this land, and the Black farmers working it, now that the war was over and plantation owners were coming home?

To Maria Child, the solution was obvious. "The large plantations ought to be confiscated by the U.S. government, divided into small farms, a certain number of acres given to the soldiers, white and Black, and the remainder sold on easy terms to the poor whites and the emancipated slaves," she wrote to Lucy Osgood and anyone else who would listen. How she wished she simply had land of her own to distribute. Short of that, she donated all the money she could spare to meet the freedpeople's needs. Grand gestures like the Shaws' orphanage for Black children, named for their martyred son, were beyond her means. But what she lacked in wealth, she tried to make up for with a ferocious work ethic and a kind of exultant frugality. "If I have written a story, it has been to create a fund for *them*; if I have taxed my ingenuity to spend the least possible for food and clothing, it has been for the same purpose," she wrote to the Shaws. "Mr Child says he believes I counterfeit money in some corner of the house, for if I don't, he can't see where it all comes from." She kept what they needed; the rest she gave away. Her contributions, by my calculations, came to the equivalent of seven thousand of today's dollars a year. Her frugality had always been a kind of activism. Now more than ever, a dress mended instead of bought was a statement of principle.[9] Meanwhile, her outmoded clothing was becoming notorious. She wore it like a badge of honor.

Aside from land, the freedpeople's other urgent desire was for education. Child heard firsthand about eager students from Harriet Jacobs, who was still running the Jacobs School for newly emancipated children in Alexandria, Virginia. Her students' desperate conditions were sobering, Jacobs reported, but their potential was exhilarating. Who knew what future Frederick Douglasses walked barefoot and hungry among her charges? Child continued to send Jacobs what she could, including seeds for the school's garden.[10] But she longed to do more. What did these students need that she could contribute? What could she do that would assist them in the unimaginably difficult transition from enslavement to freedom?

Before long, Child had a plan: she would create a primer to help them learn to read. It would not be like the primers she had learned from as a girl. Instead of stories of American presidents and Revolutionary War battles, she would fill it with biographies of famous Africans and their descendants. In its pages she would show the freedpeople that others like them had been inventors, poets, scientists, politicians, and military leaders. As they read the stories, spelling out one word after another, they would learn facts that would raise their hopes and arm them against prejudice. The more she thought about the idea, the more she liked it. Soon she was "resolving my poor brain into a Committee of Ways and Means" to figure out how to publish it at her own expense.[11]

She began compiling the book's chapters. Harriet Jacobs agreed to contribute; Frederick Douglass granted Child permission to tell his story however she saw fit. She rewrote some of the biographical sketches of Black heroes like Toussaint L'Ouverture and Phillis Wheatley that she had included in her *Appeal* thirty years ago, recasting them in easier language for early readers. She also included stories of Africans resisting the slave trade and of fugitive slaves' daring escapes. To assure her readers that they had other white allies, she included authors like Garrison and Whittier. But perhaps most important, she quoted Douglass's eloquent outrage, the poet and orator Frances Ellen Watkins Harper's lyrical exhortations, and the agonized poetry of a slave named Mingo, written to his wife before bloodhounds tore him apart as he tried to flee. Black Americans, her anthology would make clear, had recognized the atrocities done to them, articulated them, and fought them. They had not been helpless, or submissive, or ignorant. In the table

Fig. 54. Poet and reformer Frances Ellen Watkins Harper. Child published Harper's poetry in *The Freedmen's Book*. Courtesy of the National Portrait Gallery.

of contents, Child made Black authors' accomplishments visible by putting an asterisk next to each of their names.

In addition to the compiling and editing, Child also wrote several of the book's chapters, including the last one. She called it "Advice from an Old Friend." "For many years I have felt great sympathy for you, my brethren and sisters, and I have tried to do what I could to help you to freedom," she wrote: "I have made this book to encourage you."[12] How full her heart must have been as she wrote these words: full of sympathy, fear, and a little joy mixed, as always, with trembling. In 1865, the anthology was published. She called it *The Freedmen's Book*.

Compared with other primers created for similar purposes, Child's anthology was, once again, bracingly progressive. By contrast, *The Freedmen's Third Reader*, which was published by the American Tract Society, made no effort to cultivate pride in African culture or enslaved people's resistance. Its readings were unapologetically paternalistic and patriotic, exhorting newly freed slaves to take their place as aspiring supplicants hoping to be admitted to a superior culture. It included few acknowledgments of what slaves had suffered and no entries by Black authors. By comparison, Child's anthology was, as one historian has put it, "rare indeed."[13]

But despite all Child's passionate good intentions, I have come to think of the essays she herself wrote in *The Freedmen's Book* as among her most problematic publications. This is because encouraging freedpeople "by honorable examples of men of their own color" was not Child's only aim. She had two others, and they should give us pause.

The first of these, Child acknowledged to Lucy Osgood, was to "convey moral instruction in simple, attractive form." For Child, this did not mean a discussion of the Ten Commandments or Jesus's parables. In fact, *The Freedmen's Book* also differs from other primers by the almost total absence of theology. Instead, moral instruction to her meant cultivating the habits of respectability that were, then as always, cornerstones of her worldview. So Child, now as ever the frugal housewife, set about giving advice: how to patch worn clothes, whitewash houses, treat animals, talk to children, and plant gardens "that make the poorest cabin look beautiful."[14]

Why all this homey advice? Because, quite simply, the fate of slaves everywhere depended on it. In Spanish colonies, Child reminded her readers, people were still enslaved. "If you are vicious, lazy, and careless," she warned them, "their masters will excuse themselves for continuing to hold them in bondage, by saying: 'Look at the freedmen of the United States! What idle vagabonds they are! How dirty their cabins are! How slovenly their dress! That proves that negroes cannot take care of themselves, that they are not fit to be free.'" But the reverse, Child promised her readers, was also true: "If your houses look neat, and your clothes are clean and whole, and your gardens well weeded . . . then all the world will cry out, 'You see that negroes can take care of themselves; and it is a sin and a shame to keep such men in Slavery.'" Simple cleanliness, in short, meant everyone could win: by being respectable, Black Americans could improve both their own lot and that of others. "It is a great privilege to have a chance to do extensive good by such simple means," she concluded. To this reminder of their privilege, Child added an admonition: "Your Heavenly Father," she warned, "will hold you responsible for the use you make of your influence."[15]

She meant it as encouragement. But she also knew better. Child had shown herself throughout her life to be intensely aware of the poisonous reach of racial prejudice. She knew that the simple equation of uplift suasion—act respectably and you will be respected—was false just as often as it was true. In this same essay, she admitted as much: "For a good while it will provoke many of [your former masters] to see those who were once their slaves acting like freemen," she wrote: "They will doubtless do many things to vex and discourage you."[16] This, as she well knew, was a wrenching understatement. And what, as Peter Paul Simmons had asked decades before, was the psychological cost of asking emancipated Black Americans to believe that uplift suasion would work? How could such a demand not add a crushing psychological burden to an already desperate struggle for physical survival? In looking over Child's fifty-year career in the public eye, this is one of the lessons I find most searing: white Americans must stop combining private agony about racial injustice with a desperation to convince its victims that it doesn't exist.

The second of Child's problematic aims was, as she also wrote to Lucy Osgood, to inspire her readers "with forgiving feelings towards their own masters." So while in some chapters she did include references to rapes and floggings and children sold at auction blocks, she sometimes presented a notably sanitized version of events. A case in point is Harriet Jacobs's narrative. Now called "The Good Grandmother," Jacobs's story as it appears in *The Freed-*

men's Book includes no vengeful mistresses or sadistic masters. Instead, the narrative is entirely framed by Jacobs's grandmother's humility and forgiveness. The reader is told that Jacobs now considers herself "more than repaid for all I have endured." "Glory to God in the highest!" are the story's final triumphant words.[17]

Given Child's earlier interventions in Jacobs's work, it is fair to wonder whose words these were. It appears that they were indeed Jacobs's. She is listed in the table of contents as this chapter's author, unlike Frederick Douglass, whose story Child clearly rewrote with his permission. More convincingly, Child tells her readers that the last words were from a letter to her written as Jacobs celebrated the Emancipation Proclamation. Still, their history together should make us worry that Jacobs, perhaps at Child's suggestion, had once again molded her story to suit Child's uplifting aims.

Child's desire to promote forgiveness also raises a more philosophical question: What is the value of forgiveness without repentance? Given the chance, those who had enslaved Jacobs and her students would likely re-enslave every one of them. What, in those circumstances, does it mean to forgive? And what does it do to victims of atrocity to be encouraged to forgive when the perpetrators are eager to reoffend? What does it do when their supposed allies, as in Jacobs's revised story, weaken the evidence of what they have suffered, whitewashing a darker truth?

One more episode is worth recounting here. Child's letter to Douglass asking permission to use his story in *The Freedmen's Book* does not survive, but his reply to her suggests a question she apparently raised. Child, it seems, had read somewhere that Douglass had reconciled with his former enslaver, Thomas Auld. Was this true? No, Douglass replied, it was not: "The story of an interview between us is a newspaper story for which I am in no way responsible," he wrote. "Any such meeting could not fail to be awkward," he continued in another painful understatement: "We could hardly get at each other." But then Douglass seemed to reconsider. "Still I should be glad to see him especially if I could do so simply by meeting him halfway," he wrote. Then again, maybe not: "I do not," he continued, "fancy making a journey to see a man who gave me so many reasons for wishing the greatest distance between us."

Yet again he reconsidered: "Time and events have made changes and it is just possible that the Lamb may venture into the den of the Lion without danger of being eaten up," the letter's next paragraph begins. "I learn from my sister who still lives near Master Thomas, that he says he would be glad to see me." Then came an extraordinary promise: "He has but to say so to me by letter—and considering his age, and forgetting his past, I will make him a visit."[18]

What is going on in this letter? What had Child written to prompt such vacillation by one of America's most assertive intellectuals? We will never know, but here is my guess: Child had asked him if she could assure her readers, themselves newly emancipated, that America's most famous fugitive slave had forgiven the man who had enslaved him.

In fact, Douglass and Auld did meet again. In his last autobiography, Douglass gives an account of the meeting that was all Child could have wished for. He first recounts everything Auld had done to him. It is a long list. Auld had "struck down my personality . . . reduced me to a chattel, hired me out to a noted slave breaker to be worked like a beast and flogged into submission, taken my hard earnings, sent me to prison . . . and had, without any apparent disturbance of his conscience, sold my body to his brother Hugh and pocketed the price of my flesh and blood." He then admits that his own fame had made Auld's otherwise unremarkable life the subject of international outrage: "I had by my writings made his name and his deeds familiar to the world in four different languages," Douglass acknowledged. But now Auld was an invalid, and the reunion between former master and slave took place in his bedroom. Douglass took Auld's palsied hand, and both men were overcome by emotion. Auld told Douglass he did not blame him for running away. It was not quite an apology, but it was close enough for Douglass. In return, Douglass offered a defense of Auld's behavior that was generous to the point of implausibility. "I regarded him as I did myself," he wrote, "a victim of the circumstances of birth, education, law, and custom."[19]

By the time this account was published in 1881, Lydia Maria Child was no longer alive to read it. If she had been, surely she would have rejoiced in this report of reconciliation. But Douglass was lucky, if we want to call it that. Auld had offered Douglass one of the things that makes reconciliation possible: an admission of harm by the wrongdoer. But sixteen years earlier, as *The Freedmen's Book* was published, most former slaves confronted the opposite: far from acknowledging slavery's evil, their former enslavers were doing everything in their power to re-create it. Given this reality, I am somehow glad that Douglass's reconciliation with Auld came too late for Child to use it in *The Freedmen's Book*. Quite simply: its absence kept her from telling her readers that, following Douglass's famous example, they were expected to do the same.

* * *

Meanwhile, the question of what the freedpeople should do continued. Should they flee their former homes and head North? Or gather with other refugees in Southern cities? Should they stay on the land they knew, still hoping that Congress would recognize their claim to it? Many—including Child, Jacobs, and officials in the Freedmen's Bureau—favored the third option.[20] Better to stay and work, proving their independence and industry, in the hopes of being rewarded than to join the squalor of contraband camps or risk the foreign and inhospitable North.

Ironically, the conviction that freedpeople should stay where they were was shared by two groups that Child otherwise despised: Northern speculators and Southern aristocrats. Even as *The Freedmen's Book* was published, capitalists were streaming down from the North, full of optimism and investment dollars. Surely, these investors thought, the problem was simple. The freedpeople needed work; plantation owners, now returning from wartime exile, needed workers. The two sides could cooperate, and Northern investment would soon turn a profit. Naturally there were complications: it was understandable that many freedpeople would resist working for their former enslavers, and it was probably true that former enslavers could not immediately be trusted to treat their workers as the free people they legally were. But surely mutual self-interest would overcome these obstacles and a new system of free labor would triumph. For Southern aristocrats the goal was much simpler. They simply wanted their labor force back exactly as they had left it.

It turned out, however, that many freedpeople could not be persuaded to do backbreaking work for pitiful pay in order to enrich their former enslavers. They did not want to grow cotton for capitalists to sell; they wanted to grow vegetables for their families to eat. They were not interested in new labor practices introduced by ambitious Northerners to increase productivity. What, one freedman asked, was "the use of being free . . . if he had to work harder than when he was a slave?" Determined to improve their working conditions even if they stayed, freedpeople sometimes went on strike or refused to sign contracts that re-created the conditions of slavery.[21] These efforts were, predictably, described not as admirable attempts to secure fair treatment but as evidence of dishonesty and laziness.

If formerly enslaved people did not want to work, Southern governments would have to find ways to force them. A series of laws called Black Codes was duly created, making it all but impossible for freedpeople to work anywhere but on the plantations where they had been enslaved. Black Codes required freedpeople to sign employment contracts with plantation owners for an entire year on pain of imprisonment. Once the contracts were signed, plantation owners controlled their workers' travel, socializing, and work hours. Other Black Codes set prohibitive taxes on freedpeople wanting to engage in any labor except farming. They denied freedpeople permits to sell food they had grown and prohibited them from hunting. Freedpeople could also be fined or imprisoned for "misspending" or "disorderly behavior." If they were deemed "unfit" parents, their children could be turned over to their former masters and forced to work. Again the blame here must be shared by North and South. The laws were Southern, but support from Wall Street's cotton investors was enthusiastic. The South needed to rebuild; to achieve this, it needed cotton; to harvest cotton, it needed a massive workforce; to make a profit, it needed that workforce to be stable and cheap. If that workforce could be secured only by re-creating the conditions of slavery as nearly as possible, Northern capitalists reasoned, then so be it.[22]

But Black Codes were not the worst force confronting the freedpeople. In the year after the Thirteenth Amendment was passed, anti-Black violence escalated dramatically, ranging from public whippings to lynchings to the burning down of entire Black communities. Reports of these attacks were harrowing enough that Congress convened a Joint Committee on Reconstruction to hold hearings "on conditions in the South." At enormous risk to themselves, freedpeople testified to the abuses they faced. The conclusion, after months of investigations, was that more legal protection was necessary if freedpeople were to survive. Republican politicians wrote a Civil Rights Act guaranteeing Black Americans a range of both legal and social rights. It was, as one historian has put it, the first attempt to "give meaning" to the Thirteenth Amendment's promise of freedom.[23]

President Andrew Johnson vetoed it. By 1866, this was no longer particularly surprising. It was true that Child and others had initially been optimistic that Johnson would extract justice from the Confederacy's architects. "Treason must be made odious, and traitors must be punished and impoverished," he had proclaimed in 1864. Johnson had also, early on, styled himself as a great friend to the freedpeople, promising to be the Moses who would lead them out of slavery into the promised land.[24]

But he soon showed himself to be impatient with what it would take to get there. "Damn the Negroes, I am fighting those traitorous aristocrats, their masters," he complained. Soon he stopped doing even that. In the summer of 1865, Johnson pardoned thousands of Southerners, many of them the founders and sustainers of the Confederacy. It was also becoming painfully clear that his racism was deep and venomous. He declared Black people incapable of self-government; he argued explicitly that "white men must manage the South." He was also querulous, bombastic, and a drinker. "Was there ever such a braying ass as Johnson?" Child fumed to Sarah Shaw. "Every true lover of the country must want to creep into a knot-hole and hide himself, whenever the name of our President is mentioned." Johnson yet again resurrected the idea of sending all Black residents out of the country. Child, as always, opposed the naked prejudice underlying this scheme. But she did express a wry, weary hope. Johnson had promised to be the freed-people's Moses. If they indeed decided to leave, maybe Johnson would go with them.[25]

Child took up the struggle against Johnson and for the freed-people in a series of articles in the *Independent*. When Harriet Jacobs, now nursing and teaching in Savannah, wrote to her, Child excerpted long passages of Jacobs's letters for *Independent* readers. "Don't believe the stories so often repeated the that Negroes are not willing to work," Jacobs pleaded. In fact, many had worked the abandoned land and come close to turning a profit. "But just as they were beginning to realize the blessings of freedom," she reported, "all their hopes were dashed to the ground. President Johnson has pardoned their old masters, and the poor loyal freed-men are driven off the soil, that it may be given back to traitors."[26]

Building on Jacobs's reports, Child was quick to point out a bitter irony. Did her readers remember the dire warnings from before the war about "turning the slaves loose upon the masters"? Did they remember how that frightful image had been held up as a reason to continue the barbarity of slavery itself? In fact, the mobs of avenging slaves had never materialized. Violence by former masters against their former slaves, by contrast, was sustained, vicious, and well documented. In April 1866, forty-six Black residents were massacred in a two-day pogrom in Memphis. In May, another thirty-four were murdered in riots in New Orleans. In both cities, mobs also attacked Black homes, schools, and hospitals—the very things Child had promised would win them respectability—and, in some instances, burned them to the ground. "President Johnson's policy is turning the masters loose upon their defenseless slaves, just as they were before the war," Child wrote. And those people relieved that slaveholders had survived, she mourned, "now have no compassion to spare over the frightful wrongs and outrages which those oppressors are constantly practicing on their helpless victims." "So far from rejoicing over the condition of the country," she admitted, "I am in a state of chronic rage."[27]

As she continued to raise awareness about atrocities in the South, Child also tried to fight prejudice closer to home. She befriended a young Black sculptor named Edmonia Lewis whose work was causing a sensation in Boston social circles. Lewis had sculpted a well-received bust of Voltaire, and she now wanted to sculpt Robert Gould Shaw. For the readers of the *Standard*, Child described visiting Lewis's studio and being moved by how her passionate gratitude for Shaw's martyrdom had translated into a successful sculpture. In Lewis's obvious talent, Child saw nothing less than the ascendance of the African race in art as well as in history. "Who can tell what the revolving wheel of time may bring uppermost, in the revolutions of the ages?" she asked her readers. "The Star of Africa has risen above the horizon, but what will be its splendor when it culminates no prophet can foresee."[28]

But as far as Lewis's depiction of Shaw was concerned, there was a problem. His mother, Sarah Shaw, did not like it. More to the point, she did not like Lewis, who seemed to her both arrogant and vain. Child tried to smooth things over. It was important to be patient, she urged the still-grieving mother; Lewis was simply young and inexperienced. She had potential, but it was not yet realized. Like many artists, she was not good with money. All that could be changed, and Child insisted to Sarah that it was important to try. "I doubt whether we can treat our colored brethren *exactly* as we would if they were white, though it is desirable to do so," she wrote. The laudable implication of this thought is that Child wanted to give Black Americans extra resources and opportunities to compensate for the wrongs they had suffered. But unfortunately, this is not all she meant. She also meant that Black Americans should be thought of as children, which led to a blunt paternalism encapsulated in her next sentence. "We have kept their minds in a state of infancy," she urged her friend, "and children *must* be treated with more patience and forbearance than grown people."[29]

In the interest of modeling this patience herself and promoting Lewis's development, Child wrote to her, encouraging her to take on smaller projects, to practice by copying sculptures before sculpting from life, and above all not to spend her commissions before finishing a project. Not wanting to discourage or alienate Lewis, Child agonized over these letters: writing them, she said, was like having a tooth drawn. But she felt she owed it to Lewis, for her own good, to urge restraint. Lewis resisted this advice, and Child grew frustrated both with her and with the resulting artworks, which she frankly thought were bad. Still, when Lewis left to work in Italy, Child put her in contact with other Americans there and tried to mediate when things sometimes did not go well.[30] Integrating a Black artist into high society was not easy, but she wanted to try.

This aspiration became a test of patience that Child ultimately did not pass. When her wealthy friends complained that Lewis had imposed on their goodwill once too often, Child began to withdraw her support. When a fellow reformer chided her for her cooling enthusiasm, Child erupted in a rare burst of irritation: "*Art* is sacred," she replied, "as well as *Philanthropy*; and I do not think it either wise or kind to encourage a girl, merely because she is colored, to spoil good marble by making it into poor statues." It was a sad conclusion to one of Child's well-intentioned but flawed attempts to promote racial justice. In the end, Lewis didn't need Child's support. By 1876, she was exhibiting her work at Philadelphia's Centennial Exhibition; she also created successful sculptures of Lincoln, John Brown, and Henry Wadsworth Longfellow.[31] Whether Child regretted their failed friendship she never says.

* * *

That spring, Child was undertaking the major home improvements still needed to repair the damage done by the fire. She insisted on doing much of the work herself, painting, varnishing, and wallpapering until she wore herself out. David was busy with projects too. "Mr. Child is all up in arms out of doors," she wrote to Eliza Scudder with some bemusement. "He rises at four o'clock"

and then, except for meals, "[I] don't get a glimpse of him till dark."
It was true that he remained accident-prone—spraining his wrist
on the ice, falling from a woodpile—sometimes exhausting Child's
supply of medicinal herbs with his many injuries. But soon he was
up again, constructing a cistern, making apple cider, building a
stone wall, and singing in his garden. Child was grateful for this;
as long as David was busy at home, he was less likely to get into financial trouble. The activity also helped keep his worsening rheumatism at bay and entertained the neighborhood children. One
such neighbor later recounted the joy of watching Mr. Child creating a series of fountains for his wife's amusement, all the while
lecturing his little audience on the principles of hydraulics and the
world's famous aqueducts.[32]

As Maria Child worked, she continued to turn over in her mind
the problem of Southern violence and Northern apathy. What
could she do to awaken her fellow Americans' compassion? She
had, in recent months, made argument after argument in newspapers. Were these having any effect? Would a story help? Her imagination felt rusty—"somewhat stiff in the joints," she said, perhaps
not unlike David's limbs.[33] But soon she had an idea, she confessed
to her publisher. He liked it, so she started writing.

The story grew. Before long, Child was lying awake at night,
"torturing [her] old brain" to solve the complicated scrapes her
characters found themselves in.[34] Was she writing a novel? Surely
not. Surely she was too old to conjure the energy needed to drive
a plot. But the characters kept developing in her mind, taking on
new adventures and tempting their creator to record them. So as
she tended to her aging husband, she tried to imagine the heat of
young love. As she looked out onto the austere northeastern landscape around her, she took her characters to places she longed to
see but never would: elegant Italian opera houses, plunging mountain landscapes, lush Louisiana forests. At every moment, she kept
her country's racial sins in mind, hoping to contribute yet again to
its moral reckoning.

It was certainly the most complex plot she had ever attempted,
complete with moonlight escapes, babies switched at birth, and

sisters who, long believing each other dead, are reunited by a chatty parrot with a prodigious memory. And it deftly exposed the racial hypocrisy Child wanted her readers to question. When Child's heroine—the exotic, Spanish-looking Rosa, the sensation of Boston high society—is revealed to be a former slave, admirers suddenly shun her. When a light-skinned fugitive slave and the dark-haired heir to a Boston fortune are revealed to have been switched at birth, the white mother's indifference to her biological son is chilling. Like American authors before and since, Child was using "passing" to illuminate the irrationality and arbitrariness at the heart of racial prejudice. In 1867, the novel was published. Child called it *A Romance of the Republic.*[35]

The novel's message, no doubt, was one her readers still needed to hear. But for the author, the book was the worst kind of failure. Her friends, it seems, did not like it. We know this because she cataloged their indifference in long, wounded letters. And while the book did garner some glowing reviews—including favorable comparisons to *Uncle Tom's Cabin*—her public also seemed unmoved. It's not entirely clear why. Perhaps they were simply weary of the topics Child wanted them to confront. She did not help matters by refusing to advertise the book or give public readings that would remind her large fan base why they loved her.[36] Apparently she had hoped the book would be good enough that none of this would matter. That would be a risky strategy for any writer. For an author asking her readers to engage with a topic they likely wished to forget, it was simply self-defeating.

She took her novel's failure very personally. "The book has brought me a great deal of disappointment and humiliation," she wrote to Louisa Loring. "I shall never be disappointed *again* in that way," she promised Eliza Scudder, "for I shall never again *expect* anybody to feel any interest." In fact, she began to claim, she hated writing. "The apathy of my friends took all the life out of me," she confessed, "and has made me feel as if I never wanted to put pen to paper again."[37]

* * *

No doubt by now her friends were familiar with this mood: distressed outbursts about exhaustion and perceived failure are woven throughout Child's letters. No doubt they also knew the mood would evaporate as soon as another moral outrage attracted Maria Child's attention. Indeed, it did not take long. This time her fury was directed at the injustice that had preoccupied her in her earliest days as a reformer: the United States' policy toward Native Americans.

Americans' westward expansion had continued throughout the Civil War, as had battles with native inhabitants fiercely determined to protect their homeland. In one especially violent confrontation in 1864, later called the Sand Creek Massacre, US troops engaged in such barbarity in Colorado Territory that Congress was forced to investigate. Despite Child's still-bruised ego, her pen quickly found its way to paper once the report was released in 1868. The resulting "Appeal for the Indians," first published serially in the National Anti-Slavery Standard, overwhelms the reader with evidence of abhorrent behavior toward Native Americans: treaties broken, villages razed, women raped, captives mutilated and tortured. As with slavery, Americans' treatment of native tribes was made worse, Child argued, because they claimed to know better. They had declared that all men were equal; as Christians, they preached a gospel of love. Their behavior showed these assertions to be self-serving hypocrisy. Speaking of hypocrisy: How could Americans call their rebellion against the British noble but label native attempts to defend their homeland barbarous? "How," as Child put it, "can we blame the Indians for fighting, when we ourselves should have fought with half the provocation?" Instead of force, she urged patience. America's native peoples were "simply younger members of the same great human family, who need to be protected, instructed and encouraged, till they are capable of appreciating and sharing all our advantages."[38]

There it was again: the familiar combination of progress and paternalism. While many continued to suggest extermination as the only way to deal with Native Americans, Child, to her credit, fought for them to be respected as fellow humans. But even as she

wrote, forces were gathering that would make the mandate to protect, instruct, and encourage devastating to native communities.
Toward the end of the nineteenth century, the US government increasingly implemented a policy of forced assimilation, meaning
that thousands of native children were removed from their homes
and placed in boarding schools or adopted by white families. They
were then often forbidden to see their birth parents and ordered
to abandon their languages and cultural practices.[39] In this way,
even reformers who embraced Child's ostensibly gentler approach
robbed generations of children of their identities and left native
communities on the brink of cultural, and sometimes physical, extinction. Surely Child did not intend this result; insofar as words
like hers made it possible, it is another reminder that good intentions are no guarantee of good outcomes, especially if the only
good outcomes we can imagine require others to be more like us.

But to her fellow reformers, Child's "An Appeal for the Indians" was yet another triumph of moral insight. It was reprinted
as a tract and distributed widely among activists and politicians.
Perhaps most important for its wounded author, the "Appeal"
also elicited at least one deeply grateful response. It was from a
woman named Sarah Brown, who wrote to Child from upstate New
York. "Every lover of the human race must thank you for writing
your Appeal for the Indians," Brown began. "I wish that your Appeal might be scattered in all directions, so that the thousands of
humane people, who are indifferent & silent, because they do not
know, might be informed about the injuries & barbarities which
our Indians have suffered."

Brown, it turned out, had been a lifelong student of Child's
thought. "The Juvenile Miscellany," Brown wrote, "was the delight
of my childish heart." *The Frugal Housewife*, she continued, was
"by my side" when she herself first became a wife. Child's *Appeal*
had converted her to abolitionism and a lifetime of activism; *Letters from New York* had opened her eyes to new beauty and meaning in that city's familiar streets. "Your influence over me," Brown
summed up, "has always been ennobling, & purifying, & elevating, & stimulating to benevolence & charity." "You will allow me to

subscribe myself" she concluded, "with the highest esteem & love, Sarah V. V. Brown."[40]

Child was not above complaining about fan mail. There were always so many requests for autographs and photographs to deal with, and so little time. Besides, she again insisted, she hated writing.[41] I think we should take these outbursts with a grain of salt. I don't doubt that Child sometimes felt hassled by her admirers, perhaps Brown among them. But it is also true that Brown's was one of the few letters she never burned.

*   *   *

Meanwhile, 1868 was turning out to be one of those American years with a harrowing impeachment trial at its beginning and an even more harrowing election at its end. After years of antagonizing his friends and infuriating his enemies, Andrew Johnson had been accused of high crimes and misdemeanors for his improper firing of the secretary of war. "I am glad that Andy Johnson is impeached, at last," wrote Child as the news broke. But she regretted that the impeachment had not been for the right reasons or even for enough reasons. "I wish the terms of indictment had expressed something about the slaughter of loyal whites and Blacks, and the sufferings and discouragements of the freed people, caused by his nefarious 'policy,'" she wrote.[42]

In fact, although Congress had managed to pass the Civil Rights Act of 1866 over Johnson's veto ("Thank God for such a Congress," wrote Child), its guarantee of civil and legal rights had not been enough to stem the waves of anti-Black violence in the South.[43] And unless Republicans won in the next election, the rights it enumerated could easily be rescinded by the next Congress. Indeed, former Confederates were gradually fulfilling the requirements for regaining their voting rights. Soon they would again constitute a majority of voters in the South. Their allies in the Democratic Party had already made it clear that they would use this majority to reestablish as much of their former way of life as possible. Then what would the point of the war have been? There was, Republican politicians knew, only one group of potential voters who could prevent this reversal. That constituency was the freedmen.

Many abolitionists had long argued in favor of Black suffrage. For Child and others, including Black intellectuals like Frederick Douglass and Frances Ellen Watkins Harper, it was a simple matter of fulfilling the promise of emancipation. "Slavery is not abolished until the black man has the ballot," Douglass asserted. "This is the vital question of the hour," Child wrote in the *Standard* in May 1868. "It signifies not merely justice to an oppressed class, but it also involves the question of whether we will be true to the principles of our free institutions; whether we will prove by our works that we really have faith in a government by the people."[44]

Again, many white Northerners were wary. Ending slavery increasingly felt like a proud achievement, but still: Did emancipation really imply the right to *vote*? But the electoral calculus was undeniable. Child laid it out bluntly for Lucy Osgood: "Either the government of the country must again be given up to slave-holding rebels, and their Democratic allies, or the loyal men of the South *must* vote; and nearly all the loyal men in that region are black." As usual, she mourned, there was so little moral grandeur. Black soldiers had been allowed to fight only when it became clear that the Union army could not win the war without them. Now Black men would be given the vote only because Republicans could not win the peace without them. Nevertheless, with these stark facts in mind, work began on a Fourteenth Amendment that would both give constitutional backing to the Civil Rights Act and punish Southern states that prohibited Black men from voting.[45]

But there was a catch. The proposed amendment represented the first time the word "male" would appear in the Constitution. It was true that most women could not, in fact, vote. But their suffrage was limited by state laws, not by the country's founding documents. The insertion of the word "male" in the Constitution, then, would set a federal precedent for forbidding women to vote where previously there had been none. This would most certainly set back the cause of women's suffrage. "If that word 'male' be inserted," Elizabeth Cady Stanton famously predicted, "it will take us a century at least to get it out."[46]

As the danger became clear, women began to mobilize. In 1866, Stanton, Susan B. Anthony, and Lucy Stone, together with Black leaders including Frederick Douglass, Sojourner Truth, and Frances Harper, had already founded the American Equal Rights Association, whose stated goal was to "secure Equal Rights to all American citizens, especially the right of suffrage, irrespective of race, color or sex."[47] Now the association redoubled its efforts to make sure the Fourteenth Amendment would advance voting rights for both Black men and all women.

Early on, Stanton tried to enlist Child's help. Perhaps the famous abolitionist's endorsement would lend respectability to the controversial movement. Initially, Child was enthusiastic. Gone was her youthful ambivalence about voting or about making her position on women's rights known. In December 1866, she published a letter to Stanton in the *Independent*. "I am old and, having fought through a somewhat long campaign of reform, I feel little energy for enlisting in a new war," she confessed. "But since you care to know my opinion of the cause you are advocating so zealously and ably, I will tell you frankly that I sympathize entirely with your views concerning woman's true position in society, and I cordially wish you God speed." The matter was simple, Child stated: If women could be taxed, imprisoned, and hanged according to the laws, they had a right to help make those laws. "As for our capacity to vote as intelligently as the mass of men," Child concluded, "*that* is a point I would scarcely condescend to argue."[48]

But in the next several months, Child did condescend to argue this and many other points. In two major articles in the *Independent* in January 1867, she laid out her argument in classic Child fashion: by countering objections. Yes, some women did not want to vote; neither did some men. Perhaps women would indeed be distracted from their domestic chores by voting; the same was true of men. And yes, some women were bad with money, obsessed with fashion, and too frivolous to be entrusted with the nation's future.

But what did you expect from a group that had been "systematically excluded from the professions, the trades, the arts, the sciences, the halls of legislation; in a word, from all the pursuits that are best calculated to enlarge the mind, to occupy it profitably and to raise it above mean and petty subjects of thought"? Against the argument that women did not need the vote since their husbands, in effect, were voting for them, Child was unsparing: "No human being can possibly think for me, or believe for me, any more than he can eat for me, or drink for me, or breathe for me," Child asserted. "The family is a very sacred thing," she acknowledged, "but it appears to me that in a family of true order each one would think, feel, and act as an individual."[49]

It is worth pausing here to consider how painfully ironic making these arguments must have felt to Child. Her career was a one-person repudiation of the claim that women could not reason about serious matters. And the suggestion that women could not manage money or think economically was, her own marriage made clear, equally absurd. Compared with her husband, Child was the better breadwinner, the superior manager, the more productive citizen. It was David's strange combination of idealism, restlessness, and neglect that had burdened them with losses and caused Child such pain.

It was also true, Child acknowledged as she composed her arguments in favor of women's liberation, that David kept her trapped in Wayland. She longed to be closer to friends. She longed for a cultural life that would feed her soul and nurture her writing. Over and over she tried to figure out how they could move closer to Boston. "Wayland is a miserable place, and gets more miserable every year," she confessed to Eliza Scudder. But try as she might, she could conceive of no other living arrangement that would keep David profitably occupied and healthy. "No mortal but myself knows how hard I struggle against the depressing influences of my monotonous and uncongenial life," she wrote to Sarah Shaw. "I read only 'chipper' books; I hang prisms in my windows, to fill the room with rainbows. . . . I cultivate the gayest flowers; I seek cheerfulness in every possible way."[50]

Judged by the impressions of one small neighbor, these efforts at cheerfulness worked. Alfred Wayland Cutting was one of the local children who sometimes made their way to the Childs' little home. They had, he recalled, the "most beautiful garden of flowers in the world." He also remembered the prisms that hung in their parlor, calling forth rainbows like a kind of magic from another world. Arriving at their door, he remembered being rewarded with his own flower from Mrs. Child and a lecture on its characteristics from her husband. But the real flower, he remembered, was the "beauty and joy and fragrance of [Mrs. Child's] presence." She had, he remembered, "a face as bright and fresh and sweet as one of her own roses."[51]

And despite—or perhaps because of—Wayland's limitations, David and Maria Child were often happy. At night, they studied German together or read to each other. She helped ward off his digestive attacks by ensuring that his diet was healthy and regular. He bore her occasional bursts of temper patiently; they were always quick, Child assured a friend, to "kiss and make up." "We are," she confessed, "in fact, like two old children, as much interested as ever in the birds and the wildflowers, and with sympathies as lively as ever in all that concerns the welfare of the world." This balance of harmony and engagement their small neighbor also noticed. "Here the gentle old couple lived," he later reflected, "with the love of their youth stronger and more beautiful than ever; the joys and sorrows of humanity their constant interest." Indeed, the Childs actively kept up with the news, following the corruption scandals that crippled the Republican Party, the vicious wars against the Modoc Native American tribes, the escalating tensions between France and Prussia. Whenever she could, and apparently despite herself, Child continued writing: whatever she wrote, they talked about together.[52]

So while Wayland sometimes seemed like a prison, Maria Child continued to find ways to live within its bars. Not for her was the sexual freedom that Virginia Woodhull and other more radical feminists were championing. Such women, she wrote with exasperation to Sarah Shaw, are "so wild for *freedom*, that they forget

Fig. 55. David Lee Child in 1870. Collection of the Massachusetts Historical Society.

such a thing as *duty* exists."[53] Speaking of duty: as far as finances were concerned, the Childs' remaining trapped in Wayland remained partly a matter of deliberate choice. Just how deliberate would become clear only after Maria Child's death. But for now the calculus was simple: living in a city would be more expensive, and then what could she give to the freedpeople? Given the choice between a fashionable social life and helping right her country's racial wrongs, she would always choose the latter. So Wayland it was.

* * *

Fig. 56. Lydia Maria Child, ca. 1865. Collection of the Massachusetts Historical Society.

Whatever particular forces kept Child trapped in Wayland, the general forces limiting American women were intensifying in battles over the Fourteenth Amendment. There was, it turned out, little political appetite for upending both the patriarchal and the racial hierarchy all at once. Even sympathetic men began to warn that using the Fourteenth Amendment to promote women's suffrage would doom its chances of ratification, leaving freed-people without the protections they desperately needed. It was not the first time Child had been told that fighting for her rights as a woman would injure the cause. It had been painful the first time, and it was painful now. But when Wendell Phillips and others argued that it was the "Negro's Hour" and urged women to postpone their efforts, Child agreed. "That the loyal blacks of the South should vote is a present and very imperious necessity," she wrote in the *Independent*. "The suffrage of woman can better afford to wait."[54]

The Fourteenth Amendment was passed in July 1868. It would be hard to overstate the progress it achieved. "All persons born or naturalized in the United States," it decreed, "are citizens of the United States." Millions of former slaves were, from one moment to the next, transformed into citizens. "No State shall make or enforce any law which shall abridge the privileges or immunities of citizens of the United States," read its second sentence. Black Codes across the South were, with one stroke, invalidated. Whether or not its authors intended it, the Fourteenth Amendment laid the foundation of civil rights movements for generations to come—movements that sought to guarantee Americans their rights regardless of race, gender, or sexual orientation.

In its second section, the amendment also promised to punish Southern states if they kept "male inhabitants" from voting. This still did not guarantee Black men the right to vote, but it nevertheless was enormous progress. At least in theory, the federal government was for the first time trying to promote Black male suffrage. But it was also true that, in restricting this protection to men, the amendment, as Stanton had warned, threw up a new and formidable barrier to women. "I wish they had forgotten to put up that bar," Child ruefully admitted even as she celebrated the amendment's passage, "but they didn't."[55]

* * *

The politics of progress continued to grind on in painfully familiar ways. Former Union general Ulysses S. Grant had won the contentious presidential election at the end of 1868, thanks in part to the Fourteenth Amendment's support for Black suffrage in the

South. But the popular vote had been very close. If Republicans were going to protect their agenda, simply punishing states that restricted voting would not be enough. A fifteenth amendment would be needed to expand suffrage at the federal level.[56]

But expanded to whom? Just to Black men, or to others as well? Some took this opportunity to argue in favor of universal suffrage—a full embrace of the radical equality promised in the country's founding documents. Others were less generous. Western states resolutely opposed extending the vote to the Chinese immigrants who were building railroads, tending orchards, and making Western capitalists rich. Others wanted to keep Catholics, or maybe just the Irish, from the polls.[57] The electoral calculus—who would win if which group was excluded—was mind-numbingly complicated. The racist intent of much of it, by contrast, was depressingly straightforward.

And then, again, there was the question of women. One proposed version of this new amendment promised to prohibit discrimination based on race; if that was all it said, it would implicitly permit exclusions based on gender. When it became clear that this was the version of the Fifteenth Amendment most likely to pass, Stanton and Anthony decided to oppose it. Stanton, whose combination of soaring rhetoric and biting wit had made her the movement's formidable spokesperson, settled on an argument she thought would work. How demeaning, she suggested, that all men—regardless of whether they could read, or understood politics, or supported democracy—be given the right to vote ahead of women who had demonstrated their ability to do all three. The general point was irrefutable. It *was* unjust to permit all men to vote without qualification while permitting no women to vote regardless of qualification. Child herself made this argument more than once, also in print.[58] Any woman who has watched a less-qualified male be allowed to do something she was not, simply because she was female, knows how this can sting.

But Stanton was not content to make the argument on principle. Instead, she marshaled the anti-Catholic, anti-Black, anti-

Chinese, and even anti-German sentiment brewing in postwar America and funneled it into vicious caricature. "Think of Patrick and Sambo and Hans and Yung Tung," she urged her readers, "who do not know the difference between a Monarchy and a Republic, who never read the Declaration of Independence." Now, she said, imagine this band of misfits "making laws for Lydia Maria Child."[59]

I'm not sure Child ever read this particular screed, but how she would have hated it. Soon she had read enough of Stanton's racist rhetoric to distance herself from Stanton altogether. She began declining Stanton's invitations, resisting being drawn into her circle of supporters. For her part, Stanton soon moved beyond racism to scaremongering. It was not enough to claim that excluding women was unfair; Stanton began to promise that allowing Black men to vote would lead to "fearful outrages on womanhood, especially in the southern states."[60]

Now Child was horrified. She was "vexed beyond measure" with Stanton and her allies, she wrote to Sarah Shaw. When Stanton wrote an editorial titled "All Wise Women Will Oppose the 15th Amendment," Child called it "the most impardonable of all her doings." "Surely we ought to have learned, by this time that the rights of one class of people can never be secured by taking away the rights of another," she lamented.[61]

Perhaps Stanton ought to have learned this, but she hadn't. At an infamous meeting of the American Equal Rights Association in May 1869, Stanton sparred publicly with Frederick Douglass and Frances Harper about whose rights should be honored first. "You white women speak here of rights. I speak of wrongs," Harper had admonished her white allies a few years earlier. "I tell you that if there is any class of people who need to be lifted out of their airy nothings and selfishness, it is the white women of America." But Stanton was still unmoved. Soon she was also feuding with Lucy Stone, another suffragist and a longtime ally of Child's, after Stone criticized Stanton's racism and declared her support for the Fifteenth Amendment. Eventually Stone, Harper, and others broke with Stanton, founding the American Woman Suffrage Association to compete with Stanton's National Woman Suffrage Association. Again the acronyms proliferated; again the enemies of the cause rejoiced.[62]

How exhausting it was to watch another progressive cause splinter and stall. But Child could not give up. "Though tired of battling, I cannot keep my hands off 'the woman question,'" she wrote to Sarah Shaw. "It is decidedly the most important question that has been before the world." So she continued to support women's rights in the *Independent*, in Lucy Stone's *Woman's Journal*, and in open letters to women's conventions that, in part because of David's health, she could not attend. "Society can never be established on a true and solid foundation as long as any distinction whatsoever is made between men and women with regard to the full and free exercise of their faculties on all subjects," she wrote to the Women's Rights Convention. "I believe that perfect equality of the sexes in all the departments of life would be merely the development of the original plan of Divine Providence for the ultimate perfection of the human race," she wrote in the *Independent*.[63]

Ultimately, the narrowest possible version of the Fifteenth Amendment was passed.[64] Unlike the Fourteenth Amendment, its text was brief and to the point: "The right of citizens of the United States to vote," it read, "shall not be denied or abridged by the United States or by any State on account of race, color, or previous condition of servitude." It was true that Americans throughout the country would quickly find ways to stifle the Black vote anyway: through poll taxes, literacy tests, and all too often through simple violence. It was also true that women had once again been left behind and that the battle for the vote had created a rift between white feminists and Black Americans that continues to this day.

*   *   *

Nevertheless, what an achievement the Fifteenth Amendment was, and what a cause for jubilation. In one of the world's most revolutionary political developments, millions of human beings had gone from being enslaved to being voting citizens in only five years. Black Americans throughout the country quickly mastered the political system: the Forty-First and Forty-Second Congresses included several Black representatives, some of whom had been born in slavery. "Only to *think* they have colored men in the legislature of South Carolina, now!" Child rejoiced to Henrietta Sargent. "And Mississippi sends a colored man to represent her in the Senate of the United States!"[65] With suffrage achieved, antislavery societies began to declare their work done. The Massachusetts Anti-Slavery Society was among them. There would be one last meeting, and then the society would disband forever.

David badly wanted to go. It would, he was sure, be the final "gathering of the Anti Slavery troop."[66] He had been very sick that fall, sick enough that Child worried that this wish to see his old friends might be among his last. So while she dreaded the travel, the crowds, the noise, and the risk to her husband's health, she could not bring herself to refuse. Once again the aging couple braved the January weather and made their way from Wayland to Boston via coach and rail. The next morning, they joined the crowd of victorious abolitionists downtown at Horticulture Hall.

They must have made quite an impression. By now, a few biographical sketches of Child's life had appeared. Many of the attendees were no doubt eager for a glimpse of the famous but reclusive reformer whose pen had guided so many of them to opinions that had once seemed radical but now just made sense. Perhaps necks craned to see Child greeted by Wendell Phillips or reunited with her old allies Abby Kelley Foster and Angelina Grimké Weld. Perhaps Child had on her unfashionable bonnet—the one that, as she confessed to Marianne Silsbee, by now could easily have landed her in P. T. Barnum's circus. There was plenty of the crush and confusion Child so intensely disliked.[67] But finally someone must have ushered the Childs to the front, where they took their place among other abolitionist luminaries on the stage.

The meeting began. Among the first speakers was Julia Ward Howe, the woman whose "Battle Hymn of the Republic" had provided the musical accompaniment to the North's march to war. No doubt many men in the audience had sung it on their way to Southern battlefields where they had watched their friends and brothers die. Now everyone in the audience would have the opportunity to hear the author of those stirring words speak. "Dear friends," Howe commenced as the crowd quieted. "A few of us only have had the merit and privilege of cooperating with the Anti-Slavery party through the whole long course of its experience and labors," she said. Some of the few were on that very stage with her, and it was time to honor them.

Slowly, Howe began to recount the history of the small, faithful band who had dedicated themselves to ending slavery some thirty-five years before. Theirs had seemed a "forlorn hope," she told the audience. "The world was against them," she said, recalling how names like Garrison, Kelley, and Phillips had been used to conjure monsters in her own childhood home. Nevertheless, she continued, the resolute reformers had "conquered as they went": "on the high road of Truth's eternal victories, a skirmish here, a bloody battle there, the mobs and the mud of great cities, had for them little intimidation." The audience must have been rapt as they looked from the famous speaker to the group of elderly radicals behind her. What a gift to witness these men and women, now in life's twilight: to picture them in the early days of passion and outrage, to imagine their bodies pelted with bricks and their pens letting loose the fiery words that had helped change the world.

As Child sat on the stage, listening to Howe's evocation of the struggle that had defined her life, did her mind sketch in images of the scenes Howe was evoking? Did the leering faces of threatening mobs appear in her mind's eye? Did she remember weeding beets in the early morning, watching the *Standard* emerge from the presses, opening the newspaper to find her letter to Governor Wise published for all to see? "The brave, uncompromising fight they made showed the power of a steadfast faith and will which their enemies were forced to respect," she heard Howe say: "Spring after spring of the human heart was touched by their appeals." Ah, yes, the appeals. One of them had been hers, so many years ago. Others had been Angelina Grimké's. Did Child look over at her longtime friend, near her on the stage, wondering if she was remembering too?

Howe was still talking. "And now to which of us can the word freedom have the same blessed significance as it has to them?" she asked the crowd. Only to a few, she concluded: "For we have only received it as our birthright, but they have given it. The seed of good works is indeed sown on earth in dishonor. But we of to-day have seen it raised in glory." These early radicals, she said, perhaps gesturing at the honored guests on the platform, "launched the Anti-Slavery movement and were its earliest sailors. And now," the orator said, reaching her culmination, the "weather-beaten crew, brought home with honor, may rest from this voyage. Dear shall they be to our children's children—dearer to God."[68]

I have no doubt that Howe's final words brought the crowd roaring to its feet. As the audience cheered, did the Childs also rise, perhaps somewhat stiffly, in acknowledgment? Did they stand for a moment, blinking into the crowd? Did they wave in response, David perhaps more enthusiastically than his wife? The secretary recorded no such details. Neither did Child, with the exception of one brief comment to Lucy Osgood after she and David returned home. Everyone at the meeting, Child confessed to her friend, "seemed disposed to make much of us."[69]

But when Osgood suggested that Child must have enjoyed the jubilation, Child was quick to correct her. The meeting had emphatically not, she countered, been a final "ovation." The news from the South was terrible; real racial justice was still nowhere in sight. "The colored people and the loyal white people of the South, write us too many letters describing their persecutions and their dangers, and imploring us to stand by them, and say that *for* them which they dare not say for themselves," she wrote. The danger, Child was clear, was existential. "A very large number of those masters are determined to exterminate the colored race, rather than live on terms of civil equality with them," she wrote. "No," the veteran abolitionist concluded as the Fifteenth Amendment was ratified and the American Anti-Slavery Society voted itself out of existence, "there is no time for 'ovations.'"[70]

Indeed: as if to make a mockery of these glorious achievements, anti-Black violence exploded with such fury in the next year that President Grant was forced essentially to declare martial law in parts of the South. Responsible for this violence, Child told the readers of the *Standard*, was an "extensive organization bearing the mysterious name of the Ku-Klux-Klan." Its members, she reported, were "as secret as the Inquisition, and as cruel. They are scourging, and mutilating, and murdering loyal whites and Blacks, and none give heed to the agonized cries of their victims."[71]

*　*　*

In 1870, as the Fifteenth Amendment failed to extend the vote to women, a lithographer named Louis Prang decided to issue a new print. It followed a style of popular nineteenth-century inspirational images that depicted famous men, often presidents, clustered together in stately order. But Prang's image was different. Instead of Washington, Jefferson, and Madison staring sternly into the middle distance, the viewer encountered all women: Lucretia Mott, Elizabeth Cady Stanton, Mary Livermore, Susan B. Anthony, Sara Jane Lippincott, and Anna Elizabeth Dickinson. At the bottom, grounding the circle, was an image of Lydia Maria Child. The lithograph was called *Representative Women*.

Child's reaction to this honor was to lament those who had not been included. "A group of 'Representative Women' without Lucy Stone is like Hamlet performed without the Prince of Denmark," she protested in the *National Standard*.[72] A companion image was needed to honor others, she urged, like Angelina Grimké Weld, Abby Kelley Foster, and Julia Ward Howe. As to the depiction of herself, she had something to say about that too. A Boston newspaper had recently accused women of denying that they had been pioneers in the "Woman Cause" because such a status would reveal their ages. There was no way Child was going to let this accusation stand. She therefore wished it to be known that the image now circulating had been taken when she was fifty-four. She was now sixty-eight, she reported, and she did not care who knew it. Better

Fig. 57. Louis Prang and L. Schamer, *Representative Women,* ca. 1870. Courtesy of the Library of Congress.

that than the insinuation that vanity would keep her from admitting that she had indeed, over a lifetime, represented women well.

Something else is notable about the image of Child on this print. Compared with the almost architectural combinations of collars, bows, frills, and stays that encase the other women, Child's dress is loose and gathered, fastened only by an off-center brooch. It might not occur to us now, but to Child's contemporaries it would have seemed curious. It was true that Maria Child's style choices were notoriously strange, but usually because she was too frugal to care about fashion. But frugality could not account for what viewers saw here. Just what kind of dress was Child wearing?

It turns out that there was indeed an explanation. In preparation for his print, Mr. Prang had come to Wayland to consult with Child about which image to use. As they looked through the possible candidates, David produced one that must have made Mr. Prang's eyes widen. It depicted Maria Child with a shawl wrapped low around her bare shoulders. As Child looked on, perhaps in some embarrassment, Mr. Prang declared it the best of the bunch. As far as the head was concerned, Child had to agree. So it was settled: Mr. Prang would use that one. But, Child stipulated, it would not do for the public to see her naked shoulders. Whoever in Prang's Boston studio was assigned the task of converting the photograph to a lithograph should take care to "copy merely *the head*."[73]

Mr. Prang, it seems, at least initially complied. He returned to his factory outside Boston, where his distinctive coloring techniques would soon make him famous as the "father of the Christmas card." He turned Child's photograph over to an artist who sketched Child's head—the strong nose, the narrow lips, the incomprehensible hairstyle—into the stone as best he could. And then, to cover the shoulders, he sketched in a plausible dress—the gathered material, a kind of lace border, the off-center brooch. In her place among other representative women, the unusual style is noticeable, but it is not quite shocking.

But then, somehow, the original photograph got out. Perhaps the artist could not resist making a copy and things simply got out of hand. Whatever the explanation, reproductions of it, bare shoulders and all, seem soon to have been circulating freely. A copy ended up in William Lloyd Garrison's son's collection of images of famous abolitionists; another copy hangs today in the National Museum of African American History and Culture in Washington, DC, in acknowledgment of Child's antislavery work. This would, I think, be the nineteenth-century equivalent of a beach photo circulating among one's professional colleagues and hanging in a national museum. In Child's own lifetime, it certainly raised some

Fig. 58. Lydia Maria Child, ca. 1856. Collection of the Massachusetts Historical Society.

questions. Years later, after David's death, a friend dared to ask, What in the world was Child doing in such a low-cut dress?

Child had a ready answer. "The explanation is this," she wrote: "My dear old husband was as lover-like to the last year of his life, as he was during the days of courtship. He was often saying: 'I fell in love with your *honest shoulders*; and I want you to have a photograph taken, on purpose for *me*, with the shoulders uncovered.' So, at last, I humored the lover-like whim; and having no low dress, I folded a shawl about the bust." Despite her best intentions, the "honest shoulders," she wrote wryly, "came to light" after Prang's visit. It was not worth making a fuss, she had decided. "Head, shoulders, and all will be forgotten in a few years," she predicted.[74] But in the end, all has not been forgotten: neither Child's representative status nor her husband's love for her honest shoulders.

* * *

But David was getting old. He was sometimes so ill that Child put aside all her other work to care for him. Other friends were also failing. Louisa Loring died in 1868. Months later, Child's last remaining sibling, James, passed away. Charles Sumner died not long after he and Child had had one of the only disagreements of their decades-long friendship. The idea that he had died before they could reconcile, Child mourned, would "rankle in my heart, like a barbed arrow, till I die."[75]

Some deaths were more bittersweet. When Lucy Osgood, whom she had admired as a girl in the Medford church pews, died peacefully at the age of eighty-two, Child found that Osgood had left her in charge of a sizable fund dedicated to the freedpeople. Osgood had always lagged behind her more radical friend, thoughtful but timid when it came to racial justice. Yet Child had converted her, too, to believing that resources and education would quickly convert former slaves into thriving citizens. In Osgood's honor, Child founded a scholarship at Hampton College for Black students.[76] It wasn't quite getting to play Divine Providence, but so far, it was as close as Maria Child could come.

David's good spells became fewer and further between. His rheumatism often crippled him; stomach ailments kept him from digesting even the simplest food. Child's most fervent wish became to outlive him, not to leave him alone in his suffering. He bore it all so patiently, she wrote to Harriet Sewall: never irritable, only grieved that he was causing her trouble. One night as he struggled to sleep, she sat near his bedside, putting their papers in order and burning hundreds of letters. She watched as the evidence of their shared life curled, flamed, and disappeared in smoke. What strange creatures humans were, she mused to Sarah Shaw: "Capable of discovering so much that has preceded us, and of fore-casting so much that will follow us, yet flitting across our small segment of time, and disappearing like shadows of the magic-lantern."[77]

On a day in mid-September 1874, David felt well enough to tend to his garden. But soon, familiar pains forced him back inside. Resting in his rocking chair, he asked his wife to bring a dictionary so he could look up the etymology of a word. As the afternoon wore on, the pain worsened, and Child stayed near. When, after nightfall, it became clear that his final hours had come, she took him into her arms and waited in the darkness. A few minutes past midnight, his struggle was over and he breathed his last. "Your dear, kind brother passed away last night," she wrote the next morning to his sister. "He suffered greatly during the last three days," she wrote to Sarah Shaw, "but at last sunk to sleep in my arms, as peacefully as a tired babe."[78]

There was, immediately, the comfort that his pain was over. There was also gratitude that she had been able to take care of him to the last. But most of all there were crushing waves of grief. "Oh, Sarah," Child wrote, "no tongue can tell how desolate I feel." "Oh Lydia," she wrote to his sister, "I loved him very tenderly."[79]

David had not wanted to be buried in Wayland.[80] But despite his failing health, somehow the Childs had not yet made other plans. And when he died during an early autumn heat wave, it left very little time for burial arrangements. So Wayland, for eternity, it would be.

Funeral preparations were so rushed that Child did not alert Boston friends in time for them to come. William Lloyd Garrison struggled not to be hurt. Should there really have been no gathering of the faithful to honor David's life? Should there have been no speeches to inspire others to take up the causes he had so early and earnestly championed? He himself suffered from severe rheumatism, Garrison wrote, but, had he known, he would have done whatever was necessary to be there. Child wrote to explain. Garrison relented. "You have stated the reasons why no notices to distant friends were sent," he acknowledged, "and they are perfectly satisfactory."

To his credit, Garrison channeled his disappointment into

comfort for David's grieving wife. Even if she did not want public ovations, he could still put words to paper and let them soothe her heart. So in his elegant, even handwriting, Garrison praised David's "versatility of mind, his political acumen, his ardent patriotism, and his broad philanthropy." "What disgust he cherished for everything that savored of hypocrisy or cant!" Garrison remembered. "How he loved the right and hated the wrong! How dear was his vision, how intrepid his action, how thoroughly disinterested his aspirations and aims!"

"Dear Mrs. Child," Garrison continued, "while affectionately descanting upon his sterling merit and manly independence, I cannot refrain from renewing the expression of my exalted appreciation of your character, genius, literary productions, and self-denying humanity." "Multitudes on both sides of the Atlantic have read your writings with profit and delight," he wrote, "and yours has been a conspicuous part in popular education. I honor and admire you among the very first of your sex in any age or country." He praised the Childs' marriage, too. "When you say, 'No pen can describe the loneliness and desolation that I feel—it seems as if all the world had come to an end'—it is like the ingenious utterance of youthful devotion, and evinces a love that is perennial." "Yours was indeed a true marriage," Garrison assured her: "—a connection, alas! too rare."[81] This letter, too, Child kept.

David's funeral was modest and quiet, attended mostly by the Wayland residents among whom he had lived and worked. Decades later, one of these residents wrote down a childhood memory that can perhaps stand as a memorial to David's full but uneven life. "Mr. Child," wrote Alfred Wayland Cutting, had "a theory . . . for everything that [happened] in life or nature." Among these, apparently, was the theory that a child, if thrown into the water, would swim like a puppy. Not everyone was convinced, so David had come to young Alfred's parents with a question. Could he borrow their son for a quick experiment? After some "not unnatural demurring," the parents agreed, and a group of aspiring scientists headed to a local pond. Cutting doesn't tell us if Maria Child accompanied the little party to witness the experiment. If she did,

I imagine her standing at the water's edge, laughing uncertainly, head in her hands once again. Surely her husband would not allow his peculiar combination of principle and heedlessness to drown the neighbor's little boy?

David waded confidently into the pond, small Alfred in tow. By the time David was waist-deep in the water, he seemed to have forgotten his experiment and the little boy involved in it. Shouts from the witnesses on shore jolted his attention back to the present. He looked down. "I had totally disappeared, save for one clutching hand in his—the deep had engulfed me," remembered Cutting. David, I guess to his credit, reacted swiftly: "His strong arm, however, quickly drew me back to earth and breath," Cutting concluded, "and he had to acknowledge that while the experiment had certainly failed, there was in this case not much left of the principle."[82]

Despite this boyhood brush with death, Cutting's affection for his soggy rescuer is obvious. It is not an ovation, but perhaps it is a fitting tribute to Maria Child's lifelong lover: a man in whom aspiration had often jarred painfully against reality, but whose exuberant eccentricities had inspired people, and not just his wife, to love him.

14

Truly Living Now

On a Sunday morning in October, my husband asked me over breakfast how Lydia Maria Child had died. It was a heart attack, I said, over from one minute to the next. Perhaps sometime in the fall, I thought. He asked about her funeral. I couldn't remember details, but I said I thought Wendell Phillips had spoken. Maybe Whittier too. Breakfast finished, I went up to my study to start writing. I was trying to begin the Civil War chapter. It was daunting, and I needed to focus. But thoughts of Child's death stayed with me. I picked up an earlier biography and paged to the end. Exactly when had she died? October 20, my source reported. I looked at my calendar. It was October 20.

I looked out the window. Autumn's brilliance was fading, reds and yellows giving way to browns and grays. The white trunks and bare branches of birch trees stood out against the darker woods behind them. Earlier that morning, a frost had shimmered on the meadow. Small, dense clouds patterned the sky, dark in the middle but bright at their edges. Perhaps the world had looked like this as Maria Child left it.

That day would come six years after David's death. The intervening years would, in many ways, be lonely and scattered. Despite Wayland's limitations, David had anchored Child's heart there, in their small home near the pond. Now she was alone, and the challenge would be to figure out how, and where, to live without him.

* * *

The initial weeks after David's death were a terrible rush. Cold weather was coming, and a winter alone in Wayland was unthinkable. Child began the heartrending work of "breaking up her little nest" as quickly as she could. David had never wanted to throw anything away, so she found herself weeping as she sorted through barrels full of papers, including his college essays and forty-year-old receipts for hay.[1] Whatever he had that she thought friends could use, she boxed up and sent to them. Other things she decided to store until she figured out what to do next. She could leave Wayland now if she wanted. Perhaps she could sell the house and move closer to Boston. But for now, grief made it too hard to think.

She spent the first winter with the Shaws at their Staten Island mansion, where servants outnumbered residents and Child's every wish was granted. She had a lovely room overlooking the water, where she could watch steamboats glide by. She felt loved, pampered, and grateful; she also felt miserably out of place. When Christmas came, she fled to Manhattan to avoid being surrounded by the Shaws' large, boisterous family. Instead she spent a quiet holiday with Rosa Hopper, the widow of John Hopper—the young man Child had, decades ago, feared she could not live without. Hopper had died young after a series of financial disappointments. Being in Manhattan with his widow must have brought back complicated memories. Perhaps nowhere was safe. Back at the Shaws' home, Child chafed again at the luxury and the lack of anything useful to do. She longed to be on her own, digging in her garden, getting dirt under her fingernails, watching things grow.[2]

It was a relief to return to Wayland, even in the middle of a blustery March. She spent the first night with friends, then ventured out alone to complete her journey. The familiar path was, no doubt, a classic New England spring mixture of mud and ice. There at its end was their home, silent and cold. The wood David had chopped was still neatly stacked along the wall. She went through the house opening windows and doors, starting fires to drive out the chill.

"Every room," she wrote to Sarah Shaw, "was baptized with my tears."[3]

Some relief came in the form of Lucy Ann Pickering, an impoverished but proud widow who had once worked for the Lorings. She had boarded with the Childs for a time the year before, in exchange for help with the housework. Now she too was looking for a suitable living arrangement, and she agreed to stay with Child again through the summer. The two women established a firm but limited friendship. Mrs. Pickering was warm, generous, and efficient. She was also prudish, conventional, and conservative. She disapproved of her companion's more radical opinions, forcing Child to censor herself when she could. When especially harrowing news of violence against Black Americans in the South reached them, for instance, Mrs. Pickering declared that they probably had been better off in slavery.[4] Most likely that conversation did not end well.

As Child moved through the rooms her husband had inhabited and the garden he had tended, David often seemed so near. There on the shelves were his encyclopedias and dictionaries, waiting to be consulted. The terraced garden he had constructed was emerging from the winter's snow. Sometimes Child thought she heard him coming up the path or through the door. Some nights she dreamed of him. All around her were memories of his lover-like attentions, his quick delight in her witticisms, their shared joy in the wonders of spring. "I seem to hear him now bidding a loving good morning to my flowers, as he used to do," she wrote to one friend. "Nobody but myself knew what a rich mind he had, and what a large, generous, loving heart," she wrote to another. "All this cannot have gone out of existence. *Can* it?"[5]

She was not the only one asking such questions. The Civil War had left countless Americans desperate to communicate with their slaughtered sons, brothers, and husbands. The newly invented telephone had proved that distance was no obstacle to the voice; maybe other modes of communication, recently unthinkable, were possible as well. Spirit mediums claiming to communicate with the dead were soon to be found everywhere, from intimate dining rooms to large auditoriums, thrilling their audiences with messages from the beyond. Some messages were tapped out on tables; others were declaimed by hypnotized young women speaking from public stages. Some mediums used planchettes—palm-sized pieces of wood, resting on ball bearings and with a pencil attached—to channel spirits' handwriting. Many of Child's friends, Garrison among them, were enthusiastic believers in these conduits to the world beyond.[6]

Child approached spiritualism, as this movement came to be called, with her trademark combination of skepticism and wonder. She was outraged at how many mediums were obviously frauds. But she had never lost her early conviction that there was another reality beyond this one. Otherwise what did it all *mean*? What was it all *for*?[7] And if there was another reality, why couldn't there be a way of communicating with it? As her heart ached for David, Maria Child resolved to find one.

She found an unlikely accomplice in Mrs. Pickering. Despite claiming to be resolutely opposed to spiritualism—it was, she declared, "pitiful, vulgar nonsense" that could only lead to insanity—Mrs. Pickering was curious. Plus, she told Child, she had always been "uncommonly electrical," and she had heard that "planchettes will move in the hands of electrical people." Therefore, she announced to her probably startled housemate, she "should like to try."[8]

Child did not need to be asked twice. She quickly borrowed a planchette from a neighbor and gave it to Mrs. Pickering, who duly sat with it under her hand and waited to see if any spirits would "speak." The results were intriguing: when she looked down after some time had elapsed, Mrs. Pickering, somewhat to her own alarm, found that she had written the name of a young friend who had died long ago. Based on this small triumph, Child ventured a specific request. Would Mrs. Pickering, she asked, try communicating with David? Mrs. Pickering grudgingly agreed, on the condition that Child never ask again.

That night, the two women set up their small experiment. They waited until nightfall. In the Childs' parlor, where David had so often spent his evenings in front of the fire, Mrs. Pickering sat in a chair next to a table. On the table was the planchette, with its pencil, resting on a piece of paper. Mrs. Pickering placed her hand on the planchette, and the women waited in the dark. After a few hours, Mrs. Pickering reported that her arm was tense and exhausted. But she had, she thought, written nothing. The women went to bed without lighting a candle, on account, Child said, of the mosquitoes.

What they found the next morning astonished them both. Mrs. Pickering *had* produced legible sentences. "I am very far from you, yet very near," one read: "Be content. I will help you through the contest, if I can." "Tell M. to be patient," read another. "Something good will come to her." "Pray in humility, and you will have guidance," another sentence promised. Apparently Mrs. Pickering was intrigued enough to want to try again, so the two women repeated the experiment the next night with even better results. "You call us dead. We are not dead. We truly live now," they read the next morning. "I cannot tell you, you cannot know, how bright you will find . . ."[9]

The message broke off there. But it *had been* a message, Child was sure: a message from David. By this point, Mrs. Pickering was thoroughly spooked. Insanity, no doubt, was just around the corner. True to her promise, Child never again asked her to try her medium powers. But to Sarah Shaw, she was quietly ecstatic. "There *is* a telephone between this world and another; or rather a tele*graph*," she wrote, "though it does not work very perfectly." She needed no more proof: David was near her, waiting for her to join him in a bright world, a world where they could truly live. It was a joyous thought. She never stopped telling friends how much she missed him, but her grief eased a little. In its place was a new but familiar resolve: to spend whatever time was left to her doing as much good as possible. "I shall occupy myself with performing *duties here*," she wrote to Sarah, "but I feel happier in doing so, from the assured conviction that dear departed ones are 'not dead; but truly living now.'"[10]

* * *

The summer of 1875 passed, and the next winter set in. This time
Child boarded with the family of John Burt Wight, a retired minister in Wayland who had been a cherished friend of David's. The
affection between Child and the Wight family was clearly mutual,
and she felt useful as she helped keep the genteel, erudite Reverend Wight company.[11] But as soon as it was warm enough, she
moved back into her Wayland home. By now, it had become clear
that the house was not worth enough to exchange for an acceptable
home elsewhere. That fall, much to her friends' distress, Child declined all their invitations and insisted on renting rooms in Boston with Mrs. Pickering. Boardinghouse life was dreary in all the
ways familiar from the early days of her marriage, but it was better than being dependent on others' wealth or charity, so it would
have to do. Together the two widows settled into an uneasy rhythm:
Wayland in the summer, Boston in the winter.

At least initially, Boston offered some intellectual stimulation.
If Child wanted to attend a lecture on Swedenborg, or Japanese religion, or nebular theory, she could do that. She made a point of
seeking out the "most radical preaching" she could find. She went
to the occasional theater production; at Christmas, she ventured
to the department store Jordan and Marsh to see their holiday dec-
orations and was almost trampled by the crowds.[12]

Boston also offered companionship. The Sewalls took her to
dinner every week.[13] She sometimes saw Harriet Beecher Stowe or
the Lorings' grown daughter, Anna Dresel. From Boston she could
get to Concord more easily, where she paid a memorable visit to
Abba Alcott in spring 1876. Their renewed acquaintance, after decades of living apart, was a joy to them both. Child declared herself
deeply impressed with the Alcotts' legendary house and even more
with their daughters: May, who was an accomplished painter, and
Louisa, whose novel *Little Women* had prompted some to predict
that she was becoming the next most important American female
author. Next, that is, after Lydia Maria Child.[14]

There were others in Boston who loved her quick mind and invigorating company, including Sarah Russell, Sarah Shaw's sister-in-law, and Annie Fields, the wife of Child's publisher. Between Russell and Fields, Child was the target of frequent invitations. Didn't she want to come to dinner, or go to a lecture or a women's suffrage meeting? Sometimes Child accepted, but often the answer was no. The sidewalks were icy, she protested, or her rheumatism was flaring up. Just as often, Child simply wanted to be alone. It was true that Thanksgiving with Mrs. Pickering was a lonely affair, but it was better than feeling like the object of pity among someone else's bustling family. Besides, she reminded them, she could be a dangerous guest. You never knew which of her still radical views on racial equality, or women's rights, or the treatment of Native Americans could offend some refined guest. "There have been many attempts to saddle and bridle me, and teach me to keep step in respectable processions; but they have never got the lasso over my neck *yet*," she wrote to Sarah Shaw. No, there would be no grooming or stabling at this stage of her life. "The fact is," she confessed, "my contempt for fashionable people is almost ferocious."[15]

Child liked to say she was becoming yet more radical in her old age. This was not always true—her view of the labor movement, for instance, was consistently conservative. Her imagination seemed to fail her: what, she demanded as workers went on strike against deadly factory conditions, was wrong with a little *work*? And even as she continued to argue for justice for immigrants, Catholics, women, and newly freed Black Americans, her assessment of each group's potential sometimes tracked the prejudices of her day. She worried that it had been a "tremendous mistake" to admit so many immigrants so quickly and that the United States would soon be "governed by the surplus of European jails and almshouses." She was profoundly worried about the influence of the Catholic Church, which she and many Protestant Americans regarded as antidemocratic: she was concerned enough to predict that "the Catholic question would become as vexed a question as Slavery ever was." Her paternalism toward Black Americans continued, as did her impatience with women who were not evolving quickly enough into the serious, industrious human beings she knew they could be.[16] But if there was an arena in which Child's still-growing radicalism was obvious, it was religion. It was here that she would make the final contribution of her long literary life.

Not far from where she and Mrs. Pickering boarded in Boston was Theodore Parker Memorial Hall. Here Child could attend meetings of the Free Religious Association—a relatively new group dedicated to spiritual enlightenment through the eradication of religious dogma. Its founding members came from Unitarian, Quaker, and Jewish traditions; its early supporters included several of Child's allies such as Lucretia Mott, Ralph Waldo Emerson, and Thomas Wentworth Higginson. It styled itself a "spiritual anti-slavery society," welcomed women, and encouraged its members to engage in reforms of all kinds.[17] In other words, it was a group after Child's own heart.

She began attending lectures there every Sunday. The enthusiasm was mutual. She was, after all, the author of *The Progress of Religious Ideas*, a text that could well have served as the group's Bible had they wanted one. Members of the association were inclined to "make much of her," she admitted. She added them to the list of organizations she gave money to.[18]

But their lectures, she worried, were too academic to reach a broader audience.[19] All the scholarship in the world, she knew, would never persuade the average American to forget sectional affiliations and embrace a doctrine of common humanity and reform. The old restlessness took hold of her again. Now in her middle seventies, Child asked herself one last time what she could do. One last time, the answer was clear. She could write a book.

Even better, she could collect others' thoughts into a book, showing how truth seekers everywhere had reached similar conclusions about life's most fundamental questions. So Child began to sort the world's wisdom, topic by topic, into a series of themes that soon became chapters. In one titled "Ideas of a Supreme Being," she set quotations from Mohammad next to a tenth-century Hindu text, allowing readers to see how reverence for a higher power was common to otherwise distinct traditions. A chapter titled "Prayers" combined a poem by George Eliot, a plea from an anonymous slave, and a passage attributed to "Jesus Christ, Israelite." Chinese sources mixed with German philosophy in chapters on immorality, worship, and inspiration. In chapters titled "Inward Light" and "Moral Courage," she set Emerson's insights and Benjamin Franklin's wisdom alongside the revelations of Sufi mystics and Persian sages. "The fundamental laws of morality, and the religious aspirations of mankind, have been strikingly similar always and everywhere," Child assured her readers in a long introduction. These fundamental laws had to do with honesty, decency, compassion, and equality. Everyone could play a part in disseminating these truths. "Whosoever makes diligent use of life, and strives to follow the light of reason and conscience," she promised, "helps on the progress of the world by his own individual growth."[20]

She doesn't say where she found the sources that helped her span time and place in this search for truth, but both Boston and Wayland by now had free public libraries. If indeed Child made use of either, how different it must have felt from her time in the Boston Athenæum almost half a century earlier. Despite being a woman, she could now walk confidently into either reading room and browse its shelves. She needed no one's special permission; access was hers simply because she was a curious human being. Around her were no longer only the city's powerful men but its average citizens, each on his, or her, private quest for knowledge. If her book's argument was right, that quest would bring them, however slowly, to the very truths she hoped her little book would illuminate.

Aspirations of the World: A Chain of Opals was published in 1878. Child didn't expect it to sell well, and it didn't. Reviewers complained that she should have included more theology and less Emerson. This made her smile. Hadn't they noticed that less theology was exactly what she had intended? But for those who had ears to hear, the book was welcome. The Shaws loved it; Garrison praised its "garnered testimonies from the wise and good of all ages and climes"; Sarah Russell reported reading it out loud to her daughters. "Full of power and gentle; liberal-minded, great, consistent," one reader wrote. Just, she added, like its author.[21]

* * *

During the long, often lonely winters in Boston, Child rarely received visitors. It was a familiar problem: her friends had grand houses on Louisburg Square or Charles Street. Their dinner parties abounded with sparkling literary personalities or the merry warmth of chattering grandchildren. How was she to reciprocate in her comfortless rooms with only Mrs. Pickering in the background, probably silent and vaguely disapproving?

Occasionally she made an exception. One winter, she allowed someone, probably Annie Fields, to bring the young and aspiring writer Elizabeth Stuart Phelps to visit her. Phelps vividly remembered venturing from Beacon Hill into Child's South Boston neighborhood. The area was "so much less than fashionable," she remembered, "that I felt a certain awe upon me, as if I were visiting a martyr in prison." They reached the boardinghouse where Child was living that winter. Her rooms were on an upper floor where rent was cheaper. "We climbed the steep stairs of her boardinghouse thoughtfully," Phelps recounted. "Each one of them meant some generous check which Mrs. Child had drawn for the benefit of something or somebody, choosing this restricted life as the price of her beneficence." Everyone knew, she continued, that Child had sacrificed a brilliant literary career to the cause of abolition. "It is not so well known," she told her readers, "that she had all her life expended such means as she had in private charities, denying herself every luxury and many common comforts, in order to compass the power to relieve or to prevent suffering."

They reached the door. Child welcomed them in and led them to her sitting room. "Every thing was neat, respectable, and orderly," Phelps remembered. Ah, yes, respectable. Child would have made sure of that. But otherwise, her visitor remembered, the rooms were "dreariness personified." The brown carpet was threadbare, the room "so devoid of color as to seem like a cell." For someone whose soul so longed for beauty, it sounds like a prison indeed.

But as the visitors talked, the sun suddenly broke through the dark winter clouds. Their hostess, Phelps remembered, "rose quickly and, taking a little prism which she evidently treasured, hung it in the window so that it caught the southwestern ray. Instantly the colorless room leaped with rainbows." Phelps was transfixed. "The sweet old lady stood smiling, in the midst of them," she remembered; "she directed them this way and that, and threw them all over the empty spaces and plain furniture." "I never see a prism without thinking of her noble life; and I keep one in my study windows to this day, partly in memory of this beautiful and pathetic incident. It did me good," Phelps reflected, "and I do not want to forget it."[22]

Child's last years also included one new, vibrant friendship. In spring 1877, she had received a letter from Anne Whitney. Whitney was a poet and sculptor who, having recently returned from living and studying in Rome, now had a studio on Beacon Hill. Child had long known of her and admired her work. Whitney was, in fact, in high demand: soon her statue of Samuel Adams would appear before Faneuil Hall; eventually her statue of Charles Sumner would be placed in Harvard Square. And now the famous sculptor had a question for the aging reformer. Would Child allow Whitney to sculpt her?

It was a flattering request. "I should consider it a great honor to have my bust made by you; and if it were ever to be made by anyone, I should decidedly give you the preference," Child responded. But she had never considered herself beautiful, and age did not help. "I admire your genius too much to have it employed on any but beautiful or noble forms," she wrote, "and I have too much reverence for the high mission of Art to consent to its being desecrated by the portraiture of my old visage." So she declined. But while Child usually refused to be introduced to curious admirers, encouraging her friends to ward them off by insinuating that she was no longer entirely sane, this case was different.[23] Perhaps, she suggested to Whitney, the two could become better acquainted.

It was, in some respects, an improbable friendship. Whitney was two decades younger than Child. She was well traveled and

Fig. 59. Anne Whitney. Courtesy of the Watertown Free Public Library.

well educated in ways Child was not. She cut her hair short. She lived with a woman named Abby Adeline Manning in a relationship that, whether or not it was romantic, was devoted and lifelong. She carried on a bustling transatlantic social life with all the interesting people she could collect around her. In many ways, the two women could not have been more different. But their driving curiosity and intellectual insatiability made them a joy to each other. Soon Whitney was regularly visiting Child, and Child was cautiously venturing out to Whitney's studio. There she watched Whitney's sculpture of the Viking explorer Leif Erikson come into being before taking its place on a tree-lined walkway of Common-wealth Avenue. "Give my love to Miss Manning," Child wrote after visiting. And, she sometimes added, love to Leif too.[24]

There was one more difference that drew these women together in lively, irresistible disagreement. Whitney was a materialist. She was convinced by recent scientific theories that there was noth-ing to life but matter: no souls, no spirit world, and certainly no afterlife. Child, given her messages from David, was all the more certain of the opposite and loved sparring with her. "We shall have Thursday afternoon and evening to settle the affairs of the universe; which will be abundant time for us to accomplish it; considering that one of us is so well posted up in all that relates to Matter, and the other so familiar with what relates to Spirit," she wrote in anticipation of one visit. All the science in the world, she wrote in another letter, "will never convince *me* that there is not a vital, all-pervasive force, called soul, of which matter is merely the ever-changing form." When Whitney tried to convince her anyway, Child merrily declared that the fight was on. Their disagreements seemed only to deepen their friendship. "I thank you for doing so much to make the winter pleasant to me," Child wrote after return-ing to Wayland one year, "and I love you always."[25]

Child also became one of Whitney's champions, using her con-nections to seek commissions for sculptures of John Brown and Garrison. She was ecstatic when Whitney's statue of Charles Sum-ner won a competition sponsored by the Boston Art Committee. But her jubilation was short-lived. When judges, after bestow-ing the award on Whitney's sculpture, learned that Whitney was a woman, they changed their minds and took it back. That was only right, members of the press suggested: "Think of a woman bringing her mind to bear on the legs of a man—even if those legs were inside a pair of stone trousers!" the *New York Evening Post* lamented. "The Jack-asses!" Child raged.[26]

Across her decades-long correspondence, Child's signature seldom varied. To most correspondents, she was simply "L. Ma-ria Child." To intimate friends like the Shaws, she was sometimes

"Mariequita" or "Mariechen." With Whitney, things were different. "Dear Saucebox," one of Child's letters to her new friend began. It was signed "Bird O'Freedom."[27]

*　*　*

But Child's physical world was closing in. By the time she turned seventy-seven, rheumatism had so crippled one leg that she could not get in and out of carriages. Her diminished hearing meant she no longer enjoyed lectures or concerts. This made her all the more grateful when William Lloyd Garrison, despite his own weakening health, made his way to her boardinghouse for one of the things she loved most in the world: "a long cozy chat." Together among her sparse furnishings, the friends reminisced. Perhaps they reflected on some of their triumphs; almost certainly they mourned all the evidence of work still to be done. The presidential election of 1876 had been contested; after months of wrangling, Republicans gained the presidency of Rutherford B. Hayes in exchange for a pledge that the federal government would no longer intervene on behalf of Black Americans in the South. The "Black Exodus" of 1879, in which millions of freedpeople left for points west or north, was ample evidence of how quickly and completely this pledge made life in the South unlivable for many of them.[28]

But more than anything, Garrison and Child talked about the world of spirits that lay just beyond the world they knew. Garrison had also tried to contact his wife and son through mediums after their deaths. He had no doubt that spirits were all around them and could appear and communicate when called. Perhaps Child's boardinghouse room suddenly felt more crowded as the two elderly friends imagined which spirits might be surrounding them even as they spoke. And what did all this mean about the world that they, the ones left behind, still inhabited? "The only rational solution is that it is a preparation for a larger and higher life," Child concluded.[29] As they said their good-byes, perhaps both friends sensed that their time of preparation was almost over.

A few weeks later, Garrison was dead. Flags in Boston flew at

Fig. 60. William Lloyd Garrison between 1855 and 1865. Courtesy of the Library of Congress.

half-mast. Memorial services were held up and down the coast. His funeral at the First Religious Society church in Roxbury was attended by fifteen hundred people, their carriages lining nearby Eliot Square. One speaker after another showered the deceased reformer with a grateful country's praise. Garrison had, in Wendell Phillips's words, "announced the principle, arranged the method, gathered the forces, enkindled the zeal, started the argument, and finally marshalled the nation." The tributes that flooded the newspapers were thrilling to Child. They made him seem so alive again. "How," Child wondered once more, "could such a spirit die?"

Maybe it hadn't. And if Garrison still existed, truly living on the other side of the veil, Child had one last wish for the man who had changed her life. She hoped the mediums would be good enough to let his spirit rest in peace.[30]

* * *

In the spring of 1880, Child had already started looking for a place where she and Mrs. Pickering could board in the fall. Her many efforts had turned up nothing. Still, she refused one offer after another to stay with friends. She would not again be pampered by the Shaws or burden the Wights; and she most certainly would not sully Anne Whitney's beautiful surroundings by becoming first ill, then paralyzed, then finally dying in Whitney's elegant brownstone. She wanted, she wrote to the Sewalls, simply to "drift." Whitney reproached her a little. "It must be confessed there is a little leaven of offishness in you that will not allow of the best things possible falling to you," she wrote. Surely they could find a place in Boston where Child could feel comfortable and secure. Surely she was not yet so impaired that isolation was her only option. "Make the night as short as possible," Whitney urged: "Let the gracious twilight have its hour with old friends & reminiscences." Even as she wrote this, Whitney seemed to know it would change nothing. She grieved at the thought that she might never see Child again. "Don't go altogether & at once," she entreated. But she ended her correspondence sensing, it seems, that Child might do just that. "Always yours for either or both worlds," her letter concludes, "Anne Whitney."[31]

* * *

When she rose in her Wayland home on October 20, 1880, Maria Child reported that she was feeling well.[32] A new doctor was treating her rheumatism: her condition, he predicted, would improve in a few weeks. Meanwhile she was full of plans. A "worthy young man" in the neighborhood "needs some help about learning a trade," she had recently written to Sarah Russell, "and I am go-

Fig. 61. Lydia Maria Child in the 1870s. By permission of the Beaman Memorial Library.

ing to give him a lift." That was only the beginning. "Divers other projects I have in mind, and I expect to accomplish them all by the help of Aladdin's lamp," she continued, filtering her resolve with a touch of self-irony.

Then she waxed reflective. "Oh, it is such a luxury to be able to give without being afraid," she told her friend. It was a striking statement from a woman whose financial means, her friends believed, had kept her from attaining the home she longed for. But given a choice between personal comfort and the joy of helping others, she would always choose the latter. "I try not to be Quixotic," she promised Russell, "but I want to rain down blessings on all the world, in token of thankfulness for the blessings that have been rained down upon me."[33]

So as the day began, perhaps she hoped her rheumatism would spare her enough energy to produce that rain. Perhaps there was a sick friend who needed a cheering letter, or a neighborhood child she could read to. Maybe she had received a request for funds from one of her favorite charitable organizations and was calculating how much she could send. Maybe it was time to put her garden to bed in preparation for the joyful rebirth springtime would bring.

But then she suddenly reported what her lifelong friend John Greenleaf Whittier later described as "severe pain in the region of the heart."[34] Mrs. Pickering summoned help as quickly as she could. But by the time it arrived, Lydia Maria Child's heart had stopped beating, and she was gone.

Or was she?

*　*　*

Her friends soon discovered that she had given brutally spartan instructions for her funeral. There was to be no grand memorial service in Boston, no lionizing from a pulpit, no lines of curious strangers stretching past her coffin. Speaking of coffins: she wanted the plainest one possible. Also, she wanted no flowers. To me, that is the saddest part. All her life, Child had loved flowers: grown them, tended them, spread beauty and joy to friends by giving them away. But for her own memorial she wanted none. It was, in short, to be a "very quiet and inexpensive funeral," she wrote in her will; a wish, she warned her friends, "which I trust will be scrupulously observed."[35]

A few newspapers sent reporters to her modest home where the funeral was to be held. The reporters were, it seems, a little disappointed. Given her national standing and international reputation, the *Framingham Gazette* judged, how strange that there should be a coffin without a single silver handle and not a bouquet of flowers in sight. And surely it wasn't right that the public was prohibited from paying their respects to an author so many had loved. The *Boston Sunday Herald* correspondent also noted the plain coffin and lack of flowers, although he appeared moved by how beautiful the deceased looked, laid out in a simple black dress and "neat white cap." But all in all, the *Gazette* reporter concluded, it was a "peculiar funeral."[36]

Still, the locals must have been somewhat starstruck to see Wendell Phillips and John Greenleaf Whittier arrive and enter her home. There a small group of friends and family gathered. Phillips spoke, his hand on the coffin of the woman who had, almost fifty years earlier, set him on his life's path. He remembered the early, self-imposed hardships her convictions had caused her. He reminisced about the frugality that had allowed her to give to others. But struggle and thrift had not resulted in a dreary life, he assured his listeners. On the contrary, her intelligence, wit, and love of beauty meant that, despite everything, her life had often "bubbled up with joy." He struggled to encompass the span of her attributes. "Modest, womanly, simple, sincere, solid, real, loyal; to be trusted; equal to affairs yet above them," he said: "a hand ready for fireside help and a mystic loving to wander on the edge of the actual." All this she had been, and more. Her neighbor Alfred Wayland Cutting, in his journal, put it more simply: "How we shall miss her," he wrote.[37]

Local farmers carried her to a grave freshly dug next to David's. The weather that day had mixed sun and clouds: now, as her body was lowered into the earth, a rainbow appeared to the east.[38] On her tombstone were written David's words: "You call us dead; We are not dead; We are truly living now."

*   *   *

When Wendell Phillips, as Child's executor, opened her will, he found that he had more than $36,000 to give away. As I write this, that sum equals roughly three-quarters of a million of today's dollars. But what of her protestations about her poverty and all it prevented her from doing? It seems that some combination of continued literary earnings, carefully guarded investments, and legacies from friends had accrued into this substantial figure. She had certainly known how much money she had: just months before, she had written a will distributing it all with her characteristic mix of generosity and principle. After providing bequests to Mrs. Pickering and several impoverished relations, the rest of the funds were bequeathed to causes that reflected Child's lifelong preoccupations: $1,000 went to the Home for Old Colored Women, $1,000 to aid the "elevation of the character of women" in general, $1,000 to the Free Religious Association. The $2,000 bequeathed to the Hampton Agricultural College for the education of Black students came with one caveat: "The said sum," Child specified, "is never to be used for any species of theological teaching."[39]

*   *   *

Toward the end of her life, Child imagined death in many ways. Perhaps it would simply be like falling asleep into an eternal rest. After a lifetime of struggle and sacrifice, that sometimes sounded perfect.[40] Or perhaps it would be a glorious revelation of the truth she had always longed to understand. Was the secret to the world, as she had long suspected, music? Or perhaps geology? Had Plato and Swedenborg been right that this was a world of confused shadows? Would dying dispel those shadows and allow her to see the light? Finally to know, to see, to understand: that, she had often thought, would be its own kind of heaven.

But there was one more vision of the afterlife that Child sometimes imagined: an afterlife in which she could keep working. In her last letter to Anne Whitney, she mused once more to her materialist friend about her failing body and diminished spirits. Her limbs were stiff, slow, and sore; her heart was bruised by disappointment and loss. Her powers, she knew, were ebbing. But surely if she could shed her mortal flesh, her spirit would be free and her energies renewed. "I *think* there is more work for me to do in the universe," she speculated to this new friend of her old age, "and that I shall enter upon it with renovated powers."[41]

The first time I read this, I looked up and out of the window. I wish I could say I saw a rainbow, but I didn't. That doesn't mean it wasn't there.

Imagine: Lydia Maria Child, still at work in the universe: inspiring, encouraging, exhorting, convicting, admonishing; urging those of us still bound by space and time to meet the challenges of our moral lives.

All right, I thought. Let's do this.

Epilogue

But do what?

I said that I have always loved the big questions. Big answers are harder to find.

Let me return to the beginning. Philosophy, I said, means the love of wisdom. "Mrs. Child," one of her early reviewers had written, "knows the art of living well, which is certainly the highest wisdom." Western philosophy began when Socrates insisted that the unexamined life was not worth living. Child had lived an examined life; she had always sought the highest wisdom. What does it mean to seek that wisdom, to live an examined life, now?

Here, to me, is a start: To accept the problems of American democracy as my own and never be too busy to address them. To seek out knowledge that can orient me truly about historical forces that shape the present, even when that knowledge means I have to change my life. To recognize when collective responsibility means that any pride I feel in my country must be balanced by my obligation to address its wrongs.

It means to understand the barriers that have limited others in the past and to do my best not to reproduce them today. Specifically, to understand harms committed against native peoples around me and to do what I can not to perpetuate that harm. To learn more about the effects of racism in my field and adjust my understanding of it accordingly.[1] To listen to those in my community whose experience of racial injustice is personal and whose thinking about it is better informed than mine; to let their perspective change me, and to repay them with more than thanks. To understand what it means to be a white American; to think carefully about what I benefit from and what I owe.

Living an examined life means rearranging my finances, reorienting my syllabi, recommitting to organizations that support America's radical promise of equality. It means resisting a consumerism that is both unethical and unsustainable. It means taking stock of my skills, applying them where they are needed, and cultivating new skills that push me beyond what I know.

Seeking wisdom means recognizing when my actions are in tension with my professed beliefs. It requires me to construct the patterns of my life to reflect the urgent questions of my time. It asks me to cultivate a fierce humility that recognizes that even my best intentions sometimes indict my ignorance. It demands, in short, that I not flatter myself.

As I make this list, it feels overwhelming. Indeed, Child's example does not assure us that the examined life is easy. But it does assure us that it will be worthwhile.

*   *   *

When I was finishing this book, I made one more trip to Northampton, Massachusetts, where the Childs lived in the late 1830s. Here Maria Child had experienced some of her darkest moments. She had anguished from afar as the abolitionist movement splintered and her friends were mobbed by violent crowds. She had despaired at her neighbors' reluctance to recognize the wrong of enslaving their fellow humans. She had poured herself into backbreaking work to support her husband's beet-farming scheme, then watched it fail—fail not only to make money but to undermine the economic power of slavery. She had agonized as that failure broke his spirit and imperiled their marriage.

Not far from where one of their ill-fated beet fields had been, there is now a community garden. The soil is still rich and deep; the surrounding fields are wide and flat. Among the small plots where Northampton residents tend their tomatoes and corn, there is a plot dedicated to the Childs. In it are beets.

At a small shelter close by, a local historian sometimes gives lectures describing the Childs' attempts to undermine slavery through agriculture. He also recounts how their presence laid the groundwork for a thriving abolitionist community that developed there in the decade after they left. This community, which was committed to economic justice as well as racial and gender equality, included Black abolitionists Sojourner Truth and David Ruggles. Together their efforts helped make this Massachusetts town, so far from Southern plantations, a well-used stop on the Underground Railroad.

When I arrived at the garden, the local historian led me to the plot that honors this history. In the years I was writing this book, a pandemic had interrupted the Northampton historical society's plans to develop a curriculum that would bring schoolchildren to the garden to learn this part of their community's past. But there were hopes to revive those plans soon.

We stood looking at the plants emerging from neatly mounded rows of dirt, the Holyoke mountain range somewhere in the distance. "What inspired you to write about Lydia Maria Child?" he asked. I took a deep breath.

The sun was hot; the air was still. The beets were small, but they were growing.

Acknowledgments

In acknowledgment of everything I benefit from and everything I owe, and in recognition of Child's lifelong commitment to "*earning* with one hand and *giving* with the other," the proceeds from this book will be distributed to organizations that work toward Child's hope for a more just world.

What a pleasure it is at the end of a project to thank the people and institutions who helped make it happen.

This biography would not have been possible without Deborah Pickman Clifford's gripping *Crusader for Freedom: A Life of Lydia Maria Child* and Carolyn L. Karcher's magnificent *The First Woman in the Republic: A Cultural Biography of Lydia Maria Child*, both of which offer a wealth of detail and insight about Child's world. It would also not have happened without John Kaag's vision, guidance, and example. Thank you to John for seeing potential in this story and simply telling me to write it. Thanks to my agent, Katherine Flynn, whose energy and no-nonsense confidence gave me exactly the right kind of foundation for my writing. Thanks to Alan Thomas, my editor at University of Chicago Press, for his expert counsel throughout, and for having faith that a philosopher could write a biography. Thanks also to Randy Petilos at the Press for his thorough, lightning-quick answers to my many questions; to Meredith Nini and Alice Bennett; and to my anonymous readers for their encouragement and advice. I remain steadfastly thankful for my departmental colleagues at Colby College for their collegiality and support, and I gratefully acknowledge the Colby College Faculty Research Grant that helped fund the images included in this book. Enormous thanks also to Daniel Ellison, whose quick and efficient research assistance made a crucial stage of the book's completion possible.

I am so grateful to those who offered feedback on early drafts of the book: Richard Fox, Jim Johnson, Kerry McDonald, Regan Penaluna, and Bernard Prusak. Katherine Bidwell's eagle eye combined with her sharp curiosity and ready sympathy made her the best friend-as-editor I could have imagined for this project. My brother Joseph's early encouragement, editorial insights, and intellectual companionship were a deep joy to me as I wrote. His own extraordinary ability to transform his life, and his determination to live by his conscience, inspire me every day.

Thanks to my colleagues in philosophy who provided early opportunities to explore Child as a philosophical thinker: Kristin Gjesdal, Dalia Nassar, Alison Stone, Michael Rosen, and Sean Kelly. Richard Fox generously contributed his expertise in American history to guide me through territory that was new to me; Laura Walls offered wonderful understanding and practical advice; Sebastian Currier cheerfully helped me find Child sites in New York City. All my siblings and their families supported me with eagerness and patient listening as I discovered Child's story. Thank you especially to the Moland-Sanz family for housing me during my research in New York and to the Moland-Hitchcock family for their hospitality during my archival work at Cornell University. The force field known as GNO—Katherine Bidwell, Louie Cronin, Jill Kaufman, Amy Macdonald, Mary McGrath—was a source of unyielding enthusiasm every step of the way. I told them within days of encountering LMC that this would be my next book; they swung into action and never looked back. Thanks to them for literary connections, library memberships, local contacts, writerly wisdom, and for the brilliance, ferocity, and hilarity they weave into my life.

I owe enormous gratitude to the librarians and local historians who make research like mine possible. I regret that I did not note the name of the librarian at the Schlesinger Library at Harvard's

Radcliffe Institute who put the first letter by Lydia Maria Child into my hands: whoever she is, she changed my life. Thank you to Diana Carey and Sarah Hutcheon, both at the Schlesinger Library, for their ready help over subsequent visits. Mary Warnement and Carolle Morini at the Boston Athenæum were generous and accommodating as I spent weeks reading Child's letters on microfiche on the library's second floor. Carolle Morini also provided expert advice and liberal access to records of Child's time at the Athenæum. Thanks also to Karen Gillum at Miller Library, Colby College, and Erin Fitzsimmons at Colby's Special Collections and Archives; Jamie Ross at the Maine Historical Society; Paul Friedman at the New York Public Library; Daniel Hinchen and Mary Yacovone at the Massachusetts Historical Society; Mary Kathryn Lee at the Royall House and Slave Quarters; and also to Karen and Maielle Merriam.

Kyna Hamill, whose expertise as a local historian is only one of her many talents, gave me a memorable tour of the exhibit "Gathering Up the Fragments," including a treasure trove of objects about and belonging to Child, organized by the Medford Historical Society. She also solved several puzzles about Child with great efficiency and generosity. Tom Mickewich likewise guided me through a wonderful exhibit that included Child at the Norridgewock Historical Society in Maine. Steve Strimer, every biographer's dream of a local historian, spent a morning driving my husband and me around sites in Northampton where the Childs lived and liberally shared his findings about their years there. His and others' work at the David Ruggles Center for History and Education is a model of what local history can be and do. Tom Goldscheider and Faith Deering welcomed me to their presentations on the Childs and other reformers in the Northampton area and helped expand my understanding of the region in profound ways. Marie Panik, director of Historic Northampton, gave me a tour of an exhibit on Northampton in the 1840s, made the society's records about Child available to me, and helped me locate an edition of the *National Anti-Slavery Standard* that William Holloway then generously photographed for inclusion in this book. Thank you to Betty Sharpe for her assistance as well.

Jane Sciacca at the Wayland Museum and Historical Society, also a true hero among local historians, dedicated hours to guiding me through the Lydia Maria Child treasures housed there and freely shared her vast knowledge of Child's life as well as of local history generally. She answered all my follow-up questions immediately and with great resourcefulness. In the Wayland community, I am also grateful to Molly Faulkner and Katherine Gardner-Westcott. Huge thanks to Rev. Ken Sawyer for access to his amazing collection of clippings and sermons about Child, and to Rev. Stephanie May for welcoming us to visit First Parish in Wayland, where we were able to see Child's legacy at work in that congregation and in all that the Lydia Maria Child Fund for Activism is accomplishing.

This book, like everything I do, has been a joyful collaboration with my husband, Jim Johnson. When we unexpectedly discovered, in the cemetery where Lydia Maria Child is buried, evidence that a distant relation of his named John Burt Wight had been one of the Childs' closest Wayland friends, it felt like only the latest confirmation of our deeply entwined lives. For all of it—for endless willingness to hear just one more story about LMC; for driving to historical sites from Maine to North Carolina on the coldest and hottest days of the year; for reading, editing, advising, and photographing; and, more than anything, for joining his life to mine—I owe him more than I can say.

My parents exemplify what it means to live a worthwhile life of service to others. Their shared commitment to beauty and truth has formed me in ways for which I am so thankful. Their determination to keep pondering, learning, and growing is a lifetime lesson all its own. Their patience for listening to their children's many and evolving preoccupations is apparently limitless. Once when, in the middle of some monologue, I finally paused for breath, my father said: "Lydia, we love to know what you're *thinking*." I will never stop being grateful for their nurturing of my mind and heart. This book, about another Lydia who loved to think, is dedicated to them with deep respect and gratitude, and most of all with love.

Illustration Credits

1. John Warner Barber, *Southern View of Medford* (1844). From *Historical Collections, Being a General Collection of Interesting Facts, Traditions, Biographical Sketches, Anecdotes, &c., relating to the History and Antiquities of Every Town in Massachusetts* (Worcester, MA: Warren Lazell, 1844), 414. Photograph: Boston Athenæum.

2. *Royall House and Slave Quarters* (ca. 1960). Over-mantel mural, Marble Chamber, Royall House. Photograph: Courtesy of Royall House and Slave Quarters/Theresa Kelliher.

3. C. F. Kidder, *View of the Upper Portion of the North Village* (1849). From William Allen, *The History of Norridgewock* (Norridgewock, ME: Edward J. Peet, 1849). Photograph: Boston Athenæum.

4. Photomechanical from a painting by Francis Alexander, *Lydia Maria Francis (Mrs. Child)* (ca. 1824). In Portraits of American Abolitionists. Collection of the Massachusetts Historical Society. Photograph: Massachusetts Historical Society.

5. Frederick Christian Lewis, after an engraving by Samuel Laurence, *Portrait of Nathaniel Parker Willis* (1841). Photograph © The Trustees of the British Museum.

6. *Ellis Gray Loring* (n.d.). In Portraits of American Abolitionists. Collection of the Massachusetts Historical Society. Photograph: Massachusetts Historical Society.

7. William Page, *Mrs. Ellis Gray [Louisa] Loring* (1844–49). In Portraits of American Abolitionists. Collection of the Massachusetts Historical Society. Photograph: Massachusetts Historical Society.

8. Title page of *The Juvenile Miscellany*, vol. 3, no. 1 (Boston: Putnam and Hunt, 1826). Photograph: David Ruggles Center for History and Education.

9. Francis Alexander, *David Lee Child* (ca. 1825). Photograph by permission of the Beaman Memorial Library, West Boylston, Massachusetts.

10. *Andrew Jackson as Richard III*. Lydia Maria Francis Child Papers, ca. 1827–78. MC 305. Schlesinger Library, Harvard Radcliffe Institute. Photograph: Harvard University.

11. S. S. Jocelyn, steel-plate engraving after Nathaniel Jocelyn, *William Lloyd Garrison* (1833). Lydia Maria Francis Child Papers, ca. 1827–78. MC 305. Schlesinger Library, Harvard Radcliffe Institute. Photograph: Harvard University.

12. "Slave Physical Restraints" (1833). From Lydia Maria Child, *An Appeal for That Class of Americans Called Africans* (Boston: Allen and Ticknor, 1833), 16. Schomburg Center for Research in Black Culture, Jean Blackwell Hutson Research and Reference Division, New York Public Library. Photograph: New York Public Library Digital Collections. (Accessed June 22, 2021, https://digitalcollections.nypl.org.)

13. Isaac Smith Homans, *First Independent Baptist Church, Belknap Street* (African Meeting House). From *Sketches of Boston, Past and Present* (Boston: Phillips, Sampson, 1851), 88. Photograph: Boston Athenæum.

14. Leopold Grozelier, *Wendell Phillips* (ca. 1855). National Portrait Gallery, Smithsonian Institution. Photograph: National Portrait Gallery.

15. *Francis George Shaw* (before 1863). Collection of Staten Island Museum. Photograph: Staten Island Museum.

16. *Sarah Shaw* (1863). Detail of a photograph depicting Sarah Shaw with her grandson Frank Curtis. Collection of Staten Island Museum (1863). Photograph: Staten Island Museum.

17. "To the People of the City & County of New York. Greeting" (1835). Lydia Maria Francis Child Papers, ca. 1827–78. MC 305. Schlesinger Library, Harvard Radcliffe Institute. Photograph: Harvard University.

18. *Downfal [sic] of Abolition* (1835). Photograph: Digital Commonwealth. (Accessed June 22, 2021, https://ark.digitalcommonwealth.org/ark:/50959/2z111849h.)

19. Lydia Maria Child's pocket watch (ca. 1835). Photograph: Courtesy of the Medford Historical Society & Museum.

20. *Maria Weston Chapman* (n.d.). In Portraits of American Abolitionists. Collection of the Massachusetts Historical Society. Photograph: Massachusetts Historical Society.

21. Ezra Greenleaf Weld, *Weld-Grimké Family* (n.d.). William L. Clements Library, University of Michigan. Photograph: University of Michigan.

22. *Portrait of Abby Kelley Foster*, carte de visite (ca. 1861), detail. From the collection of Worcester Historical Museum, Worcester, Massachusetts. Photograph: Worcester Historical Museum.

23. Thomas Cole, *View from Mount Holyoke, Northampton, Massachusetts, after a Thunderstorm—The Oxbow* (1836). Gift of Mrs. Russell Sage, 1908 (08.228). Image copyright © The Metropolitan Museum of Art. Image source: Art Resource, New York, NY.

24. John T. Bowen, publisher, and J. C. Wild, *Destruction by Fire of Pennsylvania Hall, the New Building of the Abolition Society, on the Night of the 17th May.* Pennsylvania Philadelphia (1838). Photograph: Library of Congress, https://www.loc.gov/item/2014645336/.

25. *Frederick Douglass* (ca. 1850). After a ca. 1847 daguerreotype. National Portrait Gallery, Smithsonian Institution. Photograph: National Portrait Gallery.

26. David Lee Child, *The Culture of the Beet, and Manufacture of Beet Sugar* (Boston: Weeks, Jordan, 1840), 86. Photograph: Boston Athenæum.

27. *National Anti-Slavery Standard* (May 20, 1841). Courtesy of Historic Northampton, Northampton, Massachusetts. Photograph: William Holloway.

28. *National Anti-Slavery Standard* (May 20, 1841), detail. Courtesy of Historic Northampton, Northampton, Massachusetts. Photograph: William Holloway.

29. *Broadway, 1840* (1840). Raphael Tuck & Sons. Museum of the City of New York. F2011.33.507. Photograph: Museum of the City of New York.

30. Auguste Edouart, *Lydia Maria Francis Child* (1841). National Portrait Gallery, Smithsonian Institution; gift of Robert L. McNeil Jr. Photograph: National Portrait Gallery.

31. "Assignee's Sale," *Hampshire Gazette*, June 6, 1843. Photograph courtesy of Steve Strimer.

32. "The New-England Boy's Song about Thanksgiving Day" (1845). From Lydia Maria Child, *Flowers for Children*, vol. 2, *For Children from Four to Six Years Old* (New York: C. S. Francis, 1845), 28. Photograph: Library of Congress, https://www.loc .gov/item/2006687231/.

33. J. M. Enzing-Miller after drawing by William Page, *Isaac Tatem Hopper* (1771–1852) (n.d.). In Portraits of American Abolitionists. Collection of the Massachusetts Historical Society. Photograph: Massachusetts Historical Society.

34. Alfred Wayland Cutting, *Residence of Lydia Maria Child* (1884). Photograph: Digital Commonwealth. (Accessed June 22, 2021, https://ark.digitalcommonwealth .org/ark:/50959/4t64gr25s.)

35. Albert Sands Southworth and Josiah Johnson Hawes, *Charles Sumner* (ca. 1850). Gift of I. N. Phelps Stokes, Edward S. Hawes, Alice Mary Hawes, and Marion Augusta Hawes. Image © The Metropolitan Museum of Art. Image source: Art Resource, New York, NY.

36. John Andrews, Engraver. *Anthony Burns*, drawn by Barry from a daguerreotype by Whipple and Black (ca. 1855). Detail. Photograph: Library of Congress, https:// www.loc.gov/item/2003689280/.

37. *Marshal's Posse with Burns Moving Down State Street* (1856). Schomburg Center for Research in Black Culture, Manuscripts, Archives and Rare Books Division, New York Public Library. Photograph: New York Public Library Digital Collections. (Accessed June 22, 2021, https://digitalcollections.nypl.org/items/510d47df-944d -a3d9-e040-e00a18064a99.)

38. *Ruins of the Free State Hotel, Lawrence.* In Sara T. L. Robinson, *Kansas: Its Exterior and Interior Life, Including a Full View of Its Settlement, Political History, Social Life, Climate, Soil, Productions, Scenery, Etc.* (Boston: Crosby, Nichols, 1857), frontispiece. Photograph: Kansas State Historical Society.

39. J. L. Magee, *Southern Chivalry—Argument versus Club's* [*sic*]. (1856). Photograph: New York Public Library/Art Resource, New York, NY.

40. *John Brown* (n.d.). Photograph: Library of Congress, https://www.loc.gov/item /2003664870/.

41. *Dangerfield Newby* (n.d.). Boyd B. Stutler Collection, West Virginia Archives and History. Photograph: West Virginia Archives and History.

42. *The Harper's Ferry Insurrection—The U.S. Marines storming the engine house—Insurgents firing through holes in the doors/from a sketch made on the spot by our special artist* (1859). Photograph: Library of Congress, https://www.loc.gov/item/00652046/.

43. *Henry A. Wise* (between 1860 and 1870). Photograph: Library of Congress, https://www.loc.gov/item/2018669364/.

44. *John Anthony Copeland* (n.d.). Boyd B. Stutler Collection, West Virginia Archives and History. Photograph: West Virginia Archives and History.

45. *Expulsion of Negroes and Abolitionists from Tremont Temple, Boston, Massachusetts, on December 3* (1860). Photograph: Library of Congress, https://www.loc.gov/item/95502932/.

46. *N. P. Willis* (between 1855 and 1865). Photograph: Library of Congress, https://www.loc.gov/item/2017897695/.

47. *A View from Idlewild* (n.d.). Stereograph. Miriam and Ira D. Wallach Division of Art, Prints and Photographs: Photography Collection, New York Public Library. Photograph: New York Public Library Digital Collections. (Accessed June 25, 2021, https://digitalcollections.nypl.org/items/510d47e1-8f8e-a3d9-e040-e00a18064a99.)

48. Otis Bass (attributed), *Dr. James Norcom* (n.d.). Photograph: North Carolina Museum of History.

49. "Advertisement for the Capture of Harriet Jacobs, June 30, 1835." State Archives of North Carolina. Photograph: State Archives of North Carolina.

50. *Harriet Jacobs* (1894). Photograph: Private Collection.

51. John Adams Whipple, *Colonel Robert Gould Shaw of 7th New York Infantry Regiment, Co. H, 2nd Massachusetts Infantry Regiment, and 54th Massachusetts Infantry Regiment in Uniform* (between 1861 and 1863). Photograph: Library of Congress, https://www.loc.gov/item/2019635472/.

52. *William Harvey Carney* (ca. 1864). From John Ritchie, Carte-de-visite album of the 54th Massachusetts Infantry Regiment. Collection of the Smithsonian National Museum of African American History and Culture, Gift of the Garrison Family in memory of George Thompson Garrison. Photograph: Smithsonian National Museum of African American History and Culture.

53. *Coloured School at Alexandria Va. 1864 Taught by Harriet Jacobs & Daughter Agents of New York Friends* (1864). Robert Langmuir African American Photograph Collection, Stuart A. Rose Manuscript, Archives, and Rare Book Library, Emory University. Photograph: Emory University.

54. *Frances Ellen Watkins Harper* (n.d.). National Portrait Gallery, Smithsonian Institution. Photograph: National Portrait Gallery.

55. *David Lee Child* (1870). In Portraits of American Abolitionists. Collection of the Massachusetts Historical Society. Photograph: Massachusetts Historical Society.

56. John Adams Whipple, photographer, *Portrait of Lydia Maria Child* (ca. 1865). Photograph: Library of Congress, https://www.loc.gov/item/2018645032/.

57. Louis Prang and L. Schamer, *Representative Women* (ca. 1870). Photograph: Library of Congress, https://www.loc.gov/item/98508687/.

58. *Lydia Maria Child* (ca. 1856). In Portraits of American Abolitionists. Collection of the Massachusetts Historical Society. Photograph: Massachusetts Historical Society.

59 *Anne Whitney* (n.d.). Photograph: Watertown Free Public Library.

60. *Wm. Lloyd Garrison* (between 1855 and 1865). Photograph: Library of Congress, https://www.loc.gov/item/2017897277/.

61. *Lydia Maria Child* (n.d.). Photograph by permission of the Beaman Memorial Library, West Boylston, Massachusetts.

Abbreviations

CC   Child, Lydia Maria. *The Collected Correspondence of Lydia Maria Child*. Edited by Patricia G. Holland and Milton Meltzer. Millwood, NY: Kraus Microform, 1980.

NASS   *National Anti-Slavery Standard*, Accessible Archives.

SL   Child, Lydia Maria. *Lydia Maria Child: Selected Letters, 1817–1880*. Edited by Milton Meltzer, Patricia G. Holland, and Francine Krasno. Amherst: University of Massachusetts Press, 1982.

Notes

Prologue

1. President: LMC to Louisa Loring, 16 June 1856, Lydia Maria Child, *The Collected Correspondence of Lydia Maria Child* (Millwood, NY: Kraus Microform, 1980), 919; harvest: LMC to John Underwood, 26 October 1860, *Lydia Maria Child: Selected Letters, 1817–1880* (Amherst: University of Massachusetts Press, 1982), 363.

Chapter One

1. unpleasant: LMC to Theodore Tilton, 27 May 1866, Child, *SL*, 460; Lydias: Kyna Hamill, "Lydia Maria Child: Author and Abolitionist," in *Gathering Up the Fragments*, ed. Medford Historical Society & Museum (Medford, MA: Medford Historical Society, 2018), 4–5; Lidian Emerson: Megan Marshall, *Margaret Fuller: A New American Life* (New York: Houghton Mifflin Harcourt, 2013), 192–94.

2. Concord: John Weiss, *Discourse Occasioned by the Death of Rev. Convers Francis, D.D.: Delivered Before the First Congregational Society, Watertown, April 19, 1863* (Cambridge, MA: Privately published, 1863), 6, Internet Archive; Bunker Hill: Anna D. Hallowell, "Lydia Maria Child," *Medford Historical Register* 3, no. 3 (1900): 96, Hathi Trust; potatoes: Carolyn Karcher, *The First Woman of the Republic: A Cultural Biography of Lydia Maria Child* (Durham, NC: Duke University Press, 1994), 53.

3. colonies: Elizabeth Varon, *Disunion! The Coming of the American Civil War, 1789–1859* (Chapel Hill: University of North Carolina Press, 2008), 17; ships: Jared Ross Hardesty, *Black Lives, Native Lands, White Worlds: A History of Slavery in New England* (Amherst: University of Massachusetts Press, 2019), 28–29; blacksmiths, animals: Hardesty, *Black Lives*, 12–13, 79.

4. increase: Hardesty, *Black Lives*, 33; newspapers: Hardesty, *Black Lives*, 70.

5. structured: Varon, *Disunion!*, 17; constitution: Varon, *Disunion!*, 24–27; escape, friendly leave: Manisha Sinha, *The Slave's Cause: A History of Abolition* (New Haven, CT: Yale University Press, 2016), 77.

6. lawsuits: Hardesty, *Black Lives*, 138; petitions: Paul J. Polgar, *Standard Bearers of Equality: America's First Abolition Movement* (Chapel Hill: University of North Carolina Press, 2019), 33; pursue: Sinha, *Slave's Cause*, 68; buying self: Sinha, *Slave's Cause*, 74; born after: Sinha, *Slave's Cause*, 82; white allies: Polgar, *Standard Bearers*; ended: Hardesty, *Black Lives*, 140.

7. Quebec: Varon, *Disunion!*, 37.

8. Harriet Hemings: Annette Gordon-Reed, *The Hemingses of Monticello: An American Family* (New York: W. W. Norton), 12, 516, 605.

9. baby: Deborah Pickman Clifford, *Crusader for Freedom: A Life of Lydia Maria Child* (Boston: Beacon Press, 1992), 7; Medford crackers: William Newell, *Memoir of the Rev. Convers Francis, D.D.* (Cambridge, MA: John Wilson, 1866), 5, Hathi Trust; biscuit: Charles Brooks and James M. Usher, *History of the Town of Medford, Middlesex County, Massachusetts, from Its Settlement in 1630 to 1855* (Boston: Rand, Avery, 1886), 357, Internet Archive; large quantities: Hallowell, "Lydia Maria Child," 96; bakery: Clifford, *Crusader*, 7.

10. oak: LMC to Peter and Susan Lesley, 9 August 1856, Child, *CC*, 935.

11. literary influence: LMC to John Weiss, 15 April 1863, Child, *SL*, 425.

12. softened: Clifford, *Crusader*, 16; Unitarianism: Barbara Packer, *The Transcendentalists* (Athens: University of Georgia Press, 2007), 5; hell: LMC to [Lucy Osgood?], 17 December 1870, Child, *CC*, 1966; catechism: T. W. Higginson, "Lydia Maria Child," in James Parton et al., *Eminent Women of the Age: Being Narratives of the Lives and Deeds of the Most Prominent Women of the Present Generation* (Hartford, CT: S. M. Betts, 1869), 41, Internet Archive.

13. doughnuts: Higginson, "Lydia Maria Child," 41.

14. detested: Weiss, *Discourse*, 63; Royall: Hardesty, *Black Lives*, xiii-xiv.

15. Belinda Sutton: Hardesty, *Black Lives*, xiv; slave quarters: C. S. Manegold, *Ten Hills Farm: The Forgotten History of Slavery in the North* (Princeton, NJ: Princeton University Press, 2010), Ebook Central; Mason-Dixon: Hardesty, *Black Lives*, xiv.

16. Caesar: Brooks and Usher, *History of Medford*, 356–57. See also Clifford, *Crusader*, 9–10.

17. approbation: Brooks and Usher, *History of Medford*, 357.

18. speeches: "Abolition of Slave Trade," *Columbian Centinel*, July 14, 1808; image at Phillip Lapansky, "Black Founders: The Free Black Community in the Early Republic," Library Company of Philadelphia, https://librarycompany.org/blackfounders /section8.htm; newspapers: LMC in *NASS*, 27 May 1871, Child, *CC*, 1995a. William Cooper Nell attributes another anecdote about these celebrations to Child. The anecdote, which has sometimes been assumed to be autobiographical on Child's part, was in fact taken from Child's anthology *Authentic Anecdotes of American Slavery*, in which she collected a range of stories not her own. See William Cooper Nell, *The Colored Patriots of the American Revolution: With Sketches of Several Distinguished Colored Persons* (Boston: Robert F. Wallcut, 1855), 25–26, Internet Archive; Lydia Maria Child, ed., *Authentic Anecdotes of American Slavery* (Newburyport, MA: Charles Whipple, 1835), 13–14, Internet Archive. I am grateful to Kyna Hamill for clarifying this point.

19. tobacco: Higginson, "Lydia Maria Child," 41; grammar school: Clifford, *Crusader*, 12; virtue: LMC to Sarah Parsons, 21 December 1871, Child, *CC*, 2022.

20. poring over: LMC to John Weiss, 15 April 1863, Child, *SL*, 425; uncle: Weiss, *Discourse*, 11–13.

21. Baptist: Weiss, *Discourse*, 12.

22. gratitude: LMC to John Weiss, 15 April 1863, Child, *SL*, 425–26.

23. unearthed: Weiss, *Discourse*, 15; labor: Newell, *Convers Francis*, 8.

24. failure: LMC to John Weiss, 15 April 1863, Child, *SL*, 425–26.

25. Adams: LMC in *Independent*, 15 July 1869, Child, *CC*, 1903.

26. mother: Newell, *Convers Francis*, 5, 7.

27. proverb: LMC to Lucy Osgood, 18 March 1870, Child, *CC*, 1936; gypsies: LMC to Lucy Osgood, 26 March 1847, Child, *CC*, 705; 48 years old: Lydia Maria Child, "Hair Clippings," in May Anti-Slavery Collection, #4601, Division of Rare and Manuscript Collections, Cornell University Library, n.d.

28. books: Hallowell, "Lydia Maria Child," 97.

29. ship: Laura Dassow Walls, *Henry David Thoreau: A Life* (Chicago: University of Chicago Press, 2017), 95.

30. first child: Clifford, *Crusader*, 23; ultimately five: Karcher, *First Woman*, 81; Norridgewock: Hallowell, "Lydia Maria Child," 97.

31. Preston: "Lydia Maria Child," 97, William Allen, *The History of Norridgewock: Comprising Memorials of the Aboriginal Inhabitants and Jesuit Missionaries, Hardships of the Pioneers, Biographical Notices of the Early Settlers, and Ecclesiastical Sketches* (Norridgewock, ME: Edward J. Peet, 1849), 163, Internet Archive.

32. librarian: Clifford, *Crusader*, 23.

33. Divinity School: Newell, *Convers Francis*, 9; genius: LMC to Convers Francis, 5 June 1817, Child, *CC*, 1.

34. kindness: LMC to Convers Francis, 5 June 1817, Child, *CC*, 1.

35. Milton: LMC to Convers Francis, [?] September 1817, Child, *SL*, 2.

36. flowers: Lydia Maria Child, *Letters from New York* (Athens: University of Georgia Press, 1998), 112; spirit: "Letter from the Editor," *NASS*, 11 November 1841.

37. lakes: LMC to Convers Francis, 3 February 1819, Child, *CC*, 3.

38. church bell: Karcher, *First Woman*, 10. The collective name for native peoples in this region is now more frequently spelled Wabanaki.

39. baskets: Karcher, *First Woman*, 12; hemlock, chief: Child, *Letters from New York*, 19; baby: Karcher, *First Woman*, 11.

40. snow: Allen, *History of Norridgewock*, 111.

41. Preston: Clifford, *Crusader*, 25; vote: Ronald F. Banks, *Maine Becomes a State: The Movement to Separate Maine from Massachusetts, 1785–1820* (Middletown, CT: Wesleyan University Press, 1970), 145.

42. pack horse: Banks, *Maine Becomes a State*, 189; wicked freight: Banks, *Maine Becomes a State*, 190.

43. ruinous: Banks, *Maine Becomes a State*, 190; majority: Banks, *Maine Becomes a State*, 243.

44. sovereignty: Banks, *Maine Becomes a State*, 192.

45. protest: Banks, *Maine Becomes a State*, 199.

46. weep: Banks, *Maine Becomes a State*, 200.

47. slaves sold: Gordon-Reed, *Hemingses of Monticello*, 635, 655; children: Gordon-Reed, *Hemingses of Monticello*, 655, 661.

48. independent: LMC to Convers Francis, 12 March 1820, Child, *CC*, 7.

49. joy: LMC to Convers Francis, 10 April 1820, 8; love: Child, *Letters from New York*, 204.

50. coherent: Emanuel Swedenborg, *True Christian Religion*, trans. John C. Ager, 2 vols. (West Chester, PA: Swedenborg Foundation, 1996), 76; heaven: Swedenborg, *True Christian Religion*, 47; Marguerite Beck Block, *The New Church in the New World: A Study of Swedenborgianism in America* (New York: Octagon Books, 1968), 35–36.

51. consolation: LMC to Convers Francis, 31 May 1820, Child, *SL*, 2.

52. christened: Hamill, "Lydia Maria Child: Author and Abolitionist," 9; Medford church: Clifford, *Crusader*, 35; growth: LMC to Theodore Tilton, 27 May 1866, Child, *SL*, 460.

53. Maria: LMC to Lydia Bigelow Child, 17 February 1828, Child, *CC*, 27.

54. become Swedenborgian: Clifford, *Crusader*, 307; crocodile: Sylvia Shaw, "Preface," in *Sampson Reed: Primary Source Material for Emerson Studies*, ed. George F. Dole (West Chester, PA: Swedenborg Foundation, 1992), iii.

55. poetry: Sampson Reed, "Oration on Genius," *Swedenborg Studies* 1 (1992): 14; laws of the mind: Reed, "Observations on the Growth of the Mind (1826)," *Swedenborg Studies* 1 (1992): 19; practical: "Growth of the Mind," 24; science: "Growth of the Mind," 32.

56. experienced religion: LMC to Parke Godwin, 20 January 1856, Child, *SL*, 274–75; first love: LMC to Louisa Loring, 20 June 1858, Child, *CC*, 1064.

57. die in: LMC to Louisa Loring, 11 June [1843], Child, *CC*, 502; childhood: LMC to Lucy and Mary Osgood, 7 August 1857, Child, *CC*, 1018.

58. microcosm: LMC to Francis Shaw, 1 April 1877, Child, *CC*, 2311; heaven: LMC to Sarah Shaw, 20 December 1856, Child, *CC*, 969.

59. parlor: Clifford, *Crusader*, 36; table: LMC to Mary Preston, 26 May 1822, Child, *CC*, 10; Kant: LMC to Lucy Osgood, [7–31 December 1862], Child, *CC*, 1447.

60. flatter: LMC to Mary Preston, 26 May 1822, Child, *CC*, 10.

61. poetical: "Yamoyden, a Tale of the Wars of King Philip, in Six Cantos by James Wallis Eastburn," *North-American Review and Miscellaneous Journal* 12, no. 31 (1821): 477.

62. touched it: "Yamoyden," 466–88.

63. writing Hobomok: LMC to Rufus Wilmot Griswold, [October 1846?], Child, *SL*, 232.

64. your own: LMC to Rufus Wilmot Griswold, [October 1846?], Child, *SL*, 232. romance: Karcher, *First Woman*, 21.

65. love him: Lydia Maria Child, *"Hobomok" and Other Writings on Indians* (New York: Rutgers University Press, 1986), 137.

66. On Native Americans in early American literature, see Karcher, *First Woman*, 35ff., 103ff.

67. Harvard: Child, *"Hobomok" and Other Writings on Indians*, 150.

68. never intended: LMC to Rufus Wilmot Griswold, [October 1846?], Child, *SL*, 232; publishing market, pricing: Karcher, *First Woman*, 38.

69. "Miscellaneous Notices," *North American Review* 19, no. 44 (1824): 265–66.

70. Jefferson: David Tyack, *George Ticknor and the Boston Brahmins* (Cambridge, MA: Harvard University Press, 1967), 40; Goethe: Tyack, *George Ticknor*, 50; Ticknorville, queen: Tyack, *George Ticknor*, 1, 184.

71. author: LMC to George Ticknor, 29 March 1825, Child, *CC*, 11.

72. instigation: Karcher, *First Woman*, 39; obtain them: "Reviewed Works," *North American Review* 21, no. 48 (1825): 87, 95.

Chapter Two

1. schoolmistress: Lucy Osgood to LMC, 8 May 1843, Child, *CC*, 493; inspiration: LMC to Mary Preston, 11 June 1826, Child, *SL*, 7; worthy: LMC to Mary Preston, [1826], Child, *CC*, 22.

2. tiger: Karcher, *First Woman*, 629.

3. faults: LMC to Mary Preston, [1825?], Child, *CC*, 17; letters: LMC to Mary Preston, [1826], Child, *CC*, 22; lion: Higginson, "Lydia Maria Child," 44.

4. children: Karcher, *First Woman*, 59.

5. personification: Lydia Maria Child, *Evenings in New England: Intended for Juvenile Amusement and Instruction. By an American Lady* (Boston: Cummings, Hilliard, 1824), 1, Internet Archive; sugar: Child, *Evenings in New England,* 69; rainbows: Child, *Evenings in New England,* 28ff.

6. approbation: LMC to Mary Preston, [1825], Child, *CC*, 15.

7. "Indian Tribes": Child, *Evenings in New England*, 73–78.

8. "Little Master": Child, *Evenings in New England*, 138–47.

9. astronomy: Child, *Evenings in New England*, 147.

10. father: Tyack, *Ticknor*, 162.

11. comb: LMC to Mary Preston, 11 June 1826, Child, *CC*, 18; dedicated: LMC to George Ticknor, 2 October 1825, Child, *CC*, 14.

12. French and drawing: LMC to Mary Preston, 11 June 1826, Child, *CC*, 18; Lafayette: Karcher, *First Woman*, 40.

13. pun: Lydia Maria Child, "Booklet of Quotations and Poems," in May Anti-Slavery Collection, #4601 (Division of Rare and Manuscript Collections, Cornell University Library).

14. Alexander: LMC to Mary Preston, 11 June 1826, Child, *CC*, 18; Willis: George Ticknor Curtis, "Reminiscences of N. P. Willis and Lydia Maria Child," *Harper's New Monthly Magazine* 81 (1890): 718, Hathi Trust; LMC to Marianne Silsbee, 5 February [1867], Child, *CC*, 1761a; ears: Karcher, *First Woman*, 134; trashy: LMC to Lucy and Mary Osgood, 20 July 1856, Child, *SL*, 289.

15. advised: LMC to Sarah Shaw, 25 August 1877, Child, *CC*, 2338; first book: LMC in the *Independent*, 15 July 1968, Child, *CC*, 1903; Hawthorne: Frank L. Mott, *Golden Multitudes* (New York: Macmillan, 1947), 122.

16. Georgia: James Traub, *John Quincy Adams: Militant Spirit* (New York: Basic Books, 2016), 319–20; cotton: Jon Meacham, *American Lion: Andrew Jackson in the White House* (New York: Random House, 2008), 91; principles: Traub, *John Quincy Adams*, 322.

17. enemies: LMC to Mary Preston, 11 June 1826, Child, *CC*, 18; Alcott: LMC to Louisa May Alcott, 19 June 1878, Child, *CC*, 2398; Ellis: LMC to Louisa Loring, [June-August? 1831?], Child, *CC*, 51.

18. Locke: Packer, *Transcendentalists*, 7; Staël: Lydia Moland, "Is She Not an Unusual Woman? Say More: Germaine de Staël and Lydia Maria Child on Progress, Art, and Abolition," in *Women and Philosophy in Eighteenth-Century Germany*, ed. Corey W. Dyck (Oxford: Oxford University Press, 2021); my heart: LMC to Margaret Fuller [after October 1827], Child, *SL*, 10; Fuller: Margaret Fuller, *The Letters of Margaret Fuller*, vol. 1, *1817–1838*, ed. Robert N. Hudspeth (Ithaca, NY: Cornell University Press, 1983), 154.

19. publishers: Hallowell, "Lydia Maria Child," 100.

20. principles: Lydia Maria Child, *The Juvenile Miscellany: For the Instruction and Amusement of Youth*, vol. 1, no. 1 (Boston: John Putnam, 1826), iii; Bacon: Child, *Juvenile Miscellany* 11 (1): 97; Dutch: Child, *Juvenile Miscellany* 11 (1): 98; *H* to *K*: Lydia Maria Child, *The Juvenile Miscellany*, vol. 1, no. 2 (Boston: John Putnam, 1826), 48; London: Child, *Juvenile Miscellany* 11 (2): 108. Why is London like the letter *E*? "It is the capital of England." When is a door not a door? "When it is a jar." Lydia Maria Child, *The Juvenile Miscellany: For the Instruction and Amusement of Youth*, vol. 1, no. 3 (Boston: John Putnam, 1827), 107.

21. no child, has come: Karcher, *First Woman*, 58, 57; delight: Karcher, *First Woman*, 171; childish heart: Sarah (Van Vechten) Brown to LMC, 2 March 1869, Child, *CC*, 1887; 850: LMC to Mary Preston, 7 January 1827, Child, *CC*, 23.

22. For analysis, see Karcher, *First Woman*, 156–58. The original traveler's account is at "Extracts from a Journal," *Juvenile Miscellany* 3 (November 1827): 227–36; quotation at 232. See Karcher, *First Woman*, 653.

23. hopes: LMC to Mary Preston, 6 January 1827, Child, *CC*, 23; Watertown: LMC to Mary Preston, 11 June 1826, Child, *CC*, 18; equal: LMC to Mary Preston, 6 January 1827, Child, *CC*, 23; gifts: LMC to Mary Preston, [1826], Child, *CC*, 22. The manuscript is distorted but seems to read "jewels."

24. recommendation: Karcher, *First Woman*, 47.

25. vanity: Lydia Maria Child, "Memorial Book for David Lee Child," in May Anti-Slavery Collection #4601 (Division of Rare and Manuscript Collections, Cornell University Library, n.d.), 1.

26. DLC in Europe: Karcher, *First Woman*, 48–49.

27. wit: Child, "Memorial Book for David Lee Child," 2.

28. adverse: Child, "Memorial Book for David Lee Child," 3.

29. politician: Karcher, *First Woman*, 81; never marry: LMC to Mary Preston, 11 June 1826, Child, *CC*, 18.

30. maiden aunt: Curtis, "Reminiscences," 719; equality: Child, "Memorial Book for

David Lee Child," 14; wide awake: LMC to Sarah Shaw, 2 February 1868, Child, *SL*, 474–75.

31. proposal: Curtis, "Reminiscences," 720.

32. happy: LMC to Mary Preston, 28 October 1827, Child, *SL*, 9; accepted: "Memorial Book for David Lee Child," 5; name: Clifford, *Crusader*, 81.

33. fear: LMC to Lydia Bigelow Child, 26 July [1828], Child, *CC*, 29.

34. Harvard Street, wedding: Karcher, *First Woman*, 85; cake: LMC to Mary Preston, undated, Child, *CC*, 32; tongues: Hallowell, "Lydia Maria Child," 103.

35. Curtis, "Reminiscences," 720.

36. rights to publications: Clifford, *Crusader*, 72; alive: LMC to George William Curtis, 30 June 1867, Child, *CC*, 1782.

37. three hundred: LMC to Lydia Bigelow Child, 14 January [1829], Child, *SL*, 13; protest fiction: Karcher, *First Woman*, 102. Her stories about Native Americans during this period include "The Lone Indian" (1827), "Adventures of a Bell" (1827), "Church in the Wilderness" (1828), "The Indian Wife" (1828), and "Choc-orua's Curse" (1830). See Karcher, *First Woman*, 107, 116, 120 for analyses of these stories.

38. "Hints": Karcher, *First Woman*, 118; assistance: Karcher, *First Woman*, 645; tender: Child, "Memorial Book for David Lee Child," 13.

39. blot: LMC to Lydia Bigelow Child, 14 November 1828, Child, *CC*, 34; slaveholder: Mark R. Cheathem, "Andrew Jackson, Slavery, and Historians," *History Compass* 9, no. 4 (2011): 326–38; Meacham, *American Lion*, xix, 302–6.

40. expectations: LMC to George Ticknor [1829?], Child, *SL*, 15–16; Cherokee, Creek: Meacham, *American Lion*, 91–96; William Nester, *The Age of Jackson and the Art of American Power, 1815–1848* (Washington, DC: Potomac Books, 2013), 112; Clifford, *Crusader*, 95; expansion: Cheathem, "Andrew Jackson, Slavery, and Historians," 329; Andrew: DLC to LMC, 7 June 1837, Child, *CC*, 124; Snelling: Karcher, *First Woman*, 213.

41. libel suits: Karcher, *First Woman*, 84; aspire to office: Clifford, *Crusader*, 69; $15: Karcher, *First Woman*, 97.

42. judgment, "Libel": Karcher, *First Woman*, 97; freedom of speech: Clifford, *Crusader*, 74; boarders: LMC to Lydia Bigelow Child, [February? 1830], Child, *SL*, 16–17.

43. Ticknor: LMC to George Ticknor [1829?], Child, *SL*, 15–16.

44. murders: Karcher, *First Woman*, 99.

45. sooner the better: Karcher, *First Woman*, 99.

46. debt: Karcher, *First Woman*, 85; queer: LMC to Lydia Bigelow Child, 14 January [1829], Child, *SL*, 13.

47. bread: Lydia Maria Child, *The American Frugal Housewife* (Boston: Marsh and Capen, 1829; repr., Kansas City, MO: Andrews McMeel, 2013), 51; teeth: Child, *Frugal Housewife,* 13–14; rum: Child, *Frugal Housewife,* 13; beer: Child, *Frugal Housewife*, 49.

48. prudence: Child, *Frugal Housewife*, 7; later edition: Karcher, *First Woman*, 130; enjoyed: Child, *Frugal Housewife*, 8.

49. taste, distaste: Nathaniel Parker Willis, "The Editor's Table," *American Monthly Magazine* 1, no. 10 (1829): 721–22, Google Books.

50. editions: Karcher, *First Woman*, 131; women: Sarah (Van Vechten) Brown to LMC, 2 March 1869, Child, *CC*, 1887; preserves: Higginson, "Lydia Maria Child," 46.

51. supplanted: Lydia Maria Child, *The First Settlers of New-England, or Conquest of the Pequods, Narragansets and Pokanokets, as Related by a Mother to Her Children* (Boston: Munroe and Francis, 1829), iv, Internet Archive; slavery: Child, *First Settlers*, 29.

52. Christians: Child, *First Settlers*, 213; destroying: Child, *First Settlers*, 30; lay aside: Child, *First Settlers*, 40–41.

53. Jesus: Child, *First Settlers*, 37.

54. inevitable: Child, *First Settlers*, 281; crisis: Child, *First Settlers*, 282; Jackson: Nester, *Age of Jackson*, 115.

55. promote: Karcher, *First Woman*, 96.

56. Trail of Tears: Russell Thornton, "Cherokee Population Losses during the Trail of Tears: A New Perspective and a New Estimate," *Ethnohistory* 31, no. 4 (1984): 289–300; soldier: Meacham, *American Lion*, 318.

57. trumpets: LMC to Mary Preston, [1826], Child, *CC*, 22.

Chapter Three

1. cheerless: Maria Weston Chapman, *Right and Wrong in Massachusetts* (Boston: Dow and Jackson's Anti-Slavery Press, 1839), 3, Internet Archive.

2. bad: Child, *The American Frugal Housewife: For Those Who Are Not Ashamed of Economy*, 22nd ed. (New York: Samuel S. and William Wood, 1839), 91, Internet Archive; *Mother's Book*: Child, *SL*, 20; $2,000: Karcher, *First Woman*, 127.

3. agitation: Bruce Mills, *Cultural Reformations: Lydia Maria Child and the Literature of Reform* (Athens: University of Georgia Press, 1994), 37; Channing on Lundy: Henry Mayer, *All on Fire: William Lloyd Garrison and the Abolition of Slavery* (New York: W. W. Norton, 1998), 53.

4. ACS: Ibram X. Kendi, *Stamped from the Beginning: The Definitive History of Racist Ideas in America* (New York: Nation Books, 2016), 154; Samantha Seeley, "Beyond the American Colonization Society," *History Compass* 14, no. 3 (2016): 94–98; Northern states: James Brewer Stewart, "The Emergence of Racial Modernity and the Rise of the White North, 1790–1840," *Journal of the Early Republic* 18, no. 2 (1998): 194; Child and ACS: Karcher, *First Woman*, 178; Hayti: Child, *Evenings in New England*, 147.

5. David Walker, *Walker's Appeal in Four Articles; Together with a Preamble, to the Coloured Citizens of the World, but in Particular, and Very Expressly, to Those of the United States of America*, 3rd ed. (Boston: David Walker, 1830), 6, 7, 12, 63, 73, 82, Internet Archive.

6. censorship: Mayer, *All on Fire*, 84; DLC investigates: Karcher, *First Woman*, 658; police declined: Mayer, *All on Fire*, 108. Later scholars have concluded that Walker died of lung disease: Mayer, *All on Fire*, 108.

7. loses appeal: Karcher, *First Woman*, 126. For Keyes's case against David, see John W. Whitman, "Trial of the Case of the Commonwealth versus David Lee Child: For Publishing in the Massachusetts Journal a Libel on the Honorable John Keyes, before the Supreme Judicial Court, holden at Cambridge, in the County of Middlesex, October Term, 1828" (Boston, 1829), Internet Archive.

8. friends: Karcher, *First Woman*, 136, Clifford, *Crusader*, 81; trips to prison: Karcher, *First Woman*, 136; *Frugal Housewife* quotation, Child, *Frugal Housewife*, 7; heart melt: DLC to LMC, 29 September, 3 October 1830, Child, *CC*, 45; homesick: LMC to DLC, 8 August [1830], Child, *SL*, 18.

9. jail: Mayer, *All on Fire*, 91–94; Black community: Mayer, *All on Fire*, 68–69, 83–84, 108–10.

10. New York, Philadelphia: Polgar, *Standard Bearers*, 52–53; Hall: Sinha, *Slave's Cause*, 43; Paul: Sinha, *Slave's Cause*, 130; Fortens: Polgar, *Standard Bearers*, 66–67; Shirley J. Yee, *Black Women Abolitionists: A Study in Activism, 1828–1860* (Knoxville: University of Tennessee Press, 1992), 13. On foundations of Black abolitionism generally, see Sinha, *Slave's Cause*, 41–47. Vigilance committees: Sinha, *Slave's Cause*, 384–85; underground railroad: Sinha, *Slave's Cause*, 396; see also Eric Foner, *Gateway to Freedom: The Hidden History of America's Fugitive Slaves* (Oxford: Oxford University Press, 2015); Lay: Marcus Rediker, *The Fearless Benjamin Lay: The Quaker Dwarf Who Became the First Revolutionary Abolitionist* (Boston: Beacon Press, 2017).

11. Black community: Peter C. Ripley et al., eds., *Witness for Freedom: African American Voices on Race, Slavery, and Emancipation* (Chapel Hill: University of North Carolina Press, 1993), 4; Forten, ink and paper: Mayer, *All on Fire*, 109–10; Garrison on LMC: Karcher, *First Woman*, 172–73.

12. Garrison: LMC to Anne Whitney, 25 May 1879, Child, *SL*, 558.

13. conversion: Karcher, *First Woman*, 175. For cultural context on conversion experience and abolition, see Julie Roy Jeffrey, *The Great Silent Army of Abolitionism: Ordinary Women in the Antislavery Movement* (Chapel Hill: University of North Carolina Press, 1998), 59.

14. dungeon: LMC to Jonathan Phillips, 26 February 1838, Child, *CC*, 2533.

15. sanctioning: *An Appeal in Favor of That Class of Americans Called Africans* (Boston: Allen and Ticknor, 1833), 223, Internet Archive; Egyptian bondage: LMC to Lydia Bigelow Child [1830–34], Child, *CC*, 67.

16. Douglass, Forten: Karcher, *First Woman*, 186.

17. Child's reading list: Karcher, *First Woman*, 186–87.

18. For a list of both David and Maria Child's antislavery writings in the *Massachusetts Journal,* see Karcher, *First Woman*, 663.

19. Garrison on intermarriage: Karcher, *First Woman*, 179.

20. I will be heard: Mayer, *All on Fire*, 112; Fuller: *New York Tribune*, June 10, 1845. Quoted in Frederick Douglass and Harriet A. Jacobs, *Narrative of the Life of Frederick Douglass, an American Slave* and *Incidents in the Life of a Slave Girl*, Modern Library ed. (New York: Modern Library, 2004), 430. On Stewart, see Martha S.

Jones, *Vanguard: How Black Women Broke Barriers, Won the Vote, and Insisted on Equality for All* (New York: Basic Books, 2020), 29–38.

21. Child, *Appeal*, preface.

22. Swedenborg: Karcher, *First Woman*, 358; accustomed: Child, *Appeal*, 99; Shadd Cary: Jeffrey, *Great Silent Army*, 191; see also Jones, *Vanguard*, 73–77, 117–20.

23. headlines: Mayer, *All on Fire*, 120.

24. butchery, $5,000: Mayer, *All on Fire*, 122; clergy to Garrison: Mayer, *All on Fire*, 105.

25. never swerve: Karcher, *First Woman*, 180.

26. execrate: Child, *Appeal*, 86; insurrections: Child, *Appeal*, 15.

27. events are God's: Child, *Appeal*, 228.

28. flame: Mayer, *All on Fire*, 214; unpopular cause: LMC to Samuel J. May, 29 September 1867, Child, *SL*, 474; smart set: LMC to Henrietta Sargent, 24 July 1870, Child, *CC*, 1953.

29. gun-shy: Mayer, *All on Fire*, 131.

30. David's involvement: Karcher, *First Woman*, 182; constitution: Arnold Buffum, *Constitution of the New-England Anti-Slavery Society, with an Address to the Public* (Boston: Garrison and Knapp, 1832), 1, Internet Archive.

31. women at the Athenæum: Barbara Adams Hebard, "The Role of Women at the Boston Athenæum," in *The Boston Athenæum Bicentennial Essays*, ed. Richard Wendorf (Hanover, NH: University Press of New England, 2009); men's reactions: Charles Knowles Bolton, *The Athenaeum Centenary: The Influence and History of the Boston Athenaeum from 1807 to 1907* (Boston: Boston Athenæum, 1907), 40–41; prize very highly: LMC to the Trustees of the Boston Athenæum, [1832], Child, *CC*, 57. Decades later, Child dated her borrowing privileges to around the time she met Garrison, which was probably 1830. Athenæum records, however, show the Trustees voting to grant these privileges in January 1832, which is also when the first records of her borrowing books occur. See LMC to Samuel J. May, 29 September 1867, Child, *SL*, 474; Trustees of the Boston Athenæum, "Trustees' Records: Record group IV," in *Archives*, ed. Boston Athenæum (1807–), Circulation Department Boston Athenæum, "Books Borrowed," ed. Boston Athenæum (1827–72).

32. let us not: Child, *Appeal*, 209; unalterable: Child, *Appeal*, 140; we made slavery, duty: Child, *Appeal*, 141; Liberia: Antonio McDaniel, "Extreme Mortality in Nineteenth-Century Africa: The Case of Liberian Immigrants," *Demography* 29, no. 4 (1992): 582.

33. direct course: Child, *Appeal*, 209; net worth: Akilah Johnson et al., "Boston. Racism. Image. Reality," *Boston Globe*, December 10, 2017.

34. "Works of Mrs. Child," *North American Review* 37 (July 1833): 163.

35. voice of conscience: Child, *Appeal*, 232. On how Child found a publisher for this book, much less one who was a relation of George Ticknor, see Carolyn Karcher, "Censorship, American Style: The Case of Lydia Maria Child," *Studies in the American Renaissance*, 1986, 283–303.

36. Martineau: Harriet Martineau, *The Martyr Age of the United States* (Boston: Weeks, Jordon, 1839), 15, Internet Archive; affairs of state: Samuel J. May, *Some Recollections of Our Antislavery Conflict* (Boston: Fields, Osgood, 1869), 99–100, Internet

Archive; avoided: LMC to Sarah Shaw, 20 May 1872, Child, *CC*, 2048; James: Alfred Sereno Hudson, "The Home of Lydia Maria Child," *New England Magazine: An Illustrated Monthly* 2 (1890): 407; tongs: Lydia Maria Child, *Letters of Lydia Maria Child, with a Biographical Introduction by John G. Whittier and an Appendix by Wendell Phillips* (Boston: Houghton, Mifflin, 1883), 264, Internet Archive.

37. Southern bookstores: May, *Some Recollections*, 100; avidity: Martineau, *Martyr Age of the United States*, 15; assailed: "L. Maria Child," *Woman's Journal*, repr. from Springfield Republican (1880); journals: Mills, *Cultural Reformations*, 45; most talented: Karcher, *First Woman*, 207–8; injury: Higginson, "Lydia Maria Child," 52; Whittier: John Greenleaf Whittier to LMC, 25 March 1876, Child, *CC*, 2270.

38. displeased, leave her: Karcher, *First Woman*, 169; discontinued: Lydia Maria Child, *Juvenile Miscellany*, 3rd ser., vol. 6 (Boston: Allen and Ticknor, 1834), 216; other form: Child, *Juvenile Miscellany*, 3rd ser. vol. 6, 323.

39. principles: George Ticknor, *Life, Letters, and Journals of George Ticknor*, 2 vols. (Boston: Houghton Mifflin, 1876), 2:235; Tyack, *Ticknor*, 185; bow: Tyack, *Ticknor*, 229; Southern guests: Tyack, *Ticknor*, 230.

40. biographers: Tyack, *Ticknor*, 229.

41. victims: Tyack, *Ticknor*, 229–30.

42. blow: May, *Some Recollections*, 98.

43. prudent: LMC to Convers Francis, 25 September 1835, Child, *SL*, 38–39.

44. schoolgirl abolitionists: Sarah (Van Vechten) Brown to LMC, 2 March 1869, Child, *CC*, 1887; Higginson: Higginson, "Lydia Maria Child," 49; Sumner: Charles Sumner to LMC, 14 January 1853, Child, *CC*, 837.

45. minister: Karcher, *First Woman*, 193.

Chapter Four

1. world: LMC to Convers Francis, 25 September 1835, Child, *SL*, 39.

2. Paradis: "Memorial Book for David Lee Child," 8; cat: LMC to Anna (Loring) Dresel [2?], 6 July 1871, Child, *CC*, 2002.

3. coat: Child, *Letters of Lydia Maria Child*, 48.

4. Channing: Child, *Letters of Lydia Maria Child*, 48; Mayer, *All on Fire*, 219.

5. afraid: LMC to Henrietta Sargent, 13 November 1836, Child, *SL*, 56; *Liberator*: Mayer, *All on Fire*, 219–20; shame: Martineau, *Martyr Age of the United States*, 16.

6. Phillips: Lydia Maria Child, "How a Very Small Mouse Helped to Gnaw open a Net That Held a Great Lion," in "Duplicity—a tale from Real Life," in May Anti-Slavery Collection #4601 (Division of Rare and Manuscript Collections, Cornell University Library, n.d.); golden trumpet: A. J. Aiséirithe and Donald Yacovone, eds., *Wendell Phillips, Social Justice, and the Power of the Past* (Baton Rouge: Louisiana State University Press, 2016), 53.

7. wealthiest: Lorien Foote, *Seeking the One Great Remedy: Francis George Shaw and Nineteenth-Century Reform* (Athens: Ohio University Press, 2003), 11, 20; West Indies: Foote, *Seeking the One Great Remedy*, 31; abolitionism: Foote, *Seeking the One Great Remedy*, 34; mud: LMC to Sarah Shaw, 24 October 1872, Child, *CC*, 2066.

8. numbers: Leonard L. Richards, *Gentlemen of Property and Standing: Anti-abolition Mobs in Jacksonian America* (New York: Oxford University Press, 1970), 10, 25, ACLS Humanities E-Book; Jeffrey, *Great Silent Army*, 53–55.

9. speakers: Jeffrey, *Great Silent Army*, 55, 59; Mayer, *All on Fire*, 103–5.

10. printing: Mayer, *All on Fire*, 195; nine times: Richards, *Gentlemen*, 73; chocolate: Richards, *Gentlemen*, 52; Douglass: Frederick Douglass, *Frederick Douglass: Autobiographies: Narrative of the Life of Frederick Douglass, an American Slave/My Bondage and My Freedom/Life and Times*, Library of America (Library of America, 1994), 43.

11. assassination: Richards, *Gentlemen*, 56; resolutions: Sinha, *Slave's Cause*, 251; meddled: Child, *SL*, 78, editors' note; postmaster: Meacham, *American Lion*, 304–6; Richards, *Gentlemen*, 74; Nester, *Age of Jackson*, 108.

12. blockheads: Richards, *Gentlemen*, 10; Lincoln: Richards, *Gentlemen*, 9. For description of the factors contributing to the violence of this period, including new understandings of racial categories and racial "uplift," see Stewart, "Racial Modernity," 181–217. Racial "uplift" will be discussed in chapter 6 below.

13. Pennsylvania Hall, orphanage: Sinha, *Slave's Cause*, 238–39; concussion, Sinha, *Slave's Cause*, 228.

14. Lovejoy: Richards, *Gentlemen*, 108–10.

15. evil: LMC to Convers Francis, 19 December 1835, Child, *SL*, 41–42; sanction: LMC to Convers Francis, 25 September 1835, Child, *SL*, 39.

16. gentlemen: Richards, *Gentlemen*, 5; Jack Tager, *Boston Riots: Three Centuries of Social Violence* (Boston: Northeastern University Press, 2019), 88–90; Project Muse; heritage: Richards, *Gentlemen*, 138–49; ACS: Richards, *Gentlemen*, 30–32.

17. strategies: Richards, *Gentlemen*, 92; un-American: Richards, *Gentlemen*, 70.

18. Judge Lynch: Richards, *Gentlemen*, 87; Adams: Richards, *Gentlemen*, 69; penalties: Richards, *Gentlemen*, 51.

19. sewing: Richards, *Gentlemen*, 58; interfere: Richards, *Gentlemen*, 58, 63.

20. amalgamation: Linda K. Kerber, "Abolitionists and Amalgamators: The New York City Race Riots of 1834," *New York History* 48, no. 1 (1967): 30; New York: Richards, *Gentlemen*, 113–21; Kerber, "Abolitionists and Amalgamators," 35.

21. cradle, laws of nature: Richards, *Gentlemen*, 33.

22. Paul: Debra Gold Hansen, *Strained Sisterhood: Gender and Class in the Boston Female Anti-Slavery Society* (Amherst: University of Massachusetts Press, 1993), 14; reparations: Sheila Jackson Lee, "H.R. 40, Commission to Study and Develop Reparation Proposals for African-Americans Act" (2020), https://www.congress.gov/bill/116th-congress/house-bill/40; precarious basis: Lydia Maria Child, ed., *The Oasis* (Boston: Benjamin C. Bacon, 1834), xiv, Internet Archive.

23. institutions: LMC in *Liberator*, 1 March 1839, Child, *CC*, 168; Thomas harassed: Richards, *Gentlemen*, 64; make me: LMC to Louisa Loring, 15 August [1835], Child, *SL*, 32.

24. threats: Mayer, *All on Fire*, 197; cart-whips: Child, *Letters from New York*, 193.

25. escaped: Child, *Letters from New York*, 194, LMC in *NASS*, 27 February 1864, Child, *CC*, 1544. The details of the story vary slightly in these two accounts.

26. neighbor: LMC to Louisa Loring, 15 August [1835], Child, *SL*, 32; There seem to have been two similar flyers: one Child describes at LMC to Ellis Loring, 22 August 1835, Child, *SL*, 34; the other at Child, *Letters from New York*, 191.

27. farm: Child, *Letters from New York*, 192; Mayer, *All on Fire*, 198; boat: Child, *Letters from New York*, 195, 192.

28. Brooklyn: Child, *Letters from New York*, 191–92; violence: LMC to Louisa Loring, 15 August [1835], Child, *SL*, 31.

29. Boston mob: Mayer, *All on Fire*, 201ff.; Tager, *Boston Riots*, 90–91.

30. die: Karcher, *First Woman*, 228. See also Caroline Weston's account of the mob in Lee V. Chambers, *The Weston Sisters: An American Abolitionist Family* (Chapel Hill: University of North Carolina Press, 2014), 211.

31. disturbing peace, autographed: Tager, *Boston Riots*, 91–92; jail cell: Mark Perry, *Lift Up Thy Voice: The Grimké Family's Journey from Slaveholders to Civil Rights Leaders* (New York: Penguin, 2001), 109; ecstatic: Mayer, *All on Fire*, 206.

32. reformers: Mayer, *All on Fire*, 206; missionary: Richards, *Gentlemen*, 97; justness: Richards, *Gentlemen*, 69.

33. fled: Hansen, *Strained Sisterhood*, 15; Dresser: Karcher, *First Woman*, 208, Sinha, *Slave's Cause*, 235, Mayer, *All on Fire*, 196–97; wept: LMC to Louisa Loring, 15 August [1835], Child, *SL*, 31.

34. watch: Karcher, *First Woman*, 214; friends raised money: Karcher, *First Woman*, 211.

35. arrested: Karcher, *First Woman*, 213, pier: Martineau, *Martyr Age of the United States*, 15.

36. *Panda:* Karcher, *First Woman*, 209–10; life: LMC to DLC, 22 May 1835, Child, *CC*, 72.

37. Washington, DC: Karcher, *First Woman*, 209–10.

38. editorship: Karcher, *First Woman*, 240; Illinois: LMC to Louisa Loring [March? 1837], Child, *SL*, 63; soldiers: Karcher, *First Woman*, 230; family: LMC to Ellis Loring, 30 January 1836, Child, *SL*, 43; scrapped: Karcher, *First Woman*, 237.

39. wife: LMC to DLC, 28 July 1836, Child, *SL*, 51.

40. love: LMC to DLC, 24 July 1836, *CC*, 101; LMC to DLC, 28 July 1836, Child, *SL*, 52.

41. niece: Lydia Maria Child, "Floral Souvenir Book" (Medford Historical Society & Museum, 1855); curls: LMC to Lydia Bigelow Child, 23 June 1831, Child, *CC*, 48.

42. to father: LMC to Ellis Loring, 30 January 1836, Child, *SL*, 44; money owed: LMC to Park Benjamin, 30 May 1836, *CC*, 97.

43. gladsome light, Loring, Thoreau, Poe: Karcher, *First Woman*, 237.

44. wished to go: LMC to Lydia Bigelow Child, 19 October 1836, Child, *SL*, 55; living with father: LMC to Louisa Loring, 27 November 1836, Child, *SL*, 58.

45. liberality: LMC in *Liberator*, 21 April 1837, Child, *CC*, 119.

46. gloomy: LMC to Louisa Loring, [March? 1837], Child, *SL*, 64; uncertainty, afire: LMC to Lydia Bigelow Child, 2 April 1837, Child, *SL*, 67; return: LMC to Lydia Bigelow Child, 19 October 1836, Child, *SL*, 55; DLC to LMC, 7 June 1837, Child, *CC*, 124. David's letters did sometimes show affection, and Child was cheered by them, but she also complained that they felt "business like." See LMC to Louisa Loring, [March? 1837], Child, *SL*, 63–64; DLC to LMC, 12, 20 February 1837, *CC*, 117.

47. shame: Karcher, *First Woman*, 197.
48. amalgamation: Child, *Oasis*, xi, 200.
49. amusement, fanaticism: Karcher, *First Woman*, 208; favor: LMC to George Thompson, 18 September 1835, Child, *SL*, 36.
50. past lives: LMC to DLC, 24 July 1836, Child, *CC*, 101; chain: LMC to Jonathon Phillips, 26 February 1838, Child, *CC*, 2533.

Chapter Five

1. This chapter's title is meant to echo W. E. B. Du Bois's searing question about Black Americans' experience at the beginning of *The Souls of Black Folk:* "How does it feel to be a problem?" W. E. B. Du Bois, *The Souls of Black Folk*, in W. E. B. Du Bois, *Writings*, Library of America (New York: Library of America, 1986), 363.
2. "Ladies' Department," constitution, "Mrs. Steward's [*sic*] Essays": *Liberator*, 7 January 1832, 2.
3. Salem: Karcher, *First Woman*, 668; twelve women: Hansen, *Strained Sisterhood*, 13.
4. sympathies: LMC to Charlotte Phelps, [2 January 1834], Child, *SL*, 28.
5. wealth: Hansen, *Strained Sisterhood*, 71; beauty: Hansen, *Strained Sisterhood*, 5, 98; socialites: Hansen, *Strained Sisterhood*, 100; Lee V. Chambers, *The Weston Sisters: An American Abolitionist Family* (Chapel Hill: University of North Carolina Press, 2014), 113–14; parties: Hansen, *Strained Sisterhood*, 101; boy's clothes: Hansen, *Strained Sisterhood*, 151.
6. unmarriageable: Chambers, *Weston Sisters*, 56. Anne Weston did receive one marriage proposal but turned it down: see Chambers, *Weston Sisters*, 61.
7. lectures: Hansen, *Strained Sisterhood*, 13–14; religious and class memberships: Hansen, *Strained Sisterhood*, 66–92.
8. Garrison: Chambers, *Weston Sisters*, 142–45; disease: Lydia Maria Child, *The History of the Condition of Women, in Various Ages and Nations* (Boston: John Allen, 1835), 1:226, Internet Archive; Roman: Child, *History of the Condition of Women*, 49.
9. West Street: Chapman, "Pinda: A True Tale," *NASS*, 29 October 1840.
10. fair items: *Liberator*, 22 October 1834; Karcher, *First Woman*, 668. See also LMC, *NASS*, 6 June 1868, Child, *CC*, 1837.
11. three hundred dollars: "Anti-Slavery Fair," *Liberator*, 20 December 1834.
12. dozens: Ira V. Brown, "'Am I Not a Woman and a Sister?' The Anti-Slavery Convention of American Women, 1837–1839," *Pennsylvania History: A Journal of Mid-Atlantic Studies* 50, no. 1 (1983): 2; storm: Karcher, *First Woman*, 217.
13. all combined: Jeffrey, *Great Silent Army*, 22; mockery: *Liberator*, 24 March 1832; activity: *Liberator*, 14 January 1832, 2.
14. farmer: Jeffrey, *Great Silent Army*, 20; Mrs. Child's chapter: Jeffrey, *Great Silent Army*, 58.
15. "lady," Douglass: Jeffrey, *Great Silent Army*, 64; allies: Jeffrey, *Great Silent Army*, 64–65.

16. schools: Hansen, *Strained Sisterhood*, 37; familiarly: Jeffrey, *Great Silent Army*, 126; Stewart: "Lecture. Delivered at the Franklin Hall, Boston, September 21st, 1832. By Mrs. Maria W. Stewart." *Liberator,* 17 November 1832.

17. Paul: LMC to Jonathan Phillips, 23 January 1838, Child, *SL*, 69–70.

18. signatures: Hansen, *Strained Sisterhood*, 18; gag rule: Chambers, *Weston Sisters*, 25; Traub, *John Quincy Adams*, 433–35.

19. silent: 1 Corinthians 14:34; prophetesses: May, *Some Recollections*, 101.

20. good: LMC in *Liberator*, 6 March 1840, Child, *SL*, 128; ashes, socks: LMC to Louisa Loring, [March? 1837], Child, *SL*, 64.

21. reasons: Karcher, *First Woman*, 215–16; Clifford, *Crusader*, 86–87; ashamed: Karcher, *First Woman*, 216.

22. refuge: Chambers, *Weston Sisters*, 140, 275; Bancroft: LMC to Ellis and Louisa Loring, 5 December 1838, Child, *SL*, 96; (!!!!): Maria Weston Chapman et al., *Right and Wrong in Boston: Annual Report of the Boston Female Anti-Slavery Society: Being a Concise History of the Slave Child, Med, and of the Women Demanded as Slaves of the Supreme Judicial Court of Mass.* (Boston: Boston Female Anti-Slavery Society, 1836), Internet Archive; Joan: Hansen, *Strained Sisterhood*, 98; Lady Macbeth: Chambers, *Weston Sisters*, 213.

23. precedent: LMC to Samuel J. May, 29 September 1867, Child, *SL*, 474; disputed: Hebard, "Role of Women at the Boston Athenæum," 76–77. Whatever the truth, Hebard's inference that, because the next woman to have her privileges revoked (in 1915) was charged with damaging Athenæum property, Child must have "disgraced herself" in a similar way, is both scandalously illogical and factually unfounded (see Hebard, "Role of Women at the Boston Athenæum," 77).

24. fund-raising: LMC to Maria Weston Chapman and Other Ladies, 1 June 1834 [1835?], and editors' note, Child, *SL*, 29.

25. deeply: LMC to Maria Weston Chapman and Other Ladies, 1 June 1834 [1835?], Child, *SL*, 29. See Karcher on the publisher John Allen's taking a risk by publishing the books but being repaid by their six printings: Karcher, *First Woman*, 226.

26. Hindu: Child, *History of the Condition of Women*, 1:103; Egyptian: Child, *History of the Condition of Women*, 1:223; smallpox: Child, *History of the Condition of Women*, 2:144.

27. so little: Sarah Josepha Hale, "The History of the Condition of Women, in Various Ages and Nations. By Mrs. D. L. Child," *American Ladies' Magazine* 8 (1835): 588; see also Karcher, *First Woman*, 224.

28. argument: Child, *History of the Condition of Women*, 5th ed., preface, Hathi Trust.

29. struggle: LMC, in *NASS*, 15 July 1841.

30. sojourners: Chapman, *Right and Wrong* (1836), 40.

31. way opened, habeas corpus: LMC to Esther Carpenter, 4 September 1836, Child, *SL*, 52–53.

32. New Orleans: LMC to Esther Carpenter, 4 September 1836, Child, *SL*, 53.

33. good of child: "Case of the Slave-Child, Med: Report of the Arguments of Counsel and of the Opinions of the Court, in the Case of Commonwealth vs. Ames; Tried and

Determined in the Supreme Court of Massachusetts" (Boston, 1836), 13, Internet Archive.

34. ruling: Karen Woods Weierman, *The Case of the Slave-Child, Med: Free Soil in Antislavery Boston* (Amherst: University of Massachusetts Press, 2019), 40–49; legal protection: Hansen, *Strained Sisterhood*, 18; hotel: LMC to Esther Carpenter, 4 September 1836, Child, *SL*, 53; Chambers, *Weston Sisters*, 213.

35. proofs: Chapman, *Right and Wrong* (1836), 70; Maria: Chapman, *Right and Wrong* (1836), 67.

36. freedom: Paul Finkelman, *An Imperfect Union: Slavery, Federalism, and Comity* (Clark, NJ: Lawbook Exchange, 2013), 112; inscription: editors' note, Child, *SL*, 96; also Ellis Loring to LMC, DLC, 31 December 1838, Child, *CC*, 160; kindness: LMC to Ellis and Louisa Loring, 5 December 1838, Child, *SL*, 96.

37. For a powerful account of these and other questions related to the case, as well as details about Loring's arguments, see Weierman, *Case of the Slave-Child, Med*.

38. burned: Perry, *Lift Up Thy Voice*, 133.

39. man in audience: Mayer, *All on Fire*, 232; I have seen it: Brown, "Am I Not a Woman and a Sister?," 5; Phillips: Perry, *Lift Up Thy Voice*, 127; amazement: Stephen Browne, *Angelina Grimké: Rhetoric, Identity, and the Racial Imagination* (East Lansing: Michigan State University Press, 1999), 83.

40. sublimity: LMC to Esther Carpenter, 20 March 1838, Child, *SL*, 71–72; every word: LMC to Lydia Bigelow Child, 6 April 1838, Child, *SL*, 73.

41. mortifying: Chapman, *Right and Wrong* (1836), 61; *Liberator,* 2 June 1837, 90; *Liberator,* 2 June 1837, 62. See also Mayer, *All on Fire*, 266–68; evil: Richards, *Gentlemen*, 60; sorry: Chapman, *Right and Wrong in Boston: Annual Report of the Boston Female Anti-Slavery Society: With a Sketch of the Obstacles Thrown in the Way by Certain Clerical Abolitionists and Advocates for the Subjection of Women* (Boston: Boston Female Anti-Slavery Society, 1837), 58, Internet Archive; agony: Chapman, *Right and Wrong* (1836), 61.

42. desirable: Hansen, *Strained Sisterhood*, 22; discretions: Hansen, *Strained Sisterhood*, 21.

43. first mixed: Hansen, *Strained Sisterhood*, 19; delegates: Jeffrey, *Great Silent Army*, 94, Brown, "Am I Not a Woman and a Sister?"; and Hansen, *Strained Sisterhood*, 19; meetings, duty: LMC to Lucretia Mott, 5 March 1839, Child, *SL*, 106–7.

44. principles: Dorothy Sterling, ed., *Turning the World Upside Down: The Anti-Slavery Convention of American Women* (New York: Feminist Press, 1987), 11; repeal: Brown, "Am I Not a Woman and a Sister?," 5; jury: Sterling, *Turning the World Upside Down*, 14; seats: Karcher, *First Woman*, 246; Hansen, *Strained Sisterhood*, 19.

45. magnificence: "Ladies' Convention," *Liberator*, 2 June 1837; Douglass: Dorothy Sterling, ed., *We Are Your Sisters: Black Women in the Nineteenth Century* (New York: Norton, 1984), 102–3; upside down: Gerda Lerner, *The Grimké Sisters from South Carolina: Pioneers for Women's Rights and Abolition* (Chapel Hill: University of North Carolina Press, 2004), 10, Ebook Central.

46. unnatural: Chapman et al., "Annual Report of the Boston Female Anti-Slavery Society," 48; division: "Annual Report of the Boston Female Anti-Slavery Society," 56; see also Hansen, *Strained Sisterhood*, 83; "Appeal of Clerical Abolitionists," *Liberator—Extra,* 19 August 1837.

47. extent: *Liberator*, 15 December 1837; man-enslaving: Mayer, *All on Fire*, 235; *Liberator*, 25 August 1837; "A Layman's Reply to 'A Clerical Appeal,'" *Liberator—Extra*, 19 August 1837; pride: Hansen, *Strained Sisterhood*, 23.

48. Bible quoted: Chapman et al., "Annual Report of the Boston Female Anti-Slavery Society," 61; Grimké: Perry, *Lift Up Thy Voice*, 158; shore up: Karcher, *First Woman*, 225; "Times That Try": *Liberator*, 8 March 1839. Chapman's poem was read aloud at the Rochester Women's Convention in August 1848. See "The Times That Try Men's Souls," in *Second to None: A Document History of American Women*, vol. 1, *From the 16th Century to 1865*, ed. Ruth Barnes Moynihan, Cynthia Russett, and Laurie Crumpacker (Lincoln: University of Nebraska Press, 1993), 252.

49. mainstream: Mayer, *All on Fire*, 240.

50. twaddle: Child, *SL*, 127, editors' note.

51. absurdity: bell hooks, *Ain't I a Woman: Black Women and Feminism* (1981; reprint, New York, Routledge, 2015), 124 ff.

52. improvement: Karcher, *First Woman*, 225; encircled, interpret: Hansen, *Strained Sisterhood*, 148; upright: Sarah M. Grimké, *Letters on the Equality of the Sexes, and the Condition of Women. Addressed to Mary S. Parker, President of the Boston Female Anti-Slavery Society* (Boston: Isaac Knapp, 1838), 10.

53. jurisdiction: LMC in *Liberator*, 2 September 1839, Child, *SL*, 122–24; woman: Karcher, *First Woman*, 261.

54. sphere: Catharine E. Beecher, *An Essay on Slavery and Abolitionism, with Reference to the Duties of American Females* (Philadelphia: Henry Parkins, 1837), 102, Internet Archive; monolith: Hansen, *Strained Sisterhood*, 120.

55. The Weston sisters had written this document together: Chambers, *Weston Sisters*, 148; Hansen, *Strained Sisterhood*, 24; subtitle: Chapman et al., "Annual Report of the Boston Female Anti-Slavery Society," 1; in their place: Hansen, *Strained Sisterhood*, 24; objections: Chapman et al., "Annual Report of the Boston Female Anti-Slavery Society," 3; power struggle: Hansen, *Strained Sisterhood*, 95; degradation: LMC to Angelina Grimké Weld, [26 December 1838], Child, *CC*, 158.

56. missed: Child, "Memorial Book for David Lee Child," 9–10.

Chapter Six

1. marketed: Karcher, *First Woman*, 262; bankrupt: LMC to Lemuel Shaw, 18 August 1839, Child, *CC*, 185.

2. American women: Child, *History of the Condition of Women*, 2:265; one acre, asleep: LMC to Ellis and Louisa Loring, 10 July 1838, Child, *SL*, 76.

3. frames: LMC to Ellis Loring, 15 January 1839, Child, *CC*, 164; Karcher, *First Woman*, 252; honest, river: LMC to Louisa Loring, 12 January 1839, Child, *CC*, 162;

edge: LMC to Ellis Loring, 15 January 1839, Child, *CC*, 164; home-sick: LMC to Abigail Kelley, 1 October 1838, Child, *SL*, 89.

4. *Girl's Own,* serious matter: LMC to Samuel C. Colman, 26 July 1838, Child, *CC*, 140.

5. River Gods: Karcher, *First Woman*, 251; cooling: LMC to Caroline Weston, 13 August 1838, Child, *SL*, 83.

6. to themselves: LMC to Lydia Bigelow Child, 7 August 1838, Child, *CC*, 142.

7. hates reforms: LMC to Ellis and Louisa Loring, 10 July 1838, Child, *SL*, 77; bones: LMC to Susan Lesley, 3 August [1874], Child, *CC,* 2167; husband: LMC to Ellis and Louisa Loring, 10 July 1838, Child, *SL*, 77.

8. traitors: LMC to William Lloyd Garrison, 15 February 1839, in *Liberator*, Child, *CC*, 168; Lovejoy: LMC to Theodore Dwight Weld, 18 December 1838, Child, *SL*, 99.

9. hotels: LMC to Theodore Dwight Weld, 18 December 1838, Child, *SL*, 101; qualities: LMC to Francis and Sarah Shaw, 17 August 1838, Child, *SL*, 85.

10. salary: LMC to Theodore Dwight Weld, 18 December 1838, Child, *SL*, 100; drive out: LMC to Lydia Bigelow Child, 7 August 1838, Child, *CC*, 142; ACS: Steve Strimer, "On the Trail of the Josiah White Cottage Where Lydia Maria and David Lee Child Lived between May 1840 and May 1841 in Florence, Massachusetts," privately published, n.d., 1; neighborhood: LMC to Lydia Bigelow Child, 7 August 1838, Child, *CC*, 142.

11. autograph: LMC to Lewis J. Cist, 27 February 1838, Child, *CC*, 130; flowers: LMC to Louisa Loring, 16 August 1838, Child, *CC*, 145; Southern threat, angels: LMC to Convers Francis, 8 January 1841, Child, *CC*, 222; balloon: LMC to Louisa Loring, 9 June 1838, Child, *CC*, 136; breakfast: Ellis Loring to LMC, 22 February 1839, Child, *CC*, 170.

12. lectures: Perry, *Lift Up Thy Voice*, 173; forcibly: Dorothy Sterling, *Ahead of Her Time: Abby Kelley and the Politics of Antislavery* (New York: W. W. Norton, 1994), 63.

13. fiends: Sterling, *Ahead of Her Time*, 64; endure: Perry, *Lift Up Thy Voice*, 174–75.

14. wreck: "The Destruction of Pennsylvania Hall," *Philadelphia Inquirer*, 19 May 1838.

15. recovery: Chambers, *Weston Sisters*, 124.

16. remarkable: LMC to Lucretia Mott, 5 March 1839, Child, *SL*, 107; admired: LMC to Louisa Loring, 3 June 1838, Child, *CC*, 135.

17. Caroline: LMC to Caroline Weston, 27 July and 13 August 1838, Child, *SL*, 79–85; letters: LMC to Lydia Bigelow Child, 7 August 1838, Child, *CC*, 142; LMC to Louisa Loring, 16 August 1838, Child, *CC*, 145.

18. doctrines: Perry, *Lift Up Thy Voice*, 176; busy: Chambers, *Weston Sisters*, 125; ornaments: Hansen, *Strained Sisterhood*, 138.

19. death: Perry, *Lift Up Thy Voice*, 149.

20. rushed out: Perry, *Lift Up Thy Voice*, 176; abuses: Sterling, *Ahead of Her Time*, 116, 200, 384; second-story windows: Mayer, *All on Fire,* 304.

21. defensive: American Peace Society, *The Advocate of Peace* (Boston: Whipple and Damrell, 1837), 8–9.

22. Lovejoy: Mayer, *All on Fire*, 237; Kelly Carter Jackson, *Force and Freedom: Black*

Abolitionists and the Politics of Violence (Philadelphia: University of Pennsylvania Press, 2019), 32.

23. voting: Mayer, *All on Fire*, 250, 254–55, 257; world: Mayer, *All on Fire*, 225.

24. Non-Resistance Society: Mayer, *All on Fire*, 250; repudiate: Sterling, *Ahead of Her Time*, 72.

25. cause of peace: Mayer, *All on Fire*, 238–39.

26. spiral line: LMC to William Lloyd Garrison in *Liberator*, 6 March 1840, Child, *SL*, 127; bad foundation: LMC to Caroline Weston, 7 March 1839, Child, *SL*, 110.

27. Krishna: LMC to Ellis Loring, 7 November 1849, Child, *SL*, 252; responsibility: LMC to Abigail Kelley, 1 October 1838, Child, *SL*, 90.

28. heaven: LMC to Abigail Kelley, 1 October 1838, Child, *SL*, 90.

29. expensive: LMC to Abigail Kelley, 1 October 1838, Child, *SL*, 91.

30. war man: LMC to Abigail Hopper Gibbons, [January(?), 1840], Child, *CC*, 196; future arguments: LMC to Ellis Loring, 7 May [1840], Child, *SL*, 131; accordion: LMC to Caroline Weston, 27 July 1838, Child, *SL*, 80.

31. coax away, freedom: LMC to Caroline Weston, 27 July 1838, Child, *SL*, 79–82; blow up: LMC to Lydia Bigelow Child, 7 August 1838, Child, *CC*, 142.

32. duplicity: LMC to Caroline Weston, 27 July 1838, Child, *SL*, 82.

33. tissue: LMC to Caroline Weston, 13 August 1838, Child, *SL*, 84; dispute: LMC to Angelina Grimké Weld, 26 August 1838, Child, *SL*, 87–89.

34. good home: LMC to Angelina (Grimké) Weld, 2 October 1838, Child, *SL*, 92.

35. freedom: LMC to Angelina (Grimké) Weld, 2 October 1838, Child, *SL*, 92.

36. lie: LMC to Angelina (Grimké) Weld, 2 October 1838, Child, *SL*, 92.

37. get living: LMC to Theodore Dwight Weld, 18 December 1838, Child, *SL*, 101.

38. gag rule: Mayer, *All on Fire*, 217, 230; oppressor: Stewart, "Racial Modernity," 209; martyrdom: Karcher, *First Woman*, 255; disheartened: LMC to Theodore Dwight Weld, 29 December 1838, Child, *SL*, 104.

39. Black uplift suasion: Kendi, *Stamped from the Beginning*, 169. For a history of the changing meanings of race, respectability, and "uplift," see Stewart, "Racial Modernity," 181–217; AAS quoted in Kendi, *Stamped from the Beginning*, 176. Kendi gives a comprehensive analysis of uplift suasion in his analysis of Garrison and the abolitionist movement. See Kendi, *Stamped from the Beginning*, 124–25, 161–260. See also Ripley et al., *Witness for Freedom*, 6–7.

40. theaters: *An Address to Free Colored Americans: Issued by an Anti-Slavery Convention of American Women, Held in the City of New-York, by Adjournments from 9th to 12th May, 1837* (New York: William S. Dorr, 1837), 12.

41. Simmons speech: Peter Paul Simmons, "We Must Remain Active," *Colored American* (1839), reprinted in BlackPast, 24 September 2008; see also Jackson, *Force and Freedom*, 34–35.

42. Garnet: Sinha, *Slave's Cause*, 418; also Jackson, *Force and Freedom*, 36–40; on McCune Smith, see John Stauffer, *The Black Hearts of Men: Radical Abolitionists and the Transformation of Race* (Cambridge, MA: Harvard University Press, 2001); Jackson, *Force and Freedom*, 137–39; abject slavery: Jackson, *Force and Freedom*,

38; Jackson argues that for some of these Black intellectuals, nonviolence "could not be separated from the belief in black subordination. In other words, for many black abolitionists, moral suasion was predicated on people's acceptance of black inferiority." Jackson, *Force and Freedom*, 161. See also Stewart, "Racial Modernity," 212, Ripley et al., *Witness for Freedom*, 7–17.

43. failing: Kendi, *Stamped from the Beginning*, 187; AAS: David W. Blight, *Frederick Douglass: Prophet of Freedom* (New York: Simon and Schuster, 2018), 105; forgiveness: Blight, *Frederick Douglass*, 118; injure: Douglass, *Autobiographies*, 283. Douglass also described his battle with his enslaver in his 1845 *Narrative of the Life of Frederick Douglass, an American Slave: Written by Himself.* This earlier account in fact emphasizes Douglass's resistance: see Douglass, *Narrative*, 64–65. For a discussion of Douglass's views on violence and nonresistance, see Blight, *Frederick Douglass*, 64–66, 108, 197, 246, 261–63, and Mayer, *All on Fire*, 350, 372.

44. Garrison: Kendi, *Stamped from the Beginning*, 200–201; Blight, *Frederick Douglass*, 215–20, 225–26; Mayer, *All on Fire*, 371–75, 432–33.

45. generations: LMC to Henrietta Sargent, 18 November 1838, Child, *SL*, 93–94.

46. violence: LMC to Abigail Kelley, 1 October 1838, Child, *SL*, 90.

47. frightened: LMC to Caroline Weston, 7 March 1839, Child, *SL*, 109; necessary: LMC to Lucretia Mott, 5 March 1839, Child, *SL*, 107; injury: LMC to Maria Weston Chapman, 10 April 1839, Child, *CC*, 178.

48. guests: LMC to Louisa Loring 12 January 1839, Child, *CC*, 162, LMC to Ellis Loring, 7 May 1840, Child, *CC*, 204; alone: LMC to Henrietta Sargent, 18 November 1838, Child, *SL*, 95; fist: LMC to Ellis Loring, 9 February 1841, Child, *SL*, 136; fix your eye: LMC and DLC to the Massachusetts Anti-Slavery Society, 15 January 1839, Child, *CC*, 165.

49. Philothea, thirsty: LMC to Louisa Loring, 12 January 1839, Child, *CC*, 162; perfect sugar: LMC to Maria Weston Chapman, 10 April 1839, Child, *CC*, 178.

50. diploma: Karcher, *First Woman*, 258; manure: David Lee Child, *The Culture of the Beet, and Manufacture of Beet Sugar* (Boston: Weeks, Jordan, 1840), 22, Internet Archive.

51. spirits, maps: LMC to Louisa and Ellis Loring, 30 April 1839, Child, *SL*, 112–13; Karcher, *First Woman*, 257.

52. eyes: LMC to DLC, 18 August 1839, Child, *SL*, 116–18.

53. roses: DLC to LMC, 25 June 1839, Child, *CC*, 182; creditors: LMC to Gerrit Smith, 17 September 1836, Child, *CC*, 107; LMC to Lemuel Shaw, 18 August 1839, Child, *CC*, 185.

54. Fuller: Karcher, *First Woman*, 258; fair: LMC to Abigail Hopper Gibbons, [January? 1840], Child, *CC*, 196; talents: Karcher, *First Woman*, 259.

55. Black leaders: Mayer, *All on Fire*, 257–58, 268; Tappans: Mayer, *All on Fire*, 262, 268; mortifying: LMC to Members of the Boston Female Anti-Slavery Society, [before April 3, 1840], Child, *CC*, 201.

56. dissolved: Hansen, *Strained Sisterhood*, 27; competing fairs: Hansen, *Strained Sisterhood*, 125–26.

57. showdown, not a slave, Tappans: Mayer, *All on Fire*, 280–83.

58. Whittier: Sterling, *Ahead of Her Time*, 106.

59. executive committee: Child, *SL*, 130, editors' note.

60. inheritance: LMC to Francis Shaw, 27 May 1841, Child, *SL*, 140–41.

61. prosper: LMC to Lydia Bigelow Child, 7 June 1840, Child, *SL*, 131–32; inheritance: LMC to Ellis Loring, 17 February 1856, Child, *CC*, 905; beggary: LMC to Louisa Loring, 17 February 1841, Child, *CC*, 226; cheerfulness: LMC to Louisa Loring, 19 July 1840, Child, *CC*, 209; borrowed: Karcher, *First Woman*, 263–64.

62. dead: Perry, *Lift Up Thy Voice*, 187; see also 172, 177.

63. sorry, asking: LMC to Maria Weston Chapman, 23 August 1840, Child, *CC*, 212.

64. important service: "Beet Sugar," reprinted in *Liberator*, 13 March 1840; 30 percent: Robert M. Harveson, "History of Sugarbeets," *Cropwatch* (2015), https://cropwatch.unl.edu/history-sugarbeets.

65. suicide: LMC to Louisa Loring, 19 July 1840, Child, *CC*, 209.

Chapter Seven

1. ear: LMC to Maria Weston Chapman, 11 May [1842], Child, *SL*, 175.

2. experiment: LMC to Francis Shaw, 28 May 1841, Child, *SL*, 141–42.

3. praise: LMC to Francis Shaw, 27 May 1841, Child, *SL*, 141.

4. pleasing, oil: LMC to Ellis Loring, 6 March 1843, Child, *SL*, 192–93.

5. sunshine: LMC to Louisa Loring, 16 May 1841, Child, *CC*, 228; what has wealth: LMC to Francis Shaw, 12 October 1841, Child, *SL*, 150.

6. no house: LMC to Francis Shaw, 27 May 1841, Child, *SL*, 141; former oil mill: Strimer, "On the Trail"; hanged: LMC to Louisa Loring, 16 May 1841, Child, *CC*, 228; pilgrimage: letter from the editor, *NASS,* 11 November 1841.

7. Eldridge Street: Clifford, *Crusader*, 158; room: Child, *Letters from New York*, 17; Hopper family: LMC to Lydia Bigelow Child, 6 May 1877, Child, *CC*, 2321; dotted: Child, *Letters from New York*, 10.

8. dead hogs: Child, *Letters from New York*, 9; frightful place: LMC to Ellis Loring, 28 September 1841, Child, *SL*, 147; passage: LMC to Louisa Loring, 16 May 1841, Child, *CC*, 228.

9. printer: LMC to Ellis Loring, 28 February 1842, Child, *SL*, 162–63; first editorial: *NASS,* 20 May 1841; difficult: Ellis Loring to LMC, 29 April 1841, Child, *CC*, 227.

10. fair: "The Massachusetts Anti-Slavery Fair!" *NASS,* 11 November 1841; Rhode Island: "Letter from Abby Kelley," *NASS*, 23 December 1841; Ruggles: "Notices: Mirror of Liberty," *NASS*, 6 May 1841; Douglass: Karcher, *First Woman*, 279; vigilance: "Anti-Slavery Items," *NASS*, 1 July 1841; A, B, C: see, for instance, *NASS*, 20 January 1842.

11. DC: *NASS*, 14 July 1842; Virginia: *NASS*, 3 June 1841; Douglass: *NASS*, 14 November 1841; Mayer, *All on Fire*, 307.

12. *Creole*: Sinha, *Slave's Cause*, 411–14; New York: Foner, *Gateway to Freedom*, 44; intermarriage: *NASS*, 17 February 1842.

13. mice: *NASS*, 30 June 1842; coffee: *NASS*, 25 January 1841; slave labor: *NASS*, 3 June 1841.

14. which one: "To Abolitionists," *NASS,* 20 May 1841.

15. fear nothing: "To Abolitionists," *NASS,* 20 May 1841.

16. Webster: *NASS,* 20 May 1841; Texas: Karcher, *First Woman,* 271.

17. oversight: LMC to Maria Weston Chapman, 26 April [1842], Child, *CC,* 365; have the goodness: LMC to James Miller McKim and Philadelphia Friends, 24 [and 25] November 1841, Child, *SL,* 153–54.

18. full steam: Ellis Loring to LMC, 22 May 1841, Child, *CC,* 230; approbation: LMC to Ellis Loring, 28 September [1841], Child, *SL,* 146; doubled: Karcher, *First Woman,* 273.

19. funds: LMC to Ellis Loring, 27 May 1841, Child, *CC,* 231; crying: LMC to Ellis Loring, 17 May [1841], Child, *CC,* 229; $300: LMC to Ellis Loring, 13 December 1841, Child, *CC,* 299.

20. Smith: Child, *SL,* 148, editors' note; Garrison: LMC to Ellis Loring, 28 September [1841], Child, *SL,* 146; editing Kelley: LMC to Ellis Loring, 17 May [1841], Child, *CC,* 229; turnip: LMC to Ellis Loring, 7 March 1843, Child, *SL,* 193; Tappan: *NASS,* 2 September 1841; on Tappan see Varon, *Disunion!,* 144; Smith's speech: *NASS,* 17 February 1842. Garrison sometimes also praised Tappan, for instance in his role in the *Amistad* defense: see Mayer, *All on Fire,* 309.

21. hate it, cursed: LMC to Ellis Loring, [21 September 1841], Child, *CC,* 262; intolerable: LMC to Ellis Loring, 17 June and 27 May 1841, Child, *SL,* 143; pecuniary distress: LMC to Gerrit Smith, 28 September [1841], Child, *CC,* 266.

22. printers: LMC to Ellis Loring, 28 February 1842, Child, *SL,* 162; immigration: Clifford, *Crusader,* 172.

23. Infinite: Child, *Letters from New York,* 10.

24. soul: Child, *Letters from New York,* 10; fairy wand: Child, *Letters from New York,* 12.

25. brick wall: Child, *Letters from New York,* 16; doves: Child, *Letters from New York,* 74; outward force: Child, *Letters from New York,* 11; freewill: Child, *Letters from New York,* 133.

26. Black woman: Child, *Letters from New York,* 46–52; rabbi, Child, *Letters from New York,* 24–30; covered: Child, *Letters from New York,* 43; central ideas: Child, *Letters from New York,* 50.

27. Father: Child, *Letters from New York,* 166.

28. Native Americans, law of love: Child, *Letters from New York,* 162–63.

29. skulls: Child, *Letters from New York,* 163.

30. Douglass: Sinha, *Slave's Cause,* 313; God forgive me: Child, *Letters from New York,* 126.

31. punishing: Child, *Letters from New York,* 60; capital punishment: Child, *Letters from New York,* 137; sinners: Child, *Letters from New York,* 126.

32. matter: Child, *Letters from New York,* 102; music: Child, *Letters from New York,* 117; future: Child, *Letters from New York,* 52; beauty, death: Child, *Letters from New York,* 53.

33. Hoboken: Child, *Letters from New York,* 18; Brooklyn: Child, *Letters from New York,* 31.

34. Hopper's professions: Child, *Letters from New York*, 3 (dedication page); LMC to Ellis Loring, 22 May 1844, Child, *CC*, 557.

35. garlands: LMC to DLC, 11 July 1841, Child, *CC*, 241; gifts: LMC to Convers Francis, 17 February 1842, Child, *CC*, 336; cake, napped: LMC to DLC, 11 July 1841, Child, *CC*, 241; kindness: LMC to Ellis Loring, 28 September 1841, 10 March 1836, Child, *SL*, 47.

36. brother: Child, *Letters from New York*, dedication; daughter: LMC to Ellis Loring, 28 September [1841], Child, *SL*, 147; Zippy Damn: LMC to Susan Lyman, 9 April [1847], Child, *CC*, 707.

37. acquaintance: LMC to Ellis Loring, 27 July 1841, Child, *CC*, 244.

38. home-sick: LMC to Ellis Loring, 11 August 1841, Child, *CC*, 246; dream: LMC to DLC, 11 July 1841, Child, *CC*, 241.

39. affections: LMC to Ellis Loring, 6 March 1843, Child, *SL*, 195.

40. pain, overwhelmed: LMC to Ellis Loring, 24 November 1841, Child, *SL*, 151.

41. see a light: LMC to Ellis Loring, 24 November 1841, Child, *SL*, 151.

42. hopeful: LMC to Francis Shaw, 7 December 1841, Child, *CC*, 297.

43. tooth-ache: LMC to Ellis Loring, 25 January 1842, Child, *CC*, 327.

44. out of sorts: LMC to Ellis Loring, 15 February 1842, Child, *SL*, 159; knave: LMC to Ellis Loring, 7 March 1843, Child, *SL*, 193.

45. Kelley: Sterling, *Ahead of Her Time*, 122; dangerous: Child, *SL*, 159, editors' note; see also Sterling, *Ahead of Her Time*, 111.

46. tests: *NASS*, 31 March 1842; expelled: Karcher, *First Woman*, 372.

47. ranks: LMC to Ellis Loring, 15 February 1842, Child, *SL*, 159.

48. advocate: LMC to James Miller McKim and Philadelphia Friends, 24 [and 25] November 1841, Child, *SL*, 154.

49. should not: LMC to Ellis Loring, 9 March 1842, Child, *SL*, 164.

50. deliberately sorry, fitter: LMC to Ellis Loring, 15 February 1842, Child, *SL*, 159–60; money: LMC to Louisa Loring, 22 December 1841, Child, *CC*, 309.

51. Edouart: Child, *SL*, 149, editors' note; define my position: LMC to James Miller McKim and Philadelphia Friends, 24 [and 25] November 1841, Child, *SL*, 154; me, myself: LMC to Ellis Loring, 24 November 1841, Child, *SL*, 153.

52. shared letter: LMC to Maria Weston Chapman, 26 April [1842], Child, *CC*, 365; good wishes: LMC to Ellis Loring, 28 February 1842, Child, *SL*, 162.

53. antislavery: Madeline Hooke Rice, *Federal Street Pastor: The Life of William Ellery Channing* (New York: Bookman Associates, 1961), 245; relinquishing: Rice, *Federal Street Pastor*, 248–49.

54. Channing: William Ellery Channing to LMC, 12 March 1842, Child, *CC*, 351.

55. giant: LMC to Loring, 27 April 1842, Child, *CC*, 366; subscriptions: Karcher, *First Woman*, 273; *Liberator* circulation: William Lloyd Garrison Papers, Guide, Massachusetts Historical Society.

56. comfort: LMC to Maria Weston Chapman, 26 April [1842], Child, *CC*, 365; sunny troop: LMC to Maria Weston Chapman, 26 April 1842, Child, *SL*, 170.

Chapter Eight

1. hell: Sinha, *Slave's Cause*, 471; Mayer, *All on Fire*, 313.
2. resolved: *Liberator*, 4 February 1842 and 25 February 1842.
3. weapon: Varon, *Disunion!*, 35; Haverhill: Traub, *John Quincy Adams*, 488; Varon, *Disunion!*, 150.
4. censured: Traub, *John Quincy Adams*, 486–94; wits: Mayer, *All on Fire*, 316.
5. Child: "The Union," *NASS*, 31 March 1842.
6. reprinted: "Selections, from the *National Anti-Slavery Standard*, 'The Union,'" *Liberator*, 15 April 1842; standard: *Liberator*, 22 April 1842.
7. final question: reprinted in *Liberator*, 20 May 1842; judge: "Anniversary," *NASS*, 19 May 1842; mob fever: LMC to Wendell Phillips, 3 May 1842, Child, *SL*, 172.
8. newspapers: "CORRECTION," *Morning Courier and Enquirer*, 3 May 1842; Karcher, *First Woman*, 285, 683.
9. unfeigned surprise: *Liberator*, 6 May 1842; Ellis: LMC to Ellis Loring, 6 May 1842, Child, *SL*, 173; back out: LMC to Maria Weston Chapman, 11 May [1842], Child, *SL*, 175.
10. valuables: LMC to Wendell Phillips, 3 May 1842, Child, *SL*, 172.
11. not meddle: May 9, 1842, reprinted in *NASS*, 19 May 1842; location (Tabernacle): *NASS*, 19 May 1842.
12. disclaimer read: *NASS*, 19 May 1842.
13. tabled: *NASS*, 19 May 1842.
14. intellect: William Lloyd Garrison, "The *National Anti-Slavery Standard*," *Liberator*, 17 June 1842; respect: LMC in *NASS*, 19 May 1842.
15. tread-mill: LMC to Maria Weston Chapman, 11 May [1842], Child, *SL*, 174–76.
16. duty: editors' note, Child, *SL*, 174.
17. Long Island: Child, *Letters from New York*, 92; Staten Island: *Letters from New York*, 91ff; kaleidoscope: *Letters from New York*, 105; moonlit walks: *Letters from New York*, 104–5.
18. scathing letter: LMC to the Board of the Massachusetts Anti-Slavery Society, 21 February 1843, Child, *SL*, 190; thirty-seven cents: LMC to Ellis Loring, [29? October 1842], Child, *SL*, 179.
19. bankruptcy: Karcher, *First Woman*, xxii. The bankruptcy process was also not straightforward: see Child, *SL*, 179, editors' note, also LMC to Ellis Loring, 6 December 1842, Child, *CC*, 429; anti-slavery watch: LMC to Ellis Loring, [29? October 1842], Child, *SL*, 179.
20. come-out-ism: LMC to Ellis Loring, 16 May 1844, Child, *SL*, 207; unfavorable: "Sects and Sectarianism," *NASS*, 16 February 1843.
21. disgraced: LMC to Ellis Loring, 6 March 1843, Child, *SL*, 193.
22. LMC, "Farewell," *NASS*, 4 May 1843.
23. "The End of the Year," *NASS*, 11 May 1843.
24. Chauncey Place: Chambers, *Weston Sisters*, 24; respectfully: LMC to Maria Weston Chapman, 19 May [1843], Child, *SL*, 197. For a history of the distancing between LMC and the Weston sisters, see Chambers, *Weston Sisters*, 220.

25. revelation: Maria Weston Chapman, note on letter from LMC, 19 May 1843, Child, *CC*, 494.

26. light in me: LMC to Ellis Loring, 6 March 1843, Child, *SL*, 194; agent: LMC to Francis Shaw, 18 July 1844, Child, *SL*, 210.

27. not to follow: LMC to Louisa Loring, 28 February [1843], Child, *CC*, 459; experiment: LMC to Ellis Loring, 12 June 1843, Child, *CC*, 498; die: LMC to Ellis and Louisa Loring, 17 June and 14 August [1843], Child, *CC*, 499, 505.

28. readiness: LMC to Louisa Loring, 28 February [1843], Child, *CC*, 459.

29. liberal: LMC to Louisa Loring, 12 November 1849, Child, *CC*, 764; legal surrogate: Karcher, *First Woman*, 293; Clifford, *Crusader*, 179. For references to the separation of her finances, see also LMC to Ellis Loring, 13 April 1851, Child, *SL*, 258–59; LMC to Ellis Loring, [17 February 1856], Child, *CC*, 905; LMC to Lucy and Mary Osgood, 12 June 1858, Child, *SL*, 314; Karcher, *First Woman*, 365.

30. libel: Karcher, *First Woman*, 292; Chapman recruits David: Sterling, *Ahead of Her Time*, 176–77.

31. catastrophy [*sic*]: Karcher, *First Woman*, 292.

32. don't speak: LMC to Sarah Shaw, 20 December 1856, Child, *CC*, 969; secret causes: LMC to Ellis Loring, 12 June 1843, Child, *CC*, 498.

33. By 1846 she writes that he had "cordially assented" to the plan: see LMC to Francis Shaw, 2 August 1846, Child, *SL*, 229.

34. "Assignee's Sale," *New Hampshire Gazette*, 6 June 1843.

35. auction details: Clifford, *Crusader*, 178, 327n25. Soon Child was working on a new edition of *Philothea*, suggesting that she retained some of her rights. Since the watch remained among her possessions when she died, it seems that no one purchased it.

36. sold out: Karcher, *First Woman*, 309; Douglass: Douglass, *Autobiographies*, 904.

37. Osgood: Lucy Osgood to LMC, 8 May 1843, Child, *CC*, 493.

38. pudding: *Flowers for Children*, vol. 2 (New York: C. S. Francis, 1844), 25–28, Internet Archive.

39. antislavery themes: Karcher, *First Woman*, 170, 655; wider embrace: LMC to Francis Shaw, 2 August 1846, Child, *SL*, 228; jail: LMC to [Dear Friend], 23 April 1844, Child, *CC*, 550; prison reform: LMC in Boston *Courier*, 18 December 1844, Child, *CC*, 592; settled freedpeople: LMC to Henrietta Sargent, 23 June 1844, Child, *SL*, 208.

40. Bull: Karcher, *First Woman*, 312–19; Clifford, *Crusader*, 188–89; Fuller: Karcher, *First Woman*, 326; New York: LMC to Louisa Loring, 14 August 1843, Child, *CC*, 505.

41. toll: Perry, *Lift Up Thy Voice*, 159, 177; Chambers, *Weston Sisters*, 132.

42. Douglass: Blight, *Frederick Douglass*, 210; David Ruggles, perhaps with help from the Childs' Northampton connections, established a water cure in Northampton to treat his own shattered health. See Douglass's account of Ruggles's work in Frederick Douglass, "What I Found at the Northampton Association," in *The History of Florence, Massachusetts, Including a Complete Account of the Northampton Association of Education and Industry*, ed. Charles A. Sheffeld (Florence, MA: Published

by the editor, 1895), 129–32; conscience: LMC to Lucretia Mott, 26 February 1861, Child, *SL*, 377.

43. lobster: LMC to Francis Shaw, 2 August 1846, Child, *SL*, 228.

44. son: LMC to Francis Shaw [1843?], Child, *CC*, 497; LMC to Louisa Loring, 14 August 1843, Child, *CC*, 505; hardly care: LMC to Ellis Loring, 6 March 1843, Child, *SL*, 195; LMC to Louisa Loring, 29 May 1843, Child, *CC*, 496; LMC to Anna Loring, 6 February 1845, Child, *SL*, 217–18; dream: LMC to Louisa Loring, 14 August 1843, Child, *CC*, 505; plummeted: Karcher, *First Woman*, 288; said no: LMC to Louisa Loring, October 1844, Child, *CC*, 577.

Chapter Nine

1. origins, eloped: Karcher, *First Woman*, 355.

2. protested: LMC to Susan Lyman, 2 May 1847, Child, *CC*, 709.

3. always left: LMC to Francis Shaw, 11 July 1847, Child, *CC*, 711; California: LMC to Ellis Loring, 6 February 1852, Child, *SL*, 263; mother: LMC to Lydia Bigelow Child, 25 July 1848, Child, *CC*, 734.

4. cursing: LMC to Louisa Loring, [24?, 26? June? 1849?], Child, *CC*, 754.

5. diseased: LMC to Sarah Shaw, 3 August 1856, Child, *CC*, 933.

6. particle, men: LMC to Francis Shaw, 11 July 1847, Child, *CC*, 711; die in: LMC to Marianne Silsbee 10 July 1848, Child, *CC*, 732; envy: LMC to Sarah Parsons, 27 September 1847, Child, *CC*, 714.

7. Dolores and Hosmer: Karcher, *First Woman*, 366–67; happiness: LMC to Marianne Silsbee, 29 October 1849, Child, *CC*, 762; fugitive slave: LMC to Louisa Loring, 8 March 1849, Child, *SL*, 244; let us hope: LMC to Louisa Loring, 18 July 1852, Child, *CC*, 825.

8. human nature: LMC to Ellis Loring, 6 June 1850, Child, *CC*, 782; flowers: LMC to Sarah Shaw, 20 December 1856, Child, *CC*, 969.

9. Child did initially hope to make some money on the book, but she later predicted it would not work. See LMC to Ellis Loring, 27 October 1851, Child, *SL*, 261; growl: LMC to Convers Francis, 14 July 1849, Child, *CC*, 755a.

10. penance for love: Karcher, *First Woman*, 357.

11. burial-place: LMC to Louisa Loring, 8 March 1849, Child, *SL*, 244.

12. secede: Varon, *Disunion!*, 211–12; Fugitive Slave Act: R. J. M. Blackett, *The Captive's Quest for Freedom: Fugitive Slaves, the 1850 Fugitive Slave Law, and the Politics of Slavery* (Cambridge: Cambridge University Press, 2018), 7–13.

13. freedom: Blackett, *Captive's Quest*, xi; $200,000: Blackett, *Captive's Quest*, 5; legal fees: Blackett, *Captive's Quest*, 6.

14. commissioners' fees, testifying: Blackett, *Captive's Quest*, 8.

15. salute: Blackett, *Captive's Quest*, 29.

16. numbers fled: Blackett, *Captive's Quest*, 43–45.

17. armed: Blackett, *Captive's Quest*, 19–21; resting place, last drama: Blackett, *Captive's Quest*, 32–33; blood: Blackett, *Captive's Quest*, 66; arrested: Blackett, *Captive's Quest*, 429; women: Blackett, *Captive's Quest*, 73.

18. Indiana: Blackett, *Captive's Quest*, 104; Wisconsin, Oregon, Illinois: Blackett, *Captive's Quest*, 111; missionaries: Blackett, *Captive's Quest*, 92.

19. $1,000: Robert K. Sutton, *Stark Mad Abolitionists: Lawrence, Kansas and the Battle over Slavery in the Civil War Era* (New York: Skyhouse, 2017), xxii; average citizen: Blackett, *Captive's Quest*, 9.

20. Faneuil Hall, Syracuse: Blackett, *Captive's Quest*, 20–22.

21. Crafts, Minkins: Blackett: *Captive's Quest*, 66–67; Christiana: Stanley W. Campbell, *The Slave Catchers: Enforcement of the Fugitive Slave Law, 1850–1860* (Chapel Hill: University of North Carolina Press, 1970), 151–53.

22. Sims: Blackett, *Captive's Quest*, 413–17; Sinha, *Slave's Cause*, 509.

23. banishment: "The Society of Friends," *NASS*, 12 August 1841; love them: Lydia Maria Child, *Isaac T. Hopper: A True Life* (Boston: John P. Jewett, 1853), 480, Internet Archive.

24. other people: Child, *Isaac T. Hopper*, v.

25. notes: Child, *Isaac T. Hopper*, v–vi; toil for another: Child, *Isaac T. Hopper*, 52; Poovey: Child, *Isaac T. Hopper*, 74; try whether: Child, *Isaac T. Hopper*, 126.

26. lumberyards: Child, *Isaac T. Hopper*, 56; fled: Child, *Isaac T. Hopper*, 66; drunk: Child, *Isaac T. Hopper*, 110; tripped: Child, *Isaac T. Hopper*, 58; shoot: Child, *Isaac T. Hopper*, 64.

27. suicide: Child, *Isaac T. Hopper*, 79; children: Child, *Isaac T. Hopper*, 145; victim: Child, *Isaac T. Hopper*, 57.

28. hiding place: Child, *Isaac T. Hopper*, 96ff; amused: Child, *Isaac T. Hopper*, 102.

29. glow: Child, *Isaac T. Hopper*, vi.

30. Hopper: LMC to Ellis Loring, [1852?], Child, *CC*, 836; best-selling: Karcher, *First Woman*, 373.

31. appendix: LMC to John Hopper, 30 April [1853], Child, *CC*, 843; sentence: LMC to John Hopper, [before 30 April? 1853?], Child, *CC*, 842.

32. ability: LMC to Ellis Loring, 5 March 1854, Child, *CC*, 862.

33. consulting: LMC to Ellis Loring, 31 August 1851, Child, *CC*, 811.

34. tenderness: Child, "Memorial Book for David Lee Child," 13.

35. shirts: LMC to Louisa Loring, 21 October 1849, Child, *SL*, 250; wagon: LMC to Anna Loring Dresel, 3 December 1866, Child, *CC*, 1749; causeries: DLC to LMC, 27 June 1858, Child, *CC*, 1066; magnanimous: LMC to DLC, 19 November 1856, Child, *CC*, 959.

36. perversity: Chambers, *Weston Sisters*, 163.

37. greatest mistakes: LMC to Marianne Silsbee, 27 August 1855, Child, *CC*, 886; in duty: LMC to Marianne Silsbee, 31 October 1855, Child, *CC*, 887.

38. coach: LMC to Francis Shaw, 1 June 1858, Child, *CC*, 1059; library: "History—Wayland Free Public Library," Wayland Free Public Library, https://web.archive .org/web/20210530212731/https://waylandlibrary.org/aboutus/about-wpl /history/; yard, squirrel: LMC to Marianne Silsbee, 27 August 1855, Child, *CC*, 886; father's behavior: LMC to Sarah Shaw, 3 August 1856, Child, *CC*, 933; Sumner: LMC to Charles Sumner, 12 February 1855, Child, *CC*, 879.

39. goes to fair: LMC to Marianne Silsbee, 1 January 1854, Child, *CC*, 857a; thieving

boys: LMC to DLC, 20 December [1857], Child, *CC*, 1041; LMC to Helen Garrison, 15 December 1861, Child, *CC*, 1355; Chapman: LMC to DLC, 20 December [1857], Child, *CC*, 1041;, LMC to Louisa Loring, 8 February 1857, Child, *CC*, 990; LMC to Sarah Shaw, 12 January 1858, Child, *CC*, 1043.

40. travel: LMC to Ellis Loring, 22 January 1857, Child, *CC*, 983; chores: DLC and LMC to Henrietta Sargent, 29 January 1855, Child, *CC*, 878.

41. Hindu: Lydia Maria Child, *The Progress of Religious Ideas, through Successive Ages*, 3 vols. (New York: C. S. Francis, 1855), 1:126; Christian: Child, *Progress*, 3:23ff.; Muslims: Child, *Progress*, 3:408; absorbed: LMC to Lucy Osgood, [11?-19? February 1856], Child, *SL*, 276. Compare, for instance, Joseph B. Gross, *The Heathen Religion in Its Popular and Symbolical Development* (Boston, 1854), and F. D. Maurice, *The Religions of the World, in Their Relation to Christianity* (Boston: Gould and Lincoln, 1854), both reviewed in the *Christian Examiner*, 4th ser. 73 (March 1857): 183–99, along with Child's writings. See Karcher for an analysis of the book's main themes and its pioneering status: Karcher, *First Woman*, 374–83; penance: LMC to Lucy Osgood, [11?-19? February 1856], Child, *SL*, 276.

42. immense good: LMC to Lucy Osgood, [11?-19? February 1856], Child, *SL*, 278; time, talent: Child, *Progress*, 3:434.

43. infirmities: Child, *Progress*, 2:154; theology: Child, *Progress*, 3:451; treatment of Jews: Child, *Progress*, 3:439; caste: Child, *Progress*, 3:438.

44. ordinary readers: LMC to the editors of "Life Illustrated," 30 December 1855, Child, *CC*, 895; Karcher, *First Woman*, 383; paid for itself: LMC to [Lucy Osgood? and Mary Osgood?], 12 January 1856, Child, *CC*, 898; philosophy of religion: Lucy Osgood to LMC, 5 May 1856, Child, *CC*, 914; industry: [JFC], "Comparative Theology of Heathen Religions," *Christian Examiner and Religious Miscellany* 62 (1857); in English: Karcher, *First Woman*, 375; May: Samuel May to LMC, [January? 1856?], Child, *CC*, 900; Convers: LMC to Lucy Osgood, [11?-19? February 1856], Child, *SL*, 278; Parker: Karcher, *First Woman*, 383; on Parker's radicalism, see Richard Wightman Fox, *Jesus in America: A History* (San Francisco: HarperSanFrancisco, 2004), 232–34.

45. See Karcher's analysis at Karcher, *First Woman*, 380ff.; heathenism: [JFC], "Comparative Theology of Heathen Religions," 189.

46. Kansas-Nebraska Act: Nicole Etcheson, *Bleeding Kansas: Contested Liberty in the Civil War Era* (Lawrence: University Press of Kansas, 2004), 9–27; Andrew Delbanco, *The War Before the War: Fugitive Slaves and the Struggle for America's Soul from the Revolution to the Civil War* (New York: Penguin Press, 2018), 323–35.

47. For accounts of Burns's arrest and rendition, see Blackett, *Captive's Quest*, 422–31; Campbell, *Slave Catchers*, 124–35; Delbanco, *War Before the War*, 308–14; Sutton, *Stark Mad Abolitionists*, 3–5; scar: Mary Thacher Higginson, *Thomas Wentworth Higginson: The Story of His Life* (Boston: Houghton Mifflin, 1914), 144, Internet Archive.

48. humiliation: LMC to Charles Sumner, 12 February 1855, Child, *CC*, 879; blood: LMC to Francis Shaw, 3 June 1854, Child, *SL*, 269; ridiculous fuss: LMC to Mari-

anne Silsbee, 1 February 1857, Child, *SL*, 304; stark mad: Sutton, *Stark Mad Abolitionists*, 5.

49. cotton: Sutton, *Stark Mad Abolitionists*, 11.

50. company established: Sutton, *Stark Mad Abolitionists*, 9; fanfare: Sutton, *Stark Mad Abolitionists*, 26; valley: Sara T. L. Robinson, *Kansas: Its Exterior and Interior Life, Including a Full View of Its Settlement, Political History, Social Life, Climate, Soil, Productions, Scenery, Etc.* (Boston: Crosby, Nichols, 1857), 1–9, Internet Archive; named: Sutton, *Stark Mad Abolitionists*, 27.

51. Black residents: Varon, *Disunion!*, 260; resolution passed: Etcheson, *Bleeding Kansas*, 75.

52. stop them: Varon, *Disunion!*, 260; Etcheson, *Bleeding Kansas*, 53.

53. legislature: Sutton, *Stark Mad Abolitionists*, 51; rebuked: Sutton, *Stark Mad Abolitionists*, 59.

54. treason: Sutton, *Stark Mad Abolitionists*, 80–81; Free State Hotel: Sutton, *Stark Mad Abolitionists*, 83; rifles: Sutton, *Stark Mad Abolitionists*, 52.

55. On Sumner's speech, see Williamjames Hull Hoffer, *The Caning of Charles Sumner: Honor, Idealism and the Origins of the Civil War* (Baltimore: Johns Hopkins University Press, 2010), 60–65.

56. wiped out: Sutton, *Stark Mad Abolitionists*, 85; on the Sack of Lawrence, see 81–88; Etcheson, *Bleeding Kansas*, 100ff.; only casualty: Etcheson, *Bleeding Kansas*, 105; more at Robinson, *Kansas*, 240ff.

57. Brooks's attack: Hoffer, *Caning of Charles Sumner*, 5–11, 72–79.

58. virtually slaves: Hoffer, *Caning of Charles Sumner*, 88.

59. murders: David S. Reynolds, *John Brown, Abolitionist: The Man Who Killed Slavery, Sparked the Civil War, and Seeded Civil Rights* (New York: Vintage Books, 2006), 171–74; Frederick: Reynolds, *John Brown*, 199.

60. Joan of Arc: LMC to Charles Sumner, 7 July 1856, Child, *SL*, 285; Corday: LMC to Marianne Silsbee, 11 September 1857, Child, *SL*, 312; throbbings: LMC to Anna Loring, 8 June 1856, Child, *CC*, 918.

61. could not: LMC to Anna Loring, 8 June 1856, Child, *CC*, 918; inactive: LMC to Peter and Susan Lesley, 9 August 1856, Child, *CC*, 935; thundered: LMC to Louisa Loring, 16 June 1856, Child, *CC*, 919.

62. fabric: LMC to DLC, 27 October 1856, Child, *SL*, 295; sewing: LMC to Sarah Shaw, 27 October 1857, Child, *CC*, 952; mate: DLC to LMC, 18 October 1856, Child, *CC*, 948; letter, LMC to the Women of Kansas, published in *NASS*, 28 October 1856, Child, *CC*, 954.

63. glittering: Lydia Maria Child, "The Kansas Emigrants," in *Autumnal Leaves: Tales and Sketches in Prose and Rhyme*, by Lydia Maria Child (New York: C. S. Francis, 1857), 363, Internet Archive.

64. vote: LMC to Lucy and Mary Osgood, 20 July 1856, Child, *CC*, 932.

65. Black women: Jones, *Vanguard*, 175–202; live to see: LMC to Sarah Shaw, 14 September 1856, Child, *SL*, 292.

66. wept: LMC to Parke Godwin, 18 November 1856, Child, *CC*, 958.

67. proudly hoped, virtue: LMC to Parke Godwin, 18 November 1856, Child, *CC,* 958.

68. darkness: LMC to DLC, 19 November 1856, Child, *SL*, 295; prison: LMC to Louisa Loring, 23 [24] November 1856, Child, *CC*, 960; cried: LMC to Sarah Shaw, 8 December 1856, Child, *SL*, 301; disappointed: LMC to Ellis Loring, [27 November 1856], Child, *CC*, 961.

69. occupation: LMC to Sarah Shaw, 8 December 1856, Child, *SL*, 300.

70. Whittier: LMC to John Greenleaf Whittier, 2 December 1856, Child, *CC*, 962; John Greenleaf Whittier to LMC, [6 December 1856], Child, *CC*, 963; allowed myself: LMC to Louisa Loring, 4 May 1859, Child, *CC*, 1109.

71. twenty five: LMC to Marianne Silsbee, 11 September 1857, Child, *SL*, 312.

72. Whittier: Mary B. Claflin, *Personal Recollections of John G. Whittier* (New York: Thomas Y. Crowell, 1893), 80, Internet Archive.

73. love you truly: LMC to Marianne Silsbee, 11 September 1857, Child, *CC*, 313.

74. theater: LMC to Mary Moody Emerson, 6 January 1857, Child, *CC*, 979; Sumner: LMC to John Greenleaf Whittier, 2 January 1857, Child, *CC*, 975; overwhelmed: LMC to Mary Moody Emerson, 6 January 1857, Child, *CC*, 979; kill me: LMC to Marianne Silsbee, 9 December 1856, Child, *CC*, 965.

75. unconstitutional: Varon, *Disunion!*, 298. On *Dred Scott*, see Kendi, *Stamped from the Beginning*, 204–5; Varon, *Disunion!*, 295–304; Sinha, *Slave's Cause*, 567–68.

76. opposition, despotism: LMC to Mary and Lucy Osgood, 12 March 1857, Child, *CC*, 997; not an inch: Varon, *Disunion!*, 304; Remond: Varon, *Disunion!*, 302; hang themselves: LMC to Sarah Shaw, 20 March 1857, Child, *SL*, 308.

77. guests: LMC to Sarah Shaw, 11 October 1858, Child, *CC*, 1083; see also LMC to Sarah Shaw, 25 July 1857, Child, *CC*, 1013.

78. Venice: LMC to Sarah Shaw, 11 October 1858, Child, *CC*, 1083; Rome: LMC to Sarah Shaw, 3 August 1856, Child, *CC*, 933; Silsbee: LMC to DLC, 20 June 1858, Child, *CC*, 1063; Abigail, Sarah: LMC to Marianne Silsbee, 14 July 1858, Child, *CC*, 1068.

79. arrange: LMC to Louisa Loring, 4 May 1859, Child, *SL*, 1109.

80. collapsed: LMC to Louisa Loring, 4 May 1859, *CC*, 1109; crookedness: LMC to Lucy and Mary Osgood, 12 June 1858, Child, *SL*, 314; doing: LMC to Sarah Shaw, 21 August 1858, *CC*, 1075; silence: LMC to Lucy and Mary Osgood, 12 June 1858, Child, *SL*, 315.

81. Lincoln: Kendi, *Stamped from the Beginning*, 205–6; Varon, *Disunion!*, 315.

82. cat with mouse, never occur: LMC to Sarah Shaw, 9 November 1856, Child, *SL*, 299.

Chapter Ten

1. wealth and status: Tony Horwitz, *Midnight Rising: John Brown and the Raid That Sparked the Civil War* (New York: Henry Holt, 2011), 133–35; careful records: Horwitz, *Midnight Rising*, 134.

2. prisoner: Horwitz, *Midnight Rising*.

3. pistol and sword: Reynolds, *John Brown, Abolitionist*, 130; didn't believe: Horwitz, *Midnight Rising*, 135.

4. guardroom: Horwitz, *Midnight Rising*, 137; Osawatomie Brown: Reynolds, *John Brown, Abolitionist*, 311.

5. wanted: Horwitz, *Midnight Rising*, 90; reward: Horwitz, *Midnight Rising*, 89.

6. eternal war: Horwitz, *Midnight Rising*, 16; Sinha, *Slave's Cause*, 544; L'Ouverture and Turner: Jackson, *Force and Freedom*, 108; Garnet and Walker, Jackson, *Force and Freedom*, 110.

7. Canada: Sinha, *Slave's Cause*, 552, Horwitz, *Midnight Rising*, 89; constitution: Jackson, *Force and Freedom*, 119; see *Provisional Constitution and Ordinances for the People of the United States*, May 8, 1858, in *John Brown's Raid on Harpers Ferry: A Brief History with Documents*, ed. Jonathan Earle (Boston: Bedford/St. Martin's Press, 2008), 65–69.

8. Pleasant and Tubman: Jackson, *Force and Freedom*, 111–17.

9. bees: Jackson, *Force and Freedom*, 118; deliver: Jackson, *Force and Freedom*, 124; Garnet and Douglass: Jackson, *Force and Freedom*, 118–19.

10. hazards, Secretary of War: Horwitz, *Midnight Rising*, 142; master of transportation: Reynolds, *John Brown, Abolitionist*, 317; Horwitz, *Midnight Rising*, 173.

11. first headlines: *Wilmington Daily Herald*, 18–20 October 1859; *Daily Progress*, 19 October 1859. See Kent Blaser, "North Carolina and John Brown's Raid," *Civil War History* 24, no. 3 (1978): 197–212; Horwitz, *Midnight Rising*, 143.

12. Oliver, Watson: *Midnight Rising*, 168–70; buy me: Eugene L. Meyer, *Five for Freedom: The African-American Soldiers in John Brown's Army* (Chicago: Chicago Review Press, 2018), 24; Louisiana: Horwitz, *Midnight Rising*, 153.

13. call went up: Horwitz, *Midnight Rising*, 174.

14. alive: Horwitz, *Midnight Rising*, 177ff.; Copeland: Steven Lubet, *The "Colored Hero" of Harper's Ferry: John Anthony Copeland and the War against Slavery* (New York: Cambridge University Press, 2015), 91–97.

15. talk: F. B. Sanborn, *The Life and Letters of John Brown, Liberator of Kansas and Martyr of Virginia* (Boston: Roberts Brothers, 1885), 131, Internet Archive; Reynolds, *John Brown, Abolitionist*, 309.

16. Negro question: Horwitz, *Midnight Rising*, 186–87.

17. weapons: Horwitz, *Midnight Rising*, 181; campaign: Horwitz, *Midnight Rising*, 193.

18. force: Horwitz, *Midnight Rising*, 194; Douglass: Blight, *Frederick Douglass*, 306.

19. charges: Meyer, *Five for Freedom*, 111–13.

20. medical: Horwitz, *Midnight Rising*, 265–66.

21. respectfully: Lydia Maria Child, *Correspondence between Lydia Maria Child and Gov. Wise and Mrs. Mason, of Virginia* (Boston: American Anti-Slavery Society, 1860), 3–4, Internet Archive.

22. bless: Child, *LMC, Wise, Mason*, 14.

23. speak: Child, *LMC, Wise, Mason*, 4–6.

24. LMC to William Lloyd Garrison, 28 October 1859, Child, *CC*, 1126; no use: LMC to Sarah Shaw, 4 November 1859, Child, *CC*, 1131.

25. treason: Horwitz, *Midnight Rising*, 207.

26. be done: Horwitz, *Midnight Rising*, 212–13.

27. See Louis DeCaro Jr., *John Brown Speaks: Letters and Statements from Charlestown* (Lanham, MD: Rowman and Littlefield, 2015).

28. Brown to LMC: Child, *LMC, Wise, Mason*, 15–16; colored members: LMC to Oliver Johnson, 20 December 1859, Child, *SL*, 335.

29. November 12:, Child, *SL*, 332, editors' note; blazoned: LMC to Sarah Shaw, 4 November 1859, Child, *CC*, 1131.

30. private affair: LMC to Sarah Shaw, 4 November 1859, Child, *CC*, 1131.

31. guns: LMC to Maria Weston Chapman, 28 November 1859, Child, *CC*, 1141.

32. Child, *LMC, Wise, Mason*, 6–12.

33. Masons: Virginia Mason, *The Public Life and Diplomatic Correspondence of James M. Mason: With Some Personal History by Virginia Mason (His Daughter)* (New York: Neale, 1906), 13, 18, 39–40.

34. 1850: Varon, *Disunion!*, 213.

35. contributors: Child, *LMC, Wise, Mason*, 16–18.

36. Virginia newspapers: LMC to Horace Greeley, 18 December 1859, Child, *SL*, 333.

37. warm: Horwitz, *Midnight Rising*, 249; eyes: Reynolds, *John Brown, Abolitionist*, 395.

38. rather die: Meyer, *Five for Freedom*, 117.

39. new saint: Reynolds, *John Brown, Abolitionist*, 366; four thousand: Mayer, *All on Fire*, 501.

40. helped: Mayer, *All on Fire*, 501; amen: LMC to Sarah Shaw, 22 December 1859, Child, *CC*, 1157.

41. diligence: LMC to Marianne Silsbee, 12 January 1860, Child, *CC*, 1184.

42. letter: Child, *LMC, Wise, Mason*, 18–28.

43. Greeley: LMC to Horace Greeley, 18 December 1859, Child, *SL*, 333; Southern papers: May, *Some Recollections*, 100; numbers sold: Karcher, *First Woman*, 423; sent Mrs. Mason: LMC to Robert Folger Walcutt, [17–31 December 1859], Child, *CC*, 1170.

44. Ralph Waldo Emerson to LMC, 23 November 1859, Child, *CC*, 1139; Eliza Follen to LMC, [7 December 1859], Child, *CC*, 1144; William H. Armstrong to LMC, 25 December 1859, Child, *CC*, 1166; Hindu: LMC to [Oliver?] Johnson, 3 February 1860, Child, *CC*, 1197; used up: Sinha, *Slave's Cause*, 559; majesty: Mayer, *All on Fire*, 503; hot shot: LMC to Sarah Shaw, 16 September 1860, Child, *CC*, 1252.

45. foul: LMC to Maria Weston Chapman, 28 November 1859, Child, *CC*, 1141; womanly: Bryant Bartlett to LMC, 2 January 1860, Child, *CC*, 1175; likeness: Samuel Jackson to LMC, [before 23 December 1859], Child, *CC*, 1158.

46. soul: Eliza Follen to LMC, [7 December 1859], Child, *CC*, 1144; thank you; U. H. Fisk to LMC, 10 January 1860, Child, *CC*, 1180; praises: Lucy Osgood to LMC, 12 January 1860, Child, *CC*, 1185.

47. shock: LMC to [Maria Weston Chapman?], 22 December 1859, Child, *CC*, 1155; eagle: LMC to Parke Godwin, 27 November 1859, Child, *CC*, 1140.

48. must: *Liberator*, 23 December 1859, Child, *CC*, 1158.

49. Virginia: LMC to Robert Folger Walcutt, December [1860], Child, *CC*, 1272. These were in part expanded versions of earlier pamphlets: see Sinha, *Slave's Cause*, 559.

50. Lydia Maria Child, *The Right Way, the Safe Way, Proved by Emancipation in the British West Indies, and Elsewhere* (New York: 5 Beekman Street, 1860), Internet Archive; *The Patriarchal Institution, as Described by Members of Its Own Family* (New York: American Anti-Slavery Society, 1860), Internet Archive.

51. tracts: LMC to Robert Folger Walcutt, 15 November 1860, Child, *CC*, 1267; thousand copies: LMC to Lucretia Mott, 26 February 1861, Child, *SL*, 376.

52. blow: Child, *The Duty of Disobedience to the Fugitive Slave Act* (Boston: American Anti-Slavery Association, 1860), 11.

53. shame: Child, *Duty of Disobedience*, 5.

54. I got it: LMC to Sarah Shaw, [after 20 November] 1860, Child, *CC*, 1270; Sims: Karcher, *First Woman*, 437–8.

55. secede: Alan C. Guelzo, *Lincoln's Emancipation Proclamation: The End of Slavery in America* (New York: Simon and Schuster, 2004), 15; natural effects: Edward H. Bonekemper, *The Myth of the Lost Cause: Why the South Fought the Civil War and Why the North Won* (Washington, DC: Regnery History, 2015), 45.

56. two mobs: LMC to Charles Sumner, 28 January 1861, Child, *CC*, 1281.

57. rheumatic foot: LMC to [Sargent?] 15 July 1860, Child, *CC*, 1238; conscience: LMC to Sarah Shaw, 25 January 1861, Child, *SL*, 370.

58. all hell: LMC to Sarah Shaw, 25 January 1861, Child, *SL*, 370; mob details: Karcher, *First Woman*, 439–40; pugilist: Jackson, *Force and Freedom*, 147.

59. heart: LMC to Sarah Shaw, 25 January 1861, Child, *SL*, 370; repentance: Karcher, *First Woman*, 440.

60. thirteenth: Guelzo, *Emancipation Proclamation*, 19–20; coup and Thirteenth Amendment: Karcher, *First Woman*, 441; blood: Paul Finkelman, ed., *Defending Slavery: Proslavery Thought in the Old South; A Brief History with Documents* (Boston: Bedford/St. Martin's, 2003), 90–91.

Chapter Eleven

1. Cornwall: Jacqueline Goldsby, "'I Disguised My Hand': Writing Versions of the Truth in Harriet Jacobs's *Incidents in the Life of a Slave Girl* and John Jacobs's 'A True Tale of Slavery,'" in *Harriet Jacobs and "Incidents in the Life of a Slave Girl": New Critical Essays*, ed. Deborah M. Garfield and Rafia Zafar (Cambridge: Cambridge University Press, 2010), 18–19; Jean Fagan Yellin, *Harriet Jacobs: A Life* (New York: Basic Civitas Books, 2004), 109, 124; wife, children: Yellin, *Harriet Jacobs*, 83, 109.

2. born, mother: Harriet A. Jacobs, *Incidents in the Life of a Slave Girl: Written by Herself* (Cambridge, MA: Harvard University Press, 1987), 5–7; father: Jacobs, *Incidents*, 5, 200; death: Jacobs, *Incidents*, 10; all sold: Jacobs, *Incidents*, 8.

3. mother's death: Jacobs, *Incidents*, 6–7; fines: Christina Accomando, "'The Laws Were Laid Down to Me Anew': Harriet Jacobs and the Reframing of Legal Fictions," in *"Incidents in the Life of a Slave Girl": Contexts, Criticism*, ed. Nellie Y. McKay and Nancy Smith Foster (New York: W. W. Norton, 2001), 374; attachment: Jacobs, *Incidents*, 7.

4. three years: Jacobs, *Incidents*, 261. Jacobs, apparently incorrectly, says she was five years old: Jacobs, *Incidents*, 8.

5. cruelties: Jacobs, *Incidents*, 12–13.

6. eleven: Jacobs, *Incidents*, 35; damn you, killed her: Jacobs, *Incidents*, 13–14.

7. monster: Jacobs, *Incidents*, 27–29.

8. lewdness: Accomando, "'The Laws Were Laid Down to Me Anew,'" 375; virtuous: Jacobs, *Incidents*, 31. For recent historical work on sexual violence in slavery, see Rachel A. Feinstein, *When Rape Was Legal: The Untold History of Sexual Violence during Slavery* (New York: Routledge, 2019).

9. war, surrender: Jacobs, *Incidents*, 18–19; might: Jacobs, *Incidents*, 85; grandmother: Jacobs, *Incidents*, 28–29.

10. obvious: Jacobs, *Incidents*, 31–34; fear of grandmother: Jacobs, *Incidents*, 29; appearances: Jacobs, *Incidents*, 33; city: Jacobs, *Incidents*, 35.

11. first time, plague, cowhide: Jacobs, *Incidents*, 39–40.

12. did think: Jacobs, *Incidents*, 35.

13. heroine: Jacobs, *Incidents*, 232; cost: Jacobs, *Incidents*, 53–54.

14. trusted: Jacobs, *Incidents*, 54; akin, something sweet: Jacobs, *Incidents*, 55. For an analysis of Sands as a child predator and an analysis of the power dynamics between him and Flint, see Patricia D. Hopkins, "Seduction or Rape: Deconstructing the Black Female Body in Harriet Jacobs' *Incidents in the Life of a Slave Girl*," *Making Connections: Interdisciplinary Approaches to Cultural Diversity* 13, no. 1 (2011): 10, 16.

15. For Jacobs's reasoning, see Jacobs, *Incidents*, 55ff.

16. pity, choice: Jacobs, *Incidents*, 55–56. See also Saidiya V. Hartman, *Scenes of Subjection: Terror, Slavery, and Self-Making in Nineteenth-Century America*, Race and American Culture (New York: Oxford University Press, 1997), 103–12.

17. birth: Jacobs, *Incidents*, 60–61; kill: Jacobs, *Incidents*, 76; more terrible: Jacobs, *Incidents*, 77.

18. threw son: Jacobs, *Incidents*, 81; lover: Jacobs, *Incidents*, 83; plantation slaves: Jacobs, *Incidents*, 94; death: Jean Fagan Yellin, ed., *The Harriet Jacobs Family Papers*, 2 vols. (Chapel Hill: University of North Carolina Press, 2008), 1:302.

19. trouble: Jacobs, *Incidents*, 96; children sold: Jacobs, *Incidents*, 105–9; Sands: Jacobs, *Incidents*, 125.

20. hiding places: Jacobs, *Incidents*, 98–104, 110–11; death penalty: Yellin, *Harriet Jacobs*, 49; rats: Jacobs, *Incidents*, 49.

21. dimensions: Yellin, *Harriet Jacobs*, 49; weather, hole: Jacobs, *Incidents*, 115–16; children: Jacobs, *Incidents*, 116, 130; illness: Jacobs, *Incidents*, 122.

22. fact: Jacobs, *Incidents*, 148.

23. Philadelphia: Jacobs, *Incidents*, 159; coals: Jacobs, *Incidents*, 160–61.

24. brother: Yellin, *Harriet Jacobs*, 101–2; free to tell: Jacobs, *Incidents*, 204.

25. fugitives: Yellin, *Harriet Jacobs*, 125; see also Ann Taves, "Spiritual Purity and Sexual Shame: Religious Themes in the Writings of Harriet Jacobs," in McKay and Foster, *Contexts*, 210. Other fugitive slave narratives included Richard Hildreth's *Archy Moore, or The White Slave*, Mattie Griffiths's *Autobiography of a Female Slave*,

and James Weldon Johnson's *Autobiography of an Ex-Colored Man*. For a summary, see Sinha, *Slave's Cause*, 422ff., 430ff.; narrative by woman: Harryette Mullen, "Runaway Tongue: Resistant Orality in *Uncle Tom's Cabin, Incidents in the Life of a Slave Girl,* and *Beloved*," in McKay and Foster, *Contexts*, 254.

26. whole truth, avoiding abolitionists, unchristian: Jacobs, *Incidents*, 232.

27. final escape, friend: Jacobs, *Incidents*, 194–201; Stowe: Yellin, *Harriet Jacobs*, 119–20.

28. authenticate: *Harriet Jacobs*, 120–21; Nancy Koester, *Harriet Beecher Stowe: A Spiritual Life* (Grand Rapids, MI: Eerdmans, 2014), 144.

29. Louisa: Jacobs, *Incidents*, 233; Yellin, *Harriet Jacobs*, 120.

30. character: *Harriet Jacobs*, 120–21.

31. patronized: Jacobs, *Incidents*, 235; own work: Yellin, *Harriet Jacobs*, 21. There is some speculation that Stowe had already heard Jacobs's story and indeed appropriated it into the character of Cassie in *Uncle Tom's Cabin*. See Diane G. Scholl, "Jacobs's *Uncle Tom*, Stowe's *Incidents*: Hiding in the Attic 'Loophole,'" *ANQ: A Quarterly Journal of Short Articles, Notes and Reviews* 29, no. 2 (2016): 87–91.

32. never told: Jacobs, *Incidents*, 235; ages: Yellin, *Harriet Jacobs*, 109.

33. firmness: Yellin, *Harriet Jacobs Family Papers*, 195–96.

34. no romance, no answer: Jacobs, *Incidents*, 235–36.

35. secret, difficulties: Jacobs, *Incidents*, 236, 242.

36. foliage: Yellin, *Harriet Jacobs*, 126; paths: Nathaniel Parker Willis, "Letter from Idlewild," *Home Journal*, 21 July 1855; oracle: LMC to John Greenleaf Whittier, 4 April 1861, Child, *SL*, 378.

37. business: Nathaniel Parker Willis, *The Convalescent* (New York: Charles Scribner, 1859), 410–12, Internet Archive; trust: LMC to John Greenleaf Whittier, 4 April 1861, Child, *SL*, 378.

38. not supportive: Jacobs, *Incidents*, 232; dolls: Yellin, *Harriet Jacobs*, 129; parties: Yellin, *Harriet Jacobs*, 131; pregnancy: Yellin, *Harriet Jacobs*, 134; sympathies: Jacobs, *Incidents*, 242.

39. Toni Morrison thematizes this torturous calculation, including references to Jacobs and Child, at Toni Morrison, "The Site of Memory," in *Inventing the Truth: The Art and Craft of Memory*, ed. William Zinsser (Boston: Houghton Mifflin, 1995), 90–92.

40. For a description of this dynamic, see Alice A. Deck, "Whose Book Is This?: Authorial versus Editorial Control of Harriet Brent Jacobs' *Incidents in the Life of a Slave Girl: Written by Herself*," *Women's Studies International Forum* 10, no. 1 (1987): 34–36; Goldsby, "I Disguised My Hand," 16–18.

41. publishers: Jacobs, *Incidents*, 246–47; Jean Fagan Yellin, "Written by Herself: Harriet Jacobs' Slave Narrative," in McKay and Foster, *Contexts*, 206.

42. Stowe, Willis, preface: Jacobs, *Incidents*, 246; Yellin, *Harriet Jacobs*, 140.

43. offices: Yellin, *Harriet Jacobs*, 140; heart: Jacobs, *Incidents*, 247.

44. purpose: LMC to Harriet Jacobs, 13 August 1860, Child, *SL*, 357.

45. entertaining: LMC to Harriet Jacobs, 13 August 1860, Child, *SL*, 357.

46. Whittier: Yellin, *Harriet Jacobs*, xvi-ii; see also Albert H. Tricomi, "Harriet Jacobs' Autobiography and the Voice of Lydia Maria Child," *ESQ: A Journal of the American*

Renaissance 53, no. 3 (2007): 225, Valerie Smith, "Form and Ideology in Three Slave Narratives," in McKay and Foster, *Contexts*, 223.

47. fortnight: LMC to Harriet Jacobs, 13 August 1860, Child, *SL*, 357.

48. this time: LMC to Harriet Jacobs, 27 September 1860, Child, *CC*, 359.

49. subscription: LMC to Daniel Ricketson, 14 March 1862, Child, *CC*, 1295; LMC to John Greenleaf Whittier, 14 March 1861, Child, *CC*, 1296; LMC to John Greenleaf Whittier, 4 April 1861, Child, *SL*, 378; LMC to Sarah Shaw, [February–March? 1861], Child, *CC*, 1298; Anti-Slavery Society: LMC to Wendell Phillips, 2 December 1860 and 9 December 1860, Child, *CC*, 2549–50; run: Jacobs, *Incidents*, 247; generous arrangement: LMC to Wendell Phillips, 9 December 1860, Child, *CC*, 2550.

50. own: Jacobs, *Incidents*, 3–4.

51. For discussion of Child's language in the introduction, see Sandra Gunning, "Reading and Redemption in *Incidents in the Life of a Slave Girl*," in McKay and Foster, *Contexts*, 336–37, and Deborah M. Garfield, "Earwitness: Female Abolitionism, Sexuality, and *Incidents in the life of a Slave Girl*," in Garfield and Zafar, *Critical Essays*, 108–9.

52. small ones: Yellin, *Harriet Jacobs Family Papers*, 284. See Deck, "Whose Book Is This?," 40, for the suggestion that Jacobs perhaps never saw the final draft.

53. installments: Yellin, *Harriet Jacobs*, 142–43; see LMC to John Greenleaf Whittier, 4 April 1861, Child, *SL*, 378; Karcher, *First Woman*, 436; book was out: Yellin, *Harriet Jacobs*, 144–45, also 151–52.

54. gilt: *Harriet Jacobs*, 144.

55. not written by herself: John W. Blassingame, *The Slave Community: Plantation Life in the Antebellum South*, 2nd ed. (New York: Oxford University Press, 1979), 373. For discussion, see Yellin, *Harriet Jacobs*, xvi; Elizabeth Fox-Genovese, *Within the Plantation Household: Black and White Women of the Old South* (Chapel Hill: University of North Carolina Press, 1988), 321; Frances Smith Foster, "Resisting Incidents," in Garfield and Zafar, *Critical Essays*, 66–67; Tricomi, "Harriet Jacobs' Autobiography," 226.

56. Jean Fagan Yellin is the scholar who confirmed Jacobs's existence in the 1980s and subsequently discovered facts about her life in the years after *Incidents* was published: see Yellin's account of her research at Yellin, *Harriet Jacobs*, xv–xxi.

57. I discuss this scholarship below. All of Jacobs's letters can be found in *The Harriet Jacobs Family Papers*, edited by Jean Fagan Yellin (Chapel Hill: University of North Carolina Press, 2008).

58. Compare, for instance, the following two passages:

"I also have been very busy for an interesting Fugitive Slave, who wanted advi[c]e and assistance about her Memoirs. I was desirous to aid her, because she tells her story in a very intelligent, spirited manner, and the details seem to me well calculated to advance the cause I have so deeply at heart. It involves the reading of a good many M.S. pages, and the writing of a good many; but to help the slave is about all my life is good for now" (LMC to Lucy Osgood, 8 August 1860, Child, *CC*, 1241).

"I put the savage cruelties into one chapter, entitled 'Neighboring Planters,' in order that those who shrink from 'supping upon horrors,' might omit them, without interrupting the thread of the story.... [Her current employers] have furnished her with books to read. This accounts for the remarkably good style, in which the autobiography is written. I abridged, and struck out superfluous words sometimes; but I don't think I *altered* fifty words in the whole volume" (LMC to Lucy Searle, 4 February 1861, Child, *CC*, 1282).

59. difficulty: LMC to John Greenleaf Whittier, 4 April 1861, Child, *SL*, 378.

60. rebirth: Bruce Mills, "Lydia Maria Child and the Endings to Harriet Jacobs's *Incidents in the Life of a Slave Girl*," *American Literature* 64, no. 2 (1992): 265; bondage: Jacobs, *Incidents*, 29.

61. defiance: see Jacobs, *Incidents*, 18, 19, and her general refusal of Flint/Norcom's advances; death: Jacobs, *Incidents*, 240–41; Tricomi, "Harriet Jacobs' Autobiography," 243–44. See also Yellin, *Harriet Jacobs*, 135.

62. Child's beliefs: see, for instance, Mills, "Endings," 256ff.

63. On conventions and rhetorical strategies Jacobs used, see Jacobs, *Incidents*, xxix-xxx; Thomas Doherty, "Harriet Jacobs' Narrative Strategies," *Southern Literary Journal* 19, no. 1 (1986): 79–91; Alyssa Bellows, "Evangelicalism, Adultery, and *Incidents in the Life of a Slave Girl*," *Texas Studies in Literature and Language* 62, no. 3 (2020): 253–74. For connections between Jacobs and other literary traditions, see Michelle Burnham, "Loopholes of Resistance: Harriet Jacobs' Slave Narrative and the Critique of Agency in Foucault," in McKay and Foster, *Contexts,* 290ff.; Stephanie A. Smith, "The Tender of Memory: Restructuring Value in Harriet Jacobs's *Incidents in the Life of a Slave Girl*," in Garfield and Zafar, *Critical Essays*, 262; Carol E. Henderson, *Scarring the Black Body: Race and Representation in African American Literature* (Columbia: University of Missouri Press, 2002), 50–51; Donald B. Gibson, "Harriet Jacobs, Frederick Douglass, and the Slavery Debate: Bondage, Family, and the Discourse of Domesticity," in Garfield and Zafar, *Critical Essays*, 162–73, especially 172; Foster, "Resisting Incidents," especially 60, 62ff.; Casey Pratt, "'These Things Took the Shape of Mystery': *Incidents in the Life of a Slave Girl* as American Romance," *African American Review* 47, no. 1 (2014): 70–74; Francine L. Allen, "Sacred and Undesirable: Examining the Theological Import of Hiding Places in Exodus and Harriet Jacobs's *Incidents in the Life of a Slave Girl*," *Priscilla Papers* 29, no. 3 (2015): 21–27; Andrea Powell Wolfe, "Double-Voicedness in Incidents in the Life of a Slave Girl: 'Loud Talking' to a Northern Black Readership," *ATQ: 19th Century American Literature and Culture* 22, no. 3 (2008): 517–25. On the missing John Brown chapter, see Caleb Smith, "Harriet Jacobs among the Militants: Transformations in Abolition's Public Sphere, 1859–61," *American Literature* 84, no. 4 (2012): 743–68. For comparisons with other examples of Black literature, see Caitlin O'Neill, "'The Shape of Mystery': The Visionary Resonance of Harriet Jacobs's *Incidents in the Life of a Slave Girl*," *Journal of American Culture* 41, no. 1 (2018): 56–67.

64. P. Gabrielle Foreman, for instance, suggests that "Dr. Norcom did rape Jacobs, rather than that Linda triumphed over Dr. Flint, not only in her material escape, but in her sexual one" (P. Gabrielle Foreman, "Manifest in Signs: The Politics of Sex and Representation in *Incidents in the Life of a Slave Girl*," in Garfield and Zafar,

Critical Essays, 77). See also Novian Whitsitt, "Reading between the Lines: The Black Cultural Tradition of Masking in Harriet Jacobs's *Incidents in the Life of a Slave Girl*," *Frontiers: A Journal of Women Studies,* 31, no. 1 (2010) 73–88.

65. mockery: Foreman, "Manifest in Signs," 82; outrage, resistance: Melissa Daniels-Rauterkus, "Civil Resistance and Procreative Agency in Harriet Jacobs' *Incidents in the Life of a Slave Girl*," *Women's Studies* 48, no. 5 (2019): 498–509; Elizabeth Spelman, "The Heady Political Life of Compassion," in McKay and Foster, *Contexts*, 359–64; Clarence W. Tweedy, "Splitting the 'I': (Re)reading the Traumatic Narrative of Black Womanhood in the Autobiographies of Harriet Jacobs and Elizabeth Keckley," *Making Connections: Interdisciplinary Approaches to Cultural Diversity,* Spring (2011): 20–30; romanticizing: Henderson, *Scarring the Black Body*, 50–51; Hopkins, "Seduction or Rape," 11; Foster, "Resisting Incidents," 62.

66. shield: Sandra Gunning, "Reading and Redemption in *Incidents in the Life of a Slave Girl*," in McKay and Foster, *Contexts*, 335–36.

67. contents: LMC to Lucy Searle, 22 August 1861, Child, *CC*, 1327; LMC to Sarah Shaw, [February-March? 1861], Child, *CC*, 1298. Child also helped Jacobs try to locate her missing son in Australia: LMC to John Fraser, 20 November 1866, Child, *CC*, 1746.

68. On the author-editor relationship, Foster, for instance, writes: "That she consulted with and sometimes accepted the advice of her editor should pose no more serious concerns about authorship for Jacobs's text than it does for D. H. Lawrence's *Sons and Lovers*, certain poems signed by T. S. Eliot, or virtually any book authored by Thomas Wolfe. Neither the decision to publish the book anonymously, the reputation of Lydia Maria Child, nor the generic modifications and innovations such as changing names and creating dialogue in an autobiography account sufficiently for the resistance that *Incidents* continues to encounter" (Foster, "Resisting Incidents," 68).

69. did not: Hopkins, "Seduction or Rape," 8; Sinha, *Slave's Cause*, 457.

70. sent books: LMC to John Greenleaf Whittier, 4 April 1861, Child, *SL*, 378; copies: Yellin, *Harriet Jacobs*, 146; signed: Foster, "Resisting Incidents," 66; truly is: Yellin, *Harriet Jacobs Family Papers*, 284.

71. reviews: Yellin, *Harriet Jacobs*, 146–47.

72. market: LMC to Lucy Searle, 4 February 1861, Child, *CC*, 1282.

73. See especially Hopkins, "Seduction or Rape," 8–11.

74. good faith: Tricomi, "Harriet Jacobs' Autobiography," 245.

75. For concerns about the overexposing of *Incidents*, see Rafia Zafar, "Introduction: Over-exposed, Under-exposed: Harriet Jacobs and *Incidents in the Life of a Slave Girl*," in Garfield and Zafar, *Critical Essays*, 2, 5–7, and Garfield, "Conclusion: Vexed Alliances: Race and Female Collaborations in the Life of Harriet Jacobs," in Garfield and Zafar, *Critical Essays*, 287–89; imagined: Yellin, *Harriet Jacobs*, 126.

76. interfere: Abraham Lincoln, *The Collected Works of Abraham Lincoln*, ed. Roy P. Basler, 8 vols. (Ann Arbor: University of Michigan Digital Library Production Services, 2001), 4:250.

77. Sawyer: "SAWYER, Samuel Tredwell: 1800–1865," *Biographical Dictionary of the United States Congress*, https://bioguide.congress.gov/search/bio/S000093; curse:

LMC to Lydia Bigelow Child, 5 November 1861, Child, *CC*, 1343; suffer: LMC to Oliver Johnson, 3 June 1861, Child, *CC*, 1310.

Chapter Twelve

1. Abraham Lincoln to Horace Greely, 22 August 1862, Abraham Lincoln, *The Collected Works of Abraham Lincoln*, ed. Roy P. Basler, 8 vols. (Ann Arbor: University of Michigan Digital Library Production Services, 2001), 5:388–89.

2. hand: Chandra Manning, *Troubled Refuge: Struggling for Freedom in the Civil War* (New York: Alfred A. Knopf, 2016), 168.

3. swampland: Amy Murrell Taylor, *Embattled Freedom: Journeys through the Civil War's Slave Refugee Camps* (Chapel Hill: University of North Carolina Press, 2018), 3; teach them: Guelzo, *Emancipation Proclamation*, 17; commanded: Manning, *Troubled Refuge*, 167.

4. tyrants: LMC to Sarah Shaw, 5 May 1861, Child, *CC*, 1305.

5. balmy evening, dress: Mary Trageser, *Wayland and the Civil War* (Wayland, MA: Wayland Historical Society, 1961), 2, 4.

6. rattlesnake: LMC to Sarah Shaw, 5 May 1861, Child, *CC*, 1305; Union: LMC to Lucy Osgood, 7 May 1861, Child, *SL*, 381.

7. humanity: LMC to Lucy Searle, 5 June 1861, Child, *CC*, 1311; defeats: LMC to Henrietta Sargent, 26 July 1861, Child, *CC*, 1321; son to war: LMC to Lucy Osgood, 7 May 1861, Child, *SL*, 381; Waylanders: Trageser, "Wayland and the Civil War," 9.

8. Quartermaster: Manning, *Troubled Refuge*, 172.

9. receipts: Guelzo, *Emancipation Proclamation*, 30; oath: Manning, *Troubled Refuge*, 172.

10. contraband: Guelzo, *Emancipation Proclamation*, 30.

11. not an abolitionist: Taylor, *Embattled Freedom*, 3; Guelzo, *Emancipation Proclamation*, 29; Fort Monroe: Taylor, *Embattled Freedom*, 61; food: Taylor, *Embattled Freedom*, 140ff.

12. caps and books: LMC to Lydia Parker, 5 November 1861, Child, *CC*, 1345; Queen Victoria: LMC to Helen Frances Garrison, 5 November 1861, *SL,* 397–98.

13. chairs: LMC to Gerrit Smith, 7 January 1862, Child, *CC*, 1364; projects: LMC to Francis Shaw, 28 January 1862, Child, *SL*, 401. The use of "creatures" here, however sympathetically intended, prophesied a paternalism toward freedpeople, also among Black reformers, that would infect Northerners' attitudes at every step. This is also true of initially affectionate but ultimately derogatory terms like "Sambo," which Child also sometimes used. As the term took on its explicitly derogatory sense, her use of it, in my estimation, decreased. See, for instance, LMC to James Thomas Fields, 23 August 1865, Child, *CC*, 1678; Jacobs, "Life among the Contrabands," *Liberator*, 5 September 1862.

14. other way: LMC to Lydia Bigelow Child, 3 October 1862, Child, *CC*, 1432.

15. overconfident: Guelzo, *Emancipation Proclamation*, 35; not a short war: Barnet Schecter, *The Devil's Own Work: The Civil War Draft Riots and the Fight to Reconstruct America* (New York: Walker, 2005), 80; heart bleeds: LMC to Henrietta Sar-

gent, 26 July 1861, Child, *CC*, 1321; ruins: LMC to John Greenleaf Whittier, 21 January 1862, Child, *CC*, 1370.

16. federal property: Guelzo, *Emancipation Proclamation*, 38.

17. iniquity: LMC to Sarah Shaw, 15 December 1861, Child, *CC*, 1356.

18. free men: Guelzo, *Emancipation Proclamation*, 45.

19. report: LMC to Lucy Osgood, 1 September 1861, Child, *CC*, 1330.

20. slave states: Guelzo, *Emancipation Proclamation*, 31–32; dragged: Guelzo, *Emancipation Proclamation*, 50.

21. bomb-shell: LMC to Sarah Shaw, 24 November 1861, Child, *CC*, 1350; hanging: LMC to Mary Stearns, 30 January 1862, Child, *CC*, 1375; careful not to say: LMC to Sarah Shaw, 24 November 1861, Child, *CC*, 1350.

22. Shaw: Russell Duncan, ed. *Blue-Eyed Child of Fortune: The Civil War Letters of Robert Gould Shaw* (Athens: University of Georgia Press, 1999), 14; weak: LMC to Sarah Shaw, 24 November 1861, Child, *CC*, 1350.

23. Thanksgiving: LMC to Lucy Osgood, 1 December 1861, Child, *CC*, 1353; read aloud: LMC to Sarah Shaw, 15 December 1861, Child, *CC*, 1356; straps: LMC to Mary Stearns, 15 December 1961, Child, *SL*, 399; Jacobs: LMC to Robert Folger Walcutt, 15 December 1861, Child, *CC*, 1358.

24. example: LMC to Lydia Bigelow Child, 5 November 1861, Child, *CC*, 1343.

25. fair: LMC to Anna Loring, 15 January 1863, Child, *CC*, 1455; coppery: LMC to William Lloyd Garrison, 8 February 1864, Child, *CC*, 1532; kill: LMC to Lucy Osgood, 20 April 1862, Child, *CC*, 1403.

26. elm tree: LMC to Sarah Shaw, 14 July 1862, Child, *CC*, 1413; torturing: LMC to Gerrit Smith, 7 January 1862, Child, *CC*, 1364; body carried past: LMC in *New York Tribune* [before 5 April 1862], Child, *CC*, 1400; gentlemanly: LMC to Sarah Shaw, 9 June 1862, Child, *CC*, 1413.

27. beautiful: LMC to Lucy Searle, 3 April 1862, Child, *CC*, 1399; mourning: LMC to Henrietta Sargent, 21 August 1862, Child, *CC*, 1424; feebler, Switzerland: LMC to Sarah Shaw, [after January 8? 1862], Child, *CC*, 1368; Tubman: LMC to John Greenleaf Whittier, 21 January 1862, Child, *CC*, 1370.

28. Black woman: LMC to Henrietta Sargent, 21 August 1862, Child, *CC*, 1424.

29. Hunter: Guelzo, *Emancipation Proclamation*, 73–74; Phelps: John David Smith, ed., *Black Soldiers in Blue: African American Troops in the Civil War Era* (Chapel Hill: University of North Carolina Press, 2005), 22.

30. widely published: Karcher, *First Woman*, 460; Lincoln: LMC to Abraham Lincoln, in *NASS*, 6 September 1862, Child, *CC*, 1426.

31. moral bayonet: LMC in *NASS*, 28 March 1868, Child, *CC*, 1822.

32. Maryland: Mayer, *All on Fire*, 541; emancipation: Gideon Welles, *Diary of Gideon Welles: Secretary of the Navy under Lincoln and Johnson* (Boston: Houghton Mifflin, 1911), 1:142–43, Hathi Trust; Guelzo, *Emancipation Proclamation*, 151–56.

33. Frederick Douglass, however, immediately saw the September Proclamation as the beginning of the end of slavery. See Blight, *Frederick Douglass*, 379. On emancipation as a military necessity, see Guelzo, *Emancipation Proclamation*, 207–8, 210–12.

34. "Address on Colonization to a Deputation of Negroes": Lincoln, *The Collected Works of Abraham Lincoln*, 5:370–75. For details about this meeting and emigration proposals, including among Black Americans, see Kate Masur, "The African American Delegation to Abraham Lincoln: A Reappraisal," *Civil War History* 56, no. 2 (2010): 117–44.

35. Black leaders: Jackson, *Force and Freedom*, 150–54; Masur, "African American Delegation to Abraham Lincoln, 119ff., 137–38; Sinha, *Slave's Cause*, 330–38; appease: Blight, *Frederick Douglass*, 373; Douglass: Frederick Douglass, "Colonization," *North Star*, 26 January 1849; "Preliminary Emancipation Proclamation," Lincoln, *Collected Works of Abraham Lincoln*, 5:433–36.

36. jubilant, deeper game: LMC to Henrietta Sargent, 30 September 1862, Child, *CC*, 1429; meanest tools: LMC in *Liberator*, 19 February 1864, Child, *CC*, 1538; no emancipation: Mayer, *All on Fire*, 542; rumor: Karcher, *First Woman*, 463.

37. bandages: LMC to Sarah Shaw, 9 June 1862, Child, *CC*, 1413.

38. Haskins: LMC to William Lloyd Garrison Haskins, 28 December 1862, Child, *SL*, 423–25.

39. Haskins: LMC to William Lloyd Garrison Haskins, 30 April 1863, Child, *SL*, 427–28.

40. Tremont Temple: Blight, *Frederick Douglass*, 382; Music Hall: Mayer, *All on Fire*, 545.

41. song: Blight, *Frederick Douglass*, 383.

42. tears: LMC to Sarah Shaw, 4 January 1863, Child, *CC*, 1450.

43. rights: LMC in *Liberator*, 19 February 1864, Child, *CC*, 1538.

44. small: LMC in *Liberator*, 19 February 1864, Child, *CC*, 1538; Fort Monroe: Taylor, *Embattled Freedom*, 55.

45. curls, fall: LMC to Sarah Shaw, 4 January 1863, Child, *CC*, 1450.

46. blessings: LMC to John Weiss, 15 April 1863, Child, *SL*, 426; opium: LMC to Lucy Osgood, 5 April 1864, Child, *SL*, 442; tore: LMC to Sarah Shaw, [April?] 1863, Child, *CC*, 1478; past sixty: LMC to Elizabeth Cady Stanton, 24 May 1863, Child, *SL*, 431.

47. mouth: LMC to Parke Godwin, 13 December 1864, Child, *CC*, 1605; old: LMC to Messrs. Ticknor and Fields, 22 January 1863, Child, *CC*, 1458.

48. chew: Lydia Maria Child, *Looking toward Sunset: From Sources New and Old, Original and Selected* (Boston: Ticknor and Fields, 1865), 431, Internet Archive; bald, Child, *Looking toward Sunset*, 238.

49. Ole Bull: LMC to Marianne Silsbee, 6 January 1860, Child, *CC*, 1176; playthings: Sarah Shaw to LMC, [21? June 1863], Child, *CC*, 1485.

50. I do: Duncan, *Blue-Eyed Child of Fortune*, 12–13; hand-delivered, Duncan, *Blue-Eyed Child of Fortune*, 22–23.

51. discipline: Duncan, *Blue-Eyed Child of Fortune*, 32–37; Delany: Jackson, *Force and Freedom*, 155.

52. punishment: Duncan, *Blue-Eyed Child of Fortune*, 32–33.

53. largest: Duncan, *Blue-Eyed Child of Fortune*, 1. For accounts of this parade, see Peter Burchard, *"We'll Stand by the Union": Robert Gould Shaw and the Black 54th Massachusetts Regiment* (New York: Facts on File, 1993), 72–75; Duncan, *Blue-Eyed*

Child of Fortune, 39–41; Peter Burchard, *One Gallant Rush: Robert Gould Shaw and His Brave Black Regiment* (New York: St. Martin's Press, 1965), 92–95.

54. playthings: LMC to Sarah Shaw, 14 July 1863, Child, *CC*, 1489.

55. weak: LMC to Francis Shaw, 25 June 1863, Child, *CC*, 1486.

56. sent it back: LMC to Sarah Shaw, 14 July 1863, Child, *CC*, 1489; LMC to Francis Shaw, [25 July 1863?], Child, *CC*, 1492.

57. Edson Davis: Edmund H. Sears, Lafayette Dudley, and James S. Draper, eds., *The Town of Wayland in the Civil War of 1861–1865, as Represented in the Army and Navy of the American Union* (Wayland, MA: Rand, Avery, and Frye, 1871), 148, 153–54, Internet Archive; Sumner Davis: Sears, Dudley, and Draper, *Town of Wayland*, 160; Wellington: Sears, Dudley, and Draper, *Town of Wayland*, 433–34.

58. "Star Spangled Banner": Alfred Wayland Cutting, *Old-Time Wayland* (Boston: Privately printed, 1926), 47.

59. peril: LMC to Sarah and Francis Shaw, 17 July 1863, Child, *CC*, 1490. For accounts of the Draft Riots, see Schecter, *Devil's Own Work*, 125–252; Iver Bernstein, *The New York City Draft Riots: Their Significance for American Society and Politics in the Age of the Civil War* (New York: Oxford University Press, 1990), 17–42.

60. choice: Russell Duncan, *Where Death and Glory Meet: Colonel Robert Gould Shaw and the 54th Massachusetts Infantry* (Athens: University of Georgia Press, 1999), 110; all night: Burchard, *"We'll Stand by the Union,"* 87.

61. symbolism: Duncan, *Blue-Eyed Child of Fortune*, 51.

62. as another: Duncan, *Death and Glory*, 110; next fight: Duncan, *Blue-Eyed Child of Fortune*, 51.

63. battle: Luis F. Emilio, *History of the Fifty-Fourth Regiment of the Massachusetts Volunteer Infantry, 1863–1865* (Boston: Boston Book Company, 1891), 89–95, Internet Archive; Burchard, *One Gallant Rush*, 130–40; Duncan, *Blue-Eyed Child of Fortune*, 52–54.

64. separate grave: Burchard, *"We'll Stand by the Union,"* 95; Emilio, *History of the Fifty-Fourth Regiment*, 102; elsewhere: LMC in *NASS*, 22 August 1863, Child, *CC*, 1499; burial place: Duncan, *Blue-Eyed Child of Fortune*, 54.

65. heart: LMC to Sarah Shaw, 25 July 1863, Child, *SL*, 433.

66. anxiety: LMC to Anna Loring, 9 August 1863, Child, *CC*, 1494. Some information about their fates is at Emilio, *History of the Fifty-Fourth Regiment*, 97.

67. write to: LMC to Lucy Searle, 21 December 1862, Child, *CC*, 1443; misery: Harriet Jacobs to LMC, 18 March [1863], in Yellin, *Harriet Jacobs Family Papers*, 468; rags: Yellin, *Harriet Jacobs*, 159.

68. letter: Harriet Jacobs and L. Jacobs to LMC, 26 March 1864, printed in *NASS*, 16 April 1864, Child, *CC*, 1552; Jacobs School: Yellin, *Harriet Jacobs*, 178.

69. goodness: Abraham Lincoln to A. G. Hodges, 4 April 1864, in Abraham Lincoln, *The Collected Works of Abraham Lincoln,* ed. Roy P. Basler, 8 vols. (Ann Arbor: University of Michigan Digital Library Production Services, 2001), 7:281–82.

70. unaffected: LMC to Sarah Shaw, [May-June 1864], Child, *CC*, 1570; best man: LMC in *Liberator*, 19 February 1864, Child, *CC*, 1538; deserve: LMC to Sarah Shaw, 18 May 1862, Child, *CC*, 1410.

71. never dreaded: LMC to Lucy Osgood, 21 March 1864, Child, *CC*, 1551.

72. rout: Smith, *Black Soldiers in Blue*, 58–60.

73. all right: Frank Draper to family, 3 August 1864, Wayland Historical Society, "Massachusetts Towns in the Civil War," http://www.msp.umb.edu/localmodels /Wayland/CivilWar/Petersburgbattle.html.

74. up at night: LMC to Eliza Scudder, 3 August 1864, Child, *CC*, 1578; heart: LMC to Sarah Shaw, [February? 1864], Child, *CC*, 1547a.

75. Richmond: LMC to John Fraser, 10 November 1864, Child, *SL*, 448; better: LMC to Eliza Scudder, 14 November 1864, Child, *CC*, 1593.

76. *Looking toward Sunset*: Karcher, *First Woman*, 481.

77. giving: LMC to Anna (Loring) Dresel, 18 January 1865, Child, *CC*, 1619.

78. sure end: LMC to Sarah Shaw, [after 15 April] 1865, Child, *SL*, 453.

79. Yet: LMC to Sarah Shaw, [after 15 April] 1865, Child, *SL*, 454.

80. fireworks: Sears, Dudley, and Draper, *Wayland in the Civil War*, 452; Wellington: Sears, Dudley, and Draper, *Wayland in the Civil War*, 438; possible: Trageser, "Wayland and the Civil War," 9; four million: Jackson, *Force and Freedom*, 156; bonnet: LMC to Annie Fields, 9 February 1865, Child, *CC*, 1631.

Chapter Thirteen

1. thankful: LMC in *NASS*, 12 December 1868, Child, *CC*, 1862; emphasis added.

2. exultation: LMC to Sarah Shaw, 11 August 1865, Child, *SL,* 458; trembling: LMC to Lucy Osgood, 13 April 1865, Child, *SL*, 451; bonnet: LMC to Eliza Scudder, 13 November 1865, Child, *CC*, 1692.

3. In 1935, W. E. B. Du Bois chronicled the lessons of Reconstruction as traditionally taught in US history courses: Reconstruction was described as having failed owing to Black Americans' inability to govern themselves. In documenting instead the systematic obstruction and violence Black Americans faced from white Americans determined to prevent them from being full citizens, Du Bois's pathbreaking work is a refutation of that narrative. See W. E. B. Du Bois, *Black Reconstruction in America* (1935; reprint, New York: Free Press, 1992), especially chap. 7.

4. one year: Eric Foner, *Reconstruction: America's Unfinished Revolution, 1863–1877* (San Francisco: Harper and Row, 1988), 69.

5. restrictions: Foner, *Reconstruction*, 185, 254; Eric Foner, *The Second Founding: How the Civil War and Reconstruction Remade the Constitution* (New York: W. W. Norton, 2019), 38.

6. apology: S. Con. Res. 26–"A concurrent resolution apologizing for the enslavement and racial segregation of African Americans" (2009).

7. rights: Foner, *Second Founding*, 6, 13; expel: Foner, *Reconstruction*, 50.

8. farms: Manning, *Troubled Refuge*, 80–84.

9. land: LMC to Lucy Osgood, 13 April 1865, Child, *SL*, 452; distribute: LMC to Abigail (Kelley) Foster, 28 March 1869, Child, *SL*, 485; LMC to Anna (Loring) Dresel, 12 August 1868, Child, *CC*, 1844; purpose: LMC to Francis Shaw, 1 October 1865, Child, *CC*, 1682; counterfeit: LMC to Louisa Loring, 12 February 1867,

Child, *CC*, 1763; mended: LMC to Henrietta Sargent, 16 March 1868, Child, *CC*, 1818.

10. education: Foner, *Reconstruction*, 96–100; Jacobs: Yellin, *Harriet Jacobs*, 186; Douglass: LMC in *NASS*, 16 April 1864, Child, *CC*, 1552; seeds: LMC to Lucy Osgood, 1 April 1866, Child, *CC*, 1715.

11. ways and means: LMC to Sarah Shaw, 3 September 1865, Child, *CC*, 1680.

12. encourage: Lydia Maria Child, *The Freedmen's Book* (Boston: Ticknor and Fields, 1865), 269.

13. *Freedmen's Third Reader*: Karcher, *First Woman*, 502; see also Anna Stewart, "Revising 'Harriet Jacobs' for 1865," *American Literature* 82, no. 4 (2010): 704–5; rare indeed: Foner, *Reconstruction*, 146.

14. LMC to Lucy Osgood, 19 June 1864, Child, *CC*, 1568; cabin: Child, *Freedmen's Book*, 271.

15. great privilege: Child, *Freedmen's Book*, 270.

16. vex: Child, *Freedmen's Book*, 273.

17. glory: Child, *Freedmen's Book*, 218.

18. visit: Frederick Douglass to LMC, 30 July 1865, Child, *CC*, 1673.

19. visit: Douglass, *Autobiographies*, 874–78.

20. Freedmen's Bureau: Foner, *Reconstruction*, 155.

21. cotton: Manning, *Troubled Refuge*, 80, 83; what was the use: Foner, *Reconstruction*, 138; refuse to sign: Foner, *Reconstruction*, 105; labor conditions: Heather Cox Richardson, *West from Appomattox: The Reconstruction of American after the Civil War* (New Haven, CT: Yale University Press, 2007), 61ff. See also Du Bois's analysis of labor conditions and their effect on Reconstruction in Du Bois, *Black Reconstruction*, especially chaps. 10–12.

22. Black Codes: Foner, *Reconstruction*, 199–201; Heather Cox Richardson, *The Death of Reconstruction: Race, Labor, and Politics in the Post–Civil War North, 1865–1901* (2004), 17–19, ProQuest Ebook Central; capitalists: Foner, *Reconstruction*, 220. See also Richardson, *Death of Reconstruction*, 9–14, 22–23.

23. violence: Foner, *Reconstruction*, 119–23; Du Bois, *Black Reconstruction*, e.g., 670–90; legal and social: Foner, *Reconstruction*, 471; Richardson, *West from Appomattox*, 69; meaning: Foner, *Reconstruction*, 244.

24. treason: Foner, *Reconstruction*, 177; Moses: Foner, *Reconstruction*, 183.

25. fighting masters: Foner, *Reconstruction*, 44; Johnson: Foner, *Reconstruction*, 159, 180, 191; Richardson, *Death of Reconstruction*, 15–17; braying ass: LMC to Sarah Shaw, 7 September 1866, Child, *CC*, 1738; Moses: LMC in *Independent*, 29 February 1866, Child, *CC*, 1710.

26. traitors: LMC in *Independent*, 5 April 1866, Child, *CC*, 1716. On Jacobs's work in the South, see also Fionnghuala Sweeney, "Letters From 'Linda Brent': Harriet Jacobs and the Work of Emancipation," in *The Edinburgh Companion to Nineteenth-Century American Letters and Letter-Writing*, ed. Celeste-Marie Bernier, Judie Newman, and Matthew Pethers (Edinburgh: Edinburgh University Press, 2016).

27. Johnson's policy, masters loose: LMC in *Independent*, 5 April 1866, Child, *CC*, 1716; lack of retribution: Foner, *Reconstruction*, 121; Memphis: Gregory P. Downs, *After*

Appomattox: Military Occupation and the Ends of War (Cambridge, MA: Harvard University Press, 2015), 128; New Orleans: Downs, *After Appomattox*, 149; rage: LMC to Maria Weston Chapman, 9 June 1867, Child, *CC*, 1778.

28. Lewis: LMC in *NASS*, 14 January 1865, Child, *CC*, 1616.

29. vain: LMC to Sarah Shaw, [August? 1870], Child, *CC*, 1958; grown: LMC to Sarah Shaw, 8 April 1866, Child, *CC*, 1717.

30. copy: LMC to Sarah Shaw, [August?] 1870, Child, *CC*, 1958; tooth: LMC to Harriett Sewall, 24 June 1868, Child, *CC*, 1839; Italy: LMC to James Thomas Fields, 13 October 1865, Child, *CC*, 1685.

31. statues: LMC to Sarah Shaw, [August] 1870, Child, *CC*, 1958; Philadelphia: Kirsten Pai Buick, *Child of the Fire: Mary Edmonia Lewis and the Problem of Art History's Black and Indian Subject* (Durham, NC: Duke University Press, 2010), 186–87; Lincoln: Buick, *Child of the Fire*, 22–24; Longfellow: Buick, *Child of the Fire*, 88; also Karcher, *First Woman*, 726. Buick describes Child's efforts on Lewis's behalf at Buick, *Child of the Fire*, 11–18, emphasizing that though Child came to be very critical of Lewis in her letters, she never criticized her publicly.

32. varnishing: LMC to Theodore Tilton, 27 May 1866, Child, *SL*, 460; dark: LMC to Eliza Scudder, 13 May 1867, Child, *CC*, 1773; sprain: LMC to Lucy Osgood, 14 January 1866, Child, *CC*, 1701; woodpile, herbs: LMC to Eliza Scudder, 29 November 1867, Child, *CC*, 1800; cistern: LMC to Eliza Scudder, 13 May 1867, Child, *CC*, 1773; cider: LMC to Lydia Bigelow Child, 18 October 1867, Child, *CC*, 1795; singing: LMC to Lucy Osgood, [November ? 1866?], Child, *CC*, 1748; aqueducts: Cutting, *Old-Time Wayland*, 46.

33. stiff: LMC to [James Thomas] Fields, 19 October 1865, Child, *CC*, 1686.

34. torturing: LMC to Eliza Scudder, 11 August 1867, Child, *CC*, 1791.

35. called it: Lydia Maria Child, *A Romance of the Republic*, ed. Dana D. Nelson (1867; reprint, Lexington: University Press of Kentucky, 1997).

36. cataloged: LMC to Louisa Loring, 1 January 1868, Child, *CC*, 1806; *Uncle Tom's Cabin*: Karcher, *First Woman*, 531; advertising: LMC to Theodore Tilton, 27 October 1867, Child, *CC*, 1797.

37. disappointment, pen to paper: LMC to Louisa Loring, 1 January 1868, Child, *CC*, 1806; never expect: LMC to Eliza Scudder, 10 July 1870, Child, *CC*, 1952.

38. blame: Lydia Maria Child, "An Appeal for the Indians," in *A Lydia Maria Child Reader*, ed. Carolyn Karcher (Durham, NC: Duke University Press, 1997), 223; younger: Child, "Appeal for the Indians," 220.

39. For this history, see David Wallace Adams, *Education for Extinction: American Indians and the Boarding School Experience, 1875–1928* (Lawrence: University Press of Kansas, 1995), chaps. 2–4. For an account of Native American parents' resistance, see 211ff.

40. Sarah Brown to LMC, 2 March 1869, Child, *CC*, 1887.

41. autographs: LMC to Sarah Parsons, 1 March 1871, Child, *CC*, 1984; LMC to Emily F. Damon, 16 February 1878, Child, *CC*, 2368; hates writing: LMC to Harriet Sewall, 19 June 1871, Child, *CC*, 1998.

42. policy: LMC to Samuel E. Sewall, 21 March 1868, Child, *SL*, 478.

43. Civil Rights Bill: Foner, *Reconstruction,* 243–51; thank God: LMC to Sarah Shaw, 8 April 1866, Child, *CC,* 1717.

44. suffrage: William Lloyd Garrison, speech recorded in *NASS,* 20 May 1865; Douglass: Blight, *Frederick Douglass,* 477; vital question: LMC in *NASS,* 23 May 1868, Child, *CC,* 1831.

45. vote: Foner, *Second Founding,* 40–41; loyal men: LMC to Lucy Osgood, 4 February 1869, Child, *SL,* 484; punish: Richardson, *Death of Reconstruction,* 32.

46. century: Ellen Carol DuBois, *Feminism and Suffrage: The Emergence of an Independent Women's Movement in America, 1848–1869* (Ithaca, NY: Cornell University Press, 1978), 61.

47. Harper: hooks, *Ain't I a Woman,* 168–71; Jones, *Vanguard,* 111–17; AERA: Rosalyn Terborg-Penn, *African American Women and the Struggle for the Vote, 1850–1920* (Bloomington: Indiana University Press, 1998), 24; DuBois, *Feminism and Suffrage,* 65–71; Constitution: Stanton, Anthony, and Gage, *History of Woman Suffrage,* 173.

48. condescend: LMC to Elizabeth Cady Stanton, [before 6 December 1866], Child, *SL,* 467–68.

49. individual: LMC in *Independent,* 10 January 1867, Child, *CC,* 1759.

50. miserable: LMC to Eliza Scudder, 13 May 1867, Child, *CC,* 1773; cheerfulness: LMC to Sarah Shaw, 18 February 1868, Child, *CC,* 1815.

51. prism: Cutting, *Old-Time Wayland,* 48–49; roses: Cutting, *Old-Time Wayland,* 42.

52. German: LMC to Eliza Scudder, 29 November 1867, Child, *CC,* 1800; kiss: LMC to Harriet Sewall, 5 January 1869, Child, *CC,* 1868; children: LMC to John Greenleaf Whittier, 18 June 1874, Child, *CC,* 2156; talked about: LMC to Susan Brownell Anthony, 25 January 1877, Child, *CC,* 2301.

53. duty: LMC to Sarah Shaw, 12 December 1871, Child, *CC,* 2018.

54. Negro's Hour: Foner, *Second Founding,* 81; DuBois, *Feminism and Suffrage,* 59; wait: LMC in *Independent,* 10 January 1867, Child, *CC,* 1759.

55. didn't: LMC in *National Standard,* 27 May 1871, Child, *CC,* 1995a. The *National Anti-Slavery Standard* had renamed itself the *National Standard* in 1870.

56. close vote: Faye E. Dudden, *Fighting Chance: The Struggle over Woman Suffrage and Black Suffrage* (New York: Oxford University Press, 2011), 162, ProQuest Ebook Central. For an economic explanation of the need for suffrage, see Richardson, *Death of Reconstruction,* 44ff.

57. Chinese, Irish: Foner, *Second Founding,* 101–2.

58. in print: LMC in *Independent,* 10 January 1867, Child, *CC,* 1759.

59. Stanton: editorial, *Revolution* 2, no. 25, 24 December 1868.

60. outrages: Foner, *Second Founding,* 113; Dudden, *Fighting Chance,* 169.

61. learned: LMC to Sarah Shaw, [September? 1869], Child, *SL,* 486–87.

62. Harper: Dudden, *Fighting Chance,* 85, 179; Terborg-Penn, *African American Women and the Struggle for the Vote,* 32 ff.; Jones, *Vanguard,* 95, 116–17; May 1869 meeting: Dudden, *Fighting Chance,* 177 ff.; Stone and AWSA: Dudden, *Fighting Chance,* 181.

63. battling: LMC to Sarah Shaw, [September? 1869], Child, *SL*, 486; convention: LMC to Caroline Maria Severance in *NASS*, 16 October 1868, Child, *CC*, 1859a; perfect equality: LMC in *Independent*, 15 July 1869, Child, *CC*, 1903.

64. narrowest: Dudden, *Fighting Chance*, 173.

65. Senate: LMC to Henrietta Sargent, 17 August 1870, Child, *CC*, 1955.

66. antislavery troop: LMC to Lucy Osgood, 14 February 1870, Child, *CC*, 1928.

67. biographies: May, *Some Recollections;* Higginson, "Lydia Maria Child"; Barnum: LMC to Marianne Silsbee, 23 August 1871, Child, *CC*, 2009; confusion: LMC to Lucy Osgood, 14 February 1870, Child, *CC*, 1928.

68. Howe: Charles K. Whipple, "Annual Meeting of the Massachusetts Anti-Slavery Society," *NASS*, 5 February 1870.

69. make much of: LMC to Lucy Osgood, 14 February 1870, Child, *CC*, 1928.

70. ovations: LMC to Lucy Osgood, 14 February 1870, Child, *SL*, 490.

71. martial law: Foner, *Reconstruction*, 457; Du Bois, *Black Reconstruction*, 683; victims: LMC in *National Standard*, 8 April 1871, Child, *CC*, 1989a.

72. In fact, there had been an earlier *Representative Women* lithograph in 1857 that had included Stone and Foster. Prang, for some reason, chose other figures. Denmark: LMC in *National Standard*, 12 November 1870, Child, *CC*, 1960a.

73. head: LMC to Anne Whitney, 22 May 1878, Child, *SL*, 550.

74. forgotten: LMC to Anne Whitney, 22 May 1878, Child, *SL*, 550.

75. arrow: LMC to Sarah Shaw, 2 April 1874, Child, *CC*, 2146.

76. Hampton: LMC to Sarah Shaw, 27 January 1876, Child, *SL*, 532; Karcher, *First Woman*, 577.

77. patient: LMC to Susan Lesley, 15 June 1873, Child, *CC*, 2105; letters: LMC to Anna (Loring) Dresel, 5 August 1874, Child, *CC*, 2168; lantern: LMC to Sarah Shaw, 30 December 1871, Child, *CC*, 2026.

78. dictionary: LMC to Susan Lesley, 7 October 1874, Child, *CC*, 2187; babe: LMC to Sarah Shaw, 18 September 1874, Child, *SL*, 527.

79. no tongue: LMC to Sarah Shaw, 18 September 1874, Child, *SL*, 527; tenderly: LMC to Lydia Bigelow Child, 24 September 1874, Child, *CC*, 2181.

80. buried: LMC to Sarah Shaw, 18 August 1874, Child, *CC*, 2172.

81. rare: William Lloyd Garrison to LMC, 25 October 1874, Child, *CC*, 2191.

82. Cutting, "Childhood Memories," unpublished paper, original at Wayland Historical Society.

Chapter Fourteen

1. barrels: LMC to Harriet Sewall, 1 July 1875, Child, *CC*, 2241.

2. servants: LMC to Emily F. Damon, 22 December 1874, Child, *CC*, 2206; steamboats: LMC to Abby Bradford Francis, 23 November 1874, Child, *CC*, 2201; Christmas: LMC to Sarah Parsons, 1 January 1875, Child, *CC*, 2211; garden: LMC to Hannah Baldwin, 6 December 1874, Child, *CC*, 2202.

3. tears: LMC to Sarah Shaw, 11 April 1875, Child, *CC*, 2227.

4. better off: LMC to Sarah Shaw, 2 March 1880, Child, *CC*, 2492.

5. near: LMC to Sarah Shaw, 13 May 1875, Child, *CC*, 2232; flowers: LMC to John Burt Wight, 12 December 1874, Child, *CC*, 2204; out of existence: LMC to George William Curtis, 30 October 1874, Child, *CC*, 2193.

6. telephone: LMC to Thomas Wentworth Higginson, 9 September 1877, Child, *CC*, 2340; trance: Ann Braude, *Radical Spirits: Spiritualism and Women's Rights in Nineteenth-Century America* (Bloomington: Indiana University Press, 2001), 85; Garrison: Braude, *Radical Spirits*, 27.

7. frauds: LMC to Sarah Shaw, 13 July 1877, Child, *CC*, 2333; LMC to Sarah Shaw, 22 July 1877, Child, *CC*, 2334; what was it for: LMC to Sarah Shaw, [November?] 1876, Child, *CC*, 2288.

8. like to try: LMC to Francis Shaw, 17 June 1875, Child, *CC*, 2240.

9. truly live: LMC to Sarah Shaw, 13 July 1877, Child, *CC*, 2333.

10. telephone: LMC to Sarah Shaw, 7 July 1877, Child, *CC*, 2331; missed him: LMC to Sarah Parsons, 21 May 1878, Child, *CC*, 2386; duties here: LMC to Sarah Shaw, 13 July 1877, Child, *CC*, 2333.

11. affection: LMC to Sarah Shaw, 9 October 1875, Child, *CC*, 2251.

12. Swedenborg: LMC to Emily F. Damon, 13 February 1877, Child, *CC*, 2305; Japan: LMC to Sarah Wight, 21 February 1878, Child, *CC*, 2370; nebular theory: LMC to Anne Whitney, 19 February 1878, Child, *CC*, 2369; radical: LMC to Sarah Wight, 21 February 1878, Child, *CC*, 2370; Jordan and Marsh: LMC to Anne Whitney, 5 August 1879, Child, *CC*, 2486.

13. Sewalls: LMC to Sarah Shaw, 2 March 1878, Child, *CC*, 2375.

14. Alcotts: LMC to Sarah Shaw, 18 June 1876, Child, *CC*, 2276; next after LMC: Franklin Benjamin Sanborn, *Literary Studies and Criticism: Evaluations of the Writers of the American Renaissance—with Fresh Approaches to Transcendentalism, Literary Influences, New-England Cultural Patterns, and the Creative Experience* (Hartford, CT: Transcendental Books, 1980), 21, Internet Archive.

15. invitations: LMC to Annie Adams Fields, 22 January 1877, Child, *CC*, 2300; women's suffrage, Sarah Russell to LMC, 21 May [1878], Child, *CC*, 2388; Thanksgiving: LMC to Sarah Parsons, 20 November 1878, Child, *CC*, 2415; offending: LMC to Sarah Shaw, 7 July 1877, Child, *CC*, 2331; lasso: LMC to Sarah Shaw, 18 June 1876, Child, *CC*, 2276; ferocious: LMC to Sarah Shaw, 20 March 1879, Child, *SL*, 557.

16. labor: LMC to Sarah Shaw, 31 July 1877, Child, *SL*, 542; Karcher, *First Woman*, 568; immigration: LMC to Sarah Shaw, 14 June 1878, Child, *CC*, 2397; Catholics: LMC in *National Standard,* 10 September 1870, Child, *CC*, 1958a; LMC to Charles Sumner, 4 July 1870, Child, *SL*, 496; LMC to Sarah Shaw, 24 March 1873, Child, *SL*, 512; Black Americans: LMC to Francis Shaw, 26 October 1879, Child, *SL*, 559; LMC to Anna (Loring) Dresel, 11 August 1878, Child, *CC*, 2403.

17. reforms: Stacey M. Robertson, *Parker Pillsbury: Radical Abolitionist, Male Feminist* (Ithaca, NY: Cornell University Press, 2007), 157–79.

18. every Sunday, Phillips: LMC to Sarah Wight, 10 December 1876, Child, *CC*, 2289; gave money: LMC to Richard P. Hallowell, 28 May 1879, Child, *CC*, 2452.

19. academic: LMC to James Thomas Fields, 28 October 1877, Child, *CC*, 2343.

20. growth: Lydia Maria Child, *Aspirations of the World: A Chain of Opals* (Boston: Roberts Brothers, 1878), 42, Internet Archive.

21. Emerson: LMC to James Thomas Fields, 9 June 1878, Child, *CC*, 2395; Garrison: William Lloyd Garrison to LMC, 25 August 1878, Child, *CC*, 2407; daughters: Sarah Russell to LMC, 21 May [1878], Child, *CC*, 2388; power: Anna (Loring) Dresel to LMC, 21 May 1878, Child, *CC*, 2387.

22. forget: Elizabeth Stuart Phelps, *Chapters from a Life* (Boston: Houghton, Mifflin, 1897), 182–85, Internet Archive.

23. visage: LMC to Anne Whitney, 8 April 1877, Child, *CC*, 2317; sane: LMC to Anne Whitney, 27 November 1878, Child, *CC*, 2417.

24. visiting Whitney: LMC to Sarah Shaw, 2 March 1878, Child, *CC*, 2375; Manning: LMC to Anne Whitney, 18 April 1878, Child, *CC*, 2383; Leif: LMC to Anne Whitney, 25 November 1878, Child, *CC*, 2416.

25. soul: LMC to Anne Whitney, 14 August 1878, Child, *CC*, 2406; love: LMC to Anne Whitney, 18 April 1878, Child, *CC*, 2383.

26. Garrison: Mayer, *All on Fire*, 623; Boston Art Committee: Elizabeth Rogers Payne, "Anne Whitney: Art and Social Justice," *Massachusetts Review* 12, no. 2 (1971): 258; legs: "'Prunes and Prisms' in Art," in *National Repository*, ed. Daniel Curry (Cincinnati: Hitchcock and Walden, 1879), 464; jackasses: LMC to Sarah Shaw, [date? 1879], Child, *CC*, 2488.

27. bird: LMC to Anne Whitney, 25 November 1878, Child, *CC*, 2416.

28. leg: LMC to Harriet Sewall, 24 August 1880, Child, *CC*, 2518; hearing: LMC to Sarah Shaw, 2 March 1880, Child, *CC*, 2492; chat: LMC to Sarah Russell, 28 May 1879, Child, *CC*, 2453; election of 1876: Foner, *Reconstruction*, 575–83; Exodus: Foner, *Reconstruction*, 600–601; Richardson, *Death of Reconstruction*, 156ff.

29. higher life: LMC to Sarah Parsons, 20 July 1879, Child, *CC*, 2463.

30. funeral: Mayer, *All on Fire*, 627–28; thrilling, spirit: LMC to Harriet Sewall, 17 June 1879, Child, *CC*, 2458; mediums: LMC to Sarah Russell, 28 May 1879, Child, *CC*, 2453.

31. Whitney's invitation: LMC to Anne Whitney, 28 September 1878, Child, *CC*, 2412; drift: LMC to Harriet Sewall, 24 August 1880, Child, *CC*, 2518; both worlds: Anne Whitney to LMC, 22 September 1880, Child, *CC*, 2521.

32. feeling well: Child, *Letters*, xxiii.

33. rain down: LMC to Sarah Russell, 23 September 1880, Child, *CC*, 2522.

34. heart: Child, *Letters*, xxiii.

35. observed: Helene G. Baer, *The Heart Is Like Heaven: The Life of Lydia Maria Child* (Philadelphia: University of Pennsylvania Press, 1964), appendix.

36. *Framingham Gazette,* 29 October 1880; *Boston Sunday Herald,* 29 October 1880.

37. Phillips: Child, *Letters*, 263–68; miss her: Alfred Wayland Cutting, diary, unpublished, Wayland Historical Society.

38. funeral: Cutting, diary, xxii-xxiii.

39. legacies: Baer, *Heart Is Like Heaven*, 315, appendix; Karcher, *First Woman*, 577.

40. falling asleep: LMC to Sarah Shaw, 22 July 1877, Child, *CC*, 2334; LMC to Anne Whitney, 28 September 1878, Child, *CC*, 2412.

41. renovated powers: LMC to Anne Whitney, 16 July 1880, Child, *CC*, 2511.

Epilogue

1. Here is an inadequate but determined start: Linda Martín Alcoff, "Philosophy and Philosophical Practice: Eurocentrism as an Epistemology of Ignorance," in *Routledge Handbook of Epistemic Injustice*, ed. Gaile Pohlhaus, Jose Medina, and Ian Kidd (New York: Routledge, 2017), 397–408; Patricia Hill Collins, "Learning from the Outsider Within: The Sociological Significance of Black Feminist Thought," *Social Problems* 33, no. 6 (1986): 14–32; Kristie Dotson, "Concrete Flowers: Contemplating the Profession of Philosophy," *Hypatia* 26, no. 2 (2011): 403–9; V. Denise James, "Musing: A Black Feminist Philosopher: Is That Possible?," *Hypatia* 29, no. 1 (2014): 189–95; Charles Mills, "Non-Cartesian *Sums*: Philosophy and the African-American Experience," in Charles Mills, *Blackness Visible: Essays on Philosophy and Race* (Ithaca, NY: Cornell University Press, 1998); Cornel West, *The American Evasion of Philosophy: A Genealogy of Pragmatism* (Madison: University of Wisconsin Press, 1989); Yolonda Y. Wilson, "How Might We Address the Factors That Contribute to the Scarcity of Philosophers Who Are Women and/or of Color?," *Hypatia* 32, no. 4 (2017): 853–61; George Yancy, *Across Black Spaces: Essays and Interviews from an American Philosopher* (New York: Rowman and Littlefield, 2020).

Bibliography

Accomando, Christina. "'The Laws Were Laid Down to Me Anew': Harriet Jacobs and the Reframing of Legal Fictions." In *"Incidents in the Life of a Slave Girl": Contexts, Criticism*, edited by Nellie Y. McKay and Nancy Smith Foster, 365–85. New York: W. W. Norton, 2001.

Adams, David Wallace. *Education for Extinction: American Indians and the Boarding School Experience, 1875–1928.* Lawrence: University Press of Kansas, 1995.

"An Address to Free Colored Americans: Issued by an Anti-Slavery Convention of American Women, Held in the City of New-York, by Adjournments from 9th to 12th May, 1837." New York: William S. Dorr, 1837.

Aiséirithe, A. J., and Donald Yacovone, eds. *Wendell Phillips, Social Justice, and the Power of the Past.* Baton Rouge: Louisiana State University Press, 2016.

Alcoff, Linda Martín. "Philosophy and Philosophical Practice: Eurocentrism as an Epistemology of Ignorance." In *Routledge Handbook of Epistemic Injustice*, edited by Gaile Pohlhaus, Jose Medina, and Ian Kidd, 397–408. New York: Routledge, 2017.

Allen, Francine L. "Sacred and Undesirable: Examining the Theological Import of Hiding Places in Exodus and Harriet Jacobs's *Incidents in the Life of a Slave Girl.*" *Priscilla Papers* 29, no. 3 (2015): 21–27.

Allen, William. *The History of Norridgewock: Comprising Memorials of the Aboriginal Inhabitants and Jesuit Missionaries, Hardships of the Pioneers, Biographical Notices of the Early Settlers, and Ecclesiastical Sketches.* Norridgewock, ME: Edward J. Peet, 1849. Internet Archive.

American Peace Society. *The Advocate of Peace.* Boston: Whipple and Damrell, 1837. Hathi Trust.

"Assignee's Sale." *Hampshire Gazette*, 6 June 1843.

Baer, Helene G. *The Heart Is Like Heaven: The Life of Lydia Maria Child.* Philadelphia: University of Pennsylvania Press, 1964.

Banks, Ronald F. *Maine Becomes a State: The Movement to Separate Maine from Massachusetts, 1785–1820.* Middletown, CT: Wesleyan University Press, 1970.

Beecher, Catharine E. *An Essay on Slavery and Abolitionism, with Reference to the Duties of American Females.* Philadelphia: Henry Parkins, 1837. Internet Archive.

Bellows, Alyssa. "Evangelicalism, Adultery, and *Incidents in the Life of a Slave Girl.*" *Texas Studies in Literature and Language* 62, no. 3 (2020): 253–74.

Bernstein, Iver. *The New York City Draft Riots: Their Significance for American Society and Politics in the Age of the Civil War.* New York: Oxford University Press, 1990.

Blackett, R. J. M. *The Captive's Quest for Freedom: Fugitive Slaves, the 1850 Fugitive Slave Law, and the Politics of Slavery.* Cambridge: Cambridge University Press, 2018.

Blaser, Kent. "North Carolina and John Brown's Raid." *Civil War History* 24, no. 3 (1978): 197–212.

Blassingame, John W. *The Slave Community: Plantation Life in the Antebellum South.* 2nd ed. New York: Oxford University Press, 1979.

Blight, David W. *Frederick Douglass: Prophet of Freedom.* New York: Simon and Schuster, 2018.

Block, Marguerite Beck. *The New Church in the New World: A Study of Swedenborgianism in America.* New York: Octagon Books, 1968.

Bolton, Charles Knowles. *The Athenaeum Centenary: The Influence and History of the Boston Athenaeum from 1807 to 1907.* Boston: Boston Athenæum, 1907.

Bonekemper, Edward H. *The Myth of the Lost Cause: Why the South Fought the Civil War and Why the North Won.* Washington, DC: Regnery History, 2015.

Boston Athenæum, Circulation Department. "Books Borrowed." Archives of the Boston Athenæum, 1827–72.

Braude, Ann. *Radical Spirits: Spiritualism and Women's Rights in Nineteenth-Century America.* Bloomington: Indiana University Press, 2001.

Brooks, Charles, and James M. Usher. *History of the Town of Medford, Middlesex County, Massachusetts, from Its Settlement in 1630 to 1855.* Boston: Rand, Avery, 1886. Internet Archive.

Brown, Ira V. "'Am I Not a Woman and a Sister?' The Anti-Slavery Convention of American Women, 1837–1839." *Pennsylvania History: A Journal of Mid-Atlantic Studies* 50, no. 1 (1983): 19.

Brown, John. "*Provisional Constitution and Ordinances for the People of the United States,* May 8, 1858." In *John Brown's Raid on Harpers Ferry: A Brief History with Documents,* ed. Jonathan Earle (Boston: Bedford/St. Martin's Press, 2008): 65–69.

Browne, Stephen. *Angelina Grimké: Rhetoric, Identity, and the Racial Imagination.* East Lansing: Michigan State University Press, 1999. ACLS Humanities E-book.

Buffum, Arnold. *Constitution of the New-England Anti-Slavery Society, with an Address to the Public.* Boston: Garrison and Knapp, 1832. Internet Archive.

Buick, Kirsten Pai. *Child of the Fire: Mary Edmonia Lewis and the Problem of Art History's Black and Indian Subject*. Durham, NC: Duke University Press, 2010.

Burchard, Peter. *One Gallant Rush: Robert Gould Shaw and His Brave Black Regiment*. New York: St. Martin's Press, 1965.

Burchard, Peter. *"We'll Stand by the Union": Robert Gould Shaw and the Black 54th Massachusetts Regiment*. New York: Facts on File, 1993.

Burnham, Michelle. "Loopholes of Resistance: Harriet Jacobs' Slave Narrative and the Critique of Agency in Foucault." In *"Incidents in the Life of a Slave Girl": Contexts, Criticism*, edited by Nellie Y. McKay and Nancy Smith Foster, 278–94. New York: W. W. Norton, 2001.

Campbell, Stanley W. *The Slave Catchers: Enforcement of the Fugitive Slave Law, 1850–1860*. Chapel Hill: University of North Carolina Press, 1970.

"Case of the Slave-Child, Med: Report of the Arguments of Counsel and of the Opinions of the Court, in the Case of *Commonwealth vs. Ames*; Tried and Determined in the Supreme Court of Massachusetts." Boston, 1836. Internet Archive.

Chambers, Lee V. *The Weston Sisters: An American Abolitionist Family*. Chapel Hill: University of North Carolina Press, 2014.

Chapman, Maria Weston. *Right and Wrong in Massachusetts*. Boston: Dow and Jackson's Anti-Slavery Press, 1839. Internet Archive.

Chapman, Maria Weston. "The Times That Try Men's Souls." In *Second to None: A Document History of American Women*, vol. 1, *From the 16th Century to 1865*, edited by Ruth Barnes Moynihan, Cynthia Russett, and Laurie Crumpacker. Lincoln: University of Nebraska Press, 1993.

Chapman, Maria Weston, et al. *Right and Wrong in Boston: Annual Report of the Boston Female Anti-Slavery Society: With a Sketch of the Obstacles Thrown in the Way by Certain Clerical Abolitionists and Advocates for the Subjection of Women*. Boston: Boston Female Anti-Slavery Society, 1837. Internet Archive.

Chapman, Maria Weston, et al. *Right and Wrong in Boston: Annual Report of the Boston Female Anti-Slavery Society: Being a Concise History of the Slave Child, Med, and of the Women Demanded as Slaves of the Supreme Judicial Court of Mass.* Boston: Boston Female Anti-Slavery Society, 1836. Internet Archive.

Cheathem, Mark R. "Andrew Jackson, Slavery, and Historians." *History Compass* 9, no. 4 (2011): 326–38.

Child, David Lee. *The Culture of the Beet, and Manufacture of Beet Sugar*. Boston: Weeks, Jordan, 1840. Internet Archive.

Child, Lydia Maria. *The American Frugal Housewife: For Those Who Are Not Ashamed of Economy*. 22nd ed. New York: Samuel S. and William Wood, 1839. Internet Archive.

Child, Lydia Maria. "The Anniversary." *National Anti-Slavery Standard*, 19 May 1842.

Child, Lydia Maria. "An Appeal for the Indians." In *A Lydia Maria Child Reader*, edited by Carolyn Karcher, 79–94. Durham, NC: Duke University Press, 1997.

Child, Lydia Maria. *An Appeal in Favor of That Class of Americans Called Africans*. Boston: Allen and Ticknor, 1833. Internet Archive.

Child, Lydia Maria. *Aspirations of the World: A Chain of Opals*. Boston: Roberts Brothers, 1878. Internet Archive.

Child, Lydia Maria, ed. *Authentic Anecdotes of American Slavery*. Newburyport, MA: Charles Whipple, 1835. Internet Archive.

Child, Lydia Maria. *Autumnal Leaves: Tales and Sketches in Prose and Rhyme*. New York: C. S. Francis, 1857. Internet Archive.

Child, Lydia Maria. "Booklet of Quotations and Poems." In *May Anti-Slavery Collection, #4601*: Division of Rare and Manuscript Collections, Cornell University Library, n.d.

Child, Lydia Maria. *Brief History of the Condition of Women, in Various Ages and Nations*. 5th ed. New York: C. S. Francis, 1845. Hathi Trust.

Child, Lydia Maria. *The Collected Correspondence of Lydia Maria Child*. Edited by Patricia G. Holland and Milton Meltzer. Millwood, NY: Kraus Microform, 1980.

Child, Lydia Maria. *Correspondence between Lydia Maria Child and Gov. Wise and Mrs. Mason, of Virginia*. Boston: American Anti-Slavery Society, 1860. Internet Archive.

Child, Lydia Maria. "Duplicity—a Tale from Real Life." In *May Anti-Slavery Collection #4601*: Division of Rare and Manuscript Collections, Cornell University Library, n.d.

Child, Lydia Maria. *The Duty of Disobedience to the Fugitive Slave Act*. Boston: American Anti-Slavery Association, 1860. Internet Archive.

Child, Lydia Maria. *Evenings in New England: Intended for Juvenile Amusement and Instruction. By an American Lady*. Boston: Cummings, Hilliard, 1824. Internet Archive.

Child, Lydia Maria. *The First Settlers of New-England, or Conquest of the Pequods, Narragansets and Pokanokets, as Related by a Mother to Her Children*. Boston: Munroe and Francis, 1829. Internet Archive.

Child, Lydia Maria. "Floral Souvenir Book." Medford Historical Society & Museum, 1855.

Child, Lydia Maria. *Flowers for Children*. Vol. 2, *For Children from Four to Six Years Old*. New York: C. S. Francis, 1844. Internet Archive.

Child, Lydia Maria. *The Freedmen's Book*. Boston: Ticknor and Fields, 1865. Internet Archive.

Child, Lydia Maria. *The Frugal Housewife*. Boston: Marsh and Capen, 1829. Reprint, Kansas City, MO: Andrews McMeel, 2013.

Child, Lydia Maria. "Hair Clippings." In *May Anti-Slavery Collection, #4601*: Division of Rare and Manuscript Collections, Cornell University Library, n.d.

Child, Lydia Maria. *The History of the Condition of Women, in Various Ages and Nations*. Boston: John Allen, 1835. Internet Archive.

Child, Lydia Maria. "*Hobomok*" *and Other Writings on Indians*. Edited by Carolyn Karcher. New York: Rutgers University Press, 1986.

Child, Lydia Maria. *Isaac T. Hopper: A True Life*. Boston: John P. Jewett, 1853. Internet Archive.

Child, Lydia Maria. *The Juvenile Miscellany: For the Instruction and Amusement of Youth*. Vol. 1, no. 1. Boston: John Putnam, 1826. Google Books.

Child, Lydia Maria. *The Juvenile Miscellany: For the Instruction and Amusement of Youth*. Vol. 1, no. 2. Boston: John Putnam, 1826. Google Books.

Child, Lydia Maria. *The Juvenile Miscellany: For the Instruction and Amusement of Youth*. Vol. 1, no. 3. Boston: John Putnam, 1827. Google Books.

Child, Lydia Maria. *The Juvenile Miscellany: Third Series*, vol. 6. Boston: Allen and Ticknor, 1834. Hathi Trust.

Child, Lydia Maria. "The Kansas Emigrants." In *Autumnal Leaves: Tales and Sketches in Prose and Rhyme*, 302–63. New York: C. S. Francis, 1857. Internet Archive.

Child, Lydia Maria. *Letters from New York*. Edited by Bruce Mills. Athens: University of Georgia Press, 1998.

Child, Lydia Maria. *Letters of Lydia Maria Child, with a Biographical Introduction by John G. Whittier and an Appendix by Wendell Phillips*. Boston: Houghton, Mifflin, 1883. Internet Archive.

Child, Lydia Maria. *Looking toward Sunset: From Sources New and Old, Original and Selected*. Boston: Ticknor and Fields, 1865. Internet Archive.

Child, Lydia Maria. *Lydia Maria Child: Selected Letters, 1817–1880*. Edited by Milton Meltzer, Patricia G. Holland, and Francine Krasno. Amherst: University of Massachusetts Press, 1982.

Child, Lydia Maria. "Memorial Book for David Lee Child." In *May Anti-Slavery Collection #4601*: Division of Rare and Manuscript Collections, Cornell University Library, n.d.

Child, Lydia Maria, ed. *The Oasis*. Boston: Benjamin C. Bacon, 1834. Internet Archive.

Child, Lydia Maria, ed. *The Patriarchal Institution, as Described by Members of Its Own Family*. New York: American Anti-Slavery Society, 1860. Internet Archive.

Child, Lydia Maria. *The Progress of Religious Ideas, through Successive Ages*. 3 vols. New York: C. S. Francis, 1855. Internet Archive.

Child, Lydia Maria. *The Right Way, the Safe Way, Proved by Emancipation in the British West Indies, and Elsewhere*. New York: 5 Beekman Street, 1860. Internet Archive.

Child, Lydia Maria. *A Romance of the Republic*. Edited by Dana D. Nelson. 1867. Reprint, Lexington: University Press of Kentucky, 1997.

Child, Lydia Maria. "Speaking in the Church." *National Anti-Slavery Standard*, 15 July 1841, 22.

Claflin, Mary B. *Personal Recollections of John G. Whittier*. New York: Thomas Y. Crowell, 1893. Internet Archive.

Clifford, Deborah Pickman. *Crusader for Freedom: A Life of Lydia Maria Child*. Boston: Beacon Press, 1992.

Collins, Patricia Hill. "Learning from the Outsider Within: The Sociological Significance of Black Feminist Thought." *Social Problems* 33, no. 6 (1986): 14–32.

"Comparative Theology of Heathen Religions." *Christian Examiner and Religious Miscellany* 62, no. 2 (1857): 183–99.

Curtis, George Ticknor. "Reminiscences of N. P. Willis and Lydia Maria Child." *Harper's New Monthly Magazine* 81 (June-November 1890): 717–20. Hathi Trust.

Cutting, Alfred Wayland. *Old-Time Wayland.* Boston: Privately printed, 1926. Internet Archive.

Daniels-Rauterkus, Melissa. "Civil Resistance and Procreative Agency in Harriet Jacobs' *Incidents in the Life of a Slave Girl.*" *Women's Studies* 48, no. 5 (July/August 2019): 498–509.

DeCaro, Louis, Jr. *John Brown Speaks: Letters and Statements from Charlestown.* Lanham, MD: Rowman and Littlefield, 2015.

Deck, Alice A. "Whose Book Is This? Authorial versus Editorial Control of Harriet Brent Jacobs' *Incidents in the Life of a Slave Girl: Written by Herself.*" *Women's Studies International Forum* 10, no. 1 (1987): 33–40.

Delbanco, Andrew. *The War before the War: Fugitive Slaves and the Struggle for America's Soul from the Revolution to the Civil War.* New York: Penguin Press, 2018.

"The Destruction of Pennsylvania Hall." *Philadelphia Inquirer*, 19 May 1838, 2.

Doherty, Thomas. "Harriet Jacobs' Narrative Strategies." *Southern Literary Journal* 19, no. 1 (Fall 1986): 79–91.

Dotson, Kristie. "Concrete Flowers: Contemplating the Profession of Philosophy." *Hypatia* 26, no. 2 (2011): 403–9.

Douglass, Frederick. "Colonization." *North Star*, 26 January 1849.

Douglass, Frederick. *Frederick Douglass: Autobiographies: Narrative of the Life of Frederick Douglass, an American Slave/My Bondage and My Freedom/Life and Times.* New York: Library of America, 1994.

Douglass, Frederick. "What I Found at the Northampton Association." In *The History of Florence, Massachusetts, Including a Complete Account of the Northampton Association of Education and Industry*, edited by Charles A. Sheffeld. Florence, MA: Published by the editor, 1895.

Douglass, Frederick, and Harriet A. Jacobs. *Narrative of the Life of Frederick Douglass, an American Slave,* and *Incidents in the Life of a Slave Girl.* New York: Modern Library, 2004.

Downs, Gregory P. *After Appomattox: Military Occupation and the Ends of War.* Cambridge, MA: Harvard University Press, 2015.

DuBois, Ellen Carol. *Feminism and Suffrage: The Emergence of an Independent Women's Movement in America, 1848–1869.* Ithaca, NY: Cornell University Press, 1978.

Du Bois, W. E. B. *Black Reconstruction in America.* 1935. Reprint, New York: Free Press, 1992.

Du Bois, W. E. B. *Writings: The Suppression of the African Slave-Trade/The Souls of Black Folk/Dusk of Dawn/Essays.* Edited by Nathan Huggins. New York: Library of America, 1986.

Dudden, Faye E. *Fighting Chance: The Struggle over Woman Suffrage and Black Suffrage.* New York: Oxford University Press, 2011. Proquest Ebook Central.

Duncan, Russell, ed. *Blue-Eyed Child of Fortune: The Civil War Letters of Robert Gould Shaw.* Athens: University of Georgia Press, 1999.

Duncan, Russell. *Where Death and Glory Meet: Colonel Robert Gould Shaw and the 54th Massachusetts Infantry.* Athens: University of Georgia Press, 1999.

Emilio, Luis F. *History of the Fifty-Fourth Regiment of the Massachusetts Volunteer Infantry, 1863–1865.* Boston: Boston Book Company, 1891. Internet Archive.

Etcheson, Nicole. *Bleeding Kansas: Contested Liberty in the Civil War Era.* Lawrence: University Press of Kansas, 2004.

Feinstein, Rachel A. *When Rape Was Legal: The Untold History of Sexual Violence during Slavery.* New York: Routledge, 2019.

Finkelman, Paul, ed. *Defending Slavery: Proslavery Thought in the Old South; A Brief History with Documents.* Boston: Bedford/St. Martin's Press, 2003.

Finkelman, Paul. *An Imperfect Union: Slavery, Federalism, and Comity.* 1949. Reprint, Clark, NJ: Lawbook Exchange, 2013.

Foner, Eric. *Gateway to Freedom: The Hidden History of America's Fugitive Slaves.* Oxford: Oxford University Press, 2015.

Foner, Eric. *Reconstruction: America's Unfinished Revolution, 1863–1877.* San Francisco: Harper and Row, 1988.

Foner, Eric. *The Second Founding: How the Civil War and Reconstruction Remade the Constitution.* New York: W. W. Norton, 2019.

Foote, Lorien. *Seeking the One Great Remedy: Francis George Shaw and Nineteenth-Century Reform.* Athens: Ohio University Press, 2003.

Foreman, P. Gabrielle. "Manifest in Signs: The Politics of Sex and Representation in *Incidents in the Life of a Slave Girl.*" In *Harriet Jacobs and "Incidents in the Life of a Slave Girl": New Critical Essays,* edited by Deborah M. Garfield and Rafia Zafar, 76–99. Cambridge: Cambridge University Press, 2010.

Foster, Frances Smith. "Resisting Incidents." In *Harriet Jacobs and "Incidents in the Life of a Slave Girl": New Critical Essays,* edited by Deborah M. Garfield and Rafia Zafar, 57–79. Cambridge: Cambridge University Press, 2010.

Fox, Richard Wightman. *Jesus in America: A History.* San Francisco: HarperSanFrancisco, 2004.

Fox-Genovese, Elizabeth. *Within the Plantation Household: Black and White Women of the Old South.* Chapel Hill: University of North Carolina Press, 1988.

Fuller, Margaret. *The Letters of Margaret Fuller,* vol. 1, *1817–1838.* Edited by Robert N. Hudspeth. 6 vols. Ithaca, NY: Cornell University Press, 1983.

Garfield, Deborah M. "Conclusion: Vexed Alliances; Race and Female Collaborations in the Life of Harriet Jacobs." In *Harriet Jacobs and "Incidents in the Life of a Slave Girl": New Critical Essays*, edited by Deborah M. Garfield and Rafia Zafar, 275–91. Cambridge: Cambridge University Press, 2010.

Garfield, Deborah M. "Earwitness: Female Abolitionism, Sexuality, and *Incidents in the Life of a Slave Girl*." In *Harriet Jacobs and "Incidents in the Life of a Slave Girl": New Critical Essays*, edited by Deborah M. Garfield and Rafia Zafar, 100–130. Cambridge: Cambridge University Press, 2010.

Garrison, William Lloyd. "The *National Anti-Slavery Standard*." *Liberator*, 17 June 1842, 94–95.

Gibson, Donald B. "Harriet Jacobs, Frederick Douglass, and the Slavery Debate: Bondage, Family, and the Discourse of Domesticity." In *Harriet Jacobs and "Incidents in the Life of a Slave Girl": New Critical Essays*, edited by Deborah M. Garfield and Rafia Zafar, 156–78. Cambridge: Cambridge University Press, 2010.

Goldsby, Jacqueline. "'I Disguised My Hand': Writing Versions of the Truth in Harriet Jacobs's *Incidents in the Life of a Slave Girl* and John Jacobs's 'A True Tale of Slavery.'" In *Harriet Jacobs and "Incidents in the Life of a Slave Girl": New Critical Essays*, edited by Deborah M. Garfield and Rafia Zafar, 11–43. Cambridge: Cambridge University Press, 2010.

Gordon-Reed, Annette. *The Hemingses of Monticello: An American Family*. New York: W. W. Norton, 2008.

Grimké, Sarah M. *Letters on the Equality of the Sexes, and the Condition of Women. Addressed to Mary S. Parker, President of the Boston Female Anti-Slavery Society*. Boston: Isaac Knapp, 1838.

Guelzo, Alan C. *Lincoln's Emancipation Proclamation: The End of Slavery in America*. New York: Simon and Schuster, 2004.

Gunning, Sandra. "Reading and Redemption in *Incidents in the Life of a Slave Girl*." In *"Incidents in the Life of a Slave Girl": Contexts, Criticism*, edited by Nellie Y. McKay and Nancy Smith Foster, 330–53. New York: W. W. Norton, 2001.

Hale, Sarah Josepha. "The History of the Condition of Women, in Various Ages and Nations, by Mrs. D. L. Child." *American Ladies' Magazine* 8 (1835).

Hallowell, Anna D. "Lydia Maria Child." *Medford Historical Register* 3, no. 3 (July 1900): 95–117. Hathi Trust.

Hamill, Kyna. "Lydia Maria Child: Author and Abolitionist." In *Gathering Up the Fragments*, edited by Medford Historical Society & Museum. Medford, MA: Medford Historical Society, 2018.

Hansen, Debra Gold. *Strained Sisterhood: Gender and Class in the Boston Female Anti-Slavery Society*. Amherst: University of Massachusetts Press, 1993.

Hardesty, Jared Ross. *Black Lives, Native Lands, White Worlds: A History of Slavery in New England*. Amherst: University of Massachusetts Press, 2019.

Hartman, Saidiya V. *Scenes of Subjection: Terror, Slavery, and Self-Making in Nineteenth-Century America*. Race and American Culture. New York: Oxford University Press, 1997.

Harveson, Robert M. "History of Sugarbeets." *Cropwatch* (2015). https://crop watch.unl.edu/history-sugarbeets.

Hebard, Barbara Adams. "The Role of Women at the Boston Athenæum." In *The Boston Athenæum Bicentennial Essays*, edited by Richard Wendorf, 69–97. Lebanon, NH: University Press of New England, 2009.

Henderson, Carol E. *Scarring the Black Body: Race and Representation in African American Literature.* Columbia: University of Missouri Press, 2002.

Higginson, Mary Thacher. *Thomas Wentworth Higginson: The Story of His Life.* Boston: Houghton Mifflin, 1914. Internet Archive.

Higginson, T. W. "Lydia Maria Child." In *Eminent Women of the Age: Being Narratives of the Lives and Deeds of the Most Prominent Women of the Present Generation*, edfited by James Parton et. al. Hartford, CT: S. M. Betts, 1869. Internet Archive.

"History—Wayland Free Public Library." Wayland Free Public Library, https://web.archive.org/web/20210530212731/https://waylandlibrary.org/aboutus /about-wpl/history/.

Hoffer, Williamjames Hull. *The Caning of Charles Sumner: Honor, Idealism and the Origins of the Civil War.* Baltimore: Johns Hopkins University Press, 2010.

hooks, bell. *Ain't I a Woman: Black Women and Feminism.* 1981. Reprint, New York: Routledge, 2015.

Hopkins, Patricia D. "Seduction or Rape: Deconstructing the Black Female Body in Harriet Jacobs' *Incidents in the Life of a Slave Girl." Making Connections: Interdisciplinary Approaches to Cultural Diversity* 13, no. 1 (2011): 4–20.

Horwitz, Tony. *Midnight Rising: John Brown and the Raid That Sparked the Civil War.* New York: Henry Holt, 2011.

Hudson, Alfred Sereno. "The Home of Lydia Maria Child." *New England Magazine: An Illustrated Monthly* 2 (1890).

Jackson, Kelly Carter. *Force and Freedom: Black Abolitionists and the Politics of Violence.* Philadelphia: University of Pennsylvania Press, 2019.

Jacobs, Harriet A. *Incidents in the Life of a Slave Girl: Written by Herself.* Cambridge, MA: Harvard University Press, 1987.

James, V. Denise. "Musing: A Black Feminist Philosopher: Is That Possible?" *Hypatia* 29, no. 1 (2014): 189–95.

Jeffrey, Julie Roy. *The Great Silent Army of Abolitionism: Ordinary Women in the Antislavery Movement.* Chapel Hill: University of North Carolina Press, 1998.

Johnson, Akilah, et al. "Boston. Racism. Image. Reality." *Boston Globe* (2017). Published electronically December 10, 2017.

Karcher, Carolyn. "Censorship, American Style: The Case of Lydia Maria Child." *Studies in the American Renaissance* 1986: 283–303.

Karcher, Carolyn. *The First Woman of the Republic: A Cultural Biography of Lydia Maria Child.* Durham, NC: Duke University Press, 1994.

Kendi, Ibram X. *Stamped from the Beginning: The Definitive History of Racist Ideas in America.* New York: Nation Books, 2016.

Kerber, Linda K. "Abolitionists and Amalgamators: The New York City Race Riots of 1834." *New York History* 48, no. 1 (1967): 28–39.

Koester, Nancy. *Harriet Beecher Stowe: A Spiritual Life.* Grand Rapids, MI: William B. Eerdmans, 2014.

"L. Maria Child." Reprinted from *Springfield Republican. Woman's Journal* 11, no. 45 (November 6, 1880): 354–55.

Lapansky, Phillip. "Black Founders: The Free Black Community in the Early Republic." Library Company of Philadelphia, https://librarycompany.org/black founders/section8.htm.

Lee, Sheila Jackson. "H.R. 40, Commission to Study and Develop Reparation Proposals for African-Americans Act." 2020. https://www.congress.gov/bill/116th -congress/house-bill/40.

Lerner, Gerda. *The Grimké Sisters from South Carolina: Pioneers for Women's Rights and Abolition.* Chapel Hill: University of North Carolina Press, 2004. Ebook Central.

Lincoln, Abraham. *The Collected Works of Abraham Lincoln.* Edited by Roy P. Basler. 8 vols. Ann Arbor: University of Michigan Digital Library Production Services, 2001.

Lubet, Steven. *The "Colored Hero" of Harper's Ferry: John Anthony Copeland and the War against Slavery.* New York: Cambridge University Press, 2015.

Manegold, C. S. *Ten Hills Farm: The Forgotten History of Slavery in the North.* Princeton, NJ: Princeton University Press, 2010. Ebook Central.

Manning, Chandra. *Troubled Refuge: Struggling for Freedom in the Civil War.* New York: Alfred A. Knopf, 2016.

Marshall, Megan. *Margaret Fuller: A New American Life.* New York: Houghton Mifflin Harcourt, 2013.

Martineau, Harriet. *The Martyr Age of the United States.* Boston: Weeks, Jordon, 1839. Internet Archive.

Mason, Virginia. *The Public Life and Diplomatic Correspondence of James M. Mason: With Some Personal History by Virginia Mason (His Daughter).* New York: Neale, 1906.

Masur, Kate. "The African American Delegation to Abraham Lincoln: A Reappraisal." *Civil War History* 56, no. 2 (June 2010): 117–44.

May, Samuel J. *Some Recollections of Our Antislavery Conflict.* Boston: Fields, Osgood, 1869. Internet Archive.

Mayer, Henry. *All on Fire: William Lloyd Garrison and the Abolition of Slavery.* New York: W. W. Norton, 1998.

McDaniel, Antonio. "Extreme Mortality in Nineteenth-Century Africa: The Case of Liberian Immigrants." *Demography* 29, no.4 (1992): 581–94.

Meacham, Jon. *American Lion: Andrew Jackson in the White House.* New York: Random House, 2008.

Meyer, Eugene L. *Five for Freedom: The African-American Soldiers in John Brown's Army.* Chicago: Chicago Review Press, 2018.

Mills, Bruce. *Cultural Reformations: Lydia Maria Child and the Literature of Reform*. Athens: University of Georgia Press, 1994.

Mills, Bruce. "Lydia Maria Child and the Endings to Harriet Jacobs's *Incidents in the Life of a Slave Girl*." *American Literature* 64, no. 2 (1992): 255–72.

Mills, Charles. *Blackness Visible: Essays on Philosophy and Race*. Ithaca, NY: Cornell University Press, 1998.

"Miscellaneous Notices." *North American Review* 19, no. 44 (July 1824): 253–63.

Moland, Lydia. "Is She Not an Unusual Woman? Say More: Germaine De Staël and Lydia Maria Child on Progress, Art, and Abolition." In *Women and Philosophy in Eighteenth-Century Germany*, edited by Corey W. Dyck. Oxford: Oxford University Press, 2021.

Morrison, Toni. "The Site of Memory." In *Inventing the Truth: The Art and Craft of Memory*, edited by William Zinsser, 88–102. Boston: Houghton Mifflin, 1995.

Mott, Frank L. *Golden Multitudes*. New York: Macmillan, 1947.

Mullen, Harryette. "Runaway Tongue: Resistant Orality in *Uncle Tom's Cabin, Incidents in the Life of a Slave Girl*, and *Beloved*." In *"Incidents in the Life of a Slave Girl": Contexts, Criticism*, edited by Nellie Y. McKay and Nancy Smith Foster, 253–78. New York: W. W. Norton, 2001.

Nell, William Cooper. *The Colored Patriots of the American Revolution: With Sketches of Several Distinguished Colored Persons*. Boston: Robert F. Wallcut, 1855. Internet Archive.

Nester, William. *The Age of Jackson and the Art of American Power, 1815–1848*. Washington, DC: Potomac Books, 2013.

Newell, William. *Memoir of the Rev. Convers Francis, D.D.* Cambridge: John Wilson and Sons, 1866. Hathi Trust.

O'Neill, Caitlin. "'The Shape of Mystery': The Visionary Resonance of Harriet Jacobs's *Incidents in the Life of a Slave Girl*." *Journal of American Culture* 41, no. 1 (2018): 56–67.

Packer, Barbara. *The Transcendentalists*. Athens: University of Georgia Press, 2007.

Payne, Elizabeth Rogers. "Anne Whitney: Art and Social Justice." *Massachusetts Review* 12, no. 2 (1971): 245–60.

Perry, Mark. *Lift Up Thy Voice: The Grimké Family's Journey from Slaveholders to Civil Rights Leaders*. New York: Penguin, 2001.

Phelps, Elizabeth Stuart. *Chapters from a Life*. Boston: Houghton, Mifflin, 1897. Internet Archive.

Polgar, Paul J. *Standard Bearers of Equality: America's First Abolition Movement*. Chapel Hill: University of North Carolina Press, 2019.

Pratt, Casey. "'These Things Took the Shape of Mystery': *Incidents in the Life of a Slave Girl* as American Romance." *African American Review* 47, no. 1 (2014): 69–81.

"'Prunes and Prisms' in Art." In *National Repository*, edited by Daniel Curry. Cincinnati: Hitchcock and Walden, 1879.

Rediker, Marcus. *The Fearless Benjamin Lay: The Quaker Dwarf Who Became the First Revolutionary Abolitionist.* Boston: Beacon Press, 2017.

Reed, Sampson. "Observations on the Growth of the Mind (1826)." *Swedenborg Studies* 1 (1992): 17–49.

Reed, Sampson. "Oration on Genius." *Swedenborg Studies* 1 (1992): 12–16.

"Reviewed Works." *North American Review* 21, no. 48 (July 1825): 78–104.

Reynolds, David S. *John Brown, Abolitionist: The Man Who Killed Slavery, Sparked the Civil War, and Seeded Civil Rights.* New York: Vintage Books, 2006.

Rice, Madeline Hooke. *Federal Street Pastor: The Life of William Ellery Channing.* New York: Bookman Associates, 1961.

Richards, Leonard L. *Gentlemen of Property and Standing: Anti-Abolition Mobs in Jacksonian America.* New York: Oxford University Press, 1970. ACLS Humanities E-book.

Richardson, Heather Cox. *The Death of Reconstruction: Race, Labor, and Politics in the Post–Civil War North, 1865–1901.* Cambridge, MA: Harvard University Press, 2004. ProQuest Ebook Central.

Richardson, Heather Cox. *West from Appomattox: The Reconstruction of American after the Civil War.* New Haven, CT: Yale University Press, 2007.

Ripley, Peter C., Roy E. Finkenbine, Michael F. Hembree, and Donald Yacovone, eds. *Witness for Freedom: African American Voices on Race, Slavery, and Emancipation.* Chapel Hill: University of North Carolina Press, 1993.

Robertson, Stacey M. *Parker Pillsbury: Radical Abolitionist, Male Feminist.* Ithaca, NY: Cornell University Press, 2007.

Robinson, Sara T. L. *Kansas: Its Exterior and Interior Life, Including a Full View of Its Settlement, Political History, Social Life, Climate, Soil, Productions, Scenery, Etc.* Boston: Crosby, Nichols, 1857. Internet Archive.

Sanborn, F[ranklin] B[enjamin]. *The Life and Letters of John Brown, Liberator of Kansas and Martyr of Virginia.* Boston: Roberts Brothers, 1885.

Sanborn, F[ranklin] B[enjamin]. *Literary Studies and Criticism: Evaluations of the Writers of the American Renaissance—with Fresh Approaches to Transcendentalism, Literary Influences, New-England Cultural Patterns, and the Creative Experience.* Hartford: Transcendental Books, 1980. Internet Archive.

"Sawyer, Samuel Tredwell: 1800–1865." *Biographical Dictionary of the United States Senate.* https://bioguide.congress.gov/search/bio/S000093.

Schecter, Barnet. *The Devil's Own Work: The Civil War Draft Riots and the Fight to Reconstruct America.* New York: Walker, 2005.

Scholl, Diane G. "Jacobs's Uncle Tom, Stowe's Incidents: Hiding in the Attic 'Loophole.'" *ANQ: A Quarterly Journal of Short Articles, Notes and Reviews* 29, no. 2 (April-June 2016): 87–91.

Sears, Edmund H., Lafayette Dudley, and James S. Draper, eds. *The Town of Wayland in the Civil War of 1861–1865, as Represented in the Army and Navy of the American Union.* Wayland, MA: Rand, Avery, and Frye, 1871. Internet Archive.

Seeley, Samantha. "Beyond the American Colonization Society." *History Compass* 14, no. 3 (2016): 93–104.

Shaw, Sylvia. "Preface." In *Sampson Reed: Primary Source Material for Emerson Studies*, edited by George F. Dole, ii–xii. West Chester, PA: Swedenborg Foundation, 1992.

Simmons, Peter Paul. "We Must Remain Active." *Colored American* (June 1, 1839). Reprinted in BlackPast, https://www.blackpast.org/african-american-history /1839-peter-paul-simmons-we-must-remain-active.

Sinha, Manisha. *The Slave's Cause: A History of Abolition.* New Haven, CT: Yale University Press, 2016.

Smith, Caleb. "Harriet Jacobs among the Militants: Transformations in Abolition's Public Sphere, 1859–61." *American Literature* 84, no. 4 (2012): 743–68.

Smith, John David, ed. *Black Soldiers in Blue: African American Troops in the Civil War Era.* Chapel Hill: University of North Carolina Press, 2005.

Smith, Martha S. *Vanguard: How Black Women Broke Barriers, Won the Vote, and Insisted on Equality for All.* New York: Basic Books, 2020.

Smith, Stephanie A. "The Tender of Memory: Restructuring Value in Harriet Jacobs's *Incidents in the Life of a Slave Girl.*" In *Harriet Jacobs and "Incidents in the Life of a Slave Girl": New Critical Essays*, edited by Deborah M. Garfield and Rafia Zafar, 251–74. Cambridge: Cambridge University Press, 2010.

Smith, Valerie. "Form and Ideology in Three Slave Narratives." In *"Incidents in the Life of a Slave Girl": Contexts, Criticism*, edited by Nellie Y. McKay and Nancy Smith Foster, 222–36. New York: W. W. Norton, 2001.

Spelman, Elizabeth V. "The Heady Political Life of Compassion." In *"Incidents in the Life of a Slave Girl": Contexts, Criticism*, edited by Nellie Y. McKay and Nancy Smith Foster, 353–64. New York: W. W. Norton, 2001.

Stauffer, John. *The Black Hearts of Men: Radical Abolitionists and the Transformation of Race.* Cambridge, MA: Harvard University Press, 2001.

Sterling, Dorothy. *Ahead of Her Time: Abby Kelley and the Politics of Antislavery.* New York: W. W. Norton, 1994.

Sterling, Dorothy, ed. *Turning the World Upside Down: The Anti-Slavery Convention of American Women.* New York: Feminist Press, 1987.

Sterling, Dorothy, ed. *We Are Your Sisters: Black Women in the Nineteenth Century.* New York: Norton, 1984.

Stewart, Anna. "Revising *Harriet Jacobs* for 1865." *American Literature* 82, no. 4 (2010): 701–24.

Stewart, James Brewer. "The Emergence of Racial Modernity and the Rise of the White North, 1790–1840." *Journal of the Early Republic* 18, no. 2 (Summer 1998): 181–217.

Strimer, Steve. "On the Trail of the Josiah White Cottage Where Lydia Maria and David Lee Child Lived between May 1840 and May 1841 in Florence, Massachusetts." Privately published, n.d.

Sutton, Robert K. *Stark Mad Abolitionists: Lawrence, Kansas, and the Battle over Slavery in the Civil War Era.* New York: Skyhouse, 2017.

Swedenborg, Emanuel. *True Christian Religion.* Translated by John C. Ager. 2 vols. West Chester, PA: Swedenborg Foundation, 1996.

Sweeney, Fionnghuala. "Letters from 'Linda Brent': Harriet Jacobs and the Work of Emancipation." In *The Edinburgh Companion to Nineteenth-Century American Letters and Letter-Writing,* edited by Celeste-Marie Bernier, Judie Newman, and Matthew Pethers. Edinburgh: Edinburgh University Press, 2016.

Tager, Jack. *Boston Riots: Three Centuries of Social Violence.* Boston: Northeastern University Press, 2019. Project Muse.

Taves, Ann. "Spiritual Purity and Sexual Shame: Religious Themes in the Writings of Harriet Jacobs." In *"Incidents in the Life of a Slave Girl": Contexts, Criticism,* edited by Nellie Y. McKay and Nancy Smith Foster, 209–22. New York: W. W. Norton, 2001.

Taylor, Amy Murrell. *Embattled Freedom: Journeys through the Civil War's Slave Refugee Camps.* Chapel Hill: University of North Carolina Press, 2018.

Terborg-Penn, Rosalyn. *African American Women and the Struggle for the Vote, 1850–1920.* Bloomington: Indiana University Press, 1998.

Thornton, Russell. "Cherokee Population Losses during the Trail of Tears: A New Perspective and a New Estimate." *Ethnohistory* 31, no. 4 (1984): 289–300.

Ticknor, George. *Life, Letters, and Journals of George Ticknor.* 2 vols. Boston: Houghton Mifflin, 1876.

Trageser, Mary. *Wayland and the Civil War.* Wayland, MA: Wayland Historical Society, 1961.

Traub, James. *John Quincy Adams: Militant Spirit.* New York: Basic Books, 2016.

Tricomi, Albert H. "Harriet Jacobs' Autobiography and the Voice of Lydia Maria Child." *ESQ: A Journal of the American Renaissance* 53, no. 3 (2007): 216–52.

Trustees of the Boston Athenæum. "Trustees' Records: Record Group IV." Archives of the Boston Athenæum, 1807–.

Tweedy, Clarence W. "Splitting the 'I': (Re)reading the Traumatic Narrative of Black Womanhood in the Autobiographies of Harriet Jacobs and Elizabeth Keckley." *Making Connections: Interdisciplinary Approaches to Cultural Diversity,* Spring 2011, 20–30.

Tyack, David. *George Ticknor and the Boston Brahmins.* Cambridge, MA: Harvard University Press, 1967.

United States Senate. "S. Con. Res. 26—a Concurrent Resolution Apologizing for the Enslavement and Racial Segregation of African Americans." 2009.

Varon, Elizabeth. *Disunion! The Coming of the American Civil War, 1789–1859.* Chapel Hill: University of North Carolina Press, 2008.

Walker, David. *Walker's Appeal in Four Articles; Together with a Preamble, to the Coloured Citizens of the World, but in Particular, and Very Expressly, to Those of the United States of America.* 3rd ed. Boston: David Walker, 1830. Internet Archive.

Walls, Laura Dassow. *Henry David Thoreau: A Life.* Chicago: University of Chicago Press, 2017.

Wayland Historical Society. "Massachusetts Towns in the Civil War." http://www
.msp.umb.edu/localmodels/Wayland/CivilWar/Petersburgbattle.html.

Weierman, Karen Woods. *The Case of the Slave-Child, Med: Free Soil in Anti-*
slavery Boston. Amherst: University of Massachusetts Press, 2019.

Weiss, John. *Discourse Occasioned by the Death of Rev. Convers Francis, D.D.:*
Delivered before the First Congregational Society, Watertown, April 19, 1863.
Cambridge, MA: Privately published, 1863. Internet Archive.

Welles, Gideon. *Diary of Gideon Welles: Secretary of the Navy under Lincoln and*
Johnson. Vol. 1, Boston: Houghton Mifflin, 1911. Hathi Trust.

West, Cornel. *The American Evasion of Philosophy: A Genealogy of Pragmatism.*
Madison: University of Wisconsin Press, 1989.

Whipple, Charles K. "Annual Meeting of the Massachusetts Anti-Slavery Society."
National Anti-Slavery Standard, 5 February 1870.

Whitman, John W. "Trial of the Case of the Commonwealth versus David Lee
Child: For Publishing in the *Massachusetts Journal* a Libel on the Honorable
John Keyes, before the Supreme Judicial Court, Holden at Cambridge, in the
County of Middlesex, October Term, 1828." Boston, 1829. Internet Archive.

Whitsitt, Novian. "Reading between the Lines: The Black Cultural Tradition of
Masking in Harriet Jacobs's *Incidents in the Life of a Slave Girl.*" *Frontiers: A*
Journal of Women Studies 31, no. 1 (2010): 73–88.

Willis, Nathaniel Parker. *The Convalescent.* New York: Charles Scribner, 1859.
Internet Archive.

Willis, Nathaniel Parker. "The Editor's Table." *American Monthly Magazine* 1, no.
10 (1829). Google Books.

Willis, Nathaniel Parker. "Letter from Idlewild." *Home Journal*, 21 July 1855,
http://www.daguerreotypearchive.org/texts/N8550001_WILLIS_HOME
_JOURN_1855-07-21.pdf.

Wilson, Yolonda Y. "How Might We Address the Factors That Contribute to the
Scarcity of Philosophers Who Are Women and/or of Color?" *Hypatia* 32, no. 4
(2017): 853–61.

Wolfe, Andrea Powell. "Double-Voicedness in *Incidents in the Life of a Slave Girl*:
'Loud Talking' to a Northern Black Readership." *ATQ: 19th Century American*
Literature and Culture 22, no. 3 (2008): 517–25.

"Works of Mrs. Child." *North American Review* 38 (July 1833): 138–64.

"Yamoyden, a Tale of the Wars of King Philip, in Six Cantos by James Wallis Eastburn." *North-American Review and Miscellaneous Journal* 12, no. 31 (1821).

Yancy, George. *Across Black Spaces: Essays and Interviews from an American Phi-*
losopher. New York: Rowman and Littlefield, 2020.

Yee, Shirley J. *Black Women Abolitionists: A Study in Activism, 1828–1860.* Knoxville: University of Tennessee Press, 1992.

Yellin, Jean Fagan. *Harriet Jacobs: A Life.* New York: Basic Civitas Books, 2004.

Yellin, Jean Fagan, ed. *The Harriet Jacobs Family Papers.* 2 vols. Chapel Hill: University of North Carolina Press, 2008.

Yellin, Jean Fagan. "*Written by Herself*: Harriet Jacobs' Slave Narrative." In "*Incidents in the Life of a Slave Girl*": Contexts, Criticism, edited by Nellie Y. McKay and Nancy Smith Foster, 203–9. New York: W. W. Norton, 2001.

Zafar, Rafia. "Introduction: Over-Exposed, Under-Exposed: Harriet Jacobs and *Incidents in the Life of a Slave Girl*." In *Harriet Jacobs and "Incidents in the Life of a Slave Girl": New Critical Essays*, edited by Deborah M. Garfield and Rafia Zafar, 1–10. Cambridge: Cambridge University Press, 2010.

Index

Page numbers in italics refer to figures.

Lewis, Edmonia, 420–21

Liberator (emancipation newspaper), 92, 95–96, 98, 101, 103, 119, 121, 129, 142, 147, 151–53, 157, 167–69, 172–73, 186–87, 192, 197–98, 204, 228, 234, 239–40, 243, 321, 324, 326, 361, 369–70, 396

liberty: and equality, 408; and independence, 405; and slavery, 235

Liberty Bell, The (Chapman), 201, 204

Liberty Party, 217

Lincoln, Abraham, xiv, 125, 300, 329–30, 332, 363–68, 371, 373, 376–83, 398–99, 401–2, 406; assassination, 320, 402; Child's letter to, 377–78; sculpture of, 421

Lippincott, Sara Jane, 440

"Little Master and His Slave, The" (Child story), 59, 89

Little Women (Alcott), 454

Livermore, Mary, 440

Longfellow, Henry Wadsworth: sculpture of, 421

Looking toward Sunset (Child), 384–85, 401

Loring, Anna. *See* Dresel, Anna (née Loring)

Loring, Ellis Gray, 64–66, *65*, 75, 95, 103–4, 118, 120, 178, 180, 188, 198, 207, 210, 215–17, 224–27, 230–32, 241, 246–52, 259, 263, 273–74, 290–91, 295, 451, 454; death, 299–300; leading lawsuit for Med's freedom, 160–63

Loring, Louisa Gilman, 64, *66*, 75, 95, 103, 118, 131–32, 140–41, 152, 156, 178, 180, 198–99, 203–5, 230, 234, 250, 263, 290–91, 295–96, 299, 423, 444, 451, 454

Louis XVIII (king), 72

Louisiana Purchase (1803), 22

L'Ouverture, Toussaint, 304–5, 410

Lovejoy, Elijah Parish, 126–27, 179, 183–84

Lowell, James Russell, 157

loyalty, and truth, 140

Lundy, Benjamin, 88, 91–93, 118, 138

Lydia Maria Child Fund for Activism, 478

Maine: Child in, 32–37, 40, 265, 286; Child's move from, 43; statehood, xiii, 37–41. *See also* Norridgewock, ME

Mallory, Charles (colonel), 368

Mallory, Shepard, 368–69

Manning, Abby Adeline, 460–61

Mansion House, hotel (Northampton, MA), 191–92

manumission societies, 22, 161

Martin, J. Stella, 307

Martineau, Harriet, 109–10

martyrdom, 134, 192, 320, 357, 420

MAS. *See* Massachusetts Anti-Slavery Society

Mason, James M. (senator), 309–10, 318, 320

Mason, Margaretta, 318–20, 322–26

Mason, Virginia, 318

Massachusetts: Child in, 31–33, 174–75, 191, 261, 328. *See also* Boston; Medford, MA; Northampton, MA; Roxbury, MA; Watertown, MA; Wayland, MA

Massachusetts Anti-Slavery Society (MAS), 135, 155, 202, 246, 309, 349, 437

Massachusetts Emigration Aid Company, 286

Massachusetts Fifty-Fourth Regiment, 386–88, 392–96

Massachusetts Journal, 70, 76, 79–80, 96, 102, 104, 113, 136, 251–52

Massachusetts Second Infantry Regiment, 386

May, Samuel, 95, 98, 103, 109, 113, 155, 258, 281–82

McClellan, George B. (general), 380